ary Movements with one of the richest available reservoirs of source-material. However, the more remarkable accomplishment is that so vast an accumulation of data from virtually the whole earth has been skillfully held in balance, and woven into a story which marches with steady rhythm and inspiring advance.

"This was one of the essential and crucial chapters in modern Christian history which was crying for treatment. Familiarity with it is the necessary premise for understanding of every other phase of the ecumenical development. Now it has been written, fully, authoritatively and interestingly. It need never be written again. But it must be read by everyone who makes a pretense of speaking or thinking about Ecumenical Christianity. I can name no other book which is, so literally, a *sine qua non* for understanding that movement."

William Richey Hogg is well qualified to write the history of the International Missionary Council. He was co-author of *Tomorrow Is Here* and *World Christian Community in Action*. At the Amsterdam Assembly of the World Council of Churches in 1948, he served as a member of the secretariat. He has also served with the Interseminary Movement and the International Missionary Council. He is an ordained minister of the Methodist Church and has received training as an overseas missionary.

Ecumenical Foundations

ECUMENICAL FOUNDATIONS

*A History of the International Missionary Council
And Its Nineteenth-Century Background*

by William Richey Hogg

Harper & Brothers, Publishers, New York

International Missionary Council

Library of Congress catalog card number: 51-11923

Dedicated to
My Mother and Father

who alone know how
much this book owes
to them

CONTENTS

vii

PREFACE

Today, in the mid-twentieth century, the non-Roman Christian churches of the world are caught up in the Ecumenical Movement. That Movement, so Christians believe, provides an example of the working of the Spirit of God in the hearts of men and women of every communion, of every nation, and of every race to bring into being a united and effectively witnessing world Christian fellowship. In this sense the Ecumenical Movement comprehends far more than all its organized expressions and the multiplying instances of church union. It stretches beyond Protestantism and embraces those within the Orthodox, Old Catholic, and ancient Eastern churches. The growing world fellowship, the increasing instruments for unity—these have sprung directly from the missionary enterprise of the past one hundred and fifty years.

What follows is the story of international missionary co-operation as it culminated in the International Missionary Council. It is neither a history of the Ecumenical Movement nor of missionary co-operation, for both those subjects open a field too vast for these pages. Yet the International Missionary Council is one of the major evidences of the Ecumenical Movement. It, too, grew out of the missionary endeavour of the last century and a half. One should not be surprised, then, to discover that the record of its history also discloses much about the genesis of the Ecumenical Movement.

The International Missionary Council's great landmarks—Edinburgh, 1910, Jerusalem, 1928, Madras, 1938, and Whitby, 1947—are familiar to many. Yet outside professional missionary circles the Council is scarcely known. Here is an agency that has established the basic working principle of ecumenical organization, that through two World Wars has saved Continental and more especially German missions from collapse, that to a remarkable degree has integrated Protestant missionary endeavour, that has advanced the younger churches and created a global network of National Christian Councils. The Council has also been the instrument through which an articulate world Christian community has been brought into being. Moreover, in unique fashion it has prepared the way for and made possible the World Council of Churches. In the chapters that follow the writer has attempted to relate the developments that led to these remarkable achievements—which became ecumenical foundations—and to suggest why the Council still remains so little known among the great majority of Christians.

In approaching an account of an international and interdenominational agency, the reader will wonder what pre-conditioning the writer brought to his task. For, strive as one may to record historical fact impartially, he is at points likely to be influenced by his background. In this case the author is a Christian, belonging to the Methodist family, who has been trained for an overseas missionary vocation. He is also an American. Moreover, he was first drawn to this study because of his interest in the Ecumenical Movement and his admiration for what the International Missionary Council has accomplished. If these pages disclose evidences of failure fully to appreciate or understand particular developments or facts, these may, at least in part, be attributable to the writer's own orientation.

For their courtesy in assisting him in his search for material the writer must indicate his great obligation to the Day Missions Library and to the Missionary Research Library, to those of the Edinburgh House staff and of the International Missionary Council's New York office who made available the Council's archives, and to Pastor E. Ramsauer who made accessible the archives of the Bremen Mission.

The writer wishes to record his gratitude to the late Ralph E. Diffendorfer through whose thoughtfulness the Board of Missions of the Methodist Church provided financial assistance toward the author's travel to Britain and the Continent in 1948. He wants also to thank Svein Hanssen-Bauer who assisted him in translating certain Scandinavian materials, Knut Westman, Joh. Blauw, and Rodolfo Anders who provided him with helpful accounts of missionary co-operation in their respective areas, and Mrs. Dorothy Ansley who typed the manuscript. Here, too, he must record his indebtedness to his wife for reasons best known to her.

The author also wishes to indicate his gratitude to the following who in conversation graciously shared with him their knowledge of international missionary co-operation—T. C. Chao, J. Merle Davis, the late Charles H. Fahs, Walter Freytag, Miss B. D. Gibson, Karl Hartenstein, John Mackenzie, Nicol Macnicol, John R. Mott, W. J. Noble, J. H. Oldham, J. H. Ritson, Miss Ruth Rouse, Martin Schlunk, Mrs. H. L. Taylor, A. L. Warnshuis, C. E. Wilson, and P. Cullen Young. Further, he must record his indebtedness to Robert S. Bilheimer, Miss B. D. Gibson, Martin Schlunk, Henry P. Van Dusen, and A. L. Warnshuis who read portions of the manuscript and offered helpful suggestions—and especially to J. H. Oldham who also prepared several lengthy and invaluable memoranda. Finally, he must express his deepest appreciation to Myrtle A. Cline, formerly librarian of the William Adams Brown Ecumenical Library, and Kenneth Scott Latourette, Sterling Professor of Missions and Oriental History in Yale University, both of whom read the entire manuscript and made numerous and valuable suggestions concerning style and content. Needless to say, for any mistakes, the writer alone is responsible. This book was presented originally in the spring of 1951 as a dissertation for the degree of Doctor of Philosophy in Yale University.

W. R. H.

New York
September 1, 1951

Ecumenical Foundations

CHAPTER I

<<<<<<<<<<<<<<<<<<<<<<<<<<<<<<<<<<<<<<>>>>>>>>>>>>>>>>>>>>>>>>>>>>>>>>>>>>

The Rise of Protestant Missions

It has become common knowledge that the nineteenth century marked Christianity's greatest period of missionary expansion. The now familiar words of the late William Temple have indelibly stamped in our minds another closely related reality: the Ecumenical Movement, "the great new fact of our era," has resulted from the missionary enterprise of the last one hundred and fifty years. While the Ecumenical Movement is greater than the sum total of the so-called "ecumenical organizations," these have helped to give what is essentially a movement of the Spirit tangible reality. One of the earliest of these bodies, world-wide in membership and outreach, was the International Missionary Council. Engaged today in an ever-broadening program, it stands as a progenitor of the World Council of Churches. While virtually unknown to most church members, the International Missionary Council affords, for one who will observe its emergence, a key for understanding the spirit of the Ecumenical Movement and its organization.

But we are anticipating our story. We must first look briefly to the rise of modern Protestant missions. Not only do they help explain and form a background for the International Missionary Council, but like it, they also are products of the Evangelical Awakening of the eighteenth and early nineteenth centuries.

PROTESTANT MISSIONS BEFORE THE EVANGELICAL AWAKENING

The non-Roman branch of Western Christianity developed its missionary spirit slowly. The Protestant reformers, among them Luther, Melanchthon, Zwingli, and Calvin, disavowed any obligation for Chris-

1

tians to carry the gospel beyond their fellow-countrymen. Moreover, theologians of the later scholastic Protestantism read into the New Testament distorted notions to throttle any attempt by their contemporaries to interpret the Great Commission as relevant for that day.[1] Equally important in retarding the rise of Protestant missions were the wars of religion resulting from the Reformation, the absence of Protestant missionary machinery, the disinterest of Protestant rulers in foreign missions, and the relative lack of contact with non-Christian peoples by predominantly Protestant countries until in the latter part of the seventeenth and in the eighteenth century.[2] These factors combined to keep Protestant Christians from thinking seriously of foreign missions and in large measure explain the relatively late rise of their program of overseas evangelization.

Despite the tardy assumption by Protestants of their missionary obligations, there were, even before the Evangelical Awakening, advocates for missions, and by the beginning of the eighteenth century the first real stirrings of Protestant missionary activity were apparent. Interestingly enough, these initial endeavours embodied the kinds of international and interdenominational co-operation today regarded as quite modern. They were begun by German Pietists and by English Christians, some of whom had been influenced by German Pietism.

German Pietism

Pietism had emerged in Germany as a reaction against Protestantism's sterile scholasticism. Its great leader, Jacob Spener, was succeeded at his death in 1705 by August Hermann Francke. Teaching at the Pietist's University of Halle, the energetic Francke imparted to others a missionary world-vision new in Lutheranism. When in 1705 Frederick IV of Denmark, urged by a Pietist-trained adviser, sought missionaries for Danish colonies, his only volunteers came from Germany—from Halle. Thus was born the Danish-Halle Mission that before long drew its strength and guidance directly from Francke.[3]

The Moravian Brethren provided Pietism's most effective missionary outreach. Remnants of the persecuted Moravians settled on the estates of Count Zinzendorf in Saxony and there in 1722 built their village, Herrnhut. Zinzendorf, educated by Francke, became their leader and contributed unstintingly of his wealth and ability to realize his, as well as their own, missionary conviction. Herrnhut soon became the centre of a new kind of world-wide missionary enterprise. The entire Moravian community made obedience to the Great Commission its chief objective. By the time Carey went to India, Moravian missions had been planted in Europe, North and South America, Africa, Asia, and the Islands of the Seas. Yet the Moravians made their greatest impact later and through others, for, among other effects, they led John Wesley to his "heart-warming" experience and thus indirectly contributed to the growth and fruitage of the Evangelical Awakening.

English Missions

In England the Society for Promoting Christian Knowledge came to birth in 1699 (1698 by the old reckoning), partly from Pietist influence. Founded largely by Anglicans, it sought not only to provide clergy for the American colonies and to supply these men with books, but also to increase the religious knowledge of British Christians. The Society regarded itself primarily as a Christian literature agency, but very soon began to support a mission in India. When in 1709 the financially-straitened Danish-Halle Mission at Tranquebar requested a subsidy, the Society for Promoting Christian Knowledge responded generously. Later it sent a printer and a printing press to Tranquebar. Before long, India had become a challenge. For the next one hundred years this Anglican society, unable to find English volunteers, supported German Lutheran clergy from Halle (though never more than a few at a time) in several stations in India. Even while continuing to aid the Danish-Halle Mission, it began missions of its own in Madras in 1728. The Society for Promoting Christian Knowledge sent out its last German missionary in 1813 and twelve years later transferred its India work (then six missionaries serving nearly 8,400 Indian Christians) to the Society for the Propagation of the Gospel.[4]

The Society for the Propagation of the Gospel in Foreign Parts was organized in 1701 by nearly the same group of men who had begun the Society for Promoting Christian Knowledge two years earlier. It was in a sense the missionary supplement to the earlier venture, for that had originally been thought of as primarily a publishing venture. The younger of the two organizations drew its support from Anglicans and sought to maintain clergy in British colonies "for the instruction of the King's loving subjects in the Christian religion." Despite its limited objective, it reached out almost from the start in the New World to Indians and Negroes. Attended by varying success, at the end of nearly a century of service the Society for the Propagation of the Gospel was weaker financially and spiritually than it had been for years.[5]

THE EVANGELICAL AWAKENING

Christian vitality in eighteenth-century Europe and Britain lay at low ebb. The rationalism of the Enlightenment proved a destructive acid to Protestantism and Roman Catholicism alike. In England the church was attacked by deists, the clergy in general were inadequate for their calling, and Hogarth's "Gin Lane" graphically depicted the depths to which morality had sunk. Yet some continued to pray for a revival of earth-quaking power. It came.

In England the renascence was designated the "Evangelical Awakening." Its chief figure and symbol, John Wesley, laboured prodigiously for more than five decades after his "heart-warming" experience in 1738. As a missionary to the Indians of Georgia, Wesley had met a group of Moravians whose certainty of faith he wanted desperately. On his return from Georgia, Wesley visited Zinzendorf at Herrnhut in 1738 and later sought spiritual guidance from a Moravian bishop in London. Largely through Moravian influence Wesley was led to his deep-going religious experience, described by Lecky as "an epoch in English history." George Whitefield, closely associated with Wesley in this revival, also received much of his evangelical nurture from German Pietism, especially from Francke's writings.[6] The American counterpart to this renewal of life in England developed in the "Great Awakening," which broke out in New Jersey in the 1720's, was symbolized in the revival begun in 1734 by Jonathan Edwards, and was furthered by the preaching of Whitefield in 1739-40.

Led by Wesley and Whitefield, the Awakening reached to all parts of Britain and was reinforced by the writings of Edwards. Emphasizing conversion and the cultivation of the spiritual life, it spread through men whose lives had been quickened by personal experience of faith in God. Moral transformation resulted. Individuals and groups reproduced their experiences in others, and new centres of evangelistic zeal multiplied in geometric progression. Indeed, the Evangelical Awakening altered the whole religious and social life of England.

The sweeping power of the Evangelical Awakening in England moved in the Baptist and Congregational fellowships and helped to pave the way for Carey's pioneering accomplishment in missionary organization.[7] It took deep root in the Church of England and greatly stirred Anglican concern for missions. Wesley had been a debtor to the German Moravians, but in the first decades of the nineteenth century cross-fertilization from the missionary flowering of the Evangelical Awakening produced new zeal and growth in German missions.

This fresh burst of Christian vigour embodied the spirit of world mission. Isaac Watt's great hymn, "Jesus shall reign where'er the sun," anticipated it in 1719. William Williams' "O'er the gloomy hills of darkness," written a few years later, became the "Marseillaise" of Carey and of the missionary movement. Thomas Coke, Methodism's "foreign minister," had proposed in 1784 a plan for a non-denominational missionary society that anticipated by more than a decade the founding of the London Missionary Society.[8] In 1786 he had taken missionaries to the West Indies and established there a flourishing work. Moreover, the Wesleyan revival, while not co-terminus with the Evangelical Awakening, was a protest against the limiting conceptions of the church and the gospel. Wesley's emphasis upon God's free grace led logically to an enlarged concern for foreign missions.[9]

William Carey

By the middle of the eighteenth century, England was caught up in the Industrial Revolution. In that Revolution, in the production of goods and new wealth, England led the rest of the world. It also led in empire, and had as one of its early builders the famous Pacific explorer, Captain James Cook. When his *Voyages* appeared in the 1770's, imaginations took fire in the Admiralty and in remote thatched roof cottages. Manufacturing, empire, and commerce blended into one picture as England grew in wealth and became the heart-centre of a network of sea roads leading to vast land areas and great populations. Spain and Portugal had once known empire and had provided their missionaries with a ready vehicle for the propagation of their faith. But, except for those few who ministered to American colonists and to the Negroes and Indians whom they touched, England had no missionaries.

In William Carey the genius of the Evangelical Awakening and the inspiration of Captain Cook's *Voyages* came together like two carbon rods. When that humble shoemaker opened his heart and mind wholly to the power of God, the resulting arc was of such brilliance that it lighted the way for thousands who came after him, believing that God's will for them was "to make disciples of all nations."

While serving as a cobbler's apprentice, Carey experienced a religious quickening. Possessed of an insatiable appetite for reading and study, he acquired several languages, including Greek and Hebrew, and gained a wide knowledge of geography. Teaching school through the week, he supported his family by making and mending shoes, and began also to preach on Sundays. Called to a Baptist chapel in Leicester, he responded, brought it new life, and laid foundations for other churches near by. Deeply influenced by the efforts of John Eliot and David Brainerd to evangelize the Indians of New England, broadened by his reading of geography, and stirred by his own faith, Carey developed a strong concern for missions to the heathen. The thought of millions without the knowledge of Christ haunted him. Leicester's thirteen thousand inhabitants included many unconverted, but they served only to make "more vivid and poignant the distress of the world's hundreds of millions."[10]

To stimulate action, Carey published in 1792 *An Enquiry into the Obligations of Christians to Use Means for the Conversion of the Heathens*.[11] Revolutionary then, his book might well be studied today as a text on missions policy. Obligation to the Great Commission, he maintained against intense opposition, did not cease with the apostles and was not meant for the few. It rests upon every Christian in every generation. "Papists" and Moravians recognized that. Why not English Christians? To set his argument against a full, factual background, Carey reviewed missions from the time of the apostles to his own day and then surveyed the peoples of his contemporary world. Seven-ninths, he showed by statistical data, were without a knowledge of Christ. In such a situation, the Christian's response should be perfectly clear.

Carey knew what had to be done. He outlined a plan for channelling the response and meeting the need. Each Christian had to be brought to recognize his personal responsibility for making the gospel known to all without Christ. Not once did Carey use the term "foreign mission." He knew only one mission entrusted to the church. Toward its fulfillment every member of each congregation should contribute. Some could give only a penny a week. Others could tithe. Wealthier members could give generously. Out of such a consecrated fund the local minister could be supported, missions could be sent to near-by villages, and funds would still remain for overseas missions. Ideally, Carey maintained, there should be one non-denominational missionary body; but in practice, because denominational differences temporarily made effective common action impossible, each church should form its own society. Yet he insisted that each society should maintain full, friendly communication with the others, and in prayer for missions the differing denominations could be one. The *Enquiry* has rightly been designated "the charter of modern missions."

The Baptist Missionary Society

In 1792 Carey prepared a special sermon which he hoped would lead to the creation of a Baptist missionary society. Using Isaiah 44:2-3 as his text, Carey besought his hearers to "Expect great things from God. Attempt great things for God." True to his own counsel, he assembled twelve village ministers to consider his plan for a missionary society. Their parishioners were illiterate and poor. Several protested that their congregations numbered less than twenty-five. Not to be dissuaded, Carey displayed the latest issue of the Moravians' *Periodical Accounts* and explained what these humble folk were doing around the world. Then he posed a searching question. "Can't we Baptists at least attempt something in fealty to the same Lord?"[12] Argument ceased, and among that little group of Baptist pastors was formed The Particular Baptist Society for the Propagation of the Gospel amongst the Heathen. In adopting a name they honoured the Anglican Society for the Propagation of the Gospel, but significantly they added "amongst the Heathen." Their society would not be colonial. It looked to the whole world.[13] Membership in it came through continuing subscription, not by occasional donation. Fittingly, the first grants went to Moravians, but in April, 1793, the society provided for Carey and John Thomas, a physician, to sail for India. It was ready to send its own missionaries.

The founding of the Baptists' missionary society in 1792 and Carey's departure for India a year later mark the dawn of modern Protestant missions. There had been, of course, English Protestant missionary efforts even before the inauguration of the Society for Promoting Christian Knowledge in 1699 and of the Society for the Propagation of the Gospel in 1701. Short-lived Dutch missions had preceded the Danish-Halle effort begun in 1705. These were all genuinely Christian endeavours, but they were limited. Colonial, they lacked any sense of obligation for world evangelization. Then came new vision. Motivated by the dynamic of the Great Commission, Zinzendorf and the Moravians planned and worked in terms of the whole world. Of even greater importance, the flame that fired their efforts later touched Wesley and Carey. Yet while they were the first Protestant body with a passion for world mission, they did not launch the modern missionary movement. When the Moravians summoned their Christian countrymen to missions, there was no response.[14] As Pietists they could find little sympathy in the churches of Germany. They spoke to the spiritual deadness of the Enlightenment. But when Carey dared his fellow-Christians to follow him, he addressed the England of the Evangelical Awakening. It proved the decisive difference. In his wake the whole missionary enterprise flourished.

Thus, one speaks of William Carey as the first of the modern missionaries and of Protestant missions as resulting from the Evangelical Awakening. Other denominations quickly followed Carey's example and copied the organizational pattern he had established. Soon American societies began to appear. These new bodies in turn encouraged the formation of still other missionary societies in Germany and elsewhere in Europe. Carey's *Enquiry* urged each Christian to contribute to the gospel's spread—without distinction between "home" and "foreign"—and advocated one mission to all the world. Yet, like so many far-seeing men, Carey was in advance of his age—a full century ahead, as we shall discover, in his program for co-operative missionary strategy.

THE EMERGENCE OF THE MISSIONARY SOCIETIES

With twentieth-century emphasis upon working together, one notes with interest that at their beginning many Protestant societies produced within themselves the earliest examples of missionary co-operation. In the last decade of the eighteenth century and the first decades of the nineteenth century, out of sheer necessity, many embodied what has come to be regarded as new, important, and laudable in present-day missionary co-operation. Yet as years passed, as missionary boards grew in strength, and as clamant denominationalism asserted itself, this noteworthy development almost wholly disappeared. Since it forms part of the background story for the International Missionary Council, we must indicate briefly those instances in which individual societies achieved a notable degree of co-operation.

England

The London Missionary Society. William Carey had helped to launch the Baptist Missionary Society in 1792, and his wide influence encouraged other ventures. Carey's first letter from India fell like a seed into fertile soil and resulted in the meeting out of which came the London Missionary Society.[15] From the start that society's inclusiveness was probably its most remarkable feature. Congregationalists predominated among its founders. Yet, not only Dissenters, but also Anglicans of "evangelical sentiments" were invited and expected to co-operate. One favourable effect of such an enterprise, it was hoped, would be an "increase of union and friendly intercourse among Christians of different denominations at home."[16] At the society's founding, an Anglican preached the sermon. The whole world, he declared, comprised the field and in the kind of united endeavour for which the London Missionary Society stood, different kinds of church order should lose their identity under the greater name "Christian."

The next year the London Missionary Society's fundamental principle was adopted. It was resolved "not to send Presbyterianism, Independency, Episcopacy, or any other form of Church Order and Government . . . but the Glorious Gospel of the blessed God to the Heathen."[17] The society's early interdenominational meetings achieved a joyous spirit of unity and were marked by international concern. Reports of the meetings went to ministers and church groups in the British Isles as well as to those overseas. Happily, these resulted in the formation of wide-spread auxiliaries and in financial contributions from the Continent.

One report reached J. T. Vanderkemp in Holland. This educated deist took pride in blaspheming the name of Christ, until the deaths of his wife and daughter brought him to a religious conversion. Upon reading the London Missionary Society's report, he went to England and offered himself for service in Africa. Returning to Holland, he translated and printed an address from the directors of the society. Widely circulated, it resulted in the formation in 1798 of the Netherlands Missionary Society which for years co-operated with and aided the London Missionary Society. Vanderkemp himself soon left for South Africa and became for future work there what Morrison was in China.[18]

The Church Missionary Society. By the 1790's within the Church of England, "Evangelicals," those who had been stirred by the Evangelical Awakening but who had remained within the Church of England, were manifesting considerable strength. Few in number, a minority scorned and strongly opposed by many, this sturdy breed stood with unflinching conviction. Their leaders, warmly disposed toward the London Missionary Society, became convinced that, loyal to the "Church-principle," Evangelicals must provide a new missionary society for Anglican outreach. Many of them were contributing to the two older Anglican societies, but these had come to a low ebb. In them the despised Evangelicals could exercise no influence. Believing as they did that the Church of England should have a missionary society embodying more of the Evangelicals' principles than did either of the two older organizations, they had only one alternative. They founded in 1799 what later became the Church Missionary Society.[19]

Henry Martyn, the well-known chaplain-missionary to India, was the first Englishman to volunteer for the Church Missionary Society. While never appointed by it, he did serve for four years as a chaplain of the British East India Company. Other Anglicans were not so eager to work abroad, and as late as 1802 the Church Missionary Society had not discovered one man whom it could send out. Yet missionaries were found. When the London Missionary Society began, an interested German baron had initiated a correspondence with its directors. In Germany he shared his enthusiasm for this new project with other Pietist friends. To promote missionary spirit and to supply workers for any new society that might emerge, they established the Berlin Missionary Seminary under the direction of a Lutheran pastor, John Jänicke. Begun in 1800, the school during its twenty-seven years of existence sent out about eighty missionaries. All these men served in English or Dutch societies. The first two candidates accepted by the

Church Missionary Society came from Jänicke's seminary, both of them German Lutheran clergymen. Of the twenty-four missionaries sent out during the new Anglican society's first fifteen years, seventeen were Germans. In later years some of the ablest Church Missionary Society men were Germans ordained by the Church of England.[20]

Non-denominational Organizations. In 1799 the Religious Tract Society was founded and in 1804 the British and Foreign Bible Society came into being, both of them strongly missionary. Particularly in the latter, a membership drawn from various church bodies was united in a common enterprise whose influence was felt in every continent.

The Wesleyan Methodist Missionary Society. Concern for the larger work of the church was early evident in Methodist societies. White-field's preaching had resulted in 1744 in special hours of prayer among Methodists "for the outpouring of the Divine Spirit upon all Christian Churches and over the whole inhabited earth." In 1786, some years before Carey departed for India, Thomas Coke, as we have already noted, had started a mission in the West Indies. In 1811 the first Methodist work was begun in Africa. Indeed, as early as 1790 the Wesleyan Conference created a committee to aid Coke in missionary affairs. With the formation of the London Missionary Society's auxiliaries, the Wesleyans, determined "with godly jealousy" not to contribute to the spread of Calvinism, created their own local missionary societies. In 1817-18 the Wesleyan Methodist Missionary Society was founded.[21] Thus the rise of the Wesleyan and Church Missionary Societies marked the partial disintegration of the co-operative endeavour so hopefully begun by the founders of the London Missionary Society.

The United States

When missionary societies arose in England, America was young, and its churches were engaged in a great home missionary effort. George Washington's first term as President was three years along when the English Baptists established their missionary society. For years Americans had supported missionary organizations reaching out to Indians, Negroes, immigrants, and frontiersmen and had even begun two small missions to foreign shores.[22] Not until 1810, however, did the first major foreign missionary society in the United States come to birth. It was distinguished by its growingly inclusive membership.

The American Board of Commissioners for Foreign Missions began largely through the missionary enthusiasm of two theological students, Samuel J. Mills and Adoniram Judson. When these two young Congregationalists presented to the General Association of Massachusetts their intention to become missionaries, that body organized a Board of Commissioners for Foreign Missions to assist them. Two years later in 1812 this became the legally incorporated American Board of Commissioners for Foreign Missions. Like the London Missionary Society it was at first interdenominational, an independent association of individuals committed to missions.[23]

In 1812, with no missionary board of its own, the General Assembly of the Presbyterian Church voted to recognize the American Board as its overseas missions society.[24] In 1817 the General Assembly of the Presbyterian Church joined with that body which eventually became the Reformed Church in America and the Associate Reformed Church to form the United Foreign Missionary Society whose object was "to spread the Gospel among the Indians of North America, the inhabitants of Mexico and South America, and in other portions of the heathen and anti-Christian world."[25] In 1826 for reasons of field comity, advantageous economic consolidation, and a generally favourable disposition among its supporters for such action, the United Society merged itself with the American Board.[26] In 1832 the Reformed Church in America arranged for its missionaries, serving under the American Board, to found churches according to their own polity and for its contributions to be designated for its own missionaries.[27] In 1838 the German Reformed Church voted to act through the American Board in similar fashion.[28] In 1837 the General Assembly of the Presbyterian Church created its own Board of Foreign Missions in which several antecedent Presbyterian missionary societies joined. Yet until the end of the "Old School" and "New School" dissension in 1870, at least some Presbyterian churches continued to operate through the American Board. Eventually the American Board of Commissioners became the missionary agency of the Congregational Church alone, but for many years it united several denominational groups in co-operative missionary endeavour.

So it was that the American Board in the United States repeated the pattern of the London Missionary Society. Broadly inclusive in its early years, it became more and more the organ of one church as other denominations determined to establish their own boards. Between 1814 and 1821 the Baptists, Methodists, and Episcopalians founded their societies. Year by year other societies emerged, but this development passes beyond the scope of our study.

Europe

Germany. The growth of missionary societies in Europe came somewhat later than in Britain or America. For the most part, German societies differed structurally from their British and American counterparts, for they were organized regionally rather than denominationally. From the first this meant that they had something of an interdenominational cast. Jänicke's mission school, which since its inception in 1800 had provided missionaries for the British and Dutch societies, declined greatly after three decades. It had, however, supplied the impulse necessary for the founding of the Berlin Mission in 1824. The Basel Society, begun in 1815, brought together in Switzerland and Germany both Lutherans and Reformed in a common task. For more than a century, although its centre remained in Basel, it retained a strong German character. With an organized ancestry going back to 1799, the Rhenish Missionary Association came into being in 1828 in the region around Cologne. It brought together Lutheran and Reformed Christians. Other societies soon arose, and by the middle of the century, in addition to the Moravian Brethren, seven large missionary societies were operating in Germany.[29] These eight, all sprung from Pietism, developed their own constituencies and, as we are to see, provided the rest of the missionary world with its first example of effective co-operation through a national missionary council.

Sweden. Among the remainder of Europe's missionary organizations, the Swedish Missionary Society in the fore-part of the nineteenth century contributes the most noteworthy example of interdenominational co-operation. During its first decade of existence (1835-45) it included on its committee—in addition to Lutherans—Moravian Brethren from Sweden and English Wesleyans. It did not operate independently, sending out its own representatives, but supported other societies through contributions of money. These grants went to Moravians, to the Basel Missionary Society, and to the London and

Wesleyan Missionary Societies. By the middle of the century a strong Lutheran confessionalism made impossible any further interdenominational endeavour by the society. This denominational exclusiveness was seen in the growing association with the strictly Lutheran Leipzig Mission and the rather dramatic break with Basel in 1866 because of the latter's Reformed coloration.[30]

Thus had the pattern emerged. Not until two and a half centuries after the Reformation did Protestant missions begin to come in strength. Heirs of the Evangelical Awakening, they had in their first years shown many examples of friendly co-operation. With rising denominational consciousness and vigour in the nineteenth century, however, most of this co-operation was surrendered. Yet, as we shall observe in the following chapter, these same societies in the second half of the century began to explore means for establishing a broad and flexible kind of missionary co-operation which eventually led to the creation of the International Missionary Council.

CHAPTER II

<<<<<<<<<<<<<<<<<<<<<<<<<<<<<<<<<<<<>>>>>>>>>>>>>>>>>>>>>>>>>>>>>>>>>>>>>>

Nineteenth-Century Missionary
Co-operation

By the middle of the nineteenth century Protestant missionary organizations in most countries were pursuing their own courses independently of all other societies. Earlier examples of co-operation as seen in individual boards largely disappeared as each missionary body, denominational or regional, advanced its own program and sent out its own missionaries. Recently, however, these societies in retrospect have been viewed as so independent and unrelated that their initial efforts in establishing co-operation have, in the main, been overlooked. These first attempts at co-operation actually provide a vast and significant background for present-day achievements, but inadequate consideration has been accorded their importance. Hence the frequent assertion has been made that international and interdenominational co-operation began at Edinburgh and belongs only to the twentieth century.

There is some factual basis for this position. For instance, the nineteenth century offers no example of truly inclusive and representative missionary co-operation. Yet, unqualified, the generalization distorts the picture, for the nineteenth century offers numerous examples of interdenominational and international co-operative ventures, foreshadowing and laying foundations for those of the twentieth century. The period after 1860 also discloses a growing momentum toward all that is associated with the World Missionary Conference at Edinburgh in 1910.

A glance at the nineteenth century to discover the antecedent forces that helped to shape the International Missionary Council reveals a twofold picture. On one hand, there were the efforts of missionary leaders through conferences, councils, and other co-operative means, to meet an ever-growing and recurring need for integrated planning and effort. On the other, limited communications, determination to maintain denominational prestige, and inability to achieve effective organization confined these efforts within a relatively small area geographically and denominationally. Yet close attention to both sides of this picture will also reveal the impelling forces that led to effective, global missionary co-operation in the twentieth century as well as those factors that determined its nature.

Four major streams of co-operation arose, increased steadily in volume, and flowed together in 1910 to make possible the famed Edinburgh Conference. The first of these was a series of conferences convened by missionaries, in the lands where they served, to explore immediate problems of theory, practice, and organization. In terms of future importance, among all these assemblies, that held at Madras in 1900 became a landmark. The second tributary comprised that series of conferences held in England and the United States beginning in New York in 1854 and culminating in New York in 1900—or, it might be argued, in Edinburgh in 1910. A third contributing stream was the development at the home base of continuing consultative groups directly concerned with problems of missionary administration and policy. In this connection little known to English-speaking peoples is the contribution made by the Continental Missions Conference, which has met regularly since 1866, and the German *Ausschuss*, begun in 1885, which stands as a prototype for all national missionary councils. The fourth, and most important, was the rise of the Student Christian Movement and the formation of the World's Student Christian Federation. The Student Movement made Edinburgh, 1910, not simply a gathering of like-minded Christians but a truly representative assembly. Thereby it set the course for the International Missionary Council and, indeed, for the Ecumenical Movement.

We must turn now to a more detailed examination of these four streams in nineteenth-century missionary co-operation.

Co-operative Missionary Conferences on the Field

Inevitably as missionaries moved into India, China, Japan, and the countries of Africa and Latin America, they encountered problems requiring joint consultation. Nearly always this meant sharing helpful information and providing mutual counsel. In a few cases it meant alleviating friction that arose when one society encroached on territory or appealed to converts of another. Conference usually sufficed to iron out the difficulties. Yet far from home, missionaries enjoyed these assemblies for the sheer joy of being together—for Christian fellowship —and significantly these conferences became a main current flowing into Edinburgh, 1910. The procedure they evolved through the years became normative for Edinburgh, 1910, and for most subsequent ecumenical conferences.

Missionary conferences in the nineteenth century were convened in Asia, Africa, and Latin America. Those in India were, over a longer period of time, more frequent than those in any other country. Thus with greater opportunity for evolving effective technique, they became most influential in shaping Edinburgh, 1910.

India

Carey's Decennial Conference Proposal. William Carey, always a man of catholic understanding and far-seeing vision, early recognized the need for a general missionary conference. It was no provincial gathering that he proposed. As one who had always thought in terms of the whole world, he wrote in May, 1806, to his friend, Andrew Fuller, recommending a decennial conference that would meet at the Cape of Good Hope regularly from 1810, or at the latest 1812. It would be a "general association of all denominations of Christians from the four quarters of the world." Carey strongly urged the proposal, recognizing that important results would likely emerge for the benefit of all missionary endeavour. From such conferences, he believed, greater understanding would result, and those present could "more entirely enter into one another's views by two hours' conversation, than by two or three years' epistolary correspondence."[1] But Carey was ahead of his time. Fuller regarded the proposed meeting as the pleasing dream of an "enlarged mind." It would have no real purpose, and so little unity would be possible that missionaries ought better to stay at home.[2] Two months later Carey outlined his plan to Henry Martyn who was very much pleased with the idea, "not on account of its practicality, but [because of] its grandeur."[3] There it seems to have died.

Local Consultative Groups. The time was not yet ripe for the fulfillment of so grand a plan. But the need to which it pointed, a need whose inevitability Carey had recognized, was felt. It was first met on the local level. Missionaries in Bombay, India, met interdenominationally in November, 1825, and constituted themselves "The Bombay Missionary Union." Represented were members of the American Board, the London Missionary Society, the Church Missionary Society, and the "Scottish Missionary Society." Membership was open to any Protestant missionary who would hold with the then members "the distinguishing doctrines of the Reformation without compromising any of those tenets, on which they may conscientiously differ." The object of the Union was to promote Christian fellowship and to provide a forum for exchanging ideas on how best to extend Christianity in India. For some years the Union continued to meet.[4]

In Calcutta on India's north-eastern shore, a similar conference came into being about 1830. William Pearce, then director of the Baptist Mission Press, had been inviting Calcutta's Protestant missionaries to breakfast in his home once each month. Informally begun, the gathering became regularized and assembled monthly to discuss practical matters of missionary work.[5] A similar body, the Madras Missionary Conference, shortly sprang up in that city.[6] These examples illustrate the early impulse to co-operation through mutual counsel so characteristic of the missionary enterprise.

The North India Conferences. Against the background of city-wide consultations, it is only natural that larger missionary conferences, embracing a whole region, soon emerged. The first of these, the General Conference of Bengal Protestant Missionaries, met at Calcutta in North India September 4 to 7, 1855. Fifty-five members attended from six missions: the Baptist Missionary Society, the London Missionary Society, the Church Missionary Society, the Cathedral Mission, the Church of Scotland Mission, and the Free Church of Scotland Mission. The conference included three Indian ministers, all listed with the Free Church of Scotland missionaries. The reading of a paper introduced each subject. Lively discussion followed, and the conference incorporated its opinions in resolutions. Among these, it is rewarding to note the following: "Respecting the Progress of the Gospel," a statement regretfully recording that "no native church has begun to support its own native pastor"; "On Vernacular Preaching," with a minority report denying that such activity is "missionary work of the highest importance"; "Respecting Female Education"; and finally an "Appeal" to the missionary societies of Europe and America for one hundred new missionaries within the next five years to raise the total number of Protestant missionaries in India to five hundred.[7]

The second conference in this succession met at Benares from January 6 to 9, 1857. No official report remains, for fire destroyed the original manuscript when the Allahabad Mission Press was burned in the Mutiny. However, *The Calcutta Christian Observer* of March, 1857, included an account of the meeting. Thirty-one missionaries, among them four Germans, and five Indian catechists came from seven missions. This conference, much like its predecessor, originated in the November, 1855, Benares annual meeting between members of the Church Missionary Society and the London Missionary Society. On one occasion when Baptist missionaries were invited to meet with this group, the ensuing discussions were so highly prized that late in 1855 the group issued a call for a conference. One year later discussion topics were circulated, and two years later in 1857 the members convened. Meeting in the mint, a large building lent by the Rajah of Benares, the assembled delegates were most impressed with the deep-going unity that pervaded the whole gathering. Among new topics not discussed earlier at Calcutta were Christian literature and the training and payment of "native workers." The conference also authorized preparation of an instruction manual for new missionaries to India.[8]

Those who assembled from December 26, 1862, until January 2, 1863, at Lahore in the third of these North India conferences could survey India's past gatherings and the three missionary conferences already held in Britain and America. In them they perceived fresh meaning and were led to preface their report with the familiar prayer of our Lord, "That they all may be one." In such assemblies they discerned a new pattern emerging: "the united action of Christian men who pray, confer, and work together, in order to advance the interests of their Master's kingdom." Moreover (and claiming the modern's interest, with intercommunion currently an issue), this conference held a service of Holy Communion in which Anglicans, Methodists, Presbyterians (American and Scottish), and English Baptists joined. From the hands of Presbyterian clergymen Baptist deacons took the elements and passed them to the assembled delegates.[9] This was the largest gathering of the kind yet held in Northern India, enlisting seventy-one persons, many of whom were laymen and eight of whom were Indians, including one rajah.

The conference provides a criterion for assaying the relationship of missionaries to the growing churches in India. A paper read by an Indian pastor produced forthright discussion between Indians and Europeans on their relations to each other. The problems of polygamy and divorce as well as comity were vigorously debated. But a paper on "An Indian Catholic Church" and the comments that followed stimulated more interest and generated more hope for what might be than did any other subject. Much that the paper advocated on church union might well have been set forth by a mid-twentieth-century leader. In it the word "ecumenical" did not appear, but there was no hesitancy to use the word "catholic." In all, the deepest impression made by the conference was its manifest spirit of unity. Symbolized in the Lord's Supper, it was seen repeatedly in the hopes expressed for a united Indian church.[10]

The South India Conferences. Missionaries in North India were not alone in coming together interdenominationally. Those in South India and Ceylon, recognizing a like need, launched a similar series of conferences. The first of these met at Ootacamund from April 19 to May 5, 1858. A small gathering of only thirty-two persons from eight societies, it included one representative from the Society for the Propagation of the Gospel and six from the German Evangelical Mission. The conference not only surveyed the history and achievements of each society working in South India, but also considered vernacular preaching, education, Bible translation and distribution, caste, and comity. On the last-named subject the sole representative of the Society for the Propagation of the Gospel addressed the group. His counsel rested on two presuppositions: first, denominational controversies may elicit truth in the West, but elsewhere they produce "nothing but *evil*"; second, through missionaries, themselves only temporary evangelizing agents, God may create a "church of India [differing], in many respects, from any of the existing Christian communities in Europe or America."[11] Resulting from this presentation, the conference sent a note of protest to the Leipzig Mission for its condonation of caste practice and its lack of regard for general rules of comity observed by other societies. Yet, in the gathering itself deep unity was felt, and all rejoiced that they could manifest "the practical Christian union" characteristic of "Evangelical Protestant Missionaries" in India."[12]

Bangalore, from June 11 to 18, 1879, served as the site of the next

South India Conference. While the first of the all-India conferences had been held seven years earlier, twenty years had passed since Ootacamund, and South India's missionaries wanted another chance to consider their own specific problems. One hundred and eighteen persons, fourteen of them Indians, were present from fifteen societies. Major attention was given to the problems of education and of "the Native Church," this latter marking a distinct advance over Ootacamund which had had no such discussion. That a church had been planted and was now growing gave cause for great rejoicing. Much of Bangalore had been anticipated at Lahore in 1862, but the conference directed its attention toward the future outward recognition in church union of an already inwardly experienced Christian unity. The illustration that carried the day likened denominations to regiments, each with its own separate colours and flags, yet all united in one army and fighting for one cause. Its fashioner also spoke of the day when there would be a "Church of Christ in India."[13] Yet, when discussing the knotty problem of lower salaries for nationals than for missionaries, delegates tempered their thinking with the fact of a relatively weak church in India. The conference did encourage "the self-support and self-government of the Native Church," but it also recognized that "any premature step would be injurious."[14]

Most important of all the South India conferences was the third, held at Madras from January 2 to 5, 1900. Its organization and consequent effect make it a watershed. The South India Missionary Association,[15] formed in 1897 and extending throughout the Madras Presidency, had rapidly achieved recognition for promoting active missionary co-operation in specific projects. In 1898 it proposed that the Madras Missionary Conference initiate a representative meeting similar to those held at Ootacamund and Bangalore. The Madras group appointed an organizing committee which faced afresh the fundamental problems of conference organization and procedure. Set against the background of the awkwardly large and unwieldy Third Decennial Conference held in Bombay in 1893, its decisions were noteworthy. To this committee of twenty-five members must be attributed the drastic change of procedure which determined the nature not only of Madras, 1900, but also of most of the subsequent missionary and ecumenical conferences.[16]

To all previous gatherings missionaries had been invited as free individuals, representing only themselves and not their missions. Thus, each meeting had been sharply limited in what it could effectively do, for conferences provide opportunity not only for discussion but also for pronouncements and legislative or executive action. To be effective, however, these last-named functions require some measure of authority inherent in the conference itself. Past missionary assemblies, therefore, had been in effective influence limited to discussion. Pronouncements and resolutions coming from them carried little weight, for they bore only the authority of a group expression of individual opinion. Consequently, the Madras organizing committee asked the missionary societies to elect or appoint for the Madras Conference 160 *official* delegates representing the societies. Thus, while none would be bound by conference decisions, an assembly would be constituted whose recommendations would carry weight with the missions and with the home societies. Furthermore, real effort was made to have as delegates the most experienced persons—men and women, European and Indian.[17] Twenty-six missions were apportioned delegates according to the number of their missionaries with more than ten years' service. All, save two, the Missouri Lutheran Mission and the Society for the Propagation of the Gospel, accepted.

Conference procedure also marked a new departure. In past meetings it had been customary to present a paper, follow it with discussion, and embody in a resolution the mind of the assembly. But, at the instance of the organizers, when delegates had been chosen, the conference executive committee divided them into committees and assigned each group a subject. That committee in turn wrestled with its problem, drafted tentative resolutions, and submitted them to the entire conference for discussion and final action. The subjects were nine: (1) the native church: its self-support, self-government, and self-propagation; (2) native agency: its selection and training; (3) education; (4) the movement among the Panchamas; (5) work among women; (6) disabilities of native Christians; (7) Christian literature; (8) comity of missions and co-operation in mission work; (9) *a.* the training of missionaries; *b.* evangelistic work among English-speaking Hindus. To one man was entrusted the work of assembling the missions' statistics. By August, 1899, the committees had been chosen and had begun their work by correspondence.[18]

The conference met for four days, beginning January 2, 1900. Committee sessions consumed the first day and a half, and the remaining time was spent in plenary session discussing committee reports.

Through and through, Madras, 1900, was a work-conference. Not a single paper was read. Preliminary thoroughness in each committee laid the foundation for its accomplishment and effectiveness. The best criterion for comparing Madras, 1900, with its predecessors in India is its report. The other meetings had produced large books, several being two-volume works, filled with speeches. In contrast stands the Madras, 1900, report, a stream-lined affair, numbering less than 110 pages including committee reports, ninety-five resolutions, and mission statistics. Moreover, this material, compiled by missionary experts and pertinent to the major problems of Christian work in South India, in almost every instance met unanimous acceptance.

The Decennial Conferences. The North India, Lahore conference of 1862 gave impetus for an all-India conference. Machinery was soon set in motion, and from December 26, 1872, until January 1, 1873, the first of these India-wide gatherings met at Allahabad with an attendance of 136. Of these twenty-eight were "native members." Nineteen societies were represented, but the conference attempted to cover too much ground in the time available. It did, however, give considerable recognition to the growing "native church" and had papers read by Indian members on this and other subjects. Its members in their coming together demonstrated a felt unity and a desire for increased co-operation. Moreover, they urged a general missionary conference every ten years.[19]

The suggestion made at Allahabad for a decennial conference became so rooted in the thinking of the missionaries that before a decade had passed, they initiated the Second Decennial Missionary Conference at Calcutta. While in a sense self-generated, the conference stood in the succession of the Allahabad meeting. Invitations were sent broadcast, and 475 persons attended, of whom forty-six were "natives." In all, twenty-seven societies were represented. Meeting from December 28, 1882, until January 2, 1883, delegates, who listened to several addresses from Indian members, had to abandon their hoped-for united communion in favour of a service held apart from the conference to which all were invited. As the largest gathering of its kind thus far held in that land, the meeting demonstrated the power of the missionary force in India.[20]

When the Third Decennial Conference met at Bombay from December 29, 1892, to January 4, 1893, it exceeded in size all its predecessors. Six hundred twenty members, including sixty-seven "Indians" (which seems to mark an advance beyond the somewhat patronizing "natives"), attended, representing forty societies. The conference itself had been arranged for by a provisional committee appointed a decade earlier at Calcutta. One fact stood out in this assembly—it was unwieldy and organizationally cumbersome. Another disconcerting factor arose when it was realized that the Decennial Conference had no constitution. If resolutions were to be proposed, who should be eligible to vote? The question was not easily answered. To circumvent difficulty, the conference was called "to *deliberate* not to *resolve*."[21] In spite of itself, on the last day the conference passed ten resolutions. One appealed to home boards for more missionaries. Another recognized the growing importance of Christian literature and urged that specially gifted people should be set apart for that work. Finally, a "Standing Committee" was appointed "with power to represent the Conference in the interim of its regular sessions, to arrange for its regular meetings and to fill vacancies."[22] Here was patent recognition of the oft-expressed desire to have an on-going body to which might be referred matters of common concern.

Bombay in 1893 had faced a twofold problem: conference representation and procedure. Madras in 1900 provided an answer. So its preparatory committee resolved that the Fourth Decennial Conference should be conducted on lines similar to those followed so successfully at Madras in 1900.[23] Delegates were allotted to particular missions in ratio to their number of missionaries. Choice of delegates— ministerial or lay, men or women, Westerners or Indians—rested with the individual mission. This conference met at Madras, December 11 to 18, 1902, with 286 delegates present from fifty-five societies. Its planners had made special efforts to enroll Indian delegates, and of these there were more than twenty. Like Madras, 1900, Madras in 1902 was built on the committee system as a working conference. Its rules were to become familiar: no theological or ecclesiastical question on which the assembled denominations differed could be raised; any member wishing to speak had to notify the chairmen by card and await recognition; and once recognized, each speaker was restricted by a time limit. As we shall later see, Madras, 1902, helped greatly to shape Edinburgh, 1910. Considerable time was given to the church in India. Increasingly, recognition came of a unity already possessed by missionaries and Indian Christians alike—an inward unity demanding vigorous concern for outward unity. The conference was shot through with this spirit. On the business side, among other things, it created a "Board of Arbitration" with power to act when the missions involved referred their case to the Board. Finally, it set up a committee to initiate the next decennial conference.[24]

Japan

Since Protestant missionary work began much later in Japan than in India, missionary conferences in the Island Empire were correspondingly fewer. While they did not contribute structurally to Edinburgh, 1910, as did the two Madras conferences, a sketch of their pre-Edinburgh development provides a valuable comparison.

Japan's first missionary conference met in Yokohama from September 20 to 25, 1872. The seventeen missionaries and two visitors present from four societies represented nearly all Protestant workers then in Japan, for missionaries had been in that land barely thirteen years. The meeting itself was called to expedite translation of the Bible into Japanese, and to that end a translation committee was organized consisting of "one member from each Mission desirous of cooperating in this work." Since not all Japan's non-Roman Catholic missionaries had been represented at the conference, it was resolved to ask the American Episcopal Mission, the Church Missionary Society (the Society for the Propagation of the Gospel arrived a year later), and Père Nicolai of the Russian Orthodox Church "to cooperate in constituting this Committee." Recognizing also that denominational divisions "obscure the oneness of the Church," the conference unanimously resolved to work for the advent in Japan of the catholic "Church of Christ." The officers of the gathering were constituted a continuing committee to call a subsequent conference.[25]

Another meeting that seemed quickly to have been forgotten and not to be recognized as in the succession of "The General Missionary Conferences" was that called by American Board missionaries from May 10 to 13, 1878. Its sole purpose was to facilitate translation of the Old Testament. It brought together forty-seven persons, the majority of them Americans and only one of them Japanese, representing fourteen societies.[26]

Japan's second "General Conference of Protestant Missionaries" convened at Osaka in 1883. From twenty-two societies, 106 missionaries, eighty-eight of whom were Americans, were present. No Japanese were included, although one session was designated for "Native and Foreign Brethren," at which time two Japanese read papers on self-support for the young church in Japan. Preparatory prayer meetings undoubtedly contributed to the feeling of revival and spirituality present in the gathering. On all sides gratitude was expressed for the unity and togetherness engendered by the conference.[27]

The third "General Conference of Protestant Missionaries" met in Tokyo from October 24 to 31, 1900. In addition to the fifteen Japanese they had invited as missionaries, 450 missionaries from forty-two societies had come together. They directed much of their attention to co-operation, comity, and church union and passed a resolution urging all Christians to pray and labour for "corporate oneness." The conference also created a "promoting committee" from which it was expected would come a "Standing Committee of the Missions" to provide for arbitration and co-operative endeavour.[28] This "Standing Committee" was organized and in turn brought into being "The Conference of Federated Missions in Japan" which met annually from 1907.[29] What later became the "Federation of Churches in Japan" was also given impetus at Tokyo, 1900.[30]

China

We turn now to the general missionary conferences held in China. The first of these met in Shanghai, from May 10 to 24, 1877, with 126 persons present from twenty missions, and with one Chinese pastor attending as an honorary member. The conference expressed concern for the unity of the growing church in China. While those present recognized a real spirit of unity among themselves, it was not gained at the expense of utter frankness, as the discussions testify. Unlike the predominantly British conferences in India, this was overwhelmingly American. The conference established a standing committee on literature and resolved that a similar gathering should be convened ten years later.[31]

The second "General Conference of the Protestant Missionaries of China" assembled in Shanghai from May 7 to 20, 1890. Four hundred forty-five persons were present from thirty-six societies. Organizationally, the second conference marked a great advance beyond the first.

Its essays and papers were distributed beforehand, and it followed the committee system, presenting in plenary session only the completed work of the committees. Considering, as it did, so many issues freighted with trouble, the conference's most distinguishing feature was its harmony and unanimity. Bible translation and revision was expected to be the most divisive issue before the conference. Yet not only did the appointed committees bring in unanimous reports, but those reports recommending specific action were also unanimously adopted by the conference. The earnest prayers of weeks and months before seemed to have been answered. In this experience delegates' joy in their oneness reached its highest pitch, and the achievement became, as the editor of the official report wrote in the introduction, "the *great* work of the Conference." The conference also passed a multitude of resolutions and set up fifteen committees to carry them out. It appealed urgently to the home boards for 1,000 workers within the next five years. Interestingly, a member of the China Inland Mission strongly attacked the illustration of the Christian church as composed of many regiments under one army flag. Apparently, the metaphor had gained wide currency. But, the speaker argued, it was a beguiling picture. Heaven's armies, the denominations, are each run by a general staff duplicating the functions of every other and ordering battles with no regard for the plans of their allied armies. Hampered by the blind desires of home churches, foreign missionaries really needed to unite![32]

The conference of 1890 had appointed among others a committee to initiate the next conference. The committee organized, filled its vacancies through the years, and made possible the "Great Conference" held at Shanghai from April 5 to May 8, 1907. This Centenary Conference of Christian misions in China was strictly delegated. Although nearly one-third of the then 3,445 Protestant missionaries in China attended, only 509 delegates from sixty-three societies could vote. In addition there were nine non-voting Chinese present. Madras, 1900, had made its impact, for it had been decided that the method adopted by that South India Conference should be followed, with important modifications.[33] Preparatory committee work and findings were printed and distributed but were not read at the conference. In similar fashion resolutions were formulated, an introductory presentation was made, then discussion proceeded on well-considered recommendations.

Christian unity was a paramount consideration. The missionaries affirmed their own unity and urged as the most immediately pressing, practical step the unification of Chinese churches holding the same ecclesiastical order.[34] Probably their most important decision concerning interdenominational co-operation was to recommend a "Christian Federation of China." Provincial councils of churches would be formed, and each council in turn would appoint representatives to a national council—a consultative and advisory body only, intended "to encourage everything that will demonstrate the existing essential unity of Christians." The national federation would have two secretaries, one Chinese and one foreign, to carry out its work. Among other committees, the 1907 conference established one to bring the federation into being.[35] But the project was not realized for some years and then was launched as a result of outside stimulus.

Africa

Missionary conferences in Africa were late in getting under way. Indeed, they began only after 1900. The First General Missionary Conference for South Africa was not held until July, 1904, at Johannesburg, where 104 members assembled from twenty-five societies. The meeting dealt in order with the subjects all missionary conferences were then considering: education, medical work, literature, the "native church," and comity and co-operation. The results of the conference and the unity it fostered were deemed so worth while that a second meeting two years later seemed wise. To this end a continuing central committee was formed.[36]

With ninety-four persons present, including four "natives," from nineteen societies, the Second General Missionary Conference for South Africa met at Johannesburg from July 5 to 11, 1906. Resolutions were passed on church comity and education, two major points of discussion, and a constitution was framed for the General Missionary Conference. The discussions made evident the considerable friction existing among the societies, and to meet this need the conference elected an unofficial Board of Arbitration to handle all inter-mission difficulties submitted to it. The constitution made explicit the aims of the conference: to promote co-operation among the missions, to speed effective evangelization, to enlighten public opinion, to protect the interests of the "Native races," and to promote self-supporting, self-propagating churches. Membership was open to all missionaries and to "one delegated Native" from each society. A continuing executive committee of officers was provided for, and the Arbitration Board became a functioning arm of the conference.[37]

The third conference in this succession convened at Bloemfontein from July 1 to 6, 1909. Seventy-five persons, three of whom were Africans, were present from twenty societies. The advances in conference technique used successfully in India and China were ignored; so the gathering was primarily a discussion group rather than a working body. Anglicans, who had been present before, did not attend this conference, presumably because their African churches had no central body with power to appoint African delegates. Consequently, the conference modified its constitution to meet Anglican needs, but members of the Church of England again remained absent in 1912.[38]

Latin America

Latin American missions were late in utilizing conferences as an aid to more effective endeavour. Mexico, however, led the way. It was probably in the early 1880's that conferences were first held in Mexico City by representatives of the different missions. These were primarily to deal with pressing matters of comity. By mutual consent, it was agreed that no mission would enter previously occupied territory, except in towns of more than 30,000. These first efforts led to a later gathering at Zacatecas which, after thoughtful deliberation, urged the home boards to establish a union college. No support came for the project, but the gatherings brought evangelical workers much closer together.[39]

Apparently, what was the first "General Assembly of Evangelical Missionaries" in Mexico convened in Mexico City from January 31 to February 3, 1888. Nearly one hundred missionaries from twelve denominations were present, and the opening service attracted 500 people. At least one Mexican pastor is mentioned in the report, and a Spanish, as well as an English, secretary was appointed; so one may assume that Mexicans were present throughout with the right to speak. Prominent on the agenda were relations with the Roman Catholic Church, Bible revision, comity, and self-support. A table of Protestant statistics for all Mexico was also presented.[40]

The second General Assembly of Evangelical Workers in Mexico gathered in Mexico City from January 27 to 31, 1897. On hand were fifty missionaries and 150 "native workers" representing twelve societies. The subjects discussed were almost identical with those of the first meeting, but medical missions were added. Speeches and papers given by Mexicans were well received. The conference, however, devoted its most pointed attention to establishing a successful comity arrangement among the societies. After a penetrating address on comity, the assembly voted unanimously to adopt the suggestions outlined, and appointed a committee of reference on which was represented nearly every mission in the country.[41]

Elsewhere in Latin America in the nineteenth century co-operation through conferences was scarcely known. The field, of course, had been entered relatively late. It was vast and claimed comparatively few labourers. All these factors militated against the growth of co-operation as it had been seen elsewhere. Nevertheless, where missionaries came in contact with one another, the questions of comity, of sharing common problems, and of seeking for solutions brought them together. When, for example, the United States took over Puerto Rico in 1898, American missions at once settled upon a policy of comity and followed it well. "The Central American Missionary Conference," meeting annually for one week and with almost no representation for nationals, was launched at roughly the same time that Edinburgh, 1910, met.[42]

The Moslem World

The first conference for those working among Moslems met at Cairo from April 4 to 9, 1906. Present were sixty-two missionaries from twenty-nine societies, serving in such countries as India, Bulgaria, Egypt, the Straits Settlements, Persia, Palestine, Syria, and Arabia. The proposal to meet to consider Moslem evangelization originated with the Reverend Samuel M. Zwemer, then serving in Arabia. Both he and H. U. Weitbrecht had attended the Madras Decennial Conference in 1902, and following that meeting, they made preparations that led to the Cairo Conference. At Cairo papers were read and discussed, but few of the proceedings found their way into print for "prudential" reasons. The assembled missionaries addressed an "Appeal" to the churches asking that workers with special training be set apart for Moslem missions, that the production and distribution of Christian literature for Moslems be more efficiently organized, and that common arrangements be made for more effective occupation in Moslem territories and for "forestalling" Islam's entrance into non-Christian territories. Cairo's discussions duplicated those of other conferences with, of course, specific orientation toward Moslem problems. The one exception to this was comity. Co-operation in the production of literature was recognized as necessary, but overlapping on the field, comity arrangements, and arbitration were no problem. The workers were too few.[43]

Observations on the Field Conferences

When one surveys the reports of these nineteenth-century conferences, he is immediately struck by several dominant themes that recur again and again. To recall these facts here will help to summarize the rather sketchy presentation of the preceding pages.

The most prominent motif through all these conferences was Christian unity—unity engendered by the situation, unity manifest by the experience itself. Where there had been no awareness of Christian unity, these meetings made it real. Where, in common purpose and effort, Christian unity had been recognized, these gatherings strengthened it. Many of these conferences had been preceded by prayer months before their members assembled. People who pray for the same end naturally tend to be drawn together in spirit. Then when these missionaries in conference joined in daily worship, they forged new bonds of shared Christian experience. The oneness of heart they all felt brought with it great joy. Furthermore, their unity, they recognized, came not from uniformity of polity, of worship, or of outlook but from something much higher in which all their diversities were comprehended and made part of a richer whole. This "something," this "stuff" of their unity they spoke of as "love," as "complete unanimity of spirit." Their conviction, frequently articulated, was that these conferences made vivid the unity that actually exists among Christians of different traditions and that its fruit was seen in ever-growing co-operation.

It is equally interesting to note that not all missions co-operated.

From most of these conferences the Anglican Society for the Propagation of the Gospel, reflecting the then High Church attitude on "co-operation," remained aloof. At the other end of the scale, a few of the so-called "faith" missions and strongly individualistic societies chose not to join in these endeavours. Thus, with all the diversity comprehended by these conferences, they brought together only the great central segment of Protestantism where the fundamental, evangelical beliefs of the different denominations were already closely akin to one another. They were not inclusive of all that is usually included in the designation "Protestant."

It is also apparent that from country to country over a half-century these conferences confronted the same situations. As years passed, problems faced by missionaries broadened. They reflected the changing times. But they remained fundamentally the same: education in all phases, the place and training of women, the development of effective literature in the vernacular, Bible translation, medical work, the evangelization of unoccupied areas, the relations between missionaries and the Christians among whom they laboured, especially between missionaries and their national co-workers, the growth of the church, its self-support and self-government, and comity and co-operation on the field.

It is equally clear that each successive conference mirrored the expansion of the younger churches. A comparison of the earliest conference reports with those at the close of the century provides a striking picture of rapidly growing young churches. Each periodic, statistical survey spelled out continuing growth. But statistics alone can be dull. Viewing them, one must pause and allow his mind to dwell on their implications. What did they signify of growing concern for the world-wide task of the church? Of increasing support for that work? Of mounting numbers of missionaries moving into strange lands? Of accumulating years of devoted but unheralded labour? Of the spreading influence of Christianity in lands where it had previously been scarcely known? These are questions that point to facts behind the statistics. Moreover, missionaries in conference invariably were concerned for the welfare of the younger churches: they should be self-governing and self-supporting. Yet independent status for these churches was always viewed as belonging to the future. When any enthusiast suggested devolution or missionary withdrawal as being shortly feasible, his voice was drowned out by a crescendoing chorus of caution. Missionary work was a long-time enterprise.

The influence of these gatherings greatly stimulated the desire for church union on the part of the younger church Christians. They, as is well known, have been especially concerned to give tangible evidence to Christian unity in church union. Each conference, in whatever land it met, gave voice to its dreams of a day when the churches of that country might be one church. Indeed, some conferences explicitly resolved to work for a "Church of Christ in India" or a "Church of Christ in Japan," or for the unity of the churches in general. In the pre-1910 period it seemed to be the missionaries, rather than the Christians among whom they worked, who took the initiative to foster concern for unity and co-operation. The difficulties and divisions occasioned by denominationalism were frankly faced. Occasional defence for the *status quo* was made. Yet the incongruity of transplanting denominations, most of whose social roots were meaningless in a new environment, was apparent. The inability to overcome this situation immediately was accepted, but all these conferences emphasized the need to achieve the greatest unity possible as quickly as possible.

With the exception of those in India and Mexico, these missionary conferences provided for virtually no representation of nationals. Present-day ecumenical gatherings emphasize adequate representation from younger churches, and the contrast with these earlier meetings is striking. In India where British societies predominated, the participation of nationals in missionary conferences was more advanced than in any other field. The ratio of missionaries to Indians was usually about ten to one, but Indians *were* invited. They shared in the deliberations, read papers, and voted. In Japan, however, where American missionaries predominated in the conferences, there was relatively little participation by the few Japanese who were admitted as visitors. A similar situation prevailed in China. Mexico was an exception to this pattern. Protestant work in India was of longer standing than in either China or Japan, and missionary conferences were further developed there. As we have seen, attempts at minimum representation for nationals in the South African conferences created some difficulty.

Comity, except for the Moslem workers' conference, was an ever-present consideration. In itself a somewhat negative kind of co-operation, comity is, nevertheless, a first step toward more positive joint action. Comity agreements most frequently divided territory among societies. Comity also included inter-mission agreements on the salaries of employed nationals and the qualifications for church membership and transfer. One also observes the frequent demand for a continuing board of arbitration or appeal to deal with the situation in which two or more missions might find themselves at loggerheads. Indeed, in India, Japan, China, South Africa, and Mexico boards of appeal with more or less permanency were actually established to help resolve friction when it arose.

The development of comity led invariably to discussion and action in broader co-operative ventures. Indeed, the spirit of co-operation that has so long characterized the missionary movement found some of its most effective early expression through these conferences. Some missionaries were chary about what they regarded as the dubious worth of these gatherings. But almost without exception, conference participants sensed a growing need for what these assemblies could accomplish. Brought together for worship, for fellowship, and for counsel, missionaries discovered many barriers breaking down that otherwise would have impeded their work. Men frequently declared that in common prayer a spiritual bond was formed whose ultimate worth no one could assay. In prayer and worship together these missionaries in a foreign land unanimously affirmed that they drew spiritual strength, encouragement, and new zeal for their work. Again, enjoying the pleasant social intercourse that characterized these meetings, they built friendships which prevented or overcame untold misunderstandings in future endeavour. These periods together also provided excellent opportunity to bring problems and difficulties into the open. As a result, a particular mission was not viewed in isolation, but was reckoned as part of the whole Christian enterprise in that particular country. Little wonder, then, that co-operative ventures in education, in translation, in the production of Christian literature, and in other areas grew apace. By the turn of the century, these conferences, particularly in India and China, had become real *working* sessions. Because of them missionary method and policy on the field were developed inclusively throughout the latter half of the nineteenth century. In their actions not all missions struck the same notes. Yet, for the most part, the notes sounded were harmonized to a remarkable degree. Had individual societies pursued their own ends with utter disregard for others, what was largely harmonious might well have been discordant.

Finally, these conferences frequently served a rôle beyond what their self-imposed limitations would seem to allow. Their decisions, while lacking any machinery of enforcement, carried great influence with missions on the field, with home boards, and occasionally even with governments.[44] In this they pointed the way to something beyond themselves—a permanently constituted, co-operative missionary body empowered to act for its members.

The Anglo-American Conferences, 1854-1900

Missionary conferences overseas had their counterparts at the home base. The first general conference on the field seems to have been held at Calcutta in 1855. Yet even before that time annual, interdenominational city conferences had sprung up in India in the second and third decades of the century. It is to be expected, then, that somewhat similar gatherings should emerge at the home base among those concerned for missions. However, the earliest of these assemblies were not convened in England or America but on the Continent. In Basel in 1837, inspectors (secretaries) of four German societies and of the Paris Mission met together. In 1846 a general missionary gathering for German societies convened in Berlin, and a year later a similar meeting took place at Barmen.[45] From this time forward, missionary co-operation through conferences followed a more or less organized pattern. But to this we must devote a separate section.

Most accounts of Edinburgh, 1910, which seek to delineate its historical background, place it in the succession of that series of conferences which began in New York and London in 1854 and which continued through the New York meeting in 1900. These were Edinburgh's predecessors, but too often this fact has been so magnified that a more important one has been largely obscured. Missionary conferences on the field and the growing Student Christian Movement actually shaped Edinburgh, 1910, much more than did these Anglo-American conferences. Developments in the more advanced Continental Missions Conferences, which also influenced Edinburgh, 1910, have been lost sight of almost completely. Yet to understand Edinburgh requires a survey of the Anglo-American conferences that preceded it.

The Evangelical Alliance

Any account of Anglo-American missionary co-operation through conferences in the nineteenth century must begin with the debt that is owed to the Evangelical Alliance. Only the accident of circumstance made the New York, 1854, gathering the first in this series of assemblies, for the Evangelical Alliance had been planning for several years for the meeting that convened a few months later in London.

The Alliance, begun in 1846, sought to unite in fellowship all those whose heritage was the Protestant Reformation and who believed in the Bible's full authority, the incarnation, the atonement, salvation by faith, and the word of the Holy Spirit.[46] The Alliance's primary concern was evangelical unity. From the first it was strongly missionary and tried to foster a co-operative, united missionary endeavour. The monthly journal of the Alliance, *Evangelical Christendom*, from its first issue in 1847 carried considerable news of missionary work everywhere. Missionaries in widely scattered parts of the world read the publication, especially for its global "Intelligence."[47] Each of the great Alliance conferences devoted much attention to the subject of missions and missionary co-operation.[48] There can be no doubt that through its broad appeal and that through the many missionaries who belonged to it, the Evangelical Alliance laid a foundation that greatly facilitated later developments in missionary co-operation.

The sixth annual meeting of the British Organization of the Evangelical Alliance met at Dublin in 1852. That body, acting on a recommendation from the preceding annual meeting, resolved to arrange for a general missionary conference in England, and to enlist the support of missionary secretaries, large contributors, and ministers for a more "comprehensive and catholic" missionary enterprise.[49] At the next annual session in London in October, 1853, a "Preliminary Missionary Conference"—actually a planning committee which included among its members Alexander Duff, the well-known missionary from India and a loyal supporter of the Alliance—met and constituted a committee to provide for a "General Missionary Conference" in accordance with the Dublin mandate.[50] It met a year later.

New York, 1854

Meanwhile, Alexander Duff had come to America. A well-to-do Philadelphia merchant, devoted to the Evangelical Alliance, Mr. George H. Stuart, had heard Duff in Edinburgh in 1851 and was deeply stirred. On meeting Duff the night he first heard him, he greeted the missionary with the direct proposal: "You must come to America." Letters followed, and in 1854 Duff did visit America.[51] In February, 1854, Duff so moved a group of clergymen in Philadelphia with his thrilling account of work in India that they unanimously recommended a "General Missionary Conference" to be held during Duff's visit. Plans were quickly laid for a New York meeting open to friends of missions from "all evangelical denominations." It was not intended to "form a new missionary organization," but one of the assembly's objects would be "a free interchange of information among the existing missionary organizations."[52]

The Union Missionary Convention (its name had been changed) met in New York on May 4 and 5, 1854, in "the lecture room of the Rev. Dr. Alexander's church." Only eleven of the 156 present were themselves missionaries. The whole gathering was alive with interest. A list of eight questions had been drawn up by the planning committee, and an enthusiastic audience sought Duff's personal response to each. Some points were so earnestly considered that there was time only to cover the first five. When each had been fully discussed, Duff would summarize an answer in resolution form. The conference passed each resolution unanimously.

The questions around which discussion centred not only engage the historian's attention but also indicate the perennial nature of the inquiries. They were:

I. To what extent are we authorized by the word of God to expect the conversion of the world to Christ?

II. What are the divinely appointed and most efficient means of extending the gospel of salvation to all men?

III. Is it best to concentrate laborers in the foreign field, or to scatter them?

IV. In view of the great extent of the Heathen world, and the degrees to which it is opened, is it expedient for different Missionary Boards to plant stations on the same ground?

V. How may the number of qualified laborers for the evangelization of the world be multiplied, and best prepared?

VI. How may the co-operation of all our congregations be best secured to aid in the spread of the gospel?

VII. How can missionary intelligence be most extensively circulated among the churches?

VIII. Is it expedient to hold such a meeting as this annually?[53]

Duff was a man of catholic thought and broad vision. His resolutions were sound and of more than passing worth. Indeed, nearly half a century later John R. Mott, summarizing the means for carrying on missionary work, quoted in its entirety Duff's answer to the second question.[54]

A great public service in the Broadway Tabernacle marked the Missionary Convention's close. "Some hundreds" who had come to hear Duff were turned away for lack of space. But those who listened to the great Scottish missionary were not disappointed, for he concluded the first general missionary conference in America with a tremendous challenge. Before the gathering adjourned, it had passed unanimously a resolution calling for a similar meeting a year later. A committee was appointed to carry out the instruction, but no more seems to be known of it.

London, 1854

The missionary conference, long planned by the British Organization of the Evangelical Alliance, met on October 12 and 13, 1854, in London at the close of the Alliance's annual meeting. It had been prepared for primarily by the secretaries of the London and Baptist Missionary Societies. Unfortunately, the account of the two-day meeting indicates in no way how many were present, although it includes a veiled apology for what appears to have been a relatively small gathering. Among those who had initiated the conference there was intense concern for greater unity in the whole missionary enterprise. Yet they were scrupulously careful to avoid giving the impression that the conference looked toward any amalgamation of missionary forces. They limited the assembly to British Christians only, parenthetically expressing the hope "that eventually the friends of Evangelical Missions in all lands may meet in a general assembly." Like Edinburgh's planners a half-century later, they also restricted the meeting to "friends of missions to Jews, Mohammedans, and heathen nations." Even so, they had to report sadly, "the officers of some . . . Missionary Societies did not see their way to joining this movement."[55]

The essential unity of evangelical missions was the first subject before the conference, and "A Plea for Mutual Sympathy and Practical Co-operation" launched its discussion. Second, the assembly considered means to increase "a native ministry and . . . itinerant preaching"—the preliminary paper being given by a missionary from India. The third presentation surveyed the scriptural basis for hope in the conversion of non-Christians. Throughout, it was apparent that what was said was rather formal. Fearing that any attempt to present resolutions might stifle free speech, the planning committee had carefully banned them. Discussion was conservative and dignified.[56]

Before the meeting adjourned, however, it created a small committee to correspond with those responsible for a proposed missionary conference in France the next year[57] and "to take any other steps which may seem advisable for the promotion of the general object of this Conference."[58]

Liverpool, 1860

In England on the eve of the century's seventh decade, among those concerned for missions a very real need arose for a conference so that "all Christians of the United Kingdom might be stirred up to greater zeal . . . in this work of the Lord." Heeding this counsel and judging it wise, the London Secretaries Association commissioned one man to carry out all preparatory arrangements for the conference. Yet the meeting itself was not promoted by the missionary societies but by a few earnest folk identified with the Revival of 1858-60. When the conference met in Liverpool from March 19 to 23, 1860, 126 members were present, thirty-seven of whom were missionaries. The Reverend Behari Lal Singh, a licensed preacher of the Free Church of Scotland in Calcutta, was the only person present representing the fruit of missionary endeavour. Liverpool's day-time meetings were private to facilitate work and discussion, but increasingly large crowds attended the public evening meetings.

Liverpool, 1860, differed from its two predecessors. Fifty-two of its members were directors and administrators of missionary societies. They worked in a business-like atmosphere and produced policy recommendations that influenced board secretaries for years to come. Among the papers read and subjects discussed were missionary recruiting, Christian education on the field, the development of native leadership, Christian giving, and the development of "native churches."[59] Much more of a "working" conference than either of its predecessors—or than of its successors—Liverpool was organizationally more closely akin to Edinburgh, 1910, than any of the other Anglo-American conferences.

Several of Liverpool's resolutions prove interesting today. While grateful for existing missionary publications, the conference declared that a real need existed for a "high class" journal to "treat of Christian missions at large." As to missionaries, since in the past the great majority had come from "the lower ranks of the middle classes, and the classes immediately below them," the conference urged that "the sons of the wealthy and learned" should be claimed for missions. In contrast with this, the members agreed that the European missionary as the founder of mission churches should be their instructor, not their pastor. "The higher Christian civilization from which he has come; his position as a messenger of foreign Churches, as a man of superior social rank, and as one of a dominant race, render him unfit to be merely their pastor. . . ."[60] The conference also agreed that in mission policy those principles should be adopted which would lead to eventual self-support for all mission churches.

One cannot escape in the report the great joy released in such an interdenominational gathering. This new-found experience of spiritual unity was exhilarating for all. Indeed, Lord Shaftesbury, who chaired the final public meeting, exclaimed that the conference appeared to him to be an "Œcumenical Council" of the dominions. All these conferences were producing similar results. People were thrilled to discover the sheer joy of Christian unity that came in fellowship together.

London, 1878

Liverpool's successor met in London from October 21 to 26, 1878, as the General Conference on Foreign Missions. The proposal and the initiative that had brought it into being had come from the London

Secretaries' Association. When the conference convened, it included more than 160 delegates from thirty-four societies, six of the societies being American and five Continental. The American Baptists brought with them a Burmese pastor who turned out to be the only non-Occidental in the meeting. Unlike Liverpool, in the London assembly of 1878 missionary problems as such were not discussed. Instead, country by country, accounts of missionary work were presented. Such a geographic survey naturally gave an impression of the tremendous outreach that Christianity's world mission had already attained. Another trend away from the Liverpool pattern was seen in the sessions: they were not private but met before a public audience that averaged about 450 persons.

An impressive group of missionaries was present, among them James Stewart of Lovedale, Donald Fraser from Africa, James Legge, then at Oxford, and Hudson Taylor of China. Departing further from its predecessor, this gathering had invited women and devoted one session to "Female Education in the East," and part of another to women's work in India. A Señora Liva from Mexico gave a brief account of Christian missions in her homeland.

The one conference address on co-operation came in a preliminary session. The note it sounded had been and was to be repeated often in similar assemblies: growing unity in missionary endeavour was a blessing. Yet denominational variety in itself did not constitute an evil situation. The growing "togetherness" transcended organizational lines and was infinitely richer precisely because it did not require organic uniformity and allowed for diversity of organization. Dr. Stewart of Africa underscored this fact and further pointed out the need for frequent, regular meetings of similar conferences. They were necessary, he urged, to consider broad questions of mission policy—particularly comity. In fulfilling this function, each conference should base its decisions on world-wide missionary statistics that should themselves be compiled every ten years.[61]

It would be an all too easy pitfall, looking back, to assume that these early gatherings aroused and influenced the Christian public's interest. Such was not the case, however, as an eminent historian of missions, Eugene Stock, tells us. In referring to this 1878 conference, he wrote soberly:

The attendance was at no time nearly equal to what the chief societies are wont to gather at their own anniversaries. Joint meetings, whether within the Church of England or on a broader platform, have never yet attracted the crowds that rally round their own particular societies.[62]

Missionary co-operation through conference was still too much of a child to arouse much attention.

London, 1888

The most representative of these Anglo-American assemblies to that time was the "Centenary Conference" on foreign missions. "Centenary," it should be noted, was used only as the rough approximation of a hundred years' work for many societies. To the conference came 1,319 people from Great Britain and the "Colonies," representing fifty-five societies; 219 from North America, representing sixty-six societies; and forty-one from Europe, representing eighteen societies. In all there were 1,579 persons from 139 missionary societies. Obviously, this meeting was overwhelmingly British, but the idea of wider representation was growing. Among the conference members listed, no non-Occidental names appear. But Dr. A. T. Pierson, in *The Missionary Review of the World*, wrote of "natives who have been converted and transformed into evangelists, pastors, and teachers—these are here."[63] The conference claimed its share of famous names, among them Professor Henry Drummond, Hudson Taylor of the China Inland Mission, Dr. Frank F. Ellinwood of the American Presbyterian Board, Philip Schaff of the Evangelical Alliance, Lars Dahle, leader of the Norwegian Missionary Society, and Dr. August Schreiber of the Rhenish Society. Invitations had gone to all British societies—"from the venerable parent 'Society for the Propagation of the Gospel' to the youngest of the family —the Salvation Army." For the preparatory committee it was a source of deep regret that these two "extremes" of order and method "stood aloof." With the further exceptions of the Society for the Promotion of Christian Knowledge and the Universities' Mission to Central Africa, all the societies of the British Isles seem to have been represented.[64]

The conference had an unusual beginning. At the November, 1886, meeting of the London Secretaries' Association, a letter was read from a layman who thought it time for another great missionary conference. He wanted the Association to take action. The missionary secretaries favoured the idea, appointed a working committee, and the conference was born.[65]

The huge assembly included private section meetings with papers and discussions, open conference sessions, and great public meetings. No resolutions touching missions policy were allowed, since no authority existed for executing them. The mass of evidence accumulated by the conference would, it was expected, make its own impression and carry its own authority. Especially was this thought to be true of the results of the private sections on missionary methods, medical missions, women's work, education, literature, native churches, comity, the home base, and commerce and diplomacy.

Missionary comity, co-operation, and church union claimed their full share of attention. Missionaries, obviously, were deeply interested in proposals of organic union for the newer churches that were being established through their endeavour. Comity was a live issue. An American Congregationalist urged the creation of a committee of reference for arbitrating differences that arise among missionary societies.[66] A similar proposal had been sent to the conference by the Netherlands Missionary Society.[67] On all sides voices were raised to propose that the conference initiate some permanent committee for arbitration. Indeed, to make their point, protagonists cited such unsavoury examples of comity-breaches that Hudson Taylor, himself in favour of a "Committee of Secretaries," had to remind the conference that an utterly false impression would be had by assuming *"that these discourtesies are the rule. Brotherly love is the rule."*[68] The tempest quickly subsided. More conservative opinion favoured the establishment and continuance of such informal bodies as the London Secretaries' Association. The secretary of the conference, as editor of its report, summarized the prevailing opinion thus:

It is alien to the character of the Anglo-Saxon race to attempt to accomplish by laws and regulations movements which can only be carried out through an administrative body, and to have formed such a body at this time would have been premature. . . . It is not impossible . . . that a future conference . . . [may] pass rules and form an executive body for carrying them out.[69]

There was, however, one paper read primarily on missionary co-operation that was so far in advance of the mind of the conference that it was never referred to again. Written by the great German professor of missions, Gustav Warneck, it proves of outstanding interest today, because as far back as 1888 it outlined and proposed for that time essentially what the International Missionary Council is today.[70]

Warneck himself had been detained in Germany, and so his paper was read for him. A remarkable document then, it still makes excellent reading.

The unity given to Christians, stated Warneck, is spiritual, allowing great freedom and diversity. Yet such unity becomes "a mere pious expression" if it does not also become *"outwardly recognisable in our practical relations with one another."* Missionary policy, however, in 1888 was making of this diversity a weakness rather than a strength. To "diminish"—to say "eliminate" would be an "illusory hope"—this evil, Warneck proposed a "General Missionary Conference," meeting each decade, "to bring about gradually, by such fraternal alliances, a certain amount of unity in Protestant Missionary labours."

Organizationally, to meet the international missionary need, Warneck proposed "A Standing Central Committee, with headquarters in London, and composed of delegates from all Protestant Missionary Societies." These men in council would "not only act as leaders in matters where the united action of all Missionary Societies is desirable, but [would also] act as arbitrators where differences threaten to disturb the harmonious working of the different Missionary Societies. . . . To give the Central Committee a sound basis, Missionary Conferences should be formed in every Protestant nation, to include all existing Evangelical Missionary Societies of that nation, and elect deputies to represent them on the Central Committee." Then Warneck pointed out that such national missionary conferences already existed in Germany, Holland, and Scandinavia. Finally, "the duty of this Committee would be: (a) to organize a general Missionary Conference once in every ten years; (b) to undertake the regular publication of a general [scientific journal of missions]; (c) to initiate united action in cases which recommend themselves to the general policy of all Missionary Societies . . . (d) [and] to settle differences with regard to boundaries of spheres of labour." Finally, added Warneck, "We must learn to look upon Missions as a *common cause* . . . to kindle a Missionary *corps d'esprit* . . . to accustom ourselves to a *solidarity of missionary interests*, and to place in the foreground the *vital* truths of the Gospel common to us all."[71]

The conference proved to be a great demonstration and made graphic the responsibility and outreach of the churches. A. T. Pierson, surveying the assembly from an upper platform, wrote enthusiastically, "This is indeed the grandest ecumenical council ever assembled since the first council in Jerusalem."[72] But time often sobers exuberant first impressions, and so Eugene Stock tells us that there were hardly enough persons present to make Exeter Hall look comfortable—even the attendance of the general public was disappointing. At not a single meeting was the hall full. "Clergymen and Non-conformist ministers were conspicuous by their absence; and the thousands of friends who gather at ordinary meetings of the Societies seem to have thought that the Conference did not concern them." In the minds of many the great meeting that was London, 1888, left an impression not of failure but of incompleteness.[73]

New York, 1900

Quite different was the Ecumenical Missionary Conference that met in New York from April 21 to May 1, 1900.[74] Its daily sessions crowded more than 4,000 people into Carnegie Hall, and overflow meetings were necessary. In all, between 170,000 and 200,000 people are estimated to have attended its various meetings. The word "ecumenical" had been employed increasingly to describe past missionary conferences. Now for the first time, it appeared in the title. "Ecumenical" was used, however, not because the conference represented every branch of the Christian church, but "because the plan of campaign which it proposes covers the whole area of the inhabited globe." For sheer size, it was the largest missionary conference that has ever been held. It claimed for its president a former Chief Executive of the United States, Benjamin Harrison, and it was opened with an address from the President of the United States, William McKinley.

The conference demonstrated as nothing before had ever done the outreach of the missionary enterprise around the world and the popular interest that it claimed. A year before the conference, invitations went out to every missionary whose name could be found! Actually, however, the conference included only 2,500 "members," North American societies being limited to 1,666 delegates with each society allotted a specific delegation determined by its field expenditures. A total of 162 missionary boards (the figure would have been much higher had women's boards of each denomination been reckoned separately as in 1888)—sixty-four North American, fifty Continental, thirty-five British, and thirteen others—were represented.

Among those present were many whose names have been written into missionary history: from India Bishop James M. Thoburn, from China Hudson Taylor and Timothy Richard, and from the New Hebrides John G. Paton. John R. Mott, as chairman of the youth committee, presided over three meetings. Robert E. Speer addressed the conference on several occasions. R. Wardlaw Thompson of the London Missionary Society spoke for the British delegation and Dr. August Schreiber, who had been to the two previous London conferences, represented the German delegation. Ira Sankey, whose name is closely linked with that of Dwight L. Moody, was one of the song leaders. Among the more than 500 platform speakers, at least eight represented the younger churches—three of them women from India. Of the latter, one was the daughter of Pandita Ramabai and another was Miss Lilavati Singh. When one speaker decried the need for women's higher education in foreign lands, Miss Singh jumped to the floor and strongly defended the right of her sisters in other lands to have a full college education. This one act, with her later eloquent address on women's higher education, captured the heart of the whole conference. President Harrison afterwards said of her, "If I had given a million dollars to foreign missions, I should count it wisely invested if it led only to the conversion of that one woman."[75]

The conference had its origin in, and was prepared for by, the body which later came to be called the Foreign Missions Conference of North America. Its agenda was tremendous. Even a bare listing of its subjects (*e.g.*, medicine, education, evangelism, etc.) would require too much space here. In addition, every phase of women's work was also covered, duplicating the subject listings. Besides these "subject" considerations, the conference included a vast territorial survey of missions, region by region. Indeed, to the faithful if weary auditor, the Ecumenical Missionary Conference may well have seemed to be just one long series of addresses after another.

The conference was designed to influence a mass audience. Its press coverage across the United States was most complete. But it had moved far from what Liverpool had attempted in 1860—a creative, working conference. Whatever there was of discussion in New York in 1900 came only from a small platform panel present for the obvious benefit of the vast audience. The mammoth assembly was not designed to legislate. It did, however, demonstrate as nothing before ever had the popular appeal among church people of foreign missions.

"Such conferences," wrote Robert E. Speer, "though they serve to do little—and this Conference did much—yet serve always to reveal the great and irresistible movements of the spirit of God. . . . This Conference . . . far as it exceeded all other Christian conferences . . . was yet but promise and prophecy of more, and not the crest of a wave destined never again to rise so high."[76] These were prophetic words, indeed.

From the standpoint of our larger story, a post-conference meeting proves to be of even greater interest than the conference itself. The delegates assembled in New York in 1900 had made no resolutions and took no action regarding a future conference or any continuing co-operation. But in 1897 J. T. Gracey of the International Missionary Union had suggested that the 1900 conference consider "establishing a great World Missionary Council of an advisory character."[77] A. T. Pierson, editor of *The Missionary Review of the World*, had been advocating the same kind of body for some years.[78] In the conference itself there had been occasional private expressions of sentiment favouring some sort of international co-operation.[79]

Accordingly, in the Central Presbyterian Church of New York on the day following the conference, to an interested but unofficial group of about 200 conference delegates—missionaries and board secretaries from Scandinavia, Britain, Germany, and North America—Dr. Frank F. Ellinwood proposed:

. . . that the executive committee of the Ecumenical Conference in New York, and the corresponding committee in London, Germany, and Scandinavia, should be requested to consider the question of appointing an international committee, who by correspondence or conference, or both, shall make known the results of their deliberations to the societies which have been represented in this conference.[80]

The resolution, after debate, was unanimously adopted, but as a recommendation only.

What happened to this forward-looking proposal? The executive committee met. A letter of inquiry was sent to a representative group of board secretaries, and an account of the replies with a recommendation was made to the 1901 meeting of the Foreign Missions Conference of North America. That body judged that there was general demand for a practical expression of missionary co-operation, but that the time had "not yet come for the establishment of such an international committee as that suggested in the post-conference resolution." The Foreign

Missions Conference did, however, recommend establishing a "General Bureau of Missions" for research and information. Through it an interchange of publications and information, it was hoped, would lead to the creation of similar bodies in England and the Continent with the result that the originally hoped for international committee might be "prepared for and hastened." Within several years the project evaporated.[81]

Observations on the Anglo-American Conferences

When we come to summarize our observations, much that was said concerning the field conferences could be repeated here. Yet some features of these Anglo-American conferences were so outstanding that they must be recorded, even if this results in repetition.

The first fact for which there is abundant evidence is that the spiritual life of these conferences showed marked similarity. Each was preceded by services of intercessory prayer, and, particularly after 1860, prayer that was offered in hundreds of parishes across a whole country as well as in remote corners of the earth. Each was built upon the foundation of delegates' daily worship together. Little wonder that those who attended such gatherings, whether at New York in 1854 or in London in 1888, almost unanimously attested that the conference had produced spiritual uplift, that in common fellowship they had experienced the sense of God's presence among them, and that among those who outwardly seemed very different, they had been thrilled with the joy that comes of recognizing a common bond at the deepest level of life's allegiance. This was new—this realization that among Christians of the most diverse modes of worship there is a fundamental unity that can be experienced and which, in the experiencing, brings a joy unmatched by any other. Naturally, then, individuals in unending procession deplored the divisions so apparent among Christians. Yet any suggestion to embody this new spirit of unity in a single organizational structure met the greatest caution and reserve. The majority seemed to fear that such an embodiment would eventually destroy this new something that had been given to them, for had not this spirit and experience of unity come to them primarily through devotion to a common cause? The unity they knew transcended organizational lines. How, then, could it be contained or made more sure by any structure that might limit and that could cause new friction? But the atmosphere was unmistakable, and the gatherings came to be compared with the ancient ecumenical councils of the church. Indeed, the new spirit so evident in these meetings was increasingly referred to as "ecumenical." One can understand why the word with increasing usage was employed, even though qualified, in the title of the last of these conferences. Here also may be a real clew to the twentieth-century renascence of the word "ecumenical."

The second fact that emerges points to a clearly discernible attitude that characterizes these conferences. Perhaps it can best be described as "Kiplingesque." These missionary folk thought quite highly of their rôle as Anglo-Saxons in carrying the gospel to other lands. Implicit in many discussions was the "white man's burden" point of view.[82] The result was a benign, sometimes patronizing, attitude toward "the natives" among whom missionaries laboured. This may or may not be reflected in the very limited representation of nationals at these conferences. While many discussions pointed toward thriving indigenous churches, the missionaries generally thought of themselves as doing most of the planning in the foreseeable future. Closely allied to this kind of thinking was the attitude that almost everything worth while being done for missions was being accomplished by Anglo-Saxons. There was almost complete failure to regard Continental missions as of any consequence.[83] The language barrier loomed as the biggest obstacle. But in view of what already had been accomplished on the Continent through co-operative missionary conferences, one is astonished by the provincialism which assumed that everything important happening in missions was British or American in origin.

A third consideration becomes apparent, especially in contrast with the development of field conferences in India. In so far as these assemblies were trying to achieve results through influencing mission policy, they showed little structural improvement over the years. Indeed, Liverpool in 1860 probably influenced the decisions of missions secretaries on policy more than New York did in 1900. The preliminary papers prepared for the conferences represented the results of individual thinking. They lacked the perspective of group thought and criticism. If several speakers addressed themselves to the same subject, little if any chance existed for preliminary correspondence or co-ordination. Discussion usually followed these addresses, but as the conferences grew larger, it became less and less effective. Really creative thinking in mass meetings was impossible. The last two assemblies in London and New York were thought of primarily as great demonstrations for the education and inspiration of the church-wide constituency. From this standpoint it could be argued that structural improvement was shown. For example, a partial criterion for the success of the 1888 conference can be seen in that British missionary giving, which had totalled $4,667,000 in 1888, sharply increased the next year, and reached $6,457,000 in 1890.[84] Yet increasingly these conferences demonstrated their unwieldiness in size and agenda. With all their popular appeal, they were simply gatherings of individuals, persons who came from particular missionary societies but who could represent no one but themselves. Effective action and its implementation were impossible. This was the real obstacle that would have made their continuance difficult.

Finally, one must recognize that these conferences helped to pave the way for Edinburgh, 1910, and for the International Missionary Council. The earliest ones looked forward to the regular convening of large missionary convocations for mutual counsel and co-operation, and in the last two the idea of regular decennial meetings was firmly implanted. Each had emphasized the need for a first-class "scientific" journal of missions, one to cover the work of all societies throughout the world and to deal with larger missionary policy. Moreover, the chorus of voices that favoured some over-all board of comity or arbitration was growing. The conferences themselves, however impressive, were increasingly regarded as ineffective. More and more, missionary leaders saw that what was needed was a continuing, representative body that could act, when necessary, in the interests of the whole missionary community. Precisely what form this organization should take and how it should be constituted were points for debate. But that such a body was necessary met with growing recognition.

For the most part these conferences, their speeches, and their ineffective resolutions have been forgotten. Their reports gather dust in the less accessible stacks of libraries. But they are of interest to the student of missions for what they show about the most advanced missionary thinking in the second half of the nineteenth century in Britain and America. Their greatest value for today is in making vivid the great and growing backlog of desire for what the International Missionary Council later became.

THE GROWTH OF MISSIONARY CO-OPERATION AT THE HOME BASE

Continuing missionary co-operation, more or less formally organized, and continuing over a long period of time, developed in different forms in Europe and America. The earliest and most informal of these organizations began in London in 1819. Yet almost forgotten by English-speaking peoples is the fact that more effective and more formally organized missionary co-operation grew up in the second half of the nineteenth century on the Continent. The largest and most representative body of this kind emerged in North America in the last decade of the century. To these different manifestations of the impulse toward effective co-operation, we must now turn.

The London Secretaries' Association

The earliest and least formal of these co-operative enterprises began in England when in 1819 the secretaries of the foreign mission boards with headquarters in London agreed to come together to form an "Association" for "mutual counsel and fellowship." They assembled first at the Baptist Missionary Society House on October 29, 1819, and met regularly thereafter, except in the summer time, almost monthly until World War II. The London Secretaries' Association, however, had no legislative power or authority. Its meetings were quite informal, the mission secretaries coming together monthly simply as individuals for a cup of tea and an informative evening of discussion. The fellowship was no more than that.[85] Yet as years went by, out of this informal association there grew a mutual trust and affection so deep that the Association discovered that it could on occasion launch projects and initiate undertakings beyond what it was technically capable of doing.

Four men had founded the Association, the then secretaries of the Baptist Missionary Society, the London Missionary Society, the Church Missionary Society, and the Wesleyan Methodist Missionary Society. By the end of its first century, however, the London Secretaries' Association included as members representatives from all the societies with headquarters in London, including the British and Foreign Bible Society, the China Inland Mission, the Society for the Propagation of the Gospel, and the Society for the Promotion of Christian Knowledge.

The only extant records of this body seem to be ten volumes of carefully penned *Minutes*, the edges of which were burned in a blitz in World War II.[86]

At the last meeting each spring (usually in April) the members of the Association reviewed missionary work on the field and the effectiveness of the home base during the preceding year. Among the perennial problems was missionary financing, *e.g.*, how much should missionaries be paid? How much additional salary should they be allotted for each child? Yet in the early years the majority of questions discussed were of a more theoretical nature, *e.g.*, "What are the indications of Providence to authorise either the entering on a new mission, or the relinquishing one already undertaken?" Until 1870 conflicts and controversies with Roman missions and missionaries provided a regular topic, but after that time they were scarcely mentioned. An absence of interest in Latin America may be shown from the fact that from 1875, when the South American Missionary Society's secretary joined the Association, until the close of World War I, only three discussions are recorded in the *Minutes* on Latin America.[87]

On several occasions, especially after 1900, the Association made general appeals to the government on behalf of missions. The April 16, 1906, meeting authorized the secretary of the Association to correspond with postal authorities, "to secure, if possible, half-penny postage for the monthly magazines of Missionary Societies." The reply was a blunt, "No." The law would not allow it. Of much greater importance during that same year was the attempt to influence a delegation from the Chinese government, critical of Christian missions. Various proposals were discussed, but the only action deemed expedient for the Association was framed thus: "Resolved, that efforts be limited for the present to the influencing of the Commission which is about to visit England from China." This "influencing" was accomplished by authorizing the secretary of the Association to approach a prominent official and to "seek his advice and help with a view to the formation of a committee, the aim of which shall be to show the Commission from China something of the philanthropic and religious work carried on in England."[88]

Conversation in the Association's meetings was frank and open. But, it seems, there was an unwritten understanding that nothing said in meeting would be reported for printing in any of the church or missionary periodicals. Yet in 1887 notes of one session did appear in *The Christian*. As a result, the secretaries explicitly banned any reporting of future gatherings, lest "freedom of speech" be curtailed under the fear of publicity.[89] Caution was the watchword.

As we have already noted, England's three greatest interdenominational missionary conferences had their origin in the London Secretaries' Association. Here were launched the plans that led to Liverpool, 1860, to London, 1878, and to London, 1888. However, after the "Centenary Conference" more and more occasions arose calling for united representations to the government. Although many urged the Association to elect an executive with some power to represent the societies, general reluctance always greeted such proposals. In 1902 a motion was put to establish "an executive to take public action when necessary in the interests of the missionary cause."[90] The proposed action was defeated. The Association retained its jealously guarded informality and unofficial status.

Although lacking a constitution and any real authority, the London Secretaries' Association helped to promote missionary co-operation among the boards located in London. We shall refer again to the Association's rôle after Edinburgh, 1910, in paving the way for the Conference of Missionary Societies in Great Britain and Ireland. But here a summary appraisal of the Association may be helpful. J. H. Ritson, then its secretary, wrote in 1919:

. . . The weakness of the Association lies in its lack of executive power and of responsible officers set free from other duties and able to devote their time to organization in common tasks. On the other hand the weakness of the Association has been its strength. The very informality of its meetings has enabled Secretaries to speak with the utmost freedom and without committing their Societies. By the Missionary Conferences it has summoned, it has done something to mould the views of wider circles than its own, and both before and after the Edinburgh Conference it has been an invaluable instrument in bringing in the new era of co-operation which is working a revolution in missionary method and outlook.[91]

The Northern Lutheran Missions Conferences

We turn now to the growth of co-operative missionary conferences in Scandinavia—a development facilitated by the political movement for Scandinavian unity, by the predominantly Lutheran cast of these countries, and by a strong dash of enthusiasm among some Scandinavian missionary leaders for the Evangelical Alliance.

The background for Scandinavian co-operation is rather more complex than that of any other area. The 1840's and 1850's marked the heyday of "Scandinavianism"—a regional kind of internationalism. Norway participated in this movement, but Sweden, particularly in the South, and Denmark were the great protagonists for demonstrating concretely Scandinavian unity. Student mass meetings fanned the flames of Scandinavianism, but no practical scheme for political unity ever advanced captured the popular mind. Yet the atmosphere was charged with the idea of Scandinavian oneness. Such an intellectual climate naturally fostered a similar idea—closer unity for the churches.

Ecclesiastical Scandinavianism probably found its first expression in Denmark in 1853.[92] Christian Kalkar, a converted Danish Jew, was early won to the cause. Convinced that common Christian convictions and values are of greater importance than denominational differences, he welcomed the formation of the Evangelical Alliance and began his long association with that movement in 1853 in Berlin. There he saw that Scandinavian churches had a character and task distinctively different from those in Germany. Hoping that a "Scandinavian church" might result from Northern ecclesiastical co-operation, Kalkar set in motion forces which led to three Scandinavian church gatherings at Copenhagen in 1857, at Lund in 1859, and at Kristiania (Oslo) in 1861. Denmark and Southern Sweden were most adequately represented in these meetings which Sundkler describes as "the Evangelical Alliance translated into Scandinavian language." Baptism, religious freedom, the Evangelical Alliance—all these were discussed. But to apply conference generalities practically to diverse local situations was found to be impossible. One subject only—missions—transcended national lines and seemed to offer the initiators what they had been seeking for: "a vital issue which promised practical results."[93]

To appreciate what next developed, one must recall that in Denmark, where Kalkar had been elected president of the Danish Missionary Society in 1860, missionary interest had long been dead. As a result, the Danish government in 1847 had handed over the Danish-Halle Mission in India to the strongly confessional Leipzig Mission Society of Germany. That organization, to the chagrin of other missionaries in India, condoned caste practices among its Indian converts. But when, in the late 1850's, Denmark experienced a missionary revival and found itself without a mission field, it looked with favour upon a united Scandinavian mission concentrating on one area. If such were successful, Denmark would have a new missionary outlet. Meanwhile, Kalkar had persuaded a German missionary named Ochs, who had broken from the Leipzig Society on the caste issue and had established his own mission among the Tamils, to place his new work in the hands of the Danish Society. At the same time and at the peak of Scandinavianism, the proposal had come from Denmark for a common Scandinavian missionary venture.

A similar proposal had also come from Lund, Sweden. Both had reference to the one issue that the Scandinavian church conferences were discovering "promised practical results." So at Lund in 1859, Kalkar took up the cudgels for a common Scandinavian missionary undertaking. He advocated an "apostolic mission," subordinating the differences of confessional missions. Uppermost in Kalkar's mind, it appears, was the effect such a venture would have among the home churches as an expression of "Scandinavian ecumenical cooperation." Said Kalkar, "Through such cooperation in heathen countries the Scandinavian Church will feel even more as one." In 1861 at Kristiania in another eloquent address, he proposed for the Scandinavian countries one missionary undertaking with a common executive body, one magazine, one training school, and common missionary conferences.[94]

Then to the Danish Missions Conferences of 1862 and 1863 Kalkar invited Swedish guests. Between the Swedes and the Danes preliminary plans were laid for a Scandinavian missionary conference, to be held in Mälmo, Sweden, August 27 to 28, 1863. To that assembly were invited members of the missionary societies in Norway, Sweden, and Denmark founded "on an evangelical Lutheran basis."[95] No invitation went to Finland.

Mälmo, 1863. To Mälmo in August, 1863, came about 200 delegates. Approximately seventy-five were Danish, 125 were Swedish, and three were Norwegian. The last named, despite their number, were probably the most representative group present, they being the Director of the Norwegian Missionary Society, the Principal of the Missionary Training School, and Sven Bruun, a prominent churchman, who chaired the Mälmo Conference. The strongly confessional Swedish Missionary Society did not participate. With little interest in Scandinavianism, it greatly feared that the outcome of the conference might rupture its close tie with the Leipzig Society. This suspicion was strengthened when Kalkar, the moving power behind the conference, invited Ochs, who had just broken with Leipzig, to Mälmo.

"Missions-Scandinavianism," paralleling the wider political Scandinavianism, was limited in its effectiveness to Denmark and Southern Sweden. Northern Sweden's constituency moved in a different, more strongly confessional, theological climate and worked closely with Leipzig. But those who breathed the air of "Missions-Scandinavianism" wanted no divided loyalties. They sought one mission claiming total Scandinavian support. A letter was read from the temperance movement's leader, Peter Wieselgren, who had earlier advocated a "Union Parliament" for Scandinavian missions.[96] He now urged one Scandinavian field with no "second wife" relationship toward Leipzig. When many Norwegian and Swedish members reacted strongly against this, a fissure appeared, dividing the conference. To attempt to force a common mission now, it was apparent, would only incite greater conflict over the involved Swedish Missionary Society-Leipzig-caste question. At this point, Waldemar Rudin, leader of the pietistic Evangelical Society of the Fatherland, a recent splinter-movement from the Swedish Missionary Society, probably best represented the majority mind of the conference. Speaking firmly, he agreed to accept as feasible in the whole grand scheme only the common missionary conferences and the scientific missionary journal.[97]

A cloud had enveloped the conference: "namely, the relationship between the planned Scandinavian mission in India and the Leipzig Society. It was, for the most part, this hidden tension that destroyed [Missions-Scandinavianism]." The proposal for a united Scandinavian project was defeated. To have urged it further would have produced unfortunate consequences. Yet one practical result did emerge from Mälmo. An annual Scandinavian missionary conference was "very much desired." Plans were laid for the next meeting a year later to be held at Copenhagen.[98]

Copenhagen, 1864, was, however, never held. Through the personable, if wildly imaginative, King Charles XV, the Danes had been led to understand that in time of trouble they could count on a military alliance between Denmark and the Norway-Sweden Union, a proposition that never had the approval of the Norwegian or Swedish state councils. When the Schleswig question led to war between the German states and Denmark in 1863-64, the proffered assistance did not come.

Denmark was defeated, and bitter feelings ensued. Scandinavianism was no more. The sustaining nerve of common Scandinavian missionary action had died.

Gothenburg, 1885. After twenty-two years the Northern Lutheran Missionary Conference convened again in 1885. A major explanation for the long hiatus between the first and second meetings lies in the complete collapse of Scandinavianism and the ensuing growth in Southern Sweden of a strong, confessional Lutheranism unfavourable to all interdenominational co-operation. Yet a new development led to increasing contact during the 1880's among mission-minded folk in Scandinavia. It also provided a new and far more effective base for common Christian action than the earlier political movement. This was the Santal Mission in India, an amazingly successful effort to win the primitive Santals. Its popular appeal made it an inter-Nordic enterprise, uniting people of different countries and of different missionary constituencies by giving their interest a common focus.[99]

The 1885 meeting had been made possible through the initiative of some of Gothenburg's clergymen and laymen. They, fortunately, had been able to interest missionary leaders in Sweden, Norway, Denmark, and Finland in resuming what Mälmo had looked forward to. The conference met from September 6 to 8, 1885, with nearly 1,100 persons present. While it did not attempt to unite Scandinavian missionary efforts as its ill-fated predecessor had done, this in a sense had already partially taken place through the great appeal of the Santal Mission. The general tenor of the conference can be judged from its discussions: the meaning of the Great Commission, the creation of missionary interest, the influence of missions on the home country, the need for all missionaries to be related to a church or society at the home base, and the attributes of a good missionary.

To forestall any possible recurrence of what had happened two decades before, this was announced as a *Lutheran* conference, and its "churchly" character was evident throughout. Certainly, in this respect it was different from its predecessor. Its tone was no longer "the Evangelical Alliance translated into Scandinavian language." (Yet, interestingly enough, when the Alliance met in 1884 in Copenhagen with Christians present from all parts of the world, the "venerable patriarch" who presided was Dr. Christian Kalkar.)[100] Gothenburg's atmosphere, a pleasing surprise to the theologically more conservative members, was characterized, however, by "inner devotion, Christian fellowship, and love."[101]

The conference stimulated popular interest in foreign missions. Satisfactorily conducted, it concluded by proposing that a representative group of nine prepare for another meeting four years hence.[102]

Kristiania (Oslo), 1889. The third conference in this series met at Oslo from July 2 to 5, 1889, under the chairmanship of Sven Bruun. To excite interest preparatory committees had been established in Norway, Sweden, and Denmark. These countries sent more than 500 persons to Oslo. Finland appears not to have been represented, and the report on Finnish missions was read by a Dane.

Kristiania's discussions tended toward the theoretical: the increased Scandinavian responsibility for missions; the extent to which the gospel influences religious and moral conditions among the young congregations; and the interrelationship of foreign and inner (home) missions. H. P. Börresen, the popular Danish missionary and co-founder of the Santal Mission in India, was present. Good feeling about the closer unity of Scandinavian missions was freely expressed. The whole conference voiced its recognition of the spiritual unity of all Christians. Moreover, the experience of devotional fellowship and of having been "strengthened by grace" moved in the hearts of all present.

The succession of these conferences appears to have been quite informal, there being no guarantee that another conference would be held, a quadrennium later. That fact was taken for granted. At the close of the 1889 sessions, Sven Bruun merely expressed gratitude that the conference would probably reconvene regularly.[103]

Copenhagen, 1893. The next conference assembled at Copenhagen from August 22 to 25, 1893, and attracted more than 1,200 persons from the four Scandinavian countries. Its account states that "even two Norwegian bishops were present," the implication apparently being that in addition to the missionary societies, the *church* itself was represented. Historical surveys of the work of each Scandinavian mission since 1889 were given, and various topics were considered. The growing strength and influence of the Student Volunteer Movement in the United States and Great Britain claimed attention and resulted in the expression of hope that this example would be followed by Scandinavian students.

More and more it was becoming clear that the aim implicit in the conferences from Gothenburg on was being realized. These large meetings increased interest in and knowledge of foreign missions among all segments of the population. Such results naturally encouraged mission leaders. With furloughed missionaries participating in them, these conferences gave to those who attended a vital sense of relatedness to missionary endeavour.[104]

Stockholm, 1897. The fifth conference met at Stockholm from August 26 to 28, 1897, attracting more than 1,000 people from the four Scandinavian countries. The meeting was widely representative. In addition, there were two representatives from Germany and fifteen, of Scandinavian background, from America. Nathan Söderblom, then a young professor at Paris, had come North for the meeting and reminded those assembled that though there are many churches, they are as one in the body of Christ.

Among the subjects presented at Stockholm were: surveys of Scandinavian missions since 1893, a survey of the missionary movement at the home base, and reports from the field. Of greatest interest today is a paper read by Pastor Henry Ussing, author of a popular history of missions, and the vigorous discussion that followed. Ussing contrasted the then current thought trends in Anglo-Saxon missions—primary emphasis being on the Student Volunteer Movement watchword, "The evangelization of the world in this generation"—with German "missions theory." The American emphasis he traced back to Jonathan Edwards and early monthly prayer meetings for missions. This same zealous spirit, he pointed out, dominated the missionary conferences on the field. He saw its logical outworking in such endeavours as the China Inland Mission and the Alliance Missions. Against this understanding of missionary obligation he discussed, not without criticism, Warneck's address before the Sixth Continental Missions Conference at Bremen in that same year. According to Ussing, the Anglo-American position, while practical, activistic, and somewhat superficial would probably be modified through the years. The Scandinavians, he believed, were treading a *via media*, espousing neither extreme, but appreciating the best in both.[105]

Kristiania, 1902. The sixth conference, meeting under the chairmanship of Christian Knudsen of Norway and attracting 748 members, gathered at Oslo from June 19 to 22, 1902. In addition to reports of Scandinavian societies' work, major discussion topics included what remained to be done in missionary expansion before the final judgment (Matthew 24:14) and what distinctive contribution the Scandinavian churches had to make to missions. On the latter subject, general opinion viewed the primary task as achieving an all-Lutheran unity rather than stressing a distinctive Scandinavian contribution. That being accepted, it was generally held that in missionary work the Lutheran churches provided a "deeper approach" than others, especially where conversion was concerned. The Lutheran contribution went into the foundation rather than into the superstructure. On relations between "mother" churches in the sending countries and "missionary" churches, almost all agreed that an independent, "self-supporting Evangelical church on a national foundation" was the ultimate aim. The national members of that church alone, however, could accomplish that end. When "maturity" had been reached, there could be no more "connection" between that new church and its parent than between the "mother" church and any other church in Christendom.[106]

The next meeting of the Northern Lutheran Missions Conference was to have been held in Copenhagen in 1906, but it never assembled. Political tension had been mounting between Norway and Sweden. Each had been questioning the good faith of the other. In 1905 the Union of the two countries was broken, and resultant feelings made the conference impossible. During World War I the tension subsided and the conferences were resumed again in Copenhagen in 1922 on a broader basis. "Lutheran" was dropped from the title, and they became simply the "Scandinavian Missionary Conferences."

The Continental Missions Conference

During the long years that no Scandinavian missionary conference met, an effectively organized body for international missionary cooperation grew up on the Continent. Its purpose differed greatly from that of the Northern Lutheran Missions Conferences, and its numerically small meetings reflected that difference. It represented the most important development in home-base missionary co-operation that had been seen to that time.

As early as 1842 Inspector Hartwig Brauer of the Bremen Mission had proposed a conference meeting every four or five years to which would come representatives from all the missionary societies of the Continent.[107] Later Dr. Friedrich Fabri, Inspector of the Rhenish Mission at Barmen, tried in vain to invite representatives from all Evangelical societies to join in a conference for practical discussion and the development of closer relations among one another. In 1866 Fabri tried again. This time he was eminently successful.

The First Conference, 1866. The Continental Missions Conference first met at Bremen during Ascension Week, May 8 to 11, 1866. In issuing invitations, Dr. Fabri distinguished between Anglo-American missions and those of Germany and Scandinavia. The latter grouping he regarded as homogeneous. The Paris Mission, however, he viewed as standing midway between the two, yet a proper body to invite to a predominantly Germanic gathering. When the conference assembled, more than thirty members were present from eight German societies,* and from societies in France, Holland, Denmark (represented by Dr. Christian Kalkar), Sweden, and Norway. The group was composed of experts, the secretaries of missions societies, and the report of their sessions indicates that each made a real contribution to the issues before the conference: the preparation of a missionary atlas and survey; the pattern to follow in establishing catechists' schools; the proper form in which to present the gospel in missionary work; the relationship between mission activities and commercial enterprises on the field; and finally, the spiritual and intellectual education of missionary candidates.[108]

The Second Conference, 1868. Dr. Franz Michael Zahn of Bremen had helped Fabri in initiating the first meeting, and he joined him again in preparing for the second Continental Missions Conference. Much like its predecessor and with nearly the same persons present for four days of discussion, it met from May 19 to 22, 1868. Neither Finland nor France was represented, but several missionaries home on furlough were invited as special guests. After consulting with each society, the two planners arranged the subjects of discussion. These give some insight into the purpose of the gathering. On the agenda were such topics as the nature of missionary interest and how to stimulate it, the extent to which respect should be shown for the former customs and habits of converts, and the effect of a heathen culture on missionary effort. Here was a small group of trained missions directors who were grappling earnestly with the questions before them for the good of all present and for the societies represented. The members of the conference agreed to publish the minutes of the last

---

* Basel is here regarded as German. Hermannsburg alone of the German societies was not represented.

two meetings and to reconvene two years later. To prepare for this meeting they appointed a committee made up of the directors of the Basel, Rhenish, and North German Societies.[109]

The Third Conference, 1872. The unsettled political situation had made it infeasible to meet as previously planned in 1870, but the third conference gathered from May 7 to 10, 1872. Like its predecessors, it was a small meeting, conducive to intimate fellowship and good discussion, with German, Danish, Dutch, Swedish, and Norwegian societies represented by their directors. On the agenda for discussion were: the exercise of authority by the elder missionary on the field, the preparation of catechumens, and the creation of independent national churches as the goal for Protestant missionary endeavour. Gustav Warneck, the great teacher and missionary statesman, attended the Continental Missions Conference for the first time in 1872. His colleagues elected him recording secretary, and from that day forward he exerted great and significant influence within the Conference. But to all assembled it was clear, and by them openly recognized, that Dr. Fabri had become the spiritual "Father" of the Conference. The establishment of a tradition by the convening of three meetings also had its effect. The Conference decided that its minutes should be printed for distribution, that it should meet every two (or at most three) years during Ascension Week, and that preparations should be entrusted to the secretaries of the Bremen and Barmen Societies who could work closely together. It would meet again, "naturally, in hospitable Bremen."[110]

The Fourth Conference, 1876. Like its predecessors, the Fourth Continental Missions Conference met in Bremen from May 23 to 26, 1876, with Dr. Fabri in the chair. Attendance was small, the Paris Mission having failed to respond to its invitation and the "Northern friends" regretting that they could not come. Among subjects considered were: the benefits resulting from a mission director's travels, the execution of Bible translation in a foreign mission setting, and the development of missions groups at the home base.[111]

The Fifth Conference, 1880. The Fifth Conference assembled from May 4 to 7, 1880, at Bremen with twelve representatives from Germany, Holland, and Sweden present. The three major questions to be considered were to come up repeatedly in the future: what Continental societies could learn from America and Britain in the theory and practice of missions, what obligation rested upon Continental societies to undertake medical missions, and what provision Continental societies must make so that missionaries could marry.* Finally, the Conference voted to continue its meetings every three or four years with no change in the time or place of assembly.

Over the years these conference sessions were having a cumulative effect. Directors of societies within Germany and from other countries were being drawn into close friendship. They were not only learning to know one another personally, they were also becoming keenly aware of one another's problems. The periods of worship conducted in each conference were richly rewarding in themselves. Moreover, the conclusion of the report of this meeting joyfully notes that the conferences were demonstrating the inner unity of Evangelical missions in Germany and on the Continent. Indeed, this very manifestation of unity was seen as their outstanding achievement. Dr. Fabri's early hope was being realized.[112]

The Sixth Conference, 1884. When the Continental Missions Conference met from May 20 to 23, 1884, Dr. Fabri, affectionately described as the "traditional president," was in the chair for what was to be the last time. Fourteen societies, including those of Germany, Denmark, Holland, Sweden, and Norway, were represented. The conference met at a time when German colonial expansion was assuming major proportions, and the subject of greatest urgency was the relation of this new political situation to missions. A concern of almost equal weight was the progress of the "heathen" (corresponding to the Anglo-American usage, "native") churches toward independence.[113]

The following year, 1885, saw established the representative *Ausschuss* or "Standing Committee" of German Protestant missions, representing all Germany's Protestant societies. This body, whose growth and influence we shall later trace, was henceforth entrusted with all preparations for the quadrennial Continental Missions Conference.

The Seventh Conference, 1889. The Ascension Week meeting of the "Bremen Conference," as it was sometimes called, afforded in 1889 an interesting glimpse into the growth of missionary co-operation on the Continent. In a somewhat wistful, apologetic statement, the

---

* The marriage of a woman trained and supported by one society to a man of another society posed a knotty problem of intersocietal *pro rata* financial adjustment. The same question also concerned the Foreign Missions Conference of North America in its early years.

conference report informs the reader that since Holland and Scandinavia now had their own missionary conferences (the latter referring to the resumption in 1885 at Gothenburg of what had begun at Mälmo in 1863), the Continental Conference no longer held such appeal for the societies of these regions. But the Conference had only itself to blame! After the Mälmo disruption, association in the Continental Missions Conferences very naturally helped to bring Scandinavian secretaries to realize the need for resuming their own meetings together. Now in 1889 in addition to the ten German societies represented at this meeting, only three Dutch and one Swedish society sent delegates.

The conference proceedings include many items of interest. For the first time Roman Catholic missions found a place on the agenda. Their "growing encroachment in Evangelical fields" was feared. Colonial expansion and German nationalism forced attention upon themselves. The German administrator of the Marshall Islands, to cite one example, had denied the long-established American Board the right to hire or lease property for churches, schools, or houses. That society's steamer, *Morning Star*, had also had levied against it a yearly license tax of 1,000 marks. The Continental Missions Conference investigated this situation and would probably have asked the German government to rescind its restrictions. But, upon discovering that the American Board was approaching the proper German authorities through the American minister in Berlin, the Conference agreed to do nothing, since the American Board was following the most effective course.

This 1889 conference also affords a glimpse into what Continental directors actually thought about Anglo-American missionary attitudes and conferences. The great Centenary Conference of 1888 with nearly 1,600 persons present had just been held in London. The Bremen report for 1889, however, opens with a modestly put statement that because of its own small size and comparatively meagre agenda, it could scarcely be compared with the London meeting. On the other hand, the report strongly emphasized the fact that while the Continental Conference could send out more invitations, it was designed for only a small group of specialists and did not seek to influence a broader constituency. Those who came together actually knew missions and could discuss "objectively, fundamentally, and from all sides" any issue relating to a particular mission. The Continental secretaries were further thankful that they did not indulge in the impassioned "rhetoric" that characterized the London meeting, that took so much time, and that did so much harm. Bremen in contrast was characterized by "thoroughness, objectivity, peace, understanding, and unity."

One of the members regretted that Continental delegates had been treated like "step-children" at London. They were ignored, he thought, because the English-speaking people had no conception of the work of Continental missions. He further proposed that some member of the Bremen gathering prepare an adequate history of the Continental Missions Conference to submit to an English-language magazine, preferably *The Missionary Review of the World* published in New York. He also suggested preparing a pamphlet, "Hints to the Next Evangelical International Missionary Conference," to be sent to all English and American societies.[114] Such critical reactions as these to the large Anglo-American conferences were not atypical, did not subside, and are to be seen even more clearly in Continental—especially German—reluctance to attend the New York Conference of 1900.

The Eighth Conference, 1893. The Continental Missions Conference met next at Bremen May 9, 10 and 12, 1893, with twenty-six representatives, plus a few guests, from sixteen societies of Germany, Holland, and Denmark. A major item of business was Gustav Warneck's long report on the activities of the German *Ausschuss*. Topics discussed included: Roman missions in German Protectorates; several that reflected the impact of German imperialism on missions; and, among others, one on gaining proper and adequate coverage in the press for missions. All were delighted with the great sense of good feeling engendered by the meeting, the unity they had experienced with one another, and the expectation with which they looked forward to their next assembly.[115]

The Ninth Conference, 1897. The meeting at Bremen on May 25, 26, and 28, 1897, was the largest yet held, with more than forty present. Members attended from Germany, Holland, France, Denmark, Norway, Sweden, and Finland. From this time forward, conference delegates were numbered in the fifties and sixties rather than in the twenties. During a special session of the conference, German delegates met by themselves for a consideration of affairs relating to the *Ausschuss*. When the whole conference reassembled, it discussed such problems as the aggressive nature of Roman Catholic missions and the organization of women's missions. A long, critical paper by

Gustav Warneck severely attacking the watchword of the Student Volunteer Movement, "The evangelization of the world in this generation," precipitated considerable debate.

German reluctance to participate in the New York Ecumenical Missionary Conference of 1900 casts another instructive side-light. Warneck himself had no desire to attend. Yet, he believed, such a conference, dominated by the "world-evangelization theory" as it was advanced by the editor of *The Missionary Review of the World*, Dr. A. T. Pierson, stood sorely in need of more sober German words on the subject. Moreover, he was appalled by the scope of the program. Such an "encyclopedia of missions," he maintained, could never be encompassed in the limited time available. Others expressed their certainty that Continental representatives would be pigeon-holed and scarcely listened to. Even allowing for a good hearing, it was generally admitted that few of them could adequately express themselves in English. The atmosphere was one of resigned futility. The New York Conference was viewed as being a useless affair. That some one had to represent German societies, however, was reluctantly accepted. No one was eager to go, but Dr. Schreiber, having been to the two previous London conferences, ventured the happy thought that at least one could make new friends if he went. As it turned out, he and Dr. A. Merensky were sent.[116]

The Tenth Conference, 1901. There is little to mark this meeting of May 14, 15, and 17, 1901, apart from its predecessors. It was well attended with representatives from all the previously participating countries, except Sweden. The competition of Roman Catholic missions and their "growing danger and prevention" occupied, as it had since first introduced in 1889, a prominent place on the agenda. For the first time the Conference made an official proclamation, "To Protestant Christians of the German Tongue." At the special meeting of the *Ausschuss*, Warneck retired as its secretary, and Merensky succeeded him.[117]

The Eleventh Conference, 1905. By 1905 the agenda to be covered by the Continental Missions Conference had grown to such proportions that a five-day meeting, from May 29 to June 2, was necessary. Denmark, Sweden, Norway, Finland, Holland, Switzerland, France, and Germany were all represented. Dr. Merensky reported for the *Ausschuss*, and a growing number of subjects were covered in discussion.[118]

The Twelfth Conference, 1909. The Twelfth Continental Missions Conference met at Bremen from May 6 to 10, 1909. Edinburgh, 1910, was just one year away. Hence, in addition to the usual reports and discussions, the meeting heard Dr. Julius Richter describe the preparations for the World Missionary Conference. Because of its more "scientific" nature and because of its more adequate inclusion of Continental thought and suggestions, Edinburgh claimed a more favourable Continental response than any conference before it.

The Continental Missions Conference had achieved a status commanding the honour and respect of all the missionary societies that it touched. It had a tradition, but many had come to believe that if its position were to be preserved, the Continental Conference needed a constitution to codify what had already become practice and to establish rules for the future. What criteria for membership did it have? How did a society join? How beneficial would a constitution be in view of the prospective closer co-operation with British and American societies? These were the questions faced at Bremen in 1909.

Dr. August Schreiber, speaking for the North German Missionary Society, presented a constitution to the Conference. Explicitly envisaged was a "free association of the missions societies of the European continent," manifesting and fostering their unity and standing for the whole "apostolic Gospel of Jesus Christ" as contained in the Holy Bible. The Conference would consist of a committee, charged with responsibility for the Conference and for implementing its decisions, and an assembly, not a "missions congress" but a "working conference of mission leaders and distinguished mission experts." The Conference budget would come from gifts, profits from publications, and apportionments from the societies relative to their voting strength (one vote for each fifty active European workers).

The German *Ausschuss* advanced several amendments. The tentative constitution was then discussed, but it failed to reach a vote. Although reluctant to vote a constitution, the Conference recognized its need for and created a standing committee to care for all its interests during the four years between meetings. That body, executing the work of the Conference, was composed of the German *Ausschuss*, plus one representative from each of the non-German countries in the Continental Missions Conference. August Schreiber was made its secretary.[119]

The Standing Committee of German Protestant Missions
(Der Ausschuss der deutschen evangelischen Missionen)

Gustav Warneck. To speak of missionary co-operation in Germany one must inevitably point to Gustav Warneck. In 1862 he had entered his first assistant-pastorate and formed a close friendship with Reinhold Grundemann, a neighbouring assistant pastor, later to become famous for his missions atlases. Warneck's growing enthusiasm for missions caught the attention of Dr. Fabri in Barmen who attracted the young pastor into the service of the Rhenish Society. While working for the Rhenish Mission in 1873, Warneck founded the scholarly *Allgemeine Missions Zeitschrift*, the nineteenth century's nearest approach to *The International Review of Missions*. Through the years it became a veritable encyclopedia of missions. Ill health forced Warneck's early retirement from his strenuous work with the Rhenish Mission; so, in 1874, expecting to reduce his load of work, he went to a village near Halle and served there for twenty-two years as a pastor. During that time he gave pre-eminent leadership to German missions and unstinting labour for the Continental Missions Conference.[120] A prolific writer, Warneck is best remembered for his two great works: *A History of Protestant Missions* and *The Theory of Missions*. The wasted resources and the results of unnecessary multiplication among missionary societies constantly nettled him. A man of great vision, he thought always in terms of grand strategy. Understandable, then, was his London Conference proposal in 1888 for an organization essentially like that of today's International Missionary Council. One of Warneck's major contributions to the co-operative movement among German missions was the impetus he gave it through founding area conferences.

The Missions Conference. German missionary societies, unlike most of those in the United States, were and are independent of the churches. They solicit funds and appoint missionaries. To facilitate their work these societies formed local "associations," drawing together from several congregations supporting members with a common interest in a particular society. Inherent in this arrangement lay an obvious danger: the contributor to missions was likely to focus his attention exclusively on one society and one field of work, forgetting missions' world-outreach. To overcome this situation, Warneck conceived a plan to broaden missionary thinking and to increase interest among all congregations. To carry it out he began in 1879 his first missionary conference at Halle. Its good effects were so obvious that the idea spread quickly. Annual missions conferences were soon being held in many of Germany's provinces.

Owing its inspiration to Warneck, the Saxony Conference, continuing to this day, has served as a model for all others. With annual two- or three-day sessions, the conference has brought before its members prominent missionaries and missions specialists, presenting to the audience of pastors and laymen missionary subjects of special interest and relevance. The influence of the conferences has been far-reaching. They have educated pastors and laymen in missions. Because of the interest they arouse, with resulting excellent press coverage, they have made missions known to those who would otherwise never hear of them. They have stimulated whole congregations to their missionary responsibility. This in turn has spurred pastors to direct greater attention to missions as an integral part of the churches' life. Finally, they have provided an ecumenical approach to missions, and by bringing together from different churches the supporters of several societies and in helping them to see the extent and responsibility of their *common* task, they have furthered the development of increasing missionary co-operation in Germany.[121]

In 1906 the various regional conferences united in the "General Association of Missions Conferences," a federation whose executive committee sponsored triennially a Missions Week (*Missionswoche*) at Herrnhut to consider important missionary questions. World War II made it impossible to convene the Missions Week, but in 1939 some 13,000 members of the twenty-six provincial conferences were receiving the *Yearbook of the United German Mission Conferences*.[122]

The early provincial conferences gave a tremendous impetus to greater missionary co-operation at higher levels. Lutherans, Reformed, Moravians, and others packed the largest churches when these conferences assembled. Topics were always considered interdenominationally. This approach stirred a consciousness of the common mission of the churches at the grass-roots level. Thus, understanding and appreciating one another's work, local constituencies of the different missions societies experienced a "practical" or working (rather than a theological) unity. By providing an effective example of actual interdenominational and intersocietal co-operation, these meetings, begun by Warneck, facilitated general missionary co-operation in Germany.

The Emergence of the Ausschuss. In the Continental Missions Conference, leaders of the German societies had come to know one another well. In seeking answers to common questions, they had themselves developed a practical unity which required no definition of theological consensus. From 1868 to 1884 preparations for successive quadrennial sessions were entrusted to a small committee of German secretaries. When, after 1885, German societies discovered how imperative was a united front with a single representative voice, they had already had valuable experience in working together in the Continental Conference. It seemed a natural step, in effect, simply to enlarge the small committee that had prepared for the Continental Conference to include representatives from all German societies and to let that body, speaking with one voice, represent all.

Bismarck had united Germany and in 1871 crowned William I of Prussia as its Emperor. By 1879 German business organizations had begun to acquire privileges and concessions in the islands of the Pacific and shortly thereafter in Africa. By 1884-85 Bismarck managed to have the *Reichstag* approve formal protectorates over these far-flung territories. By 1890 the process had advanced to the point of transforming protectorates into crown colonies. Germany now possessed a colonial empire, and its appetite was whetted with each new acquisition. Increasingly, difficulties arose between the government and the missionary societies. It was obvious to missionary administrators that to be effective in dealing with the Colonial Office, the societies required a single, powerful voice.

As a result of this situation, Germany's missionary societies convened a large, special meeting at Bremen in 1885. Before that gathering Gustav Warneck proposed the establishment of a "Missions-Alliance" (*Missionsbund*) to handle common problems that confronted all societies. However, too many feared the powers that might be delegated to an alliance and, jealously independent, wanted something less binding. When a representative "standing committee" (*Ausschuss*) was proposed, it gained general acceptance and was immediately established to represent the common interests of German missionary societies, especially in their relations with colonial governments. It was to proceed on all missionary questions of current importance without interfering in the internal affairs of the missions societies themselves. The *Ausschuss* was thus regarded as no more than a free body to serve for the common good. To it were appointed three members—Doctors Fabri, Warneck, and Zahn.[123]

Again in 1890 at Halle the German societies convened in a special, large meeting. The government and the Prussian Church Council (*Oberkirchenrats*) had given orders that interfered with, and complicated the work of, the missionary societies. As a result, the *Ausschuss* was enlarged and given, without any formalization in writing, increased power to meet this new situation.[124]

By 1897 the work of the *Ausschuss* had become so formidable that a constitution became essential to its continuing effectiveness. The constitution was granted and the body became known officially as the Standing Committee of the German Protestant Missionary Societies (*Der Ausschuss der deutschen evangelischen Missionsgellschaften*). Five members of the Committee represented the fourteen German societies whose various confessional loyalties were four: Lutheran, Reformed, Moravian, and Union State Church. Entrusted to the *Ausschuss* was the right to recommend major policy on matters affecting all societies. Among these were relations between missions societies and German churches, between the societies and the German government, and between the Protestant societies and the missions of the Roman Catholic Church. It had also to provide the government with all necessary information it demanded and to communicate to the societies at once all important government actions. Recognition of the *Ausschuss'* authority remained for the societies purely "a voluntary act." Yet each assumed an equal share of its expenses.[125] In 1909 the constitution was revised, the name being modified to *Der Ausschuss der deutschen evangelischen Missionen* and the number of representatives increased from five to seven.[126]

The Work of the Ausschuss. While the *Ausschuss* did in fact, serve as the representative body for missions societies with four confessional allegiances, the predominant cast of German missions was and is Lutheran. That fact greatly facilitated close co-operation. While the *Ausschuss* had no authority whatsoever to enforce its decisions, its recommendations carried increasing weight with member societies. It was they who had to ratify in practice any suggestion made by the *Ausschuss*. Indeed, the only authority the *Ausschuss* had was the confidence increasingly placed in it as the judicious wisdom of its counsel commended itself to its member societies.

When first established, the *Ausschuss* served primarily as an agency to negotiate with the government. Its members worked diligently at this task. It averted the drafting of German missionaries for military service in the Protectorates. It opposed the government's program to deport criminals to the colonies because of the effect on those reached by missions there. It staunchly opposed the liquor trade as it was handled in Africa. And it defeated a plan of government schools in East Africa to hire certain Mohammedans as teachers with the expectation that such action might quiet some vocal Mohammedan dissatisfaction with German rule.[127]

With national and colonial feeling running high, in certain quarters use of the slogan "Only German missionaries for German colonies" was, perhaps, inevitable. The *Ausschuss* managed to defeat the spread of such an attitude. It also frequently negotiated directly with the government on behalf of missionaries from other countries working within spheres of German influence. The best illustration was that of the American Board in the Marshall Islands. The German government proposed that those missionaries then in the Marshalls be supplanted by German missionaries. The *Ausschuss* waited until the American Board appealed to the German government through the American minister, and then used the full weight of its influence on behalf of the American Board. Still later the *Ausschuss* obtained some German missionaries to work under the American Board in the Marshalls to meet the demands of the German government. That the government respected the work of the *Ausschuss* is seen from the fact that in the summer of 1903 it placed one of the members of the *Ausschuss*, a Moravian, on the Colonial Council of the government.[128]

The work of the *Ausschuss* was not all confined to relations with the government. When the evangelization of German East Africa became an issue, the *Ausschuss* divided territory among the societies willing to work there so that all overlapping and competition was avoided. It also served as a board of mediation for knotty problems that arose between societies at the home base. Undoubtedly the *Ausschuss* gained much for German missions that could never have been achieved otherwise. It also strengthened immeasurably the bonds of unity among the German societies.

The *Ausschuss*, however, unlike the provincial missionary conferences or the *Missionswoche*, claimed little public attention and was known only to the directors of missions societies and the Colonial

Office of the government. Yet, in Germany and beyond, its influence was far-reaching.[129] Indeed, the *Ausschuss* stands as the prototype for the Committee of Reference and Counsel of the Foreign Missions Conference of North America, for the Standing Committee of the Conference of Missionary Societies of Great Britain and Ireland, and for all similar bodies.

The General Dutch Missionary Conference

The General Dutch Missionary Conference (*Algemeene Neder-landsche Zendings-Conferentie*) met for the first time in Holland in 1887. Organized by the leaders of the missionary societies, this annual gathering was begun for all persons interested in missions. Meeting for one day each year in September or October, this national and interdenominational assembly usually convened in one of the great churches of Amsterdam or of some other large city. The Minister of Colonies usually attended, and those who came listened to addresses and papers on Dutch missionary work, most of which centred in the East Indies.[130]

A small committee of representatives from the different missionary societies and organizations prepared for the annual meeting.[131] E. Cêsar Segers from the Central Committee for the Seminary at Depok served as the first chairman of this interim group, and P. Van Wijk, Jr., a Lutheran, was its first secretary. Van Wijk also edited the *Nederlandsch Zendingstijdschrift*, published regularly from 1889 as an enterprise of the committee of the annual conference.

The yearly assemblies served much the same purpose as those of the Northern Missionary Conference for the education and inspiration of a wide constituency. However, the interim committee brought missionary executives together in close fellowship and on occasion was able to prepare for and bring about common action by the missionary societies.[132] Despite the measure of co-operation gained through this rather informal committee, the Dutch did not establish a missionary council until 1929, although in the meantime they had various instruments of co-operation through which they were linked with the larger sphere of international missionary co-operation.

The General Missionary Conference in Holland was preceded seven years earlier by the Netherlands Indies Missionary Conference held at the seminary in Depok, Java. In 1882 the Netherlands Indies Missionary Alliance emerged to prepare for the biennial Conference and to further mutual contact through the discussion and consideration of common problems by those at work in the area.[133]

The Foreign Missions Conference of North America*

What with the London Secretaries' Association, the Northern Lutheran Missionary Conference, the Continental Missions Conference, the German *Ausschuss*, and the Netherlands Missionary Conference, it appears rather striking that board secretaries in America did not establish some means for mutual counsel and conversation until 1893. Moreover, when they met, they did not intend to create what later came to be known as the Foreign Missions Conference of North America.

Origin. Prime mover for the Foreign Missions Conference was the Fifth General Council of the Alliance of the Reformed Churches holding the Presbyterian System, assembled at Toronto in 1892. That body, through Dr. Frank F. Ellinwood, Chairman of its Committee on Cooperation in Foreign Missions, recommended that the missionary boards of the Western Section of the Alliance should come together in conference. There they should seek for greater unity in their work, *and*, it was suggested, during one day of their sessions they should invite a broader group of representatives from the missionary societies of other Protestant churches. The date set for the enlarged gathering was January 12, 1893, in New York. Except for two oversights, invitations went to all Protestant boards in the United States and Canada to attend the January 12 session. When that meeting assembled, it kindled a spark, and the spark produced a flame.[134]

That January day in 1893, representatives from twenty-three missionary societies (including such diverse groups as the Episcopal Church, the Southern Baptist Convention, the China Inland Mission, the American Bible Society, and the International Committee of the Young Men's Christian Association) met together in the Presbyterian Mission House during the morning and afternoon. They read papers, discussed them, and were much pleased with the exchange of

---

* In November, 1950, this body became the Division of Foreign Missions of the National Council of the Churches of Christ in the U.S.A.

information and the fellowship. Among those present were three lay-men, each of whom was to play a rôle of great importance in the fu-ture of missionary co-operation: William Henry Grant, Robert E. Speer, and John R. Mott. The group regarded itself as quite informal, but recommended that another similar meeting be arranged a year later for "representatives of the various Mission boards where questions touching methods of work and kindred subjects may be more fully discussed, and the results of experience in the different boards may be made available to all." Through Dr. Ellinwood's courtesy, the "minutes" of the first meeting were published.[135]

Growth. The "Second Conference of the Officers and Representa-tives of Foreign Mission Boards and Societies in the United States and Canada" (a rather unwieldy name) met in New York January 17, 1894. Fewer societies (nineteen) were represented than in the first meet-ing, but the Universalists had been added to the list of those present. In contrast with the sixty-eight who had attended the previous year, only forty-six were now present. One notices a similarity and yet an "American" difference when comparing the subjects discussed at these conferences with those in Europe. For example, one topic covered "The Practical Provisions for Missionaries in Regard to Stipends, Out-fits, Houses, Furloughs, etc." Among others were the development of self-supporting churches and the recruiting of candidates of the highest qualifications for missionary service. The second meeting dupli-cated the first with papers followed by discussion and produced the same hearty enthusiasm for this kind of intercourse and sharing. Those present agreed to meet again in another year and appointed a com-mittee of four to make the necessary arrangements. W. Henry Grant of the Presbyterian Board was entrusted with editing the conference report.[136]

In 1895 the conference met again in New York with twenty societies represented. The Sino-Japanese War then in progress brought dis-cussion of its bearing on missions. Other topics included the develop-ment of industrial missions in foreign lands and the attitude of home boards toward the proposed National Church in India. W. Henry Grant was made the "between sessions" secretary for the conference.[137] Those present in 1895 sensed that the meetings had so justified them-selves that their future was assured. Yet, if this annual conference were to become a regular institution, it required work; so three com-mittees were set up: one on arrangements, one on editing the report, and one to study self-support in mission churches. By 1896 the three committees had become nine. One of them was established to study and make recommendations on Chinese indemnities and another, which continued for five years, was charged with the responsibility for a possible "Ecumenical Missionary Conference" to be held sometime within four years.[138] The work of this group, of course, resulted in the famous New York Conference of 1900.

In 1897 the conference created a "Committee of General Reference," consisting of seven members ". . . to whom shall be referred the Relations of Governments to Missions . . . problems of Comity . . . [and] such other matters as the Conference may commit to them." Such a body might well have become an important agency, but it made only one report in 1898. Since nothing had been referred to it, it was dissolved.[139] By 1897 "The Annual Conference of the Foreign Mission Boards" had reasonably well established itself, yet it had no defined membership. No society was obliged to attend its meetings. Each year the question was raised anew whether to meet again, and just as regularly a favourable motion was carried unanimously. There was no creedal statement nor constitution, no legislation nor binding action, and no continuing, functioning body of officers. The annual gatherings were quite unofficial and represented the desire of Christian men—missionary administrators—to counsel together on common problems. Resolutions on practical questions of missionary policy were passed, but they represented only personal opinions, recommendations of informed and responsible missions specialists to the missionary societies. Increasingly, however, boards heeded the resolutions and suggestions of this unofficial group.[140]

By 1898 the conference had grown so large that some criteria for membership became essential. A brief two paragraph "constitution" resulted, but it was simply a rule for membership. In it the conference proposed to consider only administrative questions pertaining to foreign missions. Membership, therefore, was confined to executive officers and members of foreign missionary boards and societies in the United States and Canada. In addition to sending its executive officers, each board could elect two representatives. All others, including missionaries on furlough, could be elected by the conference itself as corresponding members.[141] The sessions in 1899 were largely devoted to preparations for the Ecumenical Missionary Conference of 1900,[142] and in the year that great assembly met no special session of the Annual Conference of the Foreign Mission Boards was convened.

In 1901 the identical "constitution" that had appeared in 1898 was reprinted, and served as the only body of rules for the Conference until 1911. With the 1900 conference discussions on comity and the post-conference proposal for an international committee, comity and co-operation rather naturally occupied a major place on the 1901 agenda. Indeed, the Reverend Paul de Schweinitz of the Moravian Board (its international headquarters in Berlin gave him a knowledge of German affairs that none of the others had) offered an important bit of intelligence. The *Ausschuss*, assuming that after the 1900 Conference the American societies might create a body similar to itself, was prepared "to appoint a member at once to co-operate with any [such American] committee." De Schweinitz added, "I have the names to present just as soon as such an organization is perfected."[143] Had this resulted, it would have been the first step toward an international missionary committee.

The Influence of the Ausschuss. The permanent body that de Schweinitz was hoping for received no attention in the 1902[144] and 1903[145] meetings. Yet another issue was settled. The question was raised in 1902 whether these annual meetings should be continued. The next year the matter was settled permanently: meetings would convene annually until the conference by vote ordered otherwise.[146]

In 1904 the whole subject of a permanent committee to represent the missionary boards was reopened. De Schweinitz read a paper outlining in detail the work of the *Ausschuss*. He translated its constitution into English and described the benefits that it had brought to German societies. Then he urged that North American societies take the same course that had proved so helpful in Germany. The speaker who followed him pointed to the board of arbitration set up by the Madras Conference in 1902. The societies at home, he argued, also needed a board of reference for problems of comity and particularly in relationships with government. A committee on reference and arbitration with seven members was appointed to study the situation and to poll the boards for their official opinions on the creation of such a permanent committee.[147]

Many studied the *Ausschuss* carefully with its twenty-year history of notable accomplishment. John R. Mott, for one, saw in it an effective forward step in missionary co-operation.[148] Moreover, situations that had arisen from the Boxer Rebellion and that were arising from the Russo-Japanese War forced frank recognition that a standing committee was imperative to act and speak unitedly for all the missionary boards. From its inception this annual conference had been discussing problems of comity and co-operation. Communications on several occasions had been sent to the American and Canadian governments. Yet never had its members been able to bring themselves to establish a permanent committee with representative authority to speak unitedly for the boards themselves. In 1905[149] and 1906[150] the committee that had been appointed to pursue the question reported to the conference. A thorough process of education and consultation had been carried out. Although some were eager to establish a standing committee at once, the majority hesitated to take so important a step without first having the full confidence and conviction of the boards behind such action.

The Committee of Reference and Counsel. In 1907 the Conference of the Foreign Mission Boards in the United States and Canada considered a proposal for a "Committee On [later "Of"] Reference and Counsel." The recommendation represented three years of earnest work and was presented admirably by Dr. Arthur J. Brown. His introduction included example after example drawn from the three years just past, a period in which such a committee could have functioned to the benefit of the whole North American missionary enterprise. The lack of such an agency meant that Christian missions had suffered irreparable harm both at home and abroad. He further explained that forty boards had been polled, and that out of the forty replies, only four had actually opposed the plan. Favourable sentiment was so overwhelming that the committee had come to the belief that "this movement toward closer cooperation is in harmony with the leadings of the Spirit of God."

The proposal was adopted. The new Committee On Reference and Counsel consisted of nine members and would consider any question that a board might refer to it. Its general field, however, was thought primarily to include unoccupied areas, negotiations with governments, arbitration for problems of field comity, and the initiation of action in emergency situations not involving policy on which fundamental disagreement among the boards was likely.

The new committee's authority and limitation were clearly defined. It had no right "to interfere in any way in the internal administration of any Board or Society." It could act as arbiter only in cases referred to it. Its decisions would be received only as advice given or judgement expressed and were not binding. In any event, recognition of the committee's authority was to "remain a voluntary act." The Committee on Reference and Counsel was, then, obviously patterned on the *Ausschuss*. Whether consciously or unconsciously planned, its constitution repeated verbatim wording from the constitution of the *Ausschuss* on the all-important matter of authority.[151]

The permanent Committee On Reference and Counsel served as the *ad interim* representative of the annual conferences. Its only authority, which was not binding, derived from the fact that it represented the best wisdom of the mission boards themselves. While this was the only authority independent missionary bodies would recognize, its effectiveness grew steadily. Year after year the accumulated weight of judicious counsel commanded respect and exerted growing influence.

Summary Observations

Several points have emerged in this brief survey that may be well to recall. First of all, one is impressed with the jealously guarded independence of the missionary societies. In the London Secretaries' Association any proposal to invest representative authority in one man or in the body as a whole was resoundingly defeated. The thought that a common board of strategy might limit the full freedom of a missionary society helped to wreck the Mälmo proposals and served to keep any similar schemes out of future Northern Lutheran Missionary Conferences. While the Continental Missions Conference allowed the German *Ausschuss* after 1885 to make arrangements for its quadrennial meetings, its strictly informal nature was a highly prized possession. In 1909, although a committee was appointed to handle interim business for the conference, the attempt to adopt a constitution was put off until the next meeting. Indeed, even the German societies, which led the world in establishing a representative missions committee, carefully limited the *Ausschuss'* powers and made acceptance of its judgments purely voluntary. In North America, where since 1893 representatives of the boards had been meeting together in sessions similar to those of the Continental Missions Conference, it was not until 1907, after a thorough three-year study and with the precedent of the twenty-two-year-old German model, that the boards created a permanent Committee of Reference and Counsel, limited with restrictions identical to those governing the *Ausschuss*. It is clear that as much as their representatives appreciated fellowship and counsel with one another in conference, every missionary society feared to delegate any authority that could conceivably limit its own autonomy.

Second, one needs to remind oneself again of the impetus and leadership, long disregarded by English-speaking peoples, given to missionary co-operation by European societies. In that contribution one also sees, in turn, the influence of the Evangelical Alliance, particularly in Scandinavia through such men as Christian Kalkar and Jens Vahl. While it is true that the London Secretaries' Association had been meeting since 1819, that group preferred anonymity and never met for more than one evening a month through the winter. Its discussions were never published, and its actual influence was severely limited. Scandinavian conferences were entirely different. Large public affairs, they were meant to educate a constituency and to promote interest among pastors and laymen in missions. Meeting regularly every four or five years, they achieved an ecumenical end not met by national, denominational, or societal gatherings in Britain and America. On a much smaller scale the General Dutch Missionary Conference accomplished results similar to those of the Northern Lutheran Missionary Conference. Certainly, the Continental Missions Conference with its small group of specialists, meeting regularly after 1866 and representing different confessions and nations, was for many years unique. It approached the whole problem of missions "scientifically," as it liked to describe it, and actually laid the foundations for the so-called "science of missions." Its printed *Proceedings* were strongly influential in missionary circles. In it Gustav Warneck gained the early schooling in co-operative endeavour that helped him to initiate the German *Ausschuss*. Here, too, no doubt, he early got the insight that led him in 1888 to urge the creation of an international body for missionary co-operation. Moreover, the *Ausschuss* alone for more than two decades pointed the way to what has come to be recognized as absolutely essential at the home base of missions. In part directly, but more especially through the North American Committee of Reference and Counsel of the Foreign Missions Conference of North America modelled on it, it became normative for the standing committees of co-operative missionary agencies in the sending countries.

Finally, one's attention is arrested by the fact that missionary societies, forced to speak unitedly to governments, reached a level of representative co-operation which their independence might otherwise have delayed for years. On the several occasions when the London Secretaries' Association appointed a temporary secretary with power to act, it did so because to be effective the London societies had to speak with one voice to some government representative or agency. Clearly, what brought the *Ausschuss* into being were the problems—foreign and domestic—occasioned by colonial expansion and the pressures of one kind and another brought to bear by the government. Demands for information or the imposition of restrictions—these made imperative one body to represent or act for all the missionary societies. In the case of the Committee of Reference and Counsel in North America, circumstances arising from the Boxer Rebellion, from the Russo-Japanese War, and from representatives of foreign governments to American missions in general gave the greatest impetus to the creation of the new body. Political pressures hastened the representative co-operation that missionary societies shied away from. It was a pattern which, as we shall see, was to be repeated in the future.

The Growth of the Student Movement

We have surveyed three of the tributary streams that contributed through the nineteenth century to the emergence of Edinburgh, 1910, and the International Missionary Council. The last and most important was the rise of the Student Christian Movement, nationally and internationally. Both Dr. John R. Mott and Dr. J. H. Oldham insist that the *real* story behind the growth of international missionary co-operation was not the preceding missionary conferences but the development of the international Student Christian Movement.[152]

In characteristic fashion, Dr. Mott terms the Student Volunteer Movement and the World's Student Christian Federation "practice games in weaving together the nations and communions"—practice games in that they prepared Mott and others for the broad international and interdenominational thinking and planning without which Edinburgh, 1910, and the International Missionary Council would have been impossible.[153] We must look briefly, then, at the Student Christian Movement as that title is broadly used to refer to the American Intercollegiate Young Men's Christian Association, the Student Christian Movement and the Student Volunteer Movement in various countries, and the World's Student Christian Federation.

The great drive and organizing genius for the Student Movement came from the United States and Great Britain. Stimuli shot from one country to the other and returned again in new form. Yet it is probably accurate to say that the religious awakening among American students first influenced those in Great Britain. After that initial stimulus distinction between cause and effect becomes difficult. However, the first national Student Christian Movement was launched in the United States, and it was largely through an American, John R. Mott, that the World's Student Christian Federation was conceived and brought into being.[154]

The Intercollegiate Young Men's Christian Association

The Young Men's Christian Association began in England. Then a letter from an American student studying in Great Britain, which described the Association's work there, led to the founding in Boston in 1851 of the first Young Men's Christian Association in the United States.[155] What were probably the first college Associations were formed seven years later at the Universities of Michigan and Virginia. Within two decades, nearly forty Associations had been formed within American colleges.[156]

Among Princeton students in 1875-76 there arose a religious revival. One of the movement's leaders, Luther D. Wishard, realized the benefits to both the Young Men's Christian Association and his college Christian society if the two could be linked, each strengthening the other. At his instance the Princeton society corresponded with other college groups, urging an intercollegiate Young Men's Christian Association. The new idea took form, and in 1877 the YMCA's Louisville Convention passed favourably upon the request from twenty-five students, representing as many colleges, for an intercollegiate organization. It also made Luther D. Wishard Secretary for the Colleges in 1877-78. His task?—to help college Christian Associations band together and share their experiences and to encourage and stimulate their endeavours. Wishard, first of the student secretaries now so familiar, began his work, and the Intercollegiate Movement in the United States was under way.[157]

From the first the Intercollegiate Movement was an integral part of the YMCA's larger outreach, and from the outset its work flourished. In 1880, three years after Louisville, there were ninety-six college Associations, and by 1884 there were 181, only thirty-one of which had existed before the Intercollegiate Movement began in 1877.[158] With a new, popular approach to students' religious needs, the Movement mushroomed. Its ideas and drive came from students themselves—another powerful factor in its success. Interdenominational, and organized intercollegiately on a national scale, it projected for students a total religious program—personal and social, local and international. Its hallmarks were clear: worship, Bible study, and effective personal evangelism. After only a decade, it watched campus Association buildings going up in many places, and often with a full-time secretary for the work.

The Movement's first conferences were special student-sessions at the YMCA's international conventions. Increasingly, however, because of their own particular problems and interests, students began holding their conferences separately. By 1885 these distinct conferences, exclusively for students, had become permanent in the Intercollegiate Movement. Among the colleges, they represented the very heart of the movement.[159]

The Interseminary Missionary Alliance

The Interseminary Missionary Alliance (now the Interseminary Movement in the United States)[160] marked another branch of the Student Movement. It sprang from a Princeton Seminary student's concern for a missionary awakening among his fellows. Robert Mateer —the student, who was preparing for China—with Wishard had been at Louisville when the Intercollegiate Movement was born. Watching its effective outreach, Mateer came to believe that a similar, although exclusively missionary, organization for the seminaries could wield tremendous influence.

Mateer's initial efforts led to the convening at New Brunswick, New Jersey, in 1880 of the first meeting of the Interseminary Missionary

Alliance. Some 250 students from thirty-two seminaries attended this "First national meeting of students, whether from colleges or seminaries, *centering wholly upon the home and foreign missionary obligations of the Church and of the schools and colleges.*"[161] The meeting not only quickened missionary concern among theological students, it also influenced Wishard, who was present, and through him the whole of the Student Movement.[162] From that time on Christian missions became a paramount feature in the Student Movement.

The Alliance's annual conventions continued for some years, growing in size and influence until the Student Volunteer Movement found its strength after 1886. The latter undercut the real *raison d'être* for the Interseminary Missionary Alliance. But the Alliance, having prepared the ground for the Mount Hermon awakening in 1886, had been the Student Volunteer Movement's forerunner.[163] In 1898 in order to recognize its close tie with the Student Volunteer Movement, to enter more fully into the Student Movement as a whole, and to gain membership in the newly formed World's Student Christian Federation, the Alliance formally disbanded and at once re-formed as the Theological Section of the YMCA. Robert Wilder, a Student Volunteer Movement pioneer, became its first national secretary under the new organization.[164]

Developments in Britain

The history of the Student Christian Movement in England has already been done well and in detail.[165] Yet our story requires the retelling of certain of its high points. At a time when there were only scattered and unrelated British student Christian groups, tremendous impetus for what was to be came from an American. He was evangelist Dwight L. Moody, who, though lacking university training, appealed to and won hundreds of students. Moody's life forms another link in the chain that runs from the Evangelical Awakening, through the Student Movement, to the International Missionary Council.[166]

For years Moody had been prominent in the American YMCA when in 1873 on the invitation of a few English friends, he went with his song leader, Ira Sankey, to Britain. Unknown, they met with severe reserve—if not outright opposition. But the radiance and force of their lives so multiplied their work that when they went to Scotland, they became within six months "the strongest religious force in the country," stirring people "as they had not been since the days of Wesley and Whitefield."[167] Edinburgh students attended Moody's meetings in droves. One of these, Henry Drummond, was won so completely that he became, on Moody's urging, the latter's lieutenant in Scotland. Moody's direct effect upon students was great. But through the cultured and keen Drummond, he exercised incalculable influence on the whole Student Movement in Britain and America.[168]

Nearly a decade later Moody was in Britain again. This time the most notable outcome of his visit was the decision of C. T. Studd and Stanley Smith at Cambridge in 1882 to go as missionaries to China. These two widely known athletes were soon joined by five others, each of whom dedicated his life to missions. The effect in British student circles was electric. "The Cambridge Seven," as these athletes were known, spoke widely and stirred student religious life wherever they went. For a decade after their visit to Edinburgh, Henry Drummond, the strongest, most influential student evangelist Britain has known,[169] kept hot the fires they had kindled.

One further reference to the Cambridge Seven is in order. During the winter of 1885-86, J. E. K. Studd, a member of that group, travelled among American universities. His words at Cornell, "Seekest thou great things for thyself? Seek them not. Seek ye first the Kingdom of God," went straight to the heart of a young freshman just elected vice-president of the Cornell YMCA—John R. Mott. They resulted in the "great surrender to Christ as Lord" and a decision for life-investment. Mott's decision came in a moment, but only after months of earnest wrestling to know God's will for his life. Henceforth, he was clear: his life would be devoted "to the service of Jesus."[170] Studd later wrote: "Of all the students with whom I have come into contact during this tour among the universities, there is one man you have to keep your eye upon as a leader in your work, Mott of Cornell."[171] Prophetic words!

The Student Volunteer Movement

Several forces contributed to the Mount Hermon missionary awakening in 1886 from which came the Student Volunteer Movement. One of them was Luther D. Wishard who remained in his homeland only because he believed that God had called him to minister to students there. With his associate, C. K. Ober, he sought to infuse missionary concern in all student work. Studd's itinerary was part of that plan. Wishard himself had long wanted to assemble Christian students in a national conference, but after years of delay, in mid-April, 1886, he gained Moody's consent to meet with such a group of college men for Bible study and shared Christian living. At once, and during the few remaining weeks of the term, Wishard and Ober circularized and toured the college circuit. It is a tribute both to Moody's drawing power and to effective recruiting that 251 students, from all over the nation and representing many denominations, assembled at Mount Hermon near Northfield, Massachusetts, in July, 1886, for a month with Moody.[172]

A brother and sister, children of missionary parents in India, also contributed to the Mount Hermon awakening. Robert Wilder as a Princeton undergraduate had attended the 1883 meeting of the Inter-seminary Missionary Alliance. Its challenge so stirred him that he returned to his college to form the Princeton Foreign Missionary Society. Its members signed the following covenant: "We, the undersigned, declare ourselves willing and desirous, God permitting, to go to the unevangelized portions of the world."[173] Grace Wilder had also been a leader in the Mt. Holyoke Missionary Association which had adopted a similarly worded pledge. Throughout the academic year, 1885-86, brother and sister met to pray "for a widespread missionary movement in the colleges and universities of America."

For two weeks Moody's Mt. Hermon meeting went on with no mention of missions. But as the result of a dramatic session, brought about largely through Wilder's efforts, one hundred students from many denominations signed the Princeton declaration. One of that hundred was John R. Mott, who indicated as his chosen field "the world." Following the pattern of the Cambridge Seven, the students determined that some of their number should travel among the colleges to tell of the missionary awakening and to seek new volunteers. As it turned out, Robert Wilder and one of his classmates, John N. Forman, undertook this mission in 1886-87. Among the more than 2,100 volunteers they enrolled were Robert E. Speer and Samuel Zwemer. What had begun modestly at Princeton, Mount Hermon had made intercollegiate.[174]

In 1889 the Student Volunteer Movement was organized as a distinct movement, yet closely tied to the college YMCA's, the college YWCA's, and the Interseminary Missionary Alliance, each of which had representatives on its executive committee.[175] John R. Mott, now an associate of Ober, represented the college YMCA's on the committee and became its first chairman.[176] Ober, understanding Mott's religious fervour and missionary concern, had wisely put in his hands the Association's responsibility for the Student Volunteer Movement.[177] What seemed to be an inconsequential decision helped to determine the direction of Mott's life. From that time forward, Mott's bond with the Christian world mission was sealed. Here is further evidence of the Student Movement's importance for the International Missionary Council.

In England news of the Student Volunteer Movement spread rapidly among the universities. Its special apostles were the British students who had visited the Northfield summer conferences. They sought help from America. Robert Wilder, unable to accept their invitation to visit British universities in 1887, sent John N. Forman in his place. When Forman's visitation produced no comparable British movement, an impatient medical student in London took action that led in 1889 to the creation of the Students' Foreign Missionary Union. The Union's declaration followed closely that of the American Volunteer Movement. Yet its medical-student leaders were too closely tied to their studies to push its organization. The Union grew modestly, but showed little strength.[178]

In the summer of 1891, however, Robert Wilder reached England. His visits among the universities during the academic year galvanized British students into large-scale action. In April, 1892, in Edinburgh, the Student Volunteer Missionary Union was established on a plan similar to that which had proved so successful in America.[179]

It became immediately apparent, however, that a prior unmet need was crippling the organization of local Student Volunteer Missionary Union groups. Few universities had a Christian association of any kind. This meant that the travelling secretary had to prepare the ground and plant the seed of Christian conviction before he could even begin to present a missionary challenge. What this led to through several intermediate stages was the creation in 1898 of the Student Christian Movement of Great Britain and Ireland, of which the Student Volunteer Missionary Union became an integral part. At the same time Tissington Tatlow became general secretary of the Movement.[180]

Much of the Student Volunteer Movement's early dynamic sprang from its flaming watchword: "The evangelization of the world in this generation." The statement was adopted first by the American Movement in 1888 and eight years later by the British. The majority of its detractors (most of them Continentals) apparently failed to grasp its true meaning. It did not prophesy nor suggest as possible the *conversion* of the world in this generation. Yet many of its critics so understood it. To it they imputed naïve superficiality—worse, they viewed it as a preposterous distortion of man's rightful rôle in God's plan of salvation. Undoubtedly the watchword led some enthusiasts to believe that even the world's conversion was possible within a single generation. But the overwhelming majority of students to whom it was meaningful understood by it the *responsibility* of each generation to make the gospel known to all mankind in that generation. None other can repeat that eternal message to a particular generation. Its own members can alone do that. Understanding this, individual Christians recognized more keenly than ever the bearing of the Great Commission upon their own lives. The watchword, then, in the best sense was a call to obligation—not a prophecy of fact.[181]

The World's Student Christian Federation

The Student Movement was not limited to Britain and America. Stimulated by Anglo-American student vitality, it had been growing elsewhere from indigenous beginnings. The initial stirrings of the German student Christian life were seen in the eighties. Wishard spent the summer of 1888 in Germany and before leaving saw a secretary appointed to student work. Out of this came the German Student Christian Alliance in 1895.[182] In Scandinavia also the beginnings of a Student Movement were evident in the early 1880's. In Sweden Karl Fries, later to be Chairman of the Federation, emerged as a student leader and became the founder of a Student Missionary Association. From the little meeting of Scandinavian students that Karl Fries called together at the Northern Lutheran Missions Conference at Kristiania (Oslo) in 1889 came the beginnings of the Scandinavian Student Movement.[183] The next year the first "Scandinavian Student Meeting with a Christian Program" convened. A biennial conference, it brought together university students from Norway, Sweden, Denmark and Finland.[184]

In non-Occidental lands Luther D. Wishard had planted and nurtured many Christian Associations. Through his foresight the first student YMCA outside America was begun in 1884 in India.[185] His association with Harlan P. Beach resulted in one of the first two Associations in China.[186] Wishard himself had long dreamed and planned of a world federation of students through extending student Young Men's Christian Associations throughout the world.[187] From 1888 to 1892 he travelled through the lands of the younger churches beginning new Associations and laying foundations for national Student Movements that were later to become members of the World's Student Christian Federation. Wishard was a Federation trail blazer. Even in 1884 he had written of the need for Christian students in all lands to be united in "one world-wide movement, whose purpose shall be *Christ for the Students of the World, and the Students of the World for Christ.*"[188]

John R. Mott, however, did more than any other to found the World's Student Christian Federation.[189] He was well prepared. As president of the Cornell Christian Association, he had quadrupled its size, put one-fourth of its members (100 men) on working committees, and quickly raised from students and professors $10,000 for a new Association building. A wealthy New York publisher, immensely impressed with this feat, sent an additional check for $40,000. How typical this was of Mott's later money raising! The administrator-executive was in the making but not to the detriment of scholarship as Mott's election to Phi Beta Kappa and his selection for a European scholarship attest.[190] In the spring of 1888 upon Ober's urging, and on condition that he be required to raise no money, Mott accepted for one year only the collegiate secretaryship of the YMCA. The future proved it to be a decision freighted with significance.

Mott served for two years as Ober's associate in the YMCA's college department, travelling from one end of the country to the other and speaking and organizing conferences. In 1890 he assumed full responsibility for the work. In addition to what he had gained from the YMCA, Mott had also been moulded by Dwight L. Moody. By placing the young Iowan in charge of the Northfield Conferences, Moody launched Mott's public career as a presiding officer. Moreover, Moody deeply impressed Mott with the possibility of a growing Christian unity through large—in conception and understanding—evangelism. That idea never left Mott.[191] Other forces also helped to shape

Mott's life. As executive secretary of the Student Volunteer Movement, Mott left his impress on that organization. It, in turn, with its missionary passion and world outreach influenced him.[192] From his first days in the college Association at Cornell, he had been thinking beyond denominational lines and in terms of the "Holy Catholic Church."[193] His labours in behalf of the Student Volunteer Movement extended the bounds of his immediate concern to every nation on earth. As a secretary of the International Committee of the YMCA, and in the overseas extension of that movement, he had known work in a fellowship inclusively larger than Protestantism, for in Russia Association work took in the Orthodox and in Latin America it included Roman Catholics.

Wishard and James B. Reynolds had both thought in general terms of an international alliance of Christian students.[194] Mott himself, as an undergraduate at Cornell, had written an editorial for a college publication pointing to the need for a world movement to embrace all Christian students everywhere.[195] When in Europe for the first time in 1891 at the Amsterdam meeting of the World's Alliance of the YMCA, Mott probably gave his first serious thought to developing a world fellowship of Christian students with himself as one of those in position to help bring it about. In Amsterdam Mott called together a meeting of some of the student leaders from different lands. This meeting, explains Karl Fries, marked one stage in the development of the Federation idea.[196] He considered seriously such a plan with Professor Raoul Allier of the Sorbonne shortly after[197] and later that same year discussed it with Robert Wilder.[198] By 1894 Mott was convinced that the time was ripe for a "world-wide union of Christian Students." The optimistic hope of some Association leaders to unite students within one organization he believed to be not only inadequate but impossible. The greatest diversity, allowing for the richness of "particular genius and character," had to be allowed the developing national Student Christian Movements. These in turn needed to be linked "together in some simple and yet effective Federation."[199]

The story of the World's Student Christian Federation has been covered by its historian, Miss Ruth Rouse. But it is important to record here that during the negotiations through the summer of 1895 leading up to the historic meeting at Vadstena Castle, Sweden, it was Mott's vision, dynamic, and persuasive ability as well as the trust which he inspired that really made possible the Federation's founding.[200] Six men met together in Vadstena Castle to form the Federation in August, 1895. They represented five Student Movements: the American, the British, the German, the Scandinavian, and "The Student Christian Movement in Mission Lands"—an omnibus designation to include within the Federation all those non-Occidental Student Movements that were not closely organized at the time. The founders of this new world organization chose Karl Fries as its chairman and John R. Mott as its general secretary.

The Federation purposed to unite the Student Christian Movements of the world, to appraise the religious conditions of students in various lands the better to "lead students to become disciples of Jesus Christ as only Saviour and God," to quicken their spiritual life, and to enlist them in "extending the Kingdom of Christ throughout the whole world."[201] The Federation had no authority, save the integrity and vision of its leaders. That sufficed. The Federation could not command, but it could serve. It could lead through wise suggestion. Obviously, at its heart and core the movement was dominated by evangelistic passion. It saw the entire globe as its own, and the Student Volunteer Movement's watchword, "The evangelization of the world in this generation," had been a powerful force in its development.[202] The Federation claimed the lives of some of the ablest students of the day. It envisioned nothing less than "world conquest," and for Mott students were the "strategic points in the world's conquest."

Recognizing their responsibility for world evangelism, the Federation's founders saw also the need for greater unity at home and abroad if Christian witness were to be most effective. They sought to develop that unity which transcends national and denominational lines. Yet without consciously striving for it, those who shared in the Federation were drawn into a series of experiences which not only revealed an already present unity but also deepened it. A major strength and appeal of the American Intercollegiate Movement had sprung from its entirely interdenominational program. The Student Volunteer Movement had appealed to the world's need and Christ's command. Inevitably membership in such a committed company led to a sense of Christian oneness, transcending all lesser distinctions. In England, for example, where within the Established Church Evangelicals differed with High Churchmen, and at a time when neither had any intercourse with Free Churchmen, the Student Christian Movement laid foundations for much better understanding among them. It forged an instrument that had none of the old non-Conformist or Evangelical stigmas attached to it. It became truly inclusive.

Young Anglicans and Free Churchmen at the close of the century had no occasion to meet one another *as Christians with common concerns,* except in the Student Movement.[203] No wonder that the Movement had the full support of Dr. Mandell Creighton, Bishop of London.

The knitting-together in England from about 1898 to 1910 of Free Church, Evangelical, and Anglo-Catholic students "for the purpose of promoting missionary zeal" through the Student Movement not only provides a thrilling story, but also one filled with significance for the later development of the International Missionary Council and, indeed, of the whole Ecumenical Movement.[204] It was this heritage, this accomplishment, that was bequeathed to the World's Student Christian Federation.

With what profound and prophetic insight Mott wrote in 1895:

The Federation will be a great unifying force. . . . It will inevitably unite in spirit as never before the students of the world. And in doing this it will be achieving a yet more significant result—the hastening of the answer to our Lord's prayer, "that they may all be one." We read and hear much about Christian union. Surely there has been recently no more hopeful development towards the real spiritual union of Christendom than the World's Student Christian Federation which unites in common purpose and work the coming leaders of Church and State in all lands.[205]

The Federation came early to realize that through its international conferences it was providing a common meeting ground on which the best of each nation's contributions could be shared with others. Almost inevitably, Anglo-American students believed that they were offering to students of other lands through the Federation a tremendous amount of organizing and program genius—with accompanying feelings of superiority.[206] Yet Continental students contributed so notably to the Federation's thought life, and students from non-Occidental lands so inspired and lifted others by the zeal and buoyancy of their spirit that any sense of unilateral giving was quickly dispelled.

In keeping with this, the Federation encouraged each national Student Movement to develop along its own distinctive lines and under its own leadership. At Vadstena it had been stated as matter of principle: "Where possible, both in foreign mission and Christian lands, members of the General Committee and corresponding members should be *natives* of the country which they represent." Even though it cost much in time and money, the Federation sought always to bring nationals from overseas to its meetings rather than to economize by allowing some missionary on furlough to represent the country he served. This policy proved eminently worth while.[207]

Following Vadstena in 1895, Mott began a two-year tour among the universities of Europe, the Near East, India and Ceylon, China and Japan, and Australia, New Zealand, and Hawaii. His visits played a major share in the founding of seventy Student Associations, and he was directly responsible for organizing four national Student Christian Movements that became Federation member units. A world Christian statesman of abundant vigour and global vision was in the making. His contribution to the Federation was enormous. Its gift to him in enlarged power and insight was incalculable. He was, however, as he maintains to this day, always an appreciative student, willing and eager to "sit at the feet of the nations to learn from them."[208]

Mott's yearly journeys continued. His meetings were evangelistic, winning students of all lands to Christ. His work was organizational, resulting in new Associations, new leaders, and new national movements. Always before him was the imperative—win students to win the world. Thus in 1905, a decade after Vadstena, the general secretary could report that five national Movements (Australasia, South Africa, India and Ceylon, China, and Japan) and one international movement (uniting France, Holland, and Switzerland—all Reformed) had been organized and brought into the Federation.[209] That body was rapidly becoming a power in student life around the world.

Where lay the secret of the Federation's strength and influence? Of primary importance, believed its general secretary, the Federation had become the "servant of all the national movements and in no sense their governor. Its ambition is to decrease its authority, in order that the national organizations may increase theirs." Second, it encouraged each nation and race to strengthen its individuality so that the various national movements could share the riches of their diversity, thereby helping to increase understanding and to cement good will. Third, the Federation had sought to "promote that spirit of unity for which our Lord longed when He prayed that we all might be one." Fourth, it had given prominence in its work to the efficacy of prayer, the saving work of Christ, and the "energizing power of the Spirit and Word of God." Finally, it was strong because the Federation was above all else "practical." Conscientiously thorough in the theoretical aspects of its endeavours, it also demanded action and service— dedication to "the great work for which all our movements exist—

namely, the world-wide extension and establishment of the Kingdom of Christ."[210]

With such vision and dedicated daring behind it, the Federation's seventh conference, held in Tokyo in 1907, was understandably unique. Originally planned for 1904, because of the Russo-Japanese War it could not be held until 1907 in Japan. In that year the 700 students who assembled in Tokyo comprised the "first international conference of any kind, secular or religious, to be held in the East."[211] Against Asia's rising nationalism and Japan's recent victory, the coming of Western students to the East to meet with Eastern students on a basis of full equality and shared purpose made a tremendous impression. And in a land then viewing Christianity with a jaundiced eye, this world gathering of Christian students helped greatly to dispel anti-Christian prejudice. Japan alone sent 443 delegates. From China came seventy-four. From other lands of the East came representative delegations. John R. Mott as the Federation's secretary gave a propulsive final address and helped the conference to become itself an effective agency for evangelization in Japan.[212]

Conference plans had largely been made in Tokyo, and delegates were guests of the Japanese Student Christian Movement. The explanation for this is to be found primarily in the ideals and work of the Student YMCA, for that organization fostered and thrust forth national leadership probably more than any other missionary agency. Students actually pointed the way to their elders. The Federation conference was, for example, in striking contrast to the Centennial Conference of Christian Missions held in Shanghai in that same year, 1907. In the latter gathering there were hundreds of European and American missionaries, but the specially invited Chinese guests could be counted on the fingers of two hands. Thus did student pioneering advance beyond the limits within which missionary societies worked. This factor, gaining power at Edinburgh, 1910, came to the fore and largely determined the subsequent nature of the Continuation Committee and of the International Missionary Council.

Observations

Since the Student Movement is better known than any of the other developments here outlined, our observations may seem somewhat obvious. Certainly they can be brief.

In the first place, one notes the rapid spread and growth of the Student Movement with much of its organizational genius springing from young American and British Christian leaders. One must also record the profound influence exercised on those leaders by Dwight L. Moody. The wedding of student enthusiasm with the kind of Christian unity inherent in and resulting from Moody's presentation meant that the Student Movement took an advanced position and beckoned to the churches and missionary societies to move forward. Student leaders were dreaming of a world federation of Christian students and actually brought such a body into being at a time when the members of the London Secretaries' Association would allow no published account of their meetings lest it restrict the candour of their discussions.

Second, the Student Movement was from the first organized on a wide interdenominational basis. Such was necessary when one Christian Association had to minister to the needs of a diverse group of students on a university campus. This meant frank discussion, an honest facing of differences, a recognition of the values of diversity, and a transcending of denominational divisiveness in the common endeavour of student evangelism. International organization also characterized the Movement from an early period and was epitomized in the creation of the World's Student Christian Federation in 1895. Students knew that they belonged to a world fellowship, and their leaders learned to think and plan in terms of all denominations, all nations, and all races.

Almost inevitably, this gave rise on the part of some churchmen to a suspicion of what was disparagingly spoken of as "the YMCA mind." Presumably, according to its detractors, this led to a facile kind of artificial unity being purveyed as true Christian unity without any regard for the factors which kept the churches apart. It was also viewed with some alarm as being a "do good" sort of activism carried on without recognition of its ultimate dependence upon the organized church. Yet such a movement had to assume that Christian students, regardless of denominational affiliation, had in common the great central core of their Christian tradition and the experience of the new life in that faith. Presumably, then, students could discuss with one another any problem of their Christian faith—if not always with perfect understanding—in perfect freedom. They did. In like manner they evangelized other students together. This was new. They worked not on the fundamental basis underlying the missionary conferences, namely, that those assembled were of an "evangelical" cast, and that even within that frame of reference no point of doctrine would be discussed on which there would be disagreement. Precisely this had been one of the weaknesses of the Evangelical Alliance—that each member shared essentially the same view-point and that the whole group could not embrace within itself Christians who were more at home in a "Catholic" tradition. The Federation included widely diverse elements, and part of its genius lay in the fact that it could bring together in common cause and for brotherly conversation students from churches which, denominationally, viewed one another with suspicion.

In the fourth place, within the Student Movement, the World's Student Christian Federation was a *federation* of national movements. It was not, as the Evangelical Alliance was, a movement composed of individual members. Nor was it the crown of a monarchical structure whose will became law by fiat. It was rather a federation which linked together the national student movements of the world and advised and served them. In this it served as an example for future missionary co-operation.

Again: the Student Movement knew great strength around the world. In Britain and America, especially, its growing influence upon church leaders during the last decade of the nineteenth and the first decade of the twentieth centuries was profound. In Britain its ability to bring the so-called "High Church Wing" of the Anglican Communion within the orbit of interdenominational affairs was to have incalculable significance at Edinburgh, 1910, and upon the whole future development of the Ecumenical Movement.

Finally, the Student Movement produced a group of leaders to whom future historians must give due regard for their tremendous rôle in the life of the church during this most significant first half of the twentieth century. One needs mention only the names of Joseph H. Oldham, Nathan Söderblom, William Temple, and John R. Mott to realize the truth of this statement. Working with these men were a whole host of others, men whose names are not so widely known but without whose lives the Christian church would have been infinitely poorer.

We have surveyed those nineteenth-century developments that prepared the way for the great gathering of the missionary societies at Edinburgh in 1910. To that meeting must be ascribed the beginnings of the International Missionary Council and of the World Council of Churches, the two most important organizations that have emerged within the Ecumenical Movement during the twentieth century.

We have observed how some missionary societies early in the nineteenth century functioned interdenominationally, only to give way to more strictly denominational work. We then traced the four major movements, belonging almost wholly to the latter half of the century, that were to set the stage for Edinburgh, 1910. First, there were the co-operative field conferences, most important of which for Edinburgh was Madras in 1900. Second, there were the Anglo-American missionary conferences from 1854 to 1900 that helped to set the decennial pattern and pointed beyond themselves to the need for a permanent international missionary association. Then there were the home base organizations for missionary co-operation, most important of which for Edinburgh and what followed were the Continental Missions Conference, the German *Ausschuss*, and what came to be known as the Foreign Missions Conference of North America. Finally, there was the emergence of the Student Movement climaxed by the creation of the World's Student Christian Federation. To Edinburgh and the International Missionary Council the Federation contributed vision, daring, and leadership far out of proportion to any of the other related movements.

We must turn now to Edinburgh, 1910, to learn what forces moulded it, to discover the origin of its Continuation Committee, and to seek out its results in the years that followed.

CHAPTER III

<<<<<<<<<<<<<<<<<<<<<<<<<<<<<<<<<<<<>>>>>>>>>>>>>>>>>>>>>>>>>>>>>>>>>>

The World Missionary Conference, Edinburgh, 1910

"Edinburgh, 1910" has become a landmark. Increasingly, historians are recording that judgment. As a result of Edinburgh's far-reaching influence, it has also become customary to speak of 1910 as the beginning of modern missionary co-operation, indeed, of the Ecumenical Movement itself—a largely justifiable argument. Yet when unqualified, it may create misconceptions, for Edinburgh, 1910, was neither an ending nor a beginning. It was both. To assume that Edinburgh, as a conference, marked a wholly new departure from the past is to misunderstand its genius, for, as we shall see, it incorporated no single element that had not, in some form, been tried in previous missionary gatherings. Indeed, Edinburgh may best be described as a *lens*—a lens catching diffused beams of light from a century's attempts at missionary co-operation, focussing them, and projecting them for the future in a unified, meaningful, and determinative pattern.

Edinburgh, however, was more than a conference. It stands as an event in the life of the church. As such it is unique, for here in 1910 began a development that has distinctively characterized the Ecumenical Movement in the twentieth century. For the first time the missionary societies as such—and while not in fact, in principle the churches themselves—of America, Britain, and the Continent began to do certain things together and made organized provision for this. The process, it must quickly be added, was evolutionary and began only in indirect fashion in 1910. Yet, as nearly as one can point to a decisive event in evolutionary movement, Edinburgh marked the transition from the old to the new.

What we now call "Edinburgh, 1910" was compounded, however,

of two additional factors, and its significance can be assayed only when we view the event in its totality and from the advanced perspective of nearly half a century. Consider its position in time. First, mankind was closing behind itself the portals of the optimistic and confident nineteenth century. It was about to step through the archway of World War I into a new and distressingly different era of its history. At the same time, the Christian church, until then almost entirely a Western institution with scattered missionary colonies, was beginning to emerge as a world Christian fellowship. The tremendous significance of these two factors must be reckoned with in any appraisal of Edinburgh. They were its investiture. Yet Edinburgh's uniqueness springs from the fact that at a critical juncture in the history of the world and of the church, it released new, creative sources of power, it gave in new form to an emerging world Christian community the best of the past needed in the future, and it thrust upward leaders singularly fitted to guide that community through the perplexities of a demanding new era.

For Western Europeans and Americans the nineteenth century had been one of hopeful optimism. The Industrial Revolution and Western European expansion had brought great material wealth. The appeal of the scientific method tantalized human minds with the thought of unlimited knowledge and achievement. Evolution from lower to higher forms, so apparent in nature, was thought to apply to history and human society. Naturally, belief arose in mankind's inevitable progress. All this encouraged a frame of mind designated "the white man's burden"—an obligation assumed to rest upon European peoples to give their higher civilization to benighted races. Such an attitude became a potent factor in Western expansion—political, economic, and ecclesiastical.

The nineteenth century had also been one of comparative peace. There had been wars indeed, among them those for independence in Latin America, the Civil War in the United States, and the Franco-Prussian War of 1870. Colonial expansion brought wars in the East, and the Empire of Japan signalled the dawn of a new day among Eastern peoples when it defeated Russia in 1905. There *were* wars, but they were not the drawn out, widely ruinous kind of the preceding three centuries. From Napoleon's downfall in 1815 until the outbreak of World War I in 1914 there had probably been no comparable period so free from war's wide-spread devastation since the fourth century.[1]

The clouds that held 1914's rain of death were already in the horizon when the World Missionary Conference assembled in 1910, but to eyes accustomed to the optimism and peace of the preceding century, they were almost completely hidden from view.

It is a common-place to say that the twentieth century really dawned in 1914. It was heralded by a conflict whose equal in devastation and geographic extent mankind had never before seen—a conflict still in progress when World War II came to an end in 1945. Naturally, a century's predominant characteristics do not change overnight. Nevertheless, the twentieth century has brought a climate of opinion distinctly different from that of the last century. Industrial potential has been geared for war, and while war has brought prosperity to a few, its global legacy has been material impoverishment. The scientific method as a panacea for all of mankind's ills has been abandoned by the ablest scientists. From optimistic belief in progress, the mood of Western peoples has turned increasingly to skepticism, cynicism, and pessimism. Former advocates of "the white man's burden" have had to bow before the East's aggressive nationalism and to acknowledge the sickness of Western culture. Thus far the century has witnessed the world-wide spread of a new, aggressive and total way of life, a novel religion inspiring fanatical devotion in its zealots—Communism. The Christian church has probably not faced so powerful a contender for men's allegiance since the great conquests of Islam in the seventh and eighth and in the fifteenth and sixteenth centuries. The year 1914, then, marked a distinct break—the change of an era.

Upon turning to the Christian church, one recalls that the historian of Christianity's spread has designated the nineteenth century, "the Great Century."[2] It was a period of expansion for European peoples over the face of the globe. Imperialism, political and economic, was in the air, and it affected the missionary thinking of many Christians. In this same period and for the first time in its history, the Christian faith became world-wide. Around the world and in every country, with one or two exceptions, churches were planted. Most of them were tender seedlings, designated "missionary" or "native" churches. They were often thought of as part of the Occident's gift of itself to the non-Occident. They became, however, the hall-marks of a global faith—a new emergent in mankind's history. No other religion had ever had a comparable spread.[3]

With World War I mankind entered a new era. Remarkably enough, from the turn of the century, despite mounting conflict, suffering, and persecution, Christian churches have continued to grow numerically.[4] The rise of intense nationalism, the partitioning of the world into spheres of power and influence, and the deep divisions of two world wars all had their effect. Yet, in spite of these, most non-Roman churches around the globe could point to a growing sense of oneness in world community. The making real in practice of their common loyalty to one Lord and to one overarching task brought them to a new level of unity and co-operation on an international and an interdenominational plane. This new phenomenon was designated "the Ecumenical Movement." "Native" churches became "younger" churches, many of them independent, yet part of the one Christian community. Nevertheless, most of this world-wide Christian community viewed itself in a different light from what had obtained in the nineteenth century. It *was* a world faith. But it was a minority movement set "in the world," and for the most part "against the world."

Edinburgh, 1910, came just on the eve of the mood-change from the nineteenth to the twentieth centuries. It was part of the metamorphosis from "ecclesiastical colonialism" to global fellowship. In large measure Edinburgh and its radiating impulses helped to shape the new Christian world community with its growing recognition of inner unity and outer hostility. We must turn, then, to that pivotal meeting in Edinburgh in 1910, trace its emergence, examine its preparations, explore the conference itself, and finally seek to discover its significant results.

THE EMERGENCE OF THE WORLD MISSIONARY CONFERENCE

The Idea of Decennial Succession

Edinburgh, 1910, was first projected because the pattern of a general missionary conference every decade had become accepted and was judged to be worth while. William Carey had proposed such a plan, in 1806, envisioning the first assembly as meeting at Capetown in 1810. While no evidence appears that Carey's proposal influenced those to whom Edinburgh's origins must be traced, Gustav Warneck, who at London in 1888 urged decennial missionary conferences, may well have had Carey's suggestion in mind. In 1878 London had been host to an interdenominational missionary gathering. Ten years later it welcomed the great "Centenary Conference." The "Ecumenical Missionary Conference" of 1900 would have been held in 1898 but for the desire to convene it on the threshold of the new century.

New York in 1900 had made no provision for a further gathering. In the minds of responsible missionary leaders, however, the idea of a general, decennial, missionary assembly commended itself. London, 1888, was thought of as being the first great conference. New York, 1900, was regarded as the second. Naturally, then, suggestions for a "Third Ecumenical Conference" arose almost simultaneously in the United States, in Germany, and in Scotland.

American Overtures. Initial action came from the United States. William Henry Grant, Secretary for what later became the Foreign Missions Conference of North America, had early sought to discover what sentiment existed for another big missionary conference in 1910. On September 16, 1905, he wrote to an officer of the China Inland Mission in London to inquire whether London would be the site in 1910 of a gathering similar to that held in New York in 1900. The letter was immediately referred to the London Secretaries' Association for action.[5] A similar inquiry, it is thought, went to Scotland.[6] The small committee appointed by the Secretaries' Association to survey the matter recommended holding a conference in 1915, 1910 being thought to follow too closely on the New York meeting. Accordingly, Grant was notified.[7]

Since these preliminary inquiries indicated that additional correspondence would be required, at the January, 1906, meeting of the Foreign Missions Conference all further questions "relating to another Ecumenical Missionary Conference on Foreign Missions" were left to a special committee to which, among others, Robert E. Speer was appointed.[8] This group was instructed to "consider the feasibility of another Ecumenical Conference."[9] Since unfavourable word had already come from London regarding a 1910 assembly, Charles R. Watson opened correspondence for the Foreign Missions Conference with the British societies to see whether they would send delegates to an American meeting in 1910 if such could be arranged.[10] Sometime after these letters had gone out, Robert E. Speer received word from J. Fairley Daly, of the United Free Church of Scotland Livingstonia Mission, that because of a letter Daly had received (conceivably Watson's), he had convened a meeting in November, 1906, of Scottish missionary executives to consider the whole question of a 1910 conference.[11] The

Scottish group agreed to reconvene in late January, 1907, to decide finally whether the "Third Ecumenical Missionary Conference" could meet in Scotland. Expecting a favourable outcome, the Scots tentatively invited the Americans to come to Scotland in 1910.[12]

When the Foreign Missions Conference next met in January, 1907, it faced two alternatives. On one hand, there was an invitation from the German societies suggesting the possibility of a 1910 assembly in Germany. London and New York had had the first and second great missionary conferences. Should not the third be held in Germany?[13] On the other hand, there stood the more definite and earlier Scottish invitation. After due consideration and weighing the difficulties of the German language, the Americans voted for the Scottish proposal. Should the latter come to nought, they agreed to reconsider the German proposal.[14] With word of American approval in hand, however, the Scots determined on January 29, 1907, to advance with plans for the Third Ecumenical Missionary Conference.[15]

Scottish Initiative. Apparently, these negotiations were conducted without advising any of the English societies. When the London Secretaries' Association convened in March, 1907, it reviewed a Glasgow circular stating that the 1910 conference would be invited to Scotland. The English secretaries were piqued to realize that matters had gone so far without their being consulted.[16] Consequently, they investigated and at their next meeting in April agreed that the actual holding of a conference would be an "open question" until a scheduled assembly of British representatives settled it in Edinburgh in June.[17]

The Scottish conveners of the Edinburgh meeting in June, 1907, however, assumed a unanimous acceptance for the 1910 conference from the start. They traced each successive step from the first time the Scottish secretaries had met. Very quickly the group fixed the conference date for June, 1910, and created an executive committee to prepare for the 1910 assembly. It in turn appointed two secretaries, the Reverend James Buchanan of the United Free Church of Scotland and the Reverend A. B. Wann of the Church of Scotland.[18]

General acceptance of decennial succession gave rise to Edinburgh, 1910. Initial overtures came from America, but the decennial conviction was so strongly planted that concern for the conference arose almost at the same time in America, on the Continent, and in Britain. George Robson's "History of the Conference"[19] is substantially correct. It gives, however, an incomplete—and, therefore, a distorted—

picture of actual origins. Robson fails to record that the Scots had been stimulated by American correspondence and that the idea of a conference had sprung up elsewhere at the same time. Finally, we must note that the Third Ecumenical Missionary Conference as originally conceived was thought of as following the New York, 1900, general pattern.[20] Edinburgh's actual nature was determined later.

Other Motivations

While Edinburgh, 1910, came into being because of the solidly fixed conviction that precedent for a missionary conference every decade had been established, men looked for additional justifying reasons. These were not difficult to find.

External Factors. Abundant proof seemed to dictate the need for the new missionary conference. Enormous political changes were everywhere seen. China's Boxer Rebellion was being fought when Protestantism's missionaries had last met in New York. In that land, too, the Manchu Dynasty was on the verge of collapse, presaging Sun Yat-sen's Revolution of 1911. Japan in 1904 had defeated Russia, the first Eastern nation to overcome a Western power. All over the East and the Near East, particularly in Turkey, nationalism was stirring. In many areas Islam was pressing ahead relentlessly. Some were asking whether Africa would become Moslem or Christian. The new flowing tides in the world were racial, national, economic, and social. This meant that in many lands the missionary movement would be affected, requiring in some areas, among other things, new adjustments with governments. The sum of these factors pointed to an assembly in which counsel could be shared and plans laid for the effective prosecution of the missionary task.[21]

Internal Factors. There was further warrant for a conference in 1910. The Protestant missionary enterprise had entered its second century. A "native church" had been planted. It was growing rapidly and required wise adjustments. To some it seemed clear that missions were entering a different era, that only broad-scale study, planning, and consultation could clarify the transition within the movement and in the shifting currents of the then contemporary world. Effective "generalship" required nothing less.[22] Concern for co-operation had been growing, and church union was a recurring topic. Conference together could be a forward step in that development.[23] Moreover, American secretaries shared with their German counterparts the hope that the meeting might create an international missionary committee for the benefit of societies on both continents. All these reasons were adduced as making the assembly necessary. Their earliest rôle, however, was to justify a conference motivated by the idea of decennial succession.

The Shaping Influences

Edinburgh, 1910, was first conceived to be a great demonstration, as New York, 1900, had been. Yet it turned out quite differently. To answer the question, "What brought the change?" we must turn to the missionary conferences on the field and to the Student Christian Movement.

When the possibility was first broached for a 1910 gathering similar to that of 1900, a few declared the idea inadequate. The times, they insisted, demanded more than a demonstration of enthusiasm. Some urged consultation among a relatively small group of experts whose suggestions would guide societies' planning—an outcome which did not follow New York. Thus wrote John R. Mott in 1906: "To my mind the missionary enterprise at the present time would be much more helped by a thorough unhurried conference of the leaders of the Boards of North America and Europe than by a great popular convention. I feel strongly upon this point."[24]

In Scotland the General Committee, charged with conference preparation, met again in October, 1907. To its membership it added Joseph H. Oldham, the young secretary of the Mission Study Council, Bishop H. H. Montgomery, Secretary of the Society for the Propagation of the Gospel (and, incidentally, father of the present Field Marshal), and others. The Bishop, however, was unable to accept his election for many months. The Reverend J. H. Ritson, secretary of the British and Foreign Bible Society, was made convener of an English sub-committee, and Dr. Arthur J. Brown, Secretary of the Board of Foreign Missions of the Presbyterian Church, U.S.A., was asked to be responsible for an American "Joint Sub-Committee" appointed by the Foreign Missions Conference. Each group was to convey to Edinburgh suggestions for the conference. The machinery was moving.[25]

American Recommendations. The American committee took the request seriously, added Mott and Speer, two younger men, to its number, and set about its task earnestly. The two signers of its report were Dr. Brown and Mr. Mott, and their embodied suggestions comprised a remarkable and influential document. They advocated as Edinburgh's object "thorough study and consultation" by missionary leaders. This naturally influenced the kind of conference envisioned. Two members of the committee had been at the Shanghai Missionary Conference in 1907, and the chairman had reported on that gathering to the Foreign Missions Conference. Hence, Shanghai's results and methods were much in the group's thinking. Madras, 1902, like Shanghai, had been modelled on Madras, 1900, and it also figured in the committee's deliberations. The "practical precedents" of Madras and Shanghai strongly appealed to the Americans. They urged that Edinburgh be "like" them and thought it "not impractical to contemplate carrying out the same idea on a world scale." The recommendations further proposed that the coming conference be limited to 1,000 or 1,200 "official delegates," those allotted to any one society being proportionate either to the number of its missionaries or to the size of its budget. New York, 1900, it was noted, had apportioned North American delegates by the size of the various societies' budgets.[26]

The American body advanced numerous additional suggestions. It proposed that Edinburgh's "distinctive feature" be conference consideration of "masterly" reports compiled long in advance by commissions especially chosen for the task. To insure their adequate execution, it advocated creating an international committee to appoint and instruct these commissions. "The highest efficiency of the Edinburgh Conference," it was judged, would hinge on what this international body did in launching a study program. Referring to the splendid achievements of the Madras and Shanghai conveners and commissions, the committee insisted that all reports be printed before Edinburgh's delegates assembled. Thus discussion on the assembled material could occupy most of each day. Other suggestions included: twenty minutes daily for united intercession, a plan followed at the Liverpool Student Volunteer Conference; the organization of deputations at Edinburgh's close to go all over Great Britain, a plan followed successfully a year earlier at the World's Student Christian Federation's Tokyo Conference; and a series of parallel meetings to be held as "popular missionary demonstrations." All of these suggestions were later followed. The committee concluded by saying that its members had put concisely their "strongest convictions and recommendations in the light of [their] experience with the New York Ecumenical Conference, in the light of [their] close study of the Madras and Shanghai Conferences, and in the light of [their] consideration of the present situation and outlook in the missionary world."[27]

The American memorandum was dated January 31, 1908. Four weeks earlier Mott and Oldham had been together at the Student Volunteer conference at Liverpool. There they conferred on most of the recommendations appearing in this report. The most important—that of the international committee—Robson and Oldham had held for some time as essential to advance Edinburgh beyond its Anglo-American conference predecessors. A mere hint of the idea convinced Mott of its necessity.[28] Even for an amateur at textual criticism, much of the phrasing in the American report seems obviously to be Mott's. Certainly, the Student Christian Movement's influence in these recommendations is unmistakable. Equally apparent is the important rôle played by the missionary assemblies on the field.

British Recommendations. Remarkable, too, is the document prepared independently by the British committee. While less detailed and specific than its American counterpart, it recommended the same kind of conference. The group's convener, the Reverend William H. Findlay of the Wesleyan Methodist Missionary Society, had been at Madras in 1900 and there gave the closing address, stressing the practicality of a working conference with officially appointed delegates. Knowing that, one can more readily understand the report's strong emphasis upon the recently held India meetings. The British committee devoted most of its report to contrasting New York, 1900, with Madras, 1902, concluding that no demonstrational conference in Great Britain in 1910 could be so effective as had been the earlier one in New York. Instead, it proposed a conference—required by the times and ultimately of greater effect—modelled on the Madras-Shanghai pattern, specifically for consultation, and leading to the influencing and initiation of action.[29]

The International Committee. When the General Committee met again in February, 1908, preparations for 1910 had greatly advanced. Lord Balfour of Burleigh had accepted the presidency of the Third

Ecumenical Missionary Conference, and the three proposed vice-presidents had also agreed to serve. The German *Ausschuss* had become the committee's Continental agency. The group charged with framing a conference constitution based upon the American and British suggestions was chaired by W. H. Findlay. All its recommendations were accepted. Accordingly, Edinburgh would have only 1,100 "appointed delegates" comprising a "consultative" assembly. Societies would be apportioned places on the basis of their total home income. The proposed International Committee was ordered to meet in June, 1908. Finally, Tissington Tatlow, representing the Student Volunteer Missionary Union, was elected to the Executive Committee.[30]

The International Committee met at Oxford, July 14 to 20, 1908. Among the three Continental representatives was the Chairman of the World's Student Christian Federation, Dr. Karl Fries. In place of James Buchanan, then ill, the Scottish members sent J. H. Oldham—a momentous choice. In Buchanan's place, Oldham was made secretary of the meeting. Later John R. Mott moved that a full-time salaried secretary be placed in charge of the committee's vast preparations. Having impressed the gathering with his ability and qualifications, Oldham was chosen.[31] Out of a committee of nineteen men, representing the ablest missionary statesmen of the day, the Student Movement was represented by four of its leaders: Fries, Mott, Oldham, and Tatlow. Dr. George Robson of Edinburgh, one of the chief figures in the preparations for 1910, was in a "key position" to aid the younger Student Movement men, and at every point facilitated their desire to contribute to conference planning.[32]

At Oxford, Mott and Robson together chose a list of subjects for the commissions. Their recommendations were worked over until they became those of the International Committee. They were:

1. Carrying the Gospel to all the World.
2. The Native Church and its Workers.
3. Education in Relation to the Christianization of National Life.
4. The Missionary Message in Relation to Non-Christian Religions.
5. The Preparation of Missionaries.
6. The Home Base of Missions.
7. Relation of Missions to Governments.
8. Co-operation and Promotion of Unity.

With minor verbal changes, they became the first eight titles of the nine-volume *World Missionary Conference, 1910* series. A central advisory committee was created to co-ordinate through the conveners the work of each commission. Explicit instructions were given. The information should be "up to date" and from "all parts of the world." It should be prepared with "findings" representing majority opinions. The whole task had to be completed so that reports could go on sale not later than May 1, 1910. Each chairman would have a limited time at the conference to present his report. Finally, missionary agencies throughout the world that could furnish information should be "appointed corresponding bodies."[33]

The International Committee turned last to the conference itself. Each society should send some of its "leading missionaries" and, "if practicable, one or two natives." Of greatest importance, no resolutions would be allowed involving "questions of doctrine or Church polity with regard to which the Churches or Societies taking part . . . differ among themselves." It also faced the fact that the word "Ecumenical" with its historical and technical associations had produced some misunderstanding. Associated with conciliar and legislative action, it was deemed inappropriate for a strictly deliberative conference. Therefore, the Committee designated Edinburgh the "World Missionary Conference, 1910."[34] These actions all became effective when the General Committee adopted them in September, 1908.[35]

J. H. Oldham

The one man who more than any other engineered Edinburgh and supervised its preparatory stages was Joseph Houldsworth Oldham.[36] Born in 1874 in Scotland and reared in the warmly evangelical home of his father, a lieutenant-colonel in the Royal Engineers, J. H. Oldham took his university work at Trinity College, Oxford. Here he acquired the habit of wide reading and of delving directly to the fundamental issues of any problem. To this day he is characterized by incisive thinking. Not without reason has Oldham been described as "a thinker" and "a philosopher." At Oxford Oldham was introduced to the Student Christian Movement and with Temple Gairdner and A. G. Fraser became a leading figure in the University's Christian Union. By 1896 he had become the first full-time general secretary of the Student Christian Movement in Great Britain and Ireland. In this post Oldham emphasized Bible study. To encourage it he produced

several books, among them *The Teaching of Jesus,* the "most successful" text published by the Movement to that time.[37]

Called to India in 1897, Oldham served there from 1898 to 1900 as
general secretary of the YMCA at Lahore. While in India, he married
Mary Fraser, daughter of the Lieutenant-Governor of Bengal, Sir
Andrew Fraser, and sister of A. G. Fraser. Oldham spent only two
years in India, but they were years of intensive activity and self-giving.
Every colleague with whom he worked was captured by his spiritual
depth, his drive, his keenness of mind, and his mature, well-balanced
judgment. His impact upon other lives was in depth—an impact whose
force grew with the passing of time. In 1900 with much accomplished,
but with his work scarcely begun, the youthful Scot was invalided
home with typhoid.

Upon returning to Scotland and regaining some strength, Oldham
began studying theology at New College, Edinburgh. Later he spent
a term in Halle, and did some reading under Warneck. How important this German study was later to prove! With the completion of his
theological work, he accepted a post in the Mission Study Council
and became responsible for missionary study in the United Free Church
of Scotland. Meanwhile he managed to serve part time as Missionary
Study Secretary for the Student Volunteer Missionary Union.[38] When
he was made secretary of the Edinburgh preparatory committee at
Oxford in 1908, Oldham was granted a leave of absence from his work
in Scotland, but he arranged to give six weeks out of the year to the
Volunteer Union.[39] Yet this amazingly energetic man—slight of body,
keen of mind, and deeply spiritual—was never to return to his earlier
positions. For the next three decades he was wedded to the work that
emerged from Edinburgh.

Anglican Co-operation

The International Committee had established the principle that
Edinburgh would be composed of delegates officially appointed by
their societies. Moreover, and not without some initial opposition, the
determination to make Edinburgh inclusive prevailed. These facts confronted Edinburgh's planners with a major obstacle. Could full Anglican participation—not that of the Evangelicals alone, but of the whole
Communion, "High" and "Low"—be won? Throughout the nineteenth

century High Churchmen had remained aloof from almost every interdenominational event shared in by other missionaries. But in 1910 the Church of England did co-operate and in doing so provided one of Edinburgh's most notable achievements, one fraught with significance for the whole future of the Ecumenical Movement. Thus, a present-day Anglican, listing Edinburgh's three great accomplishments, can speak of the third as "the full entry of Anglicanism into inter-Church councils."[40] On the same point, J. H. Oldham declared, "The fact that the Church of England was in [the Edinburgh Conference] is most important for the Ecumenical Movement. It could not have developed without the Anglicans."[41]

The Society for the Propagation of the Gospel and the Student Movement. Credit for this achievement must go to the Student Movement. In October, 1907, Bishop Montgomery, then general secretary for the Society for the Propagation of the Gospel, had been appointed to Edinburgh's preparatory committee. He explained his subsequent absence with the statement that his Society was investigating whether it could participate. Nearly two years later, in June, 1909, Montgomery appeared in committee for the first time.[42] Meanwhile, others had laboured to make his presence possible.

The Society for the Propagation of the Gospel, usually regarded as "High Church," had never been represented officially at the British Student Volunteer conferences. Bishop Montgomery had attended, and missionaries of the Society had spoken in these conventions, but always in a personal capacity. However, using the sheer force of youthful audacity and opportunism as levers on Montgomery's basic sympathy for the Student Volunteer Missionary Union, Tissington Tatlow won official representation for the Society for the Propagation of the Gospel at the 1908 Liverpool Conference.[43] It was a crucial step toward what that Society came to view as co-operation without compromise in non-Anglican ventures.

Student Movement Influence. The next step came early in 1908. On many counts, Edinburgh would have failed had it not enlisted representative Anglicans. Recognizing this, the preparatory committee sought for its membership a respected Anglican who it thought could achieve results otherwise impossible. George Robson wrote to the Student Christian Movement's Tissington Tatlow, "Accordingly, we want you to join the committee which has to plan the conference, and we want you to bring the Church of England with you."[44] A young, interdenominational secretary, Tatlow was dumbfounded by such trust. Although believing that his influence had been overrated, he accepted appointment, and only later discovered the kind of respect the Student Christian Movement commanded.

At Oxford in the summer of 1908 Tatlow and Prebendary H. E. Fox, a staunch Evangelical, were asked to submit Anglican names for membership on Edinburgh's study commissions. Tatlow sought a representative group and included on his list the Bishop of Birmingham, Dr. Charles Gore, the Bishop of Southwark, Dr. E. S. Talbot, Father Herbert Kelly, Director of Kelham, and Walter Frere, then Father Superior of Mirfield. Fox neither approved these names nor would he suggest them, but he allowed Tatlow to present them. The committee accepted the representative list. The only remaining problem was to claim these men, some of whom had never previously co-operated with non-Anglicans.[45]

The task was Oldham's. Being a Scot and a Presbyterian, he naturally sought Tatlow's help. They agreed upon a strategy and set out first to win two or three key men. Tatlow went straight to Dr. Armitage Robinson, then Dean of Westminster. A warm friend of the Student Movement, the Dean quickly agreed to commission membership, but utterly refused it upon realizing that this was no student gathering but a conference of missionary societies. Tatlow's persuasiveness and the Dean's fondness for him and the Movement eventually gained the desired answer. Oldham and Tatlow went next to Bishop Talbot, because of his son Neville's activities in the Student Christian Movement. They were chagrined, however, to discover so formidable a High Churchman as Father Frere with the bishop, but they presented their case and left, not knowing what decision the older men would make. Both agreed to serve! A. G. Fraser, then home on furlough, was sent to see Dr. Charles Gore, Bishop of Birmingham, but the visit was indecisive.[46]

Bishop Gore's Acceptance.   In the autumn of 1908 Bishop Gore wrote to J. H. Oldham concerning a fundamental principle of the proposed conference: that no resolution would be allowed involving "questions of doctrine or Church polity with regard to which the Churches or Societies taking part in the Conference differ among themselves." He wanted to know whether this applied to study commission recommendations. Could it be compromised by the report on co-operation and unity? Oldham wrote at once that commissions worked under conference rules, that no recommendations for co-operation would be made involving "questions of conscience or principle," and that missionary societies in conference could not formulate the terms of church union. This last was an ecclesiastical matter. American dissent to Oldham's first point was overruled by the Central Advisory Committee in Britain as representing "no real divergence of view." The British body authorized Oldham to send his letter.[47]

Oldham followed his written word to Gore with a personal visit, for he greatly wanted the bishop's participation. The two spent a whole night talking over the fundamental principles involved. When Gore became convinced that matters of faith and order would neither be presented nor discussed at Edinburgh, he consented to attend. His prestige was enormous, and his decision became a potent factor in winning all segments of the Anglican Communion for Edinburgh.[48] Meanwhile, Mott wrote an article for the influential quarterly journal of the Society for the Propagation of the Gospel, *The East and the West*, and talked with its editor. Learning the facts of Edinburgh and being told that some High Churchmen were already co-operating, the editor confessed in print to having been "converted" to the World Missionary Conference.[49] Yet, in December, 1908, despite the cordial attitude of Bishop Montgomery, who had a high regard for Mott and the Student Movement,[50] the Standing Committee of the Society for the Propagation of the Gospel declined its invitation to be represented officially at Edinburgh.[51]

The Pan-Anglican Congress. Stemming from a suggestion by Bishop Montgomery in 1902, the Pan-Anglican Congress, one part of which was devoted to foreign missions, met in London in June, 1908. Nearly 13,000 persons, half of whom were delegates, gathered daily for its sessions. Those on the work of the church abroad stimulated British interest in missions generally and in the World Missionary Conference specifically. The Congress compiled various reports prepared from information submitted by Anglicans in all parts of the world and printed them before the assembly met.[52] The difference between them and the unified, concise results of Edinburgh's commissions is striking. In the meetings devoted to missions, nothing, it appears, was said about larger co-operation, except for the "dangerous disregard" at Shanghai in 1907 for the creeds of the ancient church.[53] The Congress helped the whole Anglican communion to think of itself as a federation and strengthened the understanding of one Anglican missionary society for another.

The Archbishop of Canterbury's Acceptance. A month later the Lambeth Conference met. While Lambeth was in session, the Archbishop of Canterbury, Randall Davidson, was first asked to give his support to the forthcoming World Missionary Conference. Nothing came of this initial overture. The request, however, and the general desire for Anglican co-operation caused some "nervousness" among certain members of the Church of England.[54]

A year after Lambeth, on July 5, 1909, a delegation consisting of Mott, Oldham, Tatlow, and Prebendary Fox visited Dr. Davidson. Accompanying them in his personal capacity was Bishop Montgomery. The group asked the Archbishop to address Edinburgh's opening session. It would be no easy thing to do. Archbishop Davidson's very presence would in a sense commit the Church of England to the whole enterprise. His absence might silence otherwise vocal dissent. Yet he was interested and promised to seek counsel.[55] When hope was expressed for participation by the Society for the Propagation of the Gospel Dr. Davidson said that he was "afraid" its charter would prevent it. Tatlow at once related his success in gaining official delegates from the Society to the interdenominational Liverpool meeting. The Archbishop wheeled around and replied, "I am profoundly thankful to hear it. I am profoundly thankful to hear it."[56] In February, 1910, four months before Edinburgh, the Convocation of Canterbury passed a resolution of sympathy and interest for the World Missionary Conference. In "approving" the greetings, the Archbishop said, "It will be by far the greatest and most important missionary conference that has ever taken place."[57] But not until two months before Edinburgh convened did the Archbishop decide to attend.[58] The Society for the Propagation of the Gospel also agreed to send official delegates. The Anglicans were in.

There was no doubt in anyone's mind how this had been achieved. The Student Movement was directly responsible. Goodwill resulting from its accomplishments had gained its representatives *entre* to Anglican dignitaries. Acceptance of the Movement's "interdenominational position" (as distinguished from *un*denominationalism), allowing "co-operation without compromise," made Anglican participation possible.[59] The persuasive force and ability of the Movement's leaders actually *won* representative Anglicans. As Edinburgh met, one of them said: "'We'—meaning by this the group in the Church of which he was a distinguished representative—'would not have been here in this conference had it not been for the Student Christian Movement.'"[60] Five years later William Temple wrote: "Members of the [Student Christian] Movement ought to know that without their movement there never could have been held the Edinburgh Conference, which was the greatest event in the life of the Church for a generation."[61]

The Commissions

In the choice of members for Edinburgh's eight preparatory commissions—they were set up in the summer of 1908—personal ability outranked consideration of denominational representation. Months later, when the commissions' facts were in and when each group after thorough evaluation of its data had made its recommendations, every chairman faced the task of writing a unified and readable report. Practicality ruled. Consideration for the limited means of clergymen and missionaries who would most likely buy the reports dictated a low price and thus determined their length. Calculation based on printing costs indicated the available number of pages, and commission chairmen were instructed to stay within that limit. No publisher, however, would venture the risk; so the conference committee decided to publish the volumes itself.[62]

Financing the Commissions. Mott knew the value of broad preparation and planning. He knew the importance of the commissions for Edinburgh's success; so he raised a total of $55,000 (made up of eleven $5,000 gifts) to get preparations for Edinburgh under way.[63] Later he raised funds for the conference in Britain. Mott's resourcefulness made possible what the commissions accomplished. With limited time and finances, however, and faced with the necessity for occasional meetings, they could include only retired or furloughed missionaries at home. However, to hundreds of Christian workers overseas went carefully compiled questionnaires. Their response was remarkable. In remote sections of the globe, they took the time and pains to send in full, accurate answers to all questions. Many of these represented the fruits of a lifetime's observations. One report ran to 140 typewritten pages. Mott's commission alone enlisted the aid of 600 correspond-

ents.[64] Thus hundreds of missionaries around the world gained a sense
of actually participating in—of being a part of—Edinburgh, 1910.

Work of the Commissions. With raw data as a basis for consultation, the various commissions met in their respective lands. Membership meant long, detailed work for an already overburdened group
of the ablest and busiest executives, professors, and churchmen. The
most optimistic had dreamed that of those asked half might accept
membership. Instead, out of the nearly 160 persons invited, only eleven
declined, each with a justifiable reason. This was one of the pre-Edinburgh miracles. Every chairman, for the sake of linguistic convenience,
was an English-speaking person. Yet two of the commission's vice-
chairmen were Julius Richter and Friedrich Würz. Among the commissions' members were represented some of the Continent's ablest
missionary teachers, including Gustav Warneck, then at Halle, and
Carl Meinhof, then professor of African languages in Hamburg.

Each member had to review every reply from the field to his commission. Then came conference together, discussion, and evaluation.
Here was the prototype for what we speak of to-day as "ecumenical
conversations." Bishop Gore had his commission members convene
every day for a week in the autumn of 1909. Mott used some of the
money he had earlier raised to bring across the Atlantic the British
and Continental members of his group—among them George Robson,
Julius Richter, Bishop Montgomery, and Ruth Rouse. Richter was helpful wherever he was because of his encyclopaedic knowledge of missions and because of his ability to relate to specific situations the experience of the German *Ausschuss.*[65]

Those who have shared in similar group projects know the slowness
with which papers are received and final drafts corrected. But the
deadline was met—although not without severe strain on the chairmen. Printed reports were in delegates' hands before most of them
departed from home for Edinburgh. They were reviewed on ocean
liners and trains. Without them, the Edinburgh that was would have
been impossible. Other conferences had circulated preliminary studies,
but they were at best committee-edited compends of individual papers,
and were limited to the work of one country. Edinburgh's commissions achieved something new. From abundant data gathered on a
world-wide scale a committee of experts distilled essential facts and
conclusions. They worked these over until the chairman, reflecting
the mind and wisdom of his committee, could produce a single, uni-

form report, comprehensive and balanced beyond what any individual otherwise could have achieved. Never before had the paramount problems of the world missionary enterprise been so thoroughly surveyed, studied, and evaluated. The result was unparalleled. For the first time Protestant missions had an adequate basis on which to begin co-ordinated planning and action. Small wonder that Edinburgh's discussions proceeded on a plane and with an effectiveness never before matched. The general pattern set by Edinburgh for preliminary study has since been followed by every major international, interdenominational conference.

The Emergence of the Continuation Committee

The passing of a decade frequently obscures in nearly impenetrable haze the details of an event which itself may never be forgotten. Thus it was with the Continuation Committee, long described as "the one creative act" of the Edinburgh Conference. Many now suppose it to have been spontaneously generated in June, 1910, or to have been the special project of one or two conference leaders. Such, however, is far from fact. The idea for a continuation committee may long have been in many minds, but the first formal appeal came from Continental societies.

The Continental Proposal. A Continental memorandum, requesting an international missionary agency, reached Edinburgh's preparatory committee nearly a year before the conference. Signed by Dr. Theodore Oehler, chairman of the *Ausschuss*, and dated September 15, 1909, at Basel, it read: "The missionary societies of the Continent of Europe take the liberty to propose in the enclosed memorial the formation of an 'International Committee' dealing with international missionary questions." Reference was made to the numerous replies received by Commission One advocating such a body. Among the correspondents urging this plan, the memorandum listed Nicol Macnicol and V. S. Azariah of India.[66]

The "Proposal" or "Memorial" was brief and to the point. Its immediate motivation sprang from the British government's failure to reimburse the Berlin Society for losses of nearly $100,000 after the Boer War. Protestant Missions, it was argued, should feel "honor bound" to create a "central organization" to assist societies seeking justice in similar circumstances. Further work for such an international committee would include negotiations with governments on such issues as the liquor and opium traffic, labour conditions for subject races, and the general abolition of injustices among colonial peoples. The agency would serve "with the authority of the united body of Protestant missions" on any occasion demanding united, international representation. The organization envisaged consisted of twenty missionaries and statesmen from Great Britain, the United States, and the Continent as well as Canada, South Africa, and Australia. If five additional members were thought to be feasible, representatives from the field could be considered. Edinburgh should initiate plans for constituting the body within a year, for deciding whether it needed a paid, permanent secretary, and for determining the financial requirements. The proposed committee would work directly with such bodies as the *Ausschuss* and could act independently or delegate functions to member bodies. The new agency could report its work at the "next decennial conference." Most of the German societies had agreed to this proposal, as had also the Norwegian Missionary Society, the Swedish National Missionary Society, the Swedish Missionary Union, and the Danish Missionary Society.[67]

A Similar American Plan. In January, 1910, Julius Richter, speaking for twenty-five Continental societies, addressed the Foreign Missions Conference of North America. He outlined the Continental proposal for an international agency and sought to enlist American support for it.[68] The plan was warmly received. When Richter finished, Dr. Arthur J. Brown related that without knowledge of the Continental suggestion, the Committee on Reference and Counsel was prepared to make "substantially" the same proposal. John R. Mott grasped the situation at once and advocated that British societies be urged to form an organization similar to those in Germany and America and to unite with these other two bodies in an international missionary committee.[69]

British Caution. A month later Richter appeared before the London Secretaries' Association, presented the same proposal he had outlined in America, and heard read an American letter. The latter recommended forming a British missionary body which could unite at Edinburgh with its Continental and American counterparts "to form an international committee on missions." Long discussion followed, but the hesitant London secretaries agreed to leave all such proposals in the hands of Edinburgh's commission on co-operation. Two months later the question was reopened. Again the consensus was to wait to see what the World Missionary Conference would do.[70]

Commission Recommendations. Meanwhile, the commissions were discovering frequent endorsement for an international organization. Commission One, under the guidance of Mott and Richter, received from the field numerous requests for such a body. Recognizing this as beyond its province, the group, nevertheless, recommended an international committee for co-operative action and investigation.[71] Commission Six on the home base completely outlined its own plan for regional missionary councils united in one "International Committee."[72] But it was Commission Eight's proposal that was finally adopted by the World Missionary Conference.

Those working on "Cooperation and the Promotion of Unity" knew the extent and force of the demands for an international agency. They recognized equally the need for such a body and the difficulties attendant upon its organization. Their recommendation, therefore, was relatively conservative. Toward the end of their preliminary work they saw that they had to offer a plan for perpetuating Edinburgh's spirit and for continuing its work after its delegates disbanded. Silas McBee, editor of *The Churchman* in New York and a powerful, if quiet, figure throughout the conference, suggested that the matter be left to Dr. W. H. Frere and Dr. J. H. Ritson. Dr. Frere, Father Superior at Mirfield, and Dr. Ritson, a Methodist and the general secretary of the British and Foreign Bible Society, represented two extremes within the commission. McBee, an Episcopalian, went on, "If they agree, doubtless the Conference would accept the proposal." Frere and Ritson worked out a plan together—and they *agreed*—recommending "The Continuation Committee."[73] To that body, proposed by Commission Eight and unanimously accepted by the conference, we must return.

Final Preparations for Edinburgh

With major concerns settled, the final months of preparation were increasingly devoted to details. One of the most important actions taken in the preliminary stages, however, was the appointment of Mr. Kenneth Maclennan, then with the Laymen's Missionary Movement in

Scotland, to be Associate Secretary of the Conference and Oldham's co-worker. He was appointed in March, 1909.[74]

The Latin America Question. With official representation, Edinburgh had to state explicitly the principles by which its discussions would be determined. One major decision centred upon the term "missionary," which in some quarters connoted more at the turn of the century than it does generally today. It was often employed for any overseas endeavour by Christians whether to convert Hindus or Roman Catholics or to aid struggling congregations of Europeans or Americans in a colonial setting. On this point Edinburgh's planners discovered that if discussions were to include any work more than that to non-Christian peoples, no other limit could be found that would meet unanimous approval. That meant that unless the conference centred attention strictly upon the missionary task to the non-Christian world, some societies would absent themselves. For that reason it had been determined two years before Edinburgh assembled that only societies sending missionaries "among non-Christian peoples" would be eligible for membership in the conference.[75]

This initial precautionary principle achieved later prominence. When certain questions arose concerning the atlas being prepared for Edinburgh, the early decision was made further explicit. Would missionary statistics include missions in Latin America, viewed by some as already Christian? Would they include missionaries sent to Europe? To avoid all difficulty in definition, the title "World Missionary Conference" was qualified with the phrase, "To consider Missionary Problems in relation to the Non-Christian World."[76] This settled the question for the official atlas. Moreover, it was the only basis on which Continental societies were willing to go ahead with the conference, for many of them sharply resented the presence in Europe of missionaries to "convert" some areas already strongly Roman Catholic. Similarly, it was only with this understanding that many Anglican societies would continue. This involved the obvious exclusion of missions to Latin America, except those to the heathen Indians.[77]

The question of statistics kept cropping up. It was finally agreed to tabulate all employed missionaries but to omit converts not gathered from "non-Christian peoples." This was again judged to exclude Latin America and resulted in some strained feeling. Yet, if missions to those claimed by the Roman Catholic Church in Latin America were to be included, why not count certain Protestant missions to Belgium, to

Italy, and to Germany? Somewhere the line had to be drawn. If missions to people claimed by the Roman Catholic Church in Latin America were to be accepted by the conference, a good case, it was argued, could be made for including missions to Roman Catholics in Britain and America, if such there were. This whole difficulty arose from an inadequate understanding of the actual situation in Latin America, but under the circumstances, Edinburgh made the only decision it could. It stood rock-solid on the "among non-Christian peoples" principle as that now ambiguous phrase was then understood.[78] This seemingly necessary distinction was refused by many Americans. For evidence one needs only to examine the two atlases that appeared in connection with Edinburgh. The American edition differed from the British by the inclusion of Latin American statistics.[79]

Other Decisions.   Numerous other questions demanded attention. Plans were initiated for a simultaneous, parallel conference with popular speakers for non-conference members who wished to attend and be associated with Edinburgh. Committees to handle details were put in motion. A *News Sheet* was launched. And a plan for a popular report of Edinburgh to be written by Temple Gairdner was approved.

The International Committee met once again, January 29, 1910. Its principal decisions were: to submit no commission conclusions for veto at Edinburgh but to allow resolutions leading to action if approved by the business committee; to invite John R. Mott to become conference chairman; and to arrange a meeting of medical men at the conference to consider their special problems.[80]

The News Sheet.   Edinburgh's *News Sheet* today provides a glimpse into the ferment generated by conference preparations. Its eight monthly issues before the conference detailed for the public Edinburgh's thrilling background.[81] The little paper more than paid its own way, ending publication with a subscription list of 8,000 and a profit of $375 (£75).

The *News Sheet* carefully noted that Edinburgh's purview included only specific problems needing "careful investigation," not "the missionary work of the church as a whole." Thus it explained the omission of medical missions, Christian literature, and women's work.[82] Julius Richter used its pages to suggest that despite Anglo-American ignorance of German missionary literature, the conference would help to end a long and unfortunate isolation. Revealing something of Continental feeling, he wrote: "The happy combination of the rich material

of information and facts furnished by English and American missionaries, with the scientific methods and thoroughness of the Germans
will lead to valuable results."[83]

Finally, the *News Sheet* discloses a hint of the wide-spread prayer
offered in behalf of the conference. Prayer was sought and given in
every land. Those responsible for the conference acknowledged their
dependence upon prayer and without it would have regarded their
task as insurmountable. The first "Intercession Sheets" were distributed
in October, 1908. A year later more than 40,000 had been given out.
Six months before Edinburgh nearly 35,000 of another edition had been
circulated throughout Great Britain. The churches observed May 15,
1910, as a day of prayer for the conference. Those who prepared for
it saw in Edinburgh God's call, and through prayer they constantly
sought his guidance and his strength.

John R. Mott's Preparation. When the World Missionary Conference convened, John R. Mott had just passed his forty-fifth birthday.
Already an experienced chairman, he had long watched the masterful
Dwight L. Moody and had made Moody's art of chairing his own.[84]
From Cornell YMCA days, he had presided over increasingly larger
and more important meetings. The World's Student Christian Federation conferences that comprised so much of his journeys around the
world after 1895 schooled him in leading international gatherings.
Yet when he was asked to chair the Edinburgh Conference, Mott set
about readying himself with such thoroughness that the uninitiated
might have thought him a novice!

Chairing an international gathering strongly Anglo-Saxon in character and conducted in English presented its own complexities. At
best, it would be an arduous task. Many Europeans would be unfamiliar with British and American procedure. To facilitate their "feeling at home" and to encourage their fullest self-expression, Mott examined book after book on procedure and consulted with experienced
leaders of European assemblies. His attention to the minutest details
of conference structure is well known. He spared no pains in assuring
that his own rôle would be perfectly executed.

How much of Edinburgh's success was due to Mott's genius as a
chairman! With uncommon common sense and with intuitive insight,
he kept the discussion properly channelled. He made certain that all
points of view—national, racial, or ecclesiastical—were aired. Occasional restlessness arose when Mott granted full time to the ob-

viously inexpert. But it was precisely his knack for judging how much representative discussion it took to satisfy *all* that won admiration for his fairness. Delegates spoke of it. Results proved it. Edinburgh had been guided by "a master of assemblies."[85]

EDINBURGH, 1910

High on "The Mound," not far from Edinburgh Castle and close to St. Giles Cathedral, stands the University of Edinburgh's New College. Its buildings surround the Assembly Hall of what in 1910 was the United Free Church of Scotland. In this great room, so admirably suited for discussion, the World Missionary Conference met from June 14 to 23, 1910.

At the opening meeting, Lord Balfour of Burleigh, President of the Conference, presided. Since no service of united communion was possible, the meeting was opened simply with prayer.[86] The necessary omission of the Lord's Supper burned in many hearts. Yet, the Archbishop of Canterbury was present, and that marked a notable step along a slowly unfolding road. He was the first speaker, and his words carried the weight of his office. Almost at once he spoke of the conference as one, "which, if men be weighed rather than counted, has, I suppose, no parallel in the history either of this or of other lands." His concluding sentences underlined the theme of his whole message: "It is my single thought tonight—that the place of missions in the life of the Church must be the central place, and none other."[87] Thrilling words—yes! But of greater consequence for the whole future of the Ecumenical Movement was his presence.

Each evening the conference met to hear Christian leaders speak. The first night a young American layman, Robert E. Speer, gave the concluding address. Evening sessions during the remaining nine days included some illustrious names. Among those who spoke were Henry Sloane Coffin, Sherwood Eddy, the Archbishop of York (Cosmo Gordon Lang), R. Wardlaw Thompson, Pastor Henry Ussing, and Bishop Charles H. Brent. Representatives from the "missionary" churches were Tasuku Harada, President of Doshisha University, President K. Ibuka of Meiji Gakuin, and the Reverend V. S. Azariah from India. On Thursday evening, June 23, John R. Mott made the concluding presentation.

Prayer and Unity

The heart of Edinburgh was not its speeches but its periods of prayer. Each day opened with fifteen minutes of prayer and worship —the virtually windowless Assembly Hall with its insulating corridors shutting out all distraction. For a half-hour near noon the conference joined in the "central act" of the day's proceedings, intercession for Christian missionary work. Members of different societies and unions led these devotional periods. The Reverend K. C. Chatterji from India, the only non-Occidental to conduct a worship service, did so, significantly, on the morning when the commission on co-operation and unity reported. From the first service of prayer, in place of the Holy Communion, to the last, these united acts became increasingly meaningful and unifying. While in a few instances some were aware of a slight tension during these occasions, many declared that prayer together was "the most sacred experience" of those rich days. Bishop Brent afterwards wrote that the noontime intercessions "brought Jesus Christ so near as to mean to some of us a new vision of the Son of Man."[88] Temple Gairdner, seeking to make real these high moments, wrote that at times the very "silence of God was *heard* within the hall."[89]

Dependence upon written records makes difficult the attempt to assess the unity or spirit of Edinburgh. Here, for the first time, official representatives of Protestant societies had come together internationally. One would expect, then, some articulated regret that certain view-points were obscured or that some persons attracted too much attention. Yet delegates' post-conference reports were remarkably free from such criticism. The very purpose and nature of the gathering provided a unifying core. The periods of united intercession did much to quicken the "unity" and "brotherly love" that characterized the meetings. Indeed, Edinburgh's remarkable demonstration of unity seemed most to attract the attention of news reporters. For many of them this was Edinburgh's outstanding feature.[90]

In all, 159 missionary societies sent to Edinburgh more than 1,200 delegates. Europeans were more in evidence than ever before, with forty-one Continental societies represented by 170 delegates. Seventeen conference members were from the churches of India, Burma, China, Japan, and Korea.[91] These non-Occidentals, however, came under the quotas of Western missionary societies. Cheng Ching-yi, for example, represented the London Missionary Society. American societies brought thirteen of the younger churchmen present. The remaining four came under British auspices. The Continent sent none.

Commission Reports

Procedure. The solid core of the conference was its commission reports. Presented and discussed each morning and afternoon, they helped to create the conference's growing strength. Machinery was so well oiled that its effective operation was scarcely discernible. Business kept moving. Progress was made smooth by the detailed, meticulous planning of Edinburgh's chairman and secretary. Facilitating their efforts was the *Daily Conference Paper*.[92] Delivered early each morning to delegates' residences, it included minutes of the previous day, official notices, and a brief outline of the day's proceedings. In the Assembly Hall rules of procedure were strict. Commission chairmen took forty-five minutes to present a summary statement of their reports. Those wishing to speak submitted cards which were sifted by the chairman. Each recognized delegate was allowed seven minutes— no more. The time limit worked perfectly, but only half of those seeking recognition ever reached the floor. The procedure was *identical* with that followed at Madras in 1902.[93]

Mott chaired superbly, and the conference felt the impress of his powerful personality. It learned also to appreciate his deft humour, an effective force in allaying disruptive weariness, in avoiding awkward situations, and in speeding work. No symphony conductor in his own sphere ever surpassed in skill Mott's perfect performance. The famous seven-minute bell interrupted bishops, missionaries, and statesmen, but it was scrupulously obeyed. Equally important was the secretary's work. Small and modestly quiet, J. H. Oldham was heard by the conference only when he gave out formal notices. Yet the first time he arose to speak, the ovation thundered as though it would never end. Why? Gairdner wrote: ". . . those that knew were aware that more than any one other, the spirit that was in this very unobtrusive exterior had been at the back of that great Conference, not merely in respect of its organisation and its methods, but also of its ideals, its aspirations, and its hopes."[94]

The Reports. As chairman of the first commission, Mott made an inspiring presentation.[95] His factual material is outdated today. His conclusions and spirit remain fresh. When he reported the task too great for any but united planning and spoke of the commission's desire for a "representative International Committee," delegates broke in with applause. That morning nineteen speakers, four of them nationals, addressed themselves to the problems of evangelization. In the afternoon session sixteen additional persons spoke to the subject, with vice-chairman Richter summarizing the discussion. When he advocated an international committee, the conference applauded again. On every successive day, save one, the need for an international missionary agency was emphasized. Increasingly awed by the immensity of the work before them, delegates seemed to grasp the urgent necessity for such a body. Each new reference to an international agency brought forth more applause.

The second day's subject covered "The Church on the Mission-Field." Previous conferences referred to the "native church" or the "missionary church." Here, for the first time, the *church* itself was recognized to exist even "on the mission field." This marked a distinct advance in missionary thinking. In this connection the word "native" was denounced for its patronizing and paternalistic overtones. When no better word could be found to convey the meaning intended, "native" was accepted with the earnest attempt to remove from it all trace of condescension.[96]

Speaking on a closely related subject several nights later, a young Indian pastor delivered what was to become one of Edinburgh's two best-remembered speeches. With utter candour and with assurance from Mott that he should bare his heart, V. S. Azariah urged missionaries to face the patronizing attitudes so often prevalent in India. He asked not for "condescending love" from missionaries, but for their "friendship" and for the real "*love*" that permits two Christians to shake hands and eat together. These were not easy words, and Azariah had been urged against his will to speak them. Their frankness roused some ire, but the address marked a high point of courageous, Christian honesty and will be remembered as long as Edinburgh.[97]

"By common consent" the report on the missionary message in relation to non-Christian religions was one of the finest if, indeed, not "the most remarkable" of all those delivered at Edinburgh.[98] With Professor D. S. Cairns of Aberdeen and Robert E. Speer as its leaders, one would expect the commission to produce a sterling report. It described the non-Christian religions and contrasted their best with the best in Christianity. Its stimulus encouraged missionary training in comparative religion probably more than had any previous work.

Thus reports were given day after day. With the chairman's summary concluded, initiative passed to the delegates. Men who had studied the reports now spoke to emphasize, modify, or relate findings to immediate needs. To appreciate the scene, one must imagine himself in Assembly Hall—a great, square room, conducive to discussion, and crowded with men accustomed themselves to lead assemblies. Many of them had prepared for two years for this meeting and were eager to share information and points of view. Representing their mission boards, they had come to Edinburgh from all over the world.

On assembling, they knew keen anticipation within themselves. They felt the very air charged with expectant hope and daring. They thrilled to be part of something new, to be on the verge of creating something permanent. The atmosphere was one of power. It filled men with the realistic buoyancy that comes of daring great things for God and expecting great things of him. The assembly had risen at its first meeting to hear read a message from the King of England. It had received greetings from the Imperial German Colonial Office and a letter from Theodore Roosevelt, then only recently President of the United States. It had found in its own midst distinguished statesmen. Moreover, the assembly came to realize that it was no huge and unwieldy group, for it had discovered the cohesion and dynamic that belong to 1,200 Christians drawn from around the world and committed to one end.

It was an assembly that generated power—all the more impressive because it was harnessed power, controlled and guided by the ablest Christian statesmen of the era. Day after day the surging force was felt as it resulted in new and effective accomplishment. Men with well-known names stood in far corners of the hall when recognized by the chair. They made their points briefly and sat down as another from the Continent or from Asia stood to speak. Here was vast preparation, organizing genius, and tremendous personal and group energy all moving in a steady crescendo. Yet morning and noon this great assembly came to a complete halt to recognize in prayer and worship him from whom all power is given. With every ecclesiastical shade represented from Anglo-Catholic to Quaker, some tensions, some differences were bound to arise, but they were minor and few. The dominant impression was one of growing strength and unity together. The paramount realization—that what had been set in motion dare not be stopped.

The Continuation Committee

Daily the conviction went deeper that what Edinburgh had begun must go on. Mott's first-day declaration that only an international missionary committee could grapple with the vast problems of unoccupied areas had driven home. In an instant there had come a group-intuition. An idea had been planted. Each repetition made it grow and deepened conviction.

For the first time in official assembly the whole gamut of non-Roman, non-Orthodox opinion was represented. This was a source of wonder and gratitude. Widely differing view-points were offered without compromise. They were respected, and the conviction grew that harmonious co-operation was possible. Yet even amid so exalted an experience, men had to confront fateful differences. No society would accept dictation from any super-body. Anglicans feared that Free Churchmen might unintentionally compromise them. Continentals deplored the "superficiality" of British and especially American missions and suspected the "world evangelization" view as a creation of naïve activists. Many Americans were impatient with any and all such reservations when to them the path seemed so perfectly clear.

On the morning of the longest day in the year, June 21, Sir Andrew Fraser presented the report on co-operation and unity. Discussion was first limited to co-operation on the mission field. This psychologically effective move made clear co-operation's benefit in practice. It put in even sharper relief the need for working together "at home." This discussion produced Edinburgh's other best-remembered address. In seven argument-packed minutes, and with a perfect command of masterful English, Cheng Ching-yi, a Congregationalist, declared that Chinese Christians were looking forward to "a united Christian Church without any denominational distinctions."[99] Finally, assuming the creation of a continuation committee, he urged it to explore with Chinese pastors the best means for bringing about such a united church. Delegates were left holding their breath. This lone figure assumed massive proportions. He could not be waved aside. He and what he represented *had arrived!* He stood as a symbol of the future. Neither speech nor speaker has been forgotten.

Just before noon Sir Andrew Fraser presented the single resolution that went before the conference: "That a Continuation Committee of the World Missionary Conference be appointed, international and representative in character, to carry out, on the lines of the Conference itself," certain specific responsibilities: among them, to complete the work of investigation begun by the conference, to carry out the suggestions made by the commission reports, and in counsel with the missionary societies to work "towards the formation of such a permanent International Missionary Committee" as was suggested by the commissions and the German and American bodies before the conference.[100]

Obviously, the proposed body fell far short of the international committee envisaged by some. Yet a continuation committee was as much as the conference could realistically achieve. No one present had authority to act for his board. Any international committee would have to be the direct creation of the societies—not that of a conference. Edinburgh could have proposed no more than it did—a continuation committee entrusted to bring into being the hoped for international committee.

Ensuing discussion was frank. Each speaker, save one, urged the creation of the Continuation Committee. That one was Bishop Montgomery, who, without mentioning the proposal, referred to himself as a "High Church lion" in a "den of Daniels." The major difference between points of view represented, he maintained, was on the nature of the church. "Our contribution to you is from the Catholic basis. . . . We are Anglicans first, and Protestants in parts. . . . [We respect those who] to our great sorrow, are not yet in communion with us."[101] The Bishop was not attacking the proposed venture but was clarifying the High Anglican position. Some tension resulted,[102] partly from the fact that certain Anglicans, in defending a position new to many, had already in the minds of some people exceeded the doctrinal discussion-limits imposed upon the conference.[103] Yet the conference always heard them through.

The Continuation Committee was a new idea. A natural hesitancy to accept the untried made many wonder whether the motion for it would carry. Yet, with each succeeding speaker, desire mounted

higher for the new agency and all that it stood for. It had been trans-
muted by a "spiritual alchemy" into a symbol of something much
greater than itself.[104] Late in the afternoon Dr. Mott asked, "Shall
the vote be now taken?" Delegates were ready. The question was put,
and a tremendous "Aye" went up from the conference. The motion
carried unanimously, the conference came to its feet, and a pent-up
flood of joyous exultation was released in the Doxology's "Praise God
from whom all blessings flow."

This was Edinburgh's climactic moment. The conference, however,
was not over. Other reports and other discussions were yet to come.
But on the afternoon of 1910's longest day Edinburgh had taken one
of the longest forward steps ever made in the history of Protestant
missionary co-operation. That act, the creation of the Continuation
Committee, will be forever associated with the Edinburgh Conference.

We have dealt, obviously, only with high points of the main conference. Any adequate appreciation of the tremendous achievement
that was Edinburgh requires that one read Gairdner's book and at
least sample the last two volumes of the Edinburgh series. In addition
to the official sessions, there were the parallel meetings, nightly public
mass assemblies, gatherings in Glasgow, and post-conference deputations. Thus the conference designed for work also had a larger, more
popular outreach, demonstrating effectively the power of the whole
missionary movement.[105]

EDINBURGH'S SIGNIFICANCE

Edinburgh had distilled the best from past missionary co-operation
and offered this powerful concentrate to the churches. Yet Edinburgh
was more—did more—than this. Something new had happened. Those
present knew that from within their midst something different was
emerging. It was a desire for an inclusive togetherness unknown
before. From Edinburgh sprang a new willingness to respect and
recognize wide differences and at the same time to work together as
Christians. Here was born the kind of international and interdenominational Christian co-operation that has increasingly characterized the
twentieth century.

Edinburgh's Omissions

Women's Work, Literature, Medicine. In seeking more specifically to assess Edinburgh's significance, one turns first to its omissions. It touched not at all upon women's work—at that time a growing feature in the missionary enterprise. When this lack was first questioned, the *News Sheet* explained that Edinburgh's scope included only particular problems pressing at that moment and needing special investigation.[106] This omission produced little or no repercussions. The absence of any comprehensive study of Christian literature may be more seriously questioned. The matter was dealt with incidentally as part of the work of Commissions Two, Three, and Eight, and was briefly discussed one afternoon.[107] This particular lack was rectified by the later important work of the Continuation Committee. Moreover, Edinburgh had directed no attention to medical missions. Through the efforts of numerous concerned physicians, a separate "Medical Missionary Conference" (with three sessions) was held in conjunction with Edinburgh. It was attended by 130 members, nearly half of whom were Edinburgh delegates.[108]

Latin America. To many, Edinburgh's most important omission was Latin America. Undoubtedly the conference that was would have been impossible had it not been for the self-imposed limitation—missions "to non-Christians." The ruling excluded certain Protestant missions in Europe and English missions among white colonial people. Few regretted their omission. Many felt, however, that a valid and relatively large segment of Christian work in Latin America had been proscribed. Silas McBee had insisted from the start that full Anglican co-operation could be had only by limiting the scope of the conference to missions to the heathen.[109] On the other hand, two years before the conference, Bishop Montgomery was puzzled to know why the Anglican Communion had so long neglected South America![110] Robert E. Speer led the forces working for Latin America's inclusion at Edinburgh and was not convinced by the opposition's argument. The "non-Christian" designation he regarded a misnomer. J. H. Oldham and others sympathized with Speer's general position, but they also believed it necessary to draw the line short on coverage to extend the line of inclusiveness. The great difficulty proved to be the fact that Latin America was a "border-line" case and in the hectic pressure that was

Edinburgh there was no time to work it out. The whole question was the "gravest issue" with which J. H. Oldham as conference secretary had to cope.[111]

Speer was so keenly disturbed by this exclusion that with several delegate-friends he led a rump session at Edinburgh to discuss Latin America's needs. To a second informal meeting in that city the original group invited a number of board secretaries with responsibility for work in Latin America. Together they considered the vast area's claims and agreed that these could be appraised only by a Latin American gathering similar to the one then meeting in Edinburgh. In that second rump session a promise was made "in behalf of the churches of Great Britain and North America that these interests should not be neglected," and that provision would be made for such a meeting.[112]

The direct outgrowth of these sessions was the two-day Conference on Missions in Latin America called by the Foreign Missions Conference and held in New York in March, 1913. At that time Robert E. Speer could declare that greater attention had been drawn to missionary work and its urgency in Latin America by its omission at Edinburgh than by its possible inclusion.[113] That conference appointed the Committee on Cooperation in Latin America.[114] The new body was concerned not to convert Roman Catholics but to survey the needs of Latin America's unevangelized millions and to co-ordinate Protestant efforts to meet those needs.[115] One outcome of the new committee's efforts was the great Panama Congress in 1916. Even today, it should be noted, the Roman Catholic Church continues to send missionaries to Latin America.

Edinburgh and the Roman Catholic Church

No attempt was made to include Roman Catholic representatives at Edinburgh. Roman acceptance of any invitation was thought impossible.[116] It was regarded quite enough a feat of organization to have represented for the first time the Catholic elements of the Anglican Communion.

With no Roman Catholics present and with most of those at Edinburgh accustomed to pursue their work without reference to the Roman Church, many fell easily into speaking of "the Christian Church" in a particular land, meaning by that the sum total of Protestant churches there. On several occasions, however, and usually by Anglicans, the conference had its attention called painfully to the fact that even its own high experience of unity was partial, because the meeting did not include Roman and Orthodox representatives.[117]

Silas McBee, a "Catholic Episcopalian," had long included among his friends numerous Roman Catholics. Before Edinburgh met, he asked an old acquaintance, Bishop Bonomelli of Cremona, to write a letter to the World Missionary Conference. The bishop did, and the letter circulated widely in Italy without criticism.[118] The eighty-year-old bishop wrote, "I applaud your Conference." He outlined the areas on which all were of a common mind and saw these as sufficient and sound basis for discussion "tending to promote the union of all believers in Christ."[119] It was a remarkable document from a man reputed to be a personal friend of the Pope. Then a representative from the Society for the Propagation of the Gospel read excerpts from another letter written to a conference delegate by a Roman Catholic university professor.[120] A Congregationalist voiced a sentiment held by many. He spoke not only of having advanced in his own experience beyond what he thought would have been possible five years earlier, but now he actually longed for the time when in another conference members of the Greek Orthodox and Roman Catholic Churches would also be represented and where all could consider together their common service.[121] In catholicity of thought this marked a tremendous advance.

One must remember, however, that references to Rome were few indeed. Nevertheless, Edinburgh's "pro-Catholic" (Anglican and Roman) sentiments were strong enough to provoke "severe criticism" from many quarters.[122]

The Outgrowth of Edinburgh's Theological Limits

Edinburgh's theological inclusiveness resulted primarily from the decision to exclude matters of faith and order. When Bishop Gore was clear that this principle would be honoured, he agreed to attend. Gore's decision made Dr. Davidson's acceptance easier, and the Archbishop of Canterbury also "unqualifiedly sustained and endorsed" the principle.[123] Even though some felt that this agreement was ignored on occasion by those who most demanded it, it was essential. The fact that the conference of necessity excluded consideration of doctrinal differences, however, so moved a young missionary bishop from the Philippines, Charles H. Brent, that through him another "omission" had profound and far-reaching consequences.

Brent had experienced Edinburgh's unity, but he saw it as danger-
ously deceptive if left unexplained. Theological issues that could
have excited heated debate were as a matter of principle omitted
from this missionary gathering. Even the commission reports had
undergone a process of consensus. No one denied his convictions, but
Edinburgh's scope had been strictly limited. Without touching, except
incidentally, areas of major disagreement, it facilitated a joyous unity.
So representative a gathering could scarcely have been convened
except on missions. Nevertheless, the "magnanimity" and the "constructive temper" of the conference captivated the bishop's mind. He
thought of "the influence which a union of all the churches represented would have on the balance of the Christian World and on the
whole of mankind."[124] Brent viewed the ultimate issue before Christians as church union, and he hoped that directly or indirectly the
World Missionary Conference would lead to it.

Edinburgh worked a tremendous change in Charles H. Brent. In
his own words, he "was converted. I learned that something was
working that was not of man in that conference; that the Spirit of
God . . . was preparing a new era in the history of Christianity."[125]
Edinburgh made Brent an "apostle of Church unity." It led him to
believe that unity was attainable within a century.[126] Yet, as Brent
saw it, Edinburgh had skirted the real issue—"faith and polity." When
he later attended the General Convention of the Protestant Episcopal
Church in Cincinnati in October, 1910, his mind had had several
months to dwell on the unity of Edinburgh and on the disunity elsewhere so evident. At the early Eucharist on the opening morning of
the Convention, there came upon him vividly, his diary records, "a
conviction that a world conference should be convened to consider
matters of faith and order."[127] He explained his idea to the convention, it took hold, and the Faith and Order Movement was born. It
became one of Edinburgh's most significant direct results.[128]

A World Conference

Basically, Edinburgh was a conference of the home base of missions.
It clarified home-base relationships to the most urgent problems of
the missionary enterprise. It was representative of the home base.
That is to say—and we already know what that meant ecclesiastically

—for the first time Continentals were proportionately represented. While the greater part of missionary work was English and American, Germany's contribution to the science and theory of missions was unmatched. To English-speaking people, because of the language barrier, it had been, however, almost unknown.

One hundred seventy Continentals had come to Edinburgh. These men participated throughout, but they also had one evening to assess missions from a Continental viewpoint. For the Germans, Edinburgh became a milestone. They had shared in its planning stages. Through its commissions they had come to feel themselves actually a part of the assembly. For them this was new. They emphasized their contributions as "thoroughness" and "objective solidity," but some of them thought that they could learn even more than they taught.[129] A German Moravian bishop wrote that at Edinburgh his countrymen truly discovered the vision of the one, great, common task belonging to the disciples of Christ.[130]

Edinburgh stands, however, as the prototype for all the "world conferences" now so familiar. Unlike its predecessors, Edinburgh was what its title indicated. In co-opted personnel and in scope its commissions had been world-wide. Its purview was global. Its constituency further exemplified its world-wideness.

Out of 1,200 delegates only seventeen were from younger churches. They came not as representatives of their own communions but of Western missionary societies. Nevertheless, at Edinburgh they had an influence out of all proportion to their numbers. From an Indian, V. S. Azariah, and a Chinese, Cheng Ching-yi, came Edinburgh's two best-remembered speeches. Non-Occidentals were few in number, but they were extremely able men, and they were vocal. Unfeigned interest and enthusiasm attended their words. Only one person from Asia led a devotional service, but among the twenty-six evening presentations, three gave major addresses. The outstanding contribution of these representatives from the East came in the debates on commission reports where their insight, candour, and ability made a profound impression. Significantly, some of them had been leaders in the Student Christian Movement in their homelands.[131] They were a symbol of a world-wide church. They were also a portent of what was to be, for increasingly Western churches were to come to regard the younger churches as having equality—not of strength but of status—and increasingly the old patronizing attitudes were to diminish. The rôle of non-Occidentals at Edinburgh was an important one.

Edinburgh's Younger Leaders

Edinburgh marked the emergence of a new missionary leadership apprenticed in the Student Christian Movement. Edinburgh also made its impression upon these younger men, increasing their vision and enlarging their responsibility.

Mott. John R. Mott and Edinburgh each contributed much to the other. Mott's commission work, drawing upon what were often lifetime observations from hundreds of correspondents around the world, brought him an unsurpassed knowledge of the non-Christian world and of the attendant problems faced by missions. As chairman of the conference, he was privileged to feel the pulse of the whole missionary enterprise as no one ever before had done. In turn, one of Mott's greatest contributions through Edinburgh was inspiring men to see, to think, and to plan in terms of the total world mission. The fusion of all that Edinburgh represented with Mott's genius for grand statesmanship produced the natural and acknowledged leader for the Protestant missionary enterprise.

Oldham. No less fatefully, J. H. Oldham grew with Edinburgh and shared its rich endowment. Organizationally, it had given him an incomparable background. Strategically, it had placed him at a unique vantage point for surveying the whole missionary movement. Personally, it had made him known, admired, and trusted by missionary secretaries and personnel. Quiet and unassuming, brilliant and energetic, a thinker who focussed his whole attention on one immediate task, Oldham was marked for a unique and indispensable rôle. Oldham and Mott were distinctly different men. Yet in the larger work that grew out of Edinburgh, each was essential to the other.

Brent. We have already traced Edinburgh's influence on Bishop Charles H. Brent. It gave him vision and hope. Against his earlier pessimism it convinced him that, beyond co-operation, even unity (more properly "union") could become a reality. His vision led to the Faith and Order Movement. Thus, one of the two major components of the World Council of Churches sprang directly from Edinburgh, 1910.

Delegates from the Younger Churches. For members of the younger churches Edinburgh meant a new vision and understanding of the work that faced them. To offer only a few examples, K. C. Chatterji of India, Cheng Ching-yi of China, and Bishop Yoitsu Honda of Japan were all placed on the Continuation Committee, and each was to aid the growth of co-operation in his own land. V. S. Azariah, who had already launched the National Missionary Society in India five years before Edinburgh, became two years later the first Anglican Indian bishop. He led India's churches in unification endeavours which prepared the way for the Church of South India. All served the cause of furthering co-operation in their own homelands.

Student Leaders. Many of those who planned for Edinburgh were Student Christian Movement men. They knew the impact the conference could make on a rising generation of British student leaders, many of whom would carry its influence into the larger life of the church. Accordingly, some younger men were appointed stewards. Among them were: John Baillie, J. McLeod Campbell, Kenneth Kirk, William Manson, Walter Moberly, William Paton, Neville Talbot, and William Temple. Paton, later a secretary of the International Missionary Council, was unable to attend, but Edinburgh's influence became a force in his life. As a Student Christian Movement secretary, he extended its impact deep into the Student Movement.[132]

Temple. When he ushered in the Assembly Hall, William Temple was twenty-eight. Even before the conference was ended, he had to depart for Australia on a Student Christian Movement tour which Mott had persuaded him to make. A prime example of Edinburgh's far-reaching and ever-multiplying influence was the vision it inspired in this young Anglican. Temple "often testified that his first acquaintance with the world problems of the Church was made in 1910, in the Assembly Hall of the Church of Scotland."[133] When one considers Archbishop Temple's stature and vigorous leadership in the Ecumenical Movement, the importance of that Edinburgh-generated vision becomes impossible to assess. It is probably not too much to say, however, that the impression the World Missionary Conference made upon William Temple was one of its several results most heavily freighted with consequence for the future.

Edinburgh's Conception of Itself

Those who attended Edinburgh knew that they were part of a great assembly. How influential in the life of the churches it would become, probably no one dreamed. Those gathered in Assembly Hall recognized nationalism's rising surge around the world. They knew the great urgency of their task. Yet none intimated any awareness of the gathering war about to engulf them. The most astute among Edinburgh's leaders may have discerned the shaping pattern on the Continent. If this was the case, no trace of it appears. This had been a missionary conference, and so its delegates regarded it. One is not struck with any display of naïve optimism at Edinburgh. Most of those present well knew the forces arrayed against them. Yet they also knew unbounded hope. The urgent demand to act before doors closed further stimulated that hope.

Men first assessed Edinburgh's significance in terms of its immediate practical results. It had powerfully demonstrated Christian unity and the possibility of increasing co-operation. It had created a continuation committee to extend its spirit and to carry out its work. But no one was quite certain how effective the new body would be. It had stimulated thoughtful missionary interest as had no other gathering before it. It resulted in tremendously increased missionary giving.[134] Organizationally, its stimulus led directly to the creation of co-operative missionary bodies with varying degrees of authority in Great Britain, the Congo, Denmark, and Sweden. Educationally, its influence was felt as some seminaries and theological colleges promptly acted on the findings of the commission on missionary preparation. That group's chairman, President Douglas Mackenzie of the Hartford Seminary, was instrumental in creating the Kennedy School of Missions directly as a result of his commission's work.[135] Missionary periodicals of the time indicate that Edinburgh was valued almost wholly in terms of its direct stimulus upon missionary endeavour and interest.

Mott translated Edinburgh's "urgency" into his *Decisive Hour of Christian Missions*,[136] and wrote the book's preface before he left Edinburgh. From the vantage point of the World Missionary Conference, he outlined the missionary situation and the strategy required to meet it. Edinburgh had made the task clearer than ever before. It had provided new stimulus. The work remained to be done.

Edinburgh's Significance for the Ecumenical Movement

The passing of four decades enables one to appreciate much of Edinburgh's importance that was hidden from the eyes of its participants. Now one knows that it was more than just "the greatest missionary conference ever held." But how much more? Edinburgh, despite some voices to the contrary, did not launch the Ecumenical Movement, but it symbolized and hastened that movement's emergence. Against that background one can discern three of its additional major contributions to the larger life of the church in recent times.

Three Fundamental Principles. Although it was not first to employ them, Edinburgh established three principles of fundamental importance for the future of ecumenical organization. The second and third were contributed largely by the Student Christian Movement.

First, unlike its predecessors—simply assemblies of individuals—Edinburgh established the principle of bringing together officially appointed delegates, responsible to their boards. New York's North American delegates in 1900 had been officially-appointed only as an expedient to limit attendance. The Shanghai and the two Madras Conferences, however, enlisted official delegates as a matter of effective policy, but they were comparatively limited gatherings. Edinburgh fixed the principle of officially-designated delegates for world Christian gatherings. In effect, this was soon to mean that the churches as such had begun to work together and were making provision for such activity—a distinctive feature of the Ecumenical Movement in the present century.

Second, Edinburgh instituted the principle of broad, denominational inclusiveness. It had been easy to assemble people of like mind, but that had been the weakness of the Evangelical Alliance. Even in preparation for Edinburgh and afterwards in the Continuation Committee insistent voices demanded the exclusion of all but "evangelical" Protestants.[137] That view did not prevail, however, for Edinburgh deliberately sought to bring together people who disagreed with one another and to help them establish co-operation without compromising any of their own fundamental beliefs. This principle of broad inclusiveness, joining Catholic and Protestant elements, prevailed.

Third, and resulting from the second, Edinburgh launched international, co-operative Christian endeavour on essential tasks without demanding prior theological consensus and by agreeing to hold in abeyance theological differences.[138] In this connection, Mott's comment on preliminary commission work is revealing: "What led to action was *getting people associated in action.*"[139] Coming to know persons of quite different theological views in work for a common Christian end, so that one came to trust them implicitly, forged bonds of Christian friendship that permitted co-operative endeavour otherwise impossible. The outworking of this principle—whole-hearted co-operation on essential tasks, without any compromise of theological conviction—in years to come helped mightily in holding together the Christian movement throughout the world.

The International Missionary Council. Edinburgh marked the International Missionary Council's beginning. The Council came into being officially in 1921, but its initiation came in 1910. The line runs directly from Edinburgh, 1910, to 1921 through the difficult years of World War I. The Continuation Committee, the Emergency Committee, and the International Missionary Council all displayed outward differences. Yet, from 1910 to 1921 the chairman of organized international missionary co-operation was John R. Mott, the secretary—J. H. Oldham. The fundamental principles governing its work were the same. The missionary secretaries who comprised its functioning arms were the same men. Its journal, *The International Review of Missions*, remained the same. Regardless of outward structural changes, and composed of the same persons and guided by the same principles, international missionary co-operation remained unchanged in its essential core. In the thinking of Mott and Oldham there was no break in organizational continuity from 1910 to 1921.[140] One can speak quite properly, then, of the International Missionary Council's having its beginning in 1910.

Ecumenical Organization. The Ecumenical Movement roots back into the Evangelical Awakening. In the preceding chapter we traced some of its growing, nineteenth-century manifestations. Expressions of it were to be found in the Evangelical Alliance, in the Student Christian Movement—especially through the World's Student Christian Federation, in the World Sunday School Conventions, through the World's Alliance of YMCA's, and in the Federal Council of the Churches of Christ in America. During and after World War I, the World Alliance for International Friendship Through the Churches provided further evidence of the Movement's extent. Yet the Ecumenical Movement has been and is a *movement*, not an organization nor the sum of those organizations often designated "ecumenical." Thus, as has sometimes been done, to designate Edinburgh "the beginning of the Ecumenical Movement" is inaccurate historically and generically. Yet, in a *special* way, Edinburgh marks the twentieth-century beginning of the two most representative embodiments of the Ecumenical Movement, the International Missionary Council and the World Council of Churches.

One may define the Ecumenical Movement as that growing consciousness in all churches of the church universal conceived as a missionary community. To this end the whole of Edinburgh contributed. Three of its topics were especially relevant: "Carrying the Gospel to the Non-Christian World," "The Church on the Mission Field," and "Cooperation and the Promotion of Unity."[141] More important, it signalized the beginning of international missionary co-operation developed in the International Missionary Council.

Edinburgh also appears to have been the first conference to create a continuing body *and* to invest it with a full-time, paid secretary. The 1909 Continental proposal had hinted at this, but it was Mott who finally insisted upon its necessity for the committee's effective functioning and maintenance.[142] Another of Edinburgh's contributions, then, was the first full-time, paid secretariat in interdenominational work—an example which has been followed hundreds of times since and which has provided the operating basis for interdenominational and ecumenical organization.[143] Eight years later when the League of Nations was established with a budget and secretary, the nation-states—probably not consciously, but in fact—repeated the earlier step of the missionary societies.

Edinburgh is also uniquely responsible for the World Council of Churches, chief symbol of the Ecumenical Movement today. Here we can mention only briefly four supporting facts. First, Edinburgh brought the younger churches into the thinking orbit of the older churches. It helped to establish them in the Christian world community. It prepared their ablest members for international and interdenominational leadership. That the World Council of Churches was founded as a *world* body resulted primarily from the extension of Edinburgh's influence through four decades.

Second, as we have already seen, Edinburgh gave rise, through its impact on Bishop Charles H. Brent, to the Faith and Order Movement, one of the two parent-movements of the World Council of Churches.

Third, the principles on which Edinburgh and its developing organization were established appealed to, and were used by, Nathan Söderblom. In his earlier years the great Swedish archbishop had been profoundly influenced by the American Student Movement and its missionary emphasis. Much of his ecumenical vision must be attributed to his first student conference in America, to Mott, and especially to Dwight L. Moody.[144] Some years later the devastation of World War I stirred Söderblom anew to the need for international Christian co-operation in the social realm. Acquainted with the work of international missionary co-operation and its governing principles, he went to J. H. Oldham to get the latter's counsel on joint Christian endeavour in which those from widely diverse ecclesiastical backgrounds were united.[145] Abundant evidence of the effective outworking of one of Edinburgh's fundamental principles encouraged Söderblom to proceed with his efforts for The Universal Christian Council for Life and Work. It built on the same foundation: co-operative Christian action on demanding common problems without immediate concern for theological unanimity and without requiring any compromise of conviction. Life and Work became the other parent-movement for the World Council of Churches.

Fourth, Edinburgh first brought British, Continental, and American Christians together in the equality born of shared endeavour. World War I was later to strain severely these first tenuous ties, but without them reconciliation would have been even more difficult. It was upon this often forgotten foundation that Faith and Order and Life and Work were able to build in the 1920's.

By preparing the churches themselves—East and West—by stimulating the founding of the two constituent bodies, and by thrusting forth qualified leaders, Edinburgh led most influentially to the creation of the World Council of Churches.

We have attempted here to assess Edinburgh's significance. It marked the beginning of a new era in world missionary co-operation and thus became a singular event in the life of the whole church—the root-symbol of the Ecumenical Movement in the twentieth century. Its adequate appraisal and proper place in the history of Christianity, however, must be the work of future historians.

CHAPTER IV

<<<<<<<<<<<<<<<<<<<<<<<<<<<<<<<<<>>>>>>>>>>>>>>>>>>>>>>>>>>>>>>

From Edinburgh to Crans, 1910-20

The years from 1910 to 1920 marked a fateful period in the world's history. They exhibited successively peace, world war, and armistice. Largely forgotten by 1914, the Hague Conferences gave way after the war to the League of Nations, yet neither was adequate to cope with the revolution in which mankind was becoming increasingly embroiled. In November, 1918, the Allied Powers greeted the Armistice with frenzied joy, but few realized how well the day had been named and that the conflict whose end it supposedly signalized would continue to spread.

Mankind had probably never seen a more violent decade. Its turbulence rocked the newly forming world Christian community and threatened to shatter it. Yet from a mid-century vantage point the impartial observer must record that that fellowship, bound by spiritual ties alone, not only weathered the storm but emerged from it stronger than before. Significantly, in the League of Nations' senescent years, the sinews of world Christian community grew steadily tougher.

In binding together the world's Protestant bodies during this period, international missionary co-operation played a key rôle. Edinburgh had made it possible. Through the Continuation Committee, agencies for co-operation were established in lands of the younger churches, and the creation of similar organizations was stimulated in Europe. Then came the war. In its wake the Emergency Committee of Cooperating Missions sought to maintain necessary international missionary co-operation and to preserve large segments of missionary endeavour which Allied pressure and German prostration might have destroyed. By war's end the major demands upon the missionary enterprise were to heal the breaches, to rebuild the international structure, and to get on with the urgent tasks of the years immediately ahead. To achieve these ends the International Missionary Council was launched in 1921. This new creation of the twenties, however, can rightly be understood only as an outgrowth of its predecessors, for while it differed from them, it was built around that core of co-operative endeavour that had remained essentially the same and was continuous from 1910 through 1921.

THE CONTINUATION COMMITTEE

Its Founding

Toward the end of the World Missionary Conference, Edinburgh's late June warmth was pleasant indeed. Few had time to enjoy the out-of-doors, but when delegates did stroll, conversation turned often to the new Continuation Committee. It was not the international agency some had hoped for. Appointed by the conference, it was charged to forward Edinburgh's spirit and work and to bring into being the desired international missionary committee. The commission which had suggested it established its operating principles. It would preclude matters involving "doctrinal or ecclesiastical differences of the various denominations." It would be a purely advisory body with no authority, except that accruing through the value of its service. Nominated by Edinburgh's business committee, its members were limited to thirty-five, ten each from America, Britain, and the Continent, and one each from Australasia, China, Japan, India, and Africa.[1]

So significant a venture naturally brought considerable behind-the-scenes flurry. During Edinburgh's last days discreet conversations and the "sounding out" of those concerned were inevitable. Most logical choice for the new secretary was J. H. Oldham, but he was altogether reluctant. The job, he agreed, needed doing, but it was not at all specific, and he did not wish to commit himself to a task so large, so general, and so undefined.

Then occurred one of those little hidden dramas that so often shape the course of the future. A group of Germans and other Continentals—most hesitant, despite their 1909 memorial, to become part of this new body—approached Oldham. He had studied in Germany and knew the language well. He appreciated the Continental contribution to missions as well as the attitude of Continentals toward missionary questions. For two years these men had worked with Oldham. They trusted him implicitly and were agreed to go ahead *only* if he accepted the secretaryship. Before long and speaking on behalf of the Anglo-Catholics, Dr. W. H. Frere made a similar and equally urgent representation to Oldham. The able young Scot saw that forming a representative committee hinged largely upon his becoming its secretary. Moreover, he regarded the permanent annexing of Mott for world missionary cooperation and the provision of an adequate outlet for his energies and gifts in the service of the missionary cause as of such paramount importance that, if this depended on the formation of a continuation committee, and if his acceptance of the secretaryship would make this easier, he could not refuse the call.[2] It was a momentous choice.

The First Meeting. On June 23, 1910, the last day of the World Missionary Conference, The Continuation Committee assembled briefly to prepare for its first major meeting.[3] This gathering on June 24 to 25, which came at the close of the World Missionary Conference, elected Dr. John R. Mott (he had just received an LL.D. from the University of Edinburgh) chairman, and Eugene Stock of the Church Missionary Society and Dr. Julius Richter from Berlin vice-chairmen, and appointed J. H. Oldham its full-time, salaried secretary. Then, accepting its mandate, the Committee named nine commissions to further what Edinburgh had begun. Several of these later proved quite important—especially those on missionary preparation, chaired by Mrs. Louise Creighton, wife of the late Bishop Mandell Creighton, and on Christian Literature, chaired by Dr. George Robson. Other commissions included unoccupied fields, Christian education, statistical uniformity, missions and governments, and press relations. The Committee further agreed to circulate widely the "Message of the Conference to the Christian Church"[4] and to thank all overseas who had contributed to Edinburgh's success, informing them at the same time of its own organization. Before the group disbanded, Dr. James Barton of the American Board, Dr. H. T. Hodgkin of the Friends' Association, and Dr. Mott prepared a provisional constitution.[5]

The Continuation Committee had met, had outlined a working program through its commissions, and had agreed to reassemble a year later. But it had completely by-passed the first item on its agenda— the formation of a permanent international committee![6]

The Secretary's Work. Their immediate tasks completed, Committee members scattered to all parts of the British Isles, to the Continent, and to America. One went to South Africa, another to Australia. The three Asian members returned to their homelands—Bishop Honda to Japan, Cheng Ching-yi to China, and Dr. Chatterji to India. When the last straggler had departed from Edinburgh, only J. H. Oldham remained in the office at 100 Princes Street—his the task of conducting the Committee's unfinished business. He had objected to the secretary-ship originally with good reason, for "to carry out the work and spirit of the Edinburgh Conference" outlined no position: it opened a vast field of endeavour. Circumstances later forced Oldham to wrestle with defining the nature and scope of his work. For a half year after Edinburgh, however, that created no problem.

All post-conference details rested with the Continuation Committee. The work was Oldham's. He had the enormous task of editing Edinburgh's reports and seeing them through publication. Britain alone absorbed 15,000 sets. Widely distributed in other lands, they became influential in missionary planning. Oldham also sent out the conference "Message." His large correspondence with board secretaries invariably touched on relationships between the new international agency and the missionary societies. Most important, Oldham had to sit down in unhurried discussions with missionary executives to explain the Continuation Committee's aims and plans, to make explicit principles and policy, and in turn to seek advice on how best to serve the societies.[7] Later he helped to found the Conference of Missionary Societies in Great Britain and Ireland. During his first year's work he also spent eight weeks in North America, Germany, and Holland. All the while he was mulling over plans for an international missionary journal.

The Commissions. The Continuation Committee itself was at work through its commissions. (Within a year or two most of these were designated "committees.") These international groups began by feeling their way and seeking to discover what they could do effectively. Their reports display the difficulties involved in conceiving their assigned tasks.[8] Three of the nine did not meet during the year. Others had done considerable spade work. Several saw that their work overlapped, and some feared that their recommendations would not claim societies' serious attention.

Commissions with American, British, and Continental sections had difficulty transacting international business by correspondence. The American press relations group proposed a unified, New York office to channel missionary news to wire services, papers, and periodicals. The

Germans explained that the 1901 Continental Conference had created a German press committee which in 1911 was publishing monthly a thousand mission news-sheets, delivered almost exclusively to newspaper editors. The British commission regarded neither plan suitable for London. All were agreed that this was basically a national problem. Thus each commission found the first year one of orientation and probing in an endeavour quite new for every one concerned.[9]

On January 25, 1911, the executive body of the Continuation Committee met in London, and while British and Continental members were on hand, Dr. Mott was the only American present. In addition to many details of business, the group took two far-reaching actions: it sanctioned plans of the Continuation Committee's British members to proceed with a conference for the missionary societies in Great Britain and advocated immediate consideration of an "International Missionary Review."[10]

The Bishop Auckland Meeting, May, 1911

Nearly a year after its first session at Edinburgh the Continuation Committee met again at Auckland Castle, espiscopal home of the Bishop of Durham, Dr. H. C. G. Moule. The great castle, built in the thirteenth century, had once been the home of Bishop Joseph Butler. Now it provided pleasant living and working quarters for the Committee's members.

The meeting mirrored a year of cautious achievement. A number of British societies had joined together to set up "The Board of Study for the Preparation of Missionaries" suggested by Mrs. Creighton's commission and had selected an executive. Another proposal for an "International Committee" to negotiate with governments failed to reach a vote. Relations with governments, it was agreed, could best be handled nationally. Should unusual circumstances (*e.g.*, questions of extraterritoriality or opium) require international representation, the Continuation Committee itself could be authorized to initiate action. The meeting dissolved several commissions and created some new ones, one of which dealt with the Moslem question. Members learned that the World Missionary Conference's total income had exceeded $52,000 (£10,475), of which a $5,875 (£1,175) surplus was transferred to the Continuation Committee.[11] The Committee set its year's budget at $20,000 (£4,000) and agreed that three-sevenths would be raised in Britain, three-sevenths in America, and one-seventh on the Continent, with the expectation that missionary societies would contribute most of the amount directly. The two largest items budgeted were $7,500 (£1,500) for the chairman's and secretary's expenses and $5,500 (£1,100) for the next meeting of the Committee in America. Finally, an invitation from the Continent asked that the next world missionary conference in 1920 (here again the firmly rooted decennial idea) meet in Europe.[12]

Two paramount considerations claimed the Committee's attention. Because the missionary enterprise abroad had to be related to the Continuation Committee and because "personal touch" loomed so large in any effective presentation of aims and program, the Committee recognized its need for an emissary to Asia. Choosing the man best fitted for the task, it requested Dr. Mott in an honorary capacity to give a "considerable portion" of his time for a visit to the Christian communities of the East. As its chairman, Mott gave the Continuation Committee only a small part of his time. Many realized, of course, that even a segment of Mott's working year was an invaluable asset. His major responsibilities centred in his being general secretary of the World's Student Christian Federation, chief secretary of the Student Department of the International Committee of the YMCA, and chairman of the executive committee of the Student Volunteer Movement. In addition he held many other responsible posts. To accept the invitation obviously meant "great and difficult readjustments" in his work, but Mott promised to consider the matter carefully.[13]

The International Review of Missions. The Committee also determined to publish an *International Review of Missions.* The original proposal had come largely from Oldham, who envisaged a quarterly modelled in general on the *Hibbert Journal* with articles similar in calibre to those of *The East and the West.* With an interdenominational and international outlook, the new journal would explore principles rather than chronicle details, and year by year would foster a sense of unity in the task of world evangelism. Heartily approving, the Continuation Committee commissioned *The International Review of Missions* its official publication, but opened its scholarly pages to any suitable article. Unanimously chosen, J. H. Oldham became the new *Review*'s editor and brought out its first issue in January, 1912.[14]

Finally, "The Continuation Committee of the World Missionary

Conference, Edinburgh, 1910," as it referred to itself, accepted the provisional constitution drafted a year earlier. In so doing it simply reaffirmed the objectives set for it in the resolution by which it was established at Edinburgh.[15]

Results. The Continuation Committee's work during the succeeding year reflected the influence of the Auckland Castle meeting. Oldham spent much of his time preparing *The International Review of Missions* for publication. The first issue (January, 1912) purposed "to further the serious study of" and to contribute to the "science of missions."[16] Receiving wide acclaim, it fulfilled its supporters' hopes.

In the first number Mott described the Continuation Committee in detail and disclosed his own view of its rôle. He saw it becoming a "clearing house for the missionary societies," an agency to "facilitate closer co-operation" between them, and a vital force to spread Edinburgh's "spirit and atmosphere." Its fulfillment would come in an international committee "thoroughly representative of the vast and complex world missionary movement."[17]

Mott further expressed his conviction that the Committee's work rested on certain broad principles. While a "world's committee," it was no super-body, but rather sought to be a "servant of all." Moreover, it was independent and represented no church nor missionary society. Finally, it stood for co-operation without compromise of conviction—a fact, Mott prophesied, which would lead to a growing unity of spirit and action.[18]

The international commissions continued their work. One emphasized the great need for missionary councils in Asia, Africa, and Latin America. That on missionary preparation had already resulted in two independent agencies devoted to problems of missionary training and supported by societies in Britain and America.[19]

Yet the Continuation Committee envisioned growing difficulty in maintaining the societies' confidence, for it was independent—responsible to no missionary organization. Meanwhile, the event designated "Edinburgh, 1910" receded rapidly into the past. Naturally, this raised again cogent arguments for establishing the permanent international committee which would, presumably, unite existing national organizations. Committee members also faced the long-range ineffectiveness of most of their commissions. A battery of international groups involved unwieldiness and huge expense. Moreover, commissions represented only a handful of individuals and, like the Committee, spoke for no society. In addition, the Atlantic barrier encouraged European and British sections to emphasize India and Africa and American sections to concentrate on the Near and Far East. At first glance advantageous, this had its grave shortcomings. Distinctive contributions had been made, yet, unrelated to the boards, commission members feared that their efforts would be largely in vain.[20]

The Lake Mohonk Meeting, Autumn, 1912

The Continuation Committee assembled for its next meeting at beautiful Lake Mohonk, New York, from September 26 to October 2, 1912. Even on the boat trip up the scenic Hudson members transacted preliminary business, presaging the intense work of days ahead. When they gathered, certain very familiar faces were missing. Dr. George Robson of Scotland, Dr. Alfred Boegner of France, and Bishop Honda of Japan had died. The venerable Eugene Stock had had to resign.[21]

Commission reports claimed considerable time, and after much discussion the proposed international committee was dropped as premature. Its possible rejection by missionary societies led a majority to favour extending the Committee's work only and to omit any further plan. When the involved question of missions and governments arose, the group reaffirmed its earlier position that national organizations could best negotiate necessary action. Yet the Committee protested to the Japanese ambassador in Washington against the imprisonment of Korean Christians for their alleged plotting against the Japanese government. Uneasiness over increasingly evident threats of war was articulated for the first time as the Committee encouraged missions to promote the cause of peace in every way. Great cities, it was also discovered, were eager to have the next world missionary conference. Toronto, Berlin, and Barmen were vying with one another for the honor. Hamburg offered hospitality for 2,000 guests and a subsidy of $25,000! But the date and nature of the next great meeting were too uncertain to justify any action. Finally, since *The International Review of Missions* claimed so much of its editor's time, the Committee authorized an associate secretary for J. H. Oldham.[22]

Thus far we have omitted the Committee's most important consideration. Dr. Mott had long since agreed to serve as he had been requested a year earlier, and at Mohonk outlined the extensive preparations he had made for a tour in Asia. He had consulted missionary executives, had reviewed findings compiled by a private research secretary, and had studied all available data on the lands and churches he would be visiting. He had worked out a careful itinerary of conferences in each area, utilizing to best advantage every day from October, 1912, to May, 1913. Syllabi of questions—tentative drafts had already circulated on the field—would go to all delegates beforehand to provide a basis for discussion in all meetings. Mott was not travelling exclusively for the Continuation Committee, however, for as general secretary of the World's Student Christian Federation, he also planned an extensive program of student evangelism. In that task he had persuaded Sherwood Eddy to accompany and assist him. The two undertakings were distinctly different phases of the same tour, but nothing done for the Continuation Committee, Mott explained, would cost that body one cent.

A few generous friends had provided for the expenses of Mott and his assistants as well as the travel and conference needs of missionary and Asian delegates. As was to be the case again and again, Mott was able to enter upon a vast and effective itinerary, all of which accrued to the benefit of international missionary co-operation, without the Continuation Committee's—and later the International Missionary Council's—having to spend a dollar. Thus was much accomplished in the Committee's name which would otherwise almost certainly have been impossible.[23] How strategically important were the undisclosed benefactors who helped to lay the foundation of world-wide Christian co-operation! When the Lake Mohonk conference was over, John R. Mott set out for Asia.

The Continuation Committee Conferences in Asia

Mott went to Asia to bring the Protestant missionary movement there into first-hand touch with the spirit and aims of Edinburgh. He also offered to the East for its own use the Edinburgh technique of co-operation. A representative of the Continuation Committee, he put its developed machinery at the disposal of the younger churches.

The over-all strategy called for several sectional gatherings of leaders in each country. Usually lasting three days, these assemblies followed the general Edinburgh procedure. In addition, national conferences

with representatives appointed from the regional meetings were held
in India, China, and Japan. Each conference thoroughly discussed
eight major areas covered by the syllabus: occupation, evangelization,
the church, leadership, the training of missionaries, education, literature, and co-operation.[24] The Asian conferences replaced two Edinburgh subjects, the "home base" and "missions and governments,"
with "Christian leadership" and "Christian literature." Medical missions
and women's work, omitted in the original syllabus, emerged in nearly
every gathering as major subjects. Supplementing the Edinburgh Series
with the findings of these Asian conferences provides as nearly complete a picture of Protestant missions on the eve of World War I as one
can find.

Between November 11, 1912, and April 11, 1913, Mott convened
twenty-one conferences from Colombo to Tokyo. Of the nearly sixteen
hundred members who participated, 14 per cent were women and
35 per cent were Asians. This made the conferences much more representative than Edinburgh, and unlike that 1910 gathering, these
produced findings. Moreover, with the exception of the three national
meetings, none of these conferences had before it the results of its
predecessors. Yet throughout, almost complete unanimity prevailed in
the findings that emerged!

India.   Dr. Mott's first conference met at Colombo, Ceylon. Thereafter gatherings were held in Madras (at this meeting Mar Dionysius,
Metropolitan of the Jacobite Syrian Church, was present with several
of his fellow-churchmen), Bombay, Jubbulpore, Allahabad, Lahore,
and Calcutta. Just before Christmas in 1912, the India National Conference assembled in Calcutta. Among India's missionaries some dissatisfaction existed because no successor to past decennial meetings
had been planned for 1912. Embarrassed by "outside" initiative, they
happily accepted, nevertheless, the Continuation Committee's Calcutta
assembly as their "Decennial" gathering.[25]

The national conference built upon its regional predecessors and
became their summation. Largely through Mott's superb chairmanship,
it accomplished an enormous amount of work. It covered the full
syllabus, established a committee with a secretary for survey (Mott
accepted responsibility for raising its funds),[26] and authorized "Provincial Representative Councils of Missions" unified in a National Missionary Council.[27] The National Council was charged to assist the local
bodies, to deal with problems national in scope, and to maintain com-

munication with the Continuation Committee. Like the latter, it embodied no legislative authority but was consultative and advisory only.[28] The National Council and its member agencies began to function at once. By August, 1914, the Council had a half-time secretary, the Reverend Herbert Anderson of the Baptist Missionary Society. At the same time World War I broke in Europe and thrust upon this new organization nearly the entire burden of suspended German missions in India. The Council seemed to have been created providentially for just such an emergency. In that situation it found itself and became a solid foundation block in the world-wide network of missionary councils.[29]

Burma and Malaya. After the India National Conference Mott convened meetings at Rangoon, Burma, and at Singapore for Malaya, in mid-January, 1913. These resulted in "The Burma Council of Christian Missions," and in an "Interim Committee" to study the possibility of an "Advisory Council" for Malaya.[30] From these Mott went directly to China.

China. The 1907 China Centenary Conference with a thousand missionaries present had recommended a "Christian Federation" with a Chinese and a non-Chinese secretary. Virtually nothing had come of the proposal. Meanwhile, China had been caught up in Sun Yat-sen's Revolution of 1911. The prevalent nationalism permeated the Christian churches and resulted in strong demands for independence. This was the somewhat uneasy scene when Mott arrived in China to begin his first sectional conference at Canton in late January, 1913. By mid-March, he had conducted regional assemblies at Shanghai, Tsinan, Peking, and Hankow as well as a national meeting at Shanghai.

The National Conference, like the regional meetings, symbolized a new day for Protestant Christian churches in China. Only six years before, nine Chinese had been onlookers at a great convention of *missionaries.* Now, welcomed on a full equality, Chinese comprised nearly one-third of the membership of a conference of *Christians.* For the benefit of those without English, all discussion was translated into Chinese. Chinese laymen and women participated significantly and impressed all with their ability and devotion. The day had forever passed when Chinese Christians could be left out of any planning for the church in China.[31]

Discussions on the church aroused deepest interest. Self-support, self-government, and self-propagation were emphasized and the union of like denominations was encouraged. So strong was the feeling of existing unity that the conference urged Chinese churches of all denominations to use the designation, "The Christian Church in China" (*Chung Hua Chi Tu Chiao Hui*).[32] It likewise insisted upon the highest possible degree of co-operation and to achieve that end created a China Continuation Committee. The new national co-operative agency would act as a "board of reference" when so requested and would link Christian forces in China with the Edinburgh Continuation Committee. "Not less than one-third" of its members would be Chinese.[33]

The China Continuation Committee began to function at once and called to its Shanghai office two secretaries, the Reverend E. C. Lobenstine, a missionary of the Presbyterian Church, U.S.A., and the Reverend Cheng Ching-yi, pastor of an independent church. Established on a basis similar to that recommended in 1907, the China Continuation Committee accepted *The Chinese Recorder* as its official English organ and conducted most of its work through special subcommittees on survey, theological education, evangelism, and literature. The first annual meeting gathered at the close of the National Conference and the second convened in May, 1914.[34]

Manchuria and Korea. From China Mott went to Moukden, Manchuria, conducting there another conference with approximately seventy missionaries and one hundred nationals present. The group determined to form a "Federal Council" for Manchuria along the lines suggested by the 1907 Shanghai Conference.[35] In Korea Presbyterians and Methodists, who dominated the field, had founded in 1905 a "General Council of Evangelical Missions in Korea." An advisory body, its greatest accomplishments had been effective comity arrangements.[36] In 1911 it became the Federal Council of Protestant Evangelical Missions in Korea,[37] a delegated body with advisory and some administrative powers entrusted to it by the missions. At its first meeting in September, 1912, it acted upon Dr. Mott's scheduled visit for the spring of 1913.[38] Since the Federal Council did not represent all missionary work in Korea, the Mott conference created an inclusive "Field Advisory Committee" somewhat similar to the China Continuation Committee.[39]

Japan. Japan's situation differed from that in any other land. The zeal, initiative, and independence of able Japanese leaders produced much more "church consciousness" there than elsewhere. The distinction between the indigenous church and the foreign-guided mission, with attendant problems of relationship, had become by 1910 probably further advanced in Japan than in any other land.[40] Rather naturally, then, missionaries united after the Tokyo Conference in 1900 to form what became known in 1910 as "The Federated Missions," the most advanced body of its kind, with *The Christian Movement in Japan* its annual official organ.[41] Almost simultaneously and growing out of the Evangelical Alliance in Japan, there came into being in 1911 "The Federation of Churches in Japan," a body whose work on a much smaller scale resembled that of the Federal Council of the Churches of Christ in America. Its chairman, Dr. Hiromichi Kozaki, typified its exclusively Japanese leadership.[42]

The Continuation Committee conference in Japan included a meeting with missionaries, one with Japanese leaders, and the Japan National Conference of April 9 to 11. These all met at Tokyo and followed the regular eight-question syllabus. Preparatory commissions, usually with four Japanese and five missionaries, had thoroughly surveyed the ground beforehand and had produced a 175-page book that was distributed to delegates before they assembled.[43] Some criticisms arose over the selection of delegates by a central committee, but almost all agreed afterwards that the meetings had proved exceptionally representative. Interestingly, most missionaries came from outlying areas while the Japanese were drawn more largely from the great cities.[44] Four delegates from the Russian Orthodox Mission attended, including Archbishop Sergius.

The Continuation Committee conferences marked a high point in Protestant missions in Japan. They lifted vision of the total task to a new level. They placed major emphasis upon Japan's complete occupation and resulted in a three-year National Evangelistic Campaign, for which Dr. Mott provided one-third of the necessary finances. They emphasized the great need for a central Christian university, equal to the imperial universities, as "essential to the ultimate success" of Christianity in Japan. Finally, they resulted in a Continuation Committee of Japan with an initial membership of thirty divided equally for appointment between the two federations. These thirty later appointed fifteen others from organizations and denominations not represented in either federation. Limited to tasks referred to it by either federation, the Committee served primarily as Japan's link with the Edinburgh Continuation Committee.[45] The conferences' two great achievements included the National Evangelistic Campaign of 1914 to 1917 with its notable results[46] and the Continuation Committee whose unique rôle was to be the only body in Japan uniting missionaries and Japanese Christians from diverse traditions on a basis of equality.

Significance. Each of these conferences contributed to the emerging world Christian community. In immediately apparent results, each provided a necessary overall survey of Christian attainments and needs. Moreover, they brought missionaries and national Christians much closer to each other in their common task of evangelism in overwhelmingly non-Christian lands. This closer community came at an especially crucial time in China and Japan where some tensions between missionaries and nationals had developed. Each conference provided enormous stimulus to co-operative endeavours in medicine, evangelism, education, and literature. Finally, they produced Continuation Committees that symbolized and actually carried out nation-wide projects of Christian co-operation.

While the Continuation Committee played an indispensable rôle in their creation, these national organizations came into being through the independent action of churches and missions in Asia. In no sense were they subordinate to the Edinburgh Continuation Committee. That body was viewed rather as a first among equals, symbolizing the togetherness of all the national missionary organizations. Each continuation committee provided a voice for the thoughts of the younger churches in its land and gradually began to translate their hopes into action. All the while these national bodies were aware of being linked by an international agency with councils sharing similar problems and aspirations in other lands. The resulting growth of world-consciousness and of commitment to a common task produced in years to come the most far-reaching consequences.

One interesting side-light illustrates the importance the Continuation Committee's chairman attached to these developments. Just before Mott reached Tokyo, the newly elected President of the United States, Woodrow Wilson, cabled that he had "set [his] heart" on Mott's becoming the American ambassador to China. After much thought, Mott cabled his refusal: he could not resign from his important duties.[47] Thirty-five years later, reviewing his labours for international missionary co-operation, Dr. Mott added, "My first and my greatest contribution to the International Missionary Council was to bring about the formation of the National Christian Councils."[48] These councils were not constituted as such until the early twenties, but in almost every instance they were simply a modification of the already existing continuation committees.

The Creation of Other Missionary Councils

Mott's remarkable accomplishment in Asia was matched by other equally important, if less dramatic, achievements in Britain and elsewhere as impulses radiating from Edinburgh and its Continuation Committee resulted directly in the creation of still other missionary councils. While all these later joined in forming the International Missionary Council, from the standpoint of international missionary co-operation during the war years, that formed in Britain carried the greatest significance.

Great Britain. The London Secretaries' Association in October, 1910, asked its secretary, J. H. Ritson, to inquire whether British members of the Continuation Committee could initiate a conference similar to that held annually in North America. With favourable preliminary indications, British members in session on December 2, 1910, resolved to convene such a gathering on the Edinburgh principle of representation.[49]

That meeting, held June 14 to 15 at York, moved that "Conferences of Missionary Societies in Great Britain and Ireland be held annually." Moreover, it created a "Standing Committee" to execute the interim work of the annual meetings,[50] and immediately that permanent agency went into action. It set up a group on missions and government, met again in October and November, and framed a constitution for the annual conference whose executive body it was.[51]

When the Conference of Missionary Societies in Great Britain and Ireland first met at Swanwick, June 12 to 14, 1912, it reappointed the Standing Committee and accepted a $12,500 (£2,500) budget for the year ahead. Approximately two-thirds of that amount represented the British share of the Continuation Committee's expenses and nearly one-third was allotted to the Board of Study (for missionary training). The remaining $250 (£50) went for conference expenses. The budget bound no one but guided the Standing Committee's recommendation to each society for its proportionate contribution.[52] For seven years voluntary leadership maintained the Conference of British Missionary Societies' extensive program, and not until 1919 did it create a salaried secretariat.

Like its North American counterpart, the Conference of British Missionary Societies had no binding power over its members. Its resolutions embodied a summation of expert opinion and were submitted to the societies for what use they chose to make of them. Probably its greatest initial contribution lay in acquainting missionary executives with one another and in helping them to focus upon their common problem. The Conference of British Missionary Societies functioned through the Standing Committee, through the permanent Committee on Missions and Government, and through special sub-committees on Moslems, literature, press, etc. Fortunately, it assumed responsibility for acquainting British societies with the Continuation Committee's activities and through that international body felt itself closely linked with the missionary agencies in North America, on the Continent, and in the Far East.[53]

Europe.   Edinburgh's stimulus to missionary co-operation in Europe must also be noted. The Danish Missions Council (*Dansk Missionsraad*), organized in April, 1912, brought together eleven societies and associated itself with the work of some earlier inter-society committees. In its formation the Edinburgh Conference and Continuation Committee through Count Joachim Moltke exerted their influence.[54]

In the Netherlands, Edinburgh's impulse produced no immediate results. Earlier, at the instance of the Netherlands Bible Society, Dutch missionary societies had joined to support a missions consul in the Netherlands Indies, and from 1906 the consul's office provided necessary *liaison* between missions and government on many social and moral questions.[55] Edinburgh's spirit and its secretary's visit to Holland led the Netherlands Bible Society's secretary to propose a Dutch "Missionary Council" for "world relations" and responsibilities in the Indies. The motion, accepted in the Bible Society's executive committee in March, 1911, came to nought.[56] The Advisory Committee (*Commissie van Advies*) for the missions consulate, while not a national missionary council, served for some years from its founding in 1915 as the Dutch link in international missionary co-operation.

In Sweden, Edinburgh's influence stirred desire for a general Swedish missionary conference. Karl Fries, a Continuation Committee member, invited all Swedish missionary societies to a conference in September, 1912, at which time 300 official representatives from twelve societies met together as the "General Swedish Missionary Conference." From this gathering came the "Working Committee" (*Arbetskomité*), the Conference's executive body. In years to come the Committee increasingly influenced Swedish missionary life.[57] It convened assemblies again in 1916 and in 1920, at which time the General Conference reconstituted itself as "The Swedish Missionary Council."

Africa. Edinburgh exhibited little influence on missionary cooperation across Africa. But its sharp challenge to South Africa that lack of co-operation there was hindering effective occupation resulted in a representative gathering at King William's Town in September, 1911, to consider the charge. A commission appointed by that meeting reported at Capetown in 1912 to the Fourth General Missionary Conference of South Africa. The assembly pronounced Edinburgh's judgment too severe, replaced its old board of arbitration with an occupation commission, and did not meet again until 1921.[58]

The long-famous Kikuyu Conference of 1913 in British East Africa has sometimes been regarded as an outgrowth of Edinburgh, but this was not the case. Kikuyu referred not once to Edinburgh. Moreover, its proposal for a "Federation of Missionary Societies" had been framed in 1909 before Edinburgh. World-wide Anglican controversy over Kikuyu arose because two Church of England bishops shared in a service of Holy Communion according to the Book of Common Prayer, but in a Church of Scotland mission and with non-Anglicans participating.[59] When Lambeth finally acted, its judgement made it impossible for the dioceses of Mombasa and Uganda to enter the proposed federation. The third Kikuyu assembly in 1918 created an "Alliance of Missionary Societies in British East Africa" to negotiate with the government and to advance the cause of church union.[60] In 1924 this body was succeeded by the Kenya Missionary Council.

As a direct result of Edinburgh, the home boards of the Protestant missions serving Madagascar sent simultaneous deputations to the vast island off Africa's East Coast. Their visit culminated in a conference at Tananarive in October, 1913. From it came a "Standing Joint Consultative Board" to consider questions of education, an agreement to apportion the poorly occupied territory, and a Continuation Committee to link Christian missions in Madagascar with the Edinburgh Continuation Committee.[61]

The Moslem World. The Second Missionary Conference on Behalf of the Mohammedan World met at Lucknow, India, January 23 to 28, 1911.[62] With clear knowledge of Edinburgh's concern with Islam, it projected a Continuation Committee which wrote at once to the Edinburgh group, asking that the latter urge Great Britain, the United States, and Germany bid Turkey to insure equality and freedom of

worship as guaranteed under its constitution. Without taking this
specific action, the Edinburgh Continuation Committee appointed an
international commission for the Moslem problem.[63] In the 1920's the
Lucknow Continuation Committee abandoned thought of convening
its own conference and merged its plans with those of the International
Missionary Council.[64]

The Hague Meeting, November, 1913

Meanwhile the Continuation Committee, spurring the creation of
new co-operative missionary bodies, continued its activities "at home."
In May, 1913, shortly after Mott's return to America from Asia, the
offices of the Committee and of *The International Review of Missions*
were moved from the original quarters to 1 Charlotte Square in Edinburgh. Oldham had done a superb job with the *Review*. Its first issue
of 1913 included a world missionary survey which was to become an
annual feature. The journal's pages sometimes included articles by able
Roman Catholic writers and regularly recorded brief news notes of
Roman Catholic missions.[65]

On Mott's return from his Asia trip, he prepared for the autumn
meeting of the Continuation Committee at The Hague a full report
of his impressions. They revealed a conception and strategy of "world
church" beyond anything Mott had written before. They disclosed the
mind of a great statesman, acknowledging the limited authority of
the Continuation Committee, yet planning in bold, sweeping terms
with full expectation that his vision would commend itself to his
constituency. As never before Mott wrote as though he were actually
engaged in knitting together a world church. The Committee, he
declared, "should do everything in its power to strengthen the bonds
of union between the new Churches in non-Christian lands and the
Church Historic, the Church Universal. . . . There could be no greater
danger than for native Christianity to become separate from historical,
credal [*sic*], ecumenical, vital Christianity."[66] This in the autumn of
1913 in Holland was the thinking that confronted the small international group which symbolized missionary co-operation.

The Continuation Committee assembled near The Hague for the
week of November 14. As a meeting there was little to distinguish
it from its predecessors. Delegates lived and worked in the comfortable, old Hotel-Castle Oud-Wassanaer. At the end of the conference,

however, all agreed that in an exceptional way they had shared together a sense of God's presence.

Invitation to Mott.   When all the commissions had made their annual reports, the Committee extended a carefully considered invitation to Dr. Mott. In view of overwhelming needs revealed by Edinburgh, by the Continuation Committee, and by Mott's Asian conferences, the members declared that the church was "still far from making an adequate response to the call of God." Therefore, to place at the disposal of the church what had "been entrusted to it of experience, knowledge, and influence," the Committee asked its chairman to "devote a large part of his time and energy" to its program. It regarded Mott as uniquely able to represent the Continuation Committee to the boards, to maintain close relations with Asia's new co-operative agencies, and to organize further conferences in Africa and the Near East. Mott "intimated his acceptance of the invitation."[67]

The Hague Principle of Missionary Co-operation.   The most important action taken at The Hague described the basis for international missionary co-operation, although the fundamental policy involved had been implicitly assumed right along. The heart of "the Hague principle" declared: ". . . the only Bodies entitled to determine missionary policy are the Home Boards, the Missions, and the Churches concerned."[68] Here was notice to all that the Continuation Committee could not and would not dictate to any missionary society. Moreover, implicit was the understanding that what had been formed at Edinburgh was not, as many were inclined to think, another non-denominational body, auxiliary to the churches, as the Student Christian Movement and the YMCA were, but an *interdenominational* agency through which the missionary societies themselves could function jointly, however limited such common effort might appear in proportion to their other activities.[69] In the formulation of specific missionary policy the Committee recognized its responsibility to invite societies to confer when occasion arose, to share with all its fund of information, and to help each mission view specific problems from an international and interdenominational perspective.

When the question arose of relationship to the newly formed agencies in India, China, and Japan, the Committee emphasized that it was neither organically related to them nor responsible for what they did. Nevertheless, it hoped for a growing "relation of mutual understanding and helpfulness, and [desired] to assist them in plans they may develop for the extension of Christ's Kingdom." Whenever it did so, it agreed to consult with all home boards concerned.[70] Here again the Committee sought to stress its advisory nature and to reassert its rôle as servant, not master.

The Committee had felt called to go forward. With its world purview, with its wide experience, and with the service of a battery of missionary experts it naturally desired on occasion to suggest missionary policy to the boards. Long and serious deliberation took place before the Committee enunciated its fundamental principle: that only missions and churches could determine missionary policy. That principle, as we shall see, still honoured and maintained in a spirit of complete trust and understanding by all concerned, provides the key to the nature of international missionary co-operation.

Unsuccessful in its first attempt to find an associate for Oldham and aware that its program had expanded beyond what one man could carry, the Continuation Committee at The Hague invited Kenneth Maclennan to its staff. Maclennan, then general secretary of the Laymen's Missionary Movement in Scotland, became a full-time associate secretary with Oldham in December, 1913, with primary responsibility for administrative duties.

An Experiment in International Missionary Co-operation

The Continuation Committee had planned to meet next at Oxford, England, in September, 1914, but it never assembled again. Officially, the Committee continued until 1921. Actually, the advent of World War I sounded its death knell. True, international missionary co-operation surmounted its first crisis during the war and grew strong. But the Continuation Committee of the four post-Edinburgh years with its annual conferences and its international commissions died in the summer of 1914.

The passing of that Committee as it had been known affords opportunity for a retrospective, assaying view. Perhaps the best appraisal can be made in terms of its secretary, for Oldham had been at its very heart. Befitting his position, he was the Committee's servant. But the personality and accomplishments of a superb secretary infuse themselves into the very nature of the organization he serves—and Oldham was a superb secretary.

Originally, Oldham had not wanted the Continuation Committee's secretaryship, but he had been prevailed upon to accept it. Month by month the work mushroomed and the new secretary grew with it. A man who recognized fundamental principles and acted upon them, Oldham inspired increasing confidence among missionary executives. Implicit in all that he did was devotion to that basic principle of co-operation later articulated at The Hague. Moreover, he knew that as secretary he could only carry out his committee's desires—not initiate action to which it would be bound. No legalist, however, Oldham recognized that rigid adherence to this fundamental would not only hobble action but also prove the principle unworkable. He saw that the confidence placed in him by Continuation Committee members and by missionary secretaries not only allowed him but required him to move ahead, initiating action even before he had his entire committee's full consent. This was possible because he recognized and respected the convictions and view-points of each Committee member and never compromised them. In other words, Oldham's complete sensitivity to his committee's feelings enabled him to know that he could act, when necessary, in the belief that the Continuation Committee would later approve his judgement. Should the slightest demur arise, he was immediately ready to move back to a position that found unanimous acceptance. In his "heart of hearts," Oldham firmly held the first principle of international missionary co-operation (the Hague formulation) to be *"true and essential."*[71]

On the opening night of the Edinburgh Conference, the Archbishop of Canterbury had referred to men being "weighed rather than counted." Thus pungent phrase pegged a principle in a young Scot's mind. Just as Quakers defer action until the "sense of the meeting" is reached, so Oldham learned that the surest way to speed effective missionary co-operation lay not in a majority vote, but in a group's unanimous conviction. A committee composed of representatives from boards (even though the Continuation Committee was technically without members representing any missionary society, it had to proceed for its own good as though this were the case) could not, as a committee of individuals might, make decisions by majority vote. That, in effect, would have been issuing instructions to a particular board which, unconvinced by the action, might have had to withdraw. This meant, rather than counting favourable votes, weighing men as representing the thoughts of a much larger group and being certain that everyone fully understood and agreed to a particular course before it was undertaken.[72] This also meant that whenever a member's absence left a particular view-point unrepresented, the secretary would speak for the absentee's position to insure a hearing for all sides and to prevent precipitous action. How natural that those for whom he laboured trusted Oldham so completely.

The Continuation Committee's secretary was a philosopher—a personalist. To speak of organizations apart from specific individuals meant little, for to him only persons were real. Thus in his later thinking the designations "Continuation Committee," "Emergency Committee," and "International Missionary Council" made little difference. Their only reality derived from the fact that through each, the same group of persons was accomplishing a necessary and continuous work. Oldham's concern lay not with organizational structure but with what men could achieve to meet the needs requiring international missionary co-operation. This helps in part to explain why Oldham and Mott worked closely with a small international group of able and representative board secretaries, trusted men whose opinions carried weight. If they agreed in principle to a particular course of action, Oldham felt reasonably assured that in his execution of that action the whole committee would agree.

Finally, it is no secret that the "least satisfying years" in Oldham's career were his first ones as the Continuation Committee's secretary. Why? Because he could not persuade himself that he had a real job. In many respects the Continuation Committee was an experiment. It went against the Scotsman's grain to have to ask overburdened board secretaries to leave their work to discuss matters that could not be directly implemented. Thus he viewed much that was done by the international commissions as unjustifiable. As it turned out, lack of time and money prevented their functioning as international bodies. When they met as national sections, it became obvious that they merely paralleled what could better be done through the Foreign Missions Conference or the Conference of British Missionary Societies. The outbreak of war only hastened abandonment of the international commissions.

In spite of its experimental nature, the Continuation Committee, as a step toward a larger, international organization, marked a tremendous advance. Its very existence helped to overcome difficulties. Moreover, the constant and growing need to negotiate with governments brought new willingness for an international, representative, missionary agency. Thus, while the war immobilized and sped the abandonment of the Continuation Committee, it propelled missionary societies toward precisely that organization Edinburgh had envisioned for the future.

The Continuation Committee achieved notable success. Most noteworthy of its accomplishments stood Mott's tour in Asia and the creation of co-operative, Christian agencies there. For itself the Committee had accumulated an invaluable treasure of experience—positive and negative—in international co-operation. It developed a powerful and able leadership, not only in Mott, Oldham, and Maclennan, but also among those missionary administrators without whose efforts nothing could have been accomplished. Moreover, it had provided a working example of an international, co-operative agency, and probably no board realized the extent of its dependence upon the Committee until war severely restricted its international outreach. However weak—however imperfect, it had filled a need no other agency could meet. Above all, it constantly pointed beyond itself to a representative agency. In this the Continuation Committee laid an indispensable foundation for future international missionary co-operation.

The War Years

The forces leading to war had long been in the making. Among them one must reckon nationalism and the growth of pan-Slavism and pan-Germanism. Likewise, the urge for commercial and colonial expansion had precipitated crisis after crisis in the years immediately before the war. The Balkans had been a constant source of trouble. Austria's annexation of Bosnia and Herzegovina in 1908 had provoked ill-feeling between Russia and Austria, and the Balkan wars of 1912-13 had left a highly volatile situation. On June 28, 1914, a Serbian nationalist assassinated the Austrian Archduke, Francis Ferdinand at Sarajevo, and exactly one month later Austria was at war with Serbia. The powder keg of World War I had been fired.

When Russia mobilized troops to quell Austria's Serbian invasion, Germany declared war on Russia. Two days later on August 3 Germany was at war with France. The next day England declared war on Germany and Austria, and by early autumn the Allied Powers were fighting Turkey. At the same time the deadlock of trench warfare had begun in Northern France. Meanwhile, most of the German colonies were seized by the French and British. The Allies quickly took Togoland, Samoa, and New Guinea. The Cameroons proved more stubborn, but within eighteen months, they had fallen. By early November, 1914, Japan had wrested Tsingtao from German control and in the meantime had occupied the German-held Marshalls, Marianas, Palau, and the Carolines. By the summer of 1915 German Southwest Africa had fallen to the British. In German East Africa, however, the opposing armies stayed in the field until the Armistice was signed. World War I was not only a war of armies but of peoples, and its tentacles stretched to every continent.

The war produced chaos and left in its wake tremendous economic and political upheavals. Its effects reached every area of life, and the Christian missionary enterprise proved no exception. Had its impact been confined to Europe and Britain, it would directly have disrupted only a large segment of the home base of missions. But the war involved colonial areas around the world where it wreaked further havoc on the missionary enterprise.

Over and above the physical impairment inflicted upon missions, the most distressing effect of the war lay in the wedge it drove into the Christian community. Attempted distinctions between love for Christian brothers and hatred for a nation's evil, as one group of Christians hurled recriminations at another, further reveal the tragedy of what was happening. With the war only one month advanced, a group of German churchmen addressed an "Appeal to Protestant Christians Abroad." Many of its signers, having attended the World Missionary Conference, referred to Edinburgh's "sacred legacy" and declared: "the guilt of [war] rests . . . not on our people." To this statement the Archbishop of Canterbury drafted a reply signed by many other widely known British Christians. Amazed by their German brothers' inability to recognize the true facts, the English churchmen replied: "Dear to us as peace is, the principles of truth and honor are yet more dear."[73] This exchange and others that followed it symbolized the tragedy that has occurred again and again when Christians of two warring nations have believed in the complete justice of their respective countries' causes. The war inflicted no greater disaster upon the Christian missionary enterprise than its rupture of the bonds of Christian love.

World War I and German Missions

It is quite beyond the scope of this study to chart the total disruptive effects of World War I on Christian missions. That has been done elsewhere.[74] Naturally, war's outbreak imposed difficulties on all missions. Even those unhindered by conflict in their homeland often found it impossible to transmit money. Much travel was halted. Markets everywhere were in confusion. German missions were drastically affected, and since international, co-operative missionary endeavour focussed upon them, we must briefly examine their plight.

German Protestant missions conducted their work very largely in British territory or in German colonies taken over by the Allied Powers. Conflicting statistics confuse the picture, but the German missionary societies' official report to the Foreign Office in Berlin shows that at the war's outbreak nearly 1,900 missionaries, including wives and single women, held the field. They ministered to approximately 630,000 baptized Christians and, of course, to a total constituency much larger than that. Approximately 215,000 pupils attended their schools.[75]

At the outset some German missionaries were immediately interned (as were some English missionaries in German East Africa), many were repatriated, while others were allowed to continue their work as before. Only in Japan (where two couples served), China, the Dutch East Indies, and the Union of South Africa were German missionaries allowed to continue. Elsewhere throughout Africa, India, and the Islands of the Pacific by 1916-17 almost all had been removed from their former fields.

The wholesale disruption of German missions affected not only missionaries but also more seriously those among whom they served. Yet a heartening story of aid to these destitute missions can be pieced together. The National Missionary Council of India and the China Continuation Committee, both supported largely by funds from Britain and America, rendered incalculable service to German missions in their respective lands. They negotiated with the governments, arranged for other missions to provide temporary support, and encouraged the interned or dislocated missionaries. Nearly all the emergency funds they distributed came from America (in China's case 98 per cent). In India the National Missionary Council defended German missionaries against reckless and damaging charges hurled at them. When in 1915 the German missionaries were removed, the Bishop of Chota Nagpur, Dr. Foss Westcott, came to the help of the Gossner Mission in India and kept much of its program intact. Lutheran societies from America assisted several German missions with money and personnel, staving off an otherwise inevitable collapse. The Church of Sweden Mission, with some help from the Danish Mission, took over the work of the Leipzig Society. The National Missionary Council assumed responsibility for the Basel Mission, largest of the societies in India affected by the war, and "farmed out" its work to different Christian bodies. The biggest segment came under the wing of the South India United Church which in turn was buttressed with financial grants from the London Missionary Society, the United Free Church of Scotland, and American boards.[76]

The war's effect on German missions was most deeply felt in Africa. All German missionaries in Togoland were repatriated in 1916, with no further provision made for their work, although one or two Swiss stayed on for awhile. Eighty-four were removed from the Cameroons in 1915, and not until 1917 was the Paris Society able to send three persons to help hold the work together. In Tanganyika the Africans, with a minimum of supervisory help, kept their Christian work going. The Basel Mission's great field on the Gold Coast had staffed thirty-three missionaries and an even larger group of Europeans in the mission's supporting commercial enterprise. When the Germans were removed, the United Free Church of Scotland supplied ten missionaries to maintain the mission. In German East Africa no really effective aid was possible, although British societies attempted to give token assistance and held some areas together with African help. With the exception of South Africa, the largest German field in Africa and where German societies continued throughout the war, the story was elsewhere much the same.[77]

International Missionary Co-operation and the War

As we have seen, war's outbreak brought an end to the Continuation Committee. The office continued, the name remained, but what had been spoken of as the Continuation Committee belonged to the past. Throughout the war it maintained in theory a non-functioning nominal existence. Yet Edinburgh's spirit remained. The essential core of international missionary co-operation, largely divested of its former covering, adapted itself to the situation.

Constitutionally the Continuation Committee had had no tie with the Conference of British Missionary Societies nor with the Foreign Missions Conference. Yet annually these bodies had made self-assessments that provided the budget for international co-operation. Their members helped to compose the Continuation Committee's membership. As secretaries of the international agency, Oldham and Maclennan held *ex-officio* status on the Conference of British Missionary Societies' committee. Mott played a large rôle in the Foreign Missions Conference. The two national bodies worked closely with the international commissions, in some instances supporting a commission's undertaking and more often merging its efforts with their own. Thus, while complete separation was acknowledged, the Continuation Committee had become in practice a binding link between the two organizations. Before the war had progressed very far, international missionary co-operation—what remained of the Continuation Committee—became no more and no less than the international functioning of the Conference of British Missionary Societies and the Foreign Missions Conference. Thus during the war in a limited but real sense, what may be spoken of as the Continuation Committee became what the International Missionary Council was later to be—a body composed of and functioning through national councils.

The Chairman's Rôle

Through the war years the Continuation Committee's chairman did relatively little within the framework of missionary co-operation. Rather he gave himself to organize the YMCA's activities among the soldiers and the prisoners of war in Europe and then among American soldiers in their homeland and abroad. In the United States he gave inspiring leadership to great financial campaigns for humanitarian projects. During the first years of the war Mott personally raised the money for YMCA work among prisoners on both sides. Before it was over Mott had led voluntary campaigns that produced nearly $260,-000,000 in America. Each year he travelled to Europe for first-hand inspection and supervision.[78]

European Mission, Autumn, 1914. Mott also found marginal time to serve the cause of international missionary co-operation. With the outbreak of hostilities, he hurried to Europe, seeking to get directly at the heart of the war's disruption. After a brief conference with the Archbishop of Canterbury, Mott went to Germany, then to Switzerland, Holland, and France, and finally back to England. Wherever he travelled, he maintained an attitude of neutrality, for he purposed to create an organization that would best meet the needs of soldiers and prisoners of war on both sides. Before leaving the United States, he agreed to survey the Continental missionary situation for the Committee of Reference and Counsel of the Foreign Missions Conference so that that American body could be most effective in meeting the demands of the hour. To this end Mott conferred in Germany among others with Adolph Harnack, Julius Richter, Karl Axenfeld, and G. Haussleiter.

The German mission leaders were deeply grateful for Mott's visit and for his personal conferences with them. For them he became the symbol of all that is best in Christian, international missionary co-operation. Most of all they appreciated his ability to enter into their thinking and to understand their problems as they viewed them.[79] Mott stood as the epitome of Christian brotherhood.

Unable to read or understand German, Mott managed with great patience and through interpreters to enter remarkably well into German thinking. The whole country's intense feeling against England had swayed the minds and hearts of her missionary leaders. Consequently, much as they might wish Mott to express himself in their favour, they accepted and respected his neutrality.[80] When Mott referred to American desire to raise a fund for continental missions, Dr. Haussleiter, speaking for the *Ausschuss*, gratefully suggested that such help would be regarded only as a loan to be repaid after the war. The Paris Mission, he pointed out, needed financial aid much more than any of the German societies, all of which sympathized with its plight. Moreover, he explained that since communication would become increasingly difficult, the *Ausschuss* had chosen the trusted pastor, Frederich Würz, who lived near Basel, intermediary for all correspondence between Germany and America.[81]

Back in England by November, 1914, Mott conferred with Sir Edward Grey, British foreign secretary, Lord Balfour of Burleigh, and missionary leaders. All listened eagerly to the arguments of the Germans Mott had interviewed and discussed their own views at length. The mood on both sides was one of holy crusade and was vented equally by self-righteous tirades against the "despicable calumny" of the enemy. When Mott returned to America and reported to the Foreign Missions Conference, it empowered its Committee of Reference and Counsel to create, if possible, a fund to help meet the most urgent needs of Continental missions in the field when such bodies could not be aided by some adjoining American mission.[82]

Appeals for Aid. In the months ahead appeal after appeal from the Continent reached Mott's desk. Some urged his stopping American munition shipments to France and England. Others requested financial aid for certain missions. Some societies sought information about missionaries long unheard from. With England and Germany at war, Mott became the remnant-symbol of the Continuation Committee. For the German societies he stood as a board of international appeal, and when petitions came, Mott had them translated and studied them carefully. Many of them dealt with the plight of German missionaries, for whom internment and repatriation sometimes brought insults, suffering, and maltreatment. This was especially so for those in the Cameroons who, taken from their stations, suffered indignities, plundering, and foul sanitary conditions.[83] The Basel Mission's vigorous protest on this incident reached the British societies and was considered by Lord Balfour's committee on missions and government. While sympathetic, the committee regarded the evidence at hand inadequate to justify protests to the Colonial Office.[84] Probably with no small amount of common sense the Continuation Committee secretaries felt it unwise to approach the government directly on many occasions with "smaller" matters. They held that "any appearance of attempting to embarrass the government in a time of military strain and crisis might prejudice [their] future influence" for the good of the missionary enterprise.[85]

Despite all his other responsibilities, Mott managed to give considerable attention to the war-time needs of Continental missions. Early in 1912 the YMCA's International Committee had asked him to become its general secretary. At the time he had been unable to give answer, but on August 10, 1915, when the burdens of war were heavy on his shoulders, Mott accepted that post.[86] Even while assuming this great added responsibility, he kept all his former commitments. Within the Foreign Missions Conference, Mott served as chairman of the

Continental Missions Relief Fund. By the end of 1915 it had distributed more than $27,000, nearly half of which went to the China Continuation Committee for Continental missions. A year later the fund had collected an additional $17,000, most of which went to the Paris Mission.[87] Up to America's entry into the war, Mott had personally raised and sent $6,500 to India for distribution through the National Missionary Council (all of it went to the Gossner Mission) and $17,000 to the China Continuation Committee for Continental missions.[88]

Mission to Russia. German missions had from 1914 looked to Mott as their neutral friend. Two war-time political appointments, however, transformed their trust into a suspicion of betrayal. In 1916 President Woodrow Wilson appointed Mott to a joint commission to discuss the settlement of American-Mexican difficulties. One periodical viewed Mott's membership as "open notice that the President expects Mexico to be dealt with not according to the dictates of worldly advantage . . . but in remembrance of this nation's brotherly obligation to be considerate, patient, and helpful."[89] The agreement reached helped to avoid war.

Again in 1917 President Wilson appointed Mott to a special diplomatic mission to Russia. Under the leadership of Elihu Root, the group reached that land in June, 1917, for the obvious purpose of strengthening ties with Russia to aid the Allies. His biographer states, however, that in accepting appointment, Mott "explicitly confined his share in the work to religious, educational, and humanitarian contacts."[90] Regardless of how his action might be interpreted, Mott believed that circumstances placed him in a unique position of Christian responsibility to serve Russia and his own homeland, but from several countries in Europe his decision brought him the severest and most bitter criticism he ever faced.

News of Mott's membership on the Russian commission produced a violent reaction in Germany. Both sides viewed the conflict as a holy and righteous defense of all that is honourable. To German missionary leaders this great world-figure, who personified supranational missionary co-operation, had entered the lists against them—against what they sincerely believed to be their just struggle for self-defense. As German subjects they could understand his accepting political appointments as natural patriotism. As Christians they believed that Mott's course required his resignation from the Continuation Committee. Baffled, dismayed, and completely shaken by what they regarded a mistaken judgement upon the rightness of their cause, they demanded that he surrender what to them was his selfishly held position of international missionary prestige since he no longer could claim the allegiance of all. Elihu Root's statements of the commission's aims further bewildered them. How could Mott be party to such plans? Their growing bitterness against Mott finally resulted in their repudiating him as head of the Continuation Committee.[91]

The Outworking of the Continuation Committee

In name the Continuation Committee continued until 1921. As a piece of international machinery it stopped functioning in 1914, although its direct influence through several of its commissions' sections continued until America's entrance into the war. Yet, as we have indicated, the Committee served, in effect, only as the technical apparatus encasing the kernel of international missionary co-operation. Thus while the Continuation Committee as an organization was suddenly halted and then slowly disintegrated, international missionary co-operation as a vital force continued through the activities of Mott, Oldham, and Maclennan, especially as they worked through the Conference of British Missionary Societies and the Foreign Missions Conference.

The Panama Congress. Requiring what almost amounts to a break in the continuity of our story, we must shift our attention back to the Southern Hemisphere of the Western World. There, remote from the war that enveloped Europe, the Congress on Christian Work in Latin America met in Panama from February 10 to 19, 1916.[92] Arranged for by the Committee on Cooperation in Latin America, it had no official tie with the Continuation Committee. Yet it had been born at Edinburgh and had been projected by men closely associated with the Continuation Committee. Organizationally it was a near replica of the World Missionary Conference, even to the eight commissions that prepared its preliminary studies.[93] At Panama Professor Eduardo Monteverde of the University of Uruguay presided over the Congress. Robert E. Speer chaired it in working sessions, and Mott chaired its business committee. The Reverend Samuel Guy Inman, who for more than a year had devoted his entire time and energy to preparations for the congress, served as its executive secretary.

Approximately half of the 304 official delegates were Latin Americans. The others were nationals from the United States, Canada, England, Spain, and Italy. Accredited visitors swelled the total to nearly 500. Roman Catholic leaders had been invited to attend, but none was present.[94] In one respect the Panama Congress marked a definite advance over Edinburgh. Rather than being a "home base" gathering of missionary experts, it was a conference of nationals and missionaries in Latin America. Moreover, Panama like Edinburgh wanted a continuing organization to perpetuate the co-operative endeavour it had initiated. It resolved unanimously that the Committee on Cooperation in Latin America should be that body.

Following Panama, congress-appointed deputations visited seven Latin American countries to convene regional conferences. Held from February through April, 1916, these gatherings met in South America's four largest republics—Peru, Chile, Argentina, and Brazil—as well as in Colombia, Cuba, and Puerto Rico.[95] Throughout Latin America the combined impact of the Panama Congress and the regional conferences greatly stimulated co-operation and more effective evangelization.

The German Repudiation.　In Europe more than a year after the Panama Congress, German members of the Continuation Committee attacked that body's policy and status. Issuing a "Declaration" in midsummer, 1917, they listed what they considered to be Mott's offenses against supranational missionary co-operation as it was symbolized in the Continuation Committee. They also listed the reported demands, gleaned from two British newspapers, of the general assemblies of the Church of Scotland and the United Free Church of Scotland to exclude German missionaries after the war from British territories and former German colonies for "a long period of years." Moreover, they noted certain unfortunate remarks (spoken in a moment of great sorrow brought on by a war-time tragedy and later much regretted) made by J. N. Ogilvie in the Assembly of the Church of Scotland.

The "Declaration" included a protest against the forcible removal of German missionaries from their stations and a refusal to recognize Mott any longer as chairman of the Continuation Committee or anything that he said or did in its name as binding on them. It also refused to recognize Ogilvie's Continuation Committee membership. On the other hand, these German members affirmed their intention to abide by the principles outlined in the statements of the English Friends' (Quakers) Foreign Missionary Board and of the Swedish Missionary Conference on the supranationality of missions. The "Declaration" included among its signers Bishop Hennig and Drs. Richter, Haussleiter, Würz, Axenfeld, and Johannes Warneck.[96]

Achievements Through the Conference of British Missionary Societies. The Continuation Committee's work as such centred in the Edinburgh office which in turn was supported by contributions from the Conference of British Missionary Societies and the Foreign Missions Conference. The most tangible effort issuing from No. 1 Charlotte Square was the quarterly *International Review of Missions*, edited by J. H. Oldham. Miss Georgina A. Gollock, who gained much of her wide knowledge of missions at the Church Missionary Society's London office, had become assistant editor in 1912, a post she filled ably for many years. In 1916 Miss Betty D. Gibson came into the office as an assistant to Mr. Oldham, and began a long and notable career in international missionary co-operation. The war's demand for manpower reduced the office staff when in December, 1916, Kenneth Maclennan accepted a government position in London for the duration. An able executive, he had administered Continuation Committee affairs for three years. His transfer to London still permitted monthly visits to Edinburgh where he retained full responsibility for the management of *The International Review of Missions* and the business side of the Committee's office.

As the great conflict dragged on, the difficulties of international communication and war-imposed restrictions of all kinds naturally led the Continuation Committee's Edinburgh office into close association with the Conference of British Missionary Societies. In many instances the latter, rather than create parallel machinery to deal, for example, with problems of literature, Moslems, and medicine, utilized the Continuation Committee's British commission-sections to which additional members were added for greater representation. In theory the Continuation Committee and its agencies maintained a separate and independent existence. In meeting the practical demands for missionary co-operation, however, the two interdependent bodies functioned so closely together that any attempt at distinction would be almost meaningless. There was much to be done, yet any attempt at international action through an impotent Continuation Committee in war-time was foredoomed. Therefore, J. H. Oldham channelled as much of his work as possible through the Conference of British Missionary Societies.

Christian Literature and Education.   The Continuation Committee's concern for Christian literature resulted in one of its outstanding contributions to the missionary enterprise. Until its literature committee went into action, no adequate survey of the field had ever been made. Under John H. Ritson's chairmanship the committee launched a thorough survey and sent questionnaires to 275 societies to discover what Christian literature they were producing and how it was being done. The resulting book not only underscored the peripheral attention most societies accorded the problem but also became the basis for the postwar development of literature enterprises in many areas.[97]

An important outgrowth of the literature committee came about almost accidentally. In its course of survey the commission invited some twenty British societies at work among the Jews to confer on their own specialized problem of literature. These societies had never before met together to consider their common concerns, and they found the conference so helpful that they appointed other committees among themselves to consider their own special problems. These led to larger meetings which prepared the way for international gatherings in the late twenties concerned with the evangelization of the Jews.[98]

In the closely allied field of education the Continuation Committee was playing an equally important rôle. Twelve societies from both sides of the Atlantic had co-operated in a common venture to establish the Christian College for Women in Madras which opened in 1915. Such an intercontinental, co-operative undertaking was unprecedented. The project had been discussed before 1910, but the Continuation Committee took considerable initiative in forwarding the enterprise. The Committee's international connections and active aid facilitated a successful culmination that would otherwise probably have been impossible.[99] The Continuation Committee also helped to initiate a thorough survey of the Christian forces in India to aid the churches and missions in that country. The Reverend W. H. Findlay reached India in November, 1915, to head this survey project for which Mott had given $5,000 to India's National Missionary Council.[100]

A major concern of the commission on Christian education overseas centred on the proposal to introduce a conscience clause in India. From that land the argument was advanced that in educational institutions supported by public funds (and many mission schools received partial government subsidies) parents, if they so wished, should have the right to withdraw their children from religious instruction.[101] The fundamental, and here conflicting, issues of missionary education's goal and of Christian respect for conscience are at once apparent. Sir Andrew Fraser's group met in January, 1917, to discuss the problems involved and submitted a helpful memorandum to the National Missionary Council in India.[102] The same group had met twice on the educational needs of the mass movement in India, but the deputation of Principal A. G. Fraser and Dr. S. K. Datta, which it had intended should go to India, was immobilized by the war. A joint American-British commission under Fraser did reach India in 1919.[103]

Missionary Preparation. Two agencies concerned with adequate training for missionaries were one of Edinburgh's earliest results. In Britain the Conference of British Missionary Societies' Board of Study, with a full-time executive, arranged summer schools and courses of lectures at Oxford, Cambridge, Birmingham, and London for missionary candidates and supplied them with quarterly bulletins, including the latest bibliographies.[104] Its companion body in North America, the Board of Missionary Preparation, less concerned with specific courses of study, concentrated on arousing boards to the preparational needs of candidates. The American group also published a series of extraordinarily helpful booklets for young missionaries.[105] The stimulus these two agencies gave to adequate missionary preparation through language schools, cultural and anthropological studies, and personal training is beyond calculation.

Oldham's Responsibilities. Maintaining the channels of world-wide Christian communication through the war and acting as missionary *liaison* with the British government became highly important tasks for the Continuation Committee's secretary. The exchange of some information with Germany through Pastor Würz of Basel and large correspondence with national missionary councils and missionaries in Asia and Africa made the Edinburgh office a war-time headquarters for Protestant missionary intelligence. The yearly "Survey of Missions" in *The International Review of Missions* reflected this fact. What this meant in helping to knit together and sustain the missionary enterprise around the world is beyond reckoning.

During the war Oldham made his greatest contribution to Protestant missions through the Conference of British Missionary Societies, for as secretary of the international Continuation Committee he had no special status with his national government. Since Britain was directly or indirectly involved in the majority of lands where Protestant missions were at work, war-time problems relating to missions and government focussed largely in London. On some of these Oldham had to speak out, and as an *ex-officio* member of the Standing Committee for several years, his voice was heard. In 1917 Oldham was made convener of the "Committee on the War and Missions."[106] Thus an international secretary, acting as an executive member of a British council, gained a respectful hearing in government offices and was, able to influence Britain's policy toward missions.

Through the war the Conference of British Missionary Societies maintained constant vigilance against threats to missionary freedom. Since the first problems arose over German missionaries in India, the India office became the point of most frequent contact between missions and government, and through it most of Britain's policy toward missions evolved.[107]

The Permanent Under-Secretary at the India office, Sir Arthur Hirtzell, was, in Oldham's words, "a keen Christian. In him the missionary enterprise had a warm friend." Somewhat chary of having to negotiate with more than forty different societies, Sir Arthur received Oldham on his first visit as a representative of the Conference of British Missionary Societies with almost unbelieving amazement. Hirtzell's grateful reply, "We can deal, then, with *one* body to represent all Protestant missionary societies!" marked the beginning of frequent conversations between Britain's government and her missionary societies.[108] This fact had far-reaching consequences for the missionary enterprise as a whole and was possible only because British societies had learned to work together and had ready the organization to act and speak for all. This again was directly attributable to Edinburgh, 1910.

Oldham, the Government, and Missions

The little-known story of J. H. Oldham's untiring labours to preserve essential freedom for the whole missionary enterprise constitutes a crucial chapter in missionary history. Probably the most important phase of international missionary co-operation during World War I and the post-war settlement period, his efforts were twofold: to shape realistic missionary policy and to guide the representations made to the government.

A Suggested Policy for Missions. Without the Conference of British Missionary Societies, effective deputations to the government would probably have been impossible. Yet the key figure was Oldham. His understanding of the approach required by circumstances helps to explain his achievement.

In general, Oldham maintained that the less missions have to do with governments the better. Frequent intrusion into the political scene, he held, would eventually spell only greater difficulty for them. On the other hand, interaction between missions and governments was inevitable and required negotiation. That being so, he viewed it as mandatory for missionary representatives to consider the practicalities of the situation in which governments have to act and to seek to understand the official's point of view. Circumstances, he argued, limit the bounds within which civil authority can adjust its policy. Any attempt to press for rights and privileges beyond that limit Oldham dismissed as futile.

The missionary representative able to encompass an issue from a political as well as a religious view-point still has to be guided by certain fundamental principles. Oldham insisted first that mission boards know all the relevant facts in any situation and establish a well-defined policy before attempting any negotiations. Only thus could they command the respect of able public officials. Moreover, their policy had to be consistent and based upon recognized principle. Allowing for circumstantially imposed modifications, he maintained that missions could not contend for a policy or action in China for which they would not stand in America. Third, he urged that mission boards make no proposals until they had surveyed the government's difficulties in trying to deal with them. If underlying counter-problems made impossible the granting of sought-for rights, missionary societies should discover these beforehand and modify their appeal. Fourth, Oldham stood for united policy, commanding respect because it represented the international consensus of Protestant missionary agencies. At the same time, he added parenthetically, "There may be some personal link—and in the last resort policy is controlled by individuals—some personal link of sympathy and understanding and support in one particular nation, and if you can work along that line, you will be more likely to be successful than working along some other line." Fifth, all missionary policy had to be based upon the spiritual independence of missions whose objectives in the long run are different from those of government. Finally, Oldham stoutly maintained, missionary policy should be one of co-operation with government, reinforcing and encouraging it wherever civil authority is striving for justice and right.[109]

Here, of course, was reflected Oldham's own personal philosophy with its emphasis upon fundamental, realistic thinking, upon persons and personal ties as the real factors in any situation, and upon a unified, grand strategy for world missions. These factors need to be kept in mind, for just as they characterized J. H. Oldham, they were also built into the foundation structure of the International Missionary Council.

Missionary Freedom. The Conference of British Missionary Societies had early accepted government regulation for missions of enemy nationalities as a war-time necessity. Since the problem focussed in India, it made representations to the Secretary of State for India to safeguard missionary interests. The India Office gave assurance that before it settled any policy involving missions, it would hear the societies and weigh their knowledge and experience.[110]

By 1917 the tides of war had strained British public opinion, and the latter was demanding severe measures against the enemy. This may serve partially to explain why in that year the British government proposed to exclude from certain parts of the Empire all nationals and organizations of enemy countries engaged in educational, medical, or philanthropic work and to license all foreigners engaged in such work. Anticipating the possible reaction, the proposal further stated that if British societies regarded this as discriminatory, in the name of equality they, too, would be licensed![111]

Oldham's first major contest for missionary freedom ensued. Since the proposal did not (or need not) affect British missions, and since their own difficulties engrossed their attention, they might readily have allowed such legislation to pass unchallenged. But largely through Oldham's alertness and a corresponding infusion of responsibility for the welfare of missionary agencies in all sending countries, the Conference of British Missionary Societies sharply objected to the whole proposal. The influence of the "non-functioning" Continuation Committee *had* made a difference!

To consider the pending legislation the Standing Committee was invited to send representatives to confer with members of the India, Colonial, and Foreign Offices on December 12, 1917. Its members had agreed beforehand not to protest exclusion, which violated missionary freedom indeed, but which under the circumstances of war and post-war adjustment appeared to be inevitable for some time to come.[112] To drive home the main objection, the Committee agreed, no voice would carry more weight than that of the Archbishop of Canterbury, and he, on invitation, agreed to be spokesman for the missionary societies. The Standing Committee strongly opposed licensure, and the Archbishop stated the case. The government's proposal discriminated against missionaries as a class (foreign traders were not to be licensed) and would provoke considerable American misapprehension—a highly undesirable political consequence at that time. Moreover, should Britain adopt licensure, other nations would undoubtedly follow suit, which in turn would hinder the protection of the liberties of British missionaries in non-British areas. Finally, to compel Christian ministers to be licensed imposed unjustifiable restraint upon religious liberty and opened wide the gate to unfair treatment of Christian missionaries by unsympathetic local officials.[113]

Positively speaking, the Standing Committee urged that government policy toward missions should proceed from a basis of welcome and not of restriction; that to give meaning to the welcome, American missionary societies should be admitted on the same terms as the British; and that the door should be left open so that with a post-war international missionary organization the missionary societies of other countries could be received in the same fashion as those from America.[114]

The deputation had its effect. The modified government policy appeared in the widely circulated *Memorandum A*. Relating only to Protestant (including Anglican) endeavour in India, it spoke appreciatively of missions and welcomed their future efforts, but excluded enemy alien missionary organizations and personnel for an indefinite period. It provided, however, that no restrictions be placed on British or American agencies recommended to the government by the Conference of British Missionary Societies or by the Foreign Missions Conference. The government further declared that it would deal only with these two representative bodies and with the National Missionary Council in India. *Memorandum B* applied to churches in communion with Rome. *Memorandum C* referred to societies of neutral and Allied countries not covered in *Memorandum A*. All missionaries of these societies were required to take out a "permit," revocable by the civil authority at its discretion, and to "cooperate loyally with the Government."[115]

One highly important point in this action was the recognition accorded the Conference of British Missionary Societies as the one responsible agent for Britain's Protestant missions. While it should be noted that the Conference of British Missionary Societies could and did recommend to the government non-member bodies (the criterion for recommendation being whether in its judgement a particular society was operated by a responsible board of experienced people), it was no accident that ten societies entered its membership between 1914 and 1919. Any government complaint went directly to the Conference of British Missionary Societies which in turn reviewed it with the society involved. This fact—that the government could deal with one responsible agency on missionary questions—kept Britain from leading other countries in an example of total missionary licensure.[116]

United, Britain's missionary societies had acted to modify otherwise disastrous legislation. Unable to appeal through press or parliament, they concentrated on personal representations to the officials involved. The revocable permit for non-Anglo-Americans *was* licensing and had not been stayed, but wholesale licensure had been blocked. Moreover, as Oldham understood it, they had secured a basic policy which, when the war psychology passed, could be expanded in the direction of freedom.[117]

THE EMERGENCY COMMITTEE

The United States entered the war against Germany on April 6, 1917. Less than a year later on January 8, 1918, President Wilson outlined his fourteen-point program for peace with its provision for a general association of nations. By the summer of 1918 American troops engaged in their first major battles, while in the autumn the dissolution of the Hapsburg monarchy coincided with Germany's collapse. With the signing of the Armistice on November 11, 1918, the cessation of hostilities opened the way to the Peace Conference which assembled at Paris in mid-January. By the end of April in 1919 the Covenant of the League of Nations had been drawn up, and by the end of June Germany had signed the Treaty of Versailles. With its signing the nations of Europe entered into the turmoil of post-war settlement and adjustment.

Formation of the Emergency Committee of Co-operating Missions

This in brief outline was the political scene against which international missionary co-operation was evolving. The Continuation Committee had ceased to function, many of its members had died, and from the standpoint of the missionary societies it no longer existed. Oldham, and Maclennan on marginal time from his government work, provided an international secretariat, but the end of the war would obviously compound the problems confronting missions on the international level. To meet this immediate need required reinvesting with new authority what Edinburgh had launched.

Initiating Action.   Concern for an effective international missionary agency rose simultaneously on both sides of the Atlantic. In Britain the Standing Committee on January 10, 1918, unanimously approved a plan to replace the Continuation Committee with an international organization based upon the national missionary agencies.[118] This action marked a distinct advance, for at Edinburgh only eight years before the same plan had been dismissed as impossible. A similar need was felt in America when the Committee of Reference and Counsel asked Dr. Mott and Dr. Charles R. Watson to visit Great Britain and France in the spring of 1918 and to suggest joint action by all English-speaking missionary societies.[119]

Mott and Watson met with the Standing Committee at the Bible House in London, April 14, 1918. That group unanimously agreed that during the war no action should be taken on the Continuation Committee's future but "that a new international committee to deal with questions demanding immediate attention and to be called the Emergency Committee of Cooperating Missions should be created" with offices in London.[120] The new agency would include eight representatives from the Foreign Missions Conference, six from the Conference of British Missionary Societies, and one each from any other country desiring representation. The group elected Mott chairman and Oldham and Maclennan secretaries and outlined the committee's functions as follows: (1) to handle all questions of governmental relations in which the societies were jointly interested; (2) to consider means to provide for war-impaired missions; (3) and to act as a clearing house and to harmonize the approach to major problems faced in common by all societies in the transition from war to peace. The Continuation

Committee, maintaining a nominal existence, would continue to publish *The International Review of Missions* under its auspices.[121] The Conference of British Missionary Societies and the Foreign Missions Conference assumed financial responsibility for the new project.

London Headquarters. There had been good reasons for having the Continuation Committee's centre in Edinburgh where that agency had been born. Away from the distraction of London meetings, there was more time for the correspondence, reading and thinking that was intended to characterize Continuation Committee headquarters. But the war made clear the need for having the machinery of co-operation in London, for government offices as well as the majority of the great societies centred in the Empire's capital. Accordingly, the Continuation Committee moved from Edinburgh to temporary quarters at 117 Victoria Street, London, in June, 1918, and there provided haven for the Emergency Committee. At the same time concerned persons advanced plans for a permanent headquarters for missionary co-operation in Great Britain and began a fund of $150,000 (£30,000) for a suitable building to be known as "Edinburgh House." The new name obviously honoured a great heritage.[122]

When the Conference of British Missionary Societies met in June, 1918, it agreed to share financial responsibility for the Emergency Committee. During its sessions a cablegram from the United States announced the Foreign Missions Conference's full approval for the Emergency Committee and its budget.[123] Moreover, since for several years the Continuation Committee's secretaries had done the greater part of their work for and on behalf of British societies, those same societies accepted financial responsibility for the Continuation Committee's staff (and, incidentally, that of the Emergency Committee) by appointing Oldham and Maclennan secretaries of the Conference of British Missionary Societies and Miss G. A. Gollock its departmental secretary for literature.[124]

Oldham's Further Efforts for Missionary Freedom

Earlier in the war Oldham had worked effectively to modify the British government's sweeping proposal for missionary licensure, but war's end brought new and larger threats. With his customary vigour and quiet effectiveness, Oldham met the challenge and devoted his energy to protect missionary freedom for all—and specifically to save

German missions. He did this through his efforts to salvage the Berlin Act, to preserve German missionary property under Article 438 of the Versailles Treaty, and to help establish the principle of missionary freedom in the peace settlements and in the League of Nations mandates.

Preserving German Mission Property. The Committee of Reference and Counsel, acting as part of the Emergency Committee, commissioned Drs. Mott, Watson, and Barton to safeguard missionary liberties in the peace negotiations. For their use Mr. Burton St. John prepared separate dossiers on British, American, and German missions for each of the countries likely to be discussed at the Paris Conference. A Columbia law professor excerpted the relevant sections of treaties and assembled the legal supports guaranteeing missionary freedom. Thus fortified the deputation enlisted British and French support so that it could present a common case with united backing.[125] When the committee reached Paris, it discovered that the treaty makers had already drafted the section with which they were primarily concerned, namely, that on German missions and the disposition of their property. Fortunately for them and for the whole missionary enterprise Article 438 saved German missions. Again the credit went to Oldham.[126] In his unobtrusive but highly effective way, respected and trusted by British government officials, he had successfully presented the case for excepting German missions from the general confiscation of German properties.

The peace treaty signed at Versailles June 28, 1919, provided for Allied appropriation of private property belonging to German subjects to satisfy German debts to nationals of Allied governments. Any balance would be retained by the Allies against the liabilities of the German government. This sweeping provision would have meant the complete disintegration of German societies. But among the treaty's final provisions stood Article 438, exempting German missions property from this claim and placing it in the hands of trustees of the same "faith" (denomination) as that of the mission involved.[127] This single article in the peace treaty saved German missions from complete dissolution. It preserved almost intact Protestant mission property estimated to be worth from fifteen to twenty million dollars.[128] What this article meant for Protestant and Catholic missions alike need not be dwelt on here. It was, to say the least, cause for heartfelt thanksgiving.

The Versailles Treaty soon proved to be quite impossible of fulfillment. In the years before this fact was widely accepted, that British historian of Versailles, H. W. V. Temperley, described it as "crushing and severe to a high degree."[129] As its provisions were made known, the treaty became the Germans' *bête noir* and among them aroused furious anger and bitterness. War-time misunderstanding and misinformation had long convinced Germany's missionary leaders that they had been repudiated by their British and American friends. When they saw Article 438, their despair led to further misunderstanding. To them their missions had been confiscated and given to non-German societies while their former friends stood by with no word of protest. As they viewed it, Mott and Oldham had watched and silently acquiesced in the dismemberment of their societies. This only compounded their distrust of these two men. Few, if any, could surmount the warping hatreds of war to realize that Article 438 had actually saved their missions.[130] As it turned out, their mission property was restored to them.

Salvaging the Berlin Act's Provisions for Missionary Freedom. Oldham also acted to preserve the important international guarantee of missionary freedom contained in the Berlin Act. Thirty-five years earlier at the height of German colonial expansion, Bismarck had invited the powers then colonizing Central Africa to meet in Berlin. Out of that three-months conference ending in February, 1885, came the General Act of Berlin, sometimes referred to as "The Congo Act." Its statutes applied to Africa's great central strip between the Atlantic and Indian Oceans and stipulated that nations holding territories in the area could proclaim their neutrality in event of war. It also provided for free trade, freedom of religion and worship, and special protection for missionaries, scientists, and explorers. In later years this international treaty was often appealed to on questions of missionary freedom.

When war broke out and German missionaries were interned in Africa, many Germans deplored what they understood to be a violation of the Congo Act: first, that neutrality had not been observed; second, that missionary freedom had been violated. This became one of the most bitter accusations made by Germans against England and against the British missionary societies for their failure to protest it.

With that background and with the clarification (through *Memoranda A, B,* and *C*) of Britain's post-war policy toward missionaries in its territories, Oldham and his colleagues turned to the policy of other nations. War's end would nullify many of the treaties to which Germany had been a party, and new treaties would be substituted for them. Of all the pre-war treaties, the most important for missions had been the Berlin Act with its explicit guarantee of religious and missionary freedom. Backed by a Standing Committee resolution, Oldham therefore went personally to the proper government officials, requesting that in any revision or replacement of the Berlin Act, the provisions of Article VI relating to religious and missionary freedom be preserved. While he received no definite promise, Oldham had reason to believe that his requests met a favourable reception and would be heeded.[131]

The Convention Revising the General Act of Berlin, signed at Saint-Germain-en-Laye, September 10, 1919, made evident the fruits of Oldham's efforts. The new Convention embodied the same rights for freedom of conscience, religion, and missionary endeavour as had the Berlin Act.[132] Directly important for Africa, the Convention's real significance lay in its guarantee of religious freedom which established internationally a powerful and noteworthy precedent for the post-war era.

Missionary Freedom and "Supranationality." As nothing before ever had done, World War I focussed attention on the Christian missionary enterprise as a movement to be reckoned with and judged beyond national lines. That the church is, indeed, a community transcending national boundaries has long been accepted among Christians. So understood, "supranationality" inheres in the very nature of Christian missions. The war spotlighted that fact and brought the term, "supranationality," to the fore.

One of the first statements came in 1915 from the Conference of Swedish Missionary Societies. The Swedes feared that war-time restrictions would curtail "what might be called the supra-nationality of missions," a status already "universally acknowledged." Moreover, they affirmed, "Mission work . . . by organizations belonging to other than ruling nations, has a claim to be continued irrespective of political conditions." In December, 1917, a conference of members of the Protestant churches of Denmark, Holland, Norway, Sweden, and Switzerland adopted the statement.[133] The Foreign Missions Conference submitted the document to a distinguished group of lawyers and asked whether it would be justifiable to press governments to recognize the supranationality of missions. The lawyers answered unanimously, "No," and pointed out the pitfalls in seeking such status, which, as stated, implied that a missionary should be treated as having no nationality.[134]

Likewise, appealing to supranationality, German missionary leaders requested the Peace Conference to allow a separate and independent commission to deal with the problem of German missions. At the same time the Danish, Dutch, Norwegian and Swedish Committees for the World Alliance for International Friendship through the Churches, as well as the Danish Missionary Council and the Conference of Swedish Missionary Societies appealed to the Versailles participants. Because of the extra-political factors involved, they asked that questions concerning missions be postponed and be settled later by a group including missionary experts from neutral countries.[135] The executive committee of the Society of Friends in Britain sent a similar appeal to the British delegates at Paris.[136] These appeals were ignored, but, as we have seen, Oldham's efforts probably served the missionary enterprise as well if not better than a post-Versailles meeting could have done.

One of the clearest statements on supranationality (with emphasis not on this, as it was being used, legally confusing term but upon "freedom") came from the first representative Christian conference in Europe after hostilities ceased. Including Germans, Hungarians, and Italians, the World Alliance for International Friendship through the Churches met at The Hague in the early autumn of 1919. One of the first questions to arise was missions. The conference immediately appointed a special committee on the subject chaired by Mrs. Louise Creighton and accepted the declaration it drew up. The first paragraph stated:

Freedom to carry the Gospel of Christ to all the nations is essential to the life of the Christian church, and is one of the fundamental claims of religious liberty. Such freedom should be granted to members of all denominations and citizens of all nationalities, provided they abstain from participation in political affairs and conduct their work in full loyalty to the government of the country in which they reside. Whatever political control is found necessary should be exercised in a way that interferes as little as possible with the religious work of the missionaries.[137]

No attempt had been made to define the legal implications of "supranationality," but what had been stressed was the right for any group to propagate the Christian faith anywhere without regulation, save that necessary for the normal welfare and order of the state. Thus on October 31, 1919, the Standing Committee reaffirmed its conviction that "freedom to carry the Gospel of Christ to all the nations is essential to the life of the Christian Church, and that such freedom should be granted to members of all denominations and citizens of all nationalities."[138] The Foreign Missions Conference in January, 1920, passed a resolution prepared by the American section of the Emergency Committee and stated, ". . . we affirm our adherence to the principle of the freedom of the whole Christian Church to carry the Gospel of Christ to all the world."[139]

Likewise, the League of Nations' mandates legally recognized the principle of missionary freedom, the heart of supranationality. The Committee of Reference and Counsel in the United States and the Standing Committee in Britain made strong representations to their respective governments, urging that the League's mandates include guarantees for religious and missionary freedom. Mott and Watson at Paris, using the legal and background materials that had been prepared for them, concentrated their efforts on this problem and were in large measure responsible for the final incorporation of these guarantees.[140] Oldham directly had had very little to do with this accomplishment, but it had been built upon the foundation-precedents he had laid. Therein the missionary enterprise was indebted to him.

The Machinery of Reconciliation

The war's end made it imperative to reopen the lines of communication between German and non-German missionary societies. The major job was to heal the breaches of war, and those breaches were wide and deep. The cumulative effect of four years of misunderstanding, misinformation, and growing distrust could not be changed overnight. Moreover, a vindictive peace and the German assumption that their missions had been confiscated by others made the difficulties of full and friendly intercourse well nigh impossible. Here the Emergency Committee had a tremendous task of reconciliation.

First Meeting of the Emergency Committee. The Emergency Committee of Cooperating Missions had been in existence a year before its first brief business meeting at the Bible House in London, March 24, 1919. Only nine British and American members were present. Correspondence had revealed that missionary councils in Europe's neutral countries were either dubious or non-committal about membership on the Emergency Committee. Those of Scandinavia, Switzerland, and Holland were by no means in sympathy with the Allied conduct of the war, and they hesitated to join a dominantly Anglo-American organization if that would hinder their intercourse with German societies. The session consisted largely of reports of political negotiations on behalf of missions. Before adjourning, the group agreed to meet again early in May after the return of Mott and Watson from Paris.[141]

Second Meeting of the Emergency Committee. The assembly of the Emergency Committee at the Bible House on May 2 and 3 marked the first nearly representative international missionary gathering after the war. Among the fourteen members present were Charles Merle d'Aubigne representing the Paris Mission, and Karl Fries, representing the Swedish missionary societies. Also present by invitation were Professor Frederik Torm and Count Joachim Moltke from Denmark, Dr. J. W. Gunning from Holland, F. H. L. Paton from Australia, and Herbert Anderson, secretary of the National Missionary Council of India.

Mott and Watson reported on their efforts at Paris to secure religious and missionary freedom in the League mandates for former German and Turkish territories.[142] In considering the problem involved in the relation of missions to governments, the Emergency Committee suggested again that most questions could best be dealt with nationally but that on some issues likely to arise in the near future the Emergency Committee, if so instructed, would act for missionary organizations in common on the international level.

The Committee surveyed the whole tangled problem of German missions. It also heard what was probably the first post-war report of an interview with German missionary leaders when Dr. Gunning told of a meeting he had had in late April (1919) in Holland with Dr. Axenfeld, Pastor Würz, and Dr. Johannes Spiecker. Dr. Henry T. Hodgkin, the Quaker, had met with them as one of the very few English persons believed by the Germans to be truly concerned for their missions. Hodgkin in turn reported on the Germans' dejection over the plight of their missions and their assertion of no evidence for the accusation of German disloyalty in British-ruled territories. Moreover, they firmly believed that temporary exclusion in reality meant permanent banishment for their missionary societies. The Germans also referred openly to the attitude of British missions during the war as one of compromise, and they urged the Standing Committee to speak out for supranationality. (It did this in the autumn of 1919. See page 189.) Constituted as it was, they viewed the Emergency Committee as a futile attempt to keep the door open for international missionary co-operation, and were especially happy when the missionary agencies of Holland, Norway, and Denmark would not accept the Committee's invitation until they had first discovered the German attitude toward it. For the near future they preferred small meetings in which to work out differences rather than big international gatherings.[143] Thus Hodgkin was able to paint in the background against which future relations with German missions would have to proceed.

From the business sessions came a request to the Standing Committee to release Oldham as much as possible from his executive duties so that he might devote himself almost wholly to the international questions confronting the Emergency Committee. It was also decided that the Emergency Committee's budget should be shared by member organizations on a proportional basis.[144] Thus the meeting ended. Four weeks later the Standing Committee unanimously agreed to free Oldham from most of his responsibility.

Efforts to Heal the Breach. With the signing of the peace treaty many British missionary folk desired at once to resume fraternal intercourse with German Christians. While frankly stating the situation as they understood it, they wrote to the German friends of missions in July, 1919, "We need you, and you need us. We must seek every opportunity of coming together. We must try to believe in one another's motives. . . . We hope in the future for full and free cooperation in this work."[145] Among the signers were Mrs. Louise Creighton, Henry T. Hodgkin, Kenneth Maclennan, William Paton, and Mary (Mrs. J. H.) Oldham. On August 19 the German societies responded with a fraternal letter. After asking for mutual confession of the fact that each country had deceived the other during the war, the German reply stated, "It was not only at the beginning of the war that we thought ourselves forced to fighting in defence of our fatherland; we still think so, and so do wide circles of our people today." Then ensues a plea to know why British societies and the Continuation Committee had not protested the interning of German missionaries, followed by the appeal to return German missionaries to their fields before becoming concerned about resuming missionary conferences. "Please have confidence in us, and we will have confidence in you."[146] The exchange helped to prepare the way for further intercourse.

The World Alliance for Promoting International Friendship Through the Churches. Largely through encouragement from the Church Peace Union, the World Alliance for Promoting International Friendship Through the Churches had been formed at Constance, Germany, on the very day World War I began.[147] It had not organized in vain, for it convened the first representative post-war conference of Christians in Europe. The Alliance met at Oud-Wassenaer near The Hague, October 1 to 3, 1919, with some sixty persons from fourteen nations attending. Among them were Archibishop Nathan Söderblom of Uppsala, Bishop Edward Stewart Talbot of Winchester, and Dr. Charles Macfarland, secretary of the Federal Council of the Churches of Christ in America.

Missions shared a prominent place on the agenda as the conference's outspoken pronouncement on missionary freedom shows. The Alliance also asked the Continuation Committee to meet as soon as possible and to speed the return of German missionaries to their work if it could do so.[148] The meeting provided the first opportunity for English and American missionary folk to share thoughts and experiences directly with five German delegates. Reconciliation proceeded further than any had thought possible, and the Germans were grateful for what was accomplished; but they refused to participate in any international missionary gathering "until the most fundamental and outstanding differences between the German members and English and American members—such as Dr. John Mott, Mr. Oldham, and Dr. Ogilvie—had been adjusted by thoroughgoing personal conferences."[149]

Continental Visitations. After initial overtures from America in the late summer of 1919, Bishop P. O. Hennig, president of the *Ausschuss*, urgently invited Dr. Arthur J. Brown to Berlin to confer with representatives of the German societies. Dr. Brown had hoped that J. H. Oldham could accompany him, but correspondence showed it best for him to go alone. As chairman of the special committee on German missions appointed by the American section of the Emergency Committee, Brown visited Holland, Germany, Belgium, France, and England during October and November, 1919. His first brief contact with German missionary folk was at the World Alliance's Hague meeting. In Germany Brown met with the *Ausschuss* and conferred with many German leaders, listening to complaints with sympathetic understanding. He returned with a full statement of aims for German and Anglo-American missions as prepared by the *Ausschuss*.[150] Later letters to Dr. Brown from those whom he met give abundant evidence of the great appreciation for his presence in Germany.

At the time of Brown's visit, several representatives of the newly formed National Lutheran Council in the United States were also in Germany to survey the full needs of the Lutheran churches, including their missions, and to assist them in any way possible. The commission went "definitely to those Lutheran Christians of Europe affected by the war who hold the faith of the Gospel as witnessed by the Unaltered Augsburg Confession." But the commissioners admitted that "Doctrinal discussion with the suffering is not entirely apropos!"[151] Aid to German Lutheran missions included loans and in some instances taking over the whole work of a society unable to send out its own missionaries. The commission informed each mission with a mixed Lutheran and Reformed constituency (and this meant most of Germany's societies) that its responsibilities could be assumed by the American branches of the Lutheran Church "only on condition that the Missionaries in the respective fields stand unreservedly on the Augustana, and that those fields sever their former connections and for all future time be considered parts of the Lutheran Church."[152] With the Lutheran proposals in mind and with the list of particulars the *Ausschuss* had given him, Brown wrote back to Berlin from Paris, inquiring whether the Germans wished to modify their requests to the Emergency Committee. Richter replied immediately that the Lutheran proposals touched only a few German societies and that the original arrangements of the *Ausschuss* with Brown should stand.[153]

In the same autumn of 1919 J. H. Oldham visited France and Switzerland. In mid-November he met with some of the Swiss missionary leaders, among them Frederick Würz and W. Oettli, at Zurich to discuss at length the problems of German missionaries.[154] Unfortunately, he was unable to reach Tübingen to confer with Bishop Hennig. While returning to England, Oldham reflected upon the resolution from the World Alliance in October and upon impressions of his own visit to Switzerland and became convinced that an international missionary meeting was imperative and should assemble if possible in April or June, 1920. With his suggestion before it, the Standing Committee passed a resolution urging immediate steps toward such a conference.[155]

Preparations for the International Meeting at Crans. By February, 1920, both the Standing Committee and the Committee of Reference and Counsel had expressed themselves in favour of a small international missionary conference. The Paris Society had verbally agreed to such a plan, and the Danish and Swedish Conferences had indicated their willingness to attend. The Germans stood adamant for a small group of about ten for intimate consultation. Their grievances, they felt, were still unmet, and they had much to be settled before they could enter into large conference.[156] Nevertheless, an international meeting, "arranged at the instance of the national missionary organizations," was launched. Whether the Germans would attend or not (and their presence was greatly desired), it would convene in June, 1920, to consider the demands of the times upon the missionary enterprise. Meanwhile, plans were under way for a small meeting between a few British and a few German representatives at Leiden, Holland, in April.[157]

All the while "war guilt" was a rankling sore. At the World Alliance meeting in October, Dr. Johannes Spiecker, director of the Rhenish Mission, had spoken in irenic terms for the German delegates. Widely reported in Germany, Spiecker's words left the impression in Christian circles there that he had publicly confessed his country's war guilt. Since missionary leaders comprised the majority of the German delegation to The Hague, they fell under grave suspicion. As one of them, Richter viewed any German participation in June, 1920, impossible. His countrymen, he argued, assumed that the British and Americans would expect another German confession before they could get on with proceedings. Moreover, the deep distrust of Mott and Oldham as men who had abused their privilege during the war still festered, and many Germans wanted to talk out their differences with them directly. In addition, there were the questions of German missionaries still interned, former German mission fields now in other hands, and the barring of German missionaries from their former posts. For the Germans all these factors made a large, international meeting undesirable. But they placed considerable hope in the small meeting scheduled for Leiden.[158]

That informal gathering assembled at Oegstgeest, a missionary centre near Leiden, on April 16 and 17, 1920. Frank Lenwood, Kenneth Maclennan, J. H. Oldham, and Miss B. D. Gibson met with Bishop P. O. Hennig, Pastor Würz, Missionsinspektor Martin Schlunk, and Missionar Lutz, with Bishop Hennig in the chair. Forthright speech was often difficult, yet frankness prevailed. The conversations revealed that the *Ausschuss* would not appoint official delegates to the proposed international missionary assembly in June, but that several Germans would probably be willing to attend in a personal capacity. In general the meeting was strained, but it achieved its purpose.[159] It established a bridge and helped German delegates to see that Oldham and many of the British missionary folk had actually been labouring on their behalf during the war and had not deserted German missions.[160] British members of the Leiden group returned home to prepare for the international meeting to be held two months later in Switzerland.

The International Missionary Meeting at Crans, June 22 to 28, 1920

The international conference held at Crans, near Geneva, Switzerland, June 22 to 28, 1920, was a meeting neither of the Continuation Committee nor of the Emergency Committee. The national missionary organizations of America, Britain, and Europe had called it *ad hoc*. Yet its personnel made it appear to be a meeting of the Continuation Committee or of the Emergency Committee, and *in one sense* it was. Actually, however, it stood alone as an independent meeting. To it came representatives from the Foreign Missions Conference, the Conference of British Missionary Societies, the Board of the Dutch Reformed Church in South Africa, the Paris Evangelical Missionary Society, the Dutch Committee of Advice, the Swedish General Missionary Conference, the Norwegian Missionary Society, the Danish Missionary Council, the Joint Missions Committee of Finland, the Belgian Society of Protestant Missions, and the Swiss missionary societies. Co-opted members, present in their personal capacity and not representing the *Ausschuss*, included Bishop Hennig, Drs. Haussleiter and Richter, and Pastor Würz, the four German members of the Continuation Committee.

The conference met at the Chateau of Crans overlooking lovely Lake Geneva as the guests of Colonel and Madame van Berchem. The van Berchems' daughter was married to Pierre de Benoit who had taken a leading part in the French-Swiss committee which had helped to carry on the Basel Mission's work in India. They had early requested the privilege of entertaining the gathering and for months had held family prayers that it might bring increased international missionary understanding and effectiveness. The assembly chose as its chairman Bishop Logan H. Roots of Hankow, China. Mott chaired the business committee, and Oldham served as conference secretary. Thirty-nine official delegates were listed, but among the few others present was Miss B. D. Gibson from the office of the Emergency Committee.

Crans was free of any affectation or feigned politeness. Men spoke without hesitancy straight to the points at issue. Naturally, this caused some strains and tensions, but it was wholesome to have them openly recognized. There was no "praying at" or "praying for" any member or group of the conference. Instead, the prayers that were offered in French, German, and English helped to unite the hearts of those assembled together. Furthermore, the conference owed much to Oldham who in his keen, clear way raised issues that had to be faced and held discussion to them.[161]

Missions and Governments.   Two major problems confronted the assembly: the relation of missions to governments and an international missionary organization. Much of the first related directly to German missions. As a basis for discussion, each delegate received J. H. Oldham's *The Missionary Situation After the War*.[162] The conference began by looking at the broad problems facing missions on an international scale. Of these, one of the most important was the increasing responsibility taken by governments for education in areas where missionaries had formerly supplied almost the only instruction available. A happy development, the new situation, nevertheless, posed serious implications for missionary policy.[163] Then Crans turned its attention to German missions. Its deliberations issued in a nine-point statement, emphasizing the need for increasing understanding on all sides and urging national missionary organizations to work to speed the return of German missionaries to their former fields.[164]

International Missionary Organization.   The other great question involved an international missionary organization. The magnitude of the problem confronted at Crans clearly made such a body imperative. The Continuation Committee, charged to create such an agency, was no longer functioning and belonged to another era. Only a handful of its original members remained. The Emergency Committee, as its name indicated, was a temporary device and was largely Anglo-American. The times demanded something new.

Oldham had prepared for Crans a remarkably thorough yet concise outline of alternative forms of international missionary organization. The intermediate and most functionable plan, as he saw it, provided for an international agency based upon national missionary bodies and co-ordinating their policy. Its itinerating officers would visit the national missionary organizations and seek to work through problems with them. This placed major responsibility upon the national co-operative agencies and avoided the expense of frequent, large international meetings. Based upon the 1913 Hague principle, the new committee would concern itself primarily with distinctively international issues. Speaking prophetically, Oldham envisioned that even this organization would soon have to give way to and become "something that may represent the beginnings of a world league of churches."[165]

After long discussion Crans' delegates unanimously recommended that the national missionary organizations create an "International Missionary Committee." Embodying the Hague principle and based upon national agencies, it would function as an international co-ordinating council through its secretaries and biennial meetings. Between its regular meetings a "Committee of Reference" would act for it, while the national missionary organizations would contribute to its budget. (As matters stood in 1920, the Foreign Missions Conference was supplying seven-tenths and the Conference of British Missionary Societies three-tenths of the budget for international missionary co-operation.) The Emergency Committee would turn over its responsibilities to the new body when it had been constituted. For officers in the International Missionary Committee, Crans recommended that Mott be chairman, that Oldham be secretary, and that Dr. A. L. Warnshuis of China be asked to become Oldham's associate.[166]

In its final instructions the conference requested J. H. Oldham to concentrate in the year ahead on two major problems—missionary freedom and education. It urged Mott to be in China in 1922 for the National Missionary Conference there and to carry out, within two years time if possible, the series of meetings in the Near East and North Africa that had been proposed just before the war.[167]

Thus the conference ended. It had helped to renew the friendships so disastrously shattered by the war and to hasten the long process of reconciliation. It had surveyed immediate needs and had plotted the immediate course for international missionary co-operation. Finally, it had set the stage for the most significant ecumenical venture yet attempted by Christians concerned for world evangelization.

Post-Crans Developments

The year following Crans was one of transition. The proposal for an International Missionary Committee had to be circulated, promoted, and explained. It then had to be acted upon by the different national organizations. The problems of the first two post-war years continued much as they had been, but added to them were the preparations necessary in shifting from the Emergency Committee as a basis for operations to that of the new International Missionary Committee.

Even at the close of the Crans meeting this process of transition was evident. The thirteen members of the Continuation Committee who had been present unanimously agreed to transfer their responsibilities, including *The International Review of Missions* and the funds at their disposal, to the International Committee when it was constituted.[168] Other Continuation Committee members not present later agreed to the resolution, and it was carried out.

Edinburgh House. In May and June, 1920, just before Crans met, the Conference of British Missionary Societies had taken possession of Edinburgh House and made provision for accommodating the Emergency Committee (and thus also the Continuation Committee). This very neat, five-story, grey stone building in London's West End was soon known around the world as the British headquarters for the International Missionary Council and for *The International Review of Missions*. In addition to the Conference of British Missionary Societies, Edinburgh House also provided space for many of the British co-operative agencies including the Council for Missionary Education, the Board of Study, and the Press Bureau.[169]

The permanent site for the London headquarters of international missionary co-operation had been well chosen. Nearly two years earlier at the conclusion of the war, Kenneth Maclennan had returned to the offices of the Emergency Committee and to his position as co-secretary with Oldham of the Conference of British Missionary Societies. When Crans nominated Oldham as secretary of the new international organization, he submitted his resignation to the Conference of British Missionary Societies, and it was accepted. Although Maclennan took no further part in the direct administration of the International Missionary Council, he continued for some twenty years as executive secretary for the Conference of Missionary Societies in Great Britain and Ireland, all the while working closely with Oldham. It was this superb executive, according to Mott, who "made Edinburgh House a model for organized cooperative activity." From 1913 Maclennan had directed all the business administration of what was soon to become the International Missionary Council. After Crans, he turned over this responsibility to Warnshuis. Recognition must also be given here to Maclennan's untiring efforts on behalf of German missions and for international missionary co-operation in every sphere.[170]

Aid for German Missions. In accord with the instructions given to him at Crans, Oldham continued to devote considerable attention to the needs of German missions and the closely allied questions of missionary freedom.[171] Some British societies by sharing counsel and personnel gave direct aid to German missions, especially to those contiguous to their own in the field, but they raised practically no money to assist them.[172] On the other hand, during 1919 American boards contributed some $7,600 for the relief of German missions in India,[173] and at the 1920 meeting of the Foreign Missions Conference, it was agreed that American boards should contribute in the next year approximately one-fifteenth of their combined budgets, which meant two million dollars, for the relief of Continental missions.[174] Undoubtedly as a result of the ill-fated Interchurch World Movement, which envisioned new millions for missionary enterprises but which collapsed leaving all boards in debt for its heavy promotional expenditures, this noble attempt was largely forgotten. During 1920, however, approximately $150,000 was sent from the United States for the use of Continental missions. One-sixth of it was given by the Moravians, and nearly all the rest came from the National Lutheran Council and several Lutheran bodies.[175] In 1921 a five-year program, somewhat comparable to the Orphaned Missions project of World War II, was begun to assist Continental missions until they could resume their fields and their full financial support.

Preparations for the International Missionary Committee. Meanwhile the Crans proposal for an International Missionary Committee had gone out to all national missionary councils for their approval.

Oldham spent the first three months of 1921 in the United States and Canada consulting with boards about the proposed new organization. Then and later he planned with Mott the arrangements for the International Missionary Committee meeting scheduled for Lake Mohonk in the autumn. In mid-June, 1921, Dr. A. L. Warnshuis arrived in England from China. He embarked at once on an orientation program by attending the annual meeting of the Conference of British Missionary Societies, speaking with British missionary executives, and journeying to Berlin with Oldham and Lenwood to gain first-hand contact with the work and problems of German missions. He also worked with a Conference of British Missionary Societies' special committee on opium, met with China's representatives in the League of Nations, and co-operated with them to frame their statements on the opium problem to be presented at the meeting of the League. In August he returned to America to prepare for the Lake Mohonk meeting.

In conclusion a brief biographical note on the newest addition to the International Missionary Committee's secretariat may be in order. Abbe Livingston Warnshuis (pronounced "Warns-hois") was born in Clymer, New York, in 1877. His grandparents had emigrated from Holland to the United States when his father was a child. Nurtured in the Reformed Church in America, he attended and was graduated from Hope College in Holland, Michigan, and later from New Brunswick Theological Seminary. In 1900 he went out to China under his church board and spent fifteen years as a missionary in Amoy. From 1915 to 1920 he served as national evangelistic secretary of the China Continuation Committee in which his outstanding work commended him to those setting up the new International Missionary Committee. In 1921 at the age of forty-four, he accepted a co-secretaryship with Oldham at Edinburgh House and began a highly significant career with the International Missionary Council that was to cover more than two decades.

Thus ended the first, and in many ways the most important, decade in the International Missionary Council's history—even though it transpired before the Council was officially founded. The World Missionary Conference in 1910 marked its beginning and was followed by the Continuation Committee. Through impulses generated by them, organized international missionary co-operation took its first exploratory steps, and national missionary councils were begun in Asia and

Europe. The Continuation Committee symbolized their oneness. It also discovered its own weaknesses.

Then came the disruptive explosion of World War I. It brought an end to the Continuation Committee as it had been known; but the essential core of international missionary co-operation which the Committee embodied, though sorely tested and at some points weakened by war's impact, adapted itself and grew stronger by overcoming successive crises with undaunted daring and creativity inspired by the vision of a world Christian fellowship. The great achievement during the years when the Emergency Committee served as a stop gap between the Continuation Committee and the International Missionary Council was the successful struggle to maintain missionary freedom and to save German missions. When the peace had been signed, the missionary societies saw clearly that what they were unready and unwilling to do in 1910 had become imperative in 1920, and they agreed to form a *representative* international council which could, when necessary, act for all.

During the war years Mott had become a giant among the world's international figures, and Oldham had become probably the best informed missionary strategist in the world. Yet their work, their accomplishments for international missionary co-operation were little known beyond a relatively small circle of well-informed missionaries, ministers, and executive-leaders of Protestant churches. Their endeavours to knit together Protestantism's world Christian community were unequalled. Mott the grand statesman and Oldham the keen strategist —together they made a perfect team. To them, for their labours during World War I, the Christian community owes a great debt.

CHAPTER V

‹‹‹‹‹‹‹‹‹‹‹‹‹‹‹‹‹‹‹‹‹‹‹‹‹‹‹‹‹‹‹›››››››››››››››››››››››››››››››

The Rise of the International
Missionary Council, 1921-27

At Lake Mohonk, New York, in the autumn of 1921 sixty-one persons from around the world assembled to found the International Missionary Council. The significance of their meeting—the progress it symbolized—can best be seen in contrast with the situation in 1910. Eleven years earlier through the foresight and courage of a handful of men the World Missionary Conference had been convened. At Edinburgh some of the most daring had suggested an international missionary council based upon national co-operative agencies. Hesitancy before the untried, however, prevented immediate entrance upon such a bold, unprecedented venture. Moreover, only two national missionary agencies for co-operation then existed, the German *Ausschuss* and the Foreign Missions Conference of North America.

Providentially, Edinburgh had taken a long, forward stride. It created a Continuation Committee whose ultimate goal was to bring into being such a body as the International Missionary Council became. Through a decade the hopes entrusted to the Continuation Committee were nurtured. They grew, took form, and in World War I surmounted the greatest crisis Protestant missions had yet faced. At last, those hopes were to be realized, for by 1921 national agencies of missionary co-operation had been created in nearly every country of the home base and in some nations of Asia as well. Now these organizations were sending their representatives to Lake Mohonk to constitute the International Missionary Council. One may wonder why forming an international organization required a period of eleven years from 1910 to 1921; but as one surveys the few similar attempts in mankind's history and as he recalls the chaotic disruption of that decade, he is more likely to marvel that it was achieved so swiftly.

THE FOUNDING OF THE INTERNATIONAL MISSIONARY COUNCIL
LAKE MOHONK, NEW YORK, 1921

Lake Mohonk is held like a rare sapphire by the mountains that encircle it. The deep blue of its water and the stillness of its bordering hills fill those who come to it with awe. Only the large Mountain House stands amidst this natural splendour as a reminder that man is also part of God's creation. Here, with autumn's beauty colouring the entire setting of silent grandeur, the International Missionary Council was born.

Establishment of the Council

Lake Mohonk stands primarily as a meeting of the home base of missions. Representatives came from Finland, Norway, Sweden, Switzerland, France, Holland, Great Britain, Canada, and the United States, as well as from Australia and South Africa. Yet the lands of the East were also represented. Dr. S. K. Datta, from the National Missionary Council of India, Burma and Ceylon, and his colleague, a woman, Dr. Ma Saw Sa of Burma, added greatly to the meeting as did also Dr. (later Bishop) Y. Y. Tsu, then a professor at St. John's University, Shanghai, and William Hung of the China Continuation Committee. From Japan came Hiromichi Kozaki, formerly president of Doshisha University, and Bishop Kogoro Uzaki of the Methodist Church, each representing the Japan Continuation Committee. Also present as co-opted members, and because of their colour thought by some to represent the churches of Africa, were Dr. James E. K. Aggrey, a native of the Gold Coast but at the time a professor at Livingstone College, North Carolina, and Dr. Robert R. Moton, Principal of Tuskegee in Alabama.

The absence of the German delegation brought deep regret to all. In March the *Ausschuss* at Halle had decided that so long as German missions were barred from Allied-held areas, German representatives could take no part in international conferences. This same position was taken by the Germans at the Continental Missions Conference at Bremen in late April and early May. There some members of neutral nations had encouraged them to accept the Mohonk invitation, and several Germans admitted their personal desire to attend; but as a matter of principle they felt that they must absent themselves in accord with the wishes of their constituencies.[1] The underlying assumption, obviously, was that certain difficulties had to be removed before Christian fellowship could be restored. Like many others, Richter was unhappy with this understanding of the situation and wrote to Oldham shortly after the Bremen meeting, "Is it not a fundamental Christian principle that differences between Christians, however deep and great, are to be resolved within the Christian fellowship and not as a precedent condition to it?"[2] As we have noted, Lenwood, Oldham, and Warnshuis met in Berlin with the *Ausschuss* in July, 1920, at which time they argued strongly for German representation at Lake Mohonk. Nevertheless, after vigorous discussion the *Ausschuss* determined to make no change in the Halle decision unless there was some demand for it from the societies themselves.[3] That did not come, and Germany went unrepresented at Lake Mohonk.

Founding Principles. Three basic principles, all of which had grown out of practical experience, were embodied in its foundation when the International Missionary Council was organized. First, the preamble to the Council's constitution included the familiar statement that "the only bodies entitled to determine missionary policy are the missionary societies and boards, or the churches which they represent, and the churches in the mission field."[4] This root principle of missionary co-operation had first been enunciated internationally by The Hague meeting of the Continuation Committee in 1913. In this connection, it is interesting to note that whereas Crans had suggested an "International Missionary Committee," Mohonk changed "Committee" to "Council" precisely to emphasize the fact that the new body had no executive function.[5]

The second principle, although not in the constitution, was made explicit by resolution. It maintained that no decision should be sought from the Council and no statement should be issued by it "on any matter involving an ecclesiastical or doctrinal question, on which the members of the Council or bodies constituting the Council may differ among themselves."[6] In no sense did this presuppose like-mindedness among the Council's diverse membership, for it was meant only to prevent discussions of faith and order within the Council. This safeguard stemmed from Edinburgh and was not so restricting as might be thought at first glance, for Edinburgh had issued a volume on the

Christian message and the Jerusalem and Madras meetings were later to do so. The guarantee was there, however, that the International Missionary Council should never usurp the field of the Faith and Order Movement nor become a theological debating society. In so far as it had a theological basis, the Council was united on the implicit belief that it is the duty of Christians to witness to the gospel of Jesus Christ among all men. In this it recognized the existence of a corporate oneness in Christian community—the unity of men bound together by devotion to one Lord in the fulfillment of a common task.

The third principle, gratefully acknowledged, recognized that any attainment, by reason of the very nature of the new venture, involved more than human capacity for achievement. Thus the constitution's preamble stated: "It is recognized that the successful working of the International Missionary Council is entirely dependent on the gift from God of the spirit of fellowship, mutual understanding and desire to cooperate."[7] In this light the Council would view any accomplishment which might be attributed to it.

Functions. A brief listing of the Council's functions will indicate its broad responsibilities. It was created "to stimulate thinking and investigation on missionary questions," enlisting in the endeavour the best knowledge and experience and making the results available to all missions; "to help coordinate" the efforts of the different national missionary organizations and their member societies and "to bring about united action where necessary"; to "help to unite Christian public opinion" in support of freedom of conscience, religion, and missionary endeavour; to bring together the world's Christian forces to achieve "justice in international and inter-racial relations"; to publish *The International Review of Missions* and any other publication contributing to the study of missionary questions; and "to call a world missionary conference" if and when desirable.[8]

The Council. The Council itself was constituted by the national missionary organizations of a number of countries. The largest was technically an international agency linking the societies of Canada and of the United States, the Foreign Missions Conference of North America. The other two large bodies were the Conference of Missionary Societies in Great Britain and Ireland and the German Protestant Missions Committee (*Ausschuss*). The latter, while not represented at Mohonk, was included among the charter organizations. The other members included the United Missionary Council of Australia, the Committee of Advice (*Commissie van Advies*) of the Netherlands, the General Swedish Missionary Conference (*Allmänna Svenska Missionskonferensen*), the Norwegian General Missions Committee (*Norske Misjoners Felleskomite*), the Danish Missions Council (*Dansk Missionsraad*), the National Joint Missions Committee of Finland (*Suomen Yleinen Lähetystoimikunta*), and three Christian organizations in Asia—the Japan Continuation Committee, the China Continuation Committee, and the National Missionary Council of India, Burma, and Ceylon. Two of the Council's first members were single missionary societies, and remain to this day the only Protestant missionary agencies in their respective countries—the Belgian Society of Protestant Missions to the Congo (*Société Belge de Missions Protestantes au Congo*) and the Paris Evangelical Missionary Society (*Société des Missions évangéliques de Paris*). Finally, among those first members were three groups of missionary societies, none of which had a co-ordinating organization of the council type—those of Switzerland, South Africa, and New Zealand.

With seventy places to be divided among its member organizations, the Council allotted twenty to the Foreign Missions Conference, fourteen to the Conference of British Missionary Societies, and six to the *Ausschuss*. The remainder were allocated among the smaller organizations. Ten additional representatives could be co-opted from areas not otherwise included—Africa, the Near East, and Latin America. The inclusion of the last-named region represented a distinct advance beyond Edinburgh.[9] Under normal circumstances the Council planned to meet every two years.

A final stipulation provided that the Council would function internationally and that its members in any country would not act as a national group, although they could assemble for consultation. This last provision stemmed from the Continuation Committee's experience that its international commissions so often duplicated needlessly what was being done or could better be done by national organizations.

The Committee of the Council. The constitution also provided that the Council at its biennial meeting should appoint a group of twelve members who, with the Council's officers, would comprise the Committee of the Council. It would act for the Council in the intervals between the latter's meetings. The smaller body would consult with the national agencies concerning its own necessary international work, but it could take no action nor make any pronouncement, except in matters of urgency and when confident that such would "commend itself to the several national missionary organizations."[10]

Lake Mohonk's Resolutions

At Lake Mohonk the International Missionary Council took no ex-executive action, but it passed a number of resolutions. A brief résumé of these may help to disclose something of "the mind of the Council" in 1921.

Church and Mission. In 1921 the International Missionary Council put itself on record concerning the relations between churches and missions in such manner that it reflected the considerable progress made on this point in only a decade. A preliminary paper by Arthur J. Brown provided a basis for the Council's discussions,[11] and although its members noted that the goal of missions—to plant an indigenous church—was not being met in many areas, they agreed that no one solution existed applicable to all situations. As a result of vigorous discussion in light of these facts, the Council sent a series of questions to many missionary societies, asking: (1) whether the time had not come for missionaries to work under the authority of nationals and with the same ecclesiastical status as their national colleagues? (2) Whether matters affecting the program of a younger church ought not to be discussed by missionaries and nationals together as representatives of the church rather than by a predominantly missionary group? (3) Whether all funds from abroad ought not to be administered jointly by the national church and the contributing agency? (4) And how best to encourage and train indigenous leadership for the different kinds of work in each country?[12] These questions were at once an admission of overlong paternalism, an indication of the degree of maturity already reached by some vigorous national churches, and an advance in missionary thinking considerably beyond that of Edinburgh. Similar questions had been asked before. They were to be asked again, for they mirrored a process of varying growth, maturity, and mutual adjustment that characterizes the process of an emerging world Christian community.

Missionary Freedom. Against a background of recent war and constant preoccupation with government restrictions, Lake Mohonk naturally centred much attention on the problem of missionary freedom. It counselled the societies concerned how best to meet and deal with certain restrictions in Portuguese Africa and in French colonies.[13]

Even more important was its detailed minute concerning restrictions on German missions, for the existing situation between German and Anglo-American missions required wisdom, tact, and Christian understanding. To help re-establish the broken fellowship and to affirm its own conviction, the International Missionary Council declared "that the wounds caused by the war cannot be fully healed until the way is opened for German missionaries to resume foreign missionary work."[14]

The bar against German missionaries in Palestine had been dropped in 1921 and in several British colonies was scheduled to be removed in the late autumn of 1922. Meanwhile, the Council urged the national missionary organizations of those countries still excluding German missionaries to discover what could be done to speed their return. Moreover, it advocated that where any non-German society had taken over German work during and after the war, such occupancy be regarded as provisional and that a final solution be arranged in conference with the original society, the national church, and the incumbent society. Then, because of repeated attacks upon the loyalty of German missionaries, the Council put itself "on record that to the best of its information the exclusion of German missionaries from Allied territory was due to general political considerations . . . [and] that speaking generally German Protestant missionaries working under the flags of other nations were not guilty of acts of disloyalty or of attempts to excite disloyalty."[15] The Council had not said that there had been no disloyalty, for it was in no position to prove that universal negative; but it had said all that it could. Had there been anyone in that gathering of men of wide experience and with a mass of detailed information before them who could have offered any evidence to the contrary, one may reasonably assume that he would have done so. Finally, the Council expressed its hope that at its next meeting, German representatives would be present.

Instructions to Officers. With reference to its past work, to the general missionary situation, and to the Lake Mohonk discussions, the Council recommended particular responsibilities for each of its officers. These not only further illuminate the Council's thinking, but also provide the determinative framework within which the International Missionary Council's program developed during the next few years.

With the Moslem world in what seemed to be a volatile state, the Council asked Dr. Mott to consider holding a series of conferences in the Near and Middle East, such as had been suggested before the war. The envisioned outcome was a co-ordination of programs for the agencies at work there. Moreover, in accord with a suggestion by Dr. Samuel Zwemer, chairman of the Lucknow [1911 Moslem Conference] Continuation Committee, the International Missionary Council proposed that the anticipated Third General Conference of Workers in Moslem Countries be merged with Mott's meetings. The Council also approved its chairman's presence at the national conferences being planned by the Japan and China Continuation Committees.

The Council encouraged Oldham's plans to visit India to confer with the National Missionary Council. It also urged him to continue his special studies on education, particularly on rapidly expanding state programs of education. This whole subject had been thoroughly, if briefly, surveyed at Mohonk. Oldham was renamed editor of *The International Review of Missions*, with Miss Gollock his associate editor. Warnshuis became the *Review's* business manager. The latter also was asked to assist national committees on Christian literature since he had had experience in that field.

The Council then charged its secretaries to give special attention to a number of matters without designating responsibility for them. Missionary freedom ranked high on the agenda. They were to continue their investigation of labour conditions in Portuguese Africa and their efforts relating to opium control and "any other moral questions of a similar character affecting the progress of Christianity in the mission field." The Council requested its officers to study the policy of the missionary movement toward the growth of industrialism in Asia and elsewhere and toward the related social problems of human welfare. It also asked them to undertake a study of race relations in so far as they bore upon missions and with special reference to the Negro community in America and in the West Indies and its relation to missions in Africa. While many missionaries had concerned themselves with these issues, here was something new in broadly organized co-operation— this concern to know what responsibilities the whole missionary enterprise has toward labour, industrialism, narcotics, race relations, and indeed, the whole broad sweep of human problems. Edinburgh and previous missionary conferences had not been blind to these issues and occasionally dealt with them, but the Lake Mohonk meeting committed the new agency of international missionary co-operation to a broad, continuing study of social issues.[16]

Before Mohonk had ended, its members agreed to recommend a budget for 1922 and 1923 of nearly $29,500 (£5,905), the largest items of which were salaries for the secretaries and grants for their travel expenses. The sessions were closed, as they had been opened—very simply—with prayer. Indeed, the spirit of prayer had been a hallmark of the entire conference. When its delegates left the serene beauty of Lake Mohonk, they felt secure in the knowledge that at long last an International Missionary Council existed and stood ready to serve a world-wide missionary enterprise.

THE GROWTH OF CO-OPERATIVE COUNCILS

Edinburgh and its Continuation Committee had given rise to a rapid increase in Europe, Asia, and Africa of national missionary councils. It is not surprising, therefore, that a similar development occurred after the Lake Mohonk meeting. Additional councils were formed in Europe so that more societies could participate in the International Missionary Council, and in Asia the councils or committees that had been formed a decade earlier, mirroring the growth of an indigenous church, were transformed into National Christian Councils.

Europe

Germany. Our attention moves first and naturally to Germany. News of Lake Mohonk's resolutions on German missions quickly reached that land and made a profound impression in missionary circles there. At a meeting of all German societies in Halle in April, 1922, Martin Schlunk and Friederich Würz were appointed delegates to the International Missionary Council.[17] In September they visited London to discuss the future of German missions, and in October they reported back to the meeting of the German societies. It was at that gathering that the German Protestant Missionary Alliance (*Der deutsche Evangelische Missionsbund*) was formed with the old *Ausschuss* becoming its standing committee.[18]

Scandinavia. As a result of Crans, Norway's missionary societies had created the Norwegian General Missions Committee in May, 1921. A year later that body became the Norwegian Missionary Council (*Norske Misjonsråd*) with membership in the International Missionary Council.[19] Shortly thereafter in Finland, the National Joint Missions Committee, which had been formed in 1918 and was represented at Lake Mohonk, became the Finnish Missionary Council (*Suomen Lähetysneuvosto*) which brought together delegates from five Finnish societies.[20]

The Northern Lutheran Missions Conferences, which had last convened at Oslo in 1902 and had been interrupted in 1906 as a result of political tensions, met again twenty years later. The assembly gathered at Copenhagen from May 11 to 14, 1922, with nearly three hundred persons present.[21] Meanwhile, missionary councils had been organized in the Northern countries. Because these included missions not only of the predominant Lutherans, but also of other churches and groups, the Copenhagen meeting resolved to create a Northern Missionary Council (*Nordiska Missionsradet*) embodying missions of all denominations. The new council was constituted at Stockholm in February, 1923, with the Reverend Jakob E. Lundahl as its secretary. Primarily an organ to develop the unity of Scandinavian missions, it did not seek independent membership in the International Missionary Council.[22]

Switzerland. At Lake Mohonk Swiss societies had been represented individually. Earlier attempts to establish a central committee among them had failed, but early in 1923 the three Swiss societies came together to form the Association of Swiss Missions for International Relations (*Delegation des Missions Suisses pour les Relations Internationales* or *Schweizerischer Missions Verband*). It served as their link with the International Missionary Council.[23]

Asia

China. The memorable National Christian Conference held in Shanghai in May, 1922, was called by the China Continuation Committee. To it came a thousand delegates, more than half of them Chinese who represented every level of the Christian church. The increase of national delegates accurately measured the growth in vigour and independence of the Chinese church. The 1913 Mott conference had been composed of selected rather than elected delegates, and the China Continuation Committee that resulted represented only the conference. Meant to be temporary, the Continuation Committee had had to serve through the years of war. The 1922 conference was charged to create a national agency directly representative of the churches and missions. That the National Christian Council actually emerged out of a welter of difficulties, including a fundamentalist controversy and an assembly composed of many persons inexperienced in the ways of such meetings, was due in no small measure to the able and patient chairmanship of the brilliant Cheng Ching-yi. Mott was present and addressed the conference, but few of the major accounts in English mention his being there. This was a Chinese conference! It not only projected the National Christian Council, but also stood as a symbol of the emergence of a strong, thoroughly capable, national leadership.[24]

T. T. Lew declared at Shanghai: "The Chinese Church shall teach her members to agree to differ and to resolve to love."[25] That very spirit enabled the conference to achieve its end. The National Christian Council it brought forth was established on the same basis as the International Missionary Council, without legislative authority and with questions of organization and doctrine, on which the churches differed, beyond its purview. Its first secretaries were Miss Y. J. Fan, the Reverend K. T. Chung, and the English Quaker, Dr. Henry T. Hodgkin, whose distinguished leadership greatly aided the Council during its formative years.[26] Thus was forged another link in the world-wide chain of councils supporting the International Missionary Council.

Japan. The Japan Continuation Committee, founded during Mott's 1913 visit, carried out a significant nation-wide evangelistic campaign in its first three years. Thereafter, dependent upon voluntary services of busy men and unable to assume specific projects because the Federated Missions or the Federation of Churches believed they could do them better, it atrophied. Such was its plight when it called the National Christian Conference in the latter half of May, 1922. When first proposed in 1919, the conference could not meet because of wartime dislocations. In 1922, however, more than two hundred members, most of them elected by churches and missions, came to the Tokyo meeting. The majority were Japanese, and a Japanese, Dr. S. Motoda, chaired the assembly. Mott gave an opening address, but like Shanghai, this was no "Mott conference" with outside inspiration and direction. Like its Chinese counterpart, it was a *National* Christian Conference.[27]

Tokyo's important outcome became the plan to establish a National Christian Council to foster unity within the church in Japan and to link it with the rest of the world Christian community. After eighteen months of preparation, the National Christian Council, based upon the International Missionary Council's Hague principle, was organized on November 13, 1923, with Bishop K. Uzaki as its chairman. The Council, with a large majority of Japanese members, elected Dr. William Axling of the American Baptist Foreign Mission and the Reverend K. Miyazaki as its secretaries. At the outset the Federation of Churches merged itself with the new Council.[28] In 1925 the Federated Missions turned over to the Council the work of five of its committees.

India. After ten years of steady, fruitful work the National Missionary Council of India, Burma, and Ceylon met at Poona in January, 1922. There it drafted a constitution for a National Christian Council to replace itself. The new constitution, incorporating several sections directly from that of the International Missionary Council, called for a membership not less than half of which was to be Indian. J. H. Oldham was present and shared an important rôle in developing plans for the new organization.[29]

A year later in January, 1923, the National Missionary Council met at Ranchi for the last time under that name and brought into being the National Christian Council. At the request of the International Missionary Council, Oldham had returned to India again and aided greatly in the new council's formation. The Reverend William Paton, formerly of the Calcutta YMCA, had been secretary of the embryonic council for a year and was made its secretary for 1923. A year later Mr. P. Ooman Philip, a member of the Mar Thoma Syrian Church in Travancore who for some time had directed the National Missionary Society of India, became joint secretary with Paton in the Council's Calcutta headquarters. The devoted labours of both Paton and Philip brought the Council great respect. Moreover, the change in name from "Missionary" to "Christian" did more than to represent a new and stronger body. It gave evidence of the growing importance of the church in India and of emphasis upon it as the centre for planning rather than the missionary movement.[30]

Korea. On March 26, 1918, Presbyterians and Methodists in Korea formed the "Korean Federal Council of Churches" on lines similar to the Federal Council of Protestant Evangelical Missions in Korea. In 1924 the Council of Churches became the Korean National Christian Council. Three years later, by amending its constitution, it opened its membership to other Protestant bodies in that country.[31] Its officers were all Koreans, and like the other national councils it held no authority to deal with matters of doctrine or polity nor to enforce its decisions. It could act, when so empowered, on behalf of its member organizations and represented them in the International Missionary Council.[32]

Africa

The Congo Protestant Council.   General missionary conferences had begun in the Congo in 1902, and nine years later a local continuation committee was formed to link them with the Edinburgh Continuation Committee. Any action taken by that group had to be approved by the Congo Missionary Conference.[33] The 1921 Bolenge meeting authorized the continuation committee's secretaries to gain representation in the International Missionary Council, and in 1924 the conference adopted a constitution for a Congo Protestant Council (*Conseil Protestant du Congo*). A year later at Léopoldville-Est the new Congo Protestant Council met for the first time with its members now representing their societies directly.[34]

The Near East Christian Council.   From February to April, 1924, the International Missionary Council convened a series of conferences in the Near East on Moslem problems. The culminating assembly at Jerusalem under Mott's chairmanship resulted in the emergence of the Council for Western Asia and Northern Africa three years later with Robert P. Wilder as its first secretary. In 1929 it became the Near East Christian Council for Missionary Cooperation.[35]

Australia and New Zealand

Australia's United Missionary Council had been formed in 1920 to promote co-operation. As a result of Mott's conference at Melbourne in April, 1926, the United Missionary Council's constitution underwent considerable revision. The "new" constitution came into effect in October, 1927, and formed the basis for the National Missionary Council of Australia.[36] From Australia Mott went to New Zealand in the latter part of April and there conducted a conference at Dunedin. That meeting's outstanding proposal called for a National Missionary Council to link New Zealand's missionary program with the International Missionary Council and to promote co-operation. Within a few months all the constituent bodies had approved it, and the Council was formed.[37]

Thus did the network of national organizations expand and grow stronger during the first years of the International Missionary Council's existence. As one quickly notes in studying their backgrounds and the needs they were designed to meet, they all fit a similar pattern. Each would provide for more effective internal co-operation and would also serve as the national tie with the growing internationalism in missionary endeavour. Moreover, their organizational structures were much the same, each being based on essentially the same foundations as the International Missionary Council itself.

Oldham had wisely spoken of these National Christian Councils as "new spiritual adventures," for they would fail or succeed "in the region of the spirit."[38] Strictly advisory, they held no authority to make decisions, except as that was granted to them on occasion by their member organizations. Each council had to lead, to give guidance and counsel, and to help its members see their problems as part of a larger whole. Each had to find its true life not independently but within existing churches and missions by helping each of them to share in a larger common life and to work more effectively. There was no visible authority holding the councils together, for any member body could withdraw support at any time. Yet they grew stronger, and despite occasional trials, more unified. Every action had to commend itself by virtue of its inherent truth and rightness. This was something new in international Christian co-operation.

THE COUNCIL FINDING ITSELF

Between the constituting of the International Missionary Council at Lake Mohonk and the renowned Jerusalem Conference in 1928, the Council met once—at Oxford, England in July, 1923.[39] The Committee of the Council, the small inner circle which conducted interim business, met three times: at Canterbury, England, in July, 1922;[40] at Atlantic City, in the United States, in January, 1925;[41] and at Rättvik, Sweden, in July, 1926.[42] Between these sessions the secretaries pursued their duties in accord with the mandates given them.

One who studies these early meetings quickly senses that in spite of the accumulated experience of the previous decade, the young Council was feeling its way, moving fearlessly but with caution, and slowly coming into its own. This was most evident in three areas: the relation of doctrinal unity to practical missionary co-operation; the Council's proper functions in terms of the kind of co-operation it represented; and the resulting proper division of responsibilities among its secretaries. We need to examine all three areas briefly.

A Theological Basis for Co-operation

Christians have differed among themselves on the interpretation of certain matters of their faith since the church's founding, and the early 1920's brought a particularly acute division among many Protestants. The basic conflict concerned the verbal inspiration and infallibility of the Bible, with lines drawn between fundamentalists and non-fundamentalists. The conflict was real and produced such widely separated manifestations as the Scopes trial in Tennessee and the Bible Union of China, a body which viewed with alarm the Continuation Committee and later the National Christian Council. In Britain and America as well as in the lands of the younger churches this rift between two large groups presented one of the greatest obstacles to co-operation. The nature of the conflict was divisive, sectarian, and exclusive. It led some groups to withdraw from common ventures, as the China Inland Mission did, and caused others to refrain from co-operating. Naturally sharp questions arose. "Is uniformity of belief essential to missionary co-operation?" "Is *any* co-operation possible with doctrinal differences?" "Does the International Missionary Council not constitute a super-board imposing doctrinal restrictions?" This was the situation the Council confronted at its Oxford meeting in 1923. Questions were being raised at many points throughout the Council's membership—questions that touched the very roots of the organization.

Two able papers by Robert E. Speer and the Bishop of Bombay, E. J. Palmer, served as background for the Council's Oxford deliberations.[43] Discussion matched the preliminary papers' high calibre and members emphasized their position by standing vote. Pointing to a Lake Mohonk resolution, the Council reaffirmed that to seek any theological consensus or to discuss or determine matters of doctrine lay beyond its province. Despite this bar, the Council obviously had a strong theological undergirding and existed because of a common theological core among its members. This consensus the Council sought to make explicit. It included "a common obligation to proclaim the Gospel of Christ in all the world," an obligation made deep because of knowledge "of the havoc wrought by sin and of the efficacy of the salvation offered by Christ"; and "a common loyalty to Jesus Himself," a loyalty which shared the confessions of Peter, "Thou art the Christ, the Son of the Living God," and of Thomas, "My Lord and my God." From these two basic affirmations flowed a whole series of agreements; yet, as the Council recognized, "our differences in doctrine, great though in some instances they are, have not hindered us from profitable co-operation in counsel. When we have gathered together, we have experienced a growing unity among ourselves, in which we recognize the influence of the Holy Spirit." Such recognition led to a common mind on many questions and made possible united recommendations whose final execution rested with the churches and missions concerned.[44]

The Council, aware that where doctrinal differences are involved some might regard co-operation in counsel considerably safer than co-operation in work, indicated a wide range of endeavours "not affected by doctrinal differences." Among others it listed negotiations with governments, the securing of religious liberty, efforts against the evils of narcotics, statistics and surveys, and problems of education. The Council also recorded with gratitude a fact noted long before by co-operative field conferences in the nineteenth century, namely, that "a still more imposing list" could be compiled of projects in which one would expect doctrinal differences to create difficulty, but in which co-operation had proved the rule. Such included translation of the scriptures, the production and distribution of Christian literature, the establishment and conduct of schools, colleges, and medical institutions, and the training of missionaries.[45]

Thus the Council affirmed its implicit theological base and, against

those who demanded a full definition of the faith and against those
who viewed its basis of co-operation as ultimately impossible, declared it adequate for its necessary functions. Finally it stated: "It
would be entirely out of harmony with the spirit of this movement to
press for such cooperation in work as would be felt to compromise
doctrinal principles or to strain consciences."[46]

Functions for an Agency of International Missionary Co-operation

Certain fundamental questions regarding the nature and function
of the Council arose during its first years. Since it was new and seeking
to find its proper rôle, its responsible officers constantly wrestled with
what at first glance might seem to be useless questions with obvious
answers. That so much conscientious attention was given to probing
the very bases of the International Missionary Council indicates,
however, the honest thoroughness with which its secretaries sought
to serve the best interests of the Council's members. This process
began at Lake Mohonk and focussed in the Atlantic City meeting in
1925. There primary attention centred on the rôle and function of the
International Missionary Council.

By 1923 it appeared to Oldham and Warnshuis that the international
organization had in many respects surrendered its envisaged functions
to the national agencies.[47] For example, most of the negotiations
with the British government, presumably carried out under the
aegis of the International Missionary Council, were actually being
conducted by the Conference of British Missionary Societies.[48] The
concerns of German missionaries in French territories were cared for
by the Paris Mission. A similar pattern seemed to be evident in other
problem areas nominally designated to the Council's oversight. In a
memorandum to the secretaries of the two largest missionary councils,
Oldham and Warnshuis made an unqualified and obviously extreme
statement to emphasize their position, declaring privately that in the
1922-23 period the Council amounted "practically to nothing more
than a conference held every two years."[49] Thus in 1925 the most
obvious query emerged first: "Is international missionary co-operation
as now conducted absolutely necessary?" The almost instinctive general reply was "Yes!" On further questioning, "Why?" and "To what
end?" positive answers came more slowly. Yet they were given—among

them, to bear witness to the universality of the Christian fellowship, to keep missions abreast of the forces shaping the lives of people whom missions serve, and to do those things that could be done only on an international basis.[50]

The secretaries also confronted two specialized kinds of work in which priority given to one or the other indicated a somewhat differing conception of the Council's function: (1) itinerating with the consequent sharing of information and points of view with all to whom they went, and (2) executive responsibilities for specifically assigned problems. The second clearly involved the recurring difficulty of respective spheres of activity for the national and international bodies. Very specific problems requiring only a limited amount of an administrator's time should, Oldham suggested, be left to national executives. On the other hand, when a comprehensive study of some broad problem was desired, such projects, he argued, should be surrendered by the national organizations as being the proper responsibility for the international body.[51] Warnshuis viewed unfavourably either one of the Council's secretaries devoting a large portion of his time to a single problem or study. He saw international missionary co-operation's future lying rather in the promotion of "helpful relations" between the national bodies.[52] Oldham also pointed out that one of the Council's most important responsibilities—it could only be hinted at, not controlled—was to be sensitive to the world's needs and those of the missionary enterprise as well as to God's will for the times. In such a position the Council might become an instrument to help bring into being those new creations or movements "which lie hid in the purpose of God for the world as it is today."[53]

The Committee of the Council, meeting in Atlantic City in 1925, devoted its major attention to these problems and helped to set the pattern of the International Missionary Council's future development. It also considered many issues confronting the missionary movement— religious liberty, race relations, indigenous churches, Christian education, opium and related social evils—and declared by unanimous vote that to confront these complex questions adequately required international missionary co-operation. Recognizing the great need to strengthen national organizations, it affirmed, nevertheless, that even at best these were inadequate for the total task. As a result, it went on record that co-operation through such a body as the International Missionary Council, constantly flexible to changing needs, was "indispensable."[54] This seemed to settle the oft-raised question whether the Council was essential or only worth while for the total missionary enterprise.

The Committee also approved the principles upon which the secretaries had been operating: that the Council should concentrate on tasks impossible for the national councils to do or to do so well as the international body could do them; that it should undertake those larger problems immediately confronting the boards and should assign them priority according to their urgency; that it should assume those endeavours that would strengthen national organizations and promote unity; that in preparing its program it should shoulder only as much as it could do well; and that the Council should also recognize certain imperatives. "There are some things which the Council must attempt to do at all costs."[55]

The Committee recognized that the Council's general sessions (*e.g.*, Mohonk and Oxford) required supplementation by "international conferences having a strictly limited purpose and dealing with a particular subject."[56] Moreover, with urgent needs in so many areas and severe demands upon the secretaries, the Committee at Atlantic City unanimously asked Dr. Mott to give his "entire time" to the Council. It was a large request! After much thought Mott gave his reply eighteen months later, expressing his conviction that he could not rightfully surrender his work with the World's Student Christian Federation and the YMCA. Yet, with the Council leaving to him the necessary adjustments in his time schedule, he agreed "as Chairman to undertake and discharge the responsibilities which the Committee have in view," giving himself to them "with full heart and conviction."[57] For the next decade and a half, Mott gave a considerable portion of each year to the International Missionary Council and assumed so many other responsibilities in addition to his normal duties as chairman that, in effect, the Council gained a full-time chief-of-staff.

Finally, it should be noted, the Atlantic City meeting gave birth to the world-famous Jerusalem Conference of 1928. The urgent circumstances that had brought the Committee's members together and led them to assert the Council's indispensability, they agreed, further required a deliberative international gathering of no more than 400 persons to consider their full implications for the missionary enterprise.

Jerusalem grew out of the conviction that the times required a "strong forward movement" by the Christian forces of the world.[58]

The Council's Staff

Between 1921 and 1928 the Council's staff reflected this process of development, adjustment, and adaptation. There were changes in personnel, the appointment of additional secretaries, and the obvious need to divide responsibilities among the officers. While in one sense the Council represented the international functioning of the national co-operative missionary bodies, in another, it was also in large measure a reflection of its chairman and its secretaries. Perhaps, as it turned out, more a strength than a weakness, the Council was built upon their personalities and abilities. If, then, we are to understand the Council's development, we must also become acquainted with the work of each officer.

Oldham. Oldham had been contributing vision to international missionary co-operation from 1908 when he became secretary for the World Missionary Conference. With a highly creative mind, Oldham made his great contribution to the thought-life of the International Missionary Council. His thinking reached out in terms of over-all strategy. Mott described him as "one of the most stimulating, thought-provocative men I have ever known."[59] Yet because of the emphasis upon his executive ability, Oldham's deep spiritual insight was often forgotten. No one who has read *A Devotional Diary* can fail to see here a man of prayer and spiritual discernment.[60] When Oldham came to a job, he concentrated on it with a single mind and with all his energy. When he had exhausted all that he could give to a particular task, he moved on to the next thing. In giving his best, he centred on one thing at a time. In this, of course, he was quite the opposite of Mott who carried on a broad range of activities simultaneously.

Oldham had edited *The International Review of Missions* from its inception and, with Miss Gollock, had made it a distinguished and respected journal. He continued as editor through 1927. After Mohonk his major attention focussed upon missionary freedom and government restrictions upon missions and the related question of the return of German missionaries to their former fields. Christian education in the post-war era, especially in Africa, became another major concern.

Closely tied to this was his work with a British government committee on East Africa in which Oldham bore special responsibility for the relation of missions to political and economic change in that area.[61] Because of his experience and continuing interest in India, Oldham naturally gave oversight to International Missionary Council affairs pertaining to that country.

Warnshuis. Warnshuis had come to the International Missionary Council from the National Christian Council in China. Entirely different from Oldham, he made an excellent co-secretary, for the talents of each man complemented the other. Large of stature, vigorous, and capable of handling effectively a tremendous volume of work, Warnshuis probably made his greatest contribution as an administrator. Able executives found they could work readily with him. Fearless, aggressive, and efficient, he commanded respect and brought the North American office of the International Missionary Council to a high position of influence and honour.

Of Dutch descent, Warnshuis rather naturally turned to issues affecting Continental missions. From the time he came on the Council's staff, he accepted responsibility for supervising American contributions to German societies. He also gave close attention to missionary concerns in French, Belgian, and Portuguese territories. To his oversight were entrusted inquiries on union institutions, women's work, student migrations, and indigenous churches. His China background led him naturally to become the Council's executive primarily responsible for Far Eastern affairs. This had also led to his early and long-continued connection with the opium question, especially as that was then being dealt with by the League of Nations. During the first three and a half years of his secretaryship, Warnshuis had his headquarters at Edinburgh House. At the time more than half the support for the whole missionary enterprise came from North America, which also made the largest yearly contribution to the Council's budget. Thus it seemed wise for the further development of international missionary co-operation to open an office in America. The Committee of the Council at Atlantic City authorized the step, and Warnshuis immediately established his headquarters at 25 Madison Avenue in New York where the offices of the Foreign Missions Conference were then located. At the same time arrangements were made by which he became a "Cooperating Secretary" of the Committee of Reference and Council.[62] One of Warnshuis' most important tasks was to help strengthen the Foreign Missions Conference. He acted as organizer for many of its field committees. Moreover, as secretary of its committee on missions and governments, and following the lessons learned from Oldham, he became known and respected in the American State Department.

Mott. The chairman of the International Missionary Council, John R. Mott, requires no further personal description here, for he had become a world-figure. As we have seen the Council was but one of many responsibilities that claimed his time. He assumed his rôle of chairman, as head and representative of the Council, quite naturally and to a remarkable degree kept himself clear of the actual administrative machinery entrusted to the secretariat. It has been suggested more than once that from 1926 on Mott was, in effect, the Council's general secretary—an idea which hints at a real truth. Stated perhaps more accurately, Mott increasingly served the Council as a full-time chairman and carried out many responsibilities impossible for the ordinary chairman which, as a result, often fall upon a secretary's shoulders. Mott's tours, for example, were not, strictly speaking, International Missionary Council functions. They cost the Council nothing although they were undertaken largely on its behalf and their results accrued to its benefit.

When at Rättvik in 1926 Mott accepted increased responsibilities within the framework of the International Missionary Council, he made it clear that his further contributions "would be in addition to the ordinary duties of the chairmanship."[63] They would be: to increase the spiritual forces of the missionary movement; to help recruit the ablest young leaders for missions; to strengthen the enterprise by "liberating" the lay forces; to encourage a fresh consideration of the distinctive Christian message in East and West; to facilitate progress in race relations; to enlist persons and institutions oustandingly qualified to contribute to the solution of major mission problems; to assist national and international "forward movements" (*e.g.*, conferences for workers among Jews); to work for closer collaboration between the national councils and the International Missionary Council so that the latter might more effectively serve them; to develop further within the Council an "enriching and truly creative international and inter-racial Christian fellowship."[64]

Miss B. D. Gibson. A Presbyterian born and reared in Scotland, Betty Gibson had come into the office of the Continuation Committee in 1916. She had taken her degree in French and German—a most useful background for a post with an international committee—and began at once translating Continental documents for the Committee's use. Her work, though little publicized, became indispensable to the on-going program of the Council. When the Oldhams went to India in 1922, Miss Gibson accompanied them at her own expense to be of whatever service she could. She shared much of Oldham's work and thus developed a great knowledge of missionary problems in Africa, a continent later to claim much of her attention. Moreover, her knowledge of Continental missions enabled her to perform invaluable service in the years after World War I, in the various efforts conducted on behalf of German missions. At Atlantic City in 1925 Oldham proposed that Miss Gibson, because of her "increasingly valuable assistance," be made an assistant secretary of the International Missionary Council. The recommendation passed, and after a decade in the Council's service, she became an official member of its secretariat.

Miss Marion J. Hunter, after distinguished war service with the Red Cross, served the Council on a voluntary basis for several years in the early twenties. She worked closely with Oldham and dealt mainly with problems of German mission property and relations with governments. She compiled *Treaties Acts and Regulations Relating to Missionary Freedom.*

Miss G. A. Gollock and Miss M. M. Underhill. Miss Georgina A. Gollock, who had assisted Oldham almost from the beginning with *The International Review of Missions,* had been appointed an associate editor in 1920 and in 1921 had become co-editor. The last recognition was indeed merited. Oldham frequently related that it was when Miss Gollock came into the office, with her wealth of experience in editing and printing and with her general organizing ability, that the *Review* really progressed upon sound and efficient lines. She shared Oldham's penchant for accuracy in detail and impressed it upon other members of the staff. To her is owed much of the credit for what *The International Review of Missions* became. Her activity and influence extended far beyond her responsibilities for this journal. As secretary of the Board of Study for the Preparation of Missionaries she galvanized that group into effective action. She was a woman of vigorous personality, wide knowledge, and sound judgment.[65]

In 1922 Miss Gollock fixed a terminal date for her service so that a successor could be found and trained. At Canterbury the Committee of the Council authorized an invitation to Miss Muriel M. Underhill, an Oxford graduate who had served for eighteen years in India with the Zenana Bible and Medical Mission, to join the *Review* with the expectation of becoming Miss Gollock's successor. Miss Underhill accepted the new post in the autumn of 1923. Nearly three and a half years later when Miss Gollock resigned in February, 1927, Miss Underhill succeeded her.[66]

Paton. Acceding to the Council's Rättvik request, William Paton came into its secretariat in 1927 and helped to usher in a new era of its life. Born in 1886, Paton had grown up in a Scottish home—religious and thoroughly Presbyterian—transplanted on English soil. At Oxford, Paton formed a lasting friendship with Frank Lenwood, then a pastor to students, which became a turning point in his life. Lenwood's influence encouraged Paton to become active in the Student Christian Movement, then emphasizing mission study, and to join in projects of local evangelism. When Mott visited Oxford in 1905, his spirit and faith so profoundly impressed Paton that the latter became convinced his own life must be given to evangelism.[67] Finishing at Oxford, Paton went on to Westminster College, Cambridge, for three years of theology.

In 1911 Paton became a secretary of the British Student Christian Movement and a year later married Grace Macdonald. In 1913 as assistant general secretary and as a man of deep faith with a passion for evangelism, he emphasized the Movement's strong missionary purpose.[68] Ordained just before his departure to India in 1917, Paton conducted YMCA work among the troops there. A year later and full of enthusiasm for India, he returned to England to become the Student Christian Movement's missionary secretary. His work brought him in touch with J. H. Oldham, and the two men began a friendship that lasted a lifetime. In 1921 Paton was on his way to India again for YMCA service that required him to travel the length and breadth of that country. A year later, after much turmoil of mind and spirit concerning the rightness of his action, Paton resigned from the YMCA to accept a secretarial post with the National Missionary Council.[69] His first task was to aid its process of transition into the National Christian Council. A man of rugged physique and indefatigable energy, Paton, in addition to editing the *National Christian Council Review,* travelled over all India, working with provincial councils, leading the fight against opium, encouraging evangelism among the Moslems, carrying through negotiations on behalf of unstaffed German missions, and stimulating the production of Christian literature.

Paton returned home on furlough in 1926 and went to the International Missionary Council's Rättvik meeting to represent the Indian National Christian Council. Meanwhile, Oldham had asked to be relieved of his administrative and executive responsibilities in the Council, for he had been approached regarding a special government service for Africa which, it was thought, might occupy his time for several years. The Committee of the Council agreed that Oldham should be freed for this new opportunity, yet should remain a secretary of the Council in an honorary capacity. At the same time it invited Paton to become a secretary of the Council. He agreed to accept on condition that a successor could be found for his post in India and that the Council there could be put on a sounder financial footing.[70] He returned to India in the autumn of 1926 and discovered that his colleagues there, while reluctant to let him go, viewed his appointment as a contribution to international work which they ought to make. Succeeded in India by Nicol Macnicol, Paton returned to London in January, 1927, and shortly began his work at Edinburgh House.

From its beginning, the International Missionary Council possessed a secretariat whose members comprised a top-flight team. Mott, as chairman, from 1926 gave an increasing amount of his time to the Council. Oldham, Warnshuis, and Paton served as co-equals. When he came on the staff, by mutual agreement with Oldham, Paton assumed the major load of administration in London. Both men had policy-making minds and shared that function together. Warnshuis had full responsibility for the Council's operation in New York. Each of the three secretaries was a man of strong and independent mind. Naturally, differences of opinion arose on occasion. Yet Mott's influence as chairman and the common desire to serve the best interests of international missionary co-operation led to a remarkably united secretariat.

THE INTERNATIONAL MISSIONARY COUNCIL'S OUTREACH

The sub-title above was deliberately chosen. "The Work of the Council" might have provided an alternate form, but "outreach" fits the facts more closely. Strictly speaking, the Council's work was limited to its secretaries' accomplishments. Its outreach, however, included the numerous enterprises its very existence stimulated among its member bodies. Indeed, it might well be said that the National Christian Council in China represented the International Missionary Council at work in that country or that the International Missionary Council symbolized the full international functioning of the Foreign Missions Conference of North Africa. The Council's nature is such that it obviously becomes difficult strictly to define its limits.

Between 1921 and 1927 several main emphases emerged. Continuing from the war years, the problem of German missions and of relief for them grew. Closely allied with this was the whole issue of missionary freedom toward which so much had been done during and just after World War I. Another major post-war emphasis was education—secular and Christian—as it related to the missionary movement. To this Oldham devoted himself whole-heartedly, and since so much of his study centred in Africa, the whole range of problems associated with that vast continent came increasingly to occupy his attention. In other areas the Council was directly concerned with such seemingly diverse questions as opium, race, labour and slavery, missionary training, and Christian literature. To these Warnshuis gave his constant attention. We turn first and naturally to that continuing responsibility from World War I, German missions.

Aid to German Missions

When the Council directed its attention to German missions, two matters at once became apparent: (1) financial aid for the few German missionaries still abroad and unable to receive support from Germany and the related need to maintain those German mission stations for so long without German personnel, and (2) the whole question of hastening the return of German missionaries as quickly as possible to their former posts.

Financial Help. In the last chapter we surveyed briefly some of the efforts made during the war and the immediate post-war period to sustain German missions. For the most part these were limited to an extension of oversight and a lending of personnel to help the depleted missions carry on. Then, during the period between Mohonk and Jerusalem, a rather informal enterprise developed similar to what during World War II was designated "Orphaned Missions." With post-war German's runaway inflation and with the mark valueless abroad, support for German missionaries still overseas had to come from sources outside Germany. The Basel Mission in China supported its work with funds from Switzerland. The National Lutheran Council in the United States supported the Berlin and Kieler Missions. Other Lutheran bodies in America maintained German missionaries elsewhere. The Dutch Reformed Church in South Africa assisted German missionaries in South and Southwest Africa. And the government of the Netherlands Indies supplied funds to support German missionaries there.[71]

In countries where German missionaries were temporarily excluded after the war, non-German societies sought to sustain their former enterprises. Usually this was done with the understanding, urged by the International Missionary Council, that such occupation was provisional and would be worked out later with the original German society and the local church. In the United States the American Board (Congregational) and the Reformed Church in America, and in England the London and Wesleyan Missionary Societies were giving a combined total of $10,000 annually to the South India United Church for support of the Malabar Mission of the Basel Society. The Augustana Synod of the Lutheran Church in the United States supported the Leipzig Mission in Tanganyika. The Evangelical Lutheran Joint Synod of Ohio conducted the Hermannsburg work in India. The Evangelical Joint Synod of Iowa supported German missions in Africa, China, India, and New Guinea. The National Lutheran Council supported German Lutheran societies at work in China, Africa, and India. The Church of Scotland, the United Free Church of Scotland, and the Universities' Mission to Central Africa attempted to care for the Moravian and Berlin Mission's program in Tanganyika. The United Free Church also undertook to aid the Basel Mission on the Gold Coast and to some extent the Bremen Mission in British Togoland. To this end it added more than $40,000 (£9,406) to its missionary budget in 1923. The Paris Mission cared for former German missions in the French Cameroons.[72] In the same year Dutch churches and societies had contributed more than $100,000 (Fl. 300,000) for the Rhenish Mission in Sumatra and for the Moravian Mission in Surinam. At the same time Swedish and Danish Societies together gave an almost comparable amount for German missions in Africa and India.[73]

Warnshuis and Miss Gibson gave much of their time to the needs of the destitute missions, urging generous giving on the part of British and American constituencies and attempting to co-ordinate those efforts. Immediately after the war French and Finnish missions also received funds, but very soon almost all financial help was going to German missions. In the United States a sustained five-year drive to aid German missions came in the period from 1921 to 1925. In 1921, 1922, and 1923, well over $300,000 yearly was given from American sources, and in 1924 and 1925 well over $200,000 yearly. The total giving in this period approximated $1,385,000, the great bulk of it from Lutheran sources, but with substantial amounts from Moravians and Seventh Day Adventists.[74] If one extends the period from America's entry into the war through 1926, total American giving to Continental missions exceeded $1,700,000.[75]

Negotiations with Government. The problems of missionary freedom—specifically, gaining permission for Germans to return to their former fields—and financial aid were directly related. With the gradual removal of restrictions first in one country and then in another, increasing numbers of German missionaries were free to resume their former work abroad; but the chaotic state of German finances forced their continuing dependence upon outside financial support. While this meant increasing its efforts to help raise money elsewhere, the International Missionary Council continued to press for the removal of government restrictions on German missionaries. Because so many of the issues involved the British government, the Conference of British Missionary Societies appointed Oldham joint secretary of a committee on government relations and invited Warnshuis to attend its meetings with the privilege of bringing matters to the committee's attention.[76]

The process of negotiating with the government on behalf of German missions evolved slowly. Most of it was undertaken in the name of the Conference of British Missionary Societies with the British government. Even by 1922 German societies encountered difficulty in having returned to them money and property retained in the hands of official government receivers. Consequently, representations were made for them with appeal to Article 438 of the Peace Treaty.[77] The transfer of properties to the original German owners, however, took a long time. Although it was for the most part accomplished by 1930, it required constant vigilance and prodding.[78] By the first three months of 1923 restrictive legislation in areas and territories controlled by Britain either had begun to lapse or the British government was willing to consider individual cases on their merit.[79] Independent of this, the British government in 1923 also adopted a policy in the colonies and protectorates of placing no restrictions upon alien missionary societies "recognized" by the Conference of British Missionary Societies or the Foreign Missions Conference. Thus India recognized certain Danish, Swedish, and Swiss societies recommended by the Conference of British Missionary Societies. German missionaries were required to obtain individual permits, and their return began as a very slow trickle.[80] In response to a request from the Conference of British Missionary Societies, the Secretary of State for the Colonies agreed in the summer of 1924 to remove the "discrimination" against German societies and to allow that agency to recommend them for "recognition" also. The Conference of British Missionary Societies in turn was guided by advice from the *Ausschuss* and submitted the names of eight societies.[81] The wheels turned slowly, however, and efforts to re-establish German missionaries were still in process after the Jerusalem meeting in 1928.

The International Missionary Council's secretaries were also alert to watch for infringements of missionary freedom in other parts of the globe and upon others than Germans. Thus they kept religious freedom constantly before British authorities during the negotiations between Britain and Egypt when the latter drew up its constitution. They also took steps to safeguard missionary freedom in French West Africa and in Angola.[82]

Africa, Education, and Christian Literature

Oldham's interest after World War I in the missionary movement's policy toward education led the Council into a general examination of that subject, with special concentration on religious education. In the process Oldham's attention was largely directed toward Africa, a fact which heightened the Council's immediate interest in that continent. At Lake Mohonk the Council had authorized Oldham to pursue further his investigations into education as it related to missions.[83] Concern was high for an educational strategy, as may be seen in the report of the Commission on Village Education in India and in the Burton Commission report on China.[84] The latter, jointly sponsored by the Committee of Reference and Counsel and the Conference of British Missionary Societies, influenced the shaping of Christian educational policies in China for some years.

The Advisory Committee. As a result of representations on African education made by the Conference of British Missionary Societies, the Colonial Office appointed an Advisory Committee on Education to deal with British African colonies.[85] Except in Mohammedan areas, nine-tenths of the education in these dependencies had been conducted by missions. Symbolizing the government's growing interest in "native education," the newly appointed agency sought to survey problems of African education and to co-ordinate the activities of regional governments and missions in a constructive educational policy. This body, in which Oldham played an important part, later became the Advisory Committee on Native Education in Tropical Africa.[86]

The Institute of African Languages and Culture. As missionary societies joined forces to consider Africa's educational needs, they encountered related problems, especially that of Christian literature. These led in England to special conferences on Africa from one of which, that held at High Leigh in September, 1924, came a suggestion (made originally by Warnshuis) for an International Institute of African Languages and Culture. Preparations got under way at once, and although it was by no means strictly a "missionary affair," Oldham and Warnshuis actively contributed to its formation and enlisted financial aid for it. The Institute, launched in London at the end of June, 1926, included in its membership government, philanthropic, and educational groups as well as representatives of missions, Protestants being represented by the International Missionary Council.[87] Through the years the Institute has helped missionary societies in their larger approach to Africa's needs.

Educational Commissions to Africa. Through initiative taken by the Foreign Missions Conference and the Phelps-Stokes Fund, a survey commission went to Central, West, and South Africa during 1920-21 to provide all necessary data on educational conditions and needs there. Its ultimate purpose was to enable missionary societies to plan a more effective strategy.[88] During 1923-24 a second commission, largely motivated by concern in Britain stimulated by Edinburgh House, went to East Africa. Oldham had been a prime mover for the commission and Miss Gollock collaborated with Thomas Jesse Jones, commission chairman, in editing the report. The commission's great service was to provide a basic program for education in harmony with the desires and aims of both government and missions.[89] These commissions had a notable influence through the years upon the thinking of government and missionary educational authorities.

Religious Education. In keeping with his concern for general education, Oldham viewed religious education as a field requiring immediate and primary exploration. Such investigation, he believed, should provide missionary societies sorely needed guidance for applying the best knowledge available in the field. The Council at Oxford had instructed its secretaries to proceed with such studies, and to this end Oldham called together small conferences in England of missionaries and religious education experts. Later on he consulted with Dr. (later Dean) Luther A. Weigle of Yale Divinity School to help integrate their findings.[90] Increasing interest in religious education becomes evident throughout the pages of *The International Review of Missions* for 1925. In these months the ground work was laid for the great emphasis put on religious education at the Jerusalem meeting of the International Missionary Council in 1928.

Christian Literature. Closely allied to these educational interests was an enlarging concern for Christian literature. Most literature projects were undertaken by national bodies, but the Council's stimulus proved a potent factor. Moreover, it served to co-ordinate and relate effectively their different efforts. Warnshuis supervised this phase of the program. Under the chairmanship of Cornelius Patton of the American Board, a committee on literature for Moslems produced a report in 1923 which surveyed the whole field of Christian literature available for Moslems.[91]

With its more than 250 languages, Africa in 1923 had only seven in which as many as seventy to one hundred books on *all* subjects existed. Providing reading material for African Christians posed a serious problem. The bibliography of existing African works compiled by C. E. Wilson and Canon F. Rowling in co-operation with the Conference of British Missionary Societies did much to clarify a vaguely appreciated situation and to stimulate the production of Christian literature for Africa.[92]

Le Zoute. "The Christian Mission in Africa," title of an international conference held in 1926, came so much to the fore during the first half of the twenties that the situation demanded a representative gathering to consider the whole Protestant Christian enterprise of that continent. The conference, arranged for by the International Missionary Council, and with Oldham as its chief planner (Warnshuis also worked closely with him on it), convened at Le Zoute, Belgium, in September, 1926, with some 200 missionaries and Africa experts present. The summer issue of *The International Review of Missions* for 1926 had been filled with preliminary papers for Le Zoute which surveyed four major areas: the church, race relations, evangelism, and education. In one form or another, the whole range of social and economic problems was covered. Probably Le Zoute's most important contribution was its able and clearly defined statement on total missionary educational policy in Africa.[93]

Shortly before Le Zoute, from January through May, Oldham had made a tour of South and East Africa. He returned to Rättvik in the summer of 1926 where the Council wisely freed him of his major administrative duties. Some time later Oldham's name appeared as a member of the Commission on Closer Union of the Eastern and Central African Dependencies, a body to deal with large questions of colonial policy with vital effects on the welfare of the African peoples.[94] The Hilton Young Commission, as it was known, was in Africa from December, 1927, to May, 1928. With the full concurrence of Mott and in the belief that he could be of great service to the missionary enterprise, Oldham accompanied the commission even though it meant his being absent from the Jerusalem Conference.

Broader Influence

Between 1921 and 1927 the International Missionary Council gave attention to a large number of social questions, among them narcotics, race, slavery, and industrialism, all of which were of imperative concern to the missionary movement. By mutual agreement most of these came under Warnshuis' surveillance.

Race. Oldham had been asked at Lake Mohonk to devote part of his time to a study of Christianity and race relations. His growing absorption in African affairs provided further background against which to conduct such a study. With the aid of Miss B. D. Gibson, who collected much of the material and saw the work through the

press, Oldham issued in 1924 his *Christianity and the Race Problem*.
While this much used book was not directly an International Missionary Council project, it was, obviously, an important outgrowth of that
body's program. It should also be noted that the Council early took a
stand advocating opportunity for Negroes in the United States and
other countries "to share in the evangelization and education of the
peoples of Africa and elsewhere."[95]

Narcotics. Narcotics, especially the opium question, claimed a
considerable amount of Warnshuis' attention. He had dealt with the
problem first as a missionary in China, but his major efforts in this
field came with the League of Nations after 1920. With Warnshuis
keeping abreast of latest developments, the International Missionary
Council became a clearing house for opium information. The League's
Opium Commission had requested the Council's collaboration in gathering information on the wide-spread traffic in the drug,[96] and the
Council in turn encouraged the national agencies to do what they
could to aid in abolishing the traffic and to get from them data helpful
to the League's commission.[97]

Slavery. By the middle of the decade several mission boards had
suggested investigating evidence of slavery and forced labour, particularly in some parts of Africa. Warnshuis spent some time on this and
established working relations with the League's International Labor
Organization. That agency's investigations of the problem led to an
exchange of information.[98]

Special Inquiries. Warnshuis was also responsible for promoting
and co-ordinating a series of special studies authorized by the Council.[99] One of these, in which he was aided by Miss Gibson, covered the
place of women in the younger churches and was summed up in a report edited by her on statements from groups in America, Britain, and
on the Continent.[100] Another investigation conducted by Ralph D.
Wellons surveyed the organization and administration of union missionary institutions.[101] Other subjects Warnshuis covered included student
migrations, missionary training schools abroad, and indigenous
churches. With his Far Eastern background he also devoted much time
to the critical situation confronted by Christian missions during the
1920's in China.[102]

Before returning to the United States in November, 1924, for the
Atlantic City meeting and to open a Council office in New York, Warnshuis itinerated for the Council on the Continent, including a visit to

the Scandinavian countries. Between that time, however, and the Jerusalem meeting, except for his journey to Le Zoute, he confined his travelling to the United States and Canada. Meanwhile, he devoted himself to the problem of indigenous churches, a paramount concern at Jerusalem.[103]

The International Missionary Council also expressed growing interest in the formulation of the Christian message. At Rättvik it initiated a world-wide inquiry into the relation of the distinctively Christian message to non-Christian theologies. The culmination of this was seen at Jerusalem.[104]

Two Conferences

At this point we must break into the natural continuity of our story to record the holding of two conferences which properly come within the orbit of the International Missionary Council's history.

North America.   In January, 1923, the Foreign Missions Conference asked the Council to consider convening another world missionary conference within two or three years. The Council's decision that the time was not yet ripe (although it encouraged the holding of national assemblies), led the Foreign Missions Conference to inaugurate a North American meeting. Its planners purposed to inform, to educate, and to inspire the churches of the United States and Canada and for that reason followed the general pattern of the Ecumenical Missionary Conference of 1900. The great meeting which convened at Washington, January 28, 1925, extended a week and registered nearly 3,500 delegates, with many more visitors attending. President Calvin Coolidge of the United States addressed the gathering, as did Mott, Oldham, and Warnshuis. To attempt to indicate the other speakers would be to catalogue the then well-known names of world Christianity, including E. Stanley Jones, Toyohiko Kagawa, and Julius Richter. The convention marked what was probably the greatest single endeavour to educate the home constituency since Edinburgh.[105]

South America.   The Congress on Christian Work in South America met in Montevideo, Uruguay, for more than a week, beginning March 29, 1925. The Panama Congress of 1916 had called for the creation of a British "Committee on Cooperation" somewhat similar to the American Committee on Cooperation in Latin America. Such a British agency got under way in 1921 with John H. Ritson as its president, but decided that because of British societies' enlarged commitments in the Orient, it ought not to assume any share in organizing the 1925 Congress. Consequently, responsibility fell largely upon the American group.[106]

The Congress reflected Protestantism's strong rooting in South America. Presided over by Erasmo Braga of Brazil, the assembly employed Spanish for its discussions (with short English summaries), which were almost wholly conducted by nationals or by missionaries. Little was said by the North American delegation. Leadership rested clearly in South American hands. These most obvious and outward differences between Panama, 1916, and Montevideo, 1925, strikingly evidenced the growing strength and ability of Protestant Christianity in South America. Moreover, the conference revealed the great diversity among South American countries and the resultant difficulty in attempting to plan for over-all co-operation by assuming a social and cultural uniformity. In part reflecting the Christian thinking of the times, the Congress heavily underscored the churches' social responsibility. It carefully surveyed educational needs and policies. Probably its most lasting impact came from the impression it gave of the energy of Protestant churches in South America *and* the need for more of them.[107]

The Chairman's Activity

While he had given it close supervision from its founding, after 1926 Mott devoted more and more of his time to the International Missionary Council. He had, while attending the Washington Conference in 1922, at the Council's request considered with certain representatives of the French government issues involving missionary freedom in French colonies in Africa.[108] In that same year he represented the Council at the national meetings held in China and Japan by the Continuation Committees there.

The Moslem Conferences. In accord with the requests made at Lake Mohonk and at Oxford Mott laid out a plan for a chain of Moslem conferences in the Near East during February, March, and April, 1924. These meetings, under the auspices of the International Missionary Council, assembled regionally in Algeria, Egypt, Lebanon, and Iraq. A general conference met in Jerusalem from April 3 to 7. With the exception of the one in Iraq, presided over by Dr. Samuel Zwemer, Mott chaired each meeting. The Jerusalem assembly, largest of all with eighty members, enlisted missionaries and Mohammedan converts from all parts of the Islamic world, including China, India, and the Dutch East Indies. At the invitation of the Greek Patriarch, it met in his church on the Mount of Olives.[109]

Eschewing formal addresses, the assembly discussed thoroughly each major barrier in the way of Moslem evangelization and produced findings accordingly.[110] Great emphasis centred on Christian literature as a means for effective evangelization with the resulting determination to create a "Coordinating Committee on Christian Literature for Moslems," a promotional rather than a producing agency.[111] Keenly aware of the growth and results of National Christian Councils elsewhere, the conference also empowered a committee to formulate plans and move, in consultation with the International Missionary Council, to create a council for Northern Africa and Western Asia which would link together Christian agencies at work in these areas.[112] These two committees met in 1925 and 1926 and determined to merge their activities in anticipation of a Christian Council with a permanent literature committee whose purview would include Moslem areas beyond the Near East. When the Council for Western Asia and Northern Africa was finally constituted in 1927, with headquarters at Cairo, Robert P. Wilder became its first secretary. In 1929 it became the Near East Christian Council.

The Pacific Basin Tour. Serving in a dual capacity as chairman of the World's Student Christian Federation and of the International Missionary Council, Mott made a tour of the Philippines, Korea, Japan, China, the Netherlands Indies, Australia, and New Zealand from December, 1925, through April, 1926. As in the past his travel cost the Council nothing but greatly extended its influence. On Mott's invitation, as chairman of the Council, some sixty Koreans met with him in conference at Seoul in late December, 1925. Attention throughout centred on an appraisal of the Christian situation in Korea, with a specific attempt to gain constructive suggestions for the forthcoming Jerusalem meeting and to discover the kind of international conference that would best aid Korea. In the long run Mott's visit undoubtedly strengthened the National Christian Council of Korea.[113]

In Japan Mott devoted much of his time to students and received a most generous reception from the Japanese. He also managed to meet with the National Christian Council for three days at Kamakura to consider its responsibilities in Japan and its rôle in the coming world missionary conference. A regular delegate at these sessions was Archbishop Sergius of the Russian Orthodox Church.[114] In China Mott met with the National Christian Council for four days early in January, 1926. Considerations included strictly Chinese problems as well as the proposed Jerusalem meeting.[115] From China Mott went for the first time in his much travelled career to the Netherlands Indies. Eager to avail itself of Mott's visit, the Missionary Union there, which met biennially, convened from February 20 to 24, 1926, on an "off" year.[116]

In Australia Mott's presence became the occasion for one of the most representative gatherings of missionaries and society representatives ever assembled there. Nearly 350 gathered in Melbourne in mid-April to consider Australia's missionary rôle, actual and potential. The conference stimulated missionary concern in Australia and through its continuation committee led to the establishment in 1927 of a National Missionary Council.[117] In the latter part of April, 1926, at Dunedin, New Zealand, the first national missionary conference ever held in that dominion met for three days. Preparations had been in progress for a year in anticipation of Mott's visit. The conference surveyed New Zealand's primary responsibilities in relation to the total missionary enterprise and resulted in the creation of a National Missionary Council.[118]

Conferences on Missions to the Jews. As a result of a discussion on the evangelization of Jews, the International Missionary Council at Oxford resolved that it would welcome and encourage conferences looking toward more effective missionary endeavour among Jews.[119] It recognized that the majority of Christians view Jewish evangelization as "off limits." It also observed that if a Christian accepts the full implications of his gospel, he must take it to "the lost sheep of the House of Israel." What was being done in Jewish missions was sporadic, little known, and unco-ordinated. Conference could do much to focus the problem and provide impetus. Consequently, the International Missionary Council encouraged the already established Committee on Work Among Jews of the Conference of British Missionary Societies to initiate arrangements. It, in turn, consulted with societies in Europe, Britain, and America and launched preparations for two conferences on the presentation of the Christian message to Jews. The meetings, under International Missionary Council auspices, were organized by Dr. J. Macdonald Webster[120] and were preceded by eighteen months of intensive preparation under his direction.

Under Mott's chairmanship, the first met at Budapest, April 7 to 13, 1927, and the second in Warsaw, April 19 to 25, 1927.[121] Each conference enrolled nearly 100 delegates from the societies engaged in Jewish missions and represented the first world meetings of that kind ever held. A Council grant of $1,000 (£200) aided the dual venture. Quite apart from financial aid, it is doubtful whether these conferences with such diverse elements represented could have been convened under any other than the International Missionary Council's auspices. Each diligently surveyed the task confronting Jewish missions and produced full findings which in many instances duplicated one another.

Declared the Budapest assembly: "Our message to the Jews is the love of God revealed in Jesus Christ . . . the fulfillment of the law and the true Messiah . . . who is bringing Israel to her destiny—viz. to become a blessing to all humanity."[122] Each pointed to the fact that the church as a whole possessed an unawakened interest in Jewish evangelization at the very time when counter-forces were leading many Jews to surrender their religion. Out of the conferences came a request, not only that committees be appointed to further co-operation among agencies doing Jewish work, but also that the International Missionary Council appoint a co-ordinating secretary to supervise the production of appropriate literature.[123] This resolution, acted on at Jerusalem, resulted in the establishment of the International Committee on the Christian Approach to the Jews.

Preparation for Jerusalem, 1928

The International Missionary Council's Jerusalem Conference sprang from the belief, voiced in Atlantic City in 1925, that the time had come for large-scale examination of the most urgent problems confronting the missionary enterprise. A corollary to this was the conviction that to meet them, the churches and missions required new determination to move forward. After reports by Mott and Oldham at Rättvik on the views of East and West concerning such a world meeting, and after full discussion, it was agreed to call the International Missionary Council's next meeting at Jerusalem from March 19 to April 1, 1928. It would be a regular deliberative session but with the Council enlarged to include representatives in large number from the so-called "receiving" countries. With 50 per cent of the personnel to come from Asia, Africa, and Latin America, it was hoped that for the first time the insight, experience, and devotion of older and younger churches could be brought together to consider questions of missionary strategy. This fact marked the difference in the genius of this assembly from that of Edinburgh, 1910.[124] Its agenda would include the very subjects then engaging the Council's attention, among them the Christian message, Christian education, indigenous churches, the presentation of the gospel to the Jews, and a number of social questions including race, industrialism in the East, and forced labour and slavery.[125]

Mott's Pacific Basin tour marked the opening round in Jerusalem's preparations. After Rättvik, Mott and Warnshuis in America devoted much of the autumn to planning for Jerusalem. They were convinced at that time that a study of the Christian message was of "supreme importance."[126] Meanwhile, co-ordinating their efforts by correspondence and conference, they and Oldham were determining what preliminary papers should be written and by whom.

Almost from the start, and especially when the preliminary outlines had been circulated, European missionary leaders expressed considerable misgiving concerning the wisdom of such a conference. Still harbouring war-born resentments, some Germans were reluctant to participate. More Europeans, however, came to regard the meeting as too heavily weighted on the "social gospel" side and its "syncretistic" approach to non-Christian religions a futile venture. Mott's firm hand and strong will were quite evident in this crisis in his determination to carry the conference forward and to use every means at his disposal to insure adequate European attendance.[127]

The Council's officers met during the last week of January, 1927, to elaborate further plans. Their consultation centred mainly on discussion subjects for Jerusalem and resulted in a prospectus-letter written by Mott to all Council members. It reaffirmed the emphasis to be placed upon "the younger churches overseas" whose participation had become "indispensable." The Council's intercession sheets, which had been issued for several years, now requested a "fellowship of prayer for spiritual revival."[128] Concerning the message, the prospectus suggested that the distinctive values of the Christian revelation would be considered in contrast to the chief insights of Buddhism, Confucianism, Hinduism, and Islam. Later that spring, Mott and Oldham together in London became convinced that another "religion," which they designated "rationalism" or "materialism," must be reckoned with. Mott suggested Rufus Jones, the Quaker mystic then teaching at Haverford, to develop the theme.[129]

During the spring of 1927 Mott travelled extensively in Europe, doing what he alone with his masterful personality could achieve, enlisting support for the Jerusalem meeting. Early the next autumn he underwent a serious sinus operation, but in November, 1927, Warnshuis, Oldham, and Paton met with Mott in his home to determine final plans for Jerusalem. Oldham's chief concern at that time for the Council's 1928 meeting was religious education, and he utilized his visit in America to confer with Luther A. Weigle who was giving considerable assistance in preparatory studies on that subject. Meanwhile, Mott and Warnshuis, having read Rufus Jones' contribution on "secularism," regarded it of sufficient importance to delay going to press until the secretaries could discuss it fully. Jones' study convinced Oldham on his first reading that Christianity's real opponent in the East was not one of the ancient religions but *secularism.* Consequently he bent every effort to make it a paramount consideration at Jerusalem. His constant attention to the issue after 1928 was in large part instrumental in leading him into the program of Life and Work and the Oxford Conference of 1937.[130]

By calling upon the wisdom and experience of all Christians around the world, Jerusalem, it was hoped, would define anew in terms relevant to the day the nature and extent of the missionary enterprise. Preparation for that task took a somewhat different course from that followed by Edinburgh. In the year before Jerusalem met, individual study groups were formed in America, Britain, on the Continent, and in Asia. That on the Christian message, for example, in Britain was under the guidance of William Temple and in America under Robert E. Speer. In America Kenyon Butterfield conducted a similar group on rural needs and Luther A. Weigle one on religious education. Many preliminary study-papers were printed and widely distributed. Their purpose was solely to stimulate thinking in preparation for Jerusalem, and no attempt as at Edinburgh was made at a group synthesis. All this was an integral part of the extensive groundwork laid for the 1928 meeting.

The secretaries laboured diligently to bring the conference to a successful culmination. Paton was new and came into the London office just a year before Jerusalem met; but the whole conception of the conference appealed to his deepest instincts, and he gave himself to its preparation with abandon.

One cannot, however, escape the impression that Mott was probably the most powerful force shaping Jerusalem. As chairman he kept constantly in touch with the secretaries' work. His own attitude toward other religions—seeking to discover in them the best they had to offer, believing that non-Christians should maintain all in their faith that reason, conscience, and experience proved to be true, yet never compromising the uniqueness of Christ as the "way, the truth, and the life"—was reflected in Jerusalem's approach to non-Christian faiths.[131] Mott undertook many and varied tasks in the Jerusalem preparations. By way of illustration, he wrote to Julius Rosenwald to enlist his aid in assuring the presence of R. R. Moton of Tuskegee. He urged Cheng Ching-yi that no responsibilities in China should keep him from Jerusalem, as it had been rumoured might be the case. He worked out with Paton a means of representation for the so-called "faith missions" which in many instances did not belong to the Council's member agencies. He wrote personal letters to those eager to attend and explained that Jerusalem was in no sense a conference as Edinburgh had been, but that it was—while enlarged—a regular meeting of the International Missionary Council to which no observers could be admitted. A towering figure held in high esteem by Continentals, Mott, it can properly be said, was largely responsible for their presence at Jerusalem in so representative a delegation.

Continental dissatisfaction with the tenor of Jerusalem's preparatory papers was marked. Their general approach toward non-Christian religions and what was understood as their undue concern with "the social gospel" provoked, even in those Europeans who agreed to attend, a highly critical attitude toward the assembly. This prevalent uneasiness led Mott to arrange for a special meeting at Cairo for Continental delegates on March 22, two days before the conference assembled in Jerusalem. There in very frank session German delegates declared to Mott and Paton that they regarded the Jerusalem approach as "entirely wrong" and discovered that they were joined in the criticism by Finns, Swedes, and Dutch.[132] The gathering fortunately clarified points of view and encouraged an airing of Continental opinion which might have been largely stifled in the larger session because of the difficulty many Continentals experienced with English.

Thus do we somewhat arbitrarily end the first period of post-war international missionary co-operation. During these seven years the International Missionary Council had been founded and had grown, with the almost simultaneous development of more effective national councils around the world. It had been a period when aid to German missions and re-establishment of full missionary freedom had been paramount. In it the Council had sought to find itself and to work out its proper function in relation to its member, national bodies. Its secretaries endeavoured to reassess their spheres of activity and welcomed Paton as a new addition to the staff. Mott, as chairman, had taken after 1925-26 a much more vigorous share in the Council's leadership. Now on the eve of a world assembly, representatives of missionary forces and indigenous churches from around the globe were gathered on the Mount of Olives to consider their common problems and in prayer to seek new vision and strength for their task. For the first time, those from Asia, Africa, and Latin America—missionaries and nationals—equalled the number of representatives from the "sending lands" of the West. That fact marked the passing of one era and the inauguration of another.

CHAPTER VI

<<<<<<<<<<<<<<<<<<<<<<<<<<<<<<<<<<>>>>>>>>>>>>>>>>>>>>>>>>>>>>>>

A Decade of Crisis and Advance,
1928-38

JERUSALEM, 1928

The time was Easter, 1928. On the Mount of Olives overlooking the spires and white domes of the Holy City had gathered men and women from fifty nations. Among them one saw a bright yellow Indian sari, the blue silk gown of a Chinese scholar, here a fez, there a turban. In the spring sunshine colourful national costumes took on added brilliance. The small company numbered no more than 250 persons, but it was unusual. Anyone could see that. But probably no one realized that here was gathered the first truly representative, global assembly of Christians in the long history of the church. From around the world, and now on a level of full equality and in numbers approaching geographically proportionate representation, Christians had drawn together to assess and renew their world mission. This was "Jerusalem, 1928."

The site itself, on the Mount of Olives where Jesus had gone apart to pray and where one could see the panorama of Jerusalem below, profoundly and inevitably influenced the mind and heart of the conference. One discovered there new depths of spiritual experience and a sacred responsibility impossible in any other surroundings. On that ground where the church had been born, no one could escape the call to apostolic mission. Awe, inspired by hallowed land, and high purpose created an atmosphere unique for Christian conference.

In such a setting accommodations mattered little. The Council met in a sanatorium, built before World War I by German Protestants, on the ridge of the Mount of Olives. Long occupied by the British, the buildings had been returned to their original owners in 1928. The Germans made them available at once to the International Missionary

244

Council. Some earthquake-weakened walls within the sanatorium led to the erection of three temporary wooden barracks and a miniature tent city as the delegates' living quarters. If one can imagine William Temple, later to become Archbishop of Canterbury, writing while prone on the floor of his tent because the drafts at table height would have extinguished his candle, one can gain a fair impression of the housing.[1] Yet no one minded the rather primitive quarters which at night time afforded a view of a moonlit alabaster city below—Jerusalem, with all its sacred associations.

Of Jerusalem's 231 members, regular and specially invited, nearly one-fourth (52) represented younger churches. Brazil had sent Professor Erasmo Braga. Cheng Ching-yi, then general secretary of the National Christian Council of China and moderator of the Church of Christ in his homeland, T. C. Chao, Francis C. M. Wei, and David Z. T. Yui stood out among the large China delegation. India's strong group included Dr. (later Bishop) Jashwant Chitambar, K. T. Paul, S. K. Datta, and P. Ooman Philip. Japan had sent, among others, Michio Kozaki, then an assistant pastor but later to become moderator of the Church of Christ in Japan, and Bishop Kogoro Uzaki. Miss Helen Kim was the only woman in the Korean delegation. Professor Davidson Jabavu spoke for his people of South Africa as did Chief Sirwano Kulubya for those of Uganda. Jerusalem's far-visioned planners had also invited leaders from the different student movements, one of whom was Augustine Ralla Ram of India. The presence of a large representative group of spokesmen from the younger churches provided the most readily apparent difference between Jerusalem and Edinburgh, held only eighteen years before. The latter had been an assembly of Westerners with a handful of specially invited guests from the younger churches. Jerusalem, on the other hand, as no other meeting before it had been, was a conference of the Protestant Christian forces from around the world.

In large measure, J. H. Oldham had been responsible for enlisting the presence of such men as Harold Grimshaw of the International Labour Office and R. H. Tawney of the London School of Economics. The determined effort to include outstanding scholars resulted also in the attendance of such men as William Ernest Hocking of Harvard, Luther A. Weigle of Yale, Karl Heim of Tübingen, and Kenyon L. Butterfield, President of Michigan State College. Among younger men achieving prominence were E. Stanley Jones from India, Hendrik

Kraemer, working in Java, John A. Mackay, then serving the YMCA in South America, Paul Sandegren of the Scandinavian Student Christian Movements, four Anglicans—William Temple, then Bishop of Manchester, Canon Oliver C. Quick, Canon Charles E. Raven, and W. Wilson Cash—and Samuel McCrea Cavert, general secretary of the Federal Council of the Churches of Christ in America.

Fortunately, because of its place of meeting, the International Missionary Council was able to establish fraternal relations with the ancient churches of the East. The Jerusalem Patriarch of the Greek Orthodox Church opened his summer palace and the Galilea Church on the Mount of Olives to the conference. Russian nuns offered hospitality in their convent to women delegates, and the cathedral choir of the Russian archbishop came and thrilled the conference at its Easter morning service.[2] The Council also entertained on one day Patriarch Damianos of the Greek Orthodox Church, Archbishop Anastassy of the Russian Orthodox Church, and leaders of the Armenian, Coptic, and Abyssinian Churches.[3]

Subsequent events have proved Jerusalem's significance, for it quickly became a landmark among the great ecumenical conferences of the first half of the twentieth century. Yet its planners insisted that it should not be viewed as a world conference but as a regularly scheduled meeting of the International Missionary Council—a way station in the steady development of international missionary cooperation. Members of a permanent organization were meeting to assess anew the most vital issues confronting Christianity's world-mission. The need was primary, and it was hoped that no one would regard the assembly called to deal with that need as an isolated event or as an end in itself.[4]

Open forum discussions largely occupied the fifteen days during which Jerusalem was in session. Main subjects, on which preparatory studies had been made, were presented in plenary session by one or two persons and were then spoken to from the floor. When the matter at hand had been thus broadly considered, delegates divided into small groups for more intensive study. Out of the diligent, painstaking work of these groups, drafting committees prepared statements which were revised and adopted by the entire Council in plenary session. They became Jerusalem's official pronouncement, *The World Mission of Christianity*.[5] Throughout, Mott's superb chairmanship guided the plenary sessions and even surpassed—if that be possible—the direction he had given at Edinburgh eighteen years earlier.

A Reflection of Its Times

The Message. Missionary conferences of the nineteenth century scarcely touched "the message." It was taken for granted. Edinburgh placed as the fourth item on its agenda "the *missionary* message," but, and reflecting the concern of many Christians, Jerusalem made "the *Christian* message" its first consideration. Those who came to the Mount of Olives generally accepted it as their most important assignment. What distinctively Christian word must the missionary proclaim? And how should he do it? Of the two distinct schools of thought, one emphasized exclusively the gospel's uniqueness, maintaining that the convert must renounce completely his former system of religious belief and any practice associated with it. The other, appealing to the comparative study of religions, saw elements of value in non-Christian religions and viewed Christianity as the fulfillment of some truths already possessed in part by other faiths.[6] The line between the two positions fairly well divided Continentals from Anglo-Saxons. Agreement upon a statement of the Christian message seemed well nigh impossible.

In large measure geographic thinking had dominated the Edinburgh, 1910, approach—a predominantly Christian West bore a gospel to the non-Christian East. Eighteen years later, Rufus Jones' keen analysis of secularism helped Jerusalem to see with clarity that the mission field could not be defined fully in geographic terms. Indeed, his concluding paragraph summarized Jerusalem's understanding of the situation to which it must address its message.

We go to Jerusalem, then, not as members of a Christian nation to convert other nations which are not Christian, but as Christians within a nation far too largely non-Christian, who face within their own borders the competition of a rival movement as powerful, as dangerous, as insidious as any of the great historic religions. We meet our fellow Christians in these other countries, therefore, on terms of equality, as fellow workers engaged in a common task.[7]

Preliminary dissent from what was judged to be Jerusalem's "syncretistic approach" and the gulf between Continental and American thought brought anxiety to many who regarded the framing of a message the main purpose of the conference. Yet, after preliminary papers had been studied and discussions completed, William Temple and Robert E. Speer set about the drafting of what they hoped would be an acceptable statement. Temple, a master at reconciling the irreconcilable, prepared the final summary. The key sentence affirmed: "Our message is Jesus Christ." Jerusalem also incorporated and made its own the statement on the Christian message prepared a year earlier by the Lausanne Conference on Faith and Order. When it referred to missionary obligation, the Jerusalem statement declared, "Christ is our motive and Christ is our end. We must give nothing less, and we can give nothing more." Underscoring deep social concern it went on: "Those who proclaim Christ's message must give evidence for it in their own lives and in the social institutions which they uphold."[8]

Temple read the entire message before the conference. When he had finished, the assembly was hushed. In the silence one thought seemed apparent to all—to such a masterfully written declaration no one could object. Let it be accepted at once and as it stood! More moderate counsel prevailed, however, and consideration was delayed until the next morning. Then, by standing vote, the message received unanimous acceptance. Silent prayer and thanksgiving followed.[9] Immediately afterwards the whole meeting thrilled with joy. The seemingly impossible had been achieved.

The formulation of the message removed considerable apprehension. A member of the German delegation happily recorded that "the fundamental note" of Jerusalem was "different from that which the [preliminary] papers had caused us to fear."[10] Karl Heim wrote: "The unanimous adoption of the Biblical message . . . was not a mere formality that was to have been fulfilled under certain limitations. On the contrary, a deep feeling of joy and thankfulness went through the whole assemblage when unity had been attained on this principal point."[11]

The emphasis placed by Jerusalem and succeeding meetings upon the Christian message could issue only in an expression of the theological thinking of the times. Yet the message is central to the mission and as stated at Jerusalem represented much more than an attempt to restate the orthodox Christian faith, thereby to prove the theological soundness of the gathering. Rather in it men from widely differing backgrounds sought to affirm what they believed to be their divinely ordained task. In it they produced an incisive call to action. It challenged the social order at points often taken for granted but maintained one insistent note: "Our message is Jesus Christ."

Moreover, in preparing to restate the Christian message, Jerusalem sharply pinpointed secularism as the greatest enemy of the faith, indeed of all religions. Everywhere, this corrosive acid compounded of humanism, scientism, and materialism, was deadening human hearts to God's claim upon them. Jerusalem thrust secularism into the consciousness of the churches as their arch foe, quite as deadly in "Christian" lands as in "non-Christian" lands.

Missions and Social Conscience. Discussion and criticism of Jerusalem have centred most frequently upon its social concern. This interest was associated by Continentals with "building the kingdom of God," a phrase they repudiated.[12] Moreover, believing the gospel to be meant for individuals and not for society, many in English-speaking countries regarded any social emphasis as "unbiblical."[13] Yet, the great majority of non-Continentals entrusted with carrying out the missionary enterprise believed that as Christians they must take into account the whole life of those to whom they ministered. To do so meant concern for the social environment in which those lives were lived. From that point of view most of Jerusalem's delegates approached the issues confronting them and in so doing mirrored Protestantism's growing social consciousness.

Jerusalem pointed out that two-thirds of the world's people dwell on and derive a living from the land. This, it indicated, called for a critical reappraisal of a missionary strategy which appeared to have been formulated largely without reference to the rural cast of Asia and Africa. Nor were rural missions to be thought of as a branch of the missionary enterprise (*e.g.,* evangelism, medicine, or literature), for an effective approach to country and village people required an accommodation of the entire range of missionary activities to a rural setting.[14] Yet the conference statement referring to the rural problem of Asia and Africa seemed to have slight effect upon the planning of missionary boards.

The Council dealt at length with race conflict and its bearing upon missions. While it condemned any discrimination because of color as a "denial of the teaching of Jesus," it confessed "with humiliation" that often even among Christian churches this principle was not realized.[15] It asked for further research to aid in a Christian solution of the problem.

Crans and Lake Mohonk had both requested study of the effects of growing industrialism in Asia and elsewhere. Rättvik viewed the issue as so acute that it insisted on its inclusion at Jerusalem. Paton's long introductory study, "Christianity and the Growth of Industrialism in Asia and Africa,"[16] and the active contributions of such men as R. H. Tawney, author of *Religion and the Rise of Capitalism*, Harold Grimshaw, and Bishop Francis J. McConnell of the United States, reflected this concern. Significantly, the consideration here given to the complexities of rising industrialism in Asia and Africa and its largely deleterious effect upon Christian missions represented the first attempt by an international missionary gathering to grapple with the problem.

The Council prefaced its official statement by affirming "with all the power at its command" that "the Gospel of Christ contains a message, not only for the individual soul, but for the world of social organization and economic relations in which individuals live." Moreover, it declared mistaken the oft-expressed antithesis between individual and social regeneration. The church's task is "both to carry the message of Christ to the individual soul, and to create a Christian civilization within which all human beings can grow to their full spiritual stature."[17] In outlining a rather detailed program for a Christian solution to the problems raised by industrialism, it called for a Bureau of Social and Economic Research and Information. This new agency, to be related to the International Missionary Council, would work with the similar bureau created by the Stockholm Conference on Life and Work, with comparable agencies of the YMCA, and with the International Labour Office.[18]

With all Jerusalem's concern for Christian responsibility in achieving social justice, the Council said almost nothing about war. Since Edinburgh, 1910, the whole world had passed through a cataclysmic upheaval, yet that fact was scarcely noted in any paper or discussion. The subject appeared at no point on Jerusalem's agenda of study, discussion, and prayer. Stirred by this omission, some delegates took initiative that led to the Council's issuing a call to all who share in the Christian mission to pray and work for the renunciation of war as an instrument of national policy, for the adoption of peaceful settlement for international differences, and for a change in the attitudes and practices that provide the roots for war.[19]

Hitherto the missionary objective had been thought of primarily in terms of geographic expansion, but Jerusalem pointed to large areas of life that must be brought effectively under the sway of Christian principle. That the gospel is meant for individuals only and that its spread can be measured by tabulating the land areas where such individuals live it rejected as false assumptions. It insisted rather that every segment of human interest and activity must be won for Christ, that Christ is Lord over all life. In this Jerusalem extended the dimensions of traditional missionary thinking.

Religious Education. Closely related to the Christian message is religious education. How can the message most effectively be taught? J. H. Oldham and Luther A. Weigle had prepared a lengthy preliminary study which formed a basis for discussion. Other contributions had come from India, Ceylon, China, Japan, and from the Le Zoute meeting of 1926. Canon Charles Raven outlined the teaching methods of Jesus in a brilliant paper, sections of which found their way into the Council's final statement.[20] Although this called for the Council to promote further study of religious education, the actual result was that with Oldham's attention increasingly fixed on secularism and the message, the Council devoted considerably less attention to religious education after Jerusalem than before.

Criticisms. Unlike Edinburgh, which received almost universal praise for its deliberations and accomplishments, Jerusalem provoked a critical reaction from many quarters. Almost all adverse comment related either to Jerusalem's theology or to its expression of social concern. Yet a sharp attack came from the Moslem world which saw in the Mount of Olives meeting the final stage of preparation for a vast assault against Islam. That Jerusalem was a closed meeting of the Council and allowed no visitors only heightened Moslem suspicions of its purpose.[21]

Many of the theologically most conservative in Britain and America sharply criticized the "modernistic" cast of the whole assembly and regarded its "syncretistic" approach to other faiths as sheer apostasy. A recent (1950) bit of conservative censure ascribes the achievement of the message to "clever ecclesiastical politics and adroit wording."[22]

From the Continent came the most far-reaching criticisms. Dr. Frederik Torm, professor of theology at the University of Copenhagen, took severe exception to the whole tenor of Jerusalem. In a paper read before the Continental Missions Conference in 1930 he expressed the views of the Northern Missionary Council. Pointing to Jerusalem's declaration that Christianity contains "not only a religious but a social message," Torm argued that not all agreed with the statement's meaning and that disagreement was "skillfully hidden in the wording."[23] In denouncing what he described as Jerusalem's "Christian sociology," Torm insisted that the church and its missions could take no responsibility for "social theories" but could only maintain that the process of individual conversion would establish justice and truth in the community.[24] This Scandinavian point of view shortly became a formidable block against establishing the Department of Social and Industrial Research.

Hendrik Kraemer, who had prepared himself thoroughly in Holland and then in Cairo for work among Moslems, was serving in Java under the Netherlands Bible Society when he attended Jerusalem. Soon afterwards he wrote a Barthian critique of Jerusalem's thought. While the Jerusalem formulation came "from totally different quarters" and was "based upon other considerations," Barthian theology, he argued, set the antithesis between Christianity and secularism in sharpest contrast. Yet he saw such international contact providing valuable cross-fertilization and opportunity to state the problem in "clearer, deeper, and more universal terms."[25] Meanwhile, the director of the Basel Mission, Karl Hartenstein, also a Barthian, appraised missionary theology as he had seen it at Jerusalem. Reviving an old quarrel, he insisted that missions could neither be nor affirm "the evangelization of the world in this generation" nor could they purvey a "social gospel" in an effort to inaugurate a new "social and political order." They can only be, he maintained, the proclamation of the revealed Word of God and must stand "midway between optimism and pessimism"—not indifferent to the needs of life, but also not seeking to bring in the kingdom of God through steady progress.[26] Thus strong differences between the Continent and Britain and America were reflected in the early stages of a theological dialogue that continues today. Those very tensions provided in the decade ahead much of the dynamic for the renewed emphasis upon the Christian message.

Jerusalem's Impact

In terms of pivotal importance for the organization of the Ecumenical Movement, Jerusalem can scarcely be ranked with Edinburgh. Yet a decade after Jerusalem, John R. Mott wrote that as a conference it had "already exerted a greater influence than that at Edinburgh in 1910."[27] In terms of impact upon the missionary movement itself, this statement, difficult to prove, might be true. If so, a major reason must be sought in the twenty-three (and their number increased after Jerusalem) National Christian Councils that in 1928 encircled the globe and could spread and implement Jerusalem's decisions. In 1910, as we have seen, only two such agencies existed.

Parity of the Younger Churches. As an event in the history of Christianity, Jerusalem will probably best be remembered for the place it accorded to those churches that had resulted from missionary labour in the preceding century in Latin America, Africa, Asia, and the Islands of the Seas. Indeed, it marked the beginning of a new era in relations between churches of "sending" and of "receiving" countries. Recognizing the proper use of the word "native," but disturbed that it so frequently denoted condescension, Jerusalem lifted to prominence the terms "older churches" and "younger churches." Here "older" obviously refers to the churches of Australasia, Europe, North America and elsewhere that have been sending out missionaries to other lands, and "younger" to those churches planted by missionaries, even though some were already sending out their own missionaries.

All those present found it a joyous experience to have representatives from Africa, Asia, and Latin America sharing fully in a common endeavour. Among that group there seemed little reason to consider relations between older and younger churches. Yet, even at Jerusalem, some tensions were noticeable, most of them resulting from a desire on the part of the younger churches for self-control and for greater freedom from the cautious trusteeship exercised by so many Western missionaries. Notwithstanding, Jerusalem marked a great advance over Edinburgh. Unlike the latter, it enlisted the full contribution of younger churches in planning for the Christian world mission. In the process it discovered that these newer churches, while the majority were still not self-supporting nor self-propagating, had achieved a degree of Christian maturity self-authoritative in its unsponsored claim for equality. Their representatives proved beyond all question that in insight, initiative, and ability to assume responsibility through comprehensive planning, they had come into their own. This single fact made it mandatory that any future gathering seeking to deal adequately with the life and faith of the world Christian community required full representation from the younger churches if it were to be truly ecumenical.

For some months, Warnshuis had been studying the problem of the indigenous church, and to that issue Jerusalem directed much of its attention. Throughout its discussions there was implied a parity—not of achievement but of status—between older and younger churches. Hence, the Council spoke of the possibility for "true partnership" in which the experience and resources of both would be pooled in an unfinished task of evangelization. With this in mind Jerusalem appealed to the younger churches for greater concern for self-support and for their developing an effective leadership and an indigenous literature. In turn, those from the younger churches urgently requested the older churches to take a "sympathetic attitude" toward "a more rapid advance in Christian reunion," probably the "greatest problem" confronting the entire church.[28]

In all this, Jerusalem marked a turning point from a widely held conception of missions as the foreign activity of Western churches. Instead, it provided a larger view of a Christian world mission carried out in partnership and full co-operation between older and younger churches. Using the term "church-centric" to describe its new approach, Jerusalem made the indigenous church the focal center for planning and action.[29] The effects were far-reaching and among younger churches helped to dispel attitudes of isolation while greatly heightening awareness of belonging to the church universal.[30] Western churches also discovered a rare treasure in this new alignment, for in mutual endeavour the younger churches brought to them the breath of first-century Christianity and the enrichment of contributions from diverse races. Jerusalem symbolized uniquely the emergence within Protestant Christianity of a world church in process of achieving spiritual unity through devotion to a common commitment.

New Evangelistic Movements. Jerusalem's insistence upon the centrality of Jesus Christ, its emphasis upon partnership, and its recognition of the universality of secularism stimulated an evangelistic impulse in the churches of Asia and resulted there in several movements of great power. None of these had been planned by the Council, but without the concern and enthusiasm generated by Jerusalem, probably none would have attained what it did.

One of these powerful evangelistic surges occurred in China. For twenty years that land had been in the throes of revolution and in the late 1920's was swept with a violent wave of anti-foreign, anti-Christian feeling. Armies from the South left many congregations leaderless and stripped bare of possessions. Christians generally suffered a period of travail, defeat, and low spiritual vigour, but Jerusalem had completely revitalized at least one Chinese Christian. Shortly after his return, Dr. Cheng Ching-yi roused the churches of China to a strong offensive with a twofold aim: a greatly quickened spiritual life and a doubled membership within five years. Begun in 1930, the Five-Year Movement turned the tide and brought new advance. By the end of the fifth year reports showed that while few local churches had doubled their membership, many had greatly increased it. Aggressive evangelism had conquered defeatism. Indeed, the Movement had so deepened the whole life of the church in China that it was continued for some time beyond its original terminal date.[31]

A similar emergent in Japan was designated the "Kingdom of God Movement." At Eastertide in 1928 when many of Asia's Christian leaders were gathered on the Mount of Olives, Toyohiko Kagawa gave himself to earnest prayer. Out of those long watches he felt the clear call of God to work for a million souls for Christ to leaven Japan as the million Huguenots in France had influenced their homeland. Soon after Kagawa and his friends launched the "Million Souls Movement," the National Christian Conference, which met in June, 1928, to hear the Jerusalem reports, projected a nation-wide evangelistic campaign through the churches. Its planners sought Kagawa, whose independent movement was already under way, to be one of the chief missioners. Conversations ensued, and within a few months the National Christian Council initiated a national evangelistic enterprise, based on Kagawa's plan. The Kingdom of God Movement was born. Conducted vigorously from 1930 to 1932, the Movement encouraged Japanese Christians to pool their funds and forces for a united approach to the nation. In it, preaching assumed a large rôle. Peasant schools were established. For a nation of voracious readers, "The Kingdom of God Weekly" became a highly effective messenger. In terms of spiritual deepening, the Movement was probably one of the most effective undertakings ever launched by the Christian churches of Japan. It was followed later by the nation-wide United Evangelistic Movement.[32]

The situation in India was somewhat different. An enlarged meeting of the National Christian Council in December, 1928, studied the

Jerusalem reports, especially as they related to the indigenous church in India. As a result of this and of other considerations, plans were made for an intensive study of the great Mass Movements toward Christianity. Such a study, it was expected, would help the churches to encourage these movements and adequately to serve their needs. Mott and Paton, both present, helped to frame the resolution by which the study was launched. Necessary funds came from the Institute of Social and Religious Research in New York. Bishop Azariah of Dornakal served as executive chairman for the project and Dr. (later Bishop) J. Waskom Pickett served as director of the survey and later prepared the report.[33]

Organizational Advance. Jerusalem brought important changes in the International Missionary Council that exerted a long-time influence. One of these appeared in the re-establishment of the Committee of the Council. Many of the International Missionary Council's member agencies, especially those from the Continent, desired greater representation. Jerusalem proved to be the minimum size to give adequate voice to all concerned, but the whole Council could meet only at lengthy intervals and at tremendous cost in time and money. Moreover, considerable vocal dissatisfaction evidenced the inadequacy, as a representative instrument, of the Committee of the Council with its less than twenty members. When the Council was founded in 1921 by seventeen member agencies, three represented younger churches. By 1928, when it included twenty-three national organizations, nine represented younger churches. Thus Jerusalem made plain the Council's nearly equally divided membership between national missionary councils representing the home base of missions and national councils representing the missionary societies and indigenous churches of Asia, Africa, and Latin America. This fact more than any other led to the decision to adjust representation in the Council.

Jerusalem's revised constitution continued national bodies as the Council's constituent members but left the size of their delegations for each Council meeting to be determined by the Committee of the Council. The latter, which since Lake Mohonk had consisted of twelve members, was now enlarged to include thirty-seven delegates allotted among each of the member bodies. With its officers and co-opted members, the Committee of the Council numbered nearly fifty and was charged with conducting the Council's business between Council meetings.[34] Instead of being appointed by the Council as formerly, the Committee of the Council was elected directly by the member organizations, and, in effect, became what the Council had been originally. Involved in this change was the conception that more than ever before the constituent national bodies now directly and actually comprised the functioning heart of the Council. When a large Council meeting became necessary, the Committee of the Council could determine its size and representative character to meet the needs of the situation.

The Committee of the Council also voted to pursue the suggestion of the Budapest and Warsaw Conferences on missions to the Jews. These had asked the International Missionary Council to appoint a co-ordinating secretary to supervise the production of appropriate literature for use in Jewish evangelization.[35] This action resulted two years later in the International Committee on the Christian Approach to the Jews. Similarly, the Council called for the establishment of a Bureau of Social and Economic Research and Information, an action brought to fruition in 1930, with the establishment of the Department of Social and Industrial Research.[36]

One of Jerusalem's least frequently mentioned and yet most important actions for the life of the International Missionary Council pertained to its chairman. The Council not only expressed its fullest gratitude to Dr. Mott for his labours on its behalf but also urgently requested him to give his time "even more fully" than had theretofore been possible. Accordingly, Mott surrendered his responsibilities for the National Council of the YMCA's of the United States and for the World's Student Christian Federation in 1928. At that time he said: "The mandates which came to the International Missionary Council during the wonderful Passiontide on Olivet are of such momentous, exacting, and urgent character as to require from its Chairman the exercise of all his powers."[37] Thereafter, Mott gave himself more fully to the International Missionary Council than ever before.

In Conclusion. Jerusalem's impact, while probably deepest and most lasting in the three areas noted above, enjoyed a much greater diffusion. It led to literally hundreds of small conferences for pastors and for laymen in most of the countries from which delegates had gone to the Mount of Olives. At the level of the local congregation these sought to make vivid the spirit and findings of Jerusalem. Tremendous interest centred in the message.[38] Leaders of theological training schools in Britain and America assembled on several occasions to relate the importance of Jerusalem and its message to theological curricula. Small groups of Christian thinkers on the Continent, in India, in Egypt, and in Latin America came together to consider the Christian message in the modern world and the problem posed to the church by secular civilization.[39] Jerusalem resulted in a representative meeting in Bombay in 1928 to review the whole field of religious education.[40] And a great conference in the Congo in the autumn of 1928, reviewing Jerusalem's findings closely, encouraged a continuing study of religious education.[41]

Jerusalem's influence permeated the missionary movement both in depth and extent. As an event in the life of the church it generated and released great power. Indeed, as we shall see, the next decade proved largely to be the outworking of its radiating impulses.

CRISIS

The decade from 1928 to 1938 was marked by crisis. Felt throughout the globe, it included a world economic depression, threats to international peace, and war. The missionary enterprise, sharply affected by these outer currents, was also experiencing inner upheaval, and the most vigorous thinking in Protestantism claimed the appropriate label, "crisis theology." This was the world-milieu in which the International Missionary Council grew and by which it was influenced.

Just two years after Jerusalem and for a period stretching almost to the beginning of World War II economic depression plagued the world. The stock market crash in the United States in October, 1929, was but the first of a whole series of untoward events which pushed many countries to the verge of bankruptcy and nearly ruined world trade. The failure of the Austrian Credit-Anstalt in May, 1931, brought financial collapse to Central Europe. In September of that year the Bank of England went off the gold standard, and in 1934 the United States revalued the dollar to little more than half its former worth. Financial crises in one country after another led to wide-spread chaos, unemployment, and domestic and international tensions which encouraged the growth of dictatorial governments. Economic instability, widespread unemployment, and the devaluation of the dollar, the pound, the mark, and other currencies not only meant that the worth of contributions to missions declined but also that giving dropped sharply. Many societies encountered great difficulty in transmitting funds.

The same decade brought the bold assertions of power that preceded World War II. Japan occupied Manchuria in the autumn of 1931. In rapid succession the Disarmament Conference of 1932 failed at Geneva and Germany withdrew from the League of Nations. In 1935 Italy invaded Ethiopia, and in less than a year had incorporated that country into Italian East Africa. In the spring of 1936 German reoccupied the Rhineland and that summer Spain plunged into Civil War. Two years later Germany had annexed Austria and as a result of Munich established German hegemony in Central Europe. Meanwhile, Japan had begun its "undeclared war" in China in 1937 and forced the removal of the Chinese capital to Chungking. The stage was set for global conflict.

Against this background a new temper was emerging in the theological world. Variously designated "Barthian," "Continental," and "Crisis," it grew out of the profound disillusionment produced by World War I and the resulting reaction from the nineteenth century's liberal optimism. This "New Orthodoxy" placed greatest emphasis upon God's wholly otherness and upon man's sinful rebellion against God and his utter inability to know God save through the decisive, unique revelation in Christ. Graphically it insisted upon the moment to moment absolute judgment of God upon man's every act and choice and thus derived its designation, "crisis." Emphasizing Christ's future return in judgment, it sharply contrasted with the dominant theological climate of Britain and America. The Barthians seriously questioned missionary motive and method, thus putting into bold relief antithetical German and American conceptions of missions. Since the proclamation of the Word alone held importance, Barthians consigned method to the background. This "foolishness to the Greeks," when proclaimed, demanded a decision. It dare not be made attractive or more "reasonable" by educational, agricultural, or medical work, necessary as these might be.[42] In no sense could the gospel be regarded as the fulfillment or crown of any other religion, for it can be accepted only by those whom God has elected. So sharp a theological division naturally produced considerable strain within the framework of the International Missionary Council's membership.[43]

World economic depression, the growing threat of large-scale war, and radical differences in theology required of the missionary enterprise severe re-evaluation of much that had hitherto been taken for granted. Moreover, further serious obstacles within and without the movement produced an internal crisis within missions.[44] Depression brought sharp curtailment in missionary giving. Budgets were reduced. Many missionary activities were severely hampered and a few ceased. In many cases the once easy flow and transfer of funds was made difficult if not impossible. The spread of war, the rise of totalitarian government, and the determination of some "non-Christian" governments to restrict missions as much as possible seriously crippled missionary endeavours both at home and abroad. Nor did the difference in views between those two positions most frequently designated "Continental" and "American" yield to ready adjustment. Moreover, younger churches severely criticized many methods employed in the missionary enterprise and especially deplored the extension of divisive sectarianism. They were keenly aware of the obstacles placed in their path through the penetration of their cultures by Western industrialism, scientism, and secularism. Growing nationalism in Asia and the pressure of State Shinto in Japan and Islam in Central Africa and Southeastern Asia provided further concern. Underlying all this, as a result of World War I, was the loss of prestige suffered by the so-called "Christian West" in the eyes of non-Occidental countries. These latter more and more viewed Christianity as an inconsequential part of Western life. Several astute observers saw the growing challenge in the Far East from communism.

Thus the decade confronted Christian missions with a complex of problems the magnitude of which had not been equalled in a century. In part to carry out its Jerusalem mandates and in part to meet the root-causes of the crisis—much of which had been foreseen at Jerusalem—the International Missionary Council developed its program in the years immediately before World War II.

GROWTH

Meetings of the Council

Between the assembling of the entire Council at Jerusalem in 1928 and at Tambaram, near Madras, in 1938 the Council as such did not meet. The Committee of the Council, composed of representatives from each constituent national council, met for periods of from ten to fourteen days three times during that period—at Williamstown in July, 1929, at Herrnhut in June and July, 1932, and at Northfield in September and October, 1935.[45] The first meeting enrolled forty representatives and the second and third some fifty-five each.

Even the Committee of the Council bulked too large for frequent assembly; so it created at Herrnhut an *Ad Interim* Committee to act for it between its meetings.[46] Thus, in effect, was repeated in 1932 the same step taken eleven years earlier when the Committee of the Council had been created to act in the interim between Council meetings. The *Ad Interim* Committee included the Council's chairman, its three vice-chairmen elected at Jerusalem, Dr. C. Y. Cheng (Cheng Ching-yi), Dr. St. Clair G. A. Donaldson, Bishop of Salisbury, and from Holland Baroness W. E. van Boetzelaer van Dubbledam, its treasurer Mr. James M. Speers, its secretaries, and the Reverend W. Wilson Cash, secretary of the Church Missionary Society, Dr. R. E. Diffendorfer, secretary of the Board of Foreign Missions of the Methodist Episcopal Church, Bishop Azariah of Dornakal, Dr. Alphonse Koechlin of Switzerland, Miss Sarah Lyon, secretary of the Foreign Division of the YWCA in the United States, Mr. Kenneth Maclennan of the Conference of British Missionary Societies, and Professor Knut B. Westman of the University of Uppsala. In 1935 the non-staff members of the *Ad Interim* Committee were increased from seven to ten, providing for greater representation of the younger churches. A few consultants were also regularly invited. Between its founding and Madras, the *Ad Interim* Committee met three times—at Salisbury for four days in July, 1934, at Old Jordans for five days in June, 1936 (at which time the then Archbishop of York, William Temple, was elected to succeed the late Bishop of Salisbury as a Council vice-chairman), and at London for three days in July, 1937.[47]

Two quite unrelated and incidental items may well be mentioned here. Displaying its growing outreach, the International Missionary Council with the World's Student Christian Federation jointly sponsored an international student missionary conference at Basel in the late summer of 1935. The conference, organized by Dr. W. A. Visser 't Hooft and chaired by William Paton, drew together nearly three hundred student delegates from some twenty-five countries.[48] In New York during the winter of 1934-35 the Council offices, which for some years had been located at 419 Madison Avenue, were moved to the Presbyterian Building at 156 Fifth Avenue where they have remained to the present.

Budget

The achievements of the missionary enterprise on a shoe-string budget represent a modern miracle. In miniature the International Missionary Council reflected this miracle and through the alchemy of devoted, selfless service transformed coppers into gold. Notorious for their limited finances, missionary societies out of funds inadequate for their own full needs supported national co-operative councils. These in turn, constantly hampered by inadequate funds, contributed from their meagre resources to maintain the International Missionary Council in its task of promoting global co-operation. It was not by accident that to meet their routine monthly operating expenses the Council offices often had to borrow against future income. This may also help to indicate why the Council was unable to launch vast projects and pay for them out of an adequate treasury and why certain of its activities were financed separately.

The budget of the Council which had reached somewhat more than $45,000 in 1929 fell to approximately $40,000 in 1930 and not quite $38,000 in 1931. During the thirties and until Madras met the budget levelled off at an average of $35,000 yearly. These figures included only the salaries of the secretaries and travel, printing, office and clerical expenses. The Council's yearly expenditures amounted to no more than those of many strong churches in numerous American cities.

In addition to the Council's regular operating expenses, yearly budgets for the auxiliary programs (Kenyon L. Butterfield's rural research, the Committee on the Christian Approach to the Jews, the Department of Social and Industrial Research, and the International Committee on Christian Literature for Africa) totalled nearly $35,000. For most of these the chairman and secretaries raised the required money. Yet even the combined total budget for special projects and Council administration was less than some large American congregations were then spending for their own programs.

The Council was uniquely blest in its chairman, for John R. Mott's services cost the Council nothing. In any business enterprise, salary for a man of Mott's stature would be reckoned in six figures. Not only did he contribute his entire time to the Council: he also conducted tours and convened conferences for which he assumed the entire financial responsibility. Thus national missionary agencies were achieving an extensive outreach through their international organization which would have cost them many additional thousands of dollars each year had it not been for Dr. Mott's extraordinary personal contribution.

Staff

No changes occurred during the decade among the Council's male secretariat, but several new faces appeared among the women on the staff. In 1928 Miss Doris H. Standley, who had been associated with the COPEC Conference and with the Life and Work Conference at Stockholm, began in the London office as William Paton's personal assistant with special responsibilities for the Council's work in India. Her ability so commended her that she was soon assuming larger and larger responsibility for general Council affairs. A special talent for administration and organization led to her being called upon frequently in setting up conferences and meetings. At Herrnhut in 1932 she was elected an assistant secretary of the Council.

Because of increasing pressure in the American office, the Jerusalem meeting approved A. L. Warnshuis' request for an aide. Shortly afterwards Miss Esther B. Strong became an assistant secretary of the Council. A Vassar graduate, she had had editorial experience with one of New York's leading publishers. While without any formal missionary service, she was well fitted for the study, research, and editorial work that demanded attention since so much of Warnshuis' energy was given to administration. Her special responsibilities included religious education, missionary studies, industry, and relations between younger and older churches. She took charge of all the Council's publishing responsibilities in New York and edited and saw through the press the *Madras Series*. During 1930-31, it should be noted, Warnshuis visited Japan, Korea, China, and the Philippines.

Oldham, who received an honorary D.D. from Edinburgh in 1929 and from Oxford in 1937, continued his oversight for the broad Africa program, including religious education, Christian literature, the liquor traffic, and missionary freedom in the Portuguese colonies. Moreover, he gave constant thought and attention to the problem of the Christian message. In all this Miss Gibson shared closely with him. From February to August, 1933, she travelled extensively through Africa with

Margaret Wrong of the International Committee on Christian Literature for Africa. In 1931 Oldham and Miss Gibson collaborated in writing *The Remaking of Man in Africa*, a study on the rôle of Christian education in moulding the African. While not a Council project and independently done, the book reflects on every page the Council background of its authors.

Paton, who was now carrying administrative responsibility for the London office, also edited *The International Review of Missions*, a task in which he was ably assisted by the quiet, hard-working Muriel Underhill. Paton carried part of the financial burden for the Committee on the Christian Approach to the Jews and for the Department of Social and Industrial Research. On his shoulders also rested the tangled problems of religious liberty in Moslem areas as well as the presentation of the Christian message to the Moslem world. For this latter work his intense interest in evangelism and his itinerary through the Near East following the Jerusalem meeting well fitted him.[49] After his first visit to the Far East in the winter of 1935-36, he visited the Near East again.[50]

Paton's major area responsibility was India and here were some of his best achievements. On his first visit to India (1928) after Jerusalem, Paton attended the World's Student Christian Federation meeting at Mysore. When the possibility of his becoming chairman of the Federation was sounded out, Paton, while moved and deeply appreciative, had to decline any consideration of the post because of his Council duties.[51] On that same visit and on the basis of a suggestion made by William Temple at Jerusalem and eagerly accepted by the Conference of British Missionary Societies, he encouraged the sending of a deputation from India to the churches of Britain. This mission, financed by Indian churches, was realized in 1933 and for England became one of Jerusalem's most significant results. In India again in 1930, Paton revealed his ability and stature in his effective handling of the so-called "Madura Case." It involved what amounted to the deportation of a missionary accused by a district magistrate of violating the pledge taken in *Memorandum A.* Paton counselled with the National Christian Council and then took up the matter with the governor of Madras and finally with the viceroy. A statement resulted, approved by the government of India, indicating that under similar circumstances a missionary could appeal to higher authority than that to which the person involved had been limited.[52] This typified the manner in which both

Oldham and Paton were accustomed to carry a case directly to top government officials. Paton gave himself whole-heartedly to India. Whenever there, he spared no pains to devote his full energies to any projects he could aid directly or indirectly.

The Chairman's Tours

To follow up Jerusalem, Mott travelled through the Near and Far East during the winter of 1928-29. From the Madras meeting of the Indian National Christian Council he went on to Thailand at the end of February and there, as chairman of the International Missionary Council, called a conference at Bangkok, from February 27 to March 4, 1929, to relate Jerusalem's findings to Thailand. The assembly not only brought together more than fifty delegates, most of them Siamese, but also decided to create a National Christian Council for Siam. Later in the year, that council was officially organized.[53]

Later in March Mott visited the Philippines where he shared in a National Christian Conference of sixty persons at Manila. Here again emphasis centred upon Jerusalem's decisions with major attention on evangelism, the financial independence of the Evangelical Church in the Philippines, and co-operation. Discussion on co-operation resulted in the determination to create a National Christian Council. Organized later that year, it succeeded the Evangelical Union of the Philippines, a missionary co-ordinating body at work in the Islands since 1901.[54]

In May, 1929, Mott attended the seventh meeting of China's National Christian Council at Hangchow. The commission on evangelism, following recommendations from five previously held regional gatherings, struck the dominant note and also called for a Five-Year Movement to quicken the life of the whole church. The commission had had Mott's assistance throughout.[55] When he returned home to the Council's Williamstown meeting in July, 1929, Mott had covered nearly the whole of the Near and Far East. He reported his considered conviction that Jerusalem's influence across Asia had been "more extensive and profound" than that of any previous world religious gathering. His "recommendations" were, in effect, that Jerusalem's proposals *had* to be carried out for Asia.[56]

The Orthodox Churches of Southeast Europe and the Near East. For years Mott had maintained not only cordial but helpful relations with leaders of the Orthodox churches. The esteem in which they held him a Western Protestant, was unique and had resulted from his efforts on behalf of students and prisoners of war. In the spring and early summer of 1933 he carried on consultations with Orthodox representatives in the capitals of the Balkans and the Near East. Huge throngs of young Orthodox students crowded most of them, and Mott steadfastly emphasized their missionary responsibility to neighbouring Moslems and other non-Christian groups.[57] In this he was carrying out the spirit and recommendations of Jerusalem.

Africa. From early April to the end of June in 1934 Dr. Mott visited one country after another in Africa, meeting with African leaders and missionaries. During the first five weeks of his tour, he met with outstanding personalities of church and state and with small groups in the Union of South Africa. At Capetown, Fort Hare, Durban, and Johannesburg he convened area conferences with church and missionary leaders and at Bloemfontein on May 15 and 16, 1934, conducted a general conference. That gathering considered evangelization, the strengthening of African Christianity, Christian literature, and relations between whites and blacks in South Africa,[58] and created a continuation committee to achieve this end. Superseding the General Missionary Conference, which was dissolved at that time, the Christian Council was begun in 1936.[59]

From South Africa Mott moved into Southern Rhodesia and then to Northern Rhodesia, convening conferences in both areas.[60] From the Rhodesias, Mott went to the Belgian Congo where he spent the month of June holding regional conferences at Elizabethville, Mutoto, and Léopoldville.[61] A final General Consultation from June 17 to 25 at Léopoldville, which enrolled more than eighty missionaries, recommended the appointment of an educational adviser by the Congo Protestant Council, the establishment of three union training schools for teachers, and the use by all Protestant churches of the common name, "Church of Christ in the Congo."[62]

The Far East. Yielding to many requests, Mott journeyed again to the Far East in the spring of 1935. From the time of his arrival in Japan on March 8, he spent a month travelling the length and breadth of that land, meeting dignitaries, addressing large groups, and conducting conferences and discussions. Of the last, the two most impor-

tant were those assembled by the National Christian Council at Kamakura and Otsu. There with more than one hundred Christian leaders,
Mott considered the task and needs of the Japanese church. Keen
enthusiasm greeted his presentation of the Council's Salisbury proposal for another world missionary conference to be held in Asia in
1938. Indeed, the Japanese responded with a unanimous vote to invite
the International Missionary Council to Japan.[63]

From Japan Mott briefly visited Korea and later journeyed to China.
In the latter country he contributed to the National Christian Council
assembly and received from it a warm invitation for the 1938 conference to meet in China.[64] He went on to the Philippines where he met
with the executive committee of the National Christian Council. In all
his consultations, the main question centred upon the 1938 Council
meeting, a proposal which everywhere received enthusiastic acclaim.[65]

New Councils

During the 1928-38 decade several new national councils came into
being and entered the International Missionary Council. A few bodies
of long standing were somewhat modified. As noted above, some of
these resulted from Mott's journeys. The National Christian Council
of the Philippines, founded in 1929, simply replaced the older Evangelical Union in the International Missionary Council's membership.
Revising its constitution and changing its name, the National Christian
Council in February, 1938, became the Philippine Federation of Evangelical Churches.[66] The National Christian Council of Siam, formed
also in 1929, was admitted to Council membership at Williamstown in
that same year. The Christian Council of South Africa, resulting from
Mott's Bloemfontein meeting and established in 1936, automatically
became the constituent agency for South Africa's missionary societies
which had been represented in the Council from its inception.

Latin America. As a result of the 1916 Panama Congress and on
a pattern similar to that of the Committee on Cooperation in Latin
America, a Committee on Cooperation in Mexico was organized in
1917. Among other responsibilities, it assembled National Conventions,
out of which in 1928 emerged a National Council of Evangelical
Churches in Mexico. In 1929 to facilitate unhindered action by the
new National Council, the Committee on Cooperation disbanded.[67] In

similar fashion the Committee on Cooperation in Brazil was organized in 1916 and produced several sub-committees which developed into autonomous bodies. Among these was the Federation of Evangelical Churches, established in 1931. In 1934 that body, the Council of Religious Education (founded in 1911 as the Brazilian Sunday School Union), and the Committee on Cooperation united in the Evangelical Confederation of Brazil.[68] The Mexican Council and the Brazilian Confederation became member organizations of the International Missionary Council at Northfield in 1935.[69]

While it resulted in no new council, the Evangelical Congress at Havana, June 20 to 30, 1929, further evidenced the coming of age of the younger churches in the Caribbean area. While the Committee on Cooperation in Latin America agreed to raise two-thirds of the assembly's budget, that meeting was organized by and was completely in the hands of Spanish-speaking Evangelicals. Preparatory papers written in Spanish were matched at Havana by a Spanish-speaking conference. Foreign representatives unfamiliar with that tongue received short English summaries of the speeches. The masterful chairmanship of the youthful Professor Gonzalo Baez-Camargo marked him for a large rôle in future gatherings. Probably never before in any "missionary conference" had the missionary voice been so silent—that of the indigenous church so pronounced.[70]

The Netherlands. The Atlantic City meeting of the Committee of the Council in 1925 had underscored the need for effective national missionary organizations. This confirmed again among Dutch leaders the fact that the Committee of Advice, related only to the missions consulate, was inadequate to represent Dutch societies in the Council. Jerusalem lent further support to the earlier Dutch feelings and gave the necessary impetus for founding the Netherlands Missionary Council (*Nederlandsche Zendings-Raad*) on February 21, 1929. Unhappily, however, the missionary agency of one of the largest segments of Dutch Protestantism, the Reformed Churches (*Zending der Gereformeerde Kerken*), while willing to co-operate in the Committee of Advice, refused to participate in the new body because of its affiliation with the International Missionary Council. In 1931, with the Christian Reformed Church, it accepted "observer" status on the Netherlands Missionary Council, and some measure of unity was restored.[71] Thus it was that by the time Madras met, the International Missionary Council consisted of twenty-six national councils, eleven of which represented missions abroad and younger churches.[72]

Crisis in German Missions

In face of severe adversity the slowly growing International Mission-ary Council once again proved its worth. Winston Churchill has desig-nated the pre-1939 period as that of "The Gathering Storm." First among the ominous clouds portending difficulty for the missionary enterprise were those associated with the rise of Hitler and National Socialism in Germany. They brought with them difficulties that plagued German societies at a time when internal upheavals rocked German churches. The government, to maintain a favourable economic position in the midst of world depression, cut off nearly all overseas transmission of money from Germany. The decrease sharply restricted German missions, which were then sending abroad approximately $1,250,000 yearly. Nearly $500,000 of this went to non-German na-tional workers and to the maintenance of institutions.[73] The remainder supported two thousand German Protestant missionaries. For a while it appeared that money could be sent to German nationals abroad; but with the tightening of Germany's economy for rearmament, the govern-ment forbade all exportation of marks. German societies became desperate.

In response to requests from Germany, non-German societies deter-mined at once to call to their aid the International Missionary Coun-cil.[74] That body, while eager to help, found itself in a difficult position. With the world depression drastically reducing incomes of all nations, to enlist support for the entire German budget was out of the question. Yet, with the arrival of a German deputation in London in November, 1934, it became clear that whatever alleviation could be offered was imperative.[75] Fortunately, German societies were still able to collect money, and their proposal, that assistance be given as a loan against which they would deposit equivalent sums in German banks for future repayment, was accepted. The result was an Emergency Fund, appeals for which went out from Edinburgh House and the International Mis-sionary Council's New York office.[76]

In India the Leipzig Mission received aid from Sweden. Germans in the Netherlands Indies were helped by Dutch societies. From Den-mark, Finland, Norway, and Switzerland came further contributions. Within a few months British societies made available nearly $34,000. The British and Foreign Bible Society, having commitments in Ger-many, arranged for German societies to finance its work there while it provided equivalent sums in sterling for transmission to their fields. This device, entirely legal at that time, freed more than $3,000 monthly. American boards gave nearly $11,000, of which more than $8,500 came from one Lutheran body. In addition, the National Lutheran Council sent more than $4,000.[77]

Eventually the German government permitted German societies to send monthly funds to missionaries at a rate representing two-thirds of their former salaries, but with nothing allowed for field budgets.[78] The Emergency Fund, intended only as an interim device until German societies could solve their problem, was dissolved in June, 1935.[79] In Germany, despite mounting obstacles, missionary giving increased steadily. But the two-thirds export restriction remained. German missions in China and India suffered financial distress, enterprises were curtailed, some formerly salaried nationals served voluntarily, and local appeals for funds were made by other missions. Thus German missions struggled along until September, 1939, when, with war's outbreak, they faced complete collapse.[80]

Outreach

Between Jerusalem and Madras much of the Council's effectiveness sprang from the activities of its departmental agencies. It had given rise to them, and they were part of its structure, even though their budgets were raised separately. They included the Department of Social and Industrial Research, the rural surveys of Dr. Kenyon L. Butterfield, the International Committee on Christian Literature for Africa, the several educational commissions, and the Committee on the Christian Approach to the Jews. To gain some appreciation of the Council's total impact on the missionary enterprise, we must examine each of these endeavours briefly.

The Department of Social and Industrial Research

The Department of Social and Industrial Research was born at Jerusalem.[81] It had been urged there by Harold Grimshaw, chief of the Native Labour Section of the International Labour Office, and by R. H. Tawney, the London economist, as a necessary and highly important arm of the missionary enterprise. In process of establishing the Department, Paton had eagerly sought Grimshaw to become its first part-time director. The latter, unable to leave his Geneva post, did agree to give as much technical counsel as possible—a contribution cut short by his untimely death. Jerusalem had provided that the Department should be supported separately from the Council's regular funds, and at Williamstown, with three dissenting votes, it was approved on this basis with a budget of $10,000 yearly. Paton shared equally with Mott in raising this amount.[82]

The office of the Department opened in Geneva in September, 1930. Its director, J. Merle Davis, had gone to Japan in 1900 and served there with the YMCA for nearly twenty years. For some time before assuming his new post in Switzerland, Mr. Davis had been general secretary of the Institute of Pacific Relations. Shortly after Davis' appointment, Dr. Otto Iserland, a young German Lutheran, was made associate director. Iserland, who had been a legal counsellor for the Transportation Trade Unions of Germany, had spent the years from 1927 to 1930 in educational work in Nagasaki, Japan. There he underwent a deep religious experience and determined to devote his life to Christian service.[83] Continentals, who had long wanted a representative on the Council's staff, welcomed Iserland's appointment.

Scandinavian resistance brought the Department its earliest difficulty. Frederik Torm of Copenhagen spoke for those who denied that the church (not individual Christians) bears responsibility for changing society. In May, 1930, as we have noted, he gave voice in Germany to the attitude of the Northern Missionary Council as that had been formulated the previous December in a memorial to the International Missionary Council. His position maintained essentially that only by the conversion of individual men could truth and justice be established in society.[84] In October, 1930, still with "misgivings concerning the establishment of the Department," the Northern Missionary Council again memorialized the International Missionary Council to the effect that if the Council continued its trend, it would ultimately minimize preaching the gospel and would likely cause some national organizations to "refuse to share responsibility" for its actions.[85] Davis endeavoured at every point to make clear that his Department served only one end—to make more effective the missionary's presentation of the gospel.[86] His irenic spirit (Mott described him as "a modest, retiring man who deserves great distinction for his work—one of the most thoughtful, creative, unselfish persons we have"),[87] Iserland's ability to make meaningful the aims of the Department, and Paton's visit to the Swedish Missionary Council in 1931 allayed suspicion, won increasing confidence and support, and prevented what might otherwise have been a serious rupture in the Council.

From September, 1930, until February, 1935, the Department maintained headquarters in Geneva in the same building with the World's Committee of the YMCA and the Bureau of the Stockholm Institute for Life and Work. The latter was doing for Europe what the Department expected to do for Africa and Asia. Thus one complemented the other. During this first period the Department pursued two major activities. First, it provided an information service for missions. Through the development of wide contacts in the League of Nations and the International Labour Office it gathered (and gave) considerable information on matters affecting the younger churches (*e.g.*, narcotics, mandated territories, forced labour, slavery, and child welfare). Reports on these concerns appeared in occasional bulletins designated *Social and Economic News*. Second, the Department conducted extensive field research. Mr. Davis led a three-man commission which during 1932 spent six months in Africa assessing the impact of industrial civilization on the life of the African. The Carnegie Corporation of New York supplied the $23,000 (£4750) required by the survey.[88] The resulting study, *Modern Industry and the African*, met with gratitude and acclaim from government officials, industrialists, educators, and mission boards. As one outcome, five British societies joined efforts in 1936 to form the United Missions in the Copper Belt in Northern Rhodesia. In 1933 the Department began its Bantu Educational Cinema Experiment to help meet the vast need for adult education among primitive tribes. So highly had the Carnegie Corporation regarded the original study that it contributed $55,000 (£11,000) for carrying out the cinema project in 1933.[89]

The Department built up a world-wide correspondence on different aspects of its work and received frequent requests for counsel. The Gossner Mission, for example, wanted a study of its work in Northern India to determine why the Indian church there had come to a stalemate. Its offer of a half-subsidy for the project was cut short by the restrictions placed on transmitting German funds overseas.

The decline in value of the pound and of the dollar, with correspondingly higher costs in Switzerland, forced the Department's removal to Edinburgh House. This brought it into much closer touch with the mission boards. It was located there from the spring of 1935 until the spring of 1936. Early in 1935 when he decided to enter the Roman Catholic Church, Dr. Otto Iserland resigned. Since he had handled the Department's information service and since the over-all budget had to be reduced, that feature was dropped. The Edinburgh House office in charge of Miss Ruth Allcock, the Department's secretary, remained open until the close of the Bantu Educational Experiment in the summer of 1937. Meanwhile, the Council at Old Jordans authorized Mr. Davis in preparation for the Council's 1938 meeting to spend the next year in the Far East studying the economic basis of the churches there. Davis again opened the Department's office in Shanghai in October, 1936, and began there an enterprise to which we must later return.

Kenyon L. Butterfield's Rural Program

Jerusalem had recommended that the Council employ a competent staff member to give full time to rural missions in all parts of the world.[90] Within a few months the Council happily accepted the services of Dr. Kenyon L. Butterfield as a volunteer missionary. For many years he had been president of the Massachusetts and then of the Michigan State Colleges of Agriculture. The Carnegie Corporation financed a South African trip so that he could study rural conditions there. His visit extended from February through August, 1929, and received enthusiastic response.[91]

Widely circulated reports of Dr. Butterfield's skill brought requests from India and China that he spend a year in each country to help relate the Christian enterprise to the life of rural peoples. As a result of these inquiries and high interest in them by a number of boards, the Committee of the Council at Williamstown appointed Dr. Butterfield for two years as its counsellor on rural missions. It was understood that he would spend a large part of each year in India and in China and would have a yearly operating budget of $10,000. Warnshuis assumed major responsibility for raising this money from interested individuals and boards, apart from the regular Council budget. From November, 1929, through April, 1930, Dr. Butterfield, under the

direction of the National Christian Council, travelled in India where
he conducted conferences, interviewed individual persons, and observed and studied the whole rural scene. His recommendations,
widely agreed to, were built upon basic "rural reconstruction units."[92]
In November, 1930, he arrived in Japan for a nine-month tour through
Japan, China, and the Philippines, with a very brief period in Korea.
His consultations issued in a well-circulated report,[93] and were greeted
with high acclaim by the younger churches.[94]

Dr. Butterfield contributed immeasurably in the Council's attempt
to make vivid to the missionary movement the fact that more than
80 per cent of the people of Asia and Africa are rural. He also helped
to clarify the conviction that rural missions constitute not a department, as medical and educational work do, but that they encompass
the entire scope of the missionary enterprise which must be adapted
to village life. Out of this endeavour the Council assisted the New
York State College of Agriculture in Cornell University to develop
a short training course for missionaries in all aspects of rural life and
work.[95] The Council's officers also shared actively in helping to
establish the Agricultural Missions Foundation in New York of which
John H. Reisner became the director.[96]

The Educational Commissions

Among the projects undertaken or stimulated by the International
Missionary Council, the educational commissions stand as among the
best known. Two of these developed in the early thirties, one to India
and one to Japan.

India. The Commission on Christian Higher Education in India
was better known as "The Lindsay Commission" after its chairman,
Dr. A. D. Lindsay, then Master of Balliol College, Oxford. With an
initial request from India, the Council at Williamstown authorized a
body to survey the field of service open to the Christian colleges under
then prevailing conditions in India and to suggest how available
resources might be used most effectively. The International Missionary
Council appointed the commission chairman and co-ordinated the
efforts of the three sponsoring bodies, the Foreign Missions Conference, the Conference of British Missionary Societies, and the
National Christian Council of India. Paton laid the groundwork by

preparing and distributing preliminary questionnaires that went to the colleges. With Miss Standley's help, he placed at the Commission's disposal all available information before the Commission even began its task in India.[97] The very ably-drafted report, while not unappreciative of the rôle of Christian colleges in India, offered some penetrating and constructive criticisms of the manner in which they functioned. In Britain its most visible accomplishment was the Indian Colleges Appeal. Although this fell short of its goal, it resulted in the formation of the Central Board of Christian Higher Education in India and enlisted gifts from many new subscribers for Indian missions. Into this enterprise Paton put his whole energy.[98] In India the report brought about the consolidation and strengthening of several colleges[99] and exerted a continuing influence on educational policy.

Japan. First suggested at Jerusalem and eagerly seized upon by the Japanese during Mott's 1929 conferences, a commission was authorized by the Council in 1929 to survey Christian higher education in Japan. Its purpose was to recommend steps to achieve Christian higher education's greater effectiveness. President Emeritus of Meiji Gakuin, Dr. Kajinosuke Ibuka, chaired the commission, which included among its members Dr. William Axling, Dr. Frank W. Padelford, who shared greatly in preparing the report, and Dr. (later Bishop) G. Bromley Oxnam. From October through December, 1931, the Commission made its survey in Japan and then prepared its report.[100] The "Ibuka-Padelford" recommendations brought some changes in Christian higher education in Japan. Yet the results scarcely approached the recommendations, a judgment which, in large measure could be applied also to the outcome of the Lindsay Commission's labours. The underlying weakness seemed to be that policies suggested by the commissions were seldom understood or acted upon as a radical revision of existing situations, but rather as exhortations to advance or to make greater financial effort, impossible in the midst of world depression.[101]

The Committee on the Christian Approach to the Jews

Acting upon suggestions from the Budapest and Warsaw conferences of 1927, Jerusalem instructed its officers to investigate the possibility for a co-ordinating committee for Jewish missions.[102] At Williamstown and as an outgrowth of these preliminary investigations, the International Missionary Council established the International Committee on the Christian Approach to the Jews, to be a central office for all Christian work related to Jews. Its functions included study and survey of the whole Jewish field, co-ordination of the work of different agencies conducting Jewish evangelization, and stimulus and production of literature for Jews and Christians on the subject.[103]

Herrnhut confirmed appointment of the Committee's director, Conrad Hoffmann, Jr., who began his work in September, 1930. Hoffmann, who had gained his Ph.D. at Wisconsin, was teaching bacteriology there when he resigned to accept a YMCA secretaryship. With the YMCA during World War I, he served prisoners of war first in England and later in Germany. Even after America's entry into the war, he was allowed to continue his work in Germany. From 1920 to 1927 he directed European Student Relief. When he returned to America, the Council's staff asked him to become executive secretary for the Committee on the Christian Approach to the Jews.

In his new post Hoffmann divided his time between New York, London, and Geneva. One of his first undertakings was a North American counterpart for the Budapest-Warsaw meetings of 1927. The conference assembled in Atlantic City, May 12 to 15, 1931, to consider the Christian approach to Jews in America.[104]

The Committee's first assembly came in England in 1932,[105] with successive gatherings in England in 1935, Holland in 1936, Austria in 1937, and England in 1938 and 1939.[106] They reflected the Committee's changing concerns in that—for Jews—especially trying decade. The Committee's initial work included efforts against anti-Semitism, studies on Palestine and the religious disintegration of Jewry, and the stimulation of new literature. Wide-spread Christian concern with Zionism and with Nazism's anti-Semitism greatly increased the Committee's outreach of service.[107] By 1937 much of its attention centred on Europe's growing Jewish refugee problem.

From the outset the Council's officers assumed financial responsibility for the Committee and raised money from outside the circles of regular contributors to the Council's program. Mott, Warnshuis, Paton, and Miss Standley worked in especially close connection with the new agency. Paton, well aware that few Christians feel any immediate responsibility for the evangelization of the Jews, gave the Committee earnest support.[108] Despite this general indifference of

Christians and the wide-spread belief that few Jewish converts are ever won to Christianity, the number of Jews who have turned to Christianity is far larger than has generally been believed. Indeed, proportionately, Jewish missions have been as successful, numerically speaking, as any other missions—if not more so.[109]

Most missions to the Jews had been conducted by those especially concerned with Biblical prophecy. Regarding the conversion of the saving remnant of Israel a precondition to the second coming of the Lord, these missions singled out Jews as a special group and received zealous support from a relatively few loyal adherents. The Committee on the Christian Approach to the Jews followed a rather different course. Building upon the work of Dr. John S. Conning, who for many years had served the Department of Jewish Evangelism in the Presbyterian Church, U. S. A., Dr. Hoffmann emphasized the "church" or "parish approach." This simply meant awakening churches to their responsibility for the Jews in their midst—neither to be singled out for special missions nor to be excluded—as persons to be included in the regular parish program of evangelism. Acknowledging the difficulty of accurate statistics, Hoffmann reported that at the outbreak of World War II probably more Jews were coming into the Christian faith through this normal approach than by way of special Jewish missions.[110]

The International Committee on Christian Literature for Africa

As early as 1923, recognizing Africa's special need for Christian literature, the Conference of British Missionary Societies established its Africa Literature Committee. Among other achievements, it produced the *Bibliography of African Christian Literature* and in 1927 the *Supplement to the Bibliography*. Le Zoute in 1926 had shown Africa's great need for printed material both in the vernacular and in the several European languages. It also demonstrated the necessity for co-operation by those agencies at work in Africa to co-ordinate and promote the production of Christian literature. Acting upon the Le Zoute recommendations, the Council at Williamstown established the International Committee on Christian Literature for Africa, a sub-committee of the International Missionary Council, whose membership included most of the non-Roman Christian missions and literature societies with work in Africa. These supported its program budget. The new agency's single aim was to "promote the production, publication, and distribution of literature for use in connection with missionary work in Africa."[111]

The Committee's secretary, Miss Margaret Wrong, assumed her duties in October, 1929. Born in a professor's home in Canada, she had had her education in Toronto and at Oxford. From 1914 to 1918 had served as student secretary of the YWCA in Toronto and in 1919 she joined the staff of the World's Student Christian Federation with responsibility for relief work in Central Europe and Russia. In 1922 she became dean of women in Toronto University and a lecturer in history. Three years after her first visit to Africa (1926) she became secretary for the International Committee on Christian Literature for Africa. At the outset a number of American and British boards, the Bible Societies, and several publishing agencies co-operated in and supported her program. The Phelps-Stokes Fund supplied money for necessary travel. The Committee itself was organized in national sections, the British being responsible for the routine administration of the Committee's activities.

Realization of the Committee's purpose required travel, interviewing, and correspondence by its secretary to discover the needs of societies in Africa, to make available to all areas news of specific projects in other regions, and to obtain new manuscripts and to stimulate their production. A quarterly bulletin, *Books for Africa*, first appeared in January, 1931, and went without cost to all missionaries in Africa to supply information on available publications and literature plans. The wide-spread demand for simple periodical material for schools and for village people resulted in the little magazine, *Listen: News from Near and Far*, used in English and in vernacular translation. Drawing upon a seven-month survey tour in Africa in 1933, Miss Wrong wrote *Africa and the Making of Books*.

Christian literature was but one reflection of the needs of an awakening Africa. Most of that vast continent South of the Sahara lacked any written language, and the reduction of local dialects to writing depended upon Christian missionaries. Though relatively few Africans could read, those able to do so were increasing rapidly. Since their own tongues had only so recently been put into writing, the problem of supplying their reading interests loomed large. Those with higher education could read books available in European languages, but the production of an indigenous literature through which Africans could read what other Africans were thinking and doing had scarcely begun. The great contribution of the Committee on Christian Literature for Africa during this period was to focus attention on these needs, to stimulate concern for adult education and for the production of native vernacular literature, and to direct attention to the whole complex of related questions on orthography, printing, and distribution of reading materials for African Christians.

Special Projects

Research Group. At Williamstown in 1929 the Council asked Kenneth Scott Latourette, professor of missions in Yale University, to undertake a world-wide survey of the then current scholarly materials being produced on missions. The study completed, Professor Latourette reported his findings at Herrnhut.[112] Convinced of the study's value, the Committee of the Council appointed a small international "Research Group" under Latourette's chairmanship to gather information on studies, wherever undertaken, related to the world missionary enterprise, and to give counsel on them whenever that was desired. The committee, which had no budget, worked closely with the editors of *The International Review of Missions* and with Miss Esther Strong in the New York office.[113] Within a year or two the Research Group became responsible for publishing certain scholarly studies.[114]

Basil Mathews. Basil Mathews, who had written the popular account of Jerusalem, was asked after Williamstown to join the Council staff for special literary assignments. His task as envisioned was to enlist youth's active interest in all lands for missions and to serve the Council in a public relations rôle with writers and publicists. In the summer of 1930 he joined the Edinburgh House group, but as a member of John R. Mott's personal staff. In this capacity he served for several years, fulfilling the Council's original intentions but without any drain on its budget.[115]

INNER LIFE

The Message

Mounting concern had been manifest before Jerusalem in the message of the Christian missionary. Jerusalem focussed on its centrality and declared, "Our message is Jesus Christ." It also urged deeper and continuing study of the Christian proclamation. Jerusalem's statement had a sound ring, but a number of Continentals believed it concealed an attitude of optimism and syncretism. Many others, sensing a changing tide of life and spirit among mankind's races, were convinced that the times required a fundamental rethinking of the Christian message in its contemporary setting. Their sole purpose was to reinvest it with penetrating power for a generation which found traditional Christian terminology devoid of meaning.

Williamstown emphasized the implementation of Jerusalem's recommendations concerning the message. Accordingly Dr. Mott twice called together some younger theologians in America, a group for which Dr. H. P. Van Dusen took primary responsibility. The Council's two British secretaries shared in these sessions. Similar groups were meeting in Switzerland, Germany, France, and Holland. Oldham, who had met with them, also brought together a few scholars in England from the fields of science, literature, history, philosophy and theology when Emil Brunner visited Britain. The group was continued. Paton had explored the question with leaders and small groups in India and in the Near East. Oldham never sought any formal organization of these gatherings nor common findings. He viewed it quite enough that the long-time stimulation and cross-fertilization of "first class minds" would have its leavening effect.[116]

Out of these conversations, Oldham drafted a preliminary statement for Herrnhut. They had pointed not only to science as a new religion transcending nation and race, but also to four dominant ideas —progress, democracy, education, and nationalism—which in many Western minds had been deified and which as modern idolatries were producing a revolution among non-Western peoples. On the other hand, it was increasingly apparent that the deification of man's reason, a growing phenomenon since the Renaissance, was being seriously questioned by many keen thinkers. Mankind was in process of long-term transition from a slowly crumbling foundation to one which might appear to give greater promise. Yet few were seeking an answer in Christianity. Thus confronted, world-wide Christianity faced its most challenging task. In this connection, Oldham pointed out, the Christian message, which had to be directed to "the common people," dare not fail to challenge the intellectual citadels which so profoundly mould the common assumptions about man, his nature, and end. "No view of the missionary task can be complete or satisfactory which does not include a vindication of the Christian understanding of God, of man and of the world against every competing view."[117]

In this situation, Oldham suggested, the International Missionary Council could play a constructive rôle. As a first priority it should seek to discover Christian thinkers with the most original and creative minds. Keeping them constantly aware of the world situation, it should bring them together as much as possible, with a full exchange between those from the East and those from the West, to the end that this quiet work behind the scenes might enable many to give a "more convincing interpretation of the relevance of the Christian message to the actual problems of today." Oldham envisaged in all this a stimulus to the younger churches, to their leaders, and to the missionaries labouring among them. Herrnhut agreed, and in large measure made Oldham's suggestions determinative for the course of the Council's action on the message and on evangelism.[118]

Evangelism

During the thirties, widely effective evangelistic endeavours spread in the East, among them the Mass Movements in India, the Five-Year Movement in China, and the Kingdom of God Movement in Japan. Northfield in 1935 pointed up these developments and called for a "thorough study" of evangelism.[119] This led to Mott's *Evangelism for the World Today*, Paton's *Studies in Evangelism*, and Kraemer's *The Christian Message in a Non-Christian World*.

The Laymen's Foreign Missions Inquiry

A self-generated movement, independent of the mission boards but dependent upon their co-operation, emerged in the United States in January, 1930. Soon known as the Laymen's Foreign Missions Inquiry, it quickly became associated with the name of its chairman, William Ernest Hocking. Concerned to re-examine the missionary enterprise, the Inquiry developed in two stages: first, the gathering of a vast amount of data in India, Burma, China, and Japan on missions there and, second, the appraisal, in light of the data, by the "Hocking Commission." The *Fact Finders' Reports*, ably produced under the guidance of the Institute of Social and Religious Research, provided the richest mine of information ever available on any field. The value and importance of the *Reports*, unfortunately, seemed quickly obscured by the sharp criticisms of the "Hocking Report."

The appraisal commission, every member of which sympathized with Christian missions, in the eyes of many lacked any absolute criterion of judgment and viewed Christian missions as joined with other religions in a common search for truth.[120] From many quarters the report's recommendations were roundly denounced as cutting at the very nerve of missionary endeavour. Tempting as the thought may be, it is not our purpose here to evaluate the strength and weakness of the appraisal. It is sufficient to point out that its unrelieved optimism and underlying relativism provoked a storm of controversy from most American mission boards.

In one sense the report symbolized the times and reflected much American Protestant thinking. Yet the volume of protest it drew upon its head testifies that it spoke for only a segment of American Protestantism. Mott drew considerable personal criticism for his share in helping to launch the Inquiry, but the International Missionary Council as an organization was little touched or influenced either by the report or by the criticism of it.

Relations Between Older and Younger Churches

Jerusalem had provided striking evidence of the rapid strides toward maturity made by the younger churches since Edinburgh, 1910. The decade that followed Jerusalem with its world-wide depression forced a withdrawal of funds from the younger churches that inevitably brought them increased independence and responsibility. Accordingly, at Herrnhut the Committee of the Council encouraged close consultation between national co-operative bodies of the sending and of the receiving countries to work out the most effective future policy for a period of increasing devolution.[121]

At Herrnhut's request, Miss Esther Strong, almost single-handedly, compiled in 1933 a *Directory of Foreign Missions*.[122] Two years later she and Warnshuis prepared for the Foreign Missions Conference *Partners in the Expanding Church*, a study of developing relations between younger and older churches since Jerusalem. The two authors charted among the younger churches a growing awareness of responsibility for their own life and advancement as attested by leadership in effective programs of evangelism taken by churches in India, China, Japan, Korea, Burma, and the Philippines. They could also point to increasing self-support.[123] This same trend, encouraged by the International Missionary Council, continued, and its results were made even more apparent at Madras in 1938.

LARGER ECUMENICITY

As indicated earlier in our study, the development of the Ecumenical Movement in its organized form after 1910 was, in many respects, the larger reflection of Edinburgh and of the International Missionary Council. For years no other body existed to knit the younger churches, through the National Christian Councils, into the organized fabric of world Christianity. In that particular sense the International Missionary Council for a time *was* the Ecumenical Movement. Increasingly, however, other movements and agencies, in whose generation the Council had shared, were achieving fuller life and were themselves becoming part of the Ecumenical Movement. In the course of time the Council had to work out its relationship with these newer bodies.

Ecumenical Contacts

During 1934 the Council's officers conversed informally with representatives of the Life and Work and of the Faith and Order Movements which were then planning to hold world conferences in 1937.

In the very nature of the case, these organizations were oriented toward Europe and America. To insure that their assemblies be *world* conferences and that the younger churches be heard, the officers of the International Missionary Council did their utmost to guarantee representation for non-Western churches. Moreover, when it early appeared that the preparatory studies for 1937 would bear direct importance for the meeting of the Council in 1938, the Council's officers determined to integrate as closely as possible their preparatory work with what was already being done.[124]

Oldham and Paton both contributed greatly to these two newer ecumenical bodies. In August, 1934, Oldham attended Life and Work's Fanø (Denmark) meeting, and a month later Paton shared in the Faith and Order Continuation Committee sessions at Hertenstein, Switzerland. In both gatherings the Council's secretaries stressed the need for an adequate voice for representatives from the East. At Fanø Oldham was placed under "great pressure" to accept the chairmanship of Life and Work's Research Commission in preparation for the 1937 Oxford Conference. Convinced that Oxford's title, "Church, Community, and State," set forth the problem confronting the church around the world and that bringing to bear keen minds on the issues involved would contribute directly to the International Missionary Council's main concern, Oldham accepted. His task, he believed, would "not mean an excessive amount of work" away from his Council duties.[125]

It soon became apparent that Oldham's new responsibility would claim considerably more of his time than had been supposed originally. For this reason Mott and Warnshuis urged him to give it up and devote himself exclusively to Council interests. Organization, however, held little place in Oldham's thinking, and he logically countered: "Fundamentally [this] is a question of what steps can most effectively be taken to meet one of the gravest situations in the history of the Christian Church."[126] He saw the new opening as an opportunity to accomplish with adequate resources that which the International Missionary Council could only do inadequately with its limited staff and finances. Through Oxford, he resolutely believed, more could be done to serve the real need of the missionary enterprise than by any other means.[127]

Paton agreed with Oldham's position, but Mott opposed it.[128] Oldham went ahead, none the less, and became more than any other person the one man responsible for the Oxford Conference of 1937. It was he, for example, who, after wide consultation, decided on the main questions Oxford should consider.[129] His choices centred on those special problems in the contemporary scene crucially involving the Christian understanding of life. Moreover, the thoroughness and depth which characterized the preliminary Oxford studies stand as a monument of ecumenical preparation.[130] Stockholm in 1925 had pointed to the individual Christian's responsibility for bringing about social reform, but Oxford emphasized the rôle of the church ("Let the church be the church.")[131] and flung out a challenge which exerts its influence even today (1950).

Paton's experience in Asia led to his writing one of Oxford's preparatory volumes, *Christianity in the Eastern Conflicts*. Oldham worked closely with W. A. Visser 't Hooft on another, *The Church and Its Function in Society*. At Oxford Mott chaired the business committee and with Paton and Oldham made a large contribution to the entire conference. Thus, through its officers, the International Missionary Conference did much to shape the Oxford Conference of 1937.

After Oxford the Second World Conference on Faith and Order met at Edinburgh in August, 1937. Fittingly, it gathered in the Assembly Hall of the Church of Scotland where the World Missionary Conference had sat in 1910. Mott, Warnshuis, and Paton shared in its proceedings. Following recommendations submitted by a "Committee of Thirty-Five" (the way for which had been prepared by a meeting called at Bishopthorpe by William Temple in 1933), both Oxford and Edinburgh approved in principle the proposal that the two movements be more closely related in a World Council of Churches.[132]

A year later at Utrecht,[133] those appointed at Oxford and Edinburgh, together with some co-opted Christian leaders, drew up a constitution for a World Council of Churches. For the period until the Council could meet, they established a Provisional Committee with Archbishop William Temple as its chairman and with W. A. Visser 't Hooft as one of its two general secretaries. For the other the Provisional Committee sought William Paton. In requesting his service, William Temple wrote to Dr. Mott:

I do not think that I am putting the matter too strongly when I say that there is no one else who in equal degree enjoys the confidence of the Churches in Great Britain, North America, and the continent of Europe, and at the same time has the invaluable touch with the younger Churches which his association with the I. M. C. has given him.[134]

At Madras the Council agreed that Paton should be allowed to accept the invitation of the World Council of Churches, just beginning its process of formation. Since his new duties would require only part of his time, the Council agreed to carry his entire salary.[135] Thus did the International Missionary Council contribute again to the emergence of the World Council of Churches.

Preparation for Madras

The 1938 Madras Conference of the International Missionary Council was launched at Salisbury in 1934. Many countries had asked the Committee of the Council to be host for this meeting. Especially behind those requests from the East, it was thought, stood a belief that in the midst of great spiritual and ideological revolution, an international Christian gathering in Asia would greatly strengthen the younger churches there. Acting on this premise, the *Ad Interim* Committee unanimously proposed a meeting of the whole Council in 1938. Its theme would be "what Professor Latourette called 'the on-going Christian community,' that is to say, the upbuilding of the younger Christian communities as living members of the universal historic Christian fellowship."[136] The financial slough of world depression made it no easy matter to proceed with a great global gathering, yet resolute determination carried the day. At Northfield the next year, Kowloon, part of the British Crown Colony of Hongkong, was chosen as the conference site, and it was agreed that nationals from the lands of the younger churches should constitute a majority of the representatives to the meeting.[137] Kowloon was not only readily accessible, but also offered the advantage, it was supposed, of neutral territory for Chinese and Japanese whose homelands were in a state of tension which verged on war.

The Council geared itself at once to prepare for 1938. Accordingly, Paton journeyed for the first (and last) time to the Far East, only to discover equally keen disappointment in China and Japan that the 1938 meeting was to be held on alien and colonial territory. The Chinese preferred attempting travel to Japan rather than to Kowloon—

a conference site which they believed would do nothing for the church in China. At least one influential Chinese refused to have anything to do with the assembly if it met on Kowloon.[138]

Desire to entertain the Council was keen. Indeed, the National Christian Councils of China, Japan, and India had all invited the Council to meet in their respective lands. With Kowloon clearly impossible, the *Ad Interim* Committee in 1936, on the advice of the National Christian Council of China, agreed upon Hangchow. At the same time it settled the meeting's central theme—the church, and the upbuilding of the younger Christian communities. It also authorized Merle Davis to transfer the office of the Department of Social and Industrial Research to Shanghai. Hendrik Kraemer was commissioned to prepare a study on evangelism with special reference to non-Christion religions.[139]

Merle Davis opened his Far Eastern office in October, 1936. With Shanghai as a base and with the assistance of the several National Christian Councils, he instituted a series of studies on the economic and social problems of Asia's churches. Davis' assignments took him to Japan, Korea, China, the Philippines, the Netherlands Indies, and India. The reports issuing from his first-hand investigations provided the basis for discussion at Madras on the economic and social environment of the church. Davis completed thirty-four studies which were embodied in twenty-two different publications.[140] In China, and especially in India, the Christian colleges assisted by providing for Davis' research the facilities of their departments of economics and of sociology. Voluntary and paid service from more than one hundred people was required, yet costs for research in the six countries totalled less than $4,000.[141] When Hangchow was later given up for Madras, Davis moved his office from Shanghai to Nagpur in March, 1938.

J. Merle Davis' studies represented one of two large-scale preparatory projects for 1938. The other was the *Statistical Survey* and the *Directory of Foreign Missions* assembled over a period of three years by Joseph Parker. In another category were the books on evangelism written by Kraemer, Mott, and Paton. In many countries Christian scholars prepared booklets and books to guide and stimulate the thinking of those interested in missions and to prepare themselves mentally and spiritually for the great meeting in the East.[142] Christian Councils in Asia and leaders of the younger churches produced a number of studies on evangelism, education, and the economic and social environ-

ment of the younger churches all of which were related to the conference. Preliminary studies for 1938 followed a quite different pattern
from the massive co-ordinated effort that had characterized Edinburgh, 1910. Instead, pamphlets, articles, and single volume studies
prepared the way for those who made the pilgrimage to the East in
1938.

The actual holding of the 1938 conference was questioned and
debated almost to the very minute of its convening. The choice of
Hangchow in place of Kowloon brought immediate repercussions.
Many Japanese leaders, sensitive to the feelings of those whom they
would represent, urged the postponing of any conference in Asia for
five years.[143] But Japan's invasion of China very soon became a full-
scale, though undeclared, war making Hangchow impossible for a
world conference. The question became more insistent: "Should the
conference be held at all?" In November, 1937, Mott called a representative meeting in New York with members present from India,
China, Korea, and Japan, in addition to the Council's officers and the
Ad Interim Committee. That group agreed that a united Christian
voice should be heard in the midst of world-wide turmoil and that the
younger churches needed to be given fuller expression in what was
emerging from the Oxford and Edinburgh meetings. An assembly in
1938 would achieve these two ends. Moreover, since the Council would
deal not with the problems of one area, but with those of the entire
Christian church, the group declared that the assembly should be
held.[144] Three weeks later the officers wrote to the constituent bodies
that the Council would gather during December, 1938, at "Tambaram,
the new site of the Madras Christian College, in the suburbs of
Madras."[145]

Even after this, grave questions arose concerning the wisdom of
"Madras." At Bremen in the summer of 1938 Mott and Paton discovered the great reluctance of German missionary leaders to participate
because of the surveillance to which they would be subjected. They
were, however, granted permission (apparently grudgingly) by Nazi
authorities to attend. Moreover, in the late summer of 1938 leading
Japanese still hesitated to go to Madras, fearing political discussion
with the Chinese would be inevitable.[146] September 29, 1938, marked
another day of difficult decision. On that date the Munich agreement
raised again the question of cancelling all plans. A series of cablegrams
between New York and London finally revealed that the officers were

of one mind. They determined to go ahead.[147] How fortunate for the entire world Christian community that Madras was held!

Here we must end another section of our account. As in the last chapter, we pause on the threshold of one of the greatest events in the Council's history, the Madras Conference of 1938. Madras had grown out of the decade just past, but it was indissolubly linked to the years of World War II and belongs with that period of our story.

Between 1928 and 1938 the Council achieved a greater effectiveness than ever before. The Jerusalem Conference in 1928 opened the decade, became the first real "world" gathering of Protestant Christians, and symbolized a new kind of global fellowship. Then, in rapid succession, economic and political upheaval on every continent compounded one difficulty after another for the missionary enterprise. Yet that movement proved its strength in community. Through its agency of international co-operation it reconciled inner differences in love and determined to advance despite seemingly impossible barriers.

Some of the Council's activities were especially noteworthy. It developed and utilized social and economic research as a foundation for more effective missionary planning among the younger churches. It brought about united action to provide Christian literature for Africa. It stimulated interest in rural missions. It encouraged a new, more effective approach to Jewish evangelization. In 1934 it came once again to the rescue of German missions. Finally, it provided a unique world-wide forum for Christian conversation—a contribution in the nature of the case difficult to assess but with the passing of time one which cannot be too strongly emphasized.

As the decade drew to a close, the International Missionary Council watched the flowering of movements to which it had contributed so much—directly and indirectly. With the spectre of world war again on the horizon, it rejoiced that two of them had joined forces to bring into being a World Council of Churches, a body which one day might make the Council's separate existence unnecessary. That time, however, had not yet come, and the Council faced an ominous future with high resolve to serve and draw together the Protestant world community as it alone could do in that hour.

CHAPTER VII

<<<<<<<<<<<<<<<<<<<<<<<<<<<<<<<<<<<<<<>>>>>>>>>>>>>>>>>>>>>>>>>>>>>>>>>>>>

World Christianity and World
Conflict, 1938-48

In the decade that followed 1938, World War II overshadowed all else. Its impact disrupted life around the globe, and that of the Christian church was no exception. Yet on this one faith which could claim universality war's net effect seemed to be the strengthening of its inner unity and the disclosure within it of a genuine world Christian community.

Uniquely and without premeditation, those who met at Madras in 1938 at the International Missionary Council's request prepared that community for trial by fire. With war's onset, support for missions cut off from their home base became the Council's chief task. With the cessation of hostilities, the Council assembled at Whitby, Ontario, in 1947 to take stock and plan for advance. A year later, crowning those forces set in motion four decades earlier at Edinburgh, the World Council of Churches was constituted in Amsterdam. In the following pages we shall attempt to survey the International Missionary Council's contribution to the building of a world Christian community during those few overcrowded years.

MADRAS[1]

The Meeting

What up until that time was probably the most representative meeting ever convened under *any* auspices assembled at Christmastide, 1938. It met in the little village of Tambaram, fifteen miles from

Madras, in India. There 471 men and women, most of them in their forties, had gathered from sixty-nine countries or areas of the world.[2] For months and from every continent people had been praying for this meeting, that in its deliberations the voice of God might be heard. The agenda was overcrowded, and those assembled were eager to get on with the strenuous task before them, but they opened their sessions with a "Quiet Day." Bishop Azariah was one of those who guided their meditations. They disclosed an attitude of penitential hope. Long before Madras ended, the quiet expectancy, born that day in prayer and never set aside, was joyously fulfilled.

Delegates worked, played, and worshipped—lived together—on the campus of the Madras Christian College. Sloping red roofs overhung its white, two-story buildings to form shady verandas. Every window and door was open, and the warm dry December breezes of South India filled each room. Everything in that setting suggested complete freedom of spirit.

The variety and colour produced by national costumes of the nearly five hundred delegates would tempt an artist's powers of description. Delicate Japanese kimonos, Indian saris, and the long skirts and bright blouses of the Burmese women vied with one another in brilliance and beauty. The men were equally resplendent and even amidst such colourful apparel brought variety. One could pick out a number of Anglican bishops in white or purple cassocks, and on special occasions an African from the Gold Coast wearing a yellow toga, Mexicans in brilliant scarlet and gold costumes, and Javanese in satin gowns with knives held in their belts. Here were government officials, students, doctors, lawyers, farmers, teachers, pastors, business men, and seventy-seven of the total number were women. Many in the group were first-generation Christians—those who had come out of a non-Christian background and had accepted Christ during their adult lifetimes. They spoke almost wholly in English, but faith in the living Christ provided their real bond of unity.

Madras drew strength from its corporate worship. A small informal group gathered by Kagawa met each morning at six-fifteen to pray for the day's sessions. After breakfast the whole conference joined in worship. Led by men and women of diverse racial and religious backgrounds, those periods early assumed special meaning and richness. Two observances of Holy Communion, many thought, provided the conference with its highest moments. On the first Sunday ten men and one woman of different races shared in administering the sacrament. On Christmas Sunday morning Bishop Azariah celebrated Communion according to the Anglican rite. Five other bishops from China, Japan, Nigeria, England, and America assisted him. The spirit of worship suffused the entire conference. During tense debate, delegates would pause—pray—and then proceed, acknowledging their trust that in the quiet moments God would speak. When the conference ended, Mott declared, "If our coming together had accomplished nothing more than what transpired in those hours of . . . standing before God . . . we would have been abundantly justified and rewarded for making our world journeys."[3]

No one who was at Madras will ever forget Christmas Day. On Christmas Eve a small group began to sing carols. One by one others joined until probably one hundred people swelled the chorus, singing Christmas songs in many tongues. Next morning the young Indian students and teachers who had foregone their holidays to serve the conference gave roses and garlands of flowers to every one. After Holy Communion, delegates gathered to hear fellow-members from different lands give their Christian testimony. Before the session began, however, John R. Mott revealed a remarkable happening. China and Japan were at war, but on Christmas Eve, and each without knowledge of the other, the delegations from those two lands had handed him similar statements of sympathy for those in areas of conflict. At Mott's suggestion a representative group worked through the night to combine them. The resulting resolution, presented jointly, quickened the heart of the entire conference and further evidenced its growing unity.[4]

During the afternoon delegates were invited into Indian homes, but that evening they came together again. Then each national group shared with the rest its finest music. Joy and pathos were mingled when the Germans sang the traditional chorales of their homeland. But the African delegation provided the evening's climax. They had chosen six of their finest singers and banked them around the one person representing all the women of Africa—Mina Soga. Their music swelled like that of a great organ while Mina Soga carried a rich obbligato. When they had finished, thunderous applause broke out.[5] The day ended on a note of perfect beauty.

Never before had a conference assembled such as this one. More than half those present represented younger churches. The Indian group outnumbered the rest, but the Chinese delegation, led by a woman, Dr. Wu Yi-fang, and absent from China at a critical time, was recognized as the ablest national group at Madras. Only the Korean delegation was missing, but the Germans had scarcely been able to come. War and oppression cast their shadows on individuals and brought the poignant reality of the world's suffering and evil into the midst of the conference. Jerusalem had marked a great advance, but Madras provided something new in the history of the human race. Men and women of every colour from nearly seventy lands had come together to plan more effectively for spreading to all people on earth knowledge of that which united them—God's love as they knew it in Christ. The conference was to that time the most widely representative assembly of Christians ever gathered.[6] Moreover, those from younger churches experienced new freedom of expression, new status. They shared full equality in every sense, not only in number, but in initiative, leadership, and responsibility with those from the older churches of the West. The agonies of a breaking world were all too evident, but much more real in the midst of this diverse group was a living, growing unity that bound men to one another. This solidarity was the most notable fact out of Madras.

The theme of the conference was the church. Emphasis centred naturally upon strengthening the younger churches as part of the on-going, universal Christian fellowship. This continued the dominant note of the Oxford and Edinburgh Conferences of 1937.[7] The latter two directed attention chiefly to Western churches, including those of Eastern Europe. It was left to Madras, much more representative of mankind's nations and races, to emphasize and define the place of the younger churches in the new world Christian community. While Madras was not an assembly of theologians, it brought together the Christian world mission's responsible leaders. To point out that it had less "ecclesiastical scholarship" than either Oxford or Edinburgh does not minimize an even more important fact. Madras, the most truly ecumenical conference yet convened, assembled more first-hand knowledge of the actual work of the church than had any previous gathering. In this sense, Madras probably more nearly caught the actual conviction of the world Christian community for an immediately relevant, working program.[8]

The Madras report discloses few questions pertinent to world evangelization to which some answer is not given. Its range is tremendous. Indeed, Madras was criticized for having undertaken too much in the available time.[9] During its first week, the conference divided into eight sections of approximately fifty-five delegates, with each section considering one subdivision of the main theme and preparing a group report. Similarly divided in the second week, the conference tackled another set of problems. In the three days remaining at the end of the conference each section presented its report in plenary session. In such limited time the conference could scarcely make each report its own through full debate and revision, but it accepted them all. Yet so nearly did each section mirror the diversity of the whole conference that this may not have been too serious a fault. The complete conference report appears in *The World Mission of the Church*.

Its Accomplishments

Any attempt to appraise Madras requires a clear understanding of its nature and setting. In part we have indicated these, but they need restatement here. Madras, a decennial meeting of the International Missionary Council, sought primarily to strengthen the upbuilding of the world Christian community. The conference directed its attention to the practical problems and program of the churches and aimed at specific recommendations for action. Moreover, it met on the eve of World War II. Each day brought fresh evidence of the frightful and continuing drift toward war. Despite this ominous cloud and much individual anxiety, the conference planned and took action on the basis that war's threat would be stayed. When World War II broke a few months later, it made largely impossible any execution of the Madras recommendations and thus shifted the point at which Madras' significance must be sought. Against this background and from the limited perspective of twelve years we must seek to outline its achievements.

Re-thinking Fundamentals. As we have seen, the founders of the Council wisely provided that it should never usurp the rôle of Faith and Order. Its primary concern was to facilitate the spread of the gospel through international co-operation. Yet, when within its membership differences in missionary method seemed to indicate variant understandings of the gospel proclaimed, a natural question arose: "What is the nature and authority of the faith?" That query had been voiced more and more insistently since before Jerusalem. It bulked large in preparation for Madras.

Consequently, the Council commissioned Hendrik Kraemer to prepare a volume on the Christian evangelistic approach to non-Christian religions.[10] His position directly opposed William Ernest Hocking's as the latter was revealed in the theological sections of *Re-thinking Missions*. Our purpose here, however, is only to indicate and not to expound Kraemer's view and the critical reaction it provoked. His widely read book, *The Christian Message in a Non-Christian World*, profoundly stimulated thinking at Madras, and his name there occupied a dominant position.

Concerned primarily with revelation, Kraemer presented what may best be described as a Barthian theology for missions. His foundation, "Biblical realism," meant acceptance of the Bible solely as a record of God's thinking and action in reference to mankind and in no sense as a story of religious pilgrimage by part of the human race. Moreover, he argued, the world of spiritual reality apprehended by Biblical realism —the truth and grace of God as known in Christ—is utterly different from and not continuous with the world of reason, nature, and history. Thus Kraemer rejected all natural theology and with it what is sometimes regarded as a preparation in non-Christian religions for receiving the gospel. This Christian revelation is unique, so utterly different from all else that "discontinuity" became his key word to emphasize the complete lack of any connection between the gospel and the world's religious aspirations.

Although a number accepted the essence of Biblical realism, few could associate themselves with what Kraemer set forth as radical discontinuity. Many from the younger churches confessed that for them Kraemer's theology required modification. Some found it impenetrable.[11] Among non-Continental Westerners Kraemer's position and contribution met with criticism tempered by gratitude.[12] Probably a majority viewed his position as a corrective and therefore likely to be extreme. Certainly, Kraemer's penetrating challenge influenced the entire conference and forced it to re-think every theological presupposition upon which it acted. Yet despite sharp theological differences, Madras' delegates unitedly declared their understanding of "The Faith by Which the Church Lives."[13]

Like Barth, Kraemer maintained that other religions offer no point of contact with Christian faith. Since they result from man's efforts, no revelation of God is to be found in them.[14] When delegates could not agree on this point, a group of three, including Kraemer, drafted a statement acceptable to the conference. It credited non-Christian religions with "values of deep religious experience, and great moral achievements" and affirmed "that everywhere and at all times [God] has been seeking to disclose Himself to men." Then it bared the main disagreement:

As to whether the non-Christian religions as total systems of thought and life may be regarded as in some sense or to some degree manifesting God's revelation Christians are not agreed. This is a matter urgently demanding thought and united study.[15]

Confronting New Rival Religions. Jerusalem in 1928 saw Christianity's chief challenge coming from secularism rather than from mankind's traditional religions. In the intervening decade and on the eve of World War II, Madras observed that a "new paganism" had arisen. Militant as secularism was not, it demanded religious devotion —absolute obedience—from its followers. The new pagan religions not only challenged Christianity's right to universality, but also sought to subjugate it or to eradicate it altogether. Of the two, nationalism then appeared the more prominent. In Europe, Asia, the Near East, and in parts of Africa and Latin America it was claiming devotion above every other allegiance. National Socialism, Fascism, and Japanese State Shinto seemed, as national religions, to be Christianity's most virile opponents.[16] The other pagan religion was communism. Appealing to youth's social idealism and promising racial equality and a more equitable distribution of wealth, communism had become the faith of many in Russia, China, the Philippines, Mexico, and other Latin American countries.[17] Madras pointed also to scientific skepticism and to the traditional religions, which were frequently adopting the methods of Christianity and at many points were re-invigorated by it, as the other rival faiths.

Madras, however, did not isolate Christianity in righteous splendour, but repented of its lethargy and sin as exposed at so many points by these contending faiths and as judged by God.[18] The reports, sectional discussions, worship, and addresses all struck this note of repentance for the sins of Christians and for the failure of the church to meet its responsibility. Especially for those from the younger churches, this was one of the most hopeful facts of the conference.[19]

Madras met at a time when many nations felt compelled to condemn the persecution of Jews in Germany, the war in Spain, the invasion of Ethiopia, the betrayal of Czechoslovakia, and Japan's conquest in

China. Because Madras did not pinpoint these national sins and condemn them explicitly, it was vigorously criticized.[20] The lack of specific judgment arose from profound conviction, not from moral timidity. Sober men reckoned that any condemnation of their government's policies might and would likely confront the German and Japanese delegations with imprisonment in their homelands. Even more decisive was the unwillingness to subject minority groups of Christians in occupied Korea, Manchuria, and China to possible retaliation or to jeopardize any Christians in Germany, Italy, and Japan. Some one had suggested that suffering could be shared vicariously but that martyrdom could not. In that spirit and after much travail of mind and heart, the conference declared:

We are unwilling that words of ours, which cost us nothing, should aggravate the problems and hazards of our fellow Christians; therefore, after careful and prayerful consideration, we have deliberately refrained from any further pronouncement which might injure them.[21]

What Madras did was to reaffirm the Christian principles that should determine judgment and action in the contemporary world. Throughout all its sessions, it borrowed heavily from the Oxford Conference of 1937. In its Christian pronouncements for the social order Madras offered little that was new. On the question of war, for example, it adopted Oxford's position.[22] Yet Madras had to face, as had no missionary conference before it, relations between church and state and the implicit question of religious liberty. Oxford had focussed attention on the issues as they appeared in traditionally "Christian" lands. Madras had to go beyond this and grapple with the problem as it was increasingly pressing in upon the younger churches. The violations might be pressure from an Islamic state, the imposition of shrine worship in Japan, or the restrictions plaguing minority groups of Evangelicals in Roman Catholic or Orthodox countries. In every case they were intensely real and were growing worse.[23] Here was the beginning of the Council's increasing attention in the next decade to religious liberty.

Discovering the Church.   Madras made the church its central concern, and a new sense of its reality runs through every statement produced there. As never before had been possible, members of the churches saw the church universal partially disclosed in their midst. In a day when many regarded the historic church as an unnecessary

appendage to "the Christian spirit," Madras brought a new awareness
of the church's importance. Some criticized this church-emphasis as
idolatrous.[24] But Madras recognized the weakness and worldliness of
the churches and saw the church itself standing under God's judgment.
Madras concentrated on the church but did not absolutize it.[25]

Madras also represented the first real world meeting of churches.
From the West missionary societies sent delegates, but from nearly
fifty lands it was the younger *churches* that sent representatives. From
first to last they were concerned with evangelism—intensive and extensive evangelism. They rejected that view which made it a "missionary" or departmental task and offered rather the church, the whole
community of believers, as the supreme instrument of total evangelism.
They focussed on the church as a witnessing community and affirmed
the Christian answer for man's need. One point they made pre-
eminently clear: the mission is not a segment of the church's life. On
the contrary, the church exists to fulfill a divinely ordained mission,
and responsibility for it rests upon every Christian. In discovering the
church, Madras found an even older word, "evangelism," and invested
it with new life.

Madras superbly demonstrated the strength of the younger churches.
It had been set up to give them a slight majority of delegates. But no
pre-arrangement could account for the fact that in conference deliberations and decisions representatives of the younger churches proved
quite as able and influential as those from the older churches.[26] Indeed,
as we noted, the Chinese delegation was freely recognized, person for
person, as the strongest and ablest group present. Jerusalem had accorded the younger churches parity, but Madras gratefully acknowledged their major contribution. Younger and older churches together
made vivid the centrality of the church for the world community of
the faithful. Perhaps this can best be illustrated by indicating what
this meant for one of China's most thoughtful Christians. He had been
at Jerusalem in 1928, but at Madras he found a new reality. Nearly a
decade later he said: "I had believed that to become a Christian meant
to follow Jesus, ethically. But Madras brought the insufficiency of this
to me and showed me my own need to be within, to be part of the
church, not a sectarian denomination, but the world church. Afterwards I became an ordained minister because of the new understanding of the church I found at Madras."[27]

Projecting a New Dimension. Madras added a new dimension to missionary thinking. In time this may prove to be its most creative contribution to the life of the church. The problem was old—the ability of the younger churches to support, govern, and propagate themselves. The approach was new. It owed its inception largely to J. Merle Davis of the Council's Department of Social and Industrial Research. For two and a half years in the Far East he had been directing a vast network of research, the results of which he brought together in readily usable form for Madras.[28] In essence the problem was this: the Western-type church transplanted by missionaries had grown up among and been supported by people accustomed to a relatively high economy. When, with its related schools and medical institutions, it was reproduced in a land of relatively low economy, it could usually be maintained only with foreign subsidy. Among folk of low economic level a few notable exceptions occurred of vigorous churches which were self-propagating and self-supporting—those of the aboriginals of Chota Nagpur in India, of the Koreans, of the Bataks in Sumatra, and of the Karens in Burma. Yet only 15 per cent of all younger church congregations were self-supporting. Regardless of some good that accrued, continuing subsidy proved debilitating.

As Davis pointed out, the missionary movement had been conceived three dimensionally—in terms of evangelistic, educational, and medical enterprises. A fourth dimension had to be reckoned with at once: the economic and social environment into which these endeavours were set.[29] Previously, he indicated, missionary architects had paid altogether too much attention to the model institution they hoped would arise but had given almost none to the adequacy of the foundations and the structural-frame. Davis' approach called for strengthening the foundation and the structure, but modifying the institution to fit them.

Following Davis' lead, Madras recognized that emphasis on support alone could be self-defeating. Basically, the problem was spiritual. Yet, without specifically condemning earlier subsidization, Madras declared that in any new fields "the principle of placing new groups of Christians upon their own resources for the support of their own work [should] be applied from the very beginning."[30] Far-sighted missionary statesmen recognized at once the permanent worth of Davis' contribution. On what many regard the most urgent problem confronting the Christian world mission today, he had assembled a mass of data and had made it meaningful. Moreover, he had clarified the general principles that must govern any sound approach to the problem. As yet Davis' work has scarely been utilized. Perhaps World War II is partially to blame, but when advance is made, it will proceed from the foundation he laid at Madras.

Advancing Two Concerns. Our account of Madras' achievements can be rounded only by mentioning here two other causes it furthered. First, Madras focussed a powerful beam on the church's ministry. Its succinct and masterful appraisal of the Christian ministry throughout the world emerged from a group under Bishop Stephen Neill's chairmanship. Its concluding affirmation pointed to theological education in the younger churches as one of the "greatest weaknesses" in world Christianity. Positively, it sought the working out of an advanced policy and program for training ministers in the younger churches.[31] War intervened, but the challenge stimulated at least two significant endeavours. The first, beginning five years later, was a comprehensive study of the Christian minister in India by Charles W. Ranson.[32] The second, coming more than a decade later, was the first part of a survey of theological education in Africa conducted by Bishop Stephen Neill, associate general secretary of the World Council of Churches, in the spring of 1950 under the auspices of the International Missionary Council.[33]

The second of these concerns advanced at Madras was Christian literature. For the first time a world conference considered literature with some thoroughness. Dr. Ralph E. Diffendorfer directed preparations of the report. Its recommendations called for a world program of co-operation and advance in the production and distribution of Christian literature.[34] To the remarkable results achieved in this sphere through the war we must presently return.

Its Significance

In light of subsequent events, what was the permanent significance of Madras? All that has been listed as accomplishment must be included in any appraisal. Madras also outlined whole programs of action in fields we have not so much as mentioned.[35] Moreover, a perspective of only twelve years from the event greatly limits our ability to discern its true meaning. Yet probably its lasting importance will have to be sought beyond all these factors.

A Unifying Event in the Life of the Church. The real significance of Madras lay in what it *was* rather than in what it *did*. It was a unifying event in the life of the whole church—an event which revealed to the churches the fellowship of the church universal.

No other experience made so deep an impact on those at Madras as that of the church, of a world-wide community united in love. Africa's delegates, by way of illustration, had never been together on a continent-wide basis. On the journey from Africa they became fully aware for the first time of what it meant to be African Christians. Madras provided an even greater transformation. It made them world Christians. When in the midst of war the Madras resolutions and addresses were forgotten, this experience of global Christian solidarity remained and took on a deeper meaning. Men and women in small, struggling churches in remote sections of the world no longer felt so isolated and weak. They belonged to a universal fellowship in whose reality they had shared. As Christians they could never again be the same. Eventually, what they had experienced would permeate the life of their home churches.[36]

Madras knew unity, but it looked out on division. It declared the church the supreme evangelizing agent, but above all else, it saw that effective evangelization requires oneness. That note runs through every pronouncement made at Madras. The conference as a whole commended spiritual unity and co-operation.[37] The statement's circumspection would satisfy every Western church participating at Madras, but in the commission that produced it, those from the younger churches were restive. To stab the conscience of the whole church and to challenge an unbelieving and torn world, they presented their own statement. "Disunion is both a stumbling block to the faithful and a mockery to those without." Among the younger churches, they declared, a "passionate longing . . . exists in all countries for visible union of the churches." For them co-operation was not enough, but loyalty would forbid their "going forward to consummate any union unless it receives the whole-hearted support and blessing of those through whom these churches have been planted." For that reason they appealed—

with all the fervor we possess, to the missionary societies and boards and the responsible authorities of the older churches, to take this matter seriously to heart, to labor with the churches in the mission field to achieve this union, to support and encourage us in all our efforts to put an end to the scandalous effects of our divisions and to lead us in the path of union—the union for which our Lord prayed, through which the world would indeed believe in the Divine Mission of the Son, our Lord Jesus Christ.[38]

Never before had so stirring an appeal been rung out by the younger churches.

The experience of lived unity amidst disintegration, the faith in the gospel's triumph over all the evil unleashed in the world by sinful men, the poignant plea for Christian unity—these can only be described as an event of singular importance in the life of the church.

Indestructible Unity for a Broken World. When Madras was first projected, no one supposed that it would prepare the world's Protestant churches for six years of devastating war and then for war's aftermath. Yet that is precisely what it did. As one looks back after scarcely more than a decade, this seems to have been its most significant contribution. "The Miracle of Madras," a phrase heard frequently at the conference, was invested with many and varied meanings. Amidst crumbling international relations, it was a miracle that Madras was held at all. In that terrifying and uncertain day only Christ's name could have drawn together men and women from sixty-nine nations of the earth.[39] It also appeared to be the first time in history when a large group of nationals from each of two warring countries came together to face unitedly a common task. Here, indeed, was a foreglimpse of the unity that strengthened Christians throughout the war.

Like the nations, the churches soon after Madras were enveloped in a cloud of darkness. Cut off from one another, often suffering persecution and hardship, they struggled on as best they could. Yet through war's most desolate days the unity born at Madras held. It proved to be a living, sustaining fire. Thus wrote a German missionary leader:

Tambaram nine months ago is like a bright star of God's promise, a signpost of the communion and fellowship of all Christian churches in the world. But now darkness has come upon us and nobody knows when the holy but terrible will of God will be changed again into mercy and love. . . . Oh our mission work, our dear and beloved mission work! . . . I shall remember the Hemmen days as the last sign of a real Christian brotherhood in this world.[40]

This was Madras. World War II cut short its projected program, but through that war its spirit served the churches indispensably, providentially. As if with premonitory vision of the trial ahead, Madras had proclaimed to the world its trust: "By faith, but in deep assurance, we declare that this body which God has fashioned through Christ cannot be destroyed."[41]

The Immediate Post-Madras Period

Follow-up. When Madras ended, the event had still to be translated into the life of the churches. This translation or follow-up continued until the outbreak of war. Most notable among the attempts to convey Madras to Western church constituencies were the Fellowship Teams made up of men and women from the younger churches. During the winter of 1939 one team crossed the United States and another travelled throughout Britain. The Foreign Missions Conference postponed its meeting from January to June and lengthened it to provide fully for "Putting Madras Into Action."[42] Delegates returning to their homelands spread its story far and wide. A whole spate of interpretive articles appeared in missionary and National Christian Council publications, and not a few books resulted.[43] Conferences in India, China, Africa, and Latin America reflected its impact. The Council's secretaries were occupied with editing and distributing *The Madras Series*. The findings volume, *The World Mission of the Church*, was translated into Arabic, Afrikaans, Chinese, Danish, French, and Spanish. By 1941 in Britain and America alone it had sold 45,000 copies. *The Madras Series* in seven volumes was translated into six languages and by 1941 in Britain and America had sold nearly 4,000 sets.

Hemmen. Madras was the last meeting of the Council before the war. However, during two days in July, 1939, the *Ad Interim* Committee with eighteen persons present met at Kasteel Hemmen, near Arnhem, Holland. The group acted on several matters growing out of Madras. Hemmen also advised the Council's departments concerning their work in the period ahead. The Madras proposal for a Far Eastern office was further discussed, and Warnshuis was asked to go at once to that area, survey the situation, and report back to the next meeting of the Committee, scheduled for August, 1940, near London.[44]

Preparation for War. By the summer of 1939 war appeared imminent. The spirit of Madras could not be broken, but in the event of conflict an emergency strategy for safeguarding missions was imperative. Hence, before the Hemmen meeting, Mott and Warnshuis went to Berlin where they met with German missionary leaders. A plan emerged and was reported at Hemmen.[45]

Out of the consultations had come four basic policies to be followed if war came: channels of communication would be kept as open as possible; National Christian Councils would care in every possible way for younger churches whose missionaries might be interned; financial help would be given to missionaries cut off from their home base but not interned; finally, the attempt would be made to protect mission property as it had been under the Versailles Treaty. The missionary community, praying and working for peace, had prepared for possible disruption by war.[46]

ORPHANED MISSIONS

Hitler's armies marched into Poland on September 1, 1939, and World War II was a fact. The repercussions were felt around the world. As one example, on the tropical island of Sumatra in the Netherlands Indies twenty-five ordained missionaries of the German Rhenish Mission were immediately affected. They were serving the Christian church in Batakland. When war broke in Europe, German missionaries in Sumatra found communication with their homeland impossible. Overnight they were cut off from the support of their parent society. Left alone, without funds and without counsel from home, they had become, like so many of their scattered colleagues, "orphaned" missionaries.

The Dutch Missions' Consul cabled the International Missionary Council at once. The Rhenish missionaries cut their working budget sharply. Bataks and straitened Dutch missionaries sacrificed to help financially. Then additional aid came through the International Missionary Council's New York office. With studied frugality and outside help, meagre though it was, the orphaned missionaries somehow maintained their work. But on May 10, 1940, Germany invaded Holland. In Sumatra prompt internment ended Rhenish work among the Bataks.

Faced with the problems of the Rhenish workers and hundreds of other missionaries in a similar plight, those responsible for world missionary co-operation faced two clamant concerns: the welfare of a younger church suddenly on its own, and the well-being of its missionaries, including their eventual re-establishment or repatriation. The self-reliant Bataks, whose effective evangelism had already won to Christianity one-third of their nation, carried on alone through the difficult years of Japanese occupation. But what of the orphaned missionaries? Throughout the war the men were interned in India while their families remained in Sumatra. By war's end the women and children were in pitiable condition. Money was forwarded to them through the International Missionary Council, but more important, that agency, aware of their difficulties, appealed on their behalf through its London office to British authorities then in charge in Indonesia. As a result their hardships were somewhat eased. In India, eighteen months after Germany's surrender, the men of the mission were being repatriated. Negotiations for repatriating the mothers and children were greatly delayed. Through months of waiting, the Rhenish families stranded in Indonesia were supported from America. Finally, after weeks in transit, they reached Germany in July, 1947.

Behind this unheralded drama, symbolic of a hundred others, lies an unparalleled example of world Christian fellowship—a story of foresight and planning, of sacrifice and solidarity. Although it was only one phase of the Christian world mission during World War II, it stands unique. Its exemplification of Christian love made tangible the real meaning of Christian unity. Undoubtedly, it was the International Missionary Council's outstanding contribution during the war. In the history of the church, its chapter title reads "Orphaned Missions." Its achievement was possible only because the Protestant missionary enterprise had become by 1939 so much a co-operative venture, and because scores of denominational societies, through their national councils, had learned the necessity of working together. In short, Orphaned Missions is the story of world Christian community in action.[47]

War in Europe

Two days after the invasion of Poland, Britain and France were at war with Germany. The plans discussed at Hemmen went into effect at once, and within two weeks the Council could announce that all missionary property would be safeguarded as it had been through World War I. The situation seemed well in hand.[48]

German Missions. Among Continental missions, those of Germany, the first affected, consituted the largest bloc. Of 3,500 Continental missionaries then on the field, nearly half came from Germany. Of the $4,500,000 then being contributed to missions by Continental societies, a full half came from Germany.[49] Furthermore, with China, Japan, and Sumatra ranking as major exceptions, the preponderant part of German missions was conducted within British territory or in areas governed by Britain or the Dominions under mandate. Again with a few notable exceptions, In British areas most of the male German missionaries were at first routinely interned and after examination sent back to their posts.

The British government, however, bearing in mind the precedents of World War I—in which Oldham had played a decisive rôle— adopted a liberal policy.[50] From the start India's ruling officers acted in consultation with the National Christian Council regarding the maintenance of German missions and very quickly released all internees. Then the British Colonial Secretary wrote to the Council's London office expressing his sincere hope that as many "enemy alien missionaries" as possible might maintain their work in Africa.[51] In Tanganyika, for example, there were five German societies with one hundred men missionaries. Interned and offered parole, all but a few returned to their work. Everywhere neighbouring missions stepped into the breach. Their immediate hearty response enabled German missions to continue.[52]

Meeting the Needs. For five years exchange regulations had hobbled German work. War's outbreak dealt the final blow. No funds could be sent to any missionary. Hence, in China, Japan, and Sumatra, where, when war first broke out, Germans had not been interned, as well as in British areas, the crucial question was financial support. Given the legal right to pursue their work, how could German missionaries continue with no money?

The International Missionary Council had to aid these distressed missions. The first gift came from Scotland in October, 1939. Unsolicited, it amounted to $1,000 (£250) and was given to be used at the discretion of the Council. Scotland was at war with Germany, but as so often during that war, the Christian community, united in love, testified anew that it transcended lines of battle, nation, and class. The Church of Sweden agreed to underwrite the Leipzig Mission in India. Dutch missionaries in the Netherlands Indies assessed themselves a small amount each month to help the German missionaries among the Bataks. Other gifts began to come in slowly. American churches contributed—most notably the Lutheran denominations, responding wonderfully to meet the needs of the almost wholly Lutheran German societies. From September, 1939, through May, 1940, the Council's New York office and the American Section of the Lutheran World Convention sent $90,000 to stranded missions needing financial support.[53]

Other Continental Missions Affected.   German missions were not alone in feeling war's first impact. The Basel Mission, long a Swiss-German organization, drawing missionaries and support from both countries, had to become a purely Swiss mission. This deprived it of much support. Yet the Paris Evangelical Missionary Society was more seriously affected. Its secretary and fifty of its ninety-eight missionaries were conscripted. Moreover, the strongest centres of Protestant giving were in Alsace-Lorraine where large-scale evacuation occurred. These facts plus the tremendous financial stress of war felt everywhere in the country made fund raising exceptionally difficult. In England an emergency committee, with the support of the Archbishop of Canterbury and others, was formed to aid the Paris Mission. Likewise, Finnish missions in Africa, China, and India were orphaned by Russia's invasion of Finland. The Scandinavian countries, Great Britain, South Africa, and the United States all came to their aid.[54]

Blitzkrieg's Aftermath

The winter of 1939-40 brought a lull in hostilities, but in the spring of 1940 German "lightning war" struck Europe. In the second week of April, Denmark and Norway were invaded. One month later German armies swept over Luxemburg, Belgium, and Holland. By June fourth Dunkirk was history. Several weeks later France surrendered. The war had entered a new phase.

Continental Missions.   Heretofore the problem had been chiefly one of German missions—the treatment of missionaries and property, the financial support of their work. Now, except for the gravely restricted Swiss and Swedish missions, the whole missionary endeavour

of Continental Protestantism faced rapid disintegration. Could international missionary co-operation meet the challenge?

On the eve of war, roughly one-half the total missionary personnel
came from North America, three-eighths came from Britain, and
slightly more than one-eighth came from the Continent. Comparison
by expenditure discloses almost identical proportions. A third criterion,
however, the nationals among whom the missionaries work, reveals
that Continental missionaries were reaching more than 22 per cent
of the entire field. One-eighth of the Protestant missionary budget
may seem inconsequential, but recognition that between one-fifth
and one-fourth of those influenced by Protestant missionaries were
reached by Continentals makes graphic the pre-war outreach of their
missions.[55]

In China nearly as many people were touched by Continental as
by British missions. In the Netherlands Indies, where Protestant
Christians outnumber those of China, Japan, Korea, the Philippines,
and Thailand combined, virtually all work belonged to Continental
societies. In India and Africa—indeed, all over the world—Continental
missions were strongly planted. Overnight more than one-fifth of the
whole Protestant missionary enterprise—3,500 missionaries in forty
countries and 168 missions—was cut off and orphaned. Communication, co-ordination, and support combined into one enormous problem.
By the summer of 1940 in British territories the majority of German
missionaries had been interned or repatriated. In the Netherlands
Indies all had been interned. But in Japan and China, while lacking
support, most of them were still free.[56]

Orphaned Missions. The sudden plight of all Continental missions
in the late spring of 1940 demanded immediate action. The Continent
was sealed off. Britain after Dunkirk was battling for existence on her
tight little island. The great load would have to be carried by North
America.

Immediately the Council's New York office enlarged its plans and
took steps to aid the "Missions Affected by War."[57] More appropriate,
it was thought, would be a fund to aid "Orphaned Missions."[58] The
designation was brief, described the actual situation, and carried
strong emotional appeal. It gained currency and came to designate
missions cut off from their home base. As it has been used, however,
the phrase connotes not only missions actually orphaned, but the
whole allied effort to assist them.

Parallel Lutheran Efforts. For months what became the United States Committee of the Lutheran World Federation (described as the "alter ego" of the National Lutheran Council) had been supporting destitute Lutheran missionaries, most of them German. When war affected all Continental missions, the Committee determined to enlarge its support. Lutheran World Action, the Lutheran fund-raising body, was directed by Dr. Ralph Long whose special concern became orphaned Lutheran missions. From the beginning American Lutherans raised, administered, and sent their money directly. But a cordial working agreement provided for close co-operation between the International Missionary Council's Orphaned Missions Fund and Lutheran World Action. Thus, while Lutheran funds were administered separately, they were always reported for inclusion in the annual totals of the Orphaned Missions Fund.

Warnshuis and Long maintained close *liaison* between the Council and Lutheran World Action both for mutual assistance and to avoid overlapping. From the start it was agreed that the Council would care primarily for non-Lutheran missions. Fifty-four of the Continent's 168 orphaned missions became the special responsibility of American Lutherans. In effect, they accepted as their special charge almost all strictly Lutheran missionary work in the world. The remaining 114 missions for the most part looked for their support to the International Missionary Council.

The Appeal for Orphaned Missions. The Council sponsored no direct relief appeal but operated through denominational relief committees and mission societies. These it supplied with information and then acted as a clearing house to channel to areas of greatest need any money they designated for orphaned missions. In the summer of 1940 Miss Gibson joined Warnshuis in New York for several months to help survey the needs of missions affected by war. In light of their similar experience during World War I both were uniquely fitted for the task they faced.

The total budgets of the orphaned missions had been about $4,500,000 annually. To sustain them on a minimal basis, it was judged, would require $2,000,000 yearly. In the autumn of 1940 an appeal for $2,000,000 was made, three-fourths of it to come from the United States. Yet never once throughout the war-time course of orphaned missions did so much as one-half of this "minimum support" come in during any one year.

Even so, by December, 1940, no Protestant mission anywhere in the world had to be suspended or abandoned.[59] Some aid had been sent to every one of the 112 missions known to be in distress. Among them many projects were dropped, but "essential" work was maintained. A year later the story was substantially the same. Understandably, England had been able to give relatively little money, but its societies were underwriting salaries for several orphaned missionaries, providing partial support for some, and giving housing to others. Moreover, some boards contributed in a way that shows in no financial report. They refrained from making additions to the budgets for their own work so that they might aid the orphaned missions.[60] Heartening gifts representing real sacrifice came from the lands of the younger churches. The Japanese Christian Fellowship Deputation that visited the United States in the spring of 1941 contributed. Christians in India and Burma gave more than $12,000 for the War Emergency Fund of their National Christian Council. Chinese churches helped as did individual congregations in the Congo, in Cameroun, and in Madagascar.

The nearly $980,000 contributed to orphaned missions in 1941 was less than half the amount thought to be absolutely necessary. Yet somehow Continental missions kept going. Gifts not counted in this total came from unexpected sources and helped immensely. Missionaries themselves sacrificed quietly to stretch each dollar given to them. Already low salaries were voluntarily cut as much as 75 per cent. Wherever possible personnel and funds of neighbouring missions were pooled for the most efficient and economical administration. The most rigorous economy was practised everywhere, and missionaries carried on with heart-breaking frugality. Meanwhile, Continental societies continued to gather money for the day when it could be used. European Christians had not abandoned their missions. They were only unable to send available funds.[61]

Despite this determination and sacrifice, had it not been for the magnificent spirit shown by the younger churches, the amounts provided for orphaned missions could never have achieved what they did. Missionaries left penniless were scattered around the world, but Christians among whom they laboured took heroic measures to help sustain them and their work. Members of the younger churches responded with vigour to support Christian enterprises in their countries. It happened thus in Madagascar, across Africa, in the Near

East, and in the Islands of the Pacific. While its nation was being drained by war and was caught in the grip of inflation, the National Christian Council of China month after month raised substantial sums for the relief of Continental missions. Similar efforts by the National Christian Council of India won for it the admiration of the missionary movement. As so often had happened in the past, disaster revealed new sources of strength in the Christian world community.[62]

War in the Pacific

War had been raging for twenty-seven months when suddenly in December, 1941, Pearl Harbor embroiled the United States and inaugurated the Japanese attack on the British Commonwealth and Empire and on the Netherlands Indies. For the first time World War II became global. Now the younger churches in Southeast Asia were completely cut off from their older colleagues.

Japanese Occupation. In the lands of Japanese occupation, orphaned Continental missions that previously had received aid were in only five areas—Japan, New Guinea, Occupied China, Manchuria, and the Netherlands Indies. The last was the largest field and, except for India, had received more orphaned missions' aid than any other area. Advance transmissions were sufficient to sustain work there until October, 1942, but as the occupation wore on, missionary casualties mounted from starvation and murder. The Indonesian church, forced at every point to display initiative, reached a high degree of self-sufficiency. When the Netherlands Indies were sealed off, China became orphaned missions' greatest responsibility under conditions of fantastic inflation. There Lutherans cared for their nine missions, and the International Missionary Council for the other six cut off from support. A similar division of responsibility occurred in India where the National Christian Council did a notable job. Yet well over 90 per cent of the financial load for orphaned missions in India was carried by American Lutherans.[63] Centres of mission work in many of the Pacific Islands also drew support from the orphaned mission funds. In the Near East saving aid went to many specific missionary projects.[64]

Africa. For Africa one can scarcely do more than enumerate those areas in which orphaned missions were maintained throughout the war. In many instances they were enabled to carry on as a result of direct aid given from near-by or related bodies. Such was the case in the Gold Coast, the British sphere of the Cameroun, and in large measure in South-west Africa and Kenya. American Lutherans provided considerable support for disrupted German work in South Africa, South-west Africa, and Tanganyika—the last, with India and Sumatra, being one of the three most important German fields supported by orphaned missions' gifts. Elsewhere, as in Nigeria, French Equatorial Africa, the French Cameroun, the Congo, Angola, Basutoland (in South Africa), and Barotseland (in Northern Rhodesia) direct grants were made from the International Missionary Council's funds.[65]

Unexpected Help.   Many gifts of inestimable benefit to orphaned missions came from unexpected sources and are not listed in the Council's records. Certain governments were particularly generous. The Norwegian Government in London between 1941 and 1945 gave $550,000 (of which $350,000 was repaid) for those missions cut off from their regular bases of support in Norway. The government of China in 1943 granted first a 50 per cent and then a 100 per cent additional allowance on currency exchange for missions, thus doubling the effectiveness of orphaned missions' aid there. The governments of Palestine and of the Congo gave aid in especially desperate cases. Elsewhere local government authorities gave occasional subsidies to struggling missions.[66] In addition to these grants, American and other soldiers, impressed by the missionary endeavour, they saw, occasionally contributed to it. The most outstanding example of such aid to an orphaned mission was the vigorous support lent the Paris Mission in Noumea.[67]

Facing the Post-war Period

As war's outcome became clearer, the significance of the orphaned missions' program became more readily assessable. The original hope had been to maintain the "essential" work of orphaned missions with aid of $2,000,000 annually. Yet in no single year was as much as $1,000,000 received and disbursed. Indeed, the yearly average during the war approximated $793,500, seven-eighths of which came from the United States (out of which a yearly average of $153,000 went directly to British missions). Of the American share, an average of $276,300 was handled through what became the United States Committee of the Lutheran World Federation.[68] Whenever had so little sustained so much? The results seem incredible until one recalls the heroic sacrifices of missionaries and the responsibilities accepted by younger churches.

Administration of the Fund. Warnshuis, who retired from the Council in 1942, had been instrumental in creating its Orphaned Missions Fund. The Council at no point desired to become a centralized administrative agency for relief. It tried primarily to co-ordinate what was being done in order to prevent overlapping and oversight. By 1945 twenty-five countries had contributed, and quite properly the United States had supplied nearly 88 per cent of the total.[69] Approximately one-third of all money given from America during the war for orphaned missions was contributed through the Lutheran World Federation.[70] The Council's London office handled some funds, but the major responsibility for orphaned missions was in New York. That office collated information on all giving for orphaned missions. From 1939 to 1945 it channelled nearly $1,160,000 in general gifts to orphaned missions. It issued monthly bulletins and annual reports and received acknowledgements from the field for all financial help sent directly through the Council. Yet administrative expenses for this whole vast enterprise were kept to almost negligible dimensions. In 1942 the Reverend (later Dr.) Leland S. Albright joined the Council's staff in New York and gave major attention to the Orphaned Missions Fund until his resignation in December, 1948.

Many sources provided the money—mission boards, denominational relief agencies, local churches, service men's groups, and individuals. Much was sent directly and reported to the Council. Contributions from within the British Commonwealth, for obvious exchange reasons, went through London. Generally, special committees of the National Christian Councils administered funds locally. In some instances, however, money had to be given directly to a specific mission.[71]

Preparation for Post-war Needs. By the end of 1943 it became clear that the needs of orphaned missions would continue for months— perhaps years—after the end of hostilities. The economies of some of the European sending countries would be so strained and some church constituencies so scattered that adequate support from them for their missionary enterprises would be impossible. These problems would be

worst in Germany, but an even greater difficulty there would be the
inability of German missionaries to return to their fields for some time.
Their former endeavours would still have to be supported financially
and with personnel. The Council prepared accordingly, and as a first
step set aside a reserve fund of $100,000 for future emergencies.[72]

The next step involved formulating a basic policy for the future of
the orphaned missions' program. This was worked out, after consultation with the North American Counsellors, by Bishop James C. Baker,
who had succeeded Mott as the Council's chairman, and by Dr. John
W. Decker, who had succeeded Warnshuis. After proposing continued
support for orphaned missions after the war, the statement of policy
listed four points bearing especially on German missions: first, the
church could not consent to the barring of missionaries from a field in
peace-time on the basis of nationality alone; second, the welfare and
progress of a younger church would be the paramount concern in any
arrangements affecting its life—moreover, that church would have to
be party to and help to carry out any decisions reached concerning it;
third, all Christian forces in a particular region would be under "heavy
obligations unselfishly to aid" in maintaining orphaned missions within
their area; finally, earnest consideration should be given to the international staffing of orphaned missions.[73]

The Receding Tide of Battle. As it turned out, neither VE Day
nor VJ Day marked war's end—only the cessation of firing. The old
dislocations continued and new problems arose. With the advance in
the Pacific area of the Allied forces toward Japan, many orphaned
missionaries, unheard from in years, were once again put in touch with
the outside world. Many of them, from Germany and elsewhere in
Europe and with no possible means of support, had to be cared for.
The orphaned enterprises in the Pacific, in Asia, and in Africa still had
to be maintained. By August, 1945, it was hoped that European societies could soon resume financial and staffing responsibilities for their
work. Every one knew this could not occur at once, but few realized
how long the process of transition would take.[74]

Evidence soon mounted that European societies would be slower in
resuming their work than had first been assumed. Those of Germany,
would be delayed beyond all the others. That great land lay pros-
trate. Despite the country's poverty, missionary zeal—in the commitment of lives and money—was marked. Occupation restrictions,

however, nullified any overseas outlet for this zeal quite as effectively as war's isolation.[75]

By the end of 1946 most of Europe's Protestant missionary societies, except Germany's, had resumed financial responsibility for almost all their enterprises. A year later, however, inflation and rising costs had become so severe that they could scarcely maintain their work even on a reduced war-time budget. By the winter of 1948 societies in some countries were unable to obtain the necessary currency exchange for overseas transmissions. Meanwhile, German missionaries were being released from internment. Small groups of them still remained at their posts in Africa, China, and the Pacific area. Almost all needed rehabilitation, but German societies could get no foreign exchange. Subsidies were desperately needed for maintenance and work budgets of German missions and for repatriation of German missionaries. Hope vanished for bringing the Orphaned Missions Fund to an early close.[76]

The situation in 1948 forced fundamental re-thinking on the whole problem. The facts were clear. The 1939-45 period was history, and only German missions remained in any sense orphaned. In the then foreseeable future German societies would be wholly unable to sustain their former work. Moreover, two large bodies, the Paris and Basel Missions would, for different reasons, require help for some time to come.[77] Responding to this need, the Lutheran World Federation in 1948 made Dr. F. A. Schiotz executive secretary of a newly created Commission on Orphaned Missions. Its first year's budget called for $750,000 to assist German Lutheran missions. Similarly, the International Missionary Council at Oegstgeest in September, 1948, focussing major attention on the hardships confronting Continental missions, projected a five-year plan for "Orphaned Missions and Intermission Aid," with a yearly budget calling for $300,000. Assistance would be given to any Continental society suffering undue financial strain, but the new project was designed primarily for non-Lutheran German missions not otherwise cared for.[78]

Orphaned Missions' Achievements

In the decade encompassing World War II huge government expenditures taught people to think in terms of billions of dollars. In contrast five *million* dollars spent for a global project during six years of war seems infinitesimal. In 1950 that amount would have paid for exactly two American B-36 bombing planes or eight of the older B-29's. Yet this was the total amount provided to maintain orphaned Protestant missions in Asia, Africa, South America, and the Pacific Islands throughout the whole war. This meant support for churches, orphanages, schools, hospitals, dispensaries, printing presses, *and missionaries,* among more than one-fifth of the younger churches of the world. The results achieved through orphaned missions and in past decades from the small sums devoted to Christian missions give pause for thoughtful reflection.

The Orphaned Missions Fund operated on an income of less than $800,000 a year during the war—money representing giving over and above regular missionary contributions. For hundreds of stranded missionaries it kept body and soul together. For members of younger churches it maintained necessary institutions, although often with their work drastically curtailed, and it bore constant testimony to the fellowship of which they are a part. Never thought of as simply a decent or friendly gesture, the whole program of orphaned missions was conceived as serving the ultimate well-being of younger churches, of an important part of the world Christian community.

In conception and achievement the project was unique in the history of the Christian church. The reality of the world Christian community in action, the manner in which it operated, indeed, the very fact of giving under the circumstances of the times had a significance that far outweighed the sums involved. Moreover, what many missionaries did in terms of personal service could never be measured financially. The majority of the orphaned missions were sustained by Christians from countries at war with the lands of those who normally supported them. Across warring lines Christians were praying for one another, working for one another, not from maudlin sentimentality, but because they were unitedly involved in a humanly overwhelming task, the evangelization of mankind. Here was actual proof of a Christian world fellowship transcending nation and denomination and uniting its members in faith and love.

The reality of this community afforded further striking evidence in the immediate resumption of planning with German societies after the war. During the holocaust one of the deepest sources of strength for German missionary leaders was their consciousness of membership in an ecumenical fellowship. In contrast with their unawareness in World

ORPHANED MISSIONS*

Summary of Contributions to Continental and British Missions
November 1, 1939, through December 31, 1949

| YEAR | To Continental Missions | | | | To British Missions | TOTALS |
| | From U.S.A.[1] | | From U.S.A. Lutheran Bodies[2] | From Other Countries | From U.S.A. | |
	Through IMC	Sent Direct	Sent Direct & Through IMC			
1940[3]	$ 119,152.25	$ 75,710.79	$ 189,940.00	$ 94,412.24	$ 187,000.00	$ 666,215.28
1941	225,445.29	88,954.98	189,852.19	101,107.94	374,013.05	979,373.45
1942	112,844.65	74,220.15	168,888.86	88,729.45	174,201.55	618,884.66
1943	161,178.44	54,294.66	247,373.43	107,487.11	142,447.18	712,780.82
1944	236,630.52	128,267.61	388,867.63	57,490.69	28,382.39	839,638.84
1945	204,656.08	110,109.65	474,554.98	135,355.97	18,913.60	943,590.28
1946	197,924.59	73,622.51	452,929.75	43,224.75	44,513.60	812,215.20
1947	159,589.92	62,348.62	507,042.47	27,017.47	64,395.80	820,394.28
1948	145,720.60	58,941.89	645,215.44	23,141.23		873,019.16
1949	183,204.38	47,067.46	752,028.59	57,220.74		1,039,521.17
	$1,746,346.72	$773,538.32	$4,016,693.34	$735,187.59	$1,033,867.17	$8,305,633.14

[1] From boards, societies, and individuals, excluding Lutheran bodies.
[2] National Lutheran Council and U.S.A. Committee for Lutheran World Federation.
[3] November 1, 1939 through December 31, 1940.

* Reproduced from Latourette and Hogg, *World Christian Community in Action* and supplemented for 1948-49 with totals from IMC *Ad Interim* Committee *Minutes*, Whitby, 1950, Appendix A, p. 49.

War I of what was being done, they knew that other Christians were caring for their missions.[79] As a result the first post-war meetings between German and British and American missionary leaders were utterly different from those following World War I. Then there had been suspicion, accusation, and tension. A decade or more was required to heal the wounds of war and to restore full fellowship. But at Hermannsburg in November, 1945,[80] while there were serious questions concerning the war-time attitudes and actions of some, there was understanding, a grateful renewal of acquaintance, and a determination to begin building together again in love and mutual trust. The next meet at which all Continental councils were represented was that of the Council's *Ad Interim Committee* at Geneva in February, 1946.[81] There was no German reluctance as at Crans in 1920. The two German representatives, Walter Freytag and Siegfried Knak, came as a matter of course to help shape plans affecting their missions. Similar gatherings met at Hermannsburg in May, 1946,[82] at Rheinfelden in October,[83] and at Baarn, Holland, in May, 1947.[84] Each of these enabled members of the Council to work at the problem of German missions as a common concern. They led naturally to the Whitby meeting of the International Missionary Council in July, 1947, and resulted in the important document there approved and published, "The Supranationality of Missions."[85]

As the story of orphaned missions shows, Christians around the world had assumed responsibility for the welfare of unknown and sometimes "enemy" missionaries. Those of other nations and churches safeguarded their property and often at great sacrifice maintained their work. Unity born of love was manifesting itself. It offered prime evidence of the inner meaning of the word "ecumenical."

THE COUNCIL DURING AND AFTER WORLD WAR II

In relating the history of orphaned missions, through a decade, we have had to anticipate bits of our larger story. Orphaned missions provided a dramatic centre for the Council's war-time program, but through the war the Council also maintained much of its regular work. To resume our narrative, we must return to the first years of the war.

Mott's Latin America Visits

At Madras the Latin American delegation urged Mott to visit the major fields of Latin America to strengthen existing National Christian Councils, to encourage new councils where they were needed, and to bring to that area his gifts of Christian statesmanship.[86] From the Continuation Committee's founding in 1910, Mott had been journeying to the four corners of the world on behalf of international missionary co-operation. He made the last of these tours as an officer of the Council to Latin America in 1940-41.

Mott went first to Mexico in January, 1940, for the meeting there of the National Council of Evangelical Churches. Dr. W. Stanley Rycroft, then recently appointed secretary of the Committee on Co-operation in Latin America, accompanied him. Mott spent March in Puerto Rico and in April visited Cuba. During May and June he and Rycroft visited Argentina, Uruguay (the River Plate area), and Brazil. They shared in the conference of the Confederation of Evangelical Churches of the River Plate Area and in June led a conference of Evangelical workers in Rio de Janeiro.[87]

A year later Mott visited Latin America, again accompanied by Stanley Rycroft. Mott convened the first of his conferences at Santiago, Chile, in late April, 1941. This was followed by a meeting at Antofagasta, Chile, early in May on Indian work. Later that month Mott convened a conference in Lima, Peru. At Barranquilla, Colombia, he met in conference with Evangelical workers from that country and from Venezuela. The Congress of Central American Evangelical Workers at Guatamala City brought together delegates from all the Central American countries—Guatamala, Honduras, Salvador, Nicaragua, and Costa Rica. Out of these gatherings several major concerns emerged. Among them were the need to bring effectively into the thinking of the United States and Canada the problems of Latin America and to increase the missionary force for that area; the need for more effective local support of the Evangelical church; the need for Christian literature; and the need to reach students.[88]

The Loss of Key Men

Six months after his return from Latin America, Mott resigned from the chairmanship of the International Missionary Council. His withdrawal came to symbolize, however, an even greater loss—the rapid dissolution of the Council's entire original secretariat. Within four years, part of them in the midst of World War II, Oldham resigned, Mott retired, Warnshuis retired, and Paton died.

Oldham. J. H. Oldham was first to go. During the mid-thirties he had increasingly devoted himself to those issues arising from the Christian confrontation of the scientific and secular civilization of the West. Oldham's interest had drawn him into organizing the Oxford Conference of 1937. More and more his concern focussed on tasks not directly within the Council's purview, and he thus felt it unwise to continue as one of its paid secretaries. Accordingly, through Mott, Oldham submitted his resignation to the Council at Madras. Exactly thirty years earlier he had agreed to organize the World Missionary Conference at Edinburgh, but he had not been present at either Jerusalem or Madras. Now, at sixty-four years of age, the man whose mind more than that of any other person had shaped the International Missionary Council was asking to be released to serve the cause of world evangelization in other ways. The Council accepted his resignation "with deep regret" and wished him and his wife God-speed.[89]

Mott. John R. Mott was next. Although he had been unanimously re-elected chairman of the Council at Madras, he stated there his wish not to continue in that position for more than three years. At the end of that time, in his seventy-seventh year, with a representative meeting of even the *Ad Interim* Committee obviously impossible, he resigned. From nearly all the Council's constituent members he had obtained written consent for his step and for appointing one of the vice-chairmen to succeed him and to serve until the Committee could meet again to elect a chairman. When he retired on January 15, 1942, Mott appointed Bishop James C. Baker of The Methodist Church as his successor, but he agreed to serve as honorary chairman.[90] The expressions of gratitude for his long service provide thrilling, heart-warming reading.[91]

Warnshuis. Probably more than anyone else, Warnshuis had facilitated the successful functioning of the Council's machinery. For some years alone, but later with Paton, he had managed its finances, had administered the complex welter of organizational details, and had established proper working relationships with other bodies. What he had done was an indispensable ingredient in the team work that made the Council. That body had early agreed that its secretaries should retire on reaching sixty-five. Because of the war, his important rôle in the orphaned missions program, and Mott's retirement, A. L. Warnshuis was strongly urged to stay on. Despite these considerations, he determined that the rule should apply in his case. Through conversation with Paton when he visited America and through correspondence with such members of the *Ad Interim* Committee as could be reached, the decision was confirmed. Warnshuis retired from the Council at the end of 1942 in his sixty-fifth year.[92]

Paton. The University of Edinburgh had honoured Paton in 1939 with a Doctorate of Divinity for his missionary statesmanship. With war's outbreak, though, except for two brief visits to America, Paton's major energies found outlet in England. He served the Council's interests at Edinburgh House[93] and gave himself to his new work with the World Council of Churches. But Paton burned himself out in carrying his international responsibilities and in providing the British churches with superhuman service during the war. Mott wrote that Paton could never say "No," and that when asked to do the impossible, he undertook it because there seemed to be no one else to do it.[94] Paton was made chairman of the Joint Committee on the Welfare of Internees and Prisoners of War. He gave himself unstintingly to Britain's wartime evangelization crusade, the "Religion and Life Weeks." In addition to his labours for war-victims of every kind, Paton also found time for religious broadcasting, helping to launch the British Council of Churches, and writing. Paton drove himself unmercifully beyond human endurance. His final illness lasted only a week, and he died on August 21, 1943, at fifty-seven years of age.

Officers. During these years there were other losses from death among the Council's officers. Dr. Cheng Ching-yi, a vice-chairman of the Council from 1928 to 1938, died in China in November, 1939. In July, 1942, Baroness Elisabeth van Boetzelaer van Dubbledam, a vice-chairman of the Council from 1928 until her death, died in Holland. In November, 1944, William Temple, Archbishop of Canterbury, died. He had helped to draft the Jerusalem message and from 1936 to 1938 served as a vice-chairman of the Council. In January, 1945, Bishop

Vedanayakam Samuel Azariah died. Vocal at Edinburgh, 1910, and spokesman at Madras for the unity of the church, he had been appointed a vice-chairman of the Council in 1938. Thus within a few short years nearly the entire older leadership of the Council passed from the scene.

Mott and Oldham had brought the International Missionary Council into existence. In the twenties they were joined by Warnshuis and Paton. In the eyes of missionary leaders everywhere this team was the International Missionary Council. One member of the quartet had dropped out on the eve of war. Then within eighteen months during the war's most trying period, Mott, Warnshuis, and Paton were withdrawn from the arena. Coming when and as it did, the blow shook the very foundations of the Council. Each member of that original team was a man of striking and vigorous personality. Each made a unique contribution. To replace them was impossible. Their successors would have to move into the gaps they had left, begin slowly to build out, and meanwhile seek to enlarge that particular contribution they could best make to the on-going life of the Council. It would not be easy, and one could only hope that transition could be made with as little dislocation as possible in the Council's work and prestige.

Organization and Personnel

The decade from 1938 to 1948 brought a complete change of personnel among the Council's officers. Within the Council the tremendous vacuum created by the loss of its chairman and three secretaries became a dominant fact. Yet from 1935 on Oldham had moved toward a peripheral position. He was irreplaceable, but in reality his successor was Paton. In the American office Miss Esther B. Strong, an assistant secretary, resigned her post at the end of 1939. No successor was appointed until August, 1942, when Leland S. Albright of the United Church of Canada, who had returned at the beginning of the war from service in Japan, came into the office. Albright began without official status, dealing primarily with orphaned missions. In 1944 by unanimous vote of the accessible members of the *Ad Interim* Committee, he was made an assistant secretary of the Council, a post he retained until the end of 1948 at which time he became director of the Canadian School of Missions in Toronto. In 1949 Dr. Glora M. Wysner was appointed in New York to the Council's staff—the first woman to be given full secretarial status.

Editors of The International Review of Missions. At Madras, Miss Muriel M. Underhill, then joint editor of *The International Review of Missions* with William Paton, presented her resignation. Although she had reached the age of retirement, she agreed to continue until a successor could be found. In October, 1939, Miss Margaret Sinclair, holder of an Oxford M.A., came into the office of the *Review* on a trial basis. She had attended the Oxford Conference and had done some editorial work on ecumenical materials in Geneva. Her name first appeared as assistant editor on the *Review* in July, 1940. Shortly thereafter, Miss Underhill's resignation became effective. Early in 1946 Miss Sinclair became associate editor of the *Review*.

The Secretaries. With Warnshuis' retirement imminent, Mott appointed a committee in America to find a successor. The accessible members of the *Ad Interim* Committee unanimously appointed its nominee, Dr. John W. Decker. Decker had spent thirteen years in China under the American Baptist Foreign Mission Society. He returned to the United States in 1935 as his Society's secretary for China, Japan, and the Philippines. In January, 1943, he succeeded Warnshuis. In similar fashion, following Paton's death, the Reverend Norman Goodall was chosen in London.[95] Mr. (later Dr.) Goodall had been in the civil service before entering the Congregational ministry. He was serving as secretary for India and the South Pacific with the London Missionary Society when he succeeded Paton in October, 1944, and became at the same time editor of the *Review*.

The Chairmanship. At the time of his retirement Mott appointed Bishop James Chamberlain Baker his successor until a meeting of the Committee of the Council could be held. For several years Baker had been resident Methodist Bishop in Japan and Korea and during that time had visited all South-east Asia. At Madras he had been elected a vice-chairman of the Council. Bishop Baker shared in the Riverside Fellowship between Japanese and American Christians just before the outbreak of war between Japan and America and immediately at the close of the war was one of the group of four churchmen who visited Japan. Through the war years, Baker counselled with the secretaries on their work, and at Whitby he presided over the Council's first post-war world meeting.[96]

At Whitby the Committee of the Council unanimously requested

Dr. John A. Mackay to become its chairman. He accepted. Born in Scotland, Dr. Mackay had been educated at the University of Aberdeen, Princeton Theological Seminary, and the University of Madrid. He had had sixteen years' experience in Latin America, serving the Free Church of Scotland and then the South American Federation of YMCA's. When he became chairman of the International Missionary Council, Mackay was president of Princeton Seminary, president of the Board of Foreign Missions of the Presbyterian Church, U.S.A., and editor of *Theology Today*.

The General Secretaryship. For years Mott had been serving without salary as a full-time executive chairman for the Council. He coordinated the work of the London and New York offices and stood uniquely as a central focus of authority. No successor could be found for the chairmanship with time to fill the large rôle which Mott so notably had served. Moreover, with the expectation of a third office in the Far East and with increasing necessity for *liaison* with the World Council of Churches, an executive head for the Council appeared necessary. Hitherto, the London and New York secretaries had arranged program details among themselves with Mott's oversight, but changed circumstances required a new structure. Both secretaries whole-heartedly agreed that the time had come when the Council needed a general secretary in addition to its chairman.[97] The Committee of the Council agreed and at Whitby unanimously chose for this important post the Reverend Charles W. Ranson. Ranson, born in an Irish Methodist manse in 1903, held his degree from Oxford. He had had sixteen years as a missionary in India and from 1942 to 1945, while serving as the National Christian Council's secretary for evangelism and theological education, had completed a thorough survey of the Christian ministry in India. At Geneva in 1946 following J. Merle Davis' retirement, he had come into the Council, as research secretary. At Whitby the Council agreed that the general secretary's office should be in New York for five years with a reconsideration of the arrangement at the end of that time.[98]

Other Officers. To fill the vacancy created by Ranson's elevation to the general secretaryship, the Council shortly after Whitby appointed the Reverend Bengt G. M. Sundkler secretary for research. Dr. Sundkler had served as a Church of Sweden missionary in Zululand and in Tanganyika.[99]

The close of the decade saw still further changes in the Council's personnel. Miss Margaret Wrong, secretary of the International Committee on Christian Literature for Africa, had set out in the spring of 1948 to visit East Africa, but her mission was left unfinished. After a sudden heart attack she died in Uganda in her sixty-first year. She was buried there in the heart of that continent for whose people she had spent her mature life.[100]

Two women who had contributed outstandingly left the Council in the two years immediately following the period of our survey. When she retired in September, 1949, Miss Betty D. Gibson had had a longer continuous association with the Council than any other secretary. A year later, also having reached retirement age, her colleague, Miss Doris H. Standley, terminated her years of service to the Council.[101] The entire staff, with the exception of Conrad Hoffmann who was to retire in late 1951, now consisted of those people who had come into the Council during or after World War II. A new period was beginning in its life.

War-time Developments

Provision for orphaned missions overshadowed all else that the International Missionary Council did during and immediately after the war. Throughout that period some of its earlier activities were curtailed, but it managed to sustain many of them. Our survey necessarily includes development of these multiform interests.

Christian Literature. Madras directed attention to the acute need for stimulating the production of Christian literature among the younger churches. Hitherto it had been paid lip service, but literature usually came out last in mission budgets. Following up the Madras recommendation, Hemmen created a special committee under the chairmanship of Dr. R. E. Diffendorfer to establish a department of literature within the Council. War led the group to foster national committees. In England Paton's greatest interest in Christian literature probably centred in the remarkable work of Miss Constance Padwick, secretary in Cairo of the Central Literature Committee for Moslems. His concern led to the creation of the Conference of British Missionary Societies' Committee on Christian Literature.[102] In North America the Foreign Missions Conference merged an already functioning agency into the new Committee on World Literacy and Christian Literature.

Everywhere, despite wide-scale destruction of libraries, paper supplies, and printing equipment, national agencies made heartening progress throughout the war.[103] By 1946 the prevailing view favoured the projection of literature programs directly from national agencies, with the Council's rôle one of exchange, advice, and co-ordination. By 1948 consideration of a permanent Council department for literature had disappeared.[104]

Publications. Closely allied to adequate production of Christian literature by the younger churches is the development of first class resource material for younger church and missionary leaders. During and immediately after the war, the Council published *The Economic and Social Basis of the Church Series,* resulting from J. Merle Davis' studies. It also printed Searle Bates' *Data on the Distribution of the Missionary Enterprise* and Bishop Ronald O. Hall's *The Missionary Artist Looks at His Job.* In line with the Madras concern for the Christian home, the Foreign Missions Conference launched a project which resulted in *The Family and Its Christian Fulfilment,* a book which appeared in 1946 as part of the Council's *Studies in the World Mission of Christianity.* Other publications in this series included *The Christian Mission Among Rural People,* edited by A. T. Mosher, Ruth Ure's *The Highway of Print,* Davis' *New Buildings on Old Foundations,* and Searle Bates' *Religious Liberty: An Inquiry.*[105]

Plans for a Far Eastern Office. At Madras the National Christian Councils of China and Japan asked the Council to consider establishing an office in the Far East. Subsequently Warnshuis was asked to investigate the situation in Asia and make recommendations. War nipped the plan in the bud. Yet to help meet what underlay the original request, the Council appointed Dr. M. Searle Bates in China and Dr. Charles W. Iglehart in Japan as unofficial consultants to the Council.[106]

In 1945 the National Christian Councils of China and India adopted a proposal for an East Asia Regional Committee of the International Missionary Council, a body operating in accord with the Council's constitution and with Dr. Rajah B. Manikam of India as its correspondent. The proposal met with "warm approval" at Geneva.[107] Meanwhile, informal discussions had been carried on concerning a joint World Council of Churches-International Missionary Council Far Eastern office, but at Whitby in 1947 representatives of the East Asian countries concluded that the proposal needed further careful consideration. They suggested a Joint Commission to plan for an East Asia conference and to consider further the possibility of a Far Eastern office.[108] Such a group met for three days in Manila in February, 1948, with Bishop Stephen Neill representing the World Council of Chuches and Dr. John W. Decker representing the International Missionary Council.[109] It proposed a conference for East Asia late in 1949 and recommended that by January, 1950, the two international bodies jointly appoint a secretary for that area. His three-year term would be experimental, his duty *liaison* rather than administration. These proposals, review at Oegstgeest, resulted in the Eastern Asia Christian Conference at Bangkok in December, 1949,[110] and the appointment, effective in January, 1951,* by the two world organizations of Rajah B. Manikam, secretary of the Christian Council of India and Pakistan, as their "roving ambassador" in East Asia.

Religious Liberty. From the Council's inception religious liberty had been a paramount concern. Madras surveyed the rapidly spreading oppression which throttled all liberty in one country after another. When Searle Bates returned from China on furlough in 1941, Warnshuis urged him to delve into the problem. Bates began in the files of the Council's New York office. In May, 1942, the Foreign Missions Conference and the Federal Council of Churches organized a Joint Committee on Religious Liberty. Within a few months a similar group was organized in Britain by the Conference of British Missionary Societies and the British Council of Churches. In the United States, over a two-year period and with world-wide correspondence and critical analysis to broaden its thinking, the Joint Committee evolved an outline for an intensive study of the subject. In choosing a person to carry it through, the Committee turned to Bates. His report appeared in the spring of 1945 as *Religious Liberty: An Inquiry*, a comprehensive study which has become a standard reference work in the field. The Joint Committee's project had behind it the "unofficial cooperation" of the International Missionary Council, indeed, as it turned out, the Council published the book.[111]

---

* On the urgent request of the Christian Council of India and Pakistan, Manikam's assumption of duty as East Asia secretary was delayed until April 1, 1951.

Re-establishing Contacts

The Post-war Fund. By 1943 it was clear that war's end would bring overwhelming needs impossible to meet unless the Council had an emergency fund to draw on. The problem of raising extra money was especially trying, because of the Council's own rapidly rising expenses. Yet the officers agreed that demands in the immediate post-war period should be met with a Post-war Fund of $100,000. Most of it was contributed by British and North American boards. By 1948 the Fund totalled more than $130,000. It was used for the larger work of the Council, Whitby's expenses being the major charge against it.[112]

Travel. After war's long blackout the Post-war Fund facilitated wide-spread travel by the officers. They brought the global network of national organizations once again into first-hand touch with the Council. Decker had first gone to England in the summer of 1943 for orientation among the British missionary organizations and for post-war planning. Between October, 1944, and May, 1945, he visited Australia, New Zealand, Ceylon, India, and China to consult with the national councils regarding their future plans. In January and February, 1945, Norman Goodall went to Sweden to renew contacts there, and in July he travelled to France and Switzerland. We have already noted the remarkable spirit in which intercourse was resumed with Germany. Miss Gibson was the first staff person to meet with the German societies in November, 1945. Thereafter, contacts were frequent, usually with Goodall and Miss Gibson together representing the Council. Bishop Baker was one of four American churchmen who visited Japan in October, 1945, to help link Japanese Christians with the outside world. After Geneva early in 1946, Goodall visited Egypt, Palestine, and Lebanon. In midsummer he and Miss Gibson were present for the West Central Africa Regional Conference at Léopold-ville, Belgian Congo. The large number of post-war planning meetings between 1945 and 1947 kept the officers on a continual round of travel. Through the winter of 1947-48, Decker journeyed to China, Thailand, and the Philippines, while Goodall visited India, Ceylon, Burma, Malaya, Australia, and New Zealand. In Australia, Goodall participated in the Morpeth Conference on Christian work in the South

Pacific. Thus the officers through wide visitation helped restore the ties of direct contact broken by war.

Geneva. Twenty-five years after the International Missionary Council's founding at Lake Mohonk, its *Ad Interim* Committee convened at Geneva, Switzerland. For the national missionary agencies this four-day session in February, 1946, marked their first post-war meeting. Including officers, consultants, and representatives from the World Council of Churches (always properly "in process of formation" until August, 1948), there were forty persons present. Geneva's greatest fact was the renewal of contact after the war. It provided opportunity for all to survey the Council's war-time work and progress and enabled the National Christian Councils isolated by war to report on what had happened to them. Geneva also briefly examined the Council's immediate program and planned for its next world meeting. One of its most important functions was to further the cooperative relationships between the World Council of Churches and the International Missionary Council, but to this we must return later.[113]

The Departments

During the war and post-war years the Council accomplished some of its most timely and effective work through its special departments. The reader will recall that the departmental directors were not officially Council secretaries, but they were always accorded equal status. A sketch of their work will help round out our picture of the Council's activities.

Social and Economic Research and Counsel. At Madras, where it contributed greatly to that outstanding conference, the old Department of Social and Industrial Research became the Department of Social and Economic Research. Four months later Davis established its office in New York. At the same time, Miss Ruth Allcock, who had worked closely with Davis, retired.

Accepting the joint request presented by the Latin American delegations at Madras, Davis spent a total of eighteen months between 1940 and 1942 conducting surveys in Mexico, Cuba, Puerto Rico, Trinidad, Barbados, Jamaica, the Dominican Republic, Argentina, Uruguay, and Brazil. Except for a grant from the Carnegie Corpora-

tion for the Caribbean area studies, North American boards bore
almost the entire cost of the research. Six printed and two mimeographed studies resulted.[114] During 1943 Davis shared in a Commission to the Indians of the High Andes and undertook a comprehensive
study of the Aymara and Quechua tribes of Ecuador, Peru, and
Bolivia. The research led to the formation of the United Andean
Mission by several North American boards.[115] In addition to interpreting the Department's findings to North American boards, seminaries, and mission schools, Davis spent most of 1945 in preparing
New Buildings on Old Foundations, a distillation from the Department's work for a decade. This book may prove to be one of the
Council's most helpful contributions to the missionary enterprise. Davis'
suggestions for "stabilizing and rooting the Younger Churches in their
environment" are so thoroughly set forth in relation to every present
day factor that any missionary planning ignoring them does so to its
own disadvantage.[116]

Davis retired in 1946 after contributing immeasurably to the fundamental strategy of the Christian world mission.[117] One of his final
recommendations was for a study of African marriage customs, so
many of which stood as formidable obstacles to the integrity of African
Christian life. The project had been requested unanimously by the
African delegation at Madras. When the Reverend Charles W. Ranson
succeeded Davis, he asked the former secretary to explore the problem
further. Davis did so with highly fruitful results. By 1948 the Council's
African marriage study was just getting under way.[118]

Ranson had scarcely had time for several months of orientation
when he was asked to undertake preparation for the July, 1947,
Whitby meeting, just a year away. Because opposition to it had died
down, Whitby agreed to end the Department's long "unofficial"
status and to make study and research an integral part of the Council's
program. The new scheme would conserve and advance its work on
even broader terms through a research secretary who would be a
full member of the Council's staff. At the same time, functions of the
Research Group, under K. S. Latourette, were transferred to the new
Research Committee, appointed to guide the Council's research
policies. Professor Latourette became its chairman. A threefold plan
of study was envisaged: first, a survey of African marriage customs;
second, a study of the ministry in the younger churches; third, a
fundamental re-thinking of the missionary obligation of the church.[119]

Dr. Bengt Sundkler, who succeeded Ranson as research secretary, took up his duties in January, 1948, and spent his first months furthering the African marriage survey and preparing for a study on the ministry. He sought also to maintain full *liaison* with the Study Department of the World Council of Churches. To achieve closer collaboration with the World Dominion Movement, which was preparing a *World Christian Handbook*, the Council in 1948 appointed Mr. E. J. Bingle of that body, and formerly of Madras Christian College, joint secretary for survey with Sundkler.[120] When Dr. Sundkler resigned in 1949 to become professor of missions and church history at the University of Uppsala, he was succeeded by the Reverend Erik W. Nielsen of Denmark.

Christian Approach to the Jews. In 1939 Dr. Conrad Hoffmann was giving three months each year as director of the Council's Committee on the Christian Approach to the Jews. The remaining nine months he served the Presbyterian Board of National Missions in its Jewish work. When war came, Hoffmann's service to the YMCA's War Prisoners' Aid program limited his time for the Council's concerns to six weeks annually. With the disruption of the Committee's European section and the temporary inactivity of its American section, the director's responsibility was limited to convening small representative groups for consultation on Jewish evangelization. For some years Hoffmann had been aiding Germany's non-Aryan refugees, and after war's outbreak, he spent much of his available time in Britain and America encouraging local committees to care for refugees.

Before his death, Paton was instrumental in setting up in London the Christian Institute of Jewish Studies with Hans Kosmala and Lev Gillet as its directors. Kosmala had been director of the Delitzschianum in Leipzig and Vienna, and the new Institute carried on its work. There was good reason for the Institute's being in an English-speaking country. When Hitler came to power, the world's Jewish population totalled 16,000,000. By 1946 only 10,000,000 remained—more than half of them in the United States. In Jewish evangelization, English would play a much more important rôle than ever before.[121]

In October, 1946, Hoffmann resumed full-time directorship of the Committee. An enlarged meeting of the Committee took place in Basel in June, 1947, and its second post-war meeting assembled at Stockholm in September, 1948.[122] Largely attributable to the Committee's influence was Amsterdam's inclusion of a section on the evangelization of the Jews.[123]

Christian Literature for Africa. At Madras Miss Gibson presented the report of the International Committee on Christian Literature for Africa for its secretary, Margaret Wrong. At the same time Miss Wrong was beginning a six-month journey across Africa. On it she made a first-hand study of the requirements of African people for literature and counselled with those producing reading materials on how best to meet the tremendous needs.[124]

The war brought thousands of African soldiers under arms and increased the demand for literacy and for reading matter. Accordingly, the Committee distributed informative materials on teaching Africans to read and write. It also produced *The African Home Library* series—small, sixteen-page booklets selling for a penny—for use in English, French, Portuguese, and African languages. Despite the war-time paper shortage, more than one hundred titles had been published by 1947. The Committee also sought to provide more advanced reading and encouraged African Christian councils in the preparation of such materials. For three years the Committee's secretary gave part of her time to preparing scripts and recordings for the BBC for broadcasting in Africa. For several months during 1939-40 and 1942-43 she visited America to consult with mission boards. Everywhere, she sought to stimulate concern for Africa's burgeoning literature needs. Additional grants enabled the Committee to publish its little magazine *Listen* monthly instead of bi-monthly. The quarterly, *Books for Africa*, circulated widely in Africa and elsewhere.[125] During 1944-45 Miss Wrong shared in an important study of rural education and agriculture in West Africa sponsored by the International Missionary Council and financed by a grant from the General Education Board of the Rockefeller Foundation through the Phelps-Stokes Fund.[126]

At Whitby Miss Wrong asked for an additional staff member to help meet the increasingly heavy demands on the Committee. As a result, early in the winter of 1948 Miss Marjorie Stewart, for fifteen years with the YWCA in Jamaica, was appointed an assistant secretary. She was to continue, however, for a period with the Christian Council of Nigeria where she had been sent some months before to develop a literature bureau. Several months later in Uganda Margaret Wrong suddenly died. No successor could be found, but Mrs. U. H. S. Snow was placed in charge of the London office. When Oegstgeest met, the future plans of the Committee were not yet clear.[127]

The National Christian Councils

The Madras *Minutes* listed twenty-five constituent agencies in the International Missionary Council. The twenty-sixth, Korea's, was omitted. The National Christian Council in that country had been dissolved by the Japanese authorities in September, 1938, and the Council subsequently dropped it from all future membership lists to avoid embarrassing any Christian group in Korea. Reconstituted in 1946, the Korean Council reorganized, sought readmission to the International Missionary Council in 1947, and was accepted in 1948.[128]

Japan offered a similar, although not quite parallel, case. During the war what had been the National Christian Council went into eclipse, although the title was continued to designate the co-ordinating organ for Protestant and Roman Catholic affairs. The National Christian Council was reorganized after the war and was readmitted to the Council in 1948.[129]

Other Councils had been formed and entered the International Missionary Council's membership during this period. The River Plate Confederation (*Confederación de Iglesias Evangélicas del Rio de La Plata*) was admitted in 1939.[130] The Swiss Association of Missionary Societies, for some years the Council's constituent body in Switzerland, united with the Committee of Missionary Societies in Switzerland in 1944 to become the Swiss Evangelical Missionary Council and automatically became that country's new member agency.[131] The Association of Evangelical Churches of Puerto Rico and the National Christian Council of Ceylon became Council members in 1947.[132]

When the Committee of the International Missionary Council met just after the formation of the World Council of Churches in Amsterdam in September, 1948, it included in its membership thirty national or regional organizations. Sixteen were councils of churches and missions representing Brazil, Ceylon, China, the Congo, India, Japan, Korea, Latin America (Committee on Cooperation in Latin America), Malaya, Mexico, the Near East, the Netherlands Indies, the Philippines, Puerto Rico, River Plate Confederation (Argentina, Uruguay, and Paraguay), and Thailand. The fourteen national or regional missionary agencies included those of Australia, Belgium, Denmark, Finland, France, Germany, Great Britain, the Netherlands, New Zealand, North America (Canada and the United States), Norway, South Africa (although this council also represented some younger churches), Sweden, and Switzerland. Of the forty-five individual members on the Committee of the Council, twenty persons or approximately 45 per cent, represented the younger churches.

The International Missionary Council was also closely linked by correspondence and occasional representation with other non-member national councils. In Africa these included organizations in Angola, French Equatorial Africa, Ethiopia, the Gold Coast, Kenya, Madagascar, Nigeria, Northern Rhodesia, Nyasaland, Mozambique (Portuguese East Africa), Sierra Leone, Southern Rhodesia, and Tanganyika. Most of these councils were functioning when Madras met and by that time or within a few years had requested membership. Since almost all lacked full-time secretaries, the Council felt justified in waiting until some effective regional representation could be worked out for Africa to avoid unduly expanding the Committee of the Council. In Latin America Honduras, Chile, and Peru had councils, and in the Caribbean area Antigua, Barbados, Cuba, Jamaica, and Trinidad and Tobago had councils.[133] These were kept very closely in touch with the International Missionary Council.

The situation in 1948 was vastly different from that in 1910. Then there had been two national missionary councils. By 1948 what had been originally two national bodies were now more than twoscore—most of them National Christian Councils in the lands of the younger churches. Some of them, like those in Great Britain, North America, China, and India, exhibited great strength and could point to a long period of varied and successful accomplishment. They represented—this whole global network of national councils—a new era in the Christian world mission.

Whitby, 1947

When the *Ad Interim* Committee met at Geneva in February, 1946, it agreed that the Council should not convene in a world meeting before 1950. War's dislocations, it then appeared, made a great world gathering in the Madras tradition impracticable before that time. Yet within a matter of weeks the urgent necessity for a world conference for stock-taking and immediate planning became apparent. Circumstances dictated that the conference assemble no later than the summer of 1947. The time factor limited both preparation and size. Although it would be comparatively small, the conference had to be representative of Christian work around the globe. Thus came the decision in the late spring of 1946 for the enlarged meeting to be held in July, 1947, at Whitby, Ontario, Canada.

The Gathering

Whitby was the first real post-war reunion of the world-wide Protestant Christian fellowship. At Geneva in 1946, only three lands of the younger churches had been represented, but Whitby brought together 112 persons from forty countries. When originally planned, it had not been thought of as standing in the same succession as Edinburgh, Jerusalem, and Madras. Unlike Jerusalem and Madras, which had been meetings of the Council, Whitby was an enlarged meeting of the Committee of the Council.[134] Yet in retrospect Whitby's importance grew large. Its significance derived from its being the first occasion after World War II when Christians from around the world could assemble in a truly representative meeting. That fact plus Whitby's spirit and accomplishment accord it a place in the succession of "the great conferences."

Whitby constantly looked forward. It planned for the future. But it grew out of the war and the experiences of the churches during the war. In that sense Whitby must always be thought of with Madras. The virtually untouched 1938 findings were still relevant in 1947, and what emerged from Whitby was meant not to supplant but to supplement them in a changing world scene. Madras had faced imminent war. Whitby began nearly nine years later with war's grim harvest— symbolized vividly but inadequately in the bomb rubble heaped from England to the Pacific Islands.

The quiet little town of Whitby lies about thirty miles east of Toronto on the shores of Lake Ontario. There, on the campus of Ontario Ladies' College, the International Missionary Council met from July 5 to July 24, 1947. Edinburgh had provided stately dignity, Jerusalem a view of the Holy City from the Mount of Olives, and

Madras a glimpse of South India. Seemingly far removed from the revoluntionary forces churning the world, Whitby provided the pleasant and peaceful quiet of shade trees and green lawns, of a small college on the edge of a lakeside village. It was a perfect haven for those who came together from a world of strife and turmoil. The homes of some had long since become rubble in London and Stuttgart. In tropical Pacific concentration camps some had watched their own bodies waste away to mere flesh and bones. Others had endured torture in prison, and still others had seen relatives bayoneted and shot. These folk had lived through enough to know that Whitby's calm was only a brief respite from their world of revolution.

At Madras, as at Edinburgh in 1910, Mott was in the chair. Others who had shared in the World Missionary Conference were also prominent at Madras, including Bishop Azariah and Cheng Ching-yi. In 1938 these men were looked on as the elder statesmen of the missionary enterprise. Whitby marked the passing of their era. There Mott was the only member who had been present at every meeting of the International Missionary Council. He sat in the front row, no longer in the chair that traditionally had been his. People spoke of "the post-Mott era." Whitby's respected elders were those who had been to Jerusalem in 1928. A new age was dawning.

Whitby was smaller than its predecessors. Its size facilitated closer, more intimate, and richer group fellowship. Its findings were more nearly the result of conference-wide discussion than those of Madras which were largely produced by small sectional groups. On the other hand, some felt that the conference's real leadership fell more than was desirable on a small group from the older churches.[135] Jerusalem and Madras had both had long periods of preparation behind them. Whitby had only eleven months. It focussed on a few fundamental concerns of Christianity as a world faith without attempting to examine the whole range of missionary policy. In this respect, all agreed that Whitby had provided a "clearer definition of the central purpose of the church's mission to the world."[136] The few who expressed disappointment that Whitby gave no more attention to specific strategy than it did, failed to realize that it was not set up for that purpose.

Whitby claimed for itself an appropriate theme: "Christian Witness in a Revolutionary World." Its delegates faced a threefold task: first, to survey the effects of war upon the church; second, to re-discover the essential gospel and its relevance for a broken world; third, to call the church again to its central task—evangelism.[137] When the meeting ended, those who had shared in its rich experience knew that evangelism—Christian witness—was their prime responsibility in a world of revolution.

Whitby's Accomplishments

Survey of the War Years. During the first three days of Whitby's sessions one delegate after another presented a survey of war's impact on his homeland and on the church there. Only Japan among the International Missionary Council's world-wide constituency was represented by a missionary rather than by a national. A Japanese delegate had been expected, but at the last minute his coming proved impossible.[138] What a tale was unfolded as one heard from Japan, China, Korea, the Philippines, Indonesia, India, Burma, the Near East, Africa, the Slavic Lands, Latin America, the South Pacific, Continental Europe, and the Anglo-American world. Through years of war, destruction, isolation, pain, and untold suffering, Christians in every walk of life had made their faith known to others. Hour after hour for three days one lived the intensely real and personal drama being disclosed. Details differed, but each story was essentially the same— some defections, but in the main steadfast, unflinching Christian witness, and always the sustaining reality of a united, world-wide fellowship in Christ.

One who sat through those days lived an aeon. He could not but identify himself with this overwhelming and repeated experience of perseverance through suffering. In that process of identity one could feel growing a powerful bond of unity. Day by day it became stronger. This solidarity of yellow men and brown men, of black men and white men, of younger churches and older churches, of victor and vanquished, of those who had suffered and those who had been spared, *of Christians*—this unity was Whitby's hallmark.

Post-war Needs. Whitby also looked ahead to the new responsibilities before the Council. In this it directed attention to the continuing needs of orphaned missions. It elected Charles W. Ranson to the newly created post of general secretary. It dealt with the need for an Office in East Asia. It reviewed the status of those National

Christian Councils which sought admission and accepted those of Ceylon and Puerto Rico. It suggested a course for future research and incorporated the work of the former Department of Social and Economic Research into the Council's program with provision for a secretary for research. Indeed, the Committee reviewed all aspects of its work—points we have already surveyed in other contexts. Whitby also gave major attention to relationships with the World Council of Churches, a consideration reserved for the next section.

Finance. The Council budget approved at Madras amounted to $36,000. Through the war with rising costs and additional responsibilities, the budget mounted. At Geneva in 1946 it was set at $55,000. Whitby made clear the fact that further increasing costs, the office of the general secretary, and the inclusion within the Council of the former work of Social and Economic Research necessitated a still higher figure. There it was agreed that the budget should be set at $93,000 yearly. This represented an amount more than two and one-half times as large as that set in 1938. Yet it should be noted that, apart from the increase due to the general rise in costs, the Council's members were simply beginning to assume as their own expense services which previously had been donated to them. The research department, hitherto supported independently, now became one of the Council's regularly budgeted responsibilities. Some realized for the first time how much Mott's contribution had stretched the slight budget of an earlier decade.

Despite the tremendous additional burden this placed on the national agencies, they agreed with the Council's past policy that its work should be "generally maintained by the regular contributions of its constituent organizations." They recognized that the abnormality of the post-war situation justified an emergency appeal for help beyond the regular sources of income. In principle, however, the constituent councils would authorize and undertake only those projects which they believed justified their financial support.[139]

Supranationality. The reader will recall the attention given after World War I to "supranationality" by those concerned with international missionary co-operation. A similar concern emerged after World War II. No one suggested this time that missionaries be placed above national law or be given the status of international citizens. Yet from the German societies came insistence that the Christian community be declared supreme over all national loyalties. At Baarn shortly before Whitby the question was thoroughly canvassed. While the resulting statement clearly evidenced the country of its origin, Whitby adopted it as applicable for the entire missionary movement. "Christian discipleship," it pointed out, demands "responsibility for and solidarity with the world," but citizenship in a heavenly kingdom means that "we are no more able unreservedly to identify ourselves with our nation, its self-willed destiny and aspirations." Missionaries must give unequivocal witness to Christ as their primary loyalty, and responsibility to "the ecumenical church" must dominate, not merely influence, their lives.[140] Only long nurture in the Ecumenical Movement made such a statement possible.

Whitby's Significance

As we have seen, Whitby did not reproduce the massive agendas of Jerusalem and Madras. Its purview included the world and the totality of the Council's program, but its significance, like its emphasis, was concentrated. Whitby will probably be best remembered for three things: its determination to make evangelism the heart and core of the missionary movement; its revelation of a new equality, a new oneness, between older and younger churches; and its demonstration of the high unity of the Protestant world Christian community.

Evangelism. Daily in its sessions and in its final documents Whitby proclaimed its conviction that the whole church must be recalled to its primary task—evangelism. In a world broken by one war and threatened by another Whitby declared that under God the task was one of "Expectant Evangelism." This was no vapid offering but bold affirmation. It did not result from weighing the possible with the impossible. It sprang out of the entire group's living conviction—a conviction heightened daily by the evidence in the lives of its own members—that evangelism is the essence of the church's mission in the world. Indeed, one of the most remarkable demonstrations of this came in a previously unscheduled session when six representatives from the younger churches shared with the conference the stories of their conversions.[141] Moreover, the conference's major addresses, in the giving of which John Baillie, Bishop Stephen Neill, Henry P. Van Dusen, and John A. Mackay played so prominent a rôle, indicate the tremendous concentration on what the church must proclaim in a chaotic world and how it can best make its witness relevant.[142]

Whitby's spirit, although emerging from different circumstances, was akin to that of the early Student Volunteer Movement. Asserting that the church must be "reconverted in every generation," Whitby confronted the church with a global responsibility. Preaching to men, it was quick to point out, is not the same as converting them; but Whitby dared

to believe it possible that, before the present generation has passed away, the Gospel should be preached to almost all the inhabitants of the world in such a way as to make clear to them the issue of faith or disbelief in Jesus Christ. If this is possible, it is the task of the Church to see that it is done.[143]

Whitby emphasized the Lordship of Christ over all life. Likewise, it insisted, the real work of evangelism in the world must be done by laymen convinced that with the aid of the Holy Spirit such a task is one they can fulfill. It further asserted that the renewal of the church's life could only come by a return to the Bible's message and to the Lord of the Bible, with the local congregation the "dwelling place of the Holy Spirit, and the spearhead of evangelism." One dare not interpret this as retreat from the world, for Whitby saw that the church had to revive concern for and give leadership in the "true social revolution." Moreover, unless the church could make clear in its own life that

the Kingdom of God made real in Christ is far more satisfying than the kingdom of man devoutly believed in and proclaimed by the Communist— there is no hope that the Gospel will verify itself as the power of God unto salvation in the present age.[144]

Partnership in Obedience. For those present at Whitby two features more than any other stood out: first, the return of evangelism to unchallenged centrality in the Christian world mission; second, the complete oneness of spirit and purpose on the part of the younger and older churches.[145] Jerusalem was the first milepost on the road to equality of spirit and shared purpose between older and younger churches. Madras had marked further significant progress. Those who had shared in all three conferences agreed that Whitby's experience of total equality was without precedent. One Chinese delegate at Whitby was overheard to say, "At Jerusalem and Madras the relationship between older and younger churches was like that between a father and his children. Here it is like that between an older brother and a younger brother."

Whitby provided a dramatic demonstration of this unity of purpose and outlook. To examine the problems involved in partnership between older and younger churches, members of the two groups met separately. Except for preliminary agreement on agenda by their chairmen, the two groups did not consult each other. Yet, when the two series of recommendations were read before the assembled conference, they proved to be almost identical! The air was charged with expectancy, and in a moment the whole gathering had come to its feet, singing the Doxology. Later these two remarkably similar documents were combined and adopted by the conference under the title, "Partners in Obedience."[146]

Partners in obedience—in obedience to the will of God in the fulfillment of a common task. This understanding united older and younger churches at Whitby in an accepted mutuality. Madras had recognized the existence of a partnership and tried to strengthen it. Whitby acknowledged an achieved mutuality and moved forward with emphasis upon the common task. So great was this sense of oneness that Whitby referred to the terms "older and younger churches" as useful distinctions with obsolete connotations. Whitby built its declaration upon a solid foundation—a partnership in total (*i.e.*, intensive and extensive) evangelism and a partnership in every area of the churches' life—in personnel, in finance, in policy and administration. One of the most striking facts arising from this partnership was the urgent plea of the younger churches for large numbers of new missionaries. Moreover, they wanted missionaries who could serve not only as top-level specialists but also as recruits for the whole range of church life and work, for pioneering as well as for institutional posts. Whitby's emphasis centred upon missionaries as agents of the church universal whose responsibilities, like those of their national colleagues with whom they should be on a par, would be determined by their training and abilities.[147]

Unity. The most memorable impression of the whole event designated "Whitby" was its remarkable demonstration of Christian unity. It depicted in miniature the restoration of Christian world fellowship that had been broken physically during the war. Whitby was neither so representative as Madras had been, nor so large as Amsterdam was to be, but it was the first inclusive world Christian gathering after the war. Many of its members had not seen one another since Christmas-tide, 1938. A few had never before been to a world conference. Yet these folk had been praying for one another—whether by name or by position, it mattered not—through the dark years of war. Their coming together, then, inevitably engendered a spirit of oneness in Christ.

This unity was realized on the Sunday when the conference first met. That morning every one joined in a service of Holy Communion according to the Anglican rite. Archbishop Mowll of Sydney, Australia, who had spent years in China, was the celebrant. He was assisted by Bishop Robin Chen of China, the Reverend R. O. C. King, a West Indian Negro, and the Reverend Mahmood Rezavi, a first-generation Christian convert from Islam. Those to whom they ministered were drawn out of every race of mankind. The service symbolized the reality of the church universal. In the plain, sunlit school assembly-room which served the conference for all its sessions, one heart united with another in the high and holy joy of that hour. From that moment on the unity of the group was sealed.[148] Moreover, every aspect of Whitby's sessions deepened it—the focus on need for vigorously re-newed world evangelization, the common acceptance of partnership in obedience to God's will, and the rich variety of daily worship. Indeed, worship's highest moments occurred when the felt bond of unity—more real than the physical surroundings—was articulated in vibrant silence. No one who shared in the living of those days could believe other than that he had experienced in part the tomorrow toward which all Christians look. This was the unity which linked Whitby with Madras—in a very real sense made them one. This was the proof that the Madras bond of Christian world community had not been broken but had been forged stronger and deeper than ever before by the fires of war. This was the living experience out of which all else at Whitby became meaningful—possible.

RELATIONS WITH THE WORLD COUNCIL OF CHURCHES

The World Council of Churches was constituted at Amsterdam in 1948. There it determined to function "in association with" the Inter-national Missionary Council. The two were already sharing jointly in several enterprises, and many viewed the formal association as a further step along the road to eventual merger. For the background of this relationship we must return to 1938 and resume our story there.

Developments to the End of World War II

Madras. We have already seen that through Mott, Oldham, and Paton the International Missionary Council contributed immeasurably to the earlier movements which led to the formation of the Provisional Committee of the World Council of Churches. At Madras, on the assumption that it shared a common ecumenical task with the nascent World Council of Churches, the International Missionary Council took four steps. First, desiring mutually helpful relations, it authorized negotiations to attain this end, but it insisted that the Council's "separate organization, autonomy and independence" be maintained. Second, until the World Council's official formation, it recommended the appointment of a Joint Committee between the two bodies. Third, it accepted the World Council's Utrecht petition to assist and counsel with the new agency in its relations with younger churches. Finally, it agreed to the Provisional Committee's request that William Paton become one of its two general secretaries.[149]

On his way to Madras H. P. Van Dusen of Union Theological Seminary in New York travelled extensively in the Far East to see at first hand the missionary enterprise at work. On his journey he stirred interest in the newly forming World Council and enlisted some of the ablest among the younger church leaders for contributions to its studies. Madras also disclosed the keen desire among representatives from the younger churches for a world-wide study of common concerns. Thus Madras assisted the World Council's Provisional Committee in laying foundations for ecumenical representation hitherto lacking in the so-called "world meetings" of Life and Work and Faith and Order.[150]

Post-Madras. The second full meeting of the Provisional Committee at St. Germain, Paris, in late January, 1939, approved the Madras recommendations and proposed Mott for chairman and Paton for secretary of the Joint Committee. The International Missionary Council's *Ad Interim* Committee gratefully accepted these developments at Hemmen in July, 1939.[151] Toward the end of July a conference on the international situation met in Geneva. Called by the Provisional Committee, this group sought to do what it could to stem the drift toward war. Paton and Visser 't Hooft prepared the lines of discussion, and Paton chaired the gathering. After examining the causal factors precipitating war, the group faced the question of the church in war-time. The meeting probably did no more than indicate to its participants their relative helplessness to stay the course of events.[152] The World Conference of Christian Youth at Amsterdam ended on August 2, 1939, and within a few weeks World War II was a reality.

The War Years. Even after war's outbreak the World Council's Administrative Committee (the inner nucleus of the Provisional Committee) convened in January, 1940, a representative gathering near Apeldoorn, Holland. The meeting, in which Paton took an important part, wrestled with the World Council's responsibility in the midst of the international crisis. It could reach no common statement, and before negotiations could proceed through correspondence, war's fury made further conversation impossible.[153]

Meanwhile, in England Paton laid the foundations for a London office of the World Council. During the war he served as *liaison* agent between the World Council and the International Missionary Council and British Council of Churches. He helped to initiate work for refugees, internees, and prisoners of war and to set up what came to be known as the "Peace Aims Group." Paton also gave time and thought to the Joint Committee's difficult responsibility for proposing a yardstick to determine which of the younger churches should properly be invited for World Council membership. The criteria were not satisfactorily settled until after the war. When Paton died in 1943, Dr. A. C. Craig assumed responsibility for the World Council's London office. In November, 1945, he was succeeded by the Reverend Oliver S. Tomkins.[154]

From War's End to Amsterdam

Geneva, 1946. The Joint Committee of the World Council of Churches and the International Missionary Council, created in 1939, first met February 14 and 15, 1946, in Geneva. Norman Goodall, as Paton's successor in the International Missionary Council, became its secretary. From February 16 to 19 the International Missionary Council's *Ad Interim* Committee met in Geneva and from February 21 to 23 the World Council's Provisional Committee was in session there. Both sponsoring agencies had appointed five members to the Joint Committee, but Bishop Azariah's death left only the Reverend George Wu of China among the ten as a representative of the younger churches.

Among the consultants, however, Mexico, India, and China each had one member. In preparation for the meeting, Mott, the chairman, through wide correspondence had collected all possible information on the two to three hundred younger churches.

The Joint Committee proceeded on the conviction that the two parent councils needed to demonstrate as fully as possible their common origin, calling, and purpose. Some things they could do together, immediately. They could relate and co-ordinate their research work. The Council could co-operate in the World Council of Churches' youth program. To create a single international agency for church reconstruction in East and West seemed impossible, but unified presentation of a common task appeared wise. The Committee also urged its sponsoring agencies to set up a common department for international affairs with special responsibility for religious liberty. It encouraged further co-operation in publishing *International Christian Press and Information Service*, shortly to become *Ecumenical Press Service*. Finally, it suggested the possibility of a joint Far Eastern Office and recommended that each Council keep the other fully informed of its proposed conferences and meetings.

In addition to suggestions for immediate joint functioning, the Committee advanced other recommendations. It proposed its own continuation. It worked out some general criteria, including a definition of autonomy, for membership in the World Council applicable to older and younger churches alike.[155] It also established a basis for future relations between the two Councils, urging that they

make clear to all their identity of purpose and concern for the evangelization of the world . . . cooperate in every possible way, and . . . draw progressively closer together in all their undertakings for Christian fellowship, witness and service.

The Committee recognized the need for the missionary endeavour of the churches to have a "functional agency" like the International Missionary Council "with its wider basis of membership and its particular responsibilities." At the same time the enlarging work of the two councils and their common Christian interest and purpose would "require that they be increasingly united in vision, plan and sacrificial action." Consequently, while cognizant of the Madras stricture, the Committee dedicated itself to discovering what relationship would best insure "that the missionary enterprise [have] its functional agency within the framework of the World Council of Churches."[156]

The Churches Commission on International Affairs. Responding to a suggestion submitted to it from the Geneva consultations, the Commission on a Just and Durable Peace of the Federal Council of Churches of Christ in America agreed to arrange for a meeting of Christian leaders on problems of peace and war.[157] The conference, enlisting some sixty persons from fifteen countries, met at Cambridge in August, 1947, under the chairmanship of John Foster Dulles. Sponsored jointly by the World Council of Churches and the International Missionary Council, the gathering established a joint permanent Commission of the Churches on International Affairs to serve the churches as a means of common counsel and action on world affairs. J. H. Oldham was present. In safeguarding religious and missionary freedom during and after World War I, he had learned the value of informal personal contacts with policy-making government officials. The Cambridge Conference leaned toward a similar informal approach in its relations with the United Nations. The gathering was sober and reckoned honestly with the desperately difficult prospects in national and international affairs.[158]

With full encouragement from the two parent bodies, the Commission's chairman, Kenneth G. Grubb, and director, Dr. O. Frederick Nolde, opened offices in London and New York respectively. The Commission was formally constituted on January 1, 1947, and was registered with the United Nations Department of Public Information which entitled it to be represented by an observer at all open meetings of the United Nations. The Commission was granted consultative status with the Economic and Social Council and maintained contact with other agencies of the United Nations and with the International Labour Office. One of the Commission's most notable achievements was its rôle in making known the views of the churches toward and its influence on the United Nations' Declaration on Human Rights. It also brought to the attention of churches in different countries relevant problems in the solution of which they could take constructive steps— *e.g.*, religious and missionary freedom, refugees, human rights, and general problems involved in the peace settlements. In 1948 the Commission gave every indication of becoming an important arm of the Ecumenical Movement.[159]

The Issues. The question of eventually incorporating the International Missionary Council within the World Council arose early in the life of the Joint Committee of the World Council of Churches and of the International Missionary Council. Here were two world Christian councils which in the very nature of the case seemed to belong together. Why could they not be fused into a stronger, more effective whole? The question—so logical and obvious—demanded real consideration from those responsible for both bodies. In 1938 Madras had stipulated preservation of the International Missionary Council's "separate organization, autonomy and independence" no matter how cordial and close the working relationships might become between the two councils. This limitation probably resulted solely from cautious desire to avoid any sweeping and premature commitments to a world organization which at the time was no more than an untried proposal.

While the World Council of Churches was still technically "in process of formation" in 1945, it had functioned through the war and was daily proving its worth and growing importance. The two agencies were co-operating closely and in the summer of 1946 had jointly established the Commission of the Churches on International Affairs. In 1947 the Joint Committee noted with satisfaction that "consultation and exchange of representatives has become a part of the procedure of the two councils."[160] When the Joint Committee declared its intention to discover what relationship would best insure "that the missionary enterprise [have] its functional agency within the framework of the World Council of Churches," it was seriously questioning the implications of the Madras mandate. The question of incorporation seemed not to be "Why?" but rather "How best?" and "When?"

Several factors were basic to any consideration of the problem. First, the International Missionary Council was made up of interdenominational national or regional councils. It was a council of councils. The World Council of Churches included only denominational churches. It was a council of churches. Any thought of integration raised at once the organizational question of fundamental structural differences between the two councils. Moreover, between the World Council of Churches and its member denominations some intermediate agency of co-operation was required. Through such a body, either national or regional, the churches could achieve in concert those national aims with which the World Council could not be concerned. In the West the Federal Council of Churches and the British Council of Churches exemplified such agencies. Elsewhere the younger churches and missions had long functioned through National Christian Councils. While fully recognizing the necessity for national co-operative organizations, the World Council of Churches intended to remain a council of churches and not to become a council of councils.[161]

Meanwhile, the International Missionary Council's secretaries were aware of the then provisional constitution of the National Council of the Churches of Christ in the United States of America. Within that Council the Foreign Missions Conference of North America would be incorporated as the Division of Foreign Missions, one of four major divisions within the council. Some saw implications for a similar relationship between the International Missionary Council and the World Council of Churches.[162]

Second, within Protestantism, the International Missionary Council's constituency was more comprehensive than that of the World Council of Churches in three ways. (1) It included many "mission churches" which could not join the World Council because of its membership qualifications. (2) The International Missionary Council's constituent councils showed a wider range of denominational inclusiveness than the World Council had, a factor not to be considered lightly. For example, one group within the International Missionary Council's constituency in 1948 and not within the World Council was the fellowship of Southern Baptists in the United States. Southern Baptists numbered more than six million members as compared with slightly less than three million Anglicans in England or a total Anglican world communicant membership of nine million.[163] (3) The International Missionary Council included in the West councils of missionary societies, some of which societies were church-related and others independent. Elsewhere, as in India and China, its councils embraced a large number of churches. Moreover, the International Missionary Council's constituent councils included such non-church-related agencies as Bible and Christian Literature Societies and different organizations within the Student Movement.

Third, as a result of its genesis the World Council of Churches had a predominantly Western outlook and was more directly involved in affairs of churches in Europe, Protestant and Orthodox, than in those of Asia, Africa, and Latin America. On the other hand, the International Missionary Council had been oriented toward, and for years had been giving a major place to, the younger churches. Their traditional experience of world-relatedness was through the International Missionary Council, but they naturally and rightly wished to join with the older churches in the World Council. Yet even with their membership in the World Council it seemed almost inevitable that the younger churches for some years would be overshadowed by that body's concern with affairs of the older churches, a situation foreshown at Amsterdam.[164] The fact here pointed to was used two ways: first, as reason for the International Missionary Council's continuing separate existence to benefit the younger churches; second, as reason for its incorporation within the World Council to give that agency a fully balanced ecumenical concern.

Fourth, some consideration was given to the International Missionary Council as a "functional" agency. As a church-related missionary society represents part of the total work of a denomination, so the International Missionary Council assumed a departmental, divisional, or functional cast in relation to the larger work of all churches. The World Council supposedly represented the total life and concern of the churches while the International Missionary Council held responsibility for the churches' overseas missionary outreach. The view contained some truth, but the oversimplification could be pushed too far. In actuality the International Missionary Council was concerned with and represented the total life and work of the younger churches and thus tended to duplicate many of the World Council's interests.[165] As was also pointed out, the World Council of Churches while not, strictly speaking, ecclesiastical in nature was "more nearly ecclesiastical" than the International Missionary Council.[166]

Fifth, the International Missionary Council had been in process of formation from 1910 to 1921 and by the time Amsterdam convened had more than a quarter-century of organized life and work. The World Council of Churches had been in process of formation from 1938 to 1948. Natural reluctance on the part of the older, established council to merge itself with a new body not yet constituted proved another factor to reckon with. The general temper within the International Missionary Council seemed to be to see how the new council would finally be organized at Amsterdam before considering integration.[167]

From the standpoint of the International Missionary Council, these were the issues that had to be faced. None made integration impossible. In the minds of judicious administrators all indicated the wisdom of proceeding without haste.

Buck Hill Falls, 1947. The International Missionary Council's Committee on Program Structure and Staffing, meeting in January, 1947, judged the Madras mandate "too rigid" and needing modification. It also regarded as a "pre-judgment" the Joint Committee's aim to insure "that the missionary enterprise [have] its functional agency within the framework of the World Council of Churches." It sought modification or removal of both statements as well as a fresh approach to the whole problem based on the premise that the two bodies were "interdependent ecumenical councils" seeking "essentially common" ends.[168] These recommendations it submitted to the Joint Committee meeting at Buck Hill Falls, Pennsylvania, in April, 1947. Under Mott's chairmanship that group amended the proposals slightly and made them its own.

Referring to the relationship between the two councils as a "process of drawing progressively closer together," the Joint Committee recognized that distinctive functions and responsibilities required their continued autonomy "for the time being." Nevertheless, it judged mutual interdependence to be quite as important as autonomy. To further effective co-operation it suggested that both use the following titles:

The International Missionary Council
In Association with
The World Council of Churches
and
The World Council of Churches
In Association with
The International Missionary Council.[169]

The Joint Committee at Buck Hill Falls also approved in principle a World Council of Churches-International Missionary Council joint office in East Asia. It recommended continuing a joint consultative committee between the two councils. It also urged that the World Council explore ways in which the International Missionary Council's constituent councils could find a recognized place within the new body.[170]

Amsterdam, 1948. The International Missionary Council at Whitby approved these suggestions, and at Amsterdam the World Council of Churches accepted them.[171] The World Council, holding that relations with national or regional councils should proceed "slowly and carefully" referred the problem to its Central Committee.[172] That body suggested that the national councils among the younger churches be invited after proper consultation to serve in promoting the World Council's activities and that its general secretary negotiate these working relationships. The Committee of the International Missionary Council welcomed this arrangement.[173] Thus the two councils began working "in association with" one another. From the outset the World Council would utilize the regional co-operative agencies of the younger churches, the National Christian Councils. The whole pattern was one to encourage interdependence and progressively closer functioning.

OEGSTGEEST, 1948

Among non-Roman Christian churches in 1948 the formation of the World Council of Churches stood as their paramount organizational achievement. Immediately after Amsterdam, the Committee of the International Missionary Council met for three days at near-by Oegstgeest. With nearly one hundred persons present, the Committee reviewed the Council's work since Whitby the summer before, and with Amsterdam in mind offered what guidance it could for future action.

Most of the Oegstgeest actions have already been noted under different headings—Christian literature, constituent councils, orphaned missions (one of Oegstgeest's major concerns), international affairs, and research. Two matters with which Oegstgeest dealt have not yet been mentioned. First, it proposed that the Council's constitution be revised with provision for enlarging what in 1948 was the Committee to one hundred members and designating it the International Missionary Council. The Council would then appoint an Administrative Committee of thirty members. In effect, this would nullify the Jerusalem decision and restore the original structure of the Council as set up at Mohonk.[174] Second, it faced as it never had before the threat of communism to the younger churches. It encouraged educating Christians to the real nature of communism, suggested four ways for churches to strengthen their witness in areas of communist penetration, and specially emphasized the need to reach with the Christian message foreign students in Western universities.[175]

Oegstgeest was brief—a convenient postscript to Amsterdam. It marked the close of one era of the International Missionary Council's life and the beginning of a new one. In all this it provides a convenient ending for our historical sketch.

None of the four decades of international missionary co-operation had been so full as that one just reviewed. The period began in the last week of 1938, encompassed World War II, and ended with two great powers drawing dividing lines over the earth's surface. What lay ahead, no one knew, but mankind trembled before an ominous future.

During Christmastide in 1938 the Council brought together at Madras what was up to that time probably the most representative gathering ever convened. With war's threat an ever-present reality, Madras fashioned a powerful bond of world Christian community. That bond never failed, and war's fires served only to temper it. During and after the war the Council served an unparalleled effort by the churches to maintain throughout the world all orphaned Protestant missions. This achievement stood as an ecumenical triumph over war's divisive hatreds. In the midst of war the Council surmounted a major crisis in its own life. Losing its chairman and two secretaries within less than two years, it went on to advance the cause of religious liberty and to strengthen the life of the younger churches.

Whitby in 1947 brought joyous confirmation of the permanent and growing strength of the unity so vividly seen at Madras and gave a propulsive thrust to the Council's work in a threatening period. Madras and Whitby enfolded nine tragic years of world history. They symbolized an invisible but indestructible unity which bound Christians to one another. A year later at Amsterdam in the constituting of the World Council of Churches the inner logic of Edinburgh, 1910, was worked out. Within slightly less than four decades what in 1910 only a few had dared to dream was realized. The great confessions of Protestantism and representative Orthodox churches had come together in a permanent council. In its ecumenical meetings they shared a "foretaste of the unity of His People."[176]

One period had come to an end. Another was beginning. The years from 1910 to 1948 were both a preparation and an achievement. In that time the International Missionary Council in a fashion too pervasive and intangible ever adequately to be measured brought reality rather than expectation to the title of the World Council of Churches. The

International Missionary Council's special task was not finished, but, so far as could be foreseen, its work would be henceforth "in association with" the World Council of Churches. For the Christian world a new era had dawned in the summer of 1948. In it, proper fulfillment of the International Missionary Council's inner purpose required breadth of vision, large statesmanship, and conviction that purpose transcends organization.

CHAPTER VIII

‹‹‹‹‹‹‹‹‹‹‹‹‹‹‹‹‹‹‹‹‹‹‹‹‹‹‹‹‹‹‹‹‹››››››››››››››››››››››››››››››

Epilogue

We have reached the end of our survey. It began with the four contributing forces in the nineteenth century leading to the World Missionary Conference in 1910—the co-operative missionary conferences on the field; the six Anglo-American conferences that met between 1854 and 1900; the growth of missionary co-operation at the home base; and the emergence of the Student Christian Movement. In that conference at Edinburgh the most notable of the contemporary agencies of the Ecumenical Movement had their inception. Directly out of that unique gathering came the International Missionary Council whose growing outreach through four decades our story has charted. Moreover, we have seen how Edinburgh and the International Missionary Council not only prepared in unique fashion the ground for the World Council of Churches but also assumed seminal importance for the whole Ecumenical Movement. Indeed, for the non-Roman churches of the world, Edinburgh and the International Missionary Council provided nothing less than the foundations upon which the organizational expressions of the Ecumenical Movement in the twentieth century have built. Since recognition of the importance of that Movement in the history of Christianity is constantly growing, the significance of those ecumenical foundations becomes at once apparent.

Out of our account, then, what generalizations can we draw? What factors were noteworthy in the emergence of the Council? What crises did it face? What obstacles stood in its way, and what weaknesses did it display? Finally, what contributions of outstanding worth did it provide for world-wide Christianity? To these questions we must address ourselves in the pages that follow.

A *Little-known Organization*

It has been observed that in the early centuries of the Christian era Roman philosophers and statesmen failed to recognize the significance of the small but growing Christian church. Some, indeed, were wholly unaware that such a movement existed. Without assuming any direct comparison between the early church and the International Missionary Council, one can see a meaningful parallel. Few non-Christians in the mid-twentieth century know that within the Christian world the Ecumenical Movement exists. And for what is probably the majority of non-Roman Christians who worship each Sunday the Ecumenical Movement still has little real meaning.

To point out, then, that the International Missionary Council—as one expression of the Ecumenical Movement—is so little known should not seem strange. Yet a great many laymen are aware of the recently formed World Council of Churches. Probably there are few, if any, ministers and Orthodox priests who have not read of it. Nevertheless, very few Western clergymen can give an accurate answer to an inquiry concerning the International Missionary Council. They have read of its great mileposts—Edinburgh, Jerusalem, Madras, and Whitby—but are otherwise uninformed on its work. This ignorance is not so thoroughgoing in the lands of the younger churches. There one finds a livelier appreciation of the International Missionary Council's endeavors. An explanation for this, at first, curious difference should be fairly obvious. Among Western Christians genuine concern for the Christian world mission has been limited to a minority. This minority seldom has had occasion to deal with other than a particular missionary society. For example, what in 1948 was the Foreign Missions Conference of North America was almost unknown among missionary-minded pastors and laymen in the United States and Canada because it was a council of missionary societies—a technical organization concerned with a range of special problems usually of little interest to the parish contributor to missions. To go a step further from a national council to the International Missionary Council, one is twice removed from the presumed interest of the local parishioner. Moreover, except for its world meetings, the Council has not attempted to make its work known among the churches. Consequently, save for those working directly in the missionary enterprise, Western Christians know virtually nothing about the International Missionary Council.

The younger churches present a different picture. Through the years the Council's main concern has centred on their life and work. It has helped to bring into being most of their National Christian Councils. Since the younger churches as churches function co-operatively through these councils and since the latter are the International Missionary Council's member agencies, it is readily apparent why leaders among the younger churches have a wider knowledge of the Council than do their Western counterparts.

As a postscript to this consideration it may be instructive to indicate the reaction of many who for the first time see the International Missionary Council's headquarters in London or in New York. The very designation "International" may convey an impression of large organization and imposing headquarters. One who knows of the Council's great world meetings and global influence is likely, on his first encounter with its offices to be surprised by their modest size. In New York the Council's headquarters are on the eleventh floor of a missionary office building. Its office probably measures no more than fifty feet square—quite adequate for inner offices for four of the Council's officers, their stenographic assistants, and a book-keeper. The Council's four or five small rooms in Edinburgh House, London, are altogether unprepossessing.

The Council has never had a large staff or budget. Perhaps its size and relative obscurity are an indirect measure of its success, for the Council, concerned with the total Christian world mission, exists primarily for the missionary societies and the younger churches. Their creation, it finds its real life in and through them by linking them more and more closely to one another, by bringing them an ecumenical perspective, and by providing them with the outline of an over-all and unified missionary policy. The Council is largely a policy-suggesting and co-ordinating body. Such functions can scarcely capture the popular imagination, but they are of fundamental importance in the Christian world mission today. Perhaps this is enough to suggest why the International Missionary Council is so little known by so many Christians.

Informal Counsel

In a policy-suggesting organization such as the International Missionary Council stimulation, suggestions, and ideas spring readily from creative conversations. This drama of the interplay of minds and personalities, seldom revealed in the researcher's documents, often provides the real clew to developing aims and action. Here we can only hint at the rôle of such interchanges.

The Council's secretaries never worked in a vacuum. Through the years they kept always in closest touch with those—and their names are scattered through these pages—who bore great responsibility for the Christian missionary enterprise: in Britain such men as C. E. Wilson, J. H. Ritson, Wilson Cash, M. A. C. Warren, and A. M. Chirgwin and in the United States such men as Arthur J. Brown, Frank Mason North, Robert E. Speer, Ralph E. Diffendorfer, Fred F. Goodsell, and Charles T. Leber. Visitation and correspondence enabled the secretaries to share in a similar though less frequent way with leaders in other countries. With these men the Council's secretaries discussed their plans, revealed their hopes, and in turn found new suggestions and ideas. Indeed, one of the most transparent reasons for the remarkable confidence of the boards—large and small—in the Council was that its secretaries knew so intimately the minds of those responsible for determining missionary policy.

In addition to this regular day to day consultation, there were also opportunities for more effectively organized, although altogether informal and unofficial thought-provoking discussions. Several times during a year the secretaries might invite, for an evening or perhaps for two days, informal and over the years changing groups of missionary leaders to consider the problems confronting the Christian world mission. In this way a wide range of informal opinion and suggestion was covered. J. H. Oldham gathered such groups in Britain. On the other side of the Atlantic the North American Counsellors represented a similar development. In the United States an independent but closely related group, which sought to remain anonymous, was also meeting. Out of these small but creative gatherings came many of the ideas and programs that were later expanded and used to great advantage by the missionary enterprise.

The Meaning of the Hague Principle

In its 1913 meeting at The Hague the Edinburgh Continuation Committee established the basic principle for all contemporary missionary co-operation. It declared that the only bodies entitled to determine missionary policy are the churches and the missionary boards and societies representing the churches. This did not mean that the Continuation Committee and later the Council were not to formulate policy in keeping with their unique international and interdenominational vantage-point but that the determination to use, modify, or reject any suggested policy rested entirely with the denominational agencies. The Council could do only what its member bodies wanted it to do and were willing to have it do. From this standpoint, on paper the Council was, as Oldham so often remarked, "demonstrably unworkable." Yet in interpreting the mandate to do only what the boards wanted done, the secretaries kept always in mind that this limited them not to what the boards might want at any given moment but what the boards would come to want as a result of the Council's vision and inspiring leadership. It was a delicate balance to maintain. That the Council achieved so much was, in a sense, a miracle. It was equally a reflection of a deep concern for unity and of a will to co-operate among its different member-bodies.

The Hague principle grew directly out of Edinburgh, 1910. It was framed primarily in terms of missionary societies, but it extended to the churches. It called for strategic leadership whose only authority derived from the inherent wisdom and integrity of its suggested policy or program. Organizationally, the principle reveals the very genius of Protestant and Protestant-Orthodox co-operation. In slightly different guise it had been embodied twenty-five years before Edinburgh in the constitution of the *Ausschuss*. There it was indicated that recognition of the *Ausschuss*' authority by the German societies remained wholly voluntary. Edinburgh stated the principle positively and wrote it large for all to see.

The Continuation Committee with its full-time secretary was new, and the missionary societies through their national councils cautiously supported it. A decade passed before they actually agreed to create and finance an International Missionary Council, but in principle they had taken the step at Edinburgh. The Continuation Committee operated on this assumption and in the knowledge that it was not an independent body apart from the churches and societies but a creation of the mission boards themselves through which they intended to conduct a small part of their work together. It also recognized their determination to guard against rearing a super-board which could thwart their autonomy, and so the Hague principle, implicit from the start, was formulated. It guaranteed that within an organ of co-operation the convictions of each denomination would be respected—not compromised. In such an organization no church group needed to fear that any coalition could by majority vote act to overturn or abrogate its fundamental principles. It guaranteed that no great monolithic structure would arise and indicated the acceptance not of an imposed uniformity but of a unity respecting diversity. This was the foundation upon which the International Missionary Council so wisely and effectually built—the foundation it offered for all future ecumenical development.

Political Pressures and Christian Co-operation

A final observation grows out of our study. In the realm of the nation-states antagonistic pressures often produce defensive solidarity among the most diverse elements of a nation or among different nations. The results of such solidarity, whatever their appearance may suggest of inherent unity, usually disappear when the pressure has been removed. Yet when defensive solidarity is forced upon diverse elements in which the potential for genuine unity is high, the resulting manifestations are likely to become more or less permanent. This same pattern seems to have been reproduced in the case of organized missionary co-operation early in the twentieth century.

Political threats to religious and missionary freedom galvanized Protestant missionary societies into collective action which their denominationalism had retarded. For two reasons, however, the result was much more than a defensive alliance. First, these same societies had shown for some time concern that their essential Christian unity should have some outward and visible expression. Second, they had exhibited increasing desire to co-operate in the interests of larger Christian strategy to accomplish together what they could not do singly. But a third factor, the implied threat or actual use of political pressures antagonistic to the interests of the societies, proved to be the catalyst that at the time produced organized missionary co-operation. The phenomenon was most apparent from 1885 to 1925, but latterly the catalytic agent, though still present, has ceased to be a potent causal factor in co-operation.

The reader will recall many examples of this observation. In 1885 the German *Ausschuss*, prototype for all future agencies of missionary co-operation, was founded to give German societies an effective voice in dealing with the German Colonial Office. Similarly, political considerations were probably the decisive factor in creating the Committee of Reference and Counsel by the Foreign Missions Conference of North America in 1907. Likewise, the initial proposal in 1909 for an Edinburgh-sponsored "International Committee" resulted from the grievances of a German society against the British government. For a decade after Edinburgh, 1910, the most important component of the Conference of British Missionary Societies was its Committee on Missions and Government. Throughout World War I it became almost indistinguishable from the Edinburgh Continuation Committee and laboured unceasingly to safeguard the freedom of Christian missions and to preserve their very existence. During the International Missionary Council's first three or four years its secretaries observed privately that several of the large missionary bodies viewed the Council as nothing more than an agency for dealing with actual or potential government infringements on their rights.

Recognition by the missionary societies of need for a common agency to represent them effectively before governments influenced and hastened their co-operative association. In the history of Christian co-operation this factor must not be disregarded. Where there had been only potential unity, it hastened solidarity. But the already present unity provides the key for understanding the continuous strengthening of that solidarity when the political pressure was no longer a factor.

CRISIS

Among those who had known and been associated with the International Missionary Council from its founding there was virtually unanimous agreement that it had faced two major crises during its first four decades—World War I and the loss of its officers in the early 1940's.

International missionary co-operation as begun in 1910 involved four major groups—the British, the Americans, the Continentals, and the younger churches. It had scarcely begun to develop when World War I broke in 1914. Throughout the war cleavages between Germans and Anglo-Americans went deep and left embittered feelings. Lack of communication produced the most distorted kind of misunderstanding. Together, these helped to bring on the German repudiation of Mott as Continuation Committee chairman and fostered mutual incrimination. The latter threatened the young organization with a disaster that could have crushed it and greatly retarded the future growth of co-operation. Fortunately, a decisive rupture was averted, and that originally tender organ, toughened by the ordeal, laboured unceasingly to save German missions from total disaster. When one considers war's bitterness and post-war suspicion and disillusionment, what it achieved was astounding. Many affirmed that only God could have strengthened it to withstand the terrible hatred of the time. War might have broken it. In reality, World War I provided this seemingly frail implement of international missionary co-operation with the opportunity for which it was created.

World War II was another severe test, but when it came, the International Missionary Council had matured and grown strong. Christians would have been shocked had it not held fast. In Mott's words the Council had turned its "stumbling blocks into stepping stones." In successfully meeting the crises presented by the two wars, the International Missionary Council offered the Christian world community one of its most magnificent achievements—the preservation of Germany's Protestant missions from total destruction and the maintenance of other Continental missions which war would have withered. Indeed, it is interesting to note during how much of its course the Council was directly occupied with the problems of German missions: from 1914 through World War I and until 1930 when the last of the German mission properties were returned; during 1934-35 when, with Hitler's rise, German societies could scarcely transmit money overseas; and from 1939 on into an unseen future. It was a proper burden that the Christian community carried for a people who had sent the first Evangelical pioneers to India nearly a century before Carey, who had made major contributions to the Protestant world in the theory, history, and science of missions, and who had given so much to the growth of co-operation.

The second great crisis came in the early 1940's. Then, after Oldham's resignation at the end of 1938, retirement took Mott and Warnshuis and death took Paton from the Council. From one point of view these men *were* the International Missionary Council. Their removal. from active service within a matter of months plunged it into a slough of insecurity. The Council was, indeed, built upon the National Christian Councils in many lands, but its leadership and functioning had revolved largely around these four unusual men. If it were objected that the Council depended wholly upon a few men for its accomplishment, the charge would have to be accepted. This was both a strength and a weakness. The Council's main concern was not vast administration but statesmanship, and that can never be advanced by mere ongoing machinery. Statesmanship always depends upon men. For the Council's officers replacements were impossible, and untried successors could not pick up where these giants had left off. In the adjustment period during which their successors endeavoured to obtain a firm grip on the Council's reins, there was naturally much uncertainty among those intimately associated with the Council, especially since this upheaval came in the midst of World War II. By 1948, however, there were clear indications that the Council was functioning efficiently and that its new secretariat promised much for the future.

OBSTACLES

Difficulties Inherent in International Co-operation

As with all similar organizations, the Council was hampered by those weaknesses that inhered in its very nature—in its purpose and organization. Among these were ignorance, provincialism, ecclesiastical differences, and the vast physical distances separating its constituent bodies. The Council was established not only to do ecumenically what was otherwise impossible, but also to foster a world-view and to encourage every element of the missionary enterprise to see its own task in terms of and related to a total global strategy. The human mind focusses so intently upon the immediate that its usual orientation acts as a tremendous drag on any movement dedicated to large purpose. Doctrinal differences and the strength of parochial and denominational loyalties offered another difficulty. The will to co-operate was strong, but the necessity for patient accommodation of very different points of view sometimes set up centrifugal forces within the Council. A further block in the way of integrating thought and action was sheer ignorance. The further the Council went, the more apparent wide-spread ignorance became—ignorance of one another, of one another's problems, and of the many facts upon which broad policy had to be founded. All these were aggravated by one of the Council's greatest handicaps—the inability to sustain really close and living contact with and among its entire membership throughout the world. Like mission boards, National Christian Councils have to concentrate upon their own particular duties. Yet without benefit of constant *liaison*, consultation, and conference, they may, to the detriment of the larger mission, fail to see beyond their national responsibilities. The small size of the Council's staff, and that staff limited by the time and resources at its disposal, added to the problem. It is clear, however, that most of these considerations arose so largely from the character of human nature that to whatever extent they may have been overcome or favourably modified, the Council may be attributed with having worked a leavening influence. There is little reason to doubt that these problems affecting international missionary co-operation—continue as they will—were noticeably diminished in 1948 from what they had been in 1910.

Anglo-American Predominance

We noted earlier that approximately seven-eighths of Protestant Christianity's missionary resources in personnel and finance have come from Anglo-American churches. Inevitably the International Missionary Council reflected that situation in its home base constituency and in the case of its younger church members. This fact largely explained Anglo-American predominance in the Council. With one brief exception, the Council's secretariat was until 1947 British and American. In the minds of many Mott, the chairman, symbolized the Council. Although an American, he was esteemed for his ability to appreciate a Continental point of view. Oldham and Miss Gibson had a remarkable grasp of the problems and attitudes of Continental missionary societies. Warnshuis was similarly oriented. Yet there was occasional feeling on this point that the Council was too much one-sided.

In the twenties Oldham indicated his wish that within the Council English should not be the only medium of intercourse. Although in Council meetings everyone was urged to speak in his mother-tongue, and despite the fact that much use was made of this privilege, the language barrier remained. Continental delegates sometimes had to say in conference or debate what they were able to say rather than what they really meant and wanted to say. They felt themselves inadequate in their inability to speak readily and fluently in English. The same factor obtained for many from younger churches, but because of their Anglo-American tutelage and their use of English as a common language among themselves, they were somewhat less hampered than those from the Continent. Moreover, their common language and cultural background made it relatively easy for the British and Americans to assemble around a committee table and reach a decision with much of the argument taken for granted. With Council secretaries in London and New York, often the only practical recourse was what appeared to be Anglo-American bilateral action submitted to and dependent upon Continental and younger church judgement.

This Anglo-American predominance came in for some critical comment, particularly among those Continental missionary leaders who had not had opportunity to share directly in the Council's meetings. Yet, so far as the writer has been able to discover, Continentals who had participated closely and actively in the Council expressed keen gratitude for its fairness toward Continental interests and problems. They recognized Anglo-American predominance, but acknowledged finding no conscious attempt at domination. Even before, but especially after Jerusalem there was manifest strong desire for a Continental secretary to represent within the secretariat a particular background and contribution.[1] Iserland's appointment in the then Department of Social and Industrial Research undoubtedly helped to fill this need. Yet that no more vigorous agitation for a Continental secretary arose after Iserland's early resignation may indicate in part the extent to which Continental societies trusted the impartiality and understanding of the Council's officers.

One other consideration—a theological difference—was involved in the Anglo-American preponderance. Continental theology had emphasized the return of Christ in a way Anglo-American theology had not. Indeed, much of the impetus for Continental missions sprang from that particular eschatological outlook which stressed man's life as one lived "between the times" of Christ's first appearance and his imminent return in judgement. Through the years the Council's Continental members defended their position as a matter of conviction and to supplement what they held to be inadequate Anglo-American theology. At Jerusalem, Madras, and Whitby they advanced their views with vigour. Jerusalem left some dissatisfaction. At Madras a minority report resulted. Beneath much of Whitby's debate there was a conceded difference of opinion on eschatology. The particular Continental understanding that was advanced was not congenial to most Anglo-American thought, which, it should be added, in no sense omitted the idea of God's final judgement. The point at issue was heard, sometimes was debated, but usually was kept in the background as a discordant and irreconcilable element. At the end of the period of our survey, at least one British missionary secretary was seeking to grapple with the implications of the so-called "Continental eschatology" for the missionary movement.[2] In this continuing debate and its implications for some areas of missionary policy there were indications that those from the Continent regarded themselves as the Council's loyal opposition.[3]

Financial Limitations

From its inception the International Missionary Council rooted itself in the missionary boards. Actively concerned with their needs, it concentrated on a limited number of central problems affecting the entire missionary enterprise and left peripheral issues for others. In effect, the Council earned its way by demonstrating to the societies that it was truly *their* agency and filled an indispensable place in their life. Each year to governing committees, board secretaries on the Continent, in Britain, and in America had to justify their society's contributing a certain amount of money through national agencies to the International Missionary Council instead of sending it to the field. The Council's central budget was small—proportionately even less than the limited budgets of most missionary societies—and had no outside donors. In principle every national organization bore financial responsibility for the Council, but in reality the missionary societies of Britain and America carried the heavy weight of its budget. Its secretaries assumed that if the Council proved its worth, the boards would support it—a powerful factor in keeping the Council and the boards close to one another and in preventing any tangential excursion by the Council.[4]

The Council's central budget, as we have noted, was no more than that of many American churches, and the secretaries constantly felt its pinch. Yet the Council often encountered resistance to requests for enlarged apportionments.[5] Relevant to this situation was Oldham's early insight that practical co-operation had to be conceived "in terms of larger and smaller concentric circles." Not all boards wished to share in every Council activity. Hence he came to think of the Council as a means for enabling (a) participating boards to counsel and act together on matters of universal concern, *e.g.*, governmental encroachment on religious liberty, and (b) a larger or smaller proportion of the boards to take common action in particular interests, *e.g.*, a survey of higher education in China.[6] In most of the projects belonging to the latter category the Council served as a common meeting ground, but expected the boards, individual persons, and foundations to finance the activities. In somewhat similar fashion the Research Department, the Committee on the Christian Approach to the Jews, and the Committee on Christian Literature for Africa grew up as sub-committees of the Council with separate budgets. Moreover, each of the world conferences—if they were to be representative—required large sums of money for travel and other expenses. They did not simply happen. For them the secretaries raised as much as they could from the boards and societies, and Mott got the rest.

Mott's money-raising ability loomed large. Some boards were willing to accede to certain projects (*e.g.*, the Scandinavian societies to the Department for Social and Industrial Research) only if they were supported outside the central budget. Under the circumstances, Mott and the secretaries found independent resources for launching these projects. Some day, they expected, these would commend themselves as necessary and integral parts of the Council's program. Mott's personal contribution in time and money and through his world journeys and regional conferences endowed the International Missionary Council with an influential outreach without which it simply would not have been the Council as it was known. Inevitably, Mott's unique position of leadership, his freedom from the Council's limiting financial resources, and his bold initiative left him open to the occasional charge that he managed "to have his own way." It was equally true that America's position as the predominant contributor to the Council's central budget was sometimes a matter of comment and criticism, but not of contention.[7] The power of the purse is tremendous. Its dedicated use is a priceless gift.

A related problem was the financing of the National Christian Councils. The Council had always been keenly alive to the need for encouraging self-support among younger churches. Yet it—with the Foreign Missions Conference and the Conference of British Missionary Societies—appeared to have aided and abetted the development of National Christian Councils of such size, program, and budget that some of them quite outstretched the supporting ability of their member churches. Two of the largest National Christian Councils, those in China and India, depended heavily upon American and British subsidies for their yearly budgets. Undoubtedly these councils served the Christian world mission magnificently—in some cases indispensably. Yet as some of them had developed, they were subject to grave weaknesses. Financed largely from abroad, they faced the constant temptation to function with something less than constant reference to their member missions and churches. Their churches in many cases could not adequately support the National Christian Council's program and hence often lost their sense of relatedness to or responsibility for the council. The implications were sobering. Nor was it healthy to maintain those conditions which encouraged local leaders to look constantly away from their normal and rightful supporting bodies to Britain and America. This whole problem of support was one of the thorniest faced by the missionary movement. It admitted no ready solution.

Knowledge without Action

Among the major obstacles confronting the International Missionary Council, "the great one," according to Mott, was the failure to take the step between recognizing, understanding, and knowing a duty and doing it.[8] In part this failure to move beyond knowing to doing resulted from some of the obstacles listed above. It also seemed to indicate lack of vision as well as excessive self-concern in maintaining old and familiar patterns. Oldham's considerable studies on Christian education in the twenties seemed to have had relatively slight effect in missionary planning and thinking. The same was true of Kenyon L. Butterfield's work which underscored the great need for Christian missions to take into account the predominant rural population of the world. Much of J. Merle Davis' extensive research, while fortunately in permanent form, appeared to have counted for little in policy guidance for missionary societies. It was, of course, too soon in 1948 to know how his studies might ultimately serve the Christian world mission.[9]

ACHIEVEMENTS

We have observed in this concluding chapter some of the notable factors attending the International Missionary Council's development. Perhaps its paramount contribution to ecumenical organization was its operating basis as formulated in the Hague principle. Its first crisis provided the initial setting for another of its greatest achievements—the preservation of German missions through two World Wars. Even in meeting some of its weaknesses the Council found strength, in the process of which it gained wisdom worthy of note by other organs of Christian co-operation. In addition to these, there were other contributions along five main lines.

The World-wide Fellowship

Heir to more than a century of Protestant missionary endeavour, the International Missionary Council within three decades brought into being a world-wide Christian fellowship. It was a fellowship comprehending widely different elements in every part of the globe. It was a world community of people who knew and who tried to understand and help one another. It grew from the warm friendships that resulted when these folk assembled together to plan their common action within the Christian world mission. In such gatherings they shared thoughts and experiences. They came to appreciate convictions and problems underlying points of view quite different from their own. They shared in the worship—made rich by the contributions of other races and cultures—of denominations not their own. They saw their horizons expanding and their Christian loyalties growing. They recognized, at least in part, their meaning for and their place in the church universal. Moreover, they invested the word "ecumenical"—so often carelessly equated in the West with "interdenominational"—with its fuller meaning. In 1948 the fellowship was still relatively small, but its influence was permeating the life of the churches. The International Missionary Council's "commonwealth" was loosely knit, indeed, in organization. It was closely knit in community.

The fellowship also brought new vigour and integration to the whole non-Roman Christian world. It was a means for bringing into the life of Western Christians the breath of first-century Christianity constantly moving through the younger churches. For the older churches this meant refreshment and invigoration. They were also forced repeatedly to consider for themselves the urgent and deep concern for Christian unity and church union so real among the younger churches. In all this the Council was the conducting nerve for vigorous stimuli to renewal of life, to obligation for world evangelism, and to new concern for Christian unity—all of which, it showed, were inseparable elements of the Lordship of Christ over all life. This cross-fertilization and strengthening of mingled strains was seen in still another area. The Council provided a forum where Continental theology enriched Anglo-American Christianity whose social concern also penetrated Continental thinking. In this particular dialogue Life and Work and Faith and Order no doubt assumed a larger rôle. But into the conversation and to the greater benefit of all, the Council was able to bring a third effective participant—the younger churches.

Part of the cohesiveness of this world fellowship resulted from its conception of itself. Edinburgh had focussed exclusively on the non-Christian world, and the Council began with the assumption of a Christian home base and a non-Christian field of endeavour overseas. Yet from within these two geographical spheres another reality was seen emerging—a world Christian community. Then at Jerusalem Rufus Jones distinguished secularism as the real religion of "the non-Christian world," thus virtually stripping the phrase of its former geographic covering. This insight into the significance and universality of secularism undoubtedly would have emerged had there been no International Missionary Council, but it probably came "with special force to minds accustomed to think in terms of the non-Christian world."[10] The realization had two immediate effects. It quickened the churches—older and younger—to the totality of their evangelistic task. It also helped to free the world community of Protestant Christianity from the stultifying notion of "Christendom" and to see itself rather as a dynamic minority movement—global and with growing unity and solidarity, indeed—but a minority movement in the world.

In the fashioning of his world fellowship one factor more than any other was pointed to by those within it as responsible for its unity and achievement. This was prayer—for the most part intercessory prayer, but also prayer of thanksgiving and penitence. It was a constant factor in every pre-1910 conference, and it was notable in every conference after 1910. Every meeting, every undertaking, was preceded by prayer. For months in advance and on every continent the world gatherings enlisted intercession. Every set of minutes discloses how each conference and meeting placed central emphasis upon prayer and worship. These were a unifying influence. Confronting tasks of almost incompassable magnitude, those who came together in prayer were forced again and again to confess their dependence upon God and their essential unity in discipleship. It was this oneness, this solidarity in world Christian community, which made possible and gave meaning to all else that the International Missionary Council did.

Advance Among Younger Churches

However it might have been phrased, the Council's real purpose was to quicken the whole church to its world-wide evangelistic responsibilities and to help the younger churches become strong members of the Body of Christ. Although neither task was likely ever to be completed, in the latter notable advance was made. The Council had created within the scattered and numerically weak younger churches an awareness of their privilege, responsibility, and oneness within the world Christian community. It provided their leaders with an ecumenical schooling whose results might not be realized for a century. In the life of the church it gave them a voice they would have lacked otherwise. The Council was the one agency steadily directing the older churches' attention to the younger churches' problems. It also provided the older churches with a means for offering their wisdom and assistance when it was desired. Yet as we have repeatedly seen, the flow of benefit had not been all one way. One of the most noteworthy contributions of the younger churches came from some of their best-known men and women. A truly great spirit cannot be meant for only one branch—denominational or geographical—of the Christian family. Such men and women, so Christians believe, are God's gift to the Christian community. And in the gift of lives to the whole church the younger bodies have shared their treasure magnificently.

The Council aided the younger churches in three other ways. Through its first chairman it helped to establish a world network of National Christian Councils. These earlier encouraged comity and latterly have served as the national interdenominational organs of the younger churches. Useful as they are, they have not been without their weaknesses, nor have they always been able to overcome real denominational separation as, for example, in Korea. The Council also kept prominently in its discussion the independence of the younger churches, and its constant attention to the problems of devolution was not without effect. Finally, the Council helped to bring into the life of the younger churches conviction of the integral relation between gospel and church and recognition that apart from the church the gospel cannot long exist. This was notably the result of Madras. It was strengthened through World War II and was seen anew at Whitby. The ultimate significance of this last consideration is incalculable.[11]

Large Strategy

That the designation "large strategy" as here used is wholly free of authoritarian overtones should be apparent from all that has gone before. Essential to the Council's life, to its "authority without authority," was the conviction that it could attempt nothing until it had a mandate from its constituents. Yet within forty years the Council brought remarkable integration into Protestant planning for the Christian world mission. One of its broadest and most remarkable demonstrations of this was the development of the Orphaned Missions' program during World War II. Through the International Missionary Council and more particularly through its regional constituent councils Protestant missionary societies and younger churches were developing a wholly new spirit of co-operation and were integrating their work and plans to an extent that would have been regarded as impossible at the turn of the century. The practical outcome of this was greater effectiveness and economy. The spiritual fruit was a heightened will to co-operate, broadened understanding, and increasing unity.

From the beginning the Council's face had been set steadily toward the problem of Christian evangelistic obligation and objective. This singleness of purpose forced the Council to centre steadily upon the Christian gospel and provided it with expansive as well as unifying power. Moreover, since the Council had been originally the creation of missionary societies rather than of churches, it was not so bound by a complex of denominational restrictions that might otherwise have hindered it. This left it somewhat freer to experiment and pioneer.

Full evidence of this larger strategy would repeat our earlier story. One or two indications may suffice for our purpose. Orphaned missions has already been mentioned. Another example was the Committee on the Christian Approach to the Jews. Through it the Council sought not only to link those societies concerned with Jewish evangelization, but to bring before all its constituent bodies the fact that the winning of the Jews to Christ is a common concern of the whole Christian enterprise. A further indication was its encouragement of joint endeavour among the boards. Outstanding results here would include the Women's Christian College in Madras, the United Missions in the Copper Belt in Northern Rhodesia, and the United Andean Indian Mission. These only hint at the Council's efforts to encourage large thinking and large planning. Among these endeavours recognition must also be given to *The International Review of Missions*. Year after year that journal served as a forum for the most scholarly and advanced thinking in the missionary enterprise and contributed immeasurably to a more unified strategy.

The Imponderables

So much of what the International Missionary Council accomplished lay in a realm which defies accurate measurement or assessment. Thus what are probably some of its most far-reaching contributions can only be intimated. The Council provided a meeting ground for minds wrestling with problems of world Christianity. This process of ecumenical conversation and friendship meant stimulation and enlargement of mind and purpose for many. It enabled secretaries and younger church leaders to see their particular tasks as integral to a global program.

Such vision generates daring and encourages unity. Who can know what unrecorded creative ideas sprang from out of the Council's many international sessions? From encounter with the pages of its journal? Who can determine what new movements of power, what new Christian enterprises, what new insights into the meaning of the Christian gospel were born in the Council's sessions?

One may ask again what impact the Council, conceived in its largest terms, may have had on a communion, on a country, or on the whole church as a result of its influence on one man, whether Indian, American, Chinese, English, Mexican, or South African. Take the case of one Englishman, William Temple, who gained his first large vision of the problems of world Christianity at Edinburgh in 1910. From that time forward his mind encompassed the church in its totality. He drafted the Council's Jerusalem message and there on the Mount of Olives saw an embodiment of the world Christian community. He served the Council several years as a vice-chairman and maintained a steadfast interest in it—and through it in the whole world mission. Is it too much to suggest that in the background of his now famous and oft-quoted Enthronement Sermon were his Edinburgh and Jerusalem experiences? The "world-fellowship," the Ecumenical Movement, "the great new fact of our era"—all this, he declared, had sprung from the recent missionary enterprise of the church. He saw it as the "one great ground of hope" for the future.[12] What did it mean for the Anglican Communion to have one of its greatest primates stress its responsibility to and for the Christian world mission? What did it mean for the Ecumenical Movement that one of its ablest leaders had had at least part of his Christian nurture within the orbit of world missionary co-operation? No precise answers to these questions can be given, but the very asking indicates much. Temple, indeed, provides an unusual example, but the list can be lengthened. In the realm of the imponderable, where one can suggest but not calculate, the Council and its fellowship had set in motion influences of large potential.

The World Council of Churches

That the roots of the World Council of Churches stretch back to Edinburgh, 1910, is everywhere acknowledged. That this newest and most striking embodiment of the Ecumenical Movement also owes much to the International Missionary Council has not been so widely recognized. Throughout our survey we have sought to indicate this contributory relationship. A few have declared enthusiastically that the World Council of Churches owes its being to the International Missionary Council. However one may choose to interpret that statement, there is adequate historical justification for suggesting that without the International Missionary Council, there could have been no World Council of Churches as it was known in 1948.

In laying the ecumenical foundations upon which the World Council of Churches was built, Edinburgh, 1910, and the International Missionary Council assumed pre-eminent importance. In its impact on the lives of five men—Brent, Mott, Oldham, Paton, and Temple—Edinburgh's significance for the World Council is at once etched sharply. Moreover, in winning the participation of the High Church or Catholic wing of the Anglican Communion, Edinburgh marked a decisive turning-point in the twentieth-century development of the Ecumenical Movement. Had the Anglo-Catholics remained aloof, their position would undoubtedly have affected the subsequent attitude of the Orthodox, Old Catholic, and Eastern Churches and would also have had a "cooling effect in other quarters."[13] On the other hand, Edinburgh's importance for Söderblom and Life and Work was rather more indirect than has sometimes been implied. What developed from Edinburgh influenced his thinking in two ways. First, with the emergence of Faith and Order in the West and with the International Missionary Council directing its attention to the life of the younger churches, Söderblom saw a gap that needed to be filled in the ecumenical development of the older churches.[14] Second, he saw in the International Missionary Council an effective precedent for associating the churches in common action without first arriving at complete theological unanimity.[15] Both these factors hastened the birth of the Universal Christian Council for Life and Work.

Faith and Order as a direct consequence of Edinburgh needs no further recital here, although we should note that the International Missionary Council's influence on that Movement was relatively slight. Such was not the case in its relation to Life and Work. Through Oldham, the International Missionary Council's Jerusalem encounter with secularism placed its stamp directly on the Oxford Conference of 1937. A year later at Utrecht Mott, Oldham, Warnshuis, and Paton were present when the World Council of Churches' first provisional constitution was drafted. They had a wealth of wisdom and practical experience accruing from nearly thirty years of international missionary co-operation to contribute. They had found answers to a wide range of technical problems that the World Council would face. They spoke for an international and interdenominational council which within three decades had vindicated itself and had won the esteem and respect of leading churchmen. These four officers provided the World Council's architects with a precedent and an example of proven worth and accomplishment.

The World Council of Churches was heir to more than the International Missionary Council's experience. A large part of the foundation on which the newer Council built was that world Christian fellowship in which the younger churches were steadily advancing. This was the International Missionary Council's incomparable gift to it. Through four decades the International Missionary Council had built solid ecumenical foundations. It had welded together in common cause Protestant Christians in every land. It had brought forth from the younger churches an ecumenically trained leadership. It was to these that the World Council of Churches, when it was constituted in the summer of 1948, owed the full meaning of its title.

Here our account must end. The International Missionary Council continues, but for the present we can trace its course no further. We have covered nearly a century of growing ecumenical experience, beginning with the rise of missionary co-operation in the mid-nineteenth century and ending in the mid-twentieth with the establishment of the World Council of Churches in association with the International Missionary Council. To the writer it is a remarkable story whose ultimate meaning lies beyond history. If as a final consideration one were to ask, "How important was this growth of international missionary co-operation?" another question would be required in answer. "Can one imagine the state of the non-Roman Christian world in the mid-twentieth century if Edinburgh, 1910, and all that followed from it had never occurred?" The thought is staggering. Perhaps only in such reflection can one discover its real significance.

© Lafayette, Ltd., 1932

J. H. Oldham

ca. 1940

A. L. Warnshuis

ca. 1935

John R. Mott

ca. 1922

Betty D. Gibson

ca. 1940

William Paton

© Bachrach, 1948

Charles W. Ranson

© Clearose Studio, 1951

John A. Mackay

© Conway Studios, Inc.,
1942

John W. Decker

© Walter Stoneman,
ca. 1945

Norman Goodall

1950

Glora M. Wysner

APPENDIX I

International Missionary Meetings

1910, **World Missionary Conference, Edinburgh**

Meetings of the Continuation Committee

1910, Edinburgh, Scotland
1911, Bishop Auckland, England
1912, Lake Mohonk, United States
1913, The Hague, Holland

Meetings of the Emergency Committee

1919, London (twice)

Meeting called ad hoc by the national missionary organizations of the Continent, Great Britain, and America

1920, Crans, Switzerland

Meetings of the International Missionary Council*

1921, Lake Mohonk, United States	**Other Ecumenical Conferences**
1922, *Canterbury, England*	
1923, Oxford, England	
1925, *Atlantic City, United States*	1925, Stockholm, Life and Work
1926, Rättvik, Sweden	1927, Lausanne, Faith and Order
1928, **Jerusalem, Palestine**	
1929, Williamstown, United States	
1932, Herrnhut, Germany	
1934, *Salisbury, England*	
1935, Northfield, United States	
1936, *Old Jordans, England*	
1937, *London, England*	1937, Oxford, Life and Work
	1937, Edinburgh, Faith and Order
1938, **Tambaram, Madras, India**	1938, Utrecht, Provisional Committee of the World Council of Churches
1939, *Kasteel Hemmen, Holland*	
1946, *Geneva, Switzerland*	
1947, **Whitby, Canada**	
1948, Oegstgeest, Holland	1948, Amsterdam, World Council of Churches
1950, *Whitby, Canada*	1949, Bangkok, Eastern Asia Christian Conference, IMC-WCC Auspices

* Meetings of the Council before 1928 and of the Committee of the Council after 1928 appear in standard type. Meetings of the Committee of the Council before 1928 and of the Ad Interim Committee after 1932 are italicized. The world meetings appear in bold-faced type.

APPENDIX II

Constitution of the International Missionary Council*

(As amended at Hemmen, 1939; Whitby, 1947; and Oegstgeest, 1948)

I. Preamble

The Council is established on the basis that the only bodies entitled to determine missionary policy are the churches and the missionary societies and boards, representing the churches.

It is recognized that the successful working of the International Missionary Council is entirely dependent on the gift from God of the spirit of fellowship, mutual understanding, and desire to co-operate.

II. Membership and Meetings

The Council is composed of the following national missionary organizations[1] and Christian councils:

National Missionary Council of Australia.
Société Belge de Missions Protestants au Congo.
Confederação Evangélica do Brasil.
Ceylon Christian Council.
National Christian Council of China.
Conseil Protestant du Congo.
Dansk Missionsraad.
Deutscher Evangelischer Missionstag.
Société des Missions Évangéliques de Paris.
Conference of Missionary Societies in Great Britain and Ireland.
National Christian Council of India, Pakistan, and Burma.
National Christian Council of Japan.
National Christian Council of Korea.
Committee on Co-operation in Latin America.
Malaya Christian Council.
Concilio Nacional de Iglesias Evangélicas do Mexico.

* Note: in 1951 the Constitution was in process of being amended to make the Council, rather than the Committee of the Council, the body to which representatives would be appointed by the national constituent organizations.

[1] The term "missionary" is used in this constitution to describe the work of presenting the Gospel to non-Christian peoples, whether carried on by the younger or by the older churches.

Near East Christian Council.
Nederlandsche Zendings-Raad.
Netherlands India.
National Missionary Council of New Zealand.
Norsk Misjonsråd.
Foreign Missions Conference of North America (United States and Canada).
Philippine Federation of Evangelical Churches.
Association of Evangelical Churches of Puerto Rico.
Confederación de Iglesias Evangélicas del Rio de la Plata.
Schweizerischer Evangelischer Missionsrat.
National Christian Council of Siam.
Christian Council of South Africa.
Suomen Lähetysneuvosto.
Svenska Missionsrådet.

National missionary organizations or Christian councils in other countries or areas may be added to those named above by the affirmative vote of the Committee of the Council, provided for later; and the Committee of the Council shall have full power to determine what qualifications shall be required of a missionary organization or a Christian council for membership in the Council. Among these qualifications the Committee would take into consideration the thoroughly representative character of the organization, its elements of stability, and the extent and nature of the area that it covers.

The meetings of the Council shall be of two kinds: namely, (a) general Council meetings, and (b) special meetings for the consideration of particular subjects. The call for these general or special meetings shall be issued by the Committee of the Council. In the case of general Council meetings, the call shall be issued only after the proposal to hold such a meeting has been approved by two-thirds of the national bodies constituting the Council. Special meetings of the Council may be called by the Committee after the proposal to hold such a meeting has been approved by two-thirds of the national bodies which will be expected to send representatives to the meeting.

The number of representatives which each national missionary organization and Christian council will be entitled to appoint for each meeting of the Council shall be as stated by the Committee in its proposal to call a meeting and as ratified by national bodies in their approval of the proposal. In arranging for the membership of any Council meeting, the Committee shall provide, in so far as it is deemed desirable, for representation from countries in which there is no national missionary organization or Christian council and shall determine the method of choosing such representatives. The Committee shall also have the right to propose in regard to any particular meeting, whenever desirable, that a limited number of persons with special knowledge of the subjects contained in the programme of the proposed meeting may be invited to attend that meeting of the Council.

III. *Functions*

The functions of the Council shall be the following:

1. To stimulate thinking and investigation on questions related to the mission and expansion of Christianity in all the world, to enlist in the solution of these questions the best knowledge and experience to be found in all countries, and to make the results available for all who share in the missionary work of the churches.

2. To help to co-ordinate the activities of the national missionary organizations and Christian councils of the different countries, and to bring about united action where necessary in missionary matters.

3. Through common consultation to help to unite Christian public opinion in support of freedom of conscience and religion and of missionary liberty.

4. To help to unite the Christian forces of the world in seeking justice in international and inter-racial relations.

5. To be responsible for the publication of *The International Review of Missions* and such other publications as in the judgment of the Council may contribute to the study of missionary questions.

6. To call a world missionary conference if and when this should be deemed desirable.

IV. The Committee of the Council

The Committee of the Council shall have the power to act for the Council in the intervals between its general Council meetings.

The membership of the Committee shall be elected by the national missionary organizations and Christian councils, and the number of representatives, except as may be determined otherwise by subsequent action, shall be as follows:

National Missionary Council of Australia	1
Société Belge de Missions Protestantes au Congo	1
Confederação Evangélica do Brasil	1
Ceylon Christian Council	1
National Christian Council of China	2
Conseil Protestant du Congo	1
Dansk Missionsraad	1
Deutscher Evangelischer Missionstag	2
Société des Missions Evangéliques de Paris	1
Conference of Missionary Societies in Great Britain and Ireland	5
National Christian Council of India, Pakistan, and Burma	2
National Christian Council of Japan	2
National Christian Council of Korea	1
Committee on Co-operation in Latin America	1
Malaya Christian Council	1
Concilio Nacional de Iglesias Evangélicas do Mexico	1
Near East Christian Council	2
Nederlandsche Zendings-Raad	1
Netherlands India	1
National Missionary Council of New Zealand	1
Norsk Misjonsråd	1
Foreign Missions Conference of North America (United States and Canada)	7
Philippine Federation of Evangelical Churches	1
Association of Evangelical Churches of Puerto Rico	1
Confederación de Iglesias Evangélicas del Rio de la Plata	1
Schweizerischer Evangelischer Missionsrat	1
National Christian Council of Siam	1
Christian Council of South Africa	1
Suomen Lähetysneuvosto	1
Svenska Missionsrådet	1

45

For each meeting the Committee may elect other members, not exceeding three in all, to be nominated by the officers, from countries not otherwise represented, who shall for each meeting have the same rights and privileges as other members. In addition to the above, the Committee may elect other members, not exceeding five in all, to be nominated by the officers, in order to supply special knowledge or experience, who shall be consultants without voting powers.

The Committee of the Council shall have the power to provide representation in the Committee of the Council for national organizations that may in the future be admitted to membership in the Council.

Each regularly established department of the Council may be represented in the Committee of the Council by its Chairman or other representative of the committee directing the department's work. Such a representative shall have for each meeting the same rights and privileges as the other delegates.

Members of the Committee shall hold office until their successors are appointed, the length of term of office and the method of appointment to be determined in each country or area by the national missionary organization or Christian council.

The officers of the Council shall be members, *ex officio*, of the Committee and shall serve as the officers of the Committee of the Council.

The Committee of the Council shall, as occasion may require, consult with the constituent organizations in regard to the work of the Committee.

The Committee of the Council shall meet at the call of the officers of the Council, or upon request of a majority of the members of the Committee (sent to the chairman or secretaries in writing), or upon the request of three or more of the constituent organizations. Ten members of the Committee other than the officers shall constitute a quorum, provided, however, that these represent national missionary organizations or Christian councils, members of the Council, in three different continents.

The Committee of the Council may appoint an *Ad Interim* Committee to serve in the period between the meetings of the Committee of the Council with such powers as that Committee may determine. The membership of the *Ad Interim* Committee shall always be on an international basis with representatives from at least five countries on at least three continents.

V. Officers

The officers of the Council shall be a Chairman, not more than eight Vice-Chairmen, of whom two shall be women, a Treasurer, and two or more Secretaries. These officers shall be elected by the Committee of the Council. Their terms of office, their respective duties, and their remuneration shall be determined by the Committee. They shall be members, *ex officio*, of the Committee. The countries from which they come shall be allowed their full representation in addition to such officials.

VI. Expenses

The Committee of the Council shall prepare annual budgets two years in advance, which shall be submitted to the constituent organizations for approval and toward which they will be invited to contribute in a proportion to be recommended by resolution of the Committee. Since in a period of two years unforeseen developments may occur requiring additional expenditure, it is understood that such emergencies may be met by special funds which the Committee of the Council may be able to secure from private sources. If the objects to be sought involve permanent or recurring expense, the approval of the constituent organizations shall be secured before such work is undertaken, even if special funds are available for its support.

VII. Procedure

It is understood that the Council and the Committee of the Council will function internationally, and that the members of the Committee of the Council in any one country will not take action as a national group, though they may be called together by the officers of the International Missionary Council for purposes of consultation if this should seem necessary.

VIII. Amendments

This constitution may be amended at any future meeting of the Committee of the Council subject to the approval of the constituent organizations.

September 1948.

NOTES

The following abbreviations have been used in the notes:

AMZ, *Allgemeine Missions Zeitschrift.*
CMSGBI *Report*, annual report of the Conference of Missionary Societies in Great Britain and Ireland.
EMM, *Evangelisches Missionsmagazin.*
FMC *Report*, annual report of the Foreign Missions Conference of North America.
IMC *Minutes*, minutes of the meetings of the International Missionary Council.
IRM, *The International Review of Missions.*
MAW, The International Missionary Council's *Bulletins*, subtitled "Orphaned Missions." (See note 57, Chap. VII.)
WCC *Minutes*, minutes of the meetings of the World Council of Churches.

Chapter I. *The Rise of Protestant Missions*

1 Gustav Warneck, *Outline of a History of Protestant Missions from the Reformation to the Present Time*, pp. 8-40.
2 Kenneth Scott Latourette, *A History of the Expansion of Christianity*, Vol. III, pp. 25-27.
3 Warneck, *op. cit.*, pp. 39-66.
4 W. O. B. Allen and Edmund McClure, *Two Hundred Years: The History of The Society for Promoting Christian Knowledge, 1698-1898, passim.*
5 C. F. Pascoe, *Two Hundred Years of the S. P. G. An Historical Account of the Society for the Propagation of the Gospel in Foreign Parts, 1701-1900, passim.*
6 Warneck, *op. cit.*, p. 71.
7 S. Pearce Carey, *William Carey, D.D., Fellow of Linnaean Society*, pp. 3, 10.
8 G. G. Findlay and W. W. Holdsworth, *The History of the Wesleyan Methodist Missionary Society*, Vol. I, p. 65.
9 *Ibid.*, pp. 30 ff.
10 Carey, *op. cit.*, p. 65.
11 William Carey, *An Enquiry into the Obligations of Christians to Use Means for the Conversion of the Heathens. In which the Religious State of the Different Nations of the World, the Success of Former Undertakings, and the Practicability of Further Undertakings, are Considered.*
12 S. Pearce Carey, *op. cit.*, p. 90.
13 *Ibid.*, pp. 90-91.
14 Warneck, *op. cit.*, p. 66.
15 Richard Lovett, *The History of the London Missionary Society*, Vol. I, pp. 3-5, 21.

16 Ibid., p. 16.
17 Ibid., pp. 49-50.
18 Ibid., pp. 481-84.
19 Eugene Stock, *The History of the Church Missionary Society: Its Environment, Its Men, and Its Work,* Vol. I, pp. 31-80.
20 Ibid., pp. 81-91.
21 Findlay and Holdsworth, *op. cit.,* Vol. I, pp. 36-80.
22 Latourette, *op. cit.,* Vol. IV, pp. 77-79.
23 Joseph Tracy, *History of the American Board of Commissioners for Foreign Missions Compiled Chiefly from the Published and Unprinted Documents of the Board.*
24 Arthur Judson Brown, *One Hundred Years. A History of the Foreign Missionary Work of the Presbyterian Church in the U. S. A., With Some Account of Countries, Peoples and the Policies and Problems of Modern Missions,* pp. 19-20.
25 Ibid., p. 16.
26 Tracy, *op. cit.,* pp. 156-60.
27 Ibid., p. 261.
28 Ibid., p. 360.
29 Warneck, *op. cit.,* pp. 116-29.
30 Bengt Sundkler, *Svenska Missionssällskapet 1835-1876,* pp. 603-4.

CHAPTER II. *Nineteenth-Century Missionary Co-operation*

Note: Facts of publication are given in the notes for the *Proceedings* of the Continental Missions Conferences, since these cannot be included in the bibliography.
1 Eustace Carey, *Memoir of William Carey, D.D., Late Missionary to Bengal; Professor of Oriental Languages in the College of Fort William, Calcutta,* p. 364.
2 S. Pearce Carey, *William Carey, D.D., Fellow of Linnaean Society,* p. 253.
3 Martyn records Carey as suggesting annual conferences. In view of Carey's letter to Fuller and Carey's great practicality, that he urged annual conferences of this kind is difficult to believe. More likely is it that when he came to write, Martyn misconstrued what Carey had urged. See S. Wilberforce, ed., *Journals and Letters of the Rev. Henry Martyn, B.D., Late Fellow of St. John's College, Cambridge; and Chaplain to the Honourable East India Company,* Vol. I, p. 466. For a fascinating account, based upon historical data, of how Carey's conference might have been carried out, see Ruth Rouse, "William Carey's 'Pleasing Dream,' " *International Review of Missions,* Vol. 38 (1949), pp. 186-92.
4 *Anecdotes of the Bombay Mission for the Conversion of the Hindoos: Exhibiting an Account of the Travels and Missionary Labours of Messrs. Hall, Newell, Judson, Mills, Richards, Rice, and Nott, in Different Districts of the East Indies, with Sketches of the Idolatrous Customs of the Native Inhabitants. Extracted from the Letters and Journals of the Rev. Gordon Hall, A.M.,* pp. 205-6. See also Tracy, *History of the American Board of Commissioners for Foreign Missions,* p. 160.
5 George Smith, *The Life of Alexander Duff, D.D., LL.D.,* Vol. I, p. 165.
6 *World Missionary Conference, 1910,* Vol. IX, pp. 28-29.
7 *Proceedings of a General Conference of Bengal Protestant Missionaries, Held at Calcutta, September 4-7, 1855.*
8 J. Gregson, "Benares Missionary Conference," *Calcutta Christian Observer,* Vol. XVIII New Series (1857), pp. 114-34.

9 Report of the Punjab Missionary Conference Held at Lahore in December and January, 1862-63. On the communion service see pp. 127, 310.

10 Ibid., pp. 310, 319, 330, 335.

11 Proceedings of the South India Missionary Conference Held at Ootacamund, Apr. 19th-May 5th, 1858, pp. 334-35.

12 Ibid., p. 341, Cf. p. 2.

13 The Missionary Conference of South India and Ceylon, 1879, Vol. I, p. 324. See also pp. 320-24, 270-84.

14 Ibid., p. 402.

15 World Missionary Conference, 1910, Vol. VIII, pp. 32-33.

16 Report of the South Indian Missionary Conference, Held at Madras, January 2-5, 1900, pp. ii-iv.

17 Report of the South Indian Missionary Conference, Held at Madras, January 2-5, 1900, pp. i ff. See also World Missionary Conference, 1910, Vol. VIII, pp. 23-29.

18 Report of the South Indian Missionary Conference, Held at Madras, January 2-5, 1900, pp. iv-viii.

19 Report of the General Missionary Conference, Held at Allahabad, 1872-73.

20 Report of the Second Decennial Missionary Conference Held at Calcutta, 1882-83, p. 462.

21 Report of the Third Decennial Missionary Conference Held at Bombay, 1892-93, Vol. I, pp. x, 4.

22 Ibid., Vol. II, pp. 744-47.

23 Report of the Fourth Decennial Indian Missionary Conference Held in Madras, December 11th-18th, 1902, p. xx.

24 Ibid., passim.

25 Report Taken from the Minutes of the Convention of Protestant Missionaries of Japan, Held at Yokohama, September 20th-25th, 1872.

26 Minutes of the Convention of Protestant Missionaries Held in Tokio, Japan, on the 10th and 13th of May, 1878.

27 Proceedings of the General Conference of the Protestant Missionaries of Japan, Held at Osaka, Japan, April, 1883.

28 Proceedings of the General Conference of Protestant Missionaries in Japan, Held in Tokyo, October 24-31, 1900, p. 42. See also pp. 660 ff. and 960 ff.

29 World Missionary Conference, 1910, Vol. VIII, pp. 35-36, 161-63.

30 Ibid., p. 115. See also Vol. I, pp. 63-64, and Tokyo, 1900, op. cit., pp. 42-43, 668-70.

31 Records of the General Conference of Protestant Missionaries of China, Held at Shanghai, May 10-24, 1877.

32 Records of the General Conference of the Protestant Missionaries of China, Held at Shanghai, May 7-20, 1890, p. 597.

33 China Centenary Missionary Conference Records. Report of the Great Conference, Held at Shanghai, April 5th to May 8th, 1907, p. iii.

34 Ibid., p. 438.

35 Ibid., pp. 719-21.

36 Report of the Proceedings of the First General Missionary Conference, Held at Johannesburg, July 13-20, 1904.

37 Report of the Proceedings of the Second General Missionary Conference for South Africa, Held at Johannesburg, July 5-11, 1906. See especially pp. 39-47 and 125-32.

38 Report of the Proceedings of the Third General Missionary Conference for

South Africa, Held at Bloemfontein, July 1-6, 1909. See also *World Missionary Conference, 1910,* Vol. VIII, p. 41.

39   *Ecumenical Missionary Conference, New York, 1900. Report of the Ecumenical Conference on Foreign Missions, Held in Carnegie Hall and Neighboring Churches, April 21 to May 1,* Vol. I, p. 257.

40   *The Missionary Review of the World,* Vol. I, New Series (1888), pp. 294-96, 376-77.

41   *Ibid.,* Vol. X, New Series (1897), pp. 302, 334-41. See also *Ecumenical Missionary Conference, New York, 1900,* Vol. I, pp. 257-58.

42   *Christian Work in Latin America* (back title, *Panama Congress, 1916*), Vol. III, pp. 48-49.

43   *Methods of Mission Work Among Moslems, Being those Papers read at the First Missionary Conference on Behalf of the Mohammedan World, Held at Cairo, April 4th-9th, 1906.* See also S. M. Zwemer, E. M. Wherry, and James L. Barton, eds., *The Mohammedan World of Today, Being Papers Read at the First Missionary Conference on Behalf of the Mohammedan World at Cairo, April 4th-9th, 1906.*

44   On this point cf. *World Missionary Conference, 1910,* Vol. VIII, pp. 44-46.

45   Martin Schlunk, *Die Weltmission des Christentums,* p. 152.

46   Philip Schaff and S. Irenaeus Prime, *History, Essays, Orations, and Other Documents of the Sixth General Conference of the Evangelical Alliance, Held in New York, October 2-12, 1873,* pp. 189-200, 760-61.

47   Cf. *Evangelical Christendom,* Vol. IX (1855), pp. 422-24.

48   For example, see Schaff and Prime, *op. cit.,* pp. 583-660.

49   *Evangelical Christendom,* Vol. VI (1852), pp. 318-19.

50   *Ibid.,* Vol. VIII (1854), p. 62. On Duff, see Vol. VI (1852), p. 31.

51   George Smith, *The Life of Alexander Duff, D.D., LL.D.,* pp. 251-52, 262.

52   *Proceedings of the Union Missionary Convention Held in New York, May 4th and 5th, 1854,* pp. 8-9.

53   *Ibid.,* p. 14.

54   John R. Mott, *The Evangelization of the World in this Generation,* p. 11.

55   *Evangelical Christendom,* Vol. IX (1855), pp. 1-6.

56   *Ibid.,* pp. 65-68.

57   On the missionary aspects of the "Paris Conference of Evangelical Christians of All Churches, 1855" see *Evangelical Christendom,* Vol. IX (1855), pp. 315, 341, 384-86.

58   *Ibid.,* Vol. VIII (1854), pp. 432-33.

59   *Conference on Missions Held in 1860 at Liverpool,* passim. See also Eugene Stock, *The History of the Church Missionary Society,* Vol. II, p. 34, and James Johnston, ed., *Report of the Centenary Conference on the Protestant Missions of the World, Held in Exeter Hall* (June 9th-19th) London, 1888, Vol. I, p. 3.

60   *Conference on Missions Held in 1860 at Liverpool,* pp. 96, 264, 310.

61   *Proceedings of the General Conference on Foreign Missions Held at the Conference Hall, in Mildmay Park, London, in October 1878.* See especially pp. 22-27, 396.

62   Stock, *The History of the Church Missionary Society,* Vol. III, p. 14.

63   *The Missionary Review of the World,* Vol. I, New Series (1888), p. 583.

64   *Centenary Conference, London,* 1888, *op. cit.,* Vol. I, p. xi.

65   "Minutes of the London Secretaries' Association," November 17, 1886. (These ten volumes of handwritten minutes covering meetings from 1819 through World War II are filed in the archives of the British and Foreign Bible Society House, London.)

66   *Centenary Conference, London,* 1888, Vol. II, p. 445.

67 *Ibid.*, p. 567.
68 *Ibid.*, pp. 455-56.
69 *Ibid.*, Vol. I, p. ix.
70 *Ibid.*, Vol. II, pp. 431-37.
71 *Ibid.*, p. 437.
72 *The Missionary Review of the World*, Vol. I, New Series (1888), p. 582.
73 Stock, *op. cit.*, Vol. III, p. 649. Cf. Vol. IV, p. 557.
74 *Ecumenical Missionary Conference, New York*, 1900.
75 *Ibid.*, Vol. I, p. 47.
76 *Ibid.*, p. 64.
77 *The Missionary Review of the World*, Vol. X, New Series (1897), pp. 522-24. The International Missionary Union, founded in 1884, met annually in the late summer. A gathering for returned missionaries, it discussed current missionary problems and encouraged co-operation through broad acquaintance. Its meetings were limited to America. See *International Missionary Index* (1884-1929).
78 *Ibid.*, Vol. XIII (1900), p. 472.
79 Cf. FMC Report, 1901, p. 25.
80 *The Missionary Review of the World*, Vol. XIII, New Series (1900), p. 472.
81 *Ibid.*, Vol. XV, New Series (1902), pp. 98-108. See also FMC *Report*, 1901, pp. 25-35.
82 Cf. *Conference on Missions Held in 1860 at Liverpool*, p. 310, and *Centenary Conference, London*, 1888, pp. xv-xvi.
83 Cf. *Centenary Conference, London*, 1888, p. 433. This is also evident throughout the report of the next conference: *Ecumenical Missionary Conference, New York*, 1900. Continentals were strongly aware of this feeling.
84 *The Christian Advocate*, Vol. 75 (1900), p. 329.
85 Statement by P. Cullen Young, personal interview, Edinburgh, July, 1948. Statement by J. H. Ritson, personal interview, Seaford, July, 1948. Cf. "Minutes of the London Secretaries' Association," *passim*.
86 See note 65. See also *Records of Missionary Secretaries, An Account of the Celebration of the Centenary of the London Secretaries' Association*. This little book with a foreword by J. H. Ritson includes a chapter giving in brief outline the history of the Association.
87 *Ibid.*, pp. 55 ff.
88 *Ibid.*, p. 63. See also "Minutes of the London Secretaries' Association," February 21, 1906.
89 "Minutes of the London Secretaries' Association," February 16, 1887.
90 *Records of Missionary Secretaries, op. cit.*, p. 64.
91 *Ibid.*, p. 64.
92 Bengt Sundkler, *Svenska Missionssälskapet 1835-1876*, p. 387.
93 *Ibid.*, pp. 388-89.
94 *Ibid.*, pp. 391-92.
95 *Ibid.*, p. 393.
96 *Ibid.*, p. 397.
97 *Ibid.*, pp. 398 ff.
98 *Ibid.*, pp. 399-400.
99 Cf. A. Kolmodin, ed., *Förhandlingarna Vid Det Femte Nordisk-Lutherska Missionsmötet I Stockholm Den* 26-29, Aug. 1897, p. 22.
100 Arnold Frank, ed., *Witnesses from Israel. Life-Stories of Jewish Converts to Christianity* (tr. from the German by Mrs. A. Fleming), p. 65.
101 Kolmodin, *op. cit.*, p. 22.

102 *Lunds Missions-Tidning*, Vol. 39 (1185), pp. 174-76, 189; Vol. 40 (1886), pp. 14-16, 29-31.
103 *Ibid.*, Vol. 41 (1889), pp. 125-27, 139-42, 149-53, 164-68.
104 *Ibid.*, Vol. 45 (1893), pp. 143-44, 170-74, 183-88. See also J. Vahl, ed., *Det fjerde Lutherska Missionsmöde i Kjöbenhaven.*
105 Kolmodin, *op. cit.* See also *Lunds Missions-Tidning*, Vol. 51 (1887), pp. 143-4, 201-8.
106 *Nordisk Missions-Tidsskrift*, Vol. IV (1902), pp. 170-85.
107 Schlunk, *Die Weltmission des Christentums*, p. 152.
108 *Verhandlungen der Allgemeinen Missionsconferenz in der Himmelfahrts-woche der Jahre 1866 und 1868* (Berlin: Wilhelm Schultze, 1868, pp. 96), pp. 1-59.
109 *Ibid.*, pp. 60-96.
110 *Verhandlungen der zu Bremen gehaltenen dritten allgemeinen Missionsconferenz in der Himmelfahrtswoche 1872* (Barmen: D. B. & T. G. Wieman, 1872, pp. 36).
111 *Verhandlungen der zu Bremen gehaltenen vierten allgemeinen Missions-Conferenz in der Himmelfahrtswoche 1876* (Gütersloh: C. Bertelsmann, 1876, pp. 35).
112 *Allgemeine Missions Zeitschrift*, Vol. VII (1880), pp. 328-36.
113 *Ibid.*, Vol. XI (1884), pp. 309-21 for an excellent account of the conference. But for the official "Die Verhandlungen der sechsten kontinentalen Missionskonferenz in Bremen," see *Evangelisches Missions-Magazin*, Vol. XXVIII, neue Folge (1884), pp. 257-346.
114 *Allgemeine Missions Zeitschrift*, Vol. XVI (1889). See supplementary report, "Bericht über die achte [this should read "siebente"] kontinentale Missionskonferenz zu Bremen in der Himmelfahrtswoche 1889." A brief but quite adequate report of this meeting also appears in English in *The Missionary Review of the World*, Vol. II, New Series (1889), pp. 840-42.
115 *Allgemeine Missions Zeitschrift*, Vol. XX (1893), pp. 308-24. The official report is: *Protokoll über die Verhandlungen der Neunten* [this should read "Achten"] *Kontinentalen Missionskonferenz zu Bremen am 9., 10. und 12. Mai 1893*, (Gütersloh: Druch von C. Bertelsmann, n. d., pp. 80).
116 *Verhandlungen der neunten Kontinentalen Missionskonferenz zu Bremen am 25., 26. und 28. Mai, 1897* (Berlin: Martin Warneck, 1897, pp. iv + 151).
117 *Verhandlungen der zehnten Kontinentalen Missions-Konferenz zu Bremen am 14., 15. und 17. Mai 1901* (Berlin: Buchhandlung der Berliner evangelischen Missionsgesellschaft, 1901, pp. 174).
118 *Verhandlungen der elften kontinentalen Missions-konferenz zu Bremen am 29., 30., 31. Mai, 1. und 2. Juni 1905* (Berlin: Buchhandlung der Berliner evangelischen Missionsgesellschaft, 1905, pp. 181).
119 *Verhandlungen der XII. kontinentalen Missions-konferenz zu Bremen vom 6. bis 10. Mai 1909* (Bremen: Komissionsverlag der Norddeutschen Missions-Gesellschaft, pp. 143), especially pp. 51-52, 110-15. For the best brief summary in German of the development of the Continental Missions Conference from its founding, see pp. 113-17.
120 Martin Schlunk, "Gustav Warneck," *The International Review of Missions*, Vol. XXIII (1934), pp. 395-404.
121 *Ibid.*, pp. 400-401. For an account in English of one of the Halle conferences see *The Missionary Review of the World*, Vol. X, New Series (1897), pp. 373-75. See also the annual reports of the Saxony Missions Conference, *Missionskonferenz in Sachsen* (1888 ff.).
122 Gerhard Brennecke, ed., *Die Träger der deutschen Weltmission*, pp. 29 ff.

See also *Allgemeine Missions Zeitschrift*, Vol. XXVI (1899), pp. 493-511, 549-66, for a complete review to that time of "Die deutschen Missionskonferenzen."

123 *Allgemeine Missions Zeitschrift*, Vol. XII (1885), pp. 545-63. See also Kontinentale Missionskonferenz, 1897, op. cit., p. 107.

124 Kontinentale Missionskonferenz, 1897, op. cit., pp. 107-8.

125 Ibid., pp. 111-13 for the 1897 constitution. It also is translated in English in FMC Report 1904, pp. 77-78.

126 *Kontinentale Missions-konferenz, 1909*, op. cit., p. 51.

127 See reports of the Ausschuss in *Kontinentale Missionskonferenz, 1897*, op. cit., pp. 106 ff; *Kontinentale Missionskonferenz, 1893*, op. cit., pp. 5 ff; Kontinentale Missions-Konferenz, 1901, op. cit., pp. 161 ff; *Kontinentale Missions-Konferenz, 1905*, op. cit., pp. 57 ff; *Kontinentale Missions-konferenz, 1909*, op. cit., pp. 107 ff.

128 Ibid., passim. See also FMC Report 1904, pp. 78-80.

129 Paul Hennig, "Abschiedsgedanken," *Evangelisches Missionsmagazin*, Vol. 58 (1924), pp. 374-76. Cf. G. A. Gollock, "Fifteen Years' Growth: A Study in Missionary Cooperation," *The International Review of Missions*, Vol. XV (1926), p. 63.

130 See *Nederlandsch Zendingstijdschrift*, Vol. I (1889), and successive issues.

131 Ibid., pp. 61-62. See also Joh. Rauws et al., *The Netherlands Indies*, p. 75.

132 Rauws, op. cit., p. 75. See also *Nederlandsch Zendingstijdschrift*, Vol. VII (1895), pp. 121 ff. This latter, for example, indicates that the committee came together in April, 1895, for an address by the Governor General of the Netherlands Indies.

133 Rauws, op. cit., p. 74. See also Ecumenical Missionary Conference, New York, 1900, Vol. I, p. 420.

134 FMC Report, 1893 (cover title: *Interdenominational Conference of Foreign Missionary Boards and Societies in the United States and Canada Held in the Presbyterian Mission House, 53 Fifth Avenue, New York, January 12, 1893*). See also Ecumenical Missionary Conference, New York, 1900, Vol. I, pp. 22-23.

135 Ecumenical Missionary Conference, New York, 1900, Vol. I, pp. 22-23.

136 FMC Report, 1894 (cover title: *Report of the Second Conference of the Officers and Representatives of Foreign Mission Boards and Societies in the United States and Canada Held in the Methodist Mission House, 150 Fifth Avenue, New York, January 17, 1894*).

137 FMC Report, 1895. On W. Henry Grant, see p. 67.

138 FMC Report, 1896.

139 FMC Report, 1897.

140 Ibid., p. 11. See also Henry Otis Dwight, "The Foreign Mission Boards in Conference," *The Missionary Review of the World*, Vol. XVIII (1905), pp. 200-204.

141 FMC Report, 1898.

142 FMC Report, 1899.

143 FMC Report, 1901, p. 18.

144 FMC Report, 1902.

145 FMC Report, 1903.

146 Ibid., p. 4.

147 FMC Report, 1904, pp. 76 ff.

148 Statement by John R. Mott, personal interview, Whitby, Canada, July, 1947.

149 FMC Report, 1905. This also contains an index to Vols. I-XII.

150 FMC Report, 1906.

151 FMC Report, 1907, pp. 79-85.

152 Statement by John R. Mott, personal interview, Whitby, Canada, July, 1947. Statement by J. H. Oldham, personal interview, London, July, 1948. This

position has also been confirmed by Ruth Rouse, in a personal interview, Amsterdam, August, 1948.

153 Statement by John R. Mott, personal interview, Whitby, Canada, July, 1947.

154 Cf. Ruth Rouse, *The World's Student Christian Federation*, p. 25.

155 Clarence P. Shedd, *Two Centuries of Student Christian Movements*, p. 93.

156 *Ibid.*, pp. 93-121.

157 *Ibid.*, pp. 137-52.

158 *Ibid.*, pp. 161, 167.

159 *Ibid.*, pp. 153-86.

160 W. Richey Hogg, *Sixty-five Years in the Seminaries. A History of the Interseminary Movement.*

161 Shedd, *op. cit.*, p. 219.

162 *Ibid.*, p. 221.

163 *Ibid.*, pp. 219, 225.

164 *Ibid.*, pp. 225-27.

165 See H. W. Oldham, *The Student Christian Movement of Great Britain and Ireland: Its Origin, Development, and Present Position*, and Tissington Tatlow, *The Story of the Student Christian Movement of Great Britain and Ireland.*

166 See William R. Moody, *The Life of Dwight L. Moody.* Shedd, *op. cit.*, Chap. XIV, also includes a good summary of Moody's relationship to the student movement.

167 Henry Drummond, *Dwight L. Moody*, pp. 3-6, quoted in Shedd, *op. cit.*, p. 233.

168 Tatlow, *op. cit.*, pp. 11-17. See also George Adam Smith, *The Life of Henry Drummond*, Chap. IV.

169 Moody, *op. cit.*, pp. 350-57. Cf. Rouse, *op. cit.*, p. 32.

170 Basil Mathews, *John R. Mott, World Citizen*, p. 35.

171 *Ibid.*, p. 34.

172 Shedd, *op. cit.*, pp. 238-52.

173 Robert P. Wilder, *The Great Commission. The Missionary Response of the Student Volunteer Movements in North America and Europe; Some Personal Reminiscences*, p. 13.

174 *Ibid.*, pp. 13-24.

175 Cf. Rouse, *op. cit.*, p. 92.

176 Shedd, *op. cit.*, pp. 268-76.

177 Mathews, *op. cit.*, pp. 83-84.

178 Tatlow, *op. cit.*, pp. 20-21.

179 *Ibid.*, pp. 28-35. Cf. Wilder, *op. cit.*, pp. 64-83.

180 Tatlow, *op cit.*, pp. 48-52, 65, 132, 177. Cf. Shedd, *op. cit.*, p. 353.

181 Cf. John R. Mott, *The Evangelization of the World in This Generation.* Even so vigorous a critic of the watchword as Gustav Warneck was taken aback when confronted by Mott and Wilder in 1898 with evidence that the watchword antedated the SVM and had come from missionaries on the field. Out of the 1877 China missionary conference had come this statement: "We want China emancipated from the thraldom of sin in this generation." See Wilder, *op. cit.*, pp. 89-90.

182 Rouse, *op. cit.*, pp. 41-42.

183 Karl Fries, *Mina Minnen*, pp. 50-51.

184 Rouse, *op. cit.*, pp. 43-45.

185 Shedd, *op. cit.*, pp. 321-22.

186 *Ibid.*, p. 323. Cf. Kenneth Scott Latourette, *A History of Christian Missions in China*, p. 404.

187 Shedd, *op. cit.*, p. 326.
188 Luther D. Wishard, *The Intercollegiate Y.M.C.A. Movement,* cited by Rouse, *op. cit.*, p. 53.
189 Shedd, *op. cit.*, pp. 357 ff., and Rouse, *op. cit.*, pp. 51-64.
190 Mathews, *op. cit.*, pp. 47-60.
191 *Ibid.*, pp. 95-96. Cf. K. S. Latourette, "Divisive and Unifying Tendencies in Revival Movements," cited by H. P. Van Dusen, *World Christianity,* p. 250.
192 Mathews, *op. cit.*, pp. 83-84.
193 *Ibid.*, p. 50.
194 Rouse, *op. cit.*, p. 53.
195 Statement by John R. Mott, personal interview, Whitby, Canada, July, 1947. This editorial probably appeared in *The Association Bulletin.*
196 Fries, *op. cit.*, p. 55.
197 Raoul Allier, "Beginnings of Federation Work in France," *Student World,* Vol. XVI (1923), p. 91.
198 Mathews, *op. cit.*, pp. 101-2.
199 John R. Mott, *The World's Student Christian Federation. Origin, Achievements, Forecast,* pp. 3-4.
200 Rouse, *op. cit.*, pp. 53-64.
201 *Ibid.*, p. 62.
202 *Ibid.*, p. 95.
203 Tatlow, *op. cit.*, p. 144.
204 Cf. *ibid.*, pp. 133-61, 389-404.
205 From a Report Letter by John R. Mott, Constantinopole, October 4, 1895, cited in Rouse, *op. cit.*, p. 64.
206 Rouse, *op. cit.*, pp. 86-87.
207 *Ibid.*, p. 87.
208 A phrase that has been typical of Dr. Mott from the time he wrote *Strategic Points in the World's Conquest* in 1897.
209 *Addresses and Papers of John R. Mott,* Vol. II, p. 59.
210 *Ibid.*, pp. 39-40.
211 Rouse, *op. cit.*, p. 124.
212 *Addresses and Papers of John R. Mott,* Vol. II, pp. 82-90.

CHAPTER III. *The World Missionary Conference, Edinburgh, 1910*

1 Kenneth Scott Latourette, *A History of the Expansion of Christianity,* Vol. IV, p. 12.
2 *Ibid.*, Vols. 4-6.
3 *Ibid.*, Vol. III, p. 489.
4 Cf. James S. Dennis, Harlan P. Beach, Charles H. Fahs, *World Atlas of Christian Missions;* Joseph L. Parker, ed., *Interpretative Statistical Survey of the World Mission of the Christian Church;* Kenneth G. Grubb, ed., E. J. Bingle, assoc. ed., *World Christian Handbook.*
5 "Minutes of the London Secretaries' Association," October 18, 1905.
6 Statement by J. H. Ritson, personal interview, Seaford, July, 1948. Cf. John H. Ritson, *The World Is Our Parish,* p. 276. In his book Ritson notes that the inquiry concerned "the advisability of holding missionary conferences decennially," although he lists its date as 1907. Arthur J. Brown in "World Missionary Conference, 1910, Report of the American Executive Committee" (reprinted in FMC

Report 1909, p. 105), wrote: "It was felt that there should be another Ecumenical Conference in 1910, and that as the last one was held in America, the next should be held in Europe. Correspondence showed that leaders in Great Britain were in sympathy with this feeling, and in November, 1906, the conveners of seven Societies of Scotland met in Glasgow and invited the Boards in Scotland to appoint three of their number as delegates to an official conference."

7 "Minutes of the London Secretaries' Association," November 15, 1905.

8 FMC *Report*, 1906, p. 6.

9 Arthur J. Brown, "World Missionary Conference, 1910, Report of the American Executive Committee," *loc. cit.*, p. 106.

10 Charles R. Watson, "Report of Committee of Arrangements on Ecumenical Conference III," FMC *Report*, 1907, pp. 101-2.

11 *Ibid.*, p. 103.

12 *Ibid.*, p. 103.

13 FMC *Report*, 1907, p. 104. See also Julius Richter, "The Opportunity of the Conference. III, From the Standpoint of the Missionary Societies on the Continent of Europe," in World Missionary Conference *News Sheet*, No. 5 (February, 1910), pp. 96-98. Richter states that the German societies wished to invite the conference, but the recognized language barrier would have made the actual carrying out of the idea impracticable.

14 FMC *Report*, 1907, p. 10.

15 *Third Ecumenical Missionary Conference (June 1910). Minutes of General Committee. I. Meeting*, 12 June 1907, pp. 4-5. (Henceforth, *General Committee*.) The printed and unbound minutes of Edinburgh's preparatory committees are on file at Edinburgh House, London, the Missionary Research Library, New York, and the Day Missions Library, Yale University, New Haven.

16 "Minutes of the London Secretaries' Association," March 20, 1907.

17 *Ibid.*, April 17, 1907.

18 *General Committee, I. Meeting*, 12th June, 1907.

19 *World Missionary Conference, 1910*, Vol. IX, pp. 3-31.

20 *Ibid.*, p. 7. Thus also had W. H. Grant written in 1905. See p. 102, note 5.

21 W. H. T. Gairdner, *Echoes from Edinburgh, 1910. An Account and Interpretation of the World Missionary Conference*, pp. 9-12. See also Arthur J. Brown, "World Missionary Conference, 1910, Report of the American Executive Committee," *loc. cit.*, p. 118. See also John R. Mott, "The Coming World Missionary Conference," *The Missionary Review of the World*, Vol. XXI, New Series (1908), especially pp. 933-34.

22 Mott, "The Coming World Missionary Conference," *loc. cit.*, p. 934.

23 *Ibid.*, p. 935.

24 Watson, "Report of Committee of Arrangements on Ecumenical Conference III," *loc. cit.*, p. 102.

25 *General Committee, II. Meeting*, 10th October 1907, pp. 7-14. *Executive Committee, I. Meeting*, 10th October 1907, pp. 1-2.

26 *Third Ecumenical Missionary Conference (June 1910). Report From North American Committee*, pp. 1-3.

27 *Ibid.*, pp. 3-7.

28 Cf. Tissington Tatlow, *The Story of the Student Christian Movement of Great Britain and Ireland*, p. 405. Oldham, however, declares that he and Robson made the recommendation to Mott verbally at Liverpool. Statement by J. H. Oldham, personal interview, London, July, 1948.

29 *Third Ecumenical Missionary Conference (June 1910). Memorandum Sug-*

gesting Constitution and Procedure of Conference, p. 7. This British report was probably submitted in January or February, 1908.

30   *Executive Committee. III. Meeting,* 13th February 1908, pp. 7-10 and *General Committee. III. Meeting* 13th February 1908, pp. 15-17.

31   *Third Ecumenical Missionary Conference (June 1910). Minutes of International Committee. Meeting,* 14th-20th July 1908, pp. 1-10. See especially Minute 11, p. 8. The World Missionary Conference *News Sheet* credits the International Committee to American origin. (See No. 6, March, 1910, pp. 118-20.) The formal proposal had come from America through Mott, but the idea (cf. note 28) had originated with Robson and Oldham. Robson had translated Warneck's *History of Protestant Missions* into English in 1901 and Oldham had studied under Warneck. Both men knew well the need to include Continental representatives in Edinburgh's preparation if it were to be in any sense a "World" conference.

32   Statement by J. H. Oldham, personal interview, London, July, 1948.

33   *Minutes of International Committee. Meeting,* 14th-20th July, 1908, pp. 5-9.

34   *Ibid.,* p. 9. See also Brown, "Report of the American Executive Committee," *loc. cit.,* p. 112.

35   *General Committee. IV. Meeting.* 23rd September 1908, p. 21. See also "World Missionary Conference, 1910. Statement of Aims and Plans," printed by the authority of the General Committee in *The Missionary Record of the United Free Church of Scotland,* Vol. IX (1909), pp. 54-57.

36   Gairdner, *op. cit.,* p. 65.

37   Tatlow, *op. cit.,* p. 320.

38   *Ibid.,* p. 324.

39   The best readily available account of Oldham's life appears in Sherwood Eddy, *Pathfinders of the World Missionary Crusade,* pp. 277-86. An Oldham biography is much needed. It would unfold the story of an amazingly productive and influential life and would shed considerable light on the growth of the Ecumenical Movement. A helpful background biography is that of J. H. Oldham's father: see H. W. Oldham, *Lt. Col. G. W. Oldham, R.E.*

40   Oliver S. Tomkins, "The Anglican Communion and the Oecumenical Movement," *The Mission of the Anglican Communion,* ed. by E. R. Morgan and Roger Lloyd, p. 103.

41   Statement by J. H. Oldham, personal interview, London, July, 1948. He qualifies this by adding, "William Temple, who had been won by the SCM, might have brought the Church of England into the Ecumenical Movement. A miss in 1910 might have been rectified when Temple became Archbishop."

42   *Executive Committee. II. Meeting,* 12th December 1907, and *Executive Committee. VIII. Meeting,* 30th June 1909.

43   Tatlow, *op. cit.,* pp. 306-9. It is helpful to note that Roger Lloyd in his *The Church of England in the Twentieth Century,* Vol. I, uses Tatlow's account exclusively for the relationships of the Student Christian Movement with the Anglican Communion. See pp. 178-84, 205-7.

44   Tatlow, *op. cit.,* p. 406.

45   *Ibid.,* pp. 406-7.

46   *Ibid.,* pp. 408-9. Lloyd, commenting on Dean Robinson's change of mind, speaks of it as a "characteristically Anglican point of view: principles don't matter when you respect and understand the people who want you to break them," *op. cit.,* p. 206.

47   *Executive Committee. VI. Meeting,* 11th December 1908, pp. 22-24.

48   Statement by J. H. Oldham, personal interview, London, July, 1948. Contrary to Roger Lloyd (cf. note 46), Oldham's personal experiences with Anglican

leaders caused him to believe that "once they knew that you fully understood and would operate in accord with the fundamental principles involved, they were willing to cooperate with you." See also J. H. Oldham, "Introductory Chapter," in A. M. Chirgwin, *Coming Together. The Churches Cooperate*, p. 7.

Gore's biographer does not mention the Bishop's decision to participate at Edinburgh. He does, however, underscore the Bishop's great influence on Anglican bodies throughout the world. The importance of Gore's Edinburgh participation for future Anglican co-operation dare not to be underestimated. G. L. Prestige, *The Life of Charles Gore—A Great Englishman*, pp. 311-12.

49 *The East and the West*, Vol. VI (1908), pp. 370-85, and pp. 459-60.

50 *Ibid.*, pp. 365-66.

51 G. K. A. Bell, *Randall Davidson, Archbishop of Canterbury*, Vol. I, p. 573.

52 *Pan-Anglican Congress 1908*, Vol. I, pp. 1-15. See also Lloyd, *op. cit.*, Chap. 10.

53 *Pan-Anglican Congress 1908*, Vol. V, Bishop Cassels, "The Comity of Missions with special Reference to China," appendix. See also pp. 162-69 and pp. 220-36. Cf. Eugene Stock, *The History of the Church Missionary Society: Its Environment, Its Men, and Its Work*, Vol. IV, pp. 549-51.

54 Bell, *op. cit.*, Vol. I, p. 572.

55 *Ibid.*, pp. 573-74.

56 Tatlow, *op. cit.*, p. 309.

57 *The East and The West*, Vol. VIII (1910), p. 226. Stock, *op. cit.*, Vol. IV, p. 574.

58 Bell, *op. cit.*, Vol. I, p. 574. Lloyd (*op. cit.*, p. 212) credits the presence of the Archbishop directly to J. H. Oldham. Oldham states that the Archbishop could not have come to Edinburgh and that the Society for the Propagation of the Gospel would not have come but for Gore's acceptance. Statement by J. H. Oldham, personal interview, London, July, 1948.

F. H. Brabant, Neville Talbot's biographer, quotes Tissington Tatlow to the effect that Neville Talbot's entrance into the Student Christian Movement and his subsequent influence on his father, the Bishop of Southwark, is the real key to Anglican participation at Edinburgh and thus to the Church of England's entry into the larger movement for co-operation. F. H. Brabant, *Neville Stuart Talbot, 1879-1943, A Memoir*. It appears to the writer that while Neville Talbot undoubtedly played a crucial rôle in "winning" the Church of England, other factors and other persons of equal importance were also involved.

59 Cf. Stock, *op cit.*, Vol. IV, p. 557; Tomkins, "The Anglican Communion and the Oecumenical Movement," *loc. cit.*, pp. 102-3, and on "cooperation without compromise," pp. 105 ff.; Ruth Rouse, *The World's Student Christian Federation: A History of the First Thirty Years*, p. 132.

60 Cited by Tatlow, *op. cit.*, p. 410.

61 William Temple, "The Baslow Retreat on Christianity and the War," *The Student Movement*, Vol. XVII (1915), p. 96.

62 Statement by J. H. Oldham, personal interview, London, July, 1948. Cf. *Executive Committee. VIII. Meeting, 30th June 1909*, Minute 99, pp. 41-42.

63 Statement by John R. Mott, personal interview, Whitby, July, 1947. Cf. Basil Mathews, *John R. Mott, World Citizen*, p. 225.

64 The material from these replies was uniformly typed and bound. Fourteen volumes of about 500 typewritten pages each are on file at Edinburgh House, London. They include replies for Commissions III, IV, VII, and VIII. Replies for Commissions I and IV are on file in Day Missions Library, New Haven, Conn.

65 Statement by the late Charles H. Fahs, former director of the Missionary Research Library, personal interview, New York, June, 1948.

66 "Memorandum on Appointment of a Standing Committee, Submitted by the Missionary Societies on the Continent of Europe" (September 15, 1909, p. 5), with a "Proposal" (p. 6). The English translation of the original document is filed in the archives at Edinburgh House, London. (See also note 68.)

67 "Proposal," *loc. cit., passim.*

68 *FMC Report*, 1910, pp. 91-96. The English translation of the "Proposal" mentioned in note 66 is repeated here.

69 *Ibid.*, pp. 96-98.

70 "Minutes of the London Secretaries' Association," February 16, 1910, and April 20, 1910.

71 *World Missionary Conference, 1910*, Vol. I, p. 368. See also pp. 404, 432.

72 *Ibid*, Vol. VI, pp. 249-53, 277-80.

73 Ritson, *The World Is Our Parish*, pp. 277-78.

74 *Executive Committee. VII. Meeting*, 25th March 1909, Minute 72, p. 28.

75 *Executive Committee. IV. Meeting*, 12th March, 1908, Minute 43, p. 14. The writer is also indebted to J. H. Oldham for a letter (June 12, 1950) on this point.

76 *Executive Committee. VII. Meeting*, 30th June, 1909, Minute 101, p. 44.

77 Statement by J. H. Oldham, personal interview, London, July, 1948. Cf. John R. Mott, *Addresses and Papers of John R. Mott*, Vol. V, p. 181.

78 Stock, *The History of the Church Missionary Society*, Vol. IV, pp. 560-61. Stock's presentation of this—for some—emotionally charged question of missions to "Christian" lands as it was involved in Edinburgh's preparations is the best the writer has seen.

79 *Statistical Atlas of Christian Missions*, p. 7. With the exception of its maps, this volume was actually printed in the United States.

Dennis, Beach, Fahs, *World Atlas of Christian Missions*, p. 9. This American atlas differs from the Edinburgh edition "by the enlargement of its scope to include in its Directory, and also some extent in its Statistical Tables, not only missions among non-Christians, but also all other foreign missionary effort."

80 *Executive Committee. VII. Meeting*, 25th March 1909, Minute 80, pp. 32-33, and *Executive Committee XI. Meeting*, 1st April 1910, pp. 68-77, *passim.*

81 *World Missionary Conference, 1910, Monthly News Sheet*, October 1909-May 1910. This volume is on file in the library of Edinburgh House, London.

82 *Ibid.* (1909), No. 2, p. 36.

83 *Ibid.* (1910), No. 5, pp. 96-98.

84 Mathews, *op. cit.*, pp. 311-12.

85 *Ibid.*, pp. 318-20. Mathews catches here the kind of thoroughness that made Mott a great chairman.

86 Gairdner, *op. cit.*, p. 87.

87 *World Missionary Conference, 1910*, Vol. IX, pp. 146-50.

88 C. H. Brent, "The World Missionary Conference—An Interpretation," *The East and the West*, Vol. VIII (1910), pp. 364-65.

89 Gairdner, *op. cit.*, p. 60. See also *Official Handbook: World Missionary Conference Edinburgh 1910*, p. 46. See also Ritson, *op. cit.*, p. 279, and *World Missionary Conference, 1910*, Vol. IX, pp. 24-25.

90 *World Missionary Conference, 1910*, Vol. IX, p. 25.

91 General uncertainty about the number of delegates at Edinburgh from the churches of Asia prompts the following list. Included are the delegate's name, the

auspices under which he came, and the page in *World Missionary Conference*, Vol. IX, on which he is officially listed. All page references below refer to Vol. IX, unless otherwise indicated.

India

1 V. S. Azariah (special by British Exec. Comm.), p. 40.*
2 K. C. Chatterji (Presbyterian, U.S.A.), p. 58.
3 J. R. Chitambar (Methodist Episcopal, U.S.A.), p. 56.
4 S. Ghose (Society Propagation of Gospel, England), p. 48.
5 Shivram Masoji (Presbyterian, U.S.A.), p. 59.
6 John Rangiah (America Baptist), p. 52. At work in Natal.**
7 R. K. Sorabji (Church Missionary Society, England), p. 43.
8 Thang Khan (American Baptist), pp. 52, 93.

Burma

9 Ah Sou (American Baptist), p. 52.

China

10 Cheng Ching-yi (London Missionary Society), p. 45.***
11 Tong Tsing-en (American Baptist), p. 52.
12 Tsang Ding Tong (Presbyterian U.S.A.), p. 59.

Korea

13 T. H. Yun (special by American Exec. Comm.), p. 51.

Japan

14 Yugoro Chiba (American Baptist), p. 52.
15 Tasuku Harada (American Board, Congregational), p. 53.
16 Yoitsu Honda (special by American Exec. Comm.), p. 51.
17 K. Ibuka (Presbyterian, U.S.A.), p. 59.

Note: C. C. Wang, a Chinese student studying in Edinburgh, presented the Chinese nationalist position from a Christian view-point to the Edinburgh Conference (p. 91). He was not "C. T. Wang," as Gairdner (*op. cit.*, pp. 164-65) has listed him. Although present at Edinburgh, he appears not to have been an official delegate.

"T. Y. Chang" (p. 78) appears to be an alternate spelling for "Tsang Ding Tong."

B. T. Sakai (Protestant Episcopal Church, U.S.A., *Official Handbook*, op. cit., p. 85) of Japan did not attend Edinburgh.

The Negro "from Liberia" mentioned by Gairdner (*op. cit.*, p. 58) appears to be Alexander P. Camphor (Methodist Episcopal, U.S.A., p. 56). Born in Louisiana, Camphor went out under the Methodist Episcopal Church to Liberia where he taught in a boys' school for some years. He returned to the United States in 1908, was elected a bishop, and was assigned to Liberia in 1916. He died in the United States in 1919.

92 A complete set of the World Missionary Conference's *Daily Conference Paper* is on file in the library of Edinburgh House, London. A similar paper had been issued each evening at the New York Conference in 1900. Cf. *Ecumenical Missionary Conference, New York, 1900*, Vol. I, p. 18.

93 Cf. *Report of the Fourth Decennial Indian Missionary Conference Held in Madras, December 11th-18th, 1902*, p. 16.

* See J. Z. Hodge, *Bishop Azariah of Dornakal.*
** Rangiah was the first foreign missionary sent out by his Telegu church to the Indians working in Africa. Sketches of the five Baptists from Asia are given in *Missions*, Vol. I (1910) pp. 189-90.
*** Cheng was of a first generation Christian family. His expenses to and from Edinburgh were borne by Chinese Christians. See W. Nelson Bitton, "Mr. Cheng Ching-yi," *The Chronicle of the London Missionary Society*, Vol. 75 (1910), p. 123.

94   Gairdner, *op. cit.*, p. 65. Cf. Tatlow, *op. cit.*, p. 411, "The conference owed its success to J. H. Oldham more than to any other one person."

95   *World Missionary Conference*, 1910, Vol. I, pp. 401-5. Cf. Gairdner, *op. cit.*, pp. 68-92.

96   Gairdner, *op. cit.*, pp. 105-6. Cf. Robert E. Speer, "The Edinburgh Missionary Conference.—II," *The East and The West*, Vol. VIII (1910), p. 375.

97   Gairdner, *op. cit.*, pp. 109-10. For an account of Azariah's speech and its aftermath at Edinburgh by a witness and long-time associate of Azariah, see Hodge, *Bishop Azariah of Dornakal*. For the speech see *World Missionary Conference*, 1910, Vol. IX, pp. 306-15. See also *The Harvest Field*, Vol. XXX (1910), pp. 345, 442-44.

98   Gairdner, *op. cit.*, pp. 134, 136.

99   *Ibid.*, pp. 183-86. Gairdner prints the whole speech. It also appears in *World Missionary Conference*, 1910, Vol. VIII, pp. 195-97. On Cheng Ching-yi see Nelson Bitton, "Cheng Ching-yi, A Christian Statesman," *International Review of Missions*, Vol. XXX (1941), pp. 513-20. See also "Dr. Cheng Ching-yi," in *The Chinese Recorder*, Vol. LXX (1939), pp. 689-98.

100   *World Missionary Conference*, 1910, Vol. VIII, pp. 202-3.

101   *Ibid.*, pp. 213-14. Interestingly enough, the witticism, "lion in a den of Daniels," has recently been attributed to a 1931 speech by Sir Willmott Lewis, long-time Washington correspondent for *The Times*, London's influential newspaper. Since then his supposed *bon mot* "has enlivened the orations of hundreds of other after-dinner speakers." Herbert Corey, "The Most Unforgettable Character I've Met," *Reader's Digest*, Vol. XXIX (March, 1950), p. 59.

102   Ritson, *op. cit.*, p. 280.

103   Cf. Gairdner, *op. cit.*, p. 197. The Anglican High Churchmen were in a difficult and precarious position at Edinburgh. They had been severely criticized by much of the High Church press, especially the *Church Times*, and they had received letters threatening loss of support and even disruption of The Society for the Propagation of the Gospel because of their participation at Edinburgh. Charles H. Fahs in *The Christian Advocate*, July 14, 1910, pp. 967-71.

104   *Ibid.*, p. 196.

105   *World Missionary Conference*, 1910, Vol. IX, pp. 28-30.

106   *News Sheet*, No. 4, January, 1910, p. 82.

107   *World Missionary Conference*, 1910, Vol. II, pp. 234-65; Vol. III, pp. 331-64; Vol. VIII, pp. 56-61. For the brief discussion see Vol. III, pp. 447-55. Cf. John H. Ritson, "Christian Literature in the Mission Field," *International Review of Missions*, Vol. IV (1915), pp. 200-220.

108   *World Missionary Conference*, 1910, Vol. IX, pp. 30, 113-20.

109   Statement by J. H. Oldham, personal interview, London, July, 1948.

110   (Bishop) H. H. Montgomery, "The Pan-Anglican Conference, and After," *The East and The West*, Vol. VI (1908), p. 366.

111   Statement by J. H. Oldham, personal interview, London, July, 1948, and a personal letter from J. H. Oldham, June 12, 1950.

112   FMC Report, 1916, pp. 195-96. Charles H. Fahs and Helen E. Davis, *Conspectus of Cooperative Missionary Enterprises*, p. 15. See also Mott, *Addresses and Papers*, Vol. V, pp. 181-83.

113   *Conference on Missions in Latin America*, p. 9.

114   *Ibid.*, p. 190.

115   *Ibid.*, p. 184.

116   Statement by J. H. Oldham, personal interview, London, July, 1948.

117   *World Missionary Conference*, 1910, Vol. VIII, pp. 198-99, 201-2.

118   Silas McBee, *An Irenic Itinerary*, pp. xiii, 48.

119 *World Missionary Conference, 1910,* Vol. VIII, pp. 220-23.

120 *Ibid.,* pp. 225-26.

121 *Ibid.,* pp. 215-16. See also Bishop Talbot on this same theme, *ibid.,* p. 234.

122 *The Missionary Review of the World,* Vol. XXIII, New Series (1910), pp. 561-62. For a critique of the World Missionary Conference from a German Catholic view-point, see G. Pietsch, "Die Edinburgher Missions Konferenz," *Zeitschrift für Missionswissenschaft,* Vol. I (1911), pp. 173 ff.

123 McBee, *op. cit.,* p. 144. McBee could say this as a result of personal conversations with Dr. Davidson.

124 Brent, "The World Missionary Conference—An Interpretation," *loc. cit.,* pp. 366-67. It has occasionally been suggested that Brent first proposed at Edinburgh a conference or movement to deal with questions of faith and order. Such a statement is not recorded in Brent's Edinburgh speeches, nor does Brent mention such an intention in his post-conference writings. See also Alexander C. Zabriskie, *Bishop Brent, Crusader for Christian Unity,* p. 147.

On this point, however, J. H. Oldham writes (personal letter, June 12, 1950): "There is in my mind no question that Bishop Brent raised this issue at the Edinburgh Conference. It is the one of two or three hundred seven-minute speeches which stands out vividly in my memory. . . . The matter is hardly one in which my memory could be at fault. Bishop Brent, in the debate, explicitly raised the question of the basis of the Edinburgh Conference. I was naturally all ears, for I had been defending the basis for two years in all sorts of quarters, and knew that if it was repudiated the Conference would disintegrate. Bishop Brent . . . went on to say that while questions of faith and order were rightly excluded from the purview of that conference they must, in a different context, be frankly and openly faced. The Edinburgh Conference was concerned with practical co-operation, but there remained the question of unity. We must not rest content with co-operation between separated bodies. The causes of separation must be examined with a view to their removal. He also made it clear that he felt this so strongly that he intended to do something about it. He did not, of course, outline a plan for a conference on faith and order. It is quite probable that he did not, at the time, know what form his action would take. But he left no doubt in my mind that he was not going to allow the matter to rest.

"I cannot forget the speech, because it showed me that the question which, up to that time, I had known could not be discussed in a body like the World Missionary Conference, could safely be taken up in another context, and ought so to be taken up. . . . I have a clear recollection of waiting expectantly, in the months which followed the Edinburgh Conference, to see in what way Bishop Brent's intention would be realised."

125 Zabriskie, *op. cit.,* p. 145.

126 *Ibid.,* p. 145.

127 *Ibid.,* p. 147.

128 Cf. H. N. Bate, ed., *Faith and Order, Proceedings of the World Conference Lausanne, August 3-21, 1927,* p. vii.

129 A. W. Schreiber, *Die Edinburger Welt-Missions-Conferenz,* see especially pp. 54-60. For a German appraisal of the theology of Edinburgh see D. Johannes Warneck, "Edinburgh—eine Rechtfertigung der freien Theologie?" *Allgemeine Missions-Zeitschrift,* Vol. 38 (1911), pp. 489-501.

130 Paul Hennig, "Abschiedsgedanken," *Evangelisches Missionsmagazine,* Vol. 68 (1924), pp. 374-6.

131 Rouse, *op. cit.,* p. 130.

132 Margaret Sinclair, *William Paton,* pp. 24-25.

133   F. A. Iremonger, *William Temple, Archbishop of Canterbury, His Life and Letters*, pp. 391-92.

134   FMC *Report*, 1916, p. 46.

135   Edward Warren Capen and Lewis Hodous. *The Kennedy School of Missions.*

136   John R. Mott, *The Decisive Hour of Christian Missions.*

137   McBee, *op. cit.*, p. 163.

138   McBee makes a moving defense of the Edinburgh principle, viewing it as the proper one for bringing about Christian unity. See McBee, *op. cit.*, pp. 132-35, 142, 144, 162-64. His criticism of his own Anglican Communion as a *via media*, pp. 185-86, and his criticism of the Chicago-Lambeth Quadrilateral as a basis for Christian unity, pp. 187-89, seem to the writer especially well taken.

139   Statement by John R. Mott, personal interview, Whitby, July, 1947.

140   Statement by J. H. Oldham, personal interview, London, July, 1948. Cf. Mott, *Addresses and Papers*, Vol. VI, p. 447.

141   See especially *World Missionary Conference*, 1910, Vol. VIII, pp. 82-88.

142   Statement by J. H. Oldham, personal interview, London, July, 1948.

143   William Henry Grant, Secretary of the Foreign Missions Conference, had only been a part-time secretary. Likewise, the Federal Council of the Churches of Christ in America was without a full-time secretary at this time. The writer regards the secretaries of the Student Christian Movement and of the YMCA as in non-denominational rather than interdenominational work.

144   Karl Fries had been instrumental in sending Söderblom to Northfield in 1890. (Karl Fries, *Mina Minnen*, pp. 55-56.) At Northfield among the younger men, John R. Mott most impressed Söderblom. The vision of the unity and universality of the faith that came through association with Christian students from around the world and Dwight L. Moody's great impact on Söderblom, inspiring his dedication to the unity of the church, were the two greatest shaping forces for the Swedish student. The importance of the American Student Christian Movement with its strong missionary emphasis cannot be over-emphasized in the genesis of Söderblom's ecumenical vision. (Nils Karlström, *Kristna Samförstandssträvanden Under Världskriget 1914-1918 Med särskild hänsyn till Nathan Söderbloms insats*, pp. 157-65; and Nathan Söderblom, Utgivna av Anna Söderblom, *Sommarminnen*, pp. 50-102.)

145   Statement by J. H. Oldham, personal interview, London, July, 1948. The conversation seems to have taken place early in 1926 after the Stockholm meeting had been held.

CHAPTER IV. *From Edinburgh to Crans, 1910-20*

1   *World Missionary Conference*, Vol. IX, pp. 95-97. African representation included only white South Africa, and not Negro Africa as a whole.

2   Letter from J. H. Oldham to John R. Mott, Mar. 16, 1942, reprinted in John R. Mott, *Addresses and Papers of John R. Mott*, Vol. V, p. 728. Statement by J. H. Oldham, personal interview, London, July, 1948. Cf. J. H. Oldham, "Introductory Chapter," in A. M. Chirgwin, *Coming Together—The Churches Cooperate*, p. 6.

3   *Minutes of the Continuation Committee of the World Missionary Conference.* I. Meeting, 23rd June 1910, pp. 2. Henceforth cited as *Continuation Committee*

Minutes. See also World Missionary Conference, Vol. IX, pp. 101-2, for the committee's members and p. 134 for an account of this first meeting at Edinburgh.

4 World Missionary Conference, Vol. IX, pp. 108-10.

5 Provisional Constitution of the Continuation Committee of the World Missionary Conference As Agreed Upon at the Meeting Held in Edinburgh, on Saturday, 25th June, 1910, To be Revised at the Next Meeting of the Continuation Committee (n.d., p. 7).

6 For all the foregoing see Continuation Committee Minutes. II. Meeting, 24th and 25th June, 1910, pp. 3-11. See also World Missionary Conference, Vol. IX, op. cit., pp. 135-38 and Mott, Addresses and Papers, Vol. V, op. cit., pp. 49-53.

7 "Report of the Continuation Committee," FMC Report, 1911, pp. 159-60. See also World Missionary Conference Minutes of General Committee. VII. Meeting, 15th July 1910, and Reports to Continuation Committee. Report of Executive Committee [April, 1911].

8 These thirteen Reports to Continuation Committee (see note 7) were prepared for the May, 1911, Bishop Auckland meeting of the Continuation Committee. Undated, they went out under a covering letter from the secretary on April 13, 1911. These are on file at Edinburgh House, London, The Missionary Research Library, New York, and Day Missions Library, Yale University, New Haven.

9 Some idea of the status of the Continuation Committee's work in its first six months can be had from the FMC Report, 1911, pp. 158-67. The commissions did not really get under way until 1911.

10 Reports to Continuation Committee. Report of Executive Committee [Apr. 1911]. Minutes of these early executive committee meetings are on file at Edinburgh House.

11 Reports to Continuation Committee. World Missionary Conference, 1910. Abstract Account of Charge and Discharge of the Intromissions of the Hon. Treasurer (H. W. Smith, W.S.) For the Period from 15th April 1908 to 24th April 1911 [April, 1911].

12 Continuation Committee Minutes. III. Meeting, 16th, 17th, 18th, and 19th May, 1911.

13 Ibid., pp. 17, 23. Minutes 41 and 54.

14 Ibid., pp. 12-14, Minute 33. See also Reports to Continuation Committee. Proposal for the Establishment of an International Missionary Review [April, 1911].

15 The Constitution of the Continuation Committee of the World Missionary Conference. As Revised at the Meeting of the Continuation Committee Held at Bishop Auckland, May 16-19, 1911. The important part of the constitution simply repeats the resolution by which the Continuation Committee was founded. See Mott, Addresses and Papers, Vol. V, pp. 46-47. A good summary of the Bishop Auckland meeting is Charles R. Watson, "The Continuation Committee of the World Missionary Conference," The Missionary Review of the World, Vol. XXIV (1911), pp. 647-54.

16 The International Review of Missions, Vol. I (1912), p. 1. J. H. Oldham set forth his conception of the magazine in a fourteen-page section, "The Editor's Notes." Henceforth, IRM.

17 John R. Mott, "The Continuation Committee," Ibid., pp. 63-64, reprinted in Mott, Addresses and Papers, Vol. V, pp. 61 ff.

18 Ibid., pp. 73-78.

19 Conference of Missionary Societies in Great Britain and Ireland. Report of the First Annual Conference Held at the Hayes, Swanwick, Derbyshire, from the 12th-14th June, 1912, p. 24. Henceforth cited as CMSGBI Report. For America see FMC Report, 1912, pp. 49-72.

20 See *Meeting of Continuation Committee, 1912.* These printed reports and memoranda are designated by letter from "A" to "S" and were circulated August 15, 1912. They are on file at Edinburgh House, Missionary Research Library, and Day Missions Library. See also CMSGBI *Report,* 1912, pp. 42-45.

21 Letter from Eugene Stock to J. H. Oldham, March 8, 1912. Stock's letter of withdrawal is instructive. Physically unable to attend this particular meeting, the vice-chairman reluctantly resigned, for only thus could a successor be appointed and the Committee be kept at full strength. England's members, he pointed out, had been chosen originally for denominational balance. With only three Anglicans and four Free Churchmen, many societies were unrepresented. Moreover, he insisted that one Chinese Congregationalist could not represent all China's missions. To remedy these inadequacies, Stock urged immediate steps to form the international missionary committee. If that proved impossible, he proposed that members assemble regionally with a large co-opted group and explore their problems. Then when these members met in Committee, they would have a representative basis for speaking.

22 *Continuation Committee Minutes. IV. Meeting, 26th, 27th, and 30th September, and 1st October 1912.* See also *Abstract of the Proceedings of the Continuation Committee of the World Missionary Conference, 1910, Lake Mohonk, September 26-October 2, 1912.* Julius Richter, "Missionary Experts in Conference," *The Missionary Review of the World,* Vol. XXV, New Series (1912), pp. 910-16; and Louise Creighton, "The Meeting of the Continuation Committee of the World Missionary Conference, Lake Mohonk, Sept. 26, to Oct. 2, 1912," IRM, Vol. II (1913), pp. 118-25. The very able statement on "Missions and Governments" appears in the IRM, Vol. II (1913), pp. 563-66.

23 John R. Mott's statement to the Continuation Committee, 1912. Reprinted in Mott, *Addresses and Papers,* Vol. V, pp. 75-79. Cf. Mathews, *John R. Mott, World Citizen,* p. 138, where Mott's biographer records that all Mott's travel expenses were covered for him by loyal friends.

24 *The Continuation Committee Conferences in Asia 1912-1913. A Brief Account of the Conferences Together With Their Findings and Lists of Members.* The eight-question syllabus appears in an appendix. This book is arranged chronologically by conferences and thus differs from *The Findings of the Continuation Committee Conferences Held in Asia, 1912-1913 Arranged by Topics,* with an introduction by Harlan P. Beach.

25 "The India National Conference of the Edinburgh Continuation Committee," *The Harvet Field,* Vol. XXXIII (1913), pp. 6-14.

26 *Ibid.,* p. 9.

27 Mott, *Addresses and Papers,* Vol. V, pp. 98-103.

28 See H. Gulliford, "The Influence of Edinburgh on India," *The Harvest Field,* XXXIV (1914), pp. 43-52.

29 *Ibid.,* pp. 110-12 prints the revised constitution of the Council and the proceedings of its first meeting. See also Herbert Anderson, "The National Missionary Council of India," *ibid.,* pp. 330-37.

30 *The Continuation Committee Conferences in Asia, 1912-1913,* pp. 157-68 for Rangoon and pp. 171-83 for Singapore.

31 E. C. Lobenstine, "The Missionary Conferences of 1913," *The China Mission Yearbook,* Vol. IV (1913), pp. 60-75. See also IRM, Vol. II (1913), pp. 501-19.

32 Mott, *Addresses and Papers,* Vol. V, p. 117. Mott reprints the findings of the National Conference, pp. 111-49.

33 *Ibid.,* pp. 143-45.

34 E. C. Lobenstine, "The First Year of the China Continuation Committee,"

The China Christian Yearbook, Vol. V (1914), pp. 484-98. See also *Proceedings of the China Continuation Committee*, Shanghai.

35 *The Continuation Committee Conferences in Asia*, pp. 371-85.

36 L. George Paik, *The History of Protestant Missions in Korea 1832-1910*, pp. 367-70.

37 *The Korea Mission Field*, Vol. VII (1911), pp. 342-45.

38 *Ibid.*, Vol. VIII (1912), pp. 340-41.

39 *The Continuation Committee Conferences in Asia, 1912-1913*, pp. 398-99.

40 Cf. Arthur Judson Brown, "The Relation of Church and Mission in Japan," *IRM*, Vol. II (1913), pp. 674-89.

41 *The Christian Movement in the Japanese Empire Including Korea and Formosa*, Vol. XIII (1915), pp. 40-46.

42 *Ibid.*, pp. 47-49.

43 *Ibid.*, Vol. XI (1913), pp. 186-283, includes abstracts of these reports.

44 *Ibid.*, pp. 178-85.

45 *The Continuation Committee Conferences in Asia, 1912-1913*, pp. 445-67.

46 *The Christian Movement in the Japanese Empire Including Korea and Formosa*, Vol. XV (1917), pp. 192 ff.

47 Mott cabled: ". . . could not fulfill serious obligations already assumed and do justice to new position." Mott, *Addresses and Papers*, Vol. VI, plate between pp. 534-35.

48 Statement by John R. Mott, personal interview, Whitby, July, 1947.

49 "Continuation Committee. Minute of Meeting of British Members, December 2nd, 1910." On file at Edinburgh House. See also note 10 above and accompanying text.

50 "Minutes of Meeting of Conference of Representatives of Missionary Societies in Great Britain and Ireland Held in the Hall of St. William's Chapel, York, on 14th and 15th June, 1911." On file at Edinburgh House. See also John H. Ritson, *The World Is Our Parish*, pp. 281-82.

51 "Standing Committee of the Conference of Missionary Societies in Great Britain and Ireland," minutes of June 15, 1911, October 26, 1911, and November 23, 1911. These handwritten minutes are on file at Edinburgh House.

52 *CMSGBI Report*, 1912.

53 *CMSGBI Report*, 1915, pp. 3-6.

54 Charles H. Fahs and Helen E. Davis, *Conspectus of Cooperative Missionary Enterprises*, p. 34.

55 Joh. Rauws et al., *The Netherlands Indies*, pp. 71-75.

56 Letter to the writer from Ds. Joh. Blauw, Secretary of the Nederlandsche Zendingsraad, October 6, 1949.

57 Jakob E. Lundahl, "Missionary Cooperation in Sweden," *IRM*, Vol. XI (1922), pp. 421-29.

58 *Report of the Proceedings of the Fourth General Missionary Conference of South Africa Held at Cape Town 3rd to 9th July, 1912*. See especially pp. 15, 41 ff. See also *IRM*, Vol. II (1913), pp. 56 ff.

59 J. J. Willis, *The Kikuyu Conference. A Study in Christian Unity*. See especially pp. 4, 15-17, 19 ff. See also *Continuation Committee Minutes. The Hague, 14th-20th November 1913*, pp. 42-43, Minute 121.

60 *Report of the United Conference of Missionary Societies in British East Africa, Kikuyu, July 23th [sic]-26th, 1918.*

61 Daniel Couve, "Cooperation in Madagascar," *IRM*, Vol. III (1914), pp. 313-22.

62 E. M. Wherry, S. M. Zwemer, C. G. Mylrea, *Islam and Missions: Being*

papers read at the Second Missionary Conference on behalf of the Mohammedan World at Lucknow, January 23-28, 1911, pp. 16-17. See also E. M. Wherry, S. M. Zwemer, and C. G. Mylrea, Lucknow, 1911: *Being papers read and discussions on the training of Missionaries, and literature for Moslems at the General Conference on Missions to Moslems held at Lucknow, January 23-28, 1911, with Committees, Programme, List of Delegates*, etc. The second of these was printed for private circulation only.

63   *Continuation Committee Minutes. III. Meeting, 16th, 17th, 18th, and 19th May, 1911*, pp. 14-15, 34, Minutes 34, 82.

64   *Mott, Addresses and Papers*, Vol. V, p. 315.

65   See IRM, Vol. II (1913), pp. 782-84 on "A Roman Catholic View of Comity"; IRM, Vol. III (1914), pp. 488-505 for F. Schwager, "Missionary Methods from a Roman Catholic Standpoint"; IRM, Vol. IV (1915), pp. 456-73, 638-49 for "A Survey of Roman Catholic Missions." This last feature was resumed after the war.

66   *Papers for Continuation Committee November 1913. B. Report of the Chairman of the Continuation Committee regarding his Journey in Asia*, pp. 8-9. These undated reports prepared for The Hague meeting are on file at Edinburgh House, Missionary Research Library, and Day Missions Library. The second half of Mott's report in slightly modified form is reproduced in the IRM, Vol. III (1914), pp. 209-24.

67   *Continuation Committee Minutes. The Hague, 14th-20th November, 1913*, pp. 48-49, Minute 138. See also *Proceedings of the Fourth Meeting of the Continuation Committee of the World Missionary Conference The Hague November 14th to 20th, 1913*. The careful reader will note that both the 1912 and 1913 meetings are described as the "fourth" in the series. This arose from the growing tendency to regard the first meeting, June 23, and the second meeting, June 24 to 25, 1910, as one. Thus there had been by 1913 four annual meetings. The call to Mott is reprinted in *Mott, Addresses and Papers*, Vol. V, pp. 177-78.

68   *Continuation Committee Minutes. The Hague. 14th-20th November, 1913*, p. 55, Minute 153. Cf. J. H. Oldham, "The Continuation Committee and the Missionary Societies," *CMSGBI Report*, 1914, pp. 31-35.

69   Letter to the writer from Dr. J. H. Oldham, June 12, 1950.

70   *Continuation Committee Minutes. The Hague. 14th-20th November, 1913*, p. 56, Minute 153.

71   Statement by J. H. Oldham, personal interview, London, July, 1948.

72   *Ibid.* "The Quaker Way Wins New Adherents," by Morris Llewellyn Cooke, sheds additional light on the growing use of this same "Quaker approach" rather than that of the "majority vote" in certain private and governmental agencies and projects (e.g., in the International Monetary Fund). *The New York Times Magazine*, June 17, 1951.

73   G. K. A. Bell, *Randall Davidson, Archbishop of Canterbury*, Vol. II, pp. 740-43.

74   IRM, Vol. VIII (1919), pp. 433-90. For a penetrating analysis of the war's disastrous effect upon world-wide evangelization, see Charles W. Iglehart, "Modern War and the World Christian Mission," *The Church, The Gospel, and War*, ed. by Rufus M. Jones.

75   J. H. Oldham, "The Position of German Missions at the Outbreak of the War." On file at Missionary Research Library. This appears to be an IRM offprint which should probably be dated in the late summer of 1921, but the writer has been unable to discover where the article was printed. It lists the authoritative German statistics and supplements Oldham's "German Missions," IRM, Vol. VIII (1919), pp. 459-78.

76 *The Harvest Field*, Vol. XXXVI (1916), pp. 460-61. Through the war years *The Harvest Field* maintained a complete account of the National Missionary Council's efforts on behalf of German missions in India. See also IRM, Vol. VIII (1919), pp. 459-65. The correspondence between Bishop Westcott and Archbishop Davidson concerning German missions in India is also instructive and is included in Bell, *op. cit.*, Vol. II, pp. 435-40.

77 IRM, Vol. VIII (1919), pp. 466-74.

78 Mathews, *op cit.*, Chapter XIV. See also Mott, *Addresses and Papers*, Vol. IV, pp. 743-908.

79 Thus wrote Julius Richter: ". . . and we were exceedingly grateful to you that you had patience and sympathy enough to work through all our presentations and documents until you saw the whole situation in our light." Letter from Julius Richter to John R. Mott, December 10, 1914. This letter is on file at the Missionary Research Library, New York.

80 An example of this came from Karl Axenfeld: "We know well that you must stay neutral consistently, and we do not wish, that you may change this position in any regard. But we felt that for all that you came as a friend and that you brought with you the earnest desire to help us in our mission work as well as is compatible with perfect neutrality. We will never forget the blessing of your visit and your brotherly assistance." Letter from K. Axenfeld to John R. Mott, November 19, 1914. Missionary Research Library.

In this same letter Axenfeld makes bitter comment upon Principal Alexander Whyte's sermon, "A Case of Kaiserism in Israel, with some of its lessons to ourselves," published in *The British Weeekly*. He further asserts that no German Christian would ever take part in any conference or Christian work of which Whyte was a part.

81 Letter from G. Haussleiter to John R. Mott, October 17, 1914. Missionary Research Library.

82 FMC *Report*, 1915, p. 52.

83 Cf. "Schriftwechsel zwischen der britischen Gesandtschaft in Bern und der Basler Mission," *Norddeutsche Allgemeine Zeitung*, March 3, 1915. See also "Britische Brutalitäten in Kamerun," *Norddeutsche Allgemeine Zeitung*, "Beiblatt," March 7, 1915. At the instance of a meeting of German and Swiss missionary executives, from among whom personal testimonies to the reported mistreatments were given, Richter, as vice-chairman of the Continuation Committee, submitted these reports to Mott.

84 Letter from Lord Balfour of Burleigh to John R. Mott, March 6, 1915. Missionary Research Library. See also the correspondence between Dr. Adolf Deissman and Dr. Randall Davidson on the maltreatment of German missionaries in Africa. This exchange touches upon the Cameroons incident and is especially illuminating. Bell, *op. cit.*, Vol. II, pp. 919-25.

85 Letter from J. H. Oldham to John R. Mott, January 6, 1915. Missionary Research Library.

86 Mott, *Addresses and Papers*, Vol. III, pp. 395-403.

87 FMC *Report*, 1916, p. 173; FMC *Report*, 1917, p. 85.

88 Letter from John R. Mott to Arthur J. Brown, July 8, 1919. Missionary Research Library.

89 Quoted in Mathews, *op. cit.*, pp. 297-98.

90 *Ibid.*, p. 294. Cf. pp. 248 ff., 275, 294-99.

91 An enormous amount of material appeared in German missionary periodicals concerning Mott's Russian venture. See for example: K. Axenfeld, "Mission, americkanische Demokratie und Kriegshetze," AMZ, Vol. 44 (1917), pp. 370 ff.; *Die Reformirte Kirchen-Zeitung*, Elberfeld, August 3, 1919 and August 27, 1919; "Der

Riss in der evangelischen Mission." (This article, "The Schism in Protestant Missions," is basically a defense of the German "Declaration," for which see note 96.) EMM, Vol. 51 (1917), pp. 403-7.

See also "Wir deutschen Missionare und die Angelsachsen," AMZ, Vol. 44 (1917), pp. 284 ff. This article is followed with a "Comment by the Editor," which, being initialed "R," undoubtedly came from Richter. In it he comments that no German mission or missionary can purchase communion with Anglo-Saxons or re-entrance into international missionary co-operation by any apology for or renunciation of the emperor, the people, or the fatherland (pp. 291-92). Further on, however (p. 293), he attempts to ameliorate some of the attacks on Mott and Oldham. "As concerns the attacks upon prominent men like Oldham and John Mott, we strongly regret their tone; they are not what these men, who have earnestly striven for a basic understanding with us, have deserved from us. Would we be able to respect Mr. Oldham if in addition to his position as general secretary of the international Edinburgh Committee he were not also a real British patriot? We often fail to understand the motives and procedures of these men; therefore we suspend judgment in so far as the positions they take do not necessitate our forming an attitude. We have had the experience that in patient discussion, a genuine understanding—if not always approval—of their modes of action resulted, which allows us to maintain our Christian fellowship in the service of the same Lord."

92 Harlan P. Beach, *Renaissant Latin America: an outline and interpretation of the Congress on Christian Work in Latin America, held at Panama, February 10-19, 1916.* A popular account.

93 The reports of the eight commissions, in addition to a history of the Congress, the minutes of the daily meetings, and other relevant data, are included in *Christian Work in Latin America.* (Cover title: *Panama Congress, 1916.*)

94 Mott, *Addresses and Papers,* Vol. V, p. 190.

95 *Regional Conferences in Latin America: The reports of a series of seven conferences following the Panama Congress in 1916,* which were held at Lima, Santiago, Buenos Aires, Rio de Janeiro, Baranquilla, Havana, and San Juan. While the book lists neither author nor editor, a foreword credits the bulk of the writing to Dr. Charles Clayton Morrison, then editor of *The Christian Century.*

96 "Erklärung," AMZ, Vol. 44 (1917), pp. 305-8. English translations of this "Declaration" are on file at Edinburgh House and Day Missions Library. The declaration by the British Board of the Society of Friends was presented to the Conference of British Missionary Societies in June, 1917, and appeared in the AMZ, Vol. 44 (1917), pp. 254-55. The Swedish statement appeared in the AMZ, Vol. 43 (1916), p. 545.

97 John H. Ritson, *Christian Literature in the Mission Field: A survey of the present situation made under the direction of the Continuation Committee of the World Missionary Conference, 1910.*

98 Ritson, *The World Is Our Parish,* pp. 285-86.

99 "Continuation Committee of the World Missionary Conference, Edinburgh, 1910. Report of the Secretaries to Members of the Continuation Committee," April 16, 1916. A four-page mimeographed letter on file at Edinburgh House.

100 *Ibid.* See also IRM, Vol. V (1916), p. 40; Vol. VII (1918), p. 32; and Vol. IX (1920), p. 169.

101 J. H. Oldham, "The Question of a Conscience Clause in India," IRM, Vol. VI (1917), pp. 126-41. See also IRM, Vol. IX (1920), p. 8.

102 A mimeographed report-letter sent out by the secretary of the Continuation

Committee on the work of that body during the preceding year. Written in April, 1917, the letter is on file at Edinburgh House.

103   FMC *Report*, 1920, pp. 45-46. See also A. G. Fraser, et al., *Village Education in India: The Report of a Commission of Inquiry.*

104   CMSGBI *Report*, 1917, pp. 37-39.

105   FMC *Report*, 1918, pp. 72-90; 1921, pp. 230-63.

106   CMSGBI *Report*, 1917, p. 19.

107   Cf. Bell, op. cit., Vol. II, pp. 931-32.

108   Statement by J. H. Oldham, personal interview, London, July, 1948. That Sir Arthur Hirtzel truly appreciated the position of the missionary societies can be seen from his own book, *The Church, the Empire, and the World. Addresses on the Work of the Church Abroad.*

109   All the foregoing is taken from J. H. Oldham, "Governmental Attitudes and How to Meet them," FMC *Report*, 1920, pp. 140-44.

110   CMSGBI *Report*, 1917, p. 19. See also J. H. Ritson, "The British Government and Missions of Alien Nationality," IRM, Vol. VIII (1919), pp. 331 ff.

111   Bell, op. cit., Vol. II, p. 932.

112   J. H. Ritson, "The British Government and Missions of Alien Nationality," loc. cit., p. 339.

113   *Ibid.*, pp. 332-33. See also, J. H. Oldham, "International Cooperation in Missions," FMC *Report*, 1920, p. 76.

114   J. H. Oldham, "International Missionary Cooperation," FMC *Report*, 1921, p. 86.

115   [J. H. Oldham] *The Missionary Situation After the War. Notes prepared for the International Missionary Meeting at Crans, near Geneva June 22-28, 1920*, pp. 18-22. See also *Treaties Acts & Regulations Relating to Missionary Freedom*, pp. 10-19. This includes *Memoranda A, B,* and *C* as revised through 1923. The German view of *Memoranda A, B,* and *C* is instructive. The British government's brief word of appreciation for missions, eagerly put forward by English missions, was regarded as ". . . insignificant—we have repeatedly heard from our government more emphatic appreciation of missionary work." The *Memoranda*, it was thought, would cause all missions at work within British territories to be "Anglicized." "Missionspolitik der britischen Regierung," AMZ, Vol. 46 (1919), p. 297.

116   Statement by J. H. Oldham, personal interview, London, July, 1948.

117   J. H. Oldham, "International Cooperation in Missions," loc. cit., p. 76.

118   "Minute of Standing Committee, January 10, 1918," Minute 56, in *Conference of Missionary Societies in Great Britain and Ireland. Minutes of Standing Committee, January, 1917, to December, 1926.* This compilation of minutes is filed at Edinburgh House.

119   FMC *Report*, 1919, p. 63.

120   "Minute of Standing Committee with Dr. John R. Mott and Dr. Charles Watson, London, April 14, 1918," in *Conference of Missionary Societies in Great Britain and Ireland. Minutes of Standing Committee, January, 1917, to December, 1926.*

121   "Proposal for the Organization of the Emergency Committee of Cooperating Missions, April 4 (this should read "April 14"), 1918," in Mott, *Addresses and Papers*, Vol. V, pp. 218-19. For a German view of the Emergency Committee see EMM, Vol. 62 (1918), pp. 418 ff.

122   John H. Ritson, "The Growth of Missionary Cooperation Since 1910," IRM, Vol. VIII (1919), p. 60.

123   CMSGBI *Report*, 1918, pp. 19-20, 23-25.

124 Ibid., p. 19.
125 Charles R. Watson, "Representations at the Peace Conference," FMC *Report*, 1920, pp. 72-73.
126 Ibid., p. 74.
127 *Treaties Acts & Regulations*, pp. 6-7. These and all other documents relating to missionary freedom were printed in the IRM as they were made public. They were then collected in this single source book.
128 Watson, "Representations at the Peace Conference," loc. cit., p. 74.
129 H. W. V. Temperley, "Treaty of Versailles," *The Encyclopedia Brittanica*, 14th ed., 1929, Vol. 23, p. 95.
130 The list of German articles deploring and castigating Article 438 is a lengthy one. See Karl Axenfeld, *Germany's Battle for the Freedom of the Christian Missions*. Axenfeld viewed Article 438 as "the outraging" of German missions, than which nothing "more immoral" had ever been demanded by a government. See also AMZ, Vol. 46 (1919), p. 163-66; and "Schriftstücke zur Missionsbewegung," AMZ, Vol. 46 (1919), pp. 193-94.
131 J. H. Oldham, "International Cooperation in Missions," FMC *Report*, 1920, p. 77. See also J. H. Oldham, "International Missionary Cooperation," FMC *Report*, 1921, p. 87, and CMSGBI *Report*, 1920, pp. 193-94.
132 *Treaties Acts & Regulations*, pp. 7-9. See also IRM, Vol. IX (1920), pp. 594-96.
133 Nathan Söderblom, "Christian Missions and National Politics," IRM, Vol. VIII, 1919, pp. 497-98.
134 FMC *Report*, 1918, pp. 42-43.
135 Ibid., pp. 498-99 includes the text of this document.
136 Arthur J. Brown, "The Problem of German Missions," *The Christian Work*, Vol. 108, April 19, 1920, pp. 454, 462. This series of articles by Dr. Brown appeared regularly in thirteen installments from January 31, 1920, to June 5, 1920, and constitutes a remarkably informative account of the relations of the missionary movement with German missions. The series resulted from the extended tour through Europe Dr. Brown took in 1919 under the auspices of the Emergency Committee and contains many otherwise almost unobtainable documents and letters relevant to the problem of German missions. Henceforth this title will be cited as "German Missions."
137 Ibid., January 31, 1920, p. 149.
138 CMSGBI *Report*, 1920, pp. 22-23.
139 FMC *Report*, 1920, p. 18.
140 IRM, Vol. XI (1922), pp. 622-23; IRM, Vol. XII (1923), pp. 150-52; *Treaties Acts & Regulations*, pp. 5-6.
141 Cf., Mott, *Addresses and Papers*, Vol. V, pp. 218-21.
142 Mott's handwritten notes of the Emergency Committee Meeting, May 2 to 3, 1919. These are on file at Missionary Research Library. Mott's jottings include the interesting note to himself that the truly important thing is "to safeguard freedom (this is a better word than supranationality) of missions." For a German view of this meeting see EMM, Vol. 63 (1919), pp. 36 ff.
143 Mott's handwritten notes.
144 "Emergency Committee of Cooperating Missions. Minutes of Meeting Held on May 2nd, 1919." These typewritten minutes are on file at Edinburgh House and Day Missions Library. The larger part of the minutes is reproduced in CMSGBI *Report*, 1919, pp. 36-37.
145 Brown, "German Missions," loc. cit., April 10, 1920, pp. 453-54.
146 Ibid., p. 454.

147 The Church Peace Union was founded February 10, 1914, at the instance of, and with a two-million-dollar endowment from, Andrew Carnegie. A month earlier the Protestant churches of Switzerland had issued an important call to the churches of Europe to meet to grapple with the problem of war's growing threat. The Swiss proposal for an officially representative congress found little favour, but wide-spread concern for the problem with the encouragement of the Church Peace Union enabled a "preliminary" conference of more than eighty delegates to meet at Constance, Germany on the day that country declared war on Russia. Two days later, having set up the organization for a World Alliance for Promoting International Friendship Through the Churches, delegates fled the land an hour before all passenger service in Germany was halted. The "preliminary" conference for Roman Catholic Churches, scheduled for August 10, 1914, at Liege, never assembled.

Six years earlier and resulting from the convictions of Mr. J. Allen Baker, M.P., that closer ties between the churches of Germany and England would strengthen international peace, leaders of all English churches invited a group of German pastors, priests, and professors to England for a week in 1908. The visit was so meaningful that a year later about two hundred British Christians accepted a similar invitation to Germany. The establishment of Councils for Promoting Friendly Relations between Great Britain and Germany took place in both countries, and keen interest was taken in the movement by the Federal Council of Churches in America. The growth of friendly relations between Christians of the two countries before the war greatly encouraged the creation of the World Alliance in 1914 and facilitated immeasurably the rapid coming together in conference of Christians from these two countries shortly after its end.

The important story of the Church Peace Union, The World Alliance for International Friendship Through the Churches, and the background movements contributing to them is given in Sidney L. Gulick and Charles S. Macfarland, *The Church and International Relations*, Vol. III of *Library of Christian Cooperation*, ed. Charles S. Macfarland.

148 Brown, "German Missions," *loc. cit.*, January 31, 1920, p. 149.

149 "Konferenz des Weltbundes für Freundschaftsarbeit der Kirchen in Oud Wassenaer bei dem Haag, Holland," AMZ, Vol. 46 (1919), pp. 294-97.

150 Brown, "German Missions," *loc. cit.*, April 3, 1920, pp. 426-27, for a summary of the *Ausschuss'* recommendations.

151 *American Lutheran Survey*, Vol. XI, January 7, 1920, p. 295.

152 *Ibid.*, February 25, 1920, p. 556. See also pp. 555-57 for the commission's relations with German missions.

153 Richter wrote: "I received your letter from Paris and answered immediately by a telegram stating that the arrangements agreed upon at our Berlin Conference seem not to be touched as far as we can see by the special negotiations of the delegates of the Social Lutheran Council with some German Lutheran missionary societies. By far the majority of German missionary societies are not Lutheran in the strict denominational sense on which American Lutheranism is based, but they are united, *i.e.*, they are combined Lutheran and Reformed congregations in the same church polity, and the American Lutherans in all their negotiations with German societies have laid stress on their strict denominationalism. So, we should be grateful to you, if you would adhere to our arrangements, and we are convinced that you will do the best to help the Germans along those lines." Letter from Julius Richter to Arthur J. Brown, November 2, 1919. This letter appears in the typewritten "Report of the Rev. Dr. Arthur J. Brown As Chairman of the Special Committee on German Missions, Appointed by the Emergency Committee of Co-

operating Missions in North America On His Conferences in October and November 1919 in Holland, Germany, Belgium, France and England." On file at Missionary Research Library.

154 "Konferenz mit Herrn. J. H. Oldham in Zürich, am 13 November 1919 in der St. Ana." This brief minute of the meeting is on file at Edinburgh House.

155 General letter from J. H. Oldham on Emergency Committee stationery, London, November 17, 1919. See also CMSGBI *Report*, 1920, pp. 22-23.

156 Letter from Karl Axenfeld to Henry Hodgkin, December 12, 1919. On file at Edinburgh House.

157 Letters from J. H. Oldham to Professor Frederik Torm, March 5, and March 19, 1920. Carbons on file at Edinburgh House.

158 Letter from Julius Richter to Arthur J. Brown, February 23, 1920, and letter from P. O. Hennig to Arthur J. Brown, February 28, 1920. Missionary Research Library.

159 CMSGBI *Report*, 1920, p. 45. See also J. H. Oldham's pencilled notes, "Leiden Meeting, April 16th and 17th, 1920." On file at Edinburgh House.

160 Thus wrote Karl Fries: "It will please you to hear that I met a person the other day who had a letter from Pastor Schlunk expressing his great satisfaction at the discussion which he and the other German delegates had with you in Holland." Letter from Karl Fries to J. H. Oldham, May 28, 1920. On file at Edinburgh House.

Years later Professor Martin Schlunk said: "We (Germans) had lacked communication. I was at Leiden. It was wonderful. Lenwood and I went home as if there had never been a war." Statement by Martin Schlunk, personal interview, Tübingen, September, 1948.

161 FMC *Report*, 1921, pp. 73-77. The discussion recorded here gives one a good glimpse into the candid impressions of Crans delegates.

162 See note 115.

163 *Minute of International Missionary Meeting Held at Crans, Near Geneva, June 22-28, 1920*, pp. 9, 12, Minutes 15, 17. Henceforth to be cited as *Crans Minutes*, 1920. See also J. H. Oldham, "A New Beginning of International Missionary Cooperation," IRM, Vol. IX (1920), pp. 486-87. The fullest discussion of this problem occurs in *The Missionary Situation After the War*, Chapter III.

164 *Crans Minutes*, 1920, pp. 9-12, Minute 16. Oldham's "A New Beginning of International Missionary Cooperation," gives the substance of this statement, *loc. cit.*, pp. 490-94.

165 J. H. Oldham, *International Missionary Organization*.

166 *Crans Minutes*, 1920, pp. 13-18, Minute 21. This is reprinted in Mott, *Addresses and Papers*, Vol. V, pp. 222-28.

167 A complete account of the Crans Conference is given by J. H. Oldham in "A New Beginning of International Missionary Cooperation," IRM, Vol. IX (1920), pp. 486-87. For a German account see "Allgemeines," EMM, Vol. 64 (1920), pp. 229-30. This brief report does not mention Mott's name.

168 General letter from J. H. Oldham on Emergency Committee stationery, July 30, 1920. On file at Edinburgh House.

169 CMSGBI *Report*, 1920, p. 46.

170 *Ibid.*, 1921, p. 28, and statement by John R. Mott, personal interview, Whitby, July, 1947. See also Kenneth Maclennan, *Twenty Years of Missionary Co-operation*. This little book gives a very good brief summary of missionary co-operation from 1910 to 1927, especially that associated with the Conference of British Missionary Societies.

171 *Ibid.*, pp. 29-31.

172 *Ibid.*, pp. 29-31.
173 FMC *Report*, 1920, p. 44.
174 *Ibid.*, pp. 22, 89-90.
175 *Ibid.*, 1921, pp. 59-60.

CHAPTER V. *The Rise of the International Missionary Council, 1921-27*

1 *Verhandlungen der XIV. Kontinentalen Missions-Konferenz zu Bremen vom 28. April bis 2. Mai 1921*, pp. 52-62.
2 The quotation from Richter is included in a letter from J. H. Oldham to G. B. A. Gerdener, May 17, 1921. On file at Edinburgh House.
3 "Report of the Conference with Messrs. J. H. Oldham, Frank Lenwood, and Dr. Warnshuis, 1st-3rd July, 1921, at the YMCA, 34 Wilhelmstrasse, Berlin." See also J. H. Oldham's personal notes on the meeting. Both these items are on file at Edinburgh House. Oldham wrote: ". . . not a word was said during these three days to which we could legitimately take exception. Throughout an unbroken spirit of fellowship was manifested notwithstanding the deep differences of view. We were treated with the utmost courtesy and came away with an enhanced respect for the character of those whom we met." Oldham's personal notes.
4 *Minutes of the International Missionary Council, Lake Mohonk, New York, U.S.A., October 1-6, 1921*, p. 34, Minute 33. Henceforth cited as IMC *Minutes*. Dr. Frank Mason North chaired the committee that drafted the constitution. With great clarity he helped all to understand what were then assumed to be necessary limitations upon the powers and functions of the council.
5 Frank Lenwood, "The International Missionary Council at Lake Mohonk, October, 1921," IRM, Vol. XI (1922), p. 36. At Crans Oldham had favoured "International Missionary Conference." Letter from J. H. Oldham to Robert E. Speer, May 5, 1921. On file at Edinburgh House. At the same time Oldham argued that the proposed International Missionary Committee would not be a committee in the usual sense of that word, for in the ordinary committee a majority decision settles policy while the new body would operate on the Hague principle. Moreover, he insisted, "the essence of a committee is that it *meets*," and the proposed agency in no sense could do that, a lesson he had learned from the international meetings of the Continuation Committee. The new body, he maintained before Mohonk, would have to be more like a conference than a committee. It also faced, according to Oldham, two impossible alternatives: (1) either to go its own way independently of the boards, or (2) to follow the Hague principle literally and never get anything done. The only solution he saw was a middle course, "vulnerable on paper," yet, "which with sufficient mutual confidence can be made to work." Full recognition of this fact, he pointed out, had led Crans to insert the clause "that the successful working of the International Missionary Committee is entirely dependent upon the gift from God of the spirit of fellowship, mutual understanding, and desire to co-operate." Letter from J. H. Oldham to the Reverend Canon Sydney Gould, May 5, 1921. On file at Edinburgh House.
6 IMC *Minutes*, Lake Mohonk, 1921, p. 40, Minute 39.
7 *Ibid.*, p. 34, Minute 33.
8 *Ibid.*, p. 36, Minute 33.
9 *Ibid.*, pp. 34-35, Minute 33.
10 *Ibid.*, pp. 36-37, Minute 33.
11 See "The Church and the Mission," IRM, Vol. X (1921), pp. 478 ff.

12 IMC *Minutes*, Lake Mohonk, 1921, pp. 46-48, Minute 48.

13 *Ibid.*, pp. 52-53, Minutes 52-53. See below, note 82.

14 *Ibid.*, pp. 51-52, Minute 51. See also Lenwood, *loc. cit.*, pp. 37-39.

15 *Ibid.*, pp. 51-52, Minute 51.

16 *Ibid.*, pp. 54-56, Minute 56.

17 CMSGBI *Minutes*, 1922, p. 34.

18 *Allgemeine Missions-Zeitschrift*, Vol. 49 (1922), pp. 344 ff.

19 Charles H. Fahs and Helen E. Davis, *Conspectus of Cooperative Missionary Enterprises*, p. 75.

20 *Ibid.*, p. 76. See also *Council Notes of the International Missionary Council*, no. 2, June 1, 1923, p. 2. Henceforth cited as *Council Notes*.

21 Ferd Munck, "Det nordiske Delegeretmøde for Ydre Mission," *Nordisk Missions-Tideskrift*, Series III, Vol. XI (1922), pp. 94 ff.

22 *Council Notes*, no. 2, June 1, 1923, p. 2.

23 *Ibid.*, p. 2. See also Fahs and Davis, *op. cit.*, p. 35.

24 F. Rawlinson, Helen Thoburn, and D. MacGillivray, eds., *The Chinese Church As Revealed in the National Christian Conference, Held in Shanghai, Tuesday, May 2, to Thursday, May 11, 1922.*

25 *The China Mission Yearbook*, 1923, Vol. XI, p. 62. IRM, Vol. XI (1922), pp. 502 ff.

26 *The China Mission Yearbook*, 1923, Vol. XI, pp. 34-65. *Ibid.*, Vol. XII (1924), pp. 147-53.

27 *The Christian Movement in Japan Korea and Formosa*, 1923, Vol. XXI, pp. 297-302.

28 *Ibid.*, pp. 303-12; 1924, Vol. XXII, pp. 269-76. See also *Council Notes* no. 2, April, 1924, p. v.

29 *The Harvest Field*, Vol. 42 (1922), pp. 41-68, 81-83, 89-108.

30 *Ibid.*, Vol. 43 (1923), pp. 85-95. See also IRM, Vol. XII (1923), pp. 272-76.

31 *Minutes of the Fourth Annual Meeting of the Korean National Christian Council Held in the First Methodist Church, Seoul, Korea, September 20, 1927,* p. 4.

32 *Ibid.*, pp. 15-18.

33 Alfred Stonelake, "The Missionary Situation in Congo," IRM, Vol. VIII (1919), p. 326.

34 Fahs and Davis, *op. cit.*, pp. 31-33.

35 John R. Mott, "The Outlook in the Moslem World," IRM, Vol. XIII (1924), pp. 321-39. See also Ruth Wilder Braisted, *In This Generation: The Story of Robert P. Wilder*, pp. 169 ff.

36 Fahs and Davis, *op. cit.*, p. 68. See also John R. Mott, *Addresses and Papers of John R. Mott*, Vol. V, pp. 405-14.

37 Fahs and Davis, *op. cit.*, p. 69. See also Mott, *Addresses and Papers*, Vol. 5, pp. 415-22.

38 J. H. Oldham, "New Spiritual Adventures in the Mission Field," IRM, Vol. XI (1922), pp. 526-50.

39 IMC *Minutes*, Oxford, 1923.

40 IMC Committee *Minutes*, Canterbury, 1922.

41 IMC Committee *Minutes*, Atlantic City, 1925.

42 IMC Committee *Minutes*, Rättvik, 1926.

43 See Robert E. Speer, "Is Identity of Doctrinal Opinion Necessary to Continued Missionary Cooperation?" and E. J. Palmer, "The Practicability of Missionary Cooperation in Face of Doctrinal Differences," IRM, Vol. XII (1923), pp. 497-514.

44 IMC *Minutes*, Oxford, 1923, pp. 37-38, Minute 64. This is reprinted in IRM, Vol. XII (1923), pp. 491-92.

45 *Ibid.*, p. 38, Minute 64.

46 *Ibid.*, p. 38, Minute 64.

47 "Memorandum from Warnshuis and Oldham to Maclennan and Turner." This six-page typewritten memorandum was signed by Oldham and should probably be dated in the 1922-23 period. It is on file at Edinburgh House and Day Missions Library.

48 Yet, commenting on this situation in another context, Oldham had been careful to explain that the Conference of British Missionary Societies' Committee on Relations with Governments was primarily an international and not a strictly British organ. "This committee was constituted at my special request, as international secretary, to provide for me a standing ground from which I could deal with these international questions insofar as they involve relationships with the British Government." Letter from J. H. Oldham to A. L. Warnshuis, November 4, 1922. On file in the International Misisonary Council office archives, New York. See also note 76 and accompanying text.

49 "Memorandum from Warnshuis and Oldham to Maclennan and Turner," *loc. cit.*

50 J. H. Oldham, *International Missionary Cooperation. A Statement of Fundamental Questions of Policy for consideration by the Committee of the International Missionary Council, January 11-15, 1925*, pp. 4-5. This paper was drafted by Oldham and revised after consultation with Mott and Warnshuis.

51 *Ibid.*, passim. See also A. L. Warnshuis, "International Missionary Cooperation. II. Some Practical Suggestions." This mimeographed seven page paper should be dated in the late winter of 1924. On file at Edinburgh House and International Missionary Council office, New York.

52 Letter from A. L. Warnshuis to John R. Mott, November 11, 1927. On file at the International Missionary Council office, New York.

53 *International Missionary Cooperation*, p. 5.

54 IMC Committee *Minutes*, Atlantic City, 1925, pp. 4, 22-23, Minutes 4, 29.

55 *Ibid.*, pp. 5-6, Minute 6.

56 *Ibid.*, p. 24, Minute 31.

57 IMC Committee *Minutes*, Rättvik, 1926, pp. 7-10, Minute 12.

58 IMC Committee *Minutes*, Atlantic City, 1925, pp. 6-7, 23-24, Minutes 8, 30.

59 Statement by John R. Mott, personal interview, Whitby, July, 1947.

60 J. H. Oldham, *A Devotional Diary*. See also by the same author *The Possibilities of Prayer*, and *The World and the Gospel*.

61 For some background on Oldham's Africa interest and for an indication of the great trust placed in him on African affairs by the Archbishop of Canterbury, see G. K. A. Bell, *Randall Davidson, Archbishop of Canterbury*, Vol. II, pp. 1229-35.

62 FMC Report, 1926, p. 83.

63 IMC Committee *Minutes*, Rättvik, 1926, p. 8, Minute 12.

64 *Ibid.*, pp. 8-9, Minute 12.

65 Letter to the writer from Miss B. D. Gibson, June 23, 1950.

66 IRM, Vol. XVI (1927), p. 127.

67 Margaret Sinclair, *William Paton*, p. 17. Miss Sinclair has provided a valuable record of Paton's life.

68 Much of this is revealed in his first book. See William Paton, *Jesus*

Christ and the World's Religions. This little text on comparative religion was reprinted several times in the course of its first decade.

69   Since Paton had gone out under the YMCA and since many of its plans centered around him, he found it most difficult to surrender his position. Yet he accepted the challenge of the new co-operative work because of his faith in the men who encouraged him to take it, not least of whom was the Metropolitan of the Church of India, Burma, and Ceylon. Sinclair, *op. cit.,* pp. 82-89. Oldham, who was also in India at the time and was instrumental in laying the groundwork for reconstructing the National Missionary Council as the National Christian Council, played an important rôle in securing Paton for the post.

70   IMC Committee *Minutes,* Rättvik, 1926, pp. 14-15, Minute 24. See also p. 21, Minute 35. Oldham, who had suggested Paton's name, felt justified in doing so—quite apart from Paton's obvious personal qualifications—because of his conviction that health and other family considerations warranted his return to England from India. Statement by J. H. Oldham, personal interview, London, July, 1948.

71   A. L. Warnshuis, "The Critical Situation in German Missions," *Missionary Review of the World,* Vol. XXXVII New Series (1924), p. 199.

72   *Ibid.,* p. 199.

73   *Quarterly Notes. Being the Bulletin of the International Missionary Council,* no. 3, July, 1924, pp. iv-v. Henceforth cited as *Quarterly Notes.*

74   FMC *Report,* 1922, pp. 49-50; 1923, pp. 45-47; 1924; p. 34; 1926, pp. 41-43 (includes reports for 1924 and 1925).

75   In addition to those listed in note 74, see also FMC *Report,* 1917, p. 85; 1919, pp. 136-37; 1920, pp. 44, 89-90; 1921, p. 59; 1927, pp. 41-42.

76   IMC Committee *Minutes,* Canterbury, 1922, p. 17, Minute 30. See also note 48 above.

77   *Ibid.,* p. 17, Minute 30.

78   Cf. CMSGBI *Report,* 1923, p. 7; 1925, p. 28; 1926, p. 29; 1927, p. 54; 1928, p. 34; 1929, p. 34.

79   *Council Notes,* no. 1, January, 1923, p. 2.

80   *Ibid.,* p. 2. German missionaries did not, however, return to French colonies.

81   CMSGBI *Report,* 1925, p. 27. See also *Quarterly Notes,* no. 11, July, 1926, pp. iv-v, and no. 15, July, 1927, pp. v-vi.

82   IMC Committee *Minutes,* Canterbury, 1922, pp. 17-20, Minute 30. See also A. L. Warnshuis, *The Relations of Missions and Governments in Belgian, French and Portuguese Colonies.*

83   See *Papers on Educational Problems in Mission Fields.*

84   On the Indian Commission see above, p. 177. On the Burton Commission see *Christian Education in China. The Report of the China Educational Commissions of 1921-1922.*

85   IMC *Minutes,* Oxford, 1923, p. 12, Minute 14. See also CMSGBI *Report,* 1924, p. 32, and *Quarterly Notes,* no. 1, January 1924, pp. i-ii.

86   See J. H. Oldham, "Educational Policy of the British Government in Africa," IRM, Vol. XIV (1925), pp. 421-27.

87   CMSGBI *Report,* 1925, p. 25. FMC *Report,* 1926, pp. 84-87. *Quarterly Notes,* no. 14, April, 1927, pp. i-iii.

Oldham's view of one aspect of the Institute casts an illuminating sidelight on the Anglo-American cast of the International Missionary Council. He wrote: "The Institute strikes me as a much more genuinely international organization than our own Council, due I think to the fact that English is not the only medium of intercourse. We owe a great deal to Vissher. There is no doubt that his complete mastery of French and German has done a great deal to make the Germans, French and Belgians feel that the enterprise is not primarily an Anglo-Saxon undertaking. It has been a great lesson to me. If I were ten years younger, I think I should make a point of trying to live for a year in France and Germany in order to try to learn to talk these languages." Letter from J. H. Oldham to A. L. Warnshuis, November 1, 1926. On file in the Council's New York office.

88 Thomas Jesse Jones, *Education in Africa. A Study of West, South, and Equatorial Africa by the African Education Commission, under the Auspices of the Phelps-Stokes Fund and Foreign Mission Societies of North America and Europe.*

89 Thomas Jesse Jones, *Education in East Africa. A Study of East, Central and South Africa by the second African Education Commission under the Auspices of the Phelps-Stokes Fund, in cooperation with the International Education Board.* See also J. H. Oldham, "The Christian Opportunity in Africa. Some Reflections on the Report of the Phelps-Stokes Commission," IRM, Vol. XIV (1925), pp. 173 ff.

90 J. H. Oldham, "Religious Education in the Mission Field," IRM, Vol. XIII (1924), pp. 500 ff. See also *Quarterly Notes,* no. 4, October, 1924, pp. v-vi.

91 *Christian Literature in Moslem Lands. A Study of the Activities of the Moslem and Christian Press in all Mohammedan Countries.*

92 C. E. Wilson, "The Provision of a Christian Literature for Africa," IRM, Vol. XV (1926), pp. 506 ff.

93 Edwin W. Smith, *The Christian Mission in Africa. A study based on the work of the International Conference at Le Zoute, Belgium, September 14th to 21st, 1926,* pp. viii, 192. See also IRM, Vol. XVI, 1927, pp. 24-25.

94 *Quarterly Notes,* no. 16, October, 1927, p. iv.

95 IMC *Minutes,* Oxford, 1923, p. 35, Minute 61.

96 IMC Committee *Minutes,* Canterbury, 1922, p. 16, Minute 29.

97 The files of the Council's office in New York contain a tremendous store of material, much of it from the League of Nations Opium Commission, on the poppy-derived narcotic. See also *Quarterly Notes,* no. 2, April, 1924, pp. iii-iv; FMC *Report,* 1926, pp. 100-101, 1927, p. 108; Sit William J. Collins, "A Review of the Geneva Opium Conferences," IRM, Vol. XV (1926), pp. 169 ff.

98 IMC Committee *Minutes,* Rättvik, 1926, p. 7, Minute 10. Also FMC *Report,* 1926, p. 100; 1927, p. 109; 1928, p. 59. The files of the Council's office in New York contain considerable material bearing on this question. See *Quarterly Notes,* no. 9, January, 1926, pp. v-vi. See also E. A. Ross, *Report on Employment of Native Labor in Portuguese Africa.* Warnshuis was instrumental in assembling a committee and in gaining financial support for the Ross survey. The report was submitted to the Secretary-General of the League of Nations.

99 IMC *Minutes,* Oxford, 1923, *passim.*

100 B. D. Gibson, ed., *The Place of Women in the Church on the Mission Field.*

101 Ralph Dillingham Wellons, *The Organizations Set Up For the Control of Mission Union Higher Educational Institutions.*

102 IMC Committee *Minutes,* Rättvik, 1926, p. 6, Minute 10. See also *Quarterly Notes,* 1924-27, *passim.* See also A. L. Warnshuis, ed., *Chinese Christian Education.*

103 *Quarterly Notes,* no. 4, October, 1924, pp. ii-iii. See also IMC Committee *Minutes,* Rättvik, 1926, p. 23, Minute 36 (g); and IRM, Vol. XVI (1927), *passim.*

104 IMC Committee *Minutes,* Rättvik, 1926, pp. 21-22, Minute 36 (b). See

also Heinrich Frick, "Is a Conviction of the Superiority of his Message Essential to the Missionary?" IRM, Vol. XV (1926), pp. 625 ff. Several other articles on missionary "appeal" and "motive" appear in the same volume.

105 Fennell P. Turner and Frank Knight Sanders, eds., *The Foreign Missions Convention at Washington, 1925. Addresses Delivered at the Foreign Missions Convention of the United States and Canada Held at Washington, D. C., January 28 to February 2, 1925.*

106 Robert E. Speer, Samuel G. Inman, and Frank K. Sanders, eds., *Christian Work in South America. Official Report of the Congress on Christian Work in South America, at Montevideo, Uruguay, April, 1926,* Vol. I, p. 8.

107 *Ibid., passim.* See also Robert E. Speer, "The Congress on Christian Work in South America," IRM, Vol. VIX (1925), pp. 499-513.

108 IMC Committee *Minutes,* Canterbury, 1922, pp. 9, 20. Minutes 13, 30 (r).

109 John R. Mott, "The Outlook in the Moslem World," IRM, Vol. XIII (1924), pp. 321 ff.

110 *Conferences of Christian Workers Among Moslems 1924. A brief account of the conferences together with their findings and lists of members.* The whole section on "Findings" in this privately printed book is reproduced in Mott, *Addresses and Papers,* Vol. V, pp. 332-57.

111 Mott, *Addresses and Papers,* Vol. V, p. 343.

112 *Ibid.,* p. 354.

113 *Ibid.,* p. 368.

114 *Ibid.,* pp. 358-67.

115 *Ibid.,* pp. 376-87.

116 *Ibid.,* pp. 393-400, 403-5.

117 *Ibid.,* pp. 405-11.

118 *Ibid.,* pp. 415-22.

119 IMC *Minutes,* Oxford, 1923, p. 33, Minute 52. This discussion resulted from the attention then being given to the question of Jewish evangelization by the Conference of British Missionary Societies. The latter's interest had sprung from Ritson's earlier literature meetings for societies at work among the Jews. Maclennan was largely responsible for drawing many of these societies into the Conference.

120 IMC Committee *Minutes,* Rättvik, 1926, p. 20, Minute 32.

121 *The Christian Approach to the Jew. Being a Report of Conferences on the Subject, Held at Budapest and Warsaw in April 1927.* See also Mott, *Addresses and Papers,* Vol. V, pp. 423 ff.

122 Mott, *Addresses and Papers,* Vol. V, p. 428.

123 *Ibid.,* pp. 433, 439, 443-44.

124 *The Jerusalem Meeting of the International Missionary Council, March 24-April 8, 1928,* Vol. VIII, p. 24.

125 IMC Committee *Minutes* Rättvik, 1926, pp. 11-13, Minutes 17-19.

126 Letter from A. L. Warnshuis to J. H. Oldham, October 26, 1926. On file in the Council's New York office.

127 See, for example, a two-page typewritten statement by Miss B. D. Gibson, October 16, 1925, "Jerusalem Conference." See also a letter from John R. Mott to A. L. Warnshuis, August 19, 1926, in which he urges Warnshuis to interview Europeans individually at Le Zoute and persuade them to attend Jerusalem. Both of these are on file at the Council's New York office.

128 IRM, Vol. XVI (1927), pp. 278 ff.

129 Letter from John R. Mott to A. L. Warnshuis, March 14, 1927. On file in the Council's New York office.

130 Statement by J. H. Oldham, personal interview, London, July, 1948.

131 Basil Mathews, *John R. Mott, World Citizen*, pp. 267-69.

132 *Jerusalem Meeting, 1928*, Vol. VIII, p. 6. See also Karl Heim, "Die Tagung des erweiterten internationalen Missionsrat in Jerusalem," *Evangelisches Missionsmagazin*, Vol. 72 (1928), pp. 161-64. In commenting finally on this Cairo meeting, Karl Heim wrote: "Despite the surprising agreement with our German standpoint which we met at Cairo, many of us, nevertheless, proceeded to Jerusalem with the fear that as representatives of the old Biblical Gospel we should find ourselves opposed by a crushing majority of others for whom the Kingdom of God means nothing more than the League of Nations, democracy, and the overcoming of militarism and capitalism." See further "Series C. 1. The Christian Message. Summary of the Meeting of Continental Delegates in Cairo on March 16, 1928, on the Subject of Religions." This two-page mimeographed document is on file at the Council's New York office. It (1) urges that Continental delegates make known their feelings in form of a communication; (2) indicates that their uneasiness about the "eventual syncretistic trend of the papers" arises not as accusation but as a question of the proper method of approach; (3) imparts a most conciliatory tone throughout.

CHAPTER VI. A Decade of Crisis and Advance, 1928-38

1 F. A. Iremonger, *William Temple, Archbishop of Canterbury, His Life and Letters*, p. 396.

2 Basil Mathews, *Roads to the City of God*, p. 17.

3 *Minutes of the International Missionary Council and of the Committee of the Council (Enlarged Meeting) Jerusalem, March 24–April 8, 1928*, p. 32, Minute 29. Henceforth cited as "IMC Minutes."

4 William Paton, *Jerusalem, 1928*, pp. 5-6.

5 *The World Mission of Christianity. Messages and Recommendations of the Enlarged Meeting of the International Missionary Council held at Jerusalem, March 24–April 8, 1928.* Henceforth cited as *World Mission of Christianity*.

6 Oliver Chase Quick, "The Jerusalem Meeting and the Christian Message," *The International Review of Missions*, Vol. XVII (1928), pp. 445-46. Henceforth cited as IRM.

7 *The Jerusalem Meeting of the International Missionary Council, March 24-April 8, 1928*, Vol. I, p. 273. Henceforth cited as *Jerusalem, 1928*.

8 *Ibid.*, Vol. I, pp. 401 ff.

9 Iremonger, *op. cit.*, pp. 396-97.

10 Karl Heim, "Die Tagung des erweiterten internationalen Missionsrats in Jerusalem," *Evangelisches Missionsmagazin*, Vol. 72 (1928), pp. 161-64.

11 *Ibid.*, p. 163. Yet see also M. M. Underhill, "A German View of the Jerusalem Meeting," IRM, Vol. XVIII (1929), pp. 266-72, for a review of Martin Schlunk's *Von den Höhen des Oelberges*. Schlunk spoke of the difficult necessity in a meeting such as Jerusalem for many Germans to accept a particular formulation of words in a theological document which may appear to establish wide agreement. He pointed out that if these were fully and adequately interpreted, the varying interpretations would disclose no unity of view at all.

12 Although Paul refers to "my fellow workers for the kingdom of God" (Col. 4:11), the New Testament nowhere speaks of "building" the kingdom of God, but of "receiving" or "entering" it. Extreme emphasis upon man's rôle as a

builder of the kingdom of God could and did result in as much distortion of the New Testament understanding of it as did the equally extreme emphasis upon man's incapacity and passivity before an omnipotent God.

13 Roland Allen, *Jerusalem: A Critical Review of "The World Mission of Christianity."*

14 *Jerusalem*, 1928, Vol. VI, *passim*.

15 *Ibid.*, Vol. IV, pp. 195-202.

16 *Ibid.*, Vol. V, pp. 3-90.

17 *Ibid.*, pp. 141-43.

18 *Ibid.*, pp. 149-50.

19 IMC *Minutes*, Jerusalem, 1928, p. 49, Minute 68; p. 58, Minute 23. Cf. Charles W. Iglehart, "Modern War and the World Christian Mission," in *The Church, the Gospel and War*, ed. Rufus M. Jones, p. 130. Iglehart was at Jerusalem as a delegate from Japan.

20 For all the foregoing see *Jerusalem*, 1928, Vol. II.

21 IRM, Vol. XVIII (1929), pp. 28-29. The story had spread among the Moslems that the Jews had enlisted the Christians in support of their cause and that the meeting was part of a plan to seize Jerusalem. Fortunately, no incidents occurred, but the government provided armed soldiers as sentry-guards at the gates of the conference grounds.

22 Chester E. Tulga, *The Case Against Modernism in Foreign Missions*, p. 9. See also Roland Allen, *op. cit.*

23 F. Torm, "The Place of Social Questions in Missionary Work," IRM, Vol. XIX (1930), p. 602.

24 *Ibid.*, p. 597.

25 H. Kraemer, "Christianity and Secularism," *ibid.*, pp. 198-99.

26 Karl Hartenstein, "The Theology of the Word and Missions," *ibid.*, Vol. XX (1931), pp. 210-27. Emil Brunner, "Secularism as a Problem for the Church," *ibid.*, Vol. XIX (1930), pp. 495-511. See also Adolf Keller, *Karl Barth and Christian Unity*, Chap. VII.

27 John R. Mott, *Addresses and Papers of John R. Mott*, Vol. V, p. 667.

28 *Jerusalem*, 1928, Vol. III, pp. 165-72.

As a sidelight on this point, it is interesting to note that during Jerusalem's sessions, two private meetings were held between members of the British delegation and members of the National Christian Council of China. The British, representing the opinion of their boards, were strongly critical of some aspects of the National Christian Council's work. That body was thought to be more concerned with "organic" than "spiritual unity," set against "conservative or fundamentalist bodies," political and "pacifist" in its interests, and not fully representative of Christianity in China. Much emphasis centered upon political statements thought to represent the National Christian Council. One Chinese pointed out that anything not "pro-British" was regarded by the British as "anti-British." Wilson Cash was the major spokesman in the first meeting and William Paton chaired the second. The two sessions clearly illustrate the fact that with all the unanimity at Jerusalem between representatives of older and younger churches, certain tensions were clearly evident. See "Minutes of Meeting held at Jerusalem—2nd April, 1928, between representatives of the British Delegation and and members of the National Christian Council of China." and "Minutes of Second meeting held at Jerusalem, 4th April, 1928, between representatives of the British Delegation and members of the N.C.C. of China." Each of these five-page mimeographed documents is on file in the Council's New York office.

29 *World Mission of Christianity*, p. 32.

30 Cf. Erasmo Braga, "Following Up the Jerusalem Meeting in Brazil," IRM, Vol. XVIII (1929), pp. 261-65. See also *China Christian Yearbook*, 1929, pp. 222-25; *Japan Christian Quarterly*, Vol. III (1928), pp. 214-70; and *National Christian Council Review*, Vol. VI New Series (1928), pp. 283-311.

31 See an interpretative article by "the Father of the Movement," Cheng Ching-yi, "An Interpretation of the Five-Year Movement in China," IRM, Vol. XX (1931), pp. 173-88. See also *China Christian Yearbook*, 1931, pp. 126-29; *ibid.*, 1932-33, pp. 203-11; *ibid.*, 1934-35, pp. 196-97.

32 Michio Kozaki, "Dr. Kagawa and 'The Kingdom of God Movement,'" IRM, Vol. XVIII (1929), pp. 573-83; Toyohiko Kagawa, "Three Main Objectives of the Kingdom of God Movement," IRM, Vol. XX (1931), pp. 333-44. See also *The Japan Mission Yearbook*, 1930, pp. 139-47; *The Japan Christian Yearbook*, 1932, pp. 91-108.

33 J. Waskom Pickett, *Christian Mass Movements in India*.

34 *Jerusalem*, 1928, Vol. VII, pp. 42-48.

35 IMC *Minutes*, Jerusalem, 1928, p. 65, Minute 3.

36 *World Mission of Christianity*, p. 52.

37 "Resignation of John R. Mott from the General Secretaryship of the National Council of the Young Men's Christian Associations of the United States of America." This four-page printed pamphlet is on file at the Council's New York office. The dinner at which Mott gave this address took place June 20, 1928. He stated at that time: "To a little band of unnamed friends who for thirty-three of the forty years of my service have provided funds so that my salary and expenses and likewise those of my personal staff have not been a charge on the budget of the Association or of the other agencies to which I have been related is due a tribute of deepest gratitude."

38 Simply as one sample of this see R. E. Diffendorfer, "The World Mission of Christianity and the Modern Preacher," IRM, Vol. XIX (1930), pp. 420-27. This account describes what the Methodist Episcopal Church in the United States did to help all its ministers utilize to best advantage the materials and findings of Jerusalem.

39 *Quarterly Notes, Being the Bulletin of the International Missionary Council*, no. 26, April, 1930, p. vii.

40 IRM, Vol. XXI (1932), p. 92.

41 *Quarterly Notes*, no. 21, January, 1929, p. i.

42 Karl Hartenstein, "The Theology of the Word and Missions," IRM, Vol. XX (1931), p. 225.

43 Cf. Adolf Keller, *Karl Barth and Christian Unity*, pp. 239-47.

44 Cf. Julius Richter, "The Missionary Crisis," IRM, Vol. XXIII (1934), pp. 313-24.

45 IMC Committee *Minutes*, Williamstown, 1929. IMC Committee *Minutes*, Herrnhut, 1932. IMC Committee *Minutes*, Northfield, 1935.

46 IMC Committee *Minutes*, Herrnhut, 1932, p. 30, Minute 38.

47 IMC Ad Interim Committee *Minutes*, Salisbury, 1934. IMC Ad Interim Committee *Minutes*, Old Jordans, 1936. IMC Interim Committee *Minutes*, London, 1937.

48 "William Paton Report Letter, September 21, 1935," on file in the Council's New York office. See also *The Student World*, Vol. XXVIII (1935), and *Quarterly Notes*, no. 49, January, 1936, p. ii.

49 Margaret Sinclair, *William Paton*, pp. 145-47.

50 *Ibid.*, pp. 175 ff. See especially pp. 199-201 for the Near East.

51 *Ibid.*, p. 143.

52   *Ibid.*, pp. 160-62.

53   Mott, *Addresses and Papers*, Vol. V, pp. 523-38. See also *Quarterly Notes*, no. 24, October, 1929, p. vii.

What appears to have been a Mott-initiated project growing out of the 1929 Bangkok Conference is Carle C. Zimmerman's study, *Siam Rural Economic Survey, 1930-31*. This survey, made by an associate professor from Harvard, was conducted with the co-operation of Siamese government officials and Buddhist priests. Although the book contains no reference to the International Missionary Council, the author's preface accords thanks to Dr. John R. Mott, Dr. and Mrs. George B. McFarland of Bangkok, and the National Christian Council of Siam for their help in initiating the survey. A letter reproduced in the front of the book from His Royal Highness, Purachatra, referring to the author says, "We have welcomed you among us because you came as a volunteer at the request of the International Council of Missions . . ."

54   Mott, *Addresses and Papers*, Vol. V, pp. 539-51.

55   *Quarterly Notes*, no. 24, October, 1929, p. v.

56   IMC Committee *Minutes*, Williamstown, 1929, pp. 7-8, Minute 9.

57   Basil Mathews, *John R. Mott, World Citizen*, p. 260.

58   Mott, *Addresses and Papers*, Vol. V, pp. 454-81.

59   Joseph I. Parker, ed., *Directory of World Missions*, p. 160.

60   *Quarterly Notes*, no. 44, October, 1934, p. iii.

61   Mott, *Addresses and Papers*, Vol. V, pp. 481-99. See also *Findings of Conferences Held Under the Leadership of Dr. John R. Mott, Chairman of the International Missionary Council at Léopoldville, Mutoto and Elizabethville, Congo Belge, 1934.*

62   Mott, *Addresses and Papers*, pp. 499-522.

63   *Ibid.*, pp. 522-76.

64   IRM, Vol. XXV (1936), p. 24.

65   *Quarterly Notes*, no. 47, July, 1935, p. i.

66   *Ibid.*, no. 59, July, 1938, p. vii.

67   Fahs and Davis, *op. cit.*, pp. 23-24.

68   *Ibid.*, p. 22. See especially Rodolfo Anders, *A Escola Dominical*, p. 28.

69   IMC Committee *Minutes*, Northfield, 1935, p. 19, Minute 32.

70   Samuel Guy Inman, *Evangelicals at Havana, Being an Account of the Hispanic American Evangelical Congress, at Havana, Cuba, June 20-30, 1929.*

71   Personal letter from Ds. Joh. Blauw, October 6, 1949. In 1946 the Reformed Churches (Reformed Synod, Zwolle) decided to participate with full membership in the Netherlands Missionary Council.

72   International Missionary Council letterhead, November, 1937.

73   *Quarterly Notes*, no. 48, October, 1935, p. v; IRM, Vol. XXV (1936), p. 91; CMSGBI *Report*, 1935, p. 30.

74   Letter from S. Knak, on behalf of the German *Missions-Tag*, to the International Missionary Council, October 9, 1934. On file at Edinburgh House and Day Missions Library.

75   "Crisis in the Work of German Missions." This three-page mimeographed statement was probably prepared in late November, 1934, by Miss B. D. Gibson. On file at Edinburgh House and Day Missions Library.

76   CMSGBI *Report*, 1935, p. 30. See also letter from S. Knak to J. H. Oldham, December 15, 1934. Mimeographed copies are on file at Edinburgh House and Day Missions Library.

77   CMSGBI *Report*, 1935, pp. 29-31; 1936, pp. 31-32. FMC *Report*, 1935, p. 33; 1936, pp. 42-43. See also *Quarterly Notes*, no. 45, January, 1935, pp. ii-iii; no. 46, April, 1935, pp. vi-vii.

78 *Quarterly Notes*, no. 48, October, 1935, p. vi.

79 FMC Report, 1936, p. 43. See also K. Appenzeller, "The Present Situation of the German Evangelical Missions at the Home Base," IRM, Vol. XXV (1936), pp. 516-25 and IMC Committee *Minutes*, Northfield, 1935, Appendix C, pp. 45-46.

80 IRM, Vol. XXVII (1938), pp. 96-97; Vol. XXVIII (1939), pp. 87-88.

81 IMC *Minutes*, Jerusalem, 1928, p. 35, Minute 42. *World Mission of Christianity*, pp. 52-53.

82 IMC Committee *Minutes*, Williamstown, 1929, pp. 22-24, Minute 27. IMC *Ad Interim* Committee *Minutes*, Salisbury, 1934, pp. 10-11, Minute 8.

83 Letter from John R. Mott to A. T. Thompson, November 19, 1930. On file at the Council's New York office.

84 F. Torm, "The Place of Social Questions in Missionary Work," IRM, Vol. XIX (1930), pp. 593-605.

85 IMC Committee *Minutes*, Herrnhut, 1932, Appendix A, pp. 47-49.

86 *Ibid.*, pp. 30-33, Minute 39, paragraph 2.

87 Statement by John R. Mott, personal interview, Whitby, July, 1947.

88 IMC Committee *Minutes*, Herrnhut, 1932, Appendix D, pp. 75-77 and IMC Committee *Minutes*, Northfield, 1935, Appendix E, p. 49.

89 IMC Committee *Minutes*, Northfield, 1935, Appendix E, p. 50. See also L. A. Notcutt and G. C. Latham, *The African and the Cinema. An Account of the work of the Bantu Educational Cinema Experiment during the period March 1935 to May 1937.*

90 *World Mission of Christianity*, p. 62.

91 FMC Report, 1930, p. 86. Warnshuis had full responsibility for financing and administering the Butterfield project.

92 Kenyon L. Butterfield, *The Christian Mission in Rural India.*

93 Kenyon L. Butterfield, *The Rural Mission of the Church in Eastern Asia. Report and Recommendations.*

94 FMC Report, 1932, pp. 66-67. See also Kenyon L. Butterfield, "Rural Work and Mission Policy," IRM, Vol. XXI (1932), pp. 412-22.

95 FMC Report, 1930, p. 87. Dean Paul Monroe of the College of Agriculture and Warnshuis were instrumental in arranging the course for missionaries.

96 *Ibid.*, 1932, p. 67. See also Mott, *Addresses and Papers*, Vol. V, pp. 750-56.

97 Sinclair, William Paton, pp. 170-73. See also *The Christian College in India. The Report of the Commission on Christian Higher Education*, p. v.

98 Sinclair, *op. cit.*, pp. 173-74.

99 IMC Committee *Minutes*, Northfield, 1935, p. 10, Minute 16.

100 *Christian Education in Japan, a Study of a Commission on Christian Education in Japan Representing the National Christian Council of Japan, the National Christian Education Association of Japan, the Foreign Missions Conference of North America and the International Missionary Council*, pp. 1-14.

101 IMC Committee *Minutes*, Northfield, 1935, pp. 10-11, Minute 16. See also William Paton, "The International Missionary Council and the Future," IRM, Vol. XXV (1936), pp. 107-8.

102 IMC *Minutes*, Jerusalem, 1928, p. 65, Minute 3.

103 IMC Committee *Minutes*, Williamstown, 1929, pp. 10-11, Minute 17.

104 *Christians and Jews. A Report of the Conference on the Christian Approach to the Jews, Atlantic City, New Jersey, May 12-15, 1931.*

105 *Minutes of the International Committee on the Christian Approach to the Jews, Digswell Park, England, June 13 and 14, 1932.* Henceforth cited as ICCAJ *Minutes*. On file in the Council's New York office.

106 ICCAJ *Minutes*, British and European Sections, Old Jordans, 1935. ICCAJ

Minutes, British and European Sections, Kasteel Hemmen, 1936. ICCAJ *Minutes,* Enlarged Meeting, Vienna, 1937. ICCAJ *Minutes,* British and European Sections, London, 1938. ICCAJ *Minutes,* British and European Sections, London, 1939. On file in the Council's New York office.

107 IMC Committee *Minutes,* Herrnut, 1932, pp. 24-25, Minute 30; and pp. 79-82 for the constitution and report of the ICCAJ. See also FMC *Report,* 1934, pp. 94-96, and IMC Committee *Minutes,* Northfield, 1935, Appendix D, pp. 47-48.

108 Sinclair, *William Paton,* p. 264.

109 Conrad Hoffmann, Jr., *The Jews Today, A Call to Christian Action,* p. 64.

110 *Ibid.,* pp. 63-64.

111 IMC Committee *Minutes,* Williamstown, 1929, p. 20, Minute 25.

112 Kenneth Scott Latourette, "Research and Christian Missions," IRM, Vol. XXI (1932), pp. 532-46. The bibliographical list is on file at the Council's New York office.

113 IMC Committee *Minutes,* Herrnhut, 1932, p. 23, Minute 28.

114 The first of these was Alfred W. Wasson's *Church Growth in Korea* and the second, James Thayer Addison's *The Medieval Missionary.*

115 IMC Committee *Minutes,* Williamstown, 1929, p. 31, Minute 37. IMC Committee *Minutes,* Herrnhut, 1932, p. 11, Minute 15. See also *Quarterly Notes,* no. 28, October, 1930, p. i.

116 J. H. Oldham, *The Christian Message in the Modern World.*

117 *Ibid.,* pp. 4-5. Oldham's devotion to this large conception of the missionary task provides the key to his determination, several years later, that he could best aid the missionary enterprise by channelling his energies through the Oxford Conference on Life and Work.

118 *Ibid.,* pp. 10-12. IMC Committee *Minutes,* Herrnhut, 1932, pp. 36-40, Minute 43.

119 IMC Committee *Minutes,* Northfield, 1934, pp. 23-26, Minute 43.

120 Cf. William Ernest Hocking, Chairman, the Commission of Appraisal, *Re-thinking Missions. A Laymen's Inquiry after One Hundred Years,* p. 326. Rufus Jones shared largely with Hocking in writing this report. A searching examination of the appraisal is given by Robert E. Speer in *"Re-thinking Missions" Examined.*

121 IMC Committee *Minutes,* Herrnhut, 1932, pp. 40-42, Minute 45.

122 Esther Boorman Strong and A. L. Warnshuis, eds., *Directory of Foreign Missions, Mission Boards, Societies, Colleges, Cooperative Councils, and Other Agencies of the Protestant Churches of the World.*

123 A. L. Warnshuis and Esther Strong, *Partners in the Expanding Church.*

124 IMC Committee *Minutes,* Northfield, 1935, p. 29, Minute 45.

125 Letter from J. H. Oldham to John R. Mott, September 21, 1934. This letter is on file in the Council's New York office.

126 Letter from J. H. Oldham to John R. Mott, November 14, 1934. On file in the Council's New York office.

127 Oldham's view of his opportunity and responsibility is so important for an adequate understanding of the organizational development of the Ecumenical Movement that we should have clearly before us the considerations that entered his thinking. He wrote:

"The opportunity . . . is not a diversion from what I have been doing in recent years or a question of passing on to something entirely new, but rather an unexpected opening for doing what, since the meeting at Jerusalem I have been trying to do, with a much larger hope of success. Though I was not present at Jerusalem that meeting had a more profound influence on my thinking and attitude than any other similar experience of my life. The contribution by Rufus Jones on Secularism opened my eyes to the realities of the world in which we are living. . . . What [secularism] means for human life has been revealed with growing clearness in the years since Jerusalem and the danger to all that gives value to human life is vastly greater than we realised at that time. . . . Consequently when the Universal Christian Council [for Life and Work] turned to me and appealed for help in the proposed undertaking, I found myself before an opportunity which for years I have been praying and looking for. It is precisely what, in all that I have written about secularism and in my efforts in connection with what we have called "the Message," I have been seeking. It is not for me a different thing connected with Life and Work, but the very thing that since Jerusalem has seemed to me to be the crucial issue in missionary work.

"I have indicated that these new responsibilities will necessarily claim a considerable part of my time, and have also recorded my own judgment that, while technically they will be discharged in a capacity unconnected with the I.M.C., they are a fulfilment of tasks which the I.M.C. ought to undertake if other provision could not be made for them.

"If, through the cooperation of the best Christian minds which the Church has at its command, a new vision of the significance of Christianity for the present situation were really to take shape, more would have been done for the missionary cause than could be done by any other means. It is the question which ever since Jerusalem we have recognized to be central—the question of the *Message*, and of the message not only in itself but in its relation and application to the modern situation." Letter from J. H. Oldham to John R. Mott, November 14, 1934. On file in the Council's New York office.

128 Letters from William Paton to John R. Mott, December 4, 1934 and from John R. Mott to J. H. Oldham, December 15, 1934. Both are on file in the Council's New York office. Mott wrote to Oldham:

"Your letter of November 14 is one of the most important you have ever written me in all these years. It has placed on me a burden of real solicitude. I would not be a true friend if I did not say quite frankly that I am not happy about what you are proposing as to your relationships and as to the use of your time and strength during the period before us." Mott goes on to point out his belief that Oldham could make the same contribution just as effectively through the International Missionary Council.

129 For an appreciative statement on Oldham's rôle in preparation for Oxford, see William Adams Brown, *Toward a United Church*, pp. 90-91. See also Henry Smith Leiper, *World Chaos or World Christianity. A Popular Interpretation of Oxford and Edinburgh, 1937*, p. 14.

130 J. H. Oldham, *The Oxford Conference (Official Report)* and *The Ten Formative Years, 1938-1948. Report on the activities of the World Council of Churches during its period of formation*, p. 27.

131 Oldham, *The Oxford Conference*, p. 45.

132 *Documents of the World Council of Churches*, p. 15.

133 Brown, *op. cit.*, pp. 144-53.

134 IMC *Minutes*, Tambaram, Madras, 1938, p. 48, Minute 52.

135 *Ibid.*, p. 50, Minute 52.

136 CMSGBI *Report*, 1935, p. 36.

137 IMC Committee *Minutes*, Northfield, 1935, pp. 31-33, Minute 48.

138 Letter from William Paton to John R. Mott, November 19, 1935, on file at the Council's New York office. See also Sinclair, *William Paton*, pp. 183-84. Two prominent Chinese delegates had been at Northfield when the original Kowloon

decision was made and apparently indicated nothing of the reaction their fellow-countrymen were to give regarding that choice.

139 IMC *Ad Interim* Committee *Minutes,* Old Jordans, 1936, pp. 5-6, Minute 4; pp. 14-18, Minute 24.

140 Volume Five of *The Madras Series* incorporates all these.

141 J. Merle Davis, *The Economic and Social Environment of the Younger Churches.* This is a briefer study than *The Madras Series,* Vol. V, but incorporates much of the same material. See also Ralph A. Felton, *The Rural Church in the Far East.*

142 Among these were Julius Richter, *Der Dienst der Kirch an der heutigen Menschheit;* J. S. Whale, *What Is A Living Church?;* and Esther B. Strong, *The Church at the Heart of the World Christian Community.* Since no consideration was given at Jerusalem to the Christian home, a small representative commission was appointed to meet this lack. Out of its deliberations came a report to be submitted to the Madras meeting. See Mrs. Robert E. Speer and Constance M. Hallock, eds., *Christian Homemaking.*

143 See considerable correspondence from William Axling to the New York office of the International Missionary Council on this subject. It covers the summer and autumn months of 1937. On file in the Council's New York office.

144 "Notes of Meeting of Officers, Members of Ad Interim Committee, and Consultants of the International Missionary Council, 156 Fifth Avenue, New York, N. Y., U.S.A., Nov. 2, 1937." This three-page mimeographed report is on file in the Council's New York office.

145 General letter from the International Missionary Council, signed by John R. Mott, William Paton, and A. L. Warnshuis, November 26, 1937. On file in the Council's New York office.

146 Letter from Fred Field Goodsell to John R. Mott, Auugst 10, 1938. On file in the Council's New York office.

147 Statement by A. L. Warnshuis, personal interview, New York, October, 1950.

Chapter VII. *World Christianity and World Conflict, 1938-48*

1 Particularly in Britain and on the Continent "Tambaram" has gained currency for the International Missionary Council's 1938 meeting. To some the "ring" of "Tambaram" fits the great event that Christmas conference was. Yet the writer prefers to designate that event as "Madras." Reared in the "Madras" tradition, he finds its ring quite as stirring as Tambaram's. His major reason for this usage is one of geographical familiarity. Beyond a small circle, few have ever heard of Tambaram. It does not appear, for example, in *Webster's Geographical Dictionary.* A majority of people know where Madras is or can readily find it in a simple atlas. Two other considerations, while scarcely decisive, might be mentioned. The conference did meet on the campus of Madras Christian College. Moreover, it seems not altogether inappropriate, in view of the lasting influence of the Madras Conferences of 1900 and 1902, to continue the use of that historically important name in missionary co-operation.

2 *Quarterly Notes,* no. 63, July, 1939, p. ii. Madras was a "younger" conference than either Edinburgh or Jerusalem.

3 *The Madras Series,* Vol. VII, pp. 159-60.

4 *Minutes of the International Missionary Council and of the Committee of the*

Council, Tambaram, Madras, December 12-19, 1938, pp. 26-27, Minute 29. Henceforth cited as IMC *Minutes* with appropriate place and year.

5   See Ruth Isabel Seabury, *Daughter of Africa*, for the delightfully told story of Mina Soga. See also Sue Weddell, *The Miracle of Madras*, for an intimate glimpse into the inner life of the conference.

6   The World Conference of Christian Youth held in Amsterdam in 1939 surpassed this record, for its membership included delegates from seventy-one countries and 220 different denominations and national churches. When the World Council of Churches was formed in Amsterdam in August, 1948, 147 churches were represented from forty-four different countries.

7   It is instructive to compare here the complementary nature of the themes of the three great conferences of 1937-38.

Oxford, July, 1937
   The Church and the Community
   Church and State
   Church, Community, and State in Relation to the Economic Order
   Church, Community, and State in Relation to Education
   The Universal Church and the World of Nations

Edinburgh, August, 1937
   The Grace of Our Lord Jesus Christ
   The Church of Christ and the Word of God
   The Communion of Saints
   The Church of Christ, Ministry and Sacraments
   The Church's Unity in Life and Worship

Madras, December, 1938
   The Faith By Which the Church Lives (sections 1-2)
   The Witness of the Church (sections 3-6)
   The Inner Life of the Church (sections 7-11)
   The Environment of the Church (sections 12-15)
   Cooperation and Unity (section 16)

8   *The World Mission of the Church. Findings and Recommendations of the International Missionary Council, Tambaram, Madras, India, December 12th to 29th, 1938*, p. 10. See also Henry P. Van Dusen, "Madras and Christian Thought," *Christendom*, Vol. IV (1939), p. 207.

9   John R. Mott, "The Tambaram Meeting and Its Significance," *Christendom*, Vol. IV (1939), p. 189.

10   H. Kraemer, *The Christian Message in a Non-Christian World*, p. v.

11   T. C. Chao, "A Chinese Delegate Looks at Tambaram," *Christendom*, Vol. IV (1939), pp. 199-200. Cf. D. G. Moses, "The Problem of Truth in Religion," *The Madras Series*, Vol. I, pp. 58-82. See also D. M. Devasahayam and A. N. Sudarisanam, eds., *Rethinking Christianity in India*, a book prepared by a group of Christian thinkers wanting to make their views known to delegates to Madras. In an appendix P. Chenchiah, who had been to Jerusalem, criticizes Kraemer from the point of view of one who would have Christianity permeate and influence Indian culture without demanding the use of the name "Christian" by all those so influenced.

12   H. P. Van Dusen suggested that Vol. I of *The Madras Series* be designated *The Authority of the Faith* and that it should incorporate a post-Madras theological dialogue with Kramer. In that volume, Walter M. Horton's "Between Hocking and Kraemer" seems well to summarize the central position of most of those at Madras.

Herbert H. Farmer's "The Authority of the Faith" provides an appreciative yet penetrating criticism of Kraemer's position.

13   *The World Mission of the Church*, pp. 13-21. The writer does not wish to suggest here that complete theological unanimity prevailed. The tensions occasioned by "Continental Theology" were everywhere present. Indeed, some members of the meeting, through Dr. Martin Schlunk, chairman of the German delegation, presented a minority report. While expressing gratitude for the fellowship of Madras and indicating their readiness to co-operate, they also stated: "We are bound by conscience to point to some vital principles of the Gospel, which must be emphasized in contrast with certain passages in the reports of some sections." Convinced that only an "eschatological attitude" could prevent the secularization of the church, they (1) disagreed with the conference's statement on communism (*World Mission of the Church*, pp. 18-19); (2) emphasized discontinuity in the Christian revelation by denying that Christianity represented an "evolutionary fulfillment"; (3) affirmed that the church as an interim-body living between the times was not concerned to inaugurate a "social program." IMC *Minutes*, Madras, 1938, pp. 32-33, Minute 35. This also appears in *World Mission of the Church*, pp. 150-51.

14   Kraemer, *op. cit.*, Chap. IV. See also, H. Kraemer, "Continuity or Discontinuity," *The Madras Series*, Vol. I, pp. 1-21.

15   *World Mission of the Church*, p. 44. H. P. Van Dusen offers a provocative discussion of this issue as it arose at Madras. He chaired Commission One there and holds a position quite different from that of Kraemer. See *World Christianity*, Chap. VII.

16   *World Mission of the Church*, pp. 17-18.

17   *Ibid.*, pp. 18-19.

18   See, for example, *World Mission of the Church*, pp. 13-21, 40-47.

19   G. Baez Camargo, "A Mexican Appraisal of Madras," *World Dominion*, Vol. 17 (1939), pp. 126-27.

20   As one example, the lead editorial in *The Shanghai Evening Post and Mercury* accused Madras of "pussy-footing" and judged it to have "failed in . . . re-establishing the Church as a living force . . . . Had Christ been present He would have felt uncomfortable." Vol. 62 (1939), February 2.

21   *World Mission of the Church*, p. 152.

22   *Ibid.*, p. 117.

23   *Ibid.*, pp. 122-27. See also *The Madras Series*, Vol. VI.

24   E. Stanley Jones argued that Madras' emphasis was misplaced, that it began with a relative factor, the church, rather than with an absolute, the kingdom of God, and thus could lead only to limiting relativities. E. Stanley Jones, "Where Madras Missed Its Way," *The Christian Century*, Vol. 56 (1939), pp. 351-52. See also Henry P. Van Dusen, "What Stanley Jones Missed at Madras," *ibid.*, pp. 410-12, and a letter from Walter M. Horton to the editor, *ibid.*, pp. 517-18.

25   *World Mission of the Church*, p. 14.

26   Cf. Henry P. Van Dusen, *For the Healing of the Nations*, pp. 121-22.

27   Statement by T. C. Chao, personal interview, Whitby, July, 1947.

28   See Chap. VI, note 140.

29   *The Madras Series*, Vol. V, pp. 519-41.

30   *World Mission of the Church*, p. 103, paragraph 5.

31   *Ibid.*, pp. 66-72.

32   C. W. Ranson, *The Christian Minister in India, His Vocation and Training*.

33   Stephen Neill, *Survey of the Training of the Ministry in Africa, Part I*.

34   *World Mission of the Church*, pp. 87-97.

35   Among these were medicine, Christian education, urban problems, women's

work, and rural problems. Of the latter, for example, Mr. John H. Reisner felt that Madras' interest was "very great," indeed, greater than the general findings would indicate. He further observed, "The increase of interest in rural work over that of the Jerusalem conference was very marked." This is a notable judgment when one recalls that Jerusalem centred special emphasis on rural work. See John H. Reisner, "The Church and Rural Problems at Madras," *Agricultural Mission Notes*, no. 30, April 1939, pp. 2-3.

36 Seabury, *Daughter of Africa*, pp. 76-77; Camargo, *op. cit.*, p. 125; C. T. Tsai, "What the Madras Conference Means to Me," *The Chinese Recorder*, Vol. 70 (1939), pp. 231-32.

37 *World Mission of the Church*, pp. 128-30.

38 *Ibid.*, pp. 130-31.

39 Compare the statement made by Herbert H. Farmer. Quoted in Weddell, *The Miracle of Madras*, p. 5.

40 Letter from Karl Hartenstein to William Paton, September 5, 1939. A copy of this letter is in the writer's files.

41 *World Mission of the Church*, p. 16.

42 FMC *Report*, 1939, p. 152; CMSGBI *Report*, 1938-39, pp. 13-15; and for a vivid account of the experiences of one member of the American team see Seabury, *Daughter of Africa*, Chap. VII. "Putting Madras into Action" was the cover title for the FMC *Report*, 1939.

43 Some of the books were: Henry P. Van Dusen, *For the Healing of the Nations*; Alberto Rembao, *Mensaje Movimento y Masa*; *Das Wunder der Kirche unter den Völkern der Erde*.

44 IMC *Ad Interim Committee Minutes*, Hemmen, 1939.

45 A. L. Warnshuis, "The Story of the Orphaned Missions," *The Student World*, Vol. 37 (1944), pp. 23-31. Nothing appears in the Hemmen *Minutes*, for the discussion was "off the record."

46 *The International Missionary Council and Continental Missions in the War* of 1939-1945, p. 3. Henceforth cited as *Continental Missions*.

47 For a fuller account of the orphaned missions see Kenneth Scott Latourette and William Richey Hogg, *World Christian Community In Action, The Story of World War II and Orphaned Missions*.

48 A. L. Warnshuis, *loc. cit.*, and *The International Review of Missions*, Vol. XXIX (1940), p. 110. Henceforth cited as IRM.

49 A. L. Warnshuis, *loc. cit.*, p. 24. A. L. Warnshuis, "The War in Europe Threatens Disaster in Missions," FMC *Report*, 1940, pp. 10-16. See also Joseph I. Parker, *Interpretative Statistical Survey of the World Mission of the Christian Church*.

50 *Continental Missions*, pp. 3-4.

51 IRM, Vol. XXIX (1940), p. 110.

52 *Ibid.*, pp. 109-16; Vol. XXX (1941), pp. 104-6; CMSGBI *Report*, 1940, pp. 9-12.

53 A. L. Warnshuis, typed, untitled, two-page statement on orphaned missions [1940]. On file in the Council's New York office.

54 IRM, Vol. XXIX (1940), pp. 116-17; Vol. XXX (1941), p. 106; CMSGBI *Report*, 1941, p. 10.

55 Eric M. North, "The Missionary Enterprise and the War," FMC *Report*, 1940, pp. 16-20.

56 CMSGBI *Report*, 1941, pp. 8, 11; A. L. Warnshuis, "The Story of the Orphaned Missions," *loc. cit.*, p. 24; and a joint statement from A. L. Warnshuis and Leland Albright entitled "Orphaned Missions." This two-page article, dated

July 9, 1943, is on file in the Council's New York office. It lists 120 missions aided by December, 1942.

57 During the war the Council's New York office put out regularly a mimeographed *Bulletin.* Frequently these *Bulletins* were entitled "Orphaned Missions" with news devoted exclusively to that subject. The code initials "MAW" (Missions Affected by War) appeared on all these "Orphaned Missions" *Bulletins.* Henceforth, these will be cited by their code initials and number.

58 Use of the term "Orphaned Missions" spread quickly and widely, but it seems first to have been suggested by Eric North of the American Bible Society. Basil Mathews at once pointed out to Warnshuis scriptural warrant for its use. The verse "I will not leave you comfortless" (John 14:18) may be translated more accurately, "I will not leave you orphans." Letters to the writer from John W. Decker enclosing correspondence on this subject from Leland S. Albright and A. L. Warnshuis, April 21, 1949, and May 9, 1949.

59 FMC Report, 1940, p. 14. See also *Financial Statement: Aid for Orphaned Missions, 1939-40,* p. 3. These printed yearly statements are on file at the Council's New York office. It has been suggested that as a result of Orphaned Missions' aid no Protestant mission had to be abandoned during World War II for want of money. The writer is unable either to prove or to disprove this contention. It is clear that individual missionaries had to leave their work because of insufficient funds in mission board treasuries.

60 Letter from A. L. Warnshuis to John W. Decker, April 21, 1949. A copy is in the writer's files.

61 Cf. Latourette and Hogg, *World Christian Community in Action,* pp. 17-20. See also IRM, Vol. XXX (1941), pp. 106-8 and *Aid for Orphaned Missions, 1941,* p. 3.

62 Latourette and Hogg, *op. cit.,* pp. 20-21.

63 *Aid for Orphaned Missions, 1939-40,* pp. 4-5; 1943, p. 11; FMC *Report,* 1944, p. 249; Latourette and Hogg, *op. cit.,* pp. 23-24.

64 *Continental Missions,* pp. 10-11. See also Latourette and Hogg. *op. cit.,* pp. 24-25.

65 *Continental Missions,* pp. 8-10.

66 *Aid For Orphaned Missions, 1941; 1942; 1943; Continental Missions,* p. 10; MAW, 81; Latourette and Hogg. *op cit.,* pp. 26-27.

67 MAW, 86; 89; 92; 96. See also Latourette and Hogg, *op. cit.,* pp. 27-28.

68 See the abridged summary of income on p. 317.

69 *Aid for Orphaned Missions, 1945,* p. 2.

70 *Ibid.,* p. 2.

71 MAW, 73.

72 MAW, 89.

73 *Ibid.*

74 MAW, 80, 86; 92; IRM, Vol. XXXIV (1945), pp. 62-63, 70; FMC *Report,* 1944, p. 249; CMSGBI *Report,* 1945, p. 10.

75 MAW, 118.

76 *Aid For Orphaned Missions, 1947,* p. 10.

77 MAW, 131; 132; 136; IMC *Committee Minutes, Oegstgeest,* 1948, pp. 39-40.

78 IMC *Committee Minutes, Oegstgeest,* 1948, pp. 39-42.

79 Thus wrote Carl Ihmels, director of the Leipzig Mission to the International Missionary Council on September 28, 1945. The letter is on file in the Council's New York Office.

"We think back with great thankfulness to the days of Tambaram. When we

separated there, we promised each other that even if war should break out, the
unity which was given to us there would never be disturbed. All the scraps of news
which we have received in the course of these last years seem to indicate to us that
this promise has been kept."

Contrast what Karl Hartenstein, director of the Basel Mission, wrote in 1940 with
what had been assumed in Germany during World War I about the treatment of
German missions.

"But the most important thing is the fact that at the moment when the German
missionaries were interned, immediately other forces arose to replace them and to
take over their work. We think with gratitude of the service of the Scots and Wesleyans in West-Africa, of the Swedes for the Indian work of the Leipzig Mission and
above all of the clearly unselfish and effectual way in which the IMC represents the
cause of German missionaries with the English government.

"Still more impressive are the witnesses from the younger churches. . . . From
different fields we know that the indigenous church bravely and resolutely has stood
in the breach.

"We know that Bishop Azariah of Dornakal immediately paid visits to the German mission fields of South India to see about continuing the work and supporting
it with new forces.

"When communications are again possible, undoubtedly a series of similar demonstrations of the younger churches will become known. They will show us that abroad
the church of Jesus Christ has emerged mentally and spiritually victorious in such a
terrible period of war." *Jahrbuch 1940 der vereiningten Deutschen Missionskon-
ferenzen*, pp. 3-4. See also FMC Report, January, 1942, p. 82.

80   *Quarterly Notes*, no. 89, January, 1946, p. 1.

81   *IMC Ad Interim Committee Minutes*, Geneva, 1946.

82   *Quarterly Notes*, no. 91, July, 1946, p. 1.

83   *Ibid.*, no. 93, January, 1947, p. 1.

84   *Ibid.*, no. 95, July, 1947 MAW, 126 "The German Missions: Report of the
Two 'Rheinfelden' Meetings." This ten-page mimeographed report is in Day Missions Library and the Council's New York office.

85   *IMC Minutes*, Whitby, 1947, pp. 40-45.

86   *World Mission of the Church*, p. 138.

87   *Quarterly Notes*, no. 67, July, 1940, p. 1; no. 68, October, 1940, p. 1; IRM,
Vol. XXX (1941), pp. 78, 82, 85-86; Mott, *Addresses and Papers*, Vol. V, pp.
577-80.

88   *Quarterly Notes*, no. 71, July, 1941, p. 1; IRM; Vol. XXXI (1942), p. 71;
Mott, *Addresses and Papers*, Vol. V, pp. 580-90 includes findings of the Chile,
Peru, and Guatamala Conferences.

89   *IMC Minutes*, Madras, 1938, pp. 40-42, Minute 48.

90   Mott, *Addresses and Papers*, Vol. V, pp. 699-701.

91   *Ibid.*, pp. 701-41.

92   *General Report of the International Missionary Council for the Years 1939-
1945*, p. 26 and *IMC Minutes*, Whitby, 1947, p. 27, Minute 9.

93   One of his major contributions was what came to be known as the "Paton
Memorandum" for India. See Sinclair, *William Paton*, pp. 253-58.

94   Mott, *op. cit.*, p. 697.

95   Norman Goodall, *One Man's Testimony*, an autobiography.

96   *IMC Committee Minutes*, Oegstgeest, 1948, pp. 7-8, Minute 6.

97   Letters from John W. Decker to Bishop James C. Baker, May 23, 1947 and
from Norman Goodall to Bishop James C. Baker, June 23, 1947. These letters were

mimeographed for the Council's Committee on Program, Structure and Staffing, Whitby, Canada, July 2 to 4, 1947. They are on file in Day Missions Library.

98 IMC *Minutes*, Whitby, 1947, p. 57, Minute 26.

99 See Sundkler's *Bantu Prophets in South Africa*.

100 *Quarterly Notes*, no. 99, July, 1948, p. 1.

101 IMC *Committee Minutes*, Oegstgeest, 1948, pp. 10-11, Minute 8; IMC *Minutes*, Whitby, 1950, pp. 7-8, Minute 8.

102 Sinclair, *op cit.*, pp. 251-53.

103 Ralph E. Diffendorfer, *Christian Literature in the Mission World*.

104 IMC *Ad Interim Committee Minutes*, Geneva, 1946, pp. 22-23, Minute 21; IMC *Minutes*, Whitby, 1947, pp. 53-56, Minute 23; IMC *Committee Minutes*, Oegstgeest, 1948, p. 21, Minute 18.

105 All these books are listed in the bibliography.

106 *General Report*, 1939-45, p. 7.

107 IMC *Ad Interim Committee Minutes*, Geneva, 1946, p. 27, Minute 30, and pp. 46-47, Appendix C.

108 IMC *Minutes*, Whitby, 1947, pp. 31-33, Minute 14.

109 *Minutes of Meeting of the Joint Commission on East Asia of the International Missionary Council and the World Council of Churches*, Manila, Philippine Republic, February 4, 6, and 7, 1948.

110 *The Christian Prospect in Eastern Asia. Papers and Minutes of the Eastern Asia Christian Conference*, Bangkok, December 3-11, 1949.

111 From a personal conversation with A. L. Warnshuis, New York, October, 1950. See also M. Searle Bates, *Religious Liberty: An Inquiry*, pp. vii-xi.

112 *General Report*, 1939-1945, p. 12, and IMC *Committee Minutes*, Oegstgeest, 1948, Appendix A, pp. 48-49.

113 IMC *Ad Interim Committee Minutes*, Geneva, 1946.

114 J. Merle Davis, *The Economic Basis of the Evangelical Church in Mexico; The Cuban Church in a Sugar Economy; The Church in Puerto Rico's Dilemma; The Church in the New Jamaica; The Evangelical Church in the River Plate Republics; How the Church Grows in Brazil*; and "The East Indian Church in Trinidad" and "Some observations upon Over-Population in Barbados." The last two mimeographed studies are on file in the Council's New York office. The reports on Cuba, Mexico and the River Plate Republics were translated into Spanish.

115 W. Stanley Rycroft, *Indians of the High Andes*. See also IRM, Vol. 36 (1947), p. 54.

116 See also J. Merle Davis' admirable study, *The Preparation of Missionaries for Work in the Post-War Era*.

117 For Davis' final recommendations to the Council, see IMC *Ad Interim Committee Minutes*, Geneva, 1946, pp. 36-39, Appendix A. See also the Council's expression of appreciation for his service, IMC *Minutes*, Whitby, 1947, p. 28.

118 IMC *Minutes*, Whitby, 1947, pp. 64-66, Minute 32; IMC *Committee Minutes*, Oegstgeest, 1948, pp. 57-58, Appendix C.

119 IMC *Minutes*, Whitby, 1947, pp. 61-66, Minute 32.

120 IMC *Committee Minutes*, Oegstgeest, pp. 17-18, Minutes 12-14. Kenneth G. Grubb and E. J. Bingle, eds., *World Christian Handbook*.

121 *General Report*, 1939-45, pp. 20-22. See also Sinclair, *William Paton*, p. 264.

122 *Minutes of the Enlarged Meeting of the International Missionary Council's Committee on the Christian Approach to the Jews*, Basle, Switzerland, June 4-7, 1947. *Minutes of the Meeting of the International Missionary Council's Committee on the Christian Approach to the Jews*, Stockholm, Sweden, September 14-19, 1948.

123 W. A. Visser 't Hooft, ed., *The First Assembly of the World Council of Churches Held at Amsterdam, August 22nd to September 4th, 1948*, pp. 160-66.

124 Margaret Wrong, *Across Africa*.

125 Diffendorfer, *Christian Literature in the Mission World*, pp. 17-18. See also *General Report, 1939-1945*, pp. 22-24, and "International Committee on Christian Literature for Africa," a two page mimeographed report given at Whitby, 1947. On file in the Council's New York office.

126 Jackson Davis, Thomas M. Campbell, Margaret Wrong, *Africa Advancing. A Study of Rural Education and Agriculture in West Africa and the Belgian Congo.*

127 *IMC Committee Minutes*, Oegstgeest, 1948, p. 23, Minute 21, and pp. 10-11, Minute 8. See also *Quarterly Notes*, no. 99, July, 1948, p. 1.

128 *Quarterly Notes*, no. 98, April, 1948, p. ii; *IMC Minutes*, Whitby, 1947, p. 51, Minute 19, and p. 60, Minute 31; *IMC Committee Minutes*, Oegstgeest, 1948, pp. 16-17, Minute 11.

129 *IMC Committee Minutes*, Oegstgeest, 1948, p. 16, Minute 11.

130 *IMC Ad Interim Committee Minutes*, Geneva, 1946, p. 18, Minute 15.

131 *Ibid.*, pp. 18-19, Minute 15. Cf. *IMC Committee Minutes*, Oegstgeest, 1948, Appendix D, p. 61.

132 *IMC Minutes*, Whitby, 1947, p. 51, Minute 19, and p. 61, Minute 31.

133 *Quarterly Notes*, no. 101, January, 1949, p. viii, and *IMC Ad Interim Committee Minutes*, Geneva, 1946, p. 19, Minute 14.

134 A distinction devoid of any, except constitutional, meaning. The Jerusalem revision of the constitution had provided for the Committee of the Council to call world meetings of the International Missionary Council when it saw fit to do so and to determine their size. A comparison between Madras and Whitby raised the question: "What distinction existed between a world meeting of the International Missionary Council and a world meeting of the Enlarged Committee of the Council?" The Council's officers recognized the confusion, but could give no satisfactory answer. At Whitby, the Council's chairman declared that "Whitby stood in the same succession and was 'quite as much a meeting of the International Missionary Council as Jerusalem and Madras.'" (See Kenneth Scott Latourette and William Richey Hogg, *Tomorrow Is Here*, p. 59.) The *IMC Minutes*, Whitby, 1947, illustrate this confusion. The cover title appears incorrectly as *Minutes of the Enlarged Meeting of the International Missionary Council and of the Committee of the Council.* The introductory sentence on page three correctly reads, "The enlarged Committee of the International Missionary Council met at Whitby . . ."

135 From answers given to a questionnaire circulated by the writer at Whitby.

136 *The Witness of a Revolutionary Church*, p. 7.

137 C. W. Ranson, ed., *Renewal and Advance. Christian Witness in a Revolutionary World*, pp. 8-9.

138 Latourette and Hogg, *Tomorrow Is Here*, p. 61.

139 *IMC Minutes*, Whitby, 1947, Appendix, pp. 70-77.

140 *Renewal and Advance*, pp. 219-21. For the German account of Whitby see Walter Freytag, Karl Hartenstein, and Carl Ihmels, *Der Grosse Auftrage*. On the background for the supranationality resolution, see pp. 72-73.

141 Latourette and Hogg, *Tomorrow Is Here*, pp. 88-104.

142 *Renewal and Advance*, passim.

143 *Ibid.*, p. 215.

144 *Ibid.*, p. 213.

145 From answers given to a questionnaire circulated by the writer at Whitby.

146 Latourette and Hogg, *Tomorrow Is Here*, pp. 67-69 and *Renewal and Advance*, pp. 173-84.

147 Latourette and Hogg, *Tomorrow Is Here*, pp. 105-20 and *Renewal and Advance*, pp. 177-8.

148 Latourette and Hogg, *Tomorrow Is Here*, pp. 46-48.

149 See above, pp. 285-86. See also IMC *Minutes*, Madras, 1938, pp. 46-50, Minute 52.

150 *The Ten Formative Years, 1938-1948*, pp. 11-12, 28.

151 *Ibid.*, p. 12. See also IMC *Ad Interim Committee Minutes*, Hemmen, 1939, pp. 7-8, Minute 8.

152 *The Ten Formative Years, 1938-1948*, p. 13. See also Sinclair, *William Paton*, pp. 223-26.

153 Sinclair, *op. cit.*, pp. 235-39. See also *The Ten Formative Years, 1938-1948*, pp. 13-14. The writer has learned from W. A. Visser 't Hooft that discussion of Bishop Berggrav's particular concern for mediation to avert total war occurred outside the Administrative Committee in another meeting at Apeldoorn.

154 Sinclair, *op. cit.*, pp. 265-66. *The Ten Formative Years, 1938-1948*, pp. 68-69. *General Report, 1939-1945*, pp. 24-25.

155 An excellent background statement showing the Council's rôle and some of the difficulties involved in providing membership for the younger churches in the World Council of Churches can be found in J. W. Decker, "The Younger Churches and the World Council," *Religion in Life*, Vol. XV (1946), pp. 548-55. See also WCC *Minutes*, Buck Hill Falls, 1947, pp. 54-57.

156 For all the foregoing see IMC *Ad Interim Committee Minutes*, Geneva, 1946, p. 20, Minute 18; Appendix B, pp. 40-45. See also *The World Council of Churches, Its Process of Formation. Minutes and reports of the meeting of the Provisional Committee of the World Council of Churches held at Geneva from February 21st to 23rd, 1946; the constitutional documents of the World Council of Churches and an introduction by W. A. Visser 't Hooft*, pp. 24-25 and pp. 99-106 which reprint the IMC *Ad Interim Committee Minutes*, Appendix B. Henceforth referred to as WCC *Minutes* with appropriate place and date included.

157 WCC *Minutes*, Geneva, 1946, pp. 43-44.

158 *Conference of Church Leaders on International Affairs at Cambridge, England, August 4-7, 1946*. For the Commission's charter see *Documents of the World Council of Churches*, pp. 85-86.

159 IMC *Committee Minutes*, Oegstgeest, 1948, pp. 25-27, Minutes 23-24; Appendix B, pp. 53-56. WCC *Minutes*, Buck Hill Falls, 1947, pp. 33-34, 62.

160 WCC *Minutes*, Buck Hill Falls, 1947, p. 62.

161 *Ibid.*, p. 56.

162 J. W. Decker Memorandum: "Present and Future Relationships of the IMC and the WCC," New York, November 1, 1946. This ten-page mimeographed memorandum is in the Day Missions Library. See also Norman Goodall's memorandum (London, February, 1947; 11 pp., mimeographed), "World Council of Churches and International Missionary Council. Some considerations bearing on their relationships." It includes a proposal that the International Missionary Council become "The Missionary Council of the World Council of Churches." See further Norman Goodall's memorandum (London, March, 1947; 10 pp., mimeographed), "World Council of Churches & International Missionary Council." This, which includes replies to his first memorandum, indicates that Norman Goodall had earlier come upon the idea of the two councils "in association with" each other. Quite independently and in reply to the first memorandum, the Archbishop of Canterbury also suggested a relationship "in association with." This conception prevailed in 1947 and 1948. Both the above are filed in the Council's New York and London offices and in the Day Missions Library.

163　*World Christian Handbook*, pp. 240, 243, 285. The Foreign Missions Conference of North America also included such diverse groups as the Church of God and the Universalist Church. See FMC *Report*, 1948, pp. 107-13.

164　From conversations with younger church leaders by the writer at Amsterdam, 1948. Cf. Decker, *Memorandum*, p. 7, and Norman Goodall, "Amsterdam and the Missionary Societies," *The Congregational Quarterly*, Vol. 27 (1949), pp. 110-15. See also Paul David Devanandan, "The Ecumenical Movement and the Younger Churches," *Man's Disorder and God's Design: The Amsterdam Assembly Series*, Vol. I, pp. 147-54. Devanandan, an Indian, suggested why the younger churches might evidence greater affection for the International Missionary Council than for the World Council of Churches at the 1948 stage of ecumenical development.

165　One notes a somewhat analagous situation with the Congregation for the Propagation of the Faith (The Propaganda), although unlike it, the Council had never had any binding authority. Rome's responsible overseer for its missionary endeavour has jurisdiction in all its territories over all matters concerning the life of the church. It does not refer any questions arising in a Roman Catholic mission field to the usually appropriate Congregation in Rome for judgment, but decides them itself because of its intimate relationship with the whole life of the mission-church.

166　Decker, *Memorandum*, p. 8.

167　From conversations by the writer with delegates at Whitby, 1947. See also Decker, *Memorandum*, p. 8.

168　IMC *Minutes*, Whitby, 1947, pp. 34-35, Minute 15.

169　WCC *Minutes*, Buck Hill Falls, 1947, pp. 18-19, 67-68.

170　*Ibid.*, pp. 59-69.

171　IMC *Minutes*, Whitby, 1947, pp. 33-39, Minute 15. *The First Assembly of the World Council of Churches*, Amsterdam, 1948, p. 130. See also a statement by Norman Goodall on the meaning of "In association with" in *The Ten Formative Years*, 1938-1948, p. 74.

172　*The First Assembly of the World Council of Churches*, Amsterdam, 1948, p. 131.

173　IMC Committee *Minutes*, Oegstgeest, 1948, p. 24, Minute 23; p. 37, Minute 33.

174　*Ibid.*, pp. 36-37, Minute 32.

175　*Ibid.*, pp. 38-39, Minute 34.

176　WCC *Minutes*, Toronto, 1950, Appendix 10, p. 90.

CHAPTER VIII. *Epilogue*

1　Memorandum-letter from Baroness Elisabeth van Boetzelaer van Dubbeldam to the Council's secretaries in September, 1929, with a typewritten summary (22 pages, plus a 5-page supplement) of the replies of Continental missionary secretaries to a questionnaire about the International Missionary Council. These are on file at Edinburgh House and Day Missions Library.

2　Max Warren, *The Truth of Vision: A Study in the Nature of the Christian Hope*.

3　Compare, for example, Siegfried Knak's reply in 1929 contained in the five-page supplement listed in note 1 above. He wrote: "When for the first time after the war a representative of the I.M.C. came to Germany (Dr. Warnshuis) I answered him to his question whether the Germans would again cooperate, 'Yes, we would, but we would be the opposition party in the I.M.C.'. . . . The development of events has shown that that actually is the task of the Germans, or, rather, of the Continental Missions . . . . As far as I can see, the attitude of opposition of the German and Continental missions has been, up till now, of a constructive character. But this will only last as long as our opposition is taken seriously. In Germany we have for the moment the impression that we are not only patiently heard, but that one earnestly tries to understand us."

4 From personal interviews with J. H. Oldham, C. E. Wilson, and A. L. Warnshuis, respectively in London, July, 1948, Seaford, July, 1948, and New York, October, 1950.

5 This was especially apparent in the replies to Baroness van Boetzelaer's questionnaire. See note 1 above.

6 J. H. Oldham in a personal letter and memorandum to the writer, June 12, 1950.

7 The facts indicated in this paragraph have been referred to by nearly every person the writer has interviewed about the Council.

8 Statement by John R. Mott, personal interview, Whitby, July, 1947.

9 In reference to Davis' work the editors of *The International Revew of Missions* commented: "It is frankly admitted that hitherto the use of this department's work has been somewhat restricted to the enthusiasm of the relatively small number of people who see its full implications for the life of the younger churches." *The International Review of Missions*, Vol. XXXVI (1947), p. 67.

10 The writer is indebted to J. H. Oldham for this thought.

11 Cf. Paul David Devanandan, "The Ecumenical Movement and the Younger Churches," *Man's Disorder and God's Design*, The Amsterdam Assembly Series, Vol. I, pp. 148-50, 153.

12 William Temple, *The Church Looks Forward*, pp. 2-3.

13 J. H. Oldham in a personal letter and memorandum to the writer, June 12, 1950.

14 *Ibid.* One should note also that at Stockholm in 1925 "the great value of the work done" at Edinburgh, 1910, and by what later came to be known as the International Missionary Council was acknowledged. The Stockholm Conference traced its beginnings, however, to the appeal for "Peace and Christian Fellowship sent out by churchmen in several neutral countries" in November, 1914. G. K. A. Bell, ed., *The Stockholm Conference 1925*, pp. 2-3.

15 Cf. pp. 141-421.

BIBLIOGRAPHY

Addison, James Thayer, *The Medieval Missionary* (New York: International Missionary Council, 1936, pp. xiv, 176).

Agricultural Missions Notes Published Quarterly by the Agricultural Missions Foundation (New York: January, 1932, ff.).

Allen, Roland, *Jerusalem: A Critical Review of "The World Mission of Christianity"* (London: World Dominion Press, 1928, pp. 38).

Allen, W. O. B., and McClure, Edmund, *Two Hundred Years: The History of the Society for Promoting Christian Knowledge, 1698-1898* (London: Society for Promoting Christian Knowledge, 1898, pp. vi+551).

Allgemeine Missions-Zeitschrift (Berlin, 1874-1923).

American Lutheran Survey (Columbia, S. C.: 1914-28).

Anders, Rodolfo, *A Escola Dominical* (Rio de Janeiro: Confederação Evangélica do Brasil, 1949, pp. 254).

Anecdotes of the Bombay Mission for the Conversion of the Hindoos: Exhibiting an Account of the Travels and Missionary Labours of Messrs. Hall, Newell, Judson, Mills, Richards, Rice, and Nott, in Different Districts of the East Indies, with Sketches of the Idolatrous Customs of the Native Inhabitants. Extracted from the Letters and Journals of the Rev. Gordon Hall, A.M. (London: Frederick J. Williamson, 1836, pp. xi+243).

Axenfeld, Karl, *Germany's Battle for the Freedom of the Christian Missions* (Berlin-Steglitz: The German Evangelical Mission Aid Society, 1919, pp. 34).

Bate, H. N., editor, *Faith and Order. Proceedings of the World Conference Lausanne, August 3-21, 1927* (New York: George H. Doran Company, 1927, pp. xxiii+534).

Bates, M. Searle, *Data on the Distribution of the Missionary Enterprise* (New York: International Missionary Council, 1943, pp. 15).

————, *Religious Liberty: An Inquiry* (New York: International Missionary Council, 1945, pp. xviii+604).

Beach, Harlan P., *Renaissant Latin America: an outline and interpretation of the Congress on Christian Work in Latin America, held at Panama, February 10-19, 1916* (New York: Missionary Education Movement of the United States and Canada, 1916, pp. iv+258).

Bell, G. K. A., *Randall Davidson, Archbishop of Canterbury* (London: Oxford University Press, 1935, 2 vols.).

Bell, G. K. A., editor, *The Stockholm Conference 1925. The Official Report of the Universal Christian Conference on Life and Work, held in Stockholm, 19-30 August, 1925* (London: Oxford University Press, 1926, pp. xvi+791).

Books for Africa. The Quarterly Bulletin of the International Committee on Christian Literature for Africa (London: 1931 ff.).

Brabant, F. H., *Neville Stuart Talbot, 1879-1943, A Memoir* (London: SCM Press, 1949, pp. 160).

Braisted, Ruth Wilder, *In This Generation. The Story of Robert P. Wilder* (New York: Friendship Press, 1941, pp. xvi+205).

Brennecke, Gerhard, editor, *Die Träger der deutschen Weltimssion* (Stuttgart, Erschienen im Evang. Missionsverlag, G. m. b. gh., 1939, pp. 36).

Brown, Arthur Judson, *One Hundred Years. A History of the Foreign Missionary Work of the Presbyterian Church in the U. S. A., With Some Account of Countries, Peoples and the Policies and Problems of Modern Missions* (New York: Fleming H. Revell Co., 1937, pp. 1140).

Brown, William Adams, *Toward A United Church* (New York: Charles Scribner's Sons, 1946, pp. xvi+264).

Butterfield, Kenyon L., *The Christian Mission in Rural India* (New York and London: International Missionary Council, 1930, pp. xv+162).

————, *The Rural Mission of the Church in Eastern Asia. Report and Recommendations* (New York: The International Missionary Council, 1931, pp. 222).

Calcutta Christian Observer (Calcutta: 1832-62?).

Capen, Edward Warren, and Hodous, Lewis, *The Kennedy School of Missions* (Hartford: The Press of the Hartford Seminary Foundation, 1936, pp. 30).

Carey, Eustace, *Memoir of William Carey, D.D., Late Missionary to Bengal; Professor of Oriental Languages in the College of Fort William, Calcutta* (Hartford: Canfield and Robins, 1837, pp. 468).

Carey, S. Pearce, *William Carey D.D., Fellow of Linnaean Society* (New York: George H. Doran Company, preface 1923, pp. xvi+428).

Carey, William, *An Inquiry into the Obligations of Christians to use Means for the Conversion of the Heathens. In which the Religious State of the Different Nations of the World, the Success of Former Undertakings, and the Practicability of Further Undertakings, are Considered* (Leicester: Ann Ireland, 1792, pp. 87).

China Centenary Missionary Conference: Addresses, Public and Devotional (Shanghai: Methodist Publishing House, 1907, pp. 192).

China Centenary Missionary Conference Records. Report of the Great Conference Held at Shanghai, April 5th to May 8, 1907 (New York: American Tract Society, n.d., pp. xxxvii+823).

The China Christian Year Book (Shanghai: Christian Literature Society, 8 vols. between 1926 and 1939, succeeding the *China Mission Year Book*).

The China Mission Year Book (Shanghai: Christian Literature Society, 1910-19, 1923-25).

The Chinese Recorder (Foochow, and later Shanghai, 1867-1941).

Chirgwin, A. M., *Coming Together. The Churches Cooperate* (London: Edinburgh House Press, 1944, pp. 84).

Christendom. A Quarterly Review (Chicago, later New York, 1935-48).

The Christian Advocate (New York: 1826 ff.).

The Christian Approach to the Jew. Being a Report of Conferences on the Subject Held at Budapest and Warsaw in April 1927 (London: Edinburgh House Press, 1927, pp. vii+208).

The Christian Century (Chicago: 1894 ff.).

The Christian College in India. The Report of the Commission on Christian Higher Education (London: Oxford University Press, 1931, pp. xiii+388).

Christian Education in China. The Report of the China Educational Commissions of 1921-1922 (Shanghai: Commercial Press, Limited, 1922, pp. iii+iii+390).

Christian Education in Japan, a Study of a Commission on Christian Education in Japan Representing the National Christian Council of Japan, the National Christian Education Association of Japan, the Foreign Missions Conference of North

America and the International Missionary Council (New York: The International Missionary Council, 1932, pp. xi+246).

Christian Literature in Moslem Lands. A Study of the Activities of the Moslem and Christian Press in all Mohammedan Countries (New York: George H. Doran Company, 1923, pp. xii+306).

The Christian Prospect in Eastern Asia. Papers and Minutes of the Eastern Asia Christian Conference. Bangkok, December 3-11, 1949 (New York: Friendship Press, 1950, pp. iv+156).

The Christian Work (New York: 1866-1926).

Christian Work in Latin America [Cover title: *Panama Congress, 1916*] New York: Missionary Education Movement, 1917, 3 vols.).

Christians and Jews. A Report of the Conference on the Christian Approach to the Jews, Atlantic City, New Jersey, May 12-15, 1931 (New York: International Committee on the Christian Approach to the Jews, International Missionary Council, 1931, pp. xi+155).

The Chronicle of the London Missionary Society (London: 1836 ff.).

Conference of Church Leaders on International Affairs at Cambridge, England, August 4-7, 1946 (New York: American Committee for the World Council of Churches, n.d., pp. 11).

Conference of Missionary Societies in Great Britain and Ireland. Minutes of Standing Committee (London: Edinburgh House, two bound volumes of mimeographed and handwritten minutes, Vol. I, June 14, 1911–May 3, 1917, Vol. II, January, 1917–December, 1926).

Conference of Missionary Societies in Great Britain and Ireland. Report of the First Annual Conference, Held at the Hayes, Swanwick, Darbyshire, from the 12th-14th June, 1912 (London: Conference of Missionary Societies in Great Britain and Ireland, 1912, pp. 184, and annually thereafter).

Conference on Missions Held in 1860 at Liverpool (London: James Nisbet & Co., 1860, pp. xi+428).

Conference on Missions in Latin America (New York: Committee on Cooperation in Latin America, 1913, pp. 192).

Conferences of Christian Workers Among Moslems 1924. A Brief Account of the conferences together with their findings and lists of members (New York: Chairman of the International Missionary Council, 1924, pp. 152).

Congregational Quarterly (London: 1923 ff.).

The Continuation Committee Conferences in Asia 1912-1913. A Brief Account of the Conferences Together With Their Findings and Lists of Members (New York: Published by the Chairman of the Continuation Committee, 1913, pp. 488).

Council Notes of the International Missionary Council (London: International Missionary Council, 1923 ff. Succeeded by Quarterly Notes).

The Cross Across the Pacific: Report of Conference of Missionary Leaders held at Morpeth, N.S.W., from February 23rd to 28th, 1948 (Sydney: The National Missionary Councils of Australia and New Zealand, n.d., pp. 64).

Davis, J. Merle, "Barbados: Some Observations upon Overpopulation" (New York: The Department of Social and Economic Research, International Missionary Council, n.d., pp. 27, mimeographed).

————, *The Church in New Jamaica* (New York: International Missionary Council, 1942, pp. x+100).

————, *The Church in Puerto Rico's Dilemma* (New York: International Missionary Council, 1942, pp. viii+80).

————, *The Cuban Church in a Sugar Economy* (New York: International Missionary Council, 1943, pp. 119).

————, "The East Indian Church in Trinidad" (New York: The Department of Social and Economic Research, International Missionary Council, 1942, pp. iv+70, mimeographed).

————, *The Economic and Social Environment of the Younger Churches* (London: The Edinburgh House Press, 1939, pp. xv+231).

————, *The Evangelical Church in the River Plate Republics* (New York: International Missionary Council, 1943, p. 119).

————, *The Economic Basis of the Evangelical Church in Mexico* (New York: International Missionary Council, 1940, pp. 133).

————, *How the Church Grows in Brazil* (New York: International Missionary Council, 1943, pp. 167).

————, *Modern Industry and the African* (London: Macmillan and Co., Limited, 1933, pp. xviii+425).

————, *New Buildings on Old Foundations. A Handbook on Stabilizing the Younger Churches in Their Environment* (New York: International Missionary Council, 1945, pp. xiv+320).

————, *The Preparation of Missionaries for Work in the Post-War Era* (New York: International Missionary Council, 1944, pp. 24).

Davis, Jackson, Campbill, Thomas M., Wrong, Margaret, *Africa Advancing. A Study of Rural Education and Agriculture in West Africa and the Belgian Congo* (New York: The Friendship Press, foreword 1945, pp. 230).

Dennis, James S., Beach, Harlan P., Fahs, Charles H., *World Atlas of Christian Missions* (New York: Student Volunteer Movement for Foreign Missions, 1911, pp. 172).

Devasahayam, D. M., and Sudarisanam, A. N., editors, *Rethinking Christianity in India* (Madras: Hogarth Press, [1938] pp. vi+267+54).

Diffendorfer, Ralph E., *Christian Literature in the Mission World* (New York: International Missionary Council, 1946, pp. 120).

Documents of the World Council of Churches (Amsterdam: First Assembly of the World Council of Churches, 1948, pp. 104).

The East and the West: A Quarterly Review for the Study of Missionary Problems (Westminster, The Society for the Propagation of the Gospel in Foreign Parts, 1903-27).

Ecumenical Missionary Conference, New York, 1900. Report of the Ecumenical Conference on Foreign Missions, Held in Carnegie Hall and Neighboring Churches, April 21 to May 1 (New York: American Tract Society, 1900, 2 vols.).

Eddy, Sherwood, *Pathfinders of the World Missionary Crusade* (New York: Abingdon-Cokesbury Press, 1945, pp. 319).

The Encyclopædia Brittanica (London: The Encyclopædia Brittanica, 14th ed., 24 vols., 1929).

Evangelical Christendom (London: 1847 ff.).

Evangelisches Missions-Magazin (Basel: New Series, 1857 ff.).

Fahs, Charles H., and Davis, Helen E., *Conspectus of Cooperative Missionary Enterprises* (New York: International Missionary Council, 1935, pp. v+252).

The Family and Its Christian Fulfilment (New York: Foreign Missions Conference of North America, 1945, pp. ix+178).

Felton, Ralph A., *The Rural Church in the Far East* (Calcutta: Department of Social and Economic Research, International Missionary Council, 1938, pp. x+258+xxxii).

Financial Statement. Aid for Orphaned Missions (New York: International Missionary Council, annually from 1939-40 to 1947).

Findings of Conferences, Held Under the Leadership of Dr. John R. Mott, Chair-

man of the International Missionary Council at Léopoldville, Mutoto and Eliza-bethville, *Congo Belge, 1934* (London: International Missionary Council, n.d., pp. 68).

The Findings of the Continuation Committee Conferences, Held in Asia, 1912-1913 *Arranged by Topics* (New York: Student Volunteer Movement for Foreign Missions, 1913, pp. 430).

Findlay, G. G., and Holdsworth, W. W., *The History of the Wesleyan Methodist Missionary Society* (London: The Epworth Press, 5 vols., 1921-24).

Foreign Missions Conference of North America Report (New York: Foreign Missions Conference of North America, 1893 ff., with varying cover titles).

Frank, Arnold, editor, *Witnesses from Israel. Life-Stories of Jewish Converts to Christianity.* Translated from the German by Mrs. A. Fleming (Edinburgh: Oliphant, Anderson and Ferrier, 1903, pp. 118).

Frazer, A. G., et al., *Village Education in India: The Report of a Commission of Inquiry* (London: Oxford University Press, 1920, pp. xii+210).

Freytag, Walter, Hartenstein, Karl, and Ihmels, Carl, *Der Grosse Auftrag* (Stuttgart and Korntal: Evangelischer Missionsverlag, 1948, pp. 96).

Freytag, Walter, editor, *Jahrbuch 1940 der Vereinigten Deutschen Missionskon-ferenzen* (Hamburg: Verlag der Deutschen Evangelischen Missionshilfe [1940], pp. 96).

Fries, Karl, *Mina Minnen* (Stockholm: Triangelförlaget A.-B., 1939, pp. 225).

Gairdner, W. H. T., *Echoes from Edinburgh, 1910. An account and Interpretation of the World Missionary Conference* (New York: Fleming H. Revell Co., preface 1910, pp. 281).

General Report of the International Missionary Council for the Years 1939-1945 (New York: International Missionary Council, foreword, 1946, pp. 30).

Gibson, B. D., editor, *The Place of Women in the Church on the Mission Field* (London and New York: The International Missionary Council, 1927, pp. 112).

Goodall, Norman, *One Man's Testimony* (London: Independent Press, 1949, pp. 128).

Grubb, Kenneth G., and Bingle, E. J., editors, *World Christian Handbook* (London: World Dominion Press, 1949, pp. xv+405).

Gulick, Sidney L., and MacFarland, Charles S., *The Church and International Relations.* Vol. III of *Library of Christian Cooperation* edited by Charles S. Mac-farland (New York: Federal Council of the Churches of Christ in America by the Missionary Education Movement, 1917, 6 vols.).

Hall, Ronald Owen, *The Missionary-Artist Looks at His Job* (New York: International Missionary Council, 1942, pp. 64).

The Harvest Field (1861, New Series, 1880 ff., continued by *The National Christian Council Review*).

Hirtzell, Sir Arthur, *The Church, the Empire, and the World. Addresses on the Work of the Church Abroad* (London: S.P.C.K., 1919, pp. xiii+128).

Hocking, William Ernest, Chairman, the Commission of Appraisal, *Re-thinking Missions. A Laymen's Inquiry after One Hundred Years* (New York: Harper & Brothers, 1932, pp. xv+349).

Hodge, J. Z., *Bishop Azariah of Dornakal* (Madras: The Christian Literature Society for India, 1946, pp. xii+112).

Hoffmann, Conrad, Jr., *The Jews Today. A Call to Christian Action* (New York: Friendship Press, 1941, pp. 80).

———, *What Now for the Jews? A Challenge to the Christian Conscience* (New York: Friendship Press, 1948, pp. 80).

Hogg, W. Richey, Sixty-five Years in the Seminaries. A History of the Interseminary Movement (New York: Interseminary Movement, [1945], pp. 15).

Inman, Samuel Guy, Evangelicals at Havana, Being an Account of the Hispanic
American Evangelical Congress, at Havana, Cuba, June 20-30, 1929 (New York:
Committee on Cooperation in Latin America, n.d., pp. 174).

The International Missionary Council and Continental Missions in the War of
1939-1945 (London: International Missionary Council, n.d., pp. 14).

The International Review of Missions (Edinburgh and later London: International
Missionary Council, 1912 ff.).

Iremonger, F. A., William Temple, Archbishop of Canterbury, His Life and Letters
(London: Oxford University Press, 1948, pp. xv+663).

The Japan Christian Quarterly (Tokyo: The Federation of Christian Missions,
and later, The Christian Literature Society of Japan, 1926-41).

The Japan Christian Year Book (Tokyo: 1927-31 as The Japan Mission Year Book
and 1932-40 The Japan Christian Year Book. Succeeded The Christian Movement in Japan).

The Jerusalem Meeting of the International Missionary Council, March 24-April 8,
1928 (New York and London: International Missionary Council, 1928, 8 vols.).

Johnston, James, editor, Report of the Centenary Conference on the Protestant Missions of the World, Held in Exeter Hall (June 9th-19th) London, 1888 (London:
James Nisbet & Co., 1888, 2 vols.).

Jones, Rufus, M., editor, The Church, the Gospel and War (New York: Harper &
Brothers, 1948, pp. xii+169).

Jones, Thomas Jesse, Education in Africa. A Study of West, South, and Equatorial
Africa by the African Education Commission under the auspices of the Phelps-
Stokes Fund and Foreign Mission Societies of North America and Europe (New
York: Phelps-Stokes Fund, n.d., pp. xxviii+323).

————, Education in East Africa. A Study of East, Central and South Africa by the
second African Education Commission under the auspices of the Phelps-Stokes
Fund, in cooperation with the International Education Board (New York: Phelps-
Stokes Fund; London: Edinburgh House Press, 1925, pp. xxviii+416).

Karlström, Nils, Kristna Samförstandssträvanden Under Världskriget 1914-1918 Med
särskild hänsyn till Nathan Söderbloms insats (Stockholm: Svenska Krykans
Diakonistyrelses Bokförlag, 1947, pp. xv+724).

Keller, Adolph, Karl Barth and Christian Unity (New York: The Macmillan Company, 1933, pp. xxii+320).

Kolmodin, A., editor, Förhandlingarna Vid Det Femte Nordisk-Lutherska Missionsmötet I Stockholm Den 26-29 Aug. 1897 (Stockholm: Fosterlands-Stiftelsans
Förlags-Expedition, 1898, pp. 229).

The Korea Mission Field (Seoul: 1905-41).

Kraemer, H., The Christian Message in a Non-Christian World (London and New
York: Harper & Brothers, 1938, pp. xvi+455).

Latourette, Kenneth Scott, A History of Christian Missions in China (New York:
The Macmillan Co., 1929, pp. xii, 930).

————, A History of the Expansion of Christianity (New York: Harper & Brothers,
1937-1945, 7 vols.).

————, and Hogg, William Richey, Tomorrow Is Here. The Mission and Work of
the Church As Seen From the Meeting of the International Missionary Council
at Whitby, Ontario, July 5-24, 1947 (New York: Friendship Press, 1948, pp.
xiv, 145).

————, and Hogg, William Richey, World Christian Community In Action. The

Story of World War II and Orphaned Missions (New York: International Missionary Council, 1949, pp. 44).

Leiper, Henry Smith, *World Chaos or World Christianity. A Popular Interpretation of Oxford and Edinburgh, 1937* (Chicago and New York: Willett, Clark & Company, 1937, pp. viii+181).

Listen (London: The International Committee on Christian Literature for Africa, 1932 ff.).

Lloyd, Roger, *The Church of England in the Twentieth Century* (London: Longmans, Green & Co., 1946, Vol. 1).

Lovett, Richard, *The History of the London Missionary Society 1795-1895* (London: Henry Frowde, 1899, 2 vols.).

Lunds Missions-Tidning (Lund: 1848 ff. Succeeded in 1920 by *Evangeliska Missionen*).

McBee, Silas, *An Irenic Itinerary* (New York: Longmans, Green, and Co., 1911, pp. xv+225).

MacLennan, Kenneth, *Twenty Years of Missionary Cooperation* (London: Edinburgh House Press, 1927, pp. 96).

"The Madras Series." *Presenting Papers Based upon the Meeting of the International Missionary Council, at Tambaram, Madras, India, December 12 to 29th, 1938* (New York: International Missionary Council, 1939, 7 vols.).

Man's Disorder and God's Design. The Amsterdam Assembly Series (New York: Harper & Brothers [1949], 4 vols.).

Mathews, Basil, *Forerunners of a New Age: An Interpretative Report of a Conference on the Training of the Ministry of the Younger Churches, Held at Newark, New Jersey, St. Andrew's-tide, 1934* (New York: International Missionary Council [and] Foreign Missions Conference of North America, 1934, pp. 90).

——, *John R. Mott, World Citizen* (New York: Harper & Brothers, pp. xiii +469).

——, *Roads to the City of God* (Garden City: Doubleday Doran & Company, Inc., 1928, pp. ix+117).

Methods of Mission Work Among Moslems. Being those Papers read at the First Missionary Conference on Behalf of the Mohammedan World, Held at Cairo, April 4th-9th, 1906 (New York: Fleming H. Revell Company, 1906, pp. 236).

Minute of International Missionary Meeting, Held at Crans, near Geneva, June 22-28, 1920 (no data [1920], pp. 20).

Minutes of the Continuation Committee of the World Missionary Conference (June 23, 1910, to November 20, 1913).

Minutes of the Convention of Protestant Missionaries Held in Tokio, Japan, on the 10th and 13th of May, 1878 (Yokohama: R. Meikle-John & Co., n.d., pp. 14).

Minutes of the Fourth Annual Meeting of the Korean National Christian Council, Held in the First Methodist Church, Seoul, Korea, September 20, 1927 (Seoul: YMCA Press, n.d., pp. 18, plus unpaginated Korean supplement).

Minutes of the International Committee on the Christian Approach to the Jews (London: International Missionary Council, 1932 ff.).

Minutes of the International Missionary Council (London: International Missionary Council, 1921 ff., including Minutes of the Committee of the Council and of the Ad Interim Committee).

"Minutes of the London Secretaries' Association" (London: British and Foreign Bible Society House, ten volumes of handwritten minutes from 1819 through World War II).

Minutes of Meeting of the Joint Commission on East Asia of the International

Missionary Council and the World Council of Churches, Manila, Philippine Republic, February 4, 6 and 7, 1948 (no data [1948], pp. 21).

Minutes and Reports of the Meeting of the Provisional Committee of the World Council of Churches, Buck Hill Falls., Penn., April 1947 (Geneva: World Council of Churches, n.d., pp. 134).

Minutes and reports of the Third Meeting of the Central Committee of the World Council of Churches, Toronto (Canada), July 9-15, 1950 (Geneva: World Council of Churches, n.d., pp. 133).

The Missionary Conference of South India and Ceylon, 1879 (Madras: Addison & Co., 1880, 2 vols.).

The Missionary Record of the United Free Church of Scotland (Edinburgh: 1901-1914).

The Missionary Review of the World (Princeton, later New York: 1878-1939).

The Missionary Situation After the War. Notes prepared for the International Missionary Meeting at Crans, Near Geneva, June 22-28, 1920 (London: Edinburgh House, preface 1920, pp. 62).

Missions (New York: 1910 ff.).

Monroe, Paul, Sadler, Michael E., and Oldham, J. H., *Papers on Educational Problems in Mission Fields* (———: International Missionary Council, foreword 1921, pp. 71).

Moody, William R., *The Life of Dwight L. Moody* (New York: Fleming H. Revell Company, 1900, pp. 590).

Morgan, E. R., and Lloyd, Roger, editors, *The Mission of the Anglican Communion* (London: S.P.C.K. & S.P.G., 1948, pp. vi+212).

Mosher, Arthur T., editor, *The Christian Mission Among Rural People* (New York: Rural Missions Cooperating Committee of the Foreign Missions Conference of North America, 1945, pp. x+334).

Mott, John R., *Addresses and Papers of John R. Mott* (New York: Association Press, 1947, 6 vols.).

———, *The Decisive Hour of Christian Missions* (New York: Student Volunteer Movement for Foreign Missions, 1910, pp. vi+251).

———, editor, *Evangelism for the World Today as Interpreted by Christian Leaders Throughout the World* (New York: Harper & Brothers, 1938, pp. 295).

———, *The Evangelization of the World in this Generation* (New York: Student Volunteer Movement for Foreign Missions, 1900, pp. 245).

———, *Strategic Points in the World's Conquest* (New York: Fleming H. Revell Company, 1897, pp. 218).

———, *The World's Student Christian Federation. Origin, Achievements, Forecast* (———: World's Student Christian Federation, 1920, pp. 92).

The National Christian Council Review (Mysore: 1924 ff., continuing *The Harvest Field*).

Nederlandsch Zendingstijdschrift (Utrecht: 1889-1901?).

Neill, Stephen, *Survey of the Training of the Ministry in Africa, Part I. Report of a survey of theological education in East and West Africa, with special reference to the training of the ordained ministry, undertaken in April to July, 1950, under the auspices of the International Missionary Council* (London: International Missionary Council, 1950, pp. 63).

The New York Times, June 17, 1951.

Norddeutsche Allgemeine Zeitung, March 3 and March 7, 1915.

Nordisk Missions-Tidsskrift (Copenhagen: 1890 ff.).

Notcutt, L. A., and Latham, G. C., *The African and the Cinema. An Account of* the Work of the Bantu Educational Cinema Experiment during the period March 1935 to May 1937 (London: Edinburgh House Press, 1937, pp. 256).

Official Handbook: World Missionary Conference Edinburgh 1910 (Edinburgh: World Missionary Conference Office, n.d., pp. 188).

Oldham, H. W., Lt. Col. G. W. Oldham, R. E. (London: Morgan & Scott, Ltd., foreword 1926, pp. xiv+127).

——, The Student Christian Movement of Great Britain and Ireland (London: British College Union, 1899, pp. 170).

Oldham, J. H., The Christian Message in the Modern World (London: International Missionary Council [1932], pp. 12). .

——, A Devotional Diary (Eighth ed., London: Student Christian Movement Press, 1930, no pagination).

——, International Missionary Cooperation. A Statement of Fundamental Questions of Policy for consideration by the Committee of the International Missionary Council, January 11-15, 1925. (Edinburgh: Morrison and Gibb Limited, n.d., pp. 20).

——, International Missionary Organization (no data [1920], pp. 8).

——, The Oxford Conference (Official Report) (Chicago and New York: Willett, Clark & Company, 1937, pp. xvi+290).

——, The Possibilities of Prayer (London & Edinburgh: T. N. Foulis, 1912, pp. 40.

——, and Gibson, B. D., The Remaking of Man in Africa (London: Oxford University Press, 1931, pp. 185).

——, The World and the Gospel (London: United Council for Missionary Education, 1916, pp. xv+224).

Paik, L. George, The History of Protestant Missions in Korea 1832-1910 (Pyeng Yang: Union Christian College Press, 1929, pp. ix+438+xiii).

Pan-Anglican Congress, 1908 (London: Society for Promoting Christian Knowledge, 1908, 7 vols.).

Papers on Educational Problems in Mission Fields (——: International Missionary Council, foreword, 1921, pp. 71).

Parker, Joseph I., editor, Interpretative Statistical Survey of the World Mission of the Christian Church (New York: International Missionary Council, 1938, pp. 323).

Pascoe, C. F., Two Hundred Years of the S. P. G.: An Historical Account of the Society for the Propagation of the Gospel in Foreign Parts, 1701-1900. (London: Published at the Society's Office, 1901, 2 vols.).

Paton, William, Christianity in the Eastern Conflicts. A Study of Christianity, Nationalism and Communism in Asia (Chicago: Willett, Clark & Co., 1937, pp. 224).

——, Jerusalem, 1928 (London: International Missionary Council, n.d., pp. 47).

——, Jesus Christ and the World's Religions (London: United Council for Missionary Education, 1916, pp. viii+102).

——, editor, Studies in Evangelism (London: International Missionary Council, 1938, pp. 299).

——, World Community (New York: The Macmillan Company, 1939, pp. 192).

Pickett, J. Waskom, Christian Mass Movements in India (New York: The Abingdon Press, 1933, pp. 382).

Prestige, G. L., The Life of Charles Gore A Great Englishman (London: William Heinemann, Ltd., 1935, pp. xi+547).

Proceedings of the China Continuation Committee, Shanghai (Shanghai: Offices of the China Continuation Committee, 1912-21).

Proceedings of a General Conference of Bengal Protestant Missionaries, Held at Calcutta, September 4-7, 1855 (Calcutta: Baptist Mission Press, 1855, pp. 183).

Proceedings of the General Conference on Foreign Missions, Held at the Conference Hall, in Mildmay Park, London, in October 1878 (London: John F. Shaw & Co., 1879, pp. viii+434).

Proceedings of the General Conference of the Protestant Missionaries of Japan Held at Osaka, Japan, April, 1883 (Yokohama: R. Meiklejohn & Co., 1883, pp. xvi+468).

Proceedings of the General Conference of Protestant Missionaries in Japan, Held in Tokyo, October 24-31, 1900 (Tokyo: Methodist Publishing House, 1901, pp. vii+1048).

Proceedings of the South India Missionary Conference, Held at Ootacamund, Apr. 19th-May 5th, 1858 (Madras: Society for Promoting Christian Knowledge, 1858, pp. vii+342+xxxiii).

Proceedings of the Union Missionary Convention, Held in New York, May 4th and 5th, 1854 (New York: Taylor & Hogg, 1854, pp. 61).

Quarterly Notes. Being the Bulletin of the International Missionary Council (London: 1923 ff. published separately at first as Council Notes of the International Missionary Council, but from January, 1924, bound with The International Review of Missions).

Ranson, C. W., The Christian Minister in India, His Vocation and Training. A study based on a Survey of Theological Education by the National Christian Council (London and Redhill: Lutterworth Press, 1945, pp. 317).

————, editor, Renewal and Advance. Christian Witness in a Revolutionary World (London: Edinburgh House Press, 1948, pp. 228).

Rauws, Joh., et al., The Netherlands Indies (London: World Dominion Press, 1935, pp. 186).

Rawlinson, F., Thoburn, Helen, and MacGillivray, D., editors, The Chinese Church As Revealed in the National Christian Conference, Held in Shanghai, Tuesday, May 2, to Thursday, May 11, 1922 (Shanghai: The Oriental Press, n.d., pp. viii+XI+724).

Records of the General Conference of Protestant Missionaries of China, Held at Shanghai, May 10-14, 1877 (Shanghai: Presbyterian Mission Press, 1878, pp. 3+492).

Records of the General Conference of the Protestant Missionaries of China, Held at Shanghai, May 7-20, 1890 (Shanghai: Presbyterian Mission Press, 1890, pp. lvxiii+744).

Records of Missionary Secretaries, An Account of the Celebration of the Centenary of the London Secretaries' Association, (Foreword by J. H. Ritson), (London: United Council for Missionary Education, 1920, pp. 79).

Die Reformirte Kirchen-Zeitung (Elberfeld: 1851 ff.).

Regional Conferences in Latin America: The reports of a series of seven conferences following the Panama Congress in 1916, which were held at Lima, Santiago, Buenos Aires, Rio de Janeiro, Baranquilla, Havana, and San Juan (New York: The Missionary Education Movement, 1917, pp. xiv+452).

Religion in Life. A Christian Quarterly (New York: Abingdon-Cokesbury Press, 1932 ff.).

Rembao, Alberto, Mensaje Movimento y Masa (Buenos Aires: Liberia "La Aurora," 1939, pp. 108).

Report of the Church History Deputation to the Orient, September 1931 to March 1932 (London: International Missionary Council, n.d., pp. 82).

Report of the Fourth Decennial Indian Missionary Conference, Held in Madras,

December 11th-18th, 1902 (Madras: Christian Literature Society, n.d., pp. xxxiv+367).

Report of the General Missionary Conference, Held at Allahabad, 1872-73 (Madras: C. Foster, 1873, pp. xxviii+548).

Report of the Proceedings of the First General Missionary Conference, Held at Johannesburg, July 13-20, 1904 (Johannesburg: The Argus Printing and Publishing Co., Limited, 1905, pp. 213).

Report of the Proceedings of the Second General Missionary Conference for South Africa, Held at Johannesburg, July 5-11, 1906 (Basutoland: Morija Printing Office, 1907, pp. 135).

Report of the Proceedings of the Third General Missionary Conference for South Africa, Held at Bloemfontein, July 1-6, 1909 (Capetown: Townshend, Taylor and Snashall, 1909, pp. iv+164).

Report of the Proceedings of the Fourth General Missionary Conference of South Africa, Held at Cape Town 3rd to 9th July, 1912 (Cape Town: Townshend, Taylor and Snashall, 1912, pp. 135).

Report of the Punjab Missionary Conference, Held at Lahore in December and January, 1862-63 (Dodiana: American Presbyterian Mission Press, 1863, pp. xix+398).

Report of the Second Decennial Missionary Conference, Held at Calcutta, 1882-83 (Calcutta: J. W. Thomas Baptist Mission Press, 1883, pp. xxx+462).

Report of the South Indian Missionary Conference, Held at Madras, January 2-5, 1900 (Madras: M. E. Publishing House, 1900, pp. xvi+108).

Report of the Third Decennial Missionary Conference, Held at Bombay, 1892-93 (Bombay: Education Society's Steam Press, 1893, 2 vols.).

Report of the United Conference of Missionary Societies in British East Africa, Kikuyu, July 23th [sic]—26th, 1918 (Nairobi: Swift Press, 1918, pp. 22).

Report Taken from the Minutes of the Convention of Protestant Missionaries of Japan, Held at Yokohama, September 20th-25th, 1872 (Yokohama: The Press of Yokohama, n.d., pp. 2).

Reports to Continuation Committee (1911 and 1912. In 1913 these preparatory materials for the Continuation Committee were designated Papers for Continuation Committee).

Richter, Julius, Der Dienst der Kirch an der heutigen Menschheit (Gütersloh: Verlag C. Bertelsmann, 1936, pp. 115).

Ritson, John H., Christian Literature in the Mission Field: A Survey of the present situation made under the direction of the Continuation Committee of the World Missionary Conference, 1910 (Edinburgh: Continuation Committee of the World Missionary Conference, 1910, preface 1915, pp. viii+152).

———, The World Is Our Parish (London: Hodder and Stoughton, 1939, pp. 336).

Ross, Edward Alsworth, Report on Employment of Native Labor in Portuguese Africa (New York: The Abbott Press, 1925, pp. 61).

Rouse, Ruth, The World's Student Christian Federation: A History of the First Thirty Years (London: S.C.M. Press Ltd., 1948, pp. 332).

Rowling, F., and Wilson, C. E., Bibliography of African Christian Literature (London: Conference of Missionary Societies in Great Britain and Ireland, 1923, pp. xvi+135).

Rycroft, W. Stanley, Indians of the High Andes: Report of the Commission appointed by the Committee on Cooperation in Latin America to Study the Indians of the Andean Highland, with a View to Establishing a Cooperative Christian Enterprise (New York: Committee on Cooperation in Latin America, 1946, pp. xiii+330).

Schaff, Philip, and Prime S. Irenaeus, *History, Essays, Orations, and Other Documents of the Sixth General Conference of the Evangelical Alliance, Held in New York, October 2-12, 1873* (New York: Harper & Brothers, 1874, pp. iv+773).

Schlunk, *Die Weltmission des Christentums* (Hamburg: Agentur des Rauhen Hauses, 1925, pp. 250).

Schreiber, A. W., *Die Edinburger Welt-Missions-Conferenz* (Basel: Verlag der Basler Missionbuchhandlung, 1910, pp. 184).

Seabury, Ruth Isabel, *Daughter of Africa* (Boston: The Pilgrim Press, 1945, pp. vii+144).

The Shanghai Evening Post and Mercury, February 2, 1939.

Shedd, Clarence P., *Two Centuries of Student Christian Movements* (New York: Association Press, 1934, pp. xxii+466).

Sinclair, Margaret, *William Paton* (London: SCM Press Ltd., 1949, pp. 272).

Smith, Edwin W., *The Christian Mission in Africa. A study based on the work of the International Conference at Le Zoute, Belgium, September 14th to 21st, 1926* (London: The International Missionary Council, 1926, pp. viii+192).

Smith, George, *The Life of Alexander Duff, D.D., LL.D.* (New York: A. C. Armstrong & Son, preface 1879, 2 vols.).

Smith, George Adam, *The Life of Henry Drummond* (New York: Doubleday & McClure Company, 1898, pp. xiii+541).

Social and Economic News (Geneva: The Department of Social and Industrial Research and Counsel of the International Missionary Council. It varied in content from 50 to 75 mimeographed pages, was referred to in reports as the "quarterly *News Sheet*," and appeared only between April, 1932, and March, 1934.).

Söderblom, Nathan (edited by Anna Söderblom), *Sommarminnen* (Stockholm: Svenska Kyrkans Diakonistyrelses Bokförlag, 1941, pp. 285).

Speer, Robert E., Inman, Samuel G., and Sanders, Frank K., editors, *Christian Work in South America. Official Report of the Congress on Christian Work in South America, at Montevideo, Uruguay, April, 1925* (New York: Fleming H. Revell Company, 1925, 2 vols.).

Speer, Robert E., *"Re-thinking Missions" Examined* (New York: Fleming H. Revel Company, 1933, pp. 64).

Speer, Mrs. Robert E., and Hallock, Constance M., editors, *Christian Homemaking* (New York: Round Table Press, Inc., 1939, pp. xii+141).

Statistical Atlas of Christian Missions (Edinburgh: World Missionary Conference, 1910, pp. 136).

Stock, Eugene, *The History of the Church Missionary Society: Its Environment, Its Men, and Its Work* (London: Church Missionary Society, 1899-1916, 4 vols.).

Strong, Esther B., *The Church at the Heart of the World Christian Community* New York: International Missionary Council, n.d., pp. iv+60).

——, and Warnshuis, A. L., editors, *Directory of Foreign Missions, Mission Boards, Societies, Colleges, Cooperative Councils, and Other Agencies of the Protestant Churches of the World* (New York: International Missionary Council, 1933, pp. xii+278).

The Student Movement (London: 1899 ff., organ of the British Student Christian Movement).

The Student World (New York and later Geneva: 1908 ff., journal of the World's Student Christian Federation).

Sundkler, Bengt G. M., *Bantu Prophets in South Africa* (London: Lutterworth Press, 1948, pp. 344).

———, *Svenska Missionssällskapet 1835-1876. Missionstankens Genombrott Och Tidigare Historia I Sverige* (Stockholm: Svenska Kyrkans Diakonistyrelses Bokförlag, 1937, pp. xxxvi+614).

Tatlow, Tissington, *The Story of the Student Christian Movement of Great Britain and Ireland* (London: Student Christian Movement Press, 1933, pp. 944).

Temple, William, *The Church Looks Forward* (New York: The Macmillan Company, 1944, pp. viii+193).

The Ten Formative Years, 1938-1948. Report on the activities of the World Council of Churches during its period of formation (Geneva: World Council of Churches, 1948, pp. 80).

Third Ecumenical Missionary Conference, June, 1910 (Printed minutes of preparatory committees for Edinburgh, 1910, from June, 1907, to July, 1908. From September, 1908 to July, 1910, they were designated World Missionary Conference, 1910).

't Hooft, W. A. Visser, editor, *The First Assembly of the World Council of Churches, Held at Amsterdam, August 22nd to September 4th, 1948* (New York: Harper & Brothers, 1949, pp. 271).

Tracy, Joseph, *History of the American Board of Commissioners for Foreign Missions Compiled chiefly from the Published and Unprinted Documents of the Board* (New York: M. W. Dodd, 2d ed., 1842, pp. viii+452).

Treaties Acts & Regulations Relating to Missionary Freedom (London: Office of the International Missionary Council, 1923, pp. 108).

Tulga, Chester E., *The Case Against Modernism in Foreign Missions* (Chicago: Conservative Baptist Fellowship, 1950, pp. 64).

Turner, Fennell P., and Sanders, Frank Knight, editors, *The Foreign Missions Convention at Washington, 1925. Addresses Delivered at the Foreign Missions Convention of the United States and Canada, Held at Washington, D. C., January 28 to February 2, 1925* (New York: Fleming H. Revell Company, 1925, pp. xiii+466).

Ure, Ruth, *The Highway of Print. A World-wide Study of the Production and Distribution of Christian Literature* (New York: Friendship Press, 1946, pp. ix+277).

Vahl, J., editor, *Det fjerde Lutherska Missionsmöde i Kjöbenhaven* (Copenhagen: Provst J. Vahl, 1893, pp. 209).

Van Dusen, Henry P., *For the Healing of the Nations. Impressions of Christianity Around the World* (New York: Charles Scribner's Sons, 1940, pp. xii+227).

———, *World Christianity, Yesterday, Today, and Tomorrow* (Nashville and New York: Abingdon-Cokesbury Press, 1947, pp. 302).

Verhandlungen der Kontinentalen Missionskonferenzen (Published regularly after 1868. For dates and places of publication, see note entries).

Warneck, Gustav, *Outline of a History of Protestant Missions from the Reformation to the Present Time.* Translated from the German by George Robson (Edinburgh: Oliphant, Anderson & Ferrier, 1901, pp. xiv+364).

Warnshuis, A. L., editor, *Chinese Christian Education: A Report of a Conference, Held in New York City, April 6th, 1925* (New York: Foreign Missions Conference of North America, 1925, pp. 103).

———, editor, *The Christian Message for the World Today* (New York: Round Table Press, Inc., 1934, pp. 203).

———, and Strong, Esther, *Partners in the Expanding Church* (New York: Foreign Missions Conference of North America and the International Missionary Council, 1935, pp. 62).

Warnshuis, A. L., *The Relations of Missions and Governments in Belgian, French and Portuguese Colonies* (London: International Missionary Council, 1923, pp. 34).

Warren, Max, *The Truth of Vision: A Study in the Nature of the Christian Hope* (London: The Canterbury Press, 1948, pp. 159).

Wasson, Alfred W., *Church Growth in Korea* (New York: International Missionary Council, 1934, pp. xii+175).

Weddell, Sue, *The Miracle of Madras* (New York: The Women's Board of Foreign Missions Reformed Church of America, n.d., pp. 52).

Wellons, Ralph Dillingham, *The Organizations Set Up For the Control of Mission Union Higher Educational Institutions* (New York: no publisher listed, 1927, pp. vi+135).

Whale, J. S., *What Is A Living Church?* (London: The Livingston Press, 1937, pp. 104).

Wherry, E. M., Zwemer, S. M., and Mylrea, C. G., *Islam and Missions: Being papers read at the Second Missionary Conference on behalf of the Mohammedan World at Lucknow, January 23-28, 1911* (New York: Fleming H. Revell Company, 1911, pp. 298).

Wherry, E. M., Zwemer, S. M., and Mylrea, C. G., *Lucknow, 1911: Being papers read and discussions on the training of Missionaries, and literature for Moslems at the General Conference on Missions to Moslems, held at Lucknow, January 23-28, 1911, with Committees, Programme, List of Delegates, etc.* (Madras: The Christian Literature Society for India, 1911, pp. 293).

Wilberforce, S., editor, *Journals and Letters of the Rev. Henry Martyn, B.D., Late Fellow of St. John's College, Cambridge; and Chaplain to the Honourable East India Company* (London: R. B. Seeley and W. Burnside, 1837, 2 vols.).

Wilder, Robert P., *The Great Commission. The Missionary Response of the Student Volunteer Movements in North America and Europe; Some Personal Reminiscences* (London: Oliphants, Ltd., preface 1936, pp. 115).

Willis, J. J., *The Kikuyu Conference. A Study in Christian Unity* (London: Longmans, Green and Co., 1914, pp. 24).

The Witness of a Revolutionary Church. Statements Issued by the Committee of the International Missionary Council, Whitby, Ontario, Canada, July 5-24, 1947 (New York: International Missionary Council [1947], pp. 45).

The World Council of Churches, Its Process of Formation. Minutes and reports of the meeting of the Provisional Committee of the World Council of Churches, held at Geneva from February 21st to 23, 1946; the constitutional documents of the World Council of Churches and an introduction by W. A. Visser 't Hooft (Geneva: World Council of Churches, n.d., pp. 205).

World Dominion. A Quarterly International Review of Christian Progress (London: World Dominion Press, 1923, ff.).

The World Mission of Christianity. Messages and Recommendations of the Enlarged Meeting of the International Missionary Council, held at Jerusalem, March 24-April 8, 1928 (New York and London: International Missionary Council, n.d., pp. 96).

The World Mission of the Church. Findings and Recommendations of the International Missionary Council, Tambaram, Madras, India, December 12th to 29th, 1938 (New York: International Missionary Council, 1939, pp. 173).

World Missionary Conference, 1910 (Edinburgh: Oliphant, Anderson & Ferrier, 9 vols. 1910).

World Missionary Conference, 1910, Daily Conference Paper (Edinburgh: World Missionary Conference, 1910).

World Missionary Conference, 1910, Monthly News Sheet, October 1909-May 1910 (Edinburgh: Morrison & Gibb Limited, n.d., pp. vii+172).

Wrong, Margaret, Across Africa (London: International Committee on Christian Literature for Africa, 1940, pp. vii+104).

Wrong, Margaret, Africa and the Making of Books: Being a Survey of Africa's Need of Literature (London: International Committee on Christian Literature for Africa, 1934, pp. 56).

Das Wunder der Kirche unter den Völkern der Erde (Stuttgart: Evang. Missions-verlag G. m. b. H., 1939, pp. 208).

Zabriskie, Alexander C., Bishop Brent, Crusader for Christian Unity, (Philadelphia: The Westminster Press, 1948, pp. 217).

Zeitschrift für Missionswissenschaft (Münster i. W.: 1911 ff.).

Zimmerman, Carle C., Siam Rural Economic Survey, 1930-31 (Bangkok: The Bang-kok Times Press, Ltd., 1931, pp. vii+321).

Zwemer, S. M., Wherry, E. M., and Barton, James L., editors, The Mohammedan World of Today, Being Papers Read at the First Missionary Conference on Behalf of the Mohammedan World at Cairo, April 4th-9th, 1906 (New York: Fleming H. Revell Company, pp. 302).

In addition to the printed sources listed above, the writer has referred to scores of letters, reports, bulletins, pamphlets, mimeographed materials and the like in the files of the Day Missions Library, New Haven, the Missionary Research Library, New York, the office of the International Missionary Council, New York, and Edinburgh House, London. References to these materials, with appropriate identifying data, will be found throughout the notes.

INDEX

[Abbreviations used: IMC *International Missionary Council*; WCC *World Council of Churches*]